MARKETING MANAGEMENT

Marketing

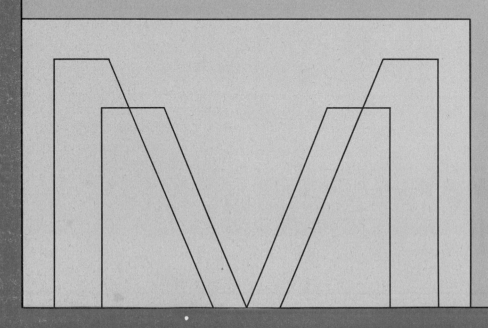

MANAGEMENT

analysis, planning, and control

FOURTH EDITION

PHILIP KOTLER

NORTHWESTERN UNIVERSITY

Prentice/Hall International, Inc.

ISBN 0–13–557983–X
Library of Congress Catalog No.:
79–21989

MARKETING MANAGEMENT   analysis, planning, and control   FOURTH EDITION
Philip Kotler

© 1980 by Prentice-Hall, Inc., Englewood Cliffs, New Jersey 07632

Printed in the United States of America

10 9 8 7 6 5 4

Editorial/Production Supervision by Maureen Wilson
Interior Design by Janet Schmid
Page Layout by Jenny Markus
Interior Illustrations by Herbert Daehnke
Acquisitions Editor: John Connolly
Manufacturing Buyer: John Hall

Prentice-Hall International, Inc., *London*

Prentice-Hall of Australia Pty. Limited, *Sydney*

Prentice-Hall of Canada, Ltd., *Toronto*

Prentice-Hall of India Private Limited, *New Delhi*

Prentice-Hall of Japan, Inc., *Tokyo*

Prentice-Hall of Southeast Asia Pte. Ltd., *Singapore*

Whitehall Books Limited, *Wellington, New Zealand*

Prentice-Hall, Inc., *Englewood Cliffs, New Jersey*

TO NANCY

Contents

PREFACE

No one knows what the 1980s will have in store for companies, consumers, and society at large. The 1970s was truly a turbulent and trying decade marked by (1) high and persistent worldwide inflation, (2) material and energy shortages, (3) economic stagnation, (4) consumerism, (5) environmentalism, (6) increased government regulation, (7) changing consumer life styles, and (8) undermarketed public sector needs. Some of these developments will continue into the 1980s and indeed intensify. New and unsuspected shocks will emerge. The challenge facing marketers in the 1980s will be to find constructive ways to reconcile company profitability, customer satisfaction, and social responsibility.

Properly viewed, these problems are also opportunities. Marketing is the link between a society's needs and its industrial responses. It is the function through which organizations adjust their offerings to the ever-changing needs and wants of the marketplace. It is through external sensors that organizations adapt and grow.

This fourth edition has been written with three objectives:

1. To bring marketing management into closer alignment with the rapidly growing practice of corporate strategic planning;

2. To enlarge the discussion of several marketing topics of increased importance, particularly the strategic planning process, competitive-marketing strategies for manufacturers and retailers, sales promotion and publicity decisions, new forces in the environment, buyer behavior theory, the marketing audit, exchange theory, organizational-buying behavior, marketing of services, product-line strategies, contents of marketing plans, marketing organization developments, and distribution-channel developments;

3. To update the text material so that it is as relevant as possible to the marketing problems of the 1980s.

The book remains true to its original principles. These principles are:

1. *A managerial orientation.* This book focuses on the major decisions facing marketing executives and top management in their attempt to harmonize the objectives and resources of the organization with the opportunities found in the marketplace.

2. *An analytical approach.* This book does not provide pat answers so much as ways of thinking about and analyzing recurrent marketing problems. Descriptive material is held to a minimum in order to permit the greatest latitude in developing the analytical content of marketing.

3. *A reliance on basic disciplines.* This book draws heavily on the basic disciplines of economics, behavioral science, and mathematics. *Economics* provides the fundamental tools and concepts for seeking optimal results in the use of scarce resources. *Behavioral science* provides fundamental concepts and findings for the interpretation of consumer and organizational buying behavior. *Mathematics* provides the means of developing explicit statements about the relationships among variables in a problem.

4. *A universal approach.* This book develops marketing thinking for the broadest of contexts. Marketing is treated as relevant to industrial as well as consumer markets, service industries as well as goods industries, small companies as well as large ones, nonprofit organizations as well as profit companies, and buyers as well as sellers.

Marketing remains one of the most difficult areas of analysis and decision making for the company. Marketing problems do not exhibit the neat quantitative properties of many of the problems in production, accounting, or finance. Psychological variables play a large role; marketing expenditures affect demand and costs simultaneously; marketing plans shape and interact with other corporate plans. Marketing decisions must be made in the face of insufficient information about processes that are dynamic, nonlinear, lagged, stochastic, interactive, and downright difficult. However, this is not taken as a case for intuitive decision making; rather it suggests the need for improved theoretical frameworks and sharper tools for analysis.

The book is organized into six parts. *Part I* develops the conceptual and strategic underpinnings of marketing. *Part II* presents concepts and tools for analyzing any market and marketing environment to discern opportunities. *Part III* presents principles for selecting target markets and planning effective marketing programs over the product's life cycle. *Part IV* deals with assembling the specific elements of the marketing mix based on their unique contributions. *Part V* develops the administrative side of marketing: organization, information handling, and control. *Part VI* broadens the discussion of marketing to cover international, nonbusiness, and contemporary issues.

ACKNOWLEDGMENTS

This fourth edition bears the imprint of many persons. My colleagues in the marketing department at Northwestern University made an important contribution through their zest in blending marketing theory with managerial practice: Bobby J. Calder, Richard M. Clewett, John Hauser, Sidney J. Levy, Louis W. Stern, Brian Sternthal, Alice Tybout, and Andris A. Zoltners. Two doctoral stu-

xi

dents in marketing, John Martin and Amy Seidel Marks, provided valuable assistance in numerous tasks connected with updating this edition. Donald P. Jacobs, dean of the Graduate School of Management, provided constant encouragement. Our secretaries, Marion Davis, Sabra Van Cleef, and Phyllis Van Hooser, provided invaluable help in manuscript preparation for the fourth edition.

I am indebted to colleagues at other universities who reviewed this edition and provided insightful suggestions: C. L. Abercrombie, Ralph Gaedeke, O. C. Ferrell, David J. Luck, Patrick E. Murphy, Edward Bonfield, and James C. Petersen.

My overriding debt is to my wife, Nancy, who provided me the time, support, and inspiration needed to regenerate this book. It is truly our book.

PHILIP KOTLER
Northwestern University
Evanston, Illinois

Understanding Marketing Management

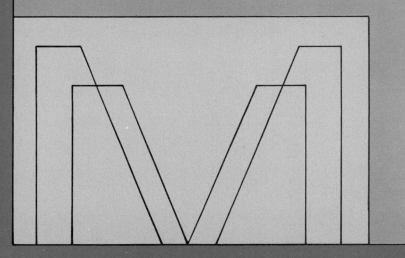

The Role of Marketing in Today's Organizations

Marketing is so basic that it cannot be considered a separate function. . . . It is the whole business seen from the point of view of its final result, that is, from the customer's point of view.
PETER DRUCKER

As human history speeds toward the year 2000, with its awe-inspiring problems and opportunities, the subject of marketing is attracting increasing attention from companies, institutions, and nations. Marketing has evolved from its early origins in distribution and selling into a comprehensive philosophy for relating any organization dynamically to its markets. Marketing is a cornerstone of policy and practice in such giant concerns as General Electric, Procter & Gamble, Sears, and IBM. Large and small business firms everywhere are beginning to appreciate the difference between selling and marketing and are organizing to do the latter. Nonprofit organizations such as museums, universities, churches, and government agencies are seeing marketing as a new way of looking at their relations with their publics. Developing nations are examining marketing principles to see how their domestic distribution system can be improved and how they can compete more effectively in world markets. Socialist nations are beginning to study how they could use marketing research, advertising, and pricing to increase their effectiveness in planning and distributing their goods.

The intensifying interest in marketing is paradoxical because while marketing is one of man's newest action disciplines, it is also one of the world's oldest professions. From the time of *simple barter* through the stage of a *money economy* to today's modern *complex marketing system, exchanges* have been taking place. But marketing—the study of exchange processes and relationships—

made its formal appearance only in the early part of the twentieth century out of questions and issues neglected by its mother science, economics.

In this short time, marketing has achieved the image of society's savior in the minds of many, and society's corrupter in the minds of others. Marketing's good deeds have been described in various ways:

> Aggressive marketing policies and practices have been largely responsible for the high material standard of living in America. Today through mass low-cost marketing we enjoy products which were once considered luxuries and which are still so classified in many foreign countries.[1]

> Advertising nourishes the consuming power of men. It creates wants for a better standard of living. It sets up before a man the goal of a better home, better clothing, better food for himself and his family. It spurs individual exertion and greater production. It brings together in fertile union those things which otherwise would not have met.[2]

Others take a dimmer view of marketing's contribution to society:

> For the past 6,000 years the field of marketing has been thought of as made up of fast-buck artists, con-men, wheeler-dealers, and shoddy-goods distributors. Too many of us have been "taken" by the tout or con-man; and all of us at times have been prodded into buying all sorts of "things" we really did not need, and which we found later on we did not even want.[3]

> What does a man need—really need? A few pounds of food each day, heat and shelter, six feet to lie down in—and some form of working activity that will yield a sense of accomplishment. That's all—in a material sense. And we know it. But we are brainwashed by our economic system until we end up in a tomb beneath a pyramid of time payments, mortgages, preposterous gadgetry, playthings that divert our attention from the sheer idiocy of the charade.[4]

It is clear that various social commentators have vastly different views on the meaning and social worth of marketing. The position taken in this book is that marketing makes a vital contribution to the advancement and satisfaction of human needs and wants. It is the means by which organizations identify unfulfilled human needs, convert them into business opportunities, and create satisfaction for others and profit for themselves. The capacity of organizations to survive and prosper depends on their ability to continuously create value for target markets in an environment of ever-changing human needs and wants.

THE AGE OF ORGANIZATIONS

To understand marketing, we must first understand organizations. Our society abounds in organizations, which stand ready to serve every need, whether large or small, good or bad, elevated or prosaic. With little effort, citizens of Chicago

[1] William J. Stanton, *Fundamentals of Marketing* (New York: McGraw-Hill Book Company, 1964), pp. 4–5.

[2] Sir Winston Churchill.

[3] Richard N. Farmer, "Would You Want Your Daughter to Marry a Marketing Man?" *Journal of Marketing*, January 1967, p. 1.

[4] Sterling Hayden, *Wanderer* (New York: Alfred A. Knopf, 1963).

can walk down Clark Street and instantly satisfy their appetite for chicken, hamburger, or pizza, courtesy of Kentucky Fried Chicken, McDonald's, or Pizza Hut. If they want new clothes, they can drive to the Old Orchard Shopping Center and rummage through racks of suits and dresses at Marshall Field's, Baskin's, or Montgomery Ward's. Their desire for recreation or entertainment can be satisfied instantaneously through the courtesy of the Touhy Tennis Club or the Biograph Theater. If the weather is too cold, they can board a 747 at O'Hare Airport and reach the balmy shores of Miami three hours later, courtesy of Delta Airlines. All said, an incredibly large number of organizations stand ready to serve human needs by holding them as business opportunities. The twentieth century is the Age of Organizations.

Organizations are so omnipresent that it is hard to believe that life ever existed without them. Yet throughout most of human history, people had to satisfy their needs through their own exertions. There was not the fast-food outlet, the health club, or the local movie theater to serve their needs.

Today's organizations come in all shapes and sizes. They may be publicly or privately owned. They may be run for profit, service, or some other goal(s). They may be organized as single proprietorships, partnerships, corporations, or conglomerates. They may range from a small private law practice to an IBM with 270,000 employees scattered throughout the world. They may have a single product line, such as paper, or sell as many as 150,000 different items, as in the case of Sears. They may operate in one locality, in a region, or nationally or internationally.

Organizations begin as ideas in the head of one or more entrepreneurs. The motivation for starting an organization could be to perform a great deed, make a great fortune, or meet an important need. The organizers must raise funds, attract personnel, establish a production or service facility, and find a market for its output. Many organizations do not survive these hurdles.

An organization can survive only if it is able to acquire the resources necessary to its sustenance. Such survival can be achieved in one of three ways. The first is through possessing legitimate or illegitimate *power*, which it uses to command resources. Thus public agencies obtain their resources through the imposition of taxes; the Mafia obtains its resources through other means. The second way is through *solicitation*, which comes about by convincing one or more persons or groups to contribute financial support freely. Opera companies and private universities survive through generous gifts that cover the large annual deficits between their normal income and cost. The third mode of survival is *exchange*, whereby an organization creates and offers goods and services that are able to attract and satisfy purchasers. This is the marketing solution to survival. The organization identifies a set of buyers and needs in the marketplace, develops a set of products and services to satisfy these needs, communicates the benefits of these products, makes them available and accessible, prices them in a reasonable manner, and convinces buyers to exchange their resources for these products.

The marketing solution calls for more than the ability of the organization to produce the needed goods and services. The organization must know how to produce better offers to the target market than its competitors. Buyers normally can buy from several sources. Their needs, preferences, and interests keep changing. The organization must keep abreast of these changes and constantly revise and improve its offer to the market. Playboy, Inc., one of the most successful publishing companies in history, has watched sales of its major magazine fall from a peak of 6.9 million copies in 1972 to 4.5 million. Kentucky Fried Chicken, one of the most successful fast-food franchisers in history, has experienced a declining market share for the past several years. Zenith, one of the most successful American manufacturers of television sets, has watched its market share erode in recent years in the face of increasing competition from Japanese television manufacturers.

The truth is that most organizations are not geared to maintain their marketing leadership in times of rapidly changing consumer wants and aggressive competition. They achieved their market positions in times when people spent more freely and when competitors were less sophisticated. They could survive by making and selling the same products year after year. These organizations can be said to lack a *marketing culture*. Only a handful of major companies— IBM, Procter & Gamble, Gillette, Eastman Kodak, Avon, McDonald's, Xerox, General Electric, and Caterpillar—are *master marketers*. The rest of them practice average marketing and are in a position of high marketing vulnerability as their markets shift and their competitors start to work harder or smarter.

The marketing function is not fully developed in most companies today for a number of reasons:

1. *Recent origins of marketing.* Marketing is a relatively new business discipline that is too often confused with one of its subfunctions, such as sales or advertising.
2. *Hostility toward marketing.* Marketing is normally resisted by vested interests in the company and must fight an uphill battle to establish its role, scope, and authority.
3. *Law of slow learning.* Marketing passes through several stages of misconception as it grows in the company.
4. *Law of fast forgetting.* Marketing principles tend to be forgotten with success, and executives have to be reminded of them periodically.

These propositions are examined in the following paragraphs.

RECENT ORIGINS OF MARKETING

How old is marketing? This question always brings about interesting speculations. Some people date marketing as beginning with earliest man and call it the world's oldest profession. Some even say marketing predates man. Consider the following case for subspecies marketing:

> I do not think it would be stretching the point too far to say that the reproductive cycle of plants is a natural exchange for profit system. After all, a flower, with its colour and perfume, is an advertisement for nectar. The exchange deal is quite straightforward—the bee has the nectar in return for pollen it has picked up elsewhere and for taking that flower's pollen onto the next one. At the next stage of the cycle the colour and perfume of the fruit is an advertisement for food. The bird eats the fruit and distributes the seeds in return.[5]

Others advance the argument that marketing began when mankind first engaged in exchange, that is, when two parties with surpluses resorted to barter as an alternative to employing force, stealing, or begging to obtain goods. Barter

[5] F.H. Elsby, in private correspondence.

evolved into the fine art of selling which received high expression in very early civilizations.

Peter Drucker thinks marketing first arose in the seventeenth century—and in Japan, not in the West.

> Marketing was invented in Japan around 1650 by the first member of the Mitsui family to settle in Tokyo as a merchant and to open what might be called the first department store. He anticipated by a full 250 years basic Sears, Roebuck policies: to be the buyer for his customers; to design the right products for them, and to develop sources for their production; the principle of your money back and no questions asked; and the idea of offering a large assortment of products to his customers rather than focusing on a craft, a product category, or a process.[6]

Drucker then suggests that marketing did not appear in the West until the middle nineteenth century at the International Harvester Company.

> The first man in the West to see marketing clearly as the unique and central function of the business enterprise, and the creation of a customer as the specific job of management, was Cyrus H. McCormick (1809–1884). The history books mention only that he invented a mechanical harvester. But he also invented the basic tools of modern marketing: market research and market analysis, the concept of market standing, pricing policies, the service salesman, parts and service supply to the customer, and installment credit.[7]

Yet another fifty years had to pass before marketing became very visible on the academic or business scene in America. The term *marketing* first appeared in college course titles in the early 1900s. In 1905, W. E. Kreusi taught a course at the University of Pennsylvania entitled "The Marketing of Products."[8] In 1910, Ralph Starr Butler offered a course entitled "Marketing Methods" at the University of Wisconsin. Butler explained how he conceived marketing:

> In considering the whole field of selling I developed the idea that personal salesmanship and advertising had to do simply with the final expression of the selling idea. My experience with the Procter & Gamble Company had convinced me that a manufacturer seeking to market a product had *to consider and solve a large number of problems* before he ever gave expression to the selling idea by sending a salesman on the road or inserting an advertisement in a publication. [italics added][9]

Marketing departments within business firms had their roots in the development of marketing research in the early twentieth century. The Curtis Publishing Company in 1911 installed the first marketing research department (called commercial research at the time) under the direction of Charles C. Parlin. Marketing research departments were subsequently established at U.S.

[6] Peter F. Drucker, *Management: Tasks, Responsibilities, Practices* (New York: Harper & Row, 1973), p. 62.

[7] Ibid.

[8] Robert Bartels, *The History of Marketing Thought,* 2nd ed. (Columbus, Ohio: Grid, 1976), p. 24.

[9] Ibid.

Rubber (1916) and Swift and Company (1917).[10] These departments were viewed as adjuncts to the sales department. Their task was to develop information that would make it easier for sales departments to sell. Over time, marketing research departments accepted additional responsibilities, such as sales analysis and marketing administration. Some time later, companies began to combine marketing research, advertising, customer services, and other miscellaneous marketing functions into marketing departments.

Marketing entered into the consciousness of different industries at different times. A few companies, such as General Electric, General Motors, Sears, and Procter & Gamble, saw its potentialities early. Marketing spread most rapidly in consumer packaged goods companies, consumer durable companies, and industrial equipment companies—in that order. Industrial commodity companies—steel, chemical, paper—came later to marketing consciousness, and still have a long way to go. In the last decade, consumer service firms—especially airlines and banks—have opened themselves to marketing. Airlines began to study travelers' attitudes toward different features of their service—schedule frequency, baggage handling, in-flight service, friendliness, seat comfort. Soon afterwards they shed the notion they were in the air carrier business and began to operate on the idea that they were in the total travel business. Bankers initially showed great resistance to marketing but in the end embraced it enthusiastically. Marketing has begun to attract interest in the insurance industry and the stock brokerage industry, although marketing is still poorly understood in these industries.

Marketing's most recent entry has been in the nonprofit sector of the economy. Such diverse organizations as colleges, hospitals, police departments, museums, and symphonies are currently taking a look at marketing. Marketing has attracted different degrees of interest and understanding in these various industries. American colleges and universities, troubled with declining enrollments, are eager to try out marketing ideas in their admissions operation. An increasing number of hospitals are beginning to look seriously into marketing as their bed counts go down. As a sign of the times, the Evanston Hospital of Evanston, Illinois, recently appointed the world's first vice president of marketing for a hospital.

What leads companies to suddenly discover marketing? An interest in marketing can be triggered by any of five circumstances:

1. *Sales decline.* This is the most common cause. For example, newspaper publishers are experiencing falling circulation as more people turn to television news. Some publishers are beginning to realize that they know very little about why people read newspapers and what they want out of newspapers. These publishers are commissioning consumer research and, on the basis of the findings, attempting to redesign newspapers to be contemporary, relevant, and interesting to readers.

2. *Slow growth.* Companies often reach the limits of their growth in their given industries and start to cast about for new markets. They recognize that they need marketing know-how if they are to successfully identify, evaluate, and select new opportunities. Dow Chemical, wanting new sources of profits, decided to enter consumer markets and invested heavily in acquiring marketing expertise to carry out the job.

3. *Changing buying patterns.* Many companies are experiencing increasingly turbulent markets marked by rapidly changing customer wants. These companies

---

[10] Ibid., pp. 124–25.

must adopt a marketing orientation in order to keep producing value for the buyers.

4. *Increasing competition.* A complacent company may suddenly be attacked by a master marketer and forced to learn marketing to meet the challenge. Consider the following:

> In the late 1950s when P&G moved into paper products, Scott Paper didn't pay much attention. From a standing start P&G has built a $1.3-billion business in toilet and facial tissues and diapers. Along the way it reduced Scott . . . to an also-ran, earning last year a paltry 4.3% on its total assets, versus P&G's 10.3%.[11]

5. *Increasing sales expenditures.* A company's expenditures for advertising, sales promotion, marketing research, and customer service, may increase without rhyme or reason. When management sees that happening, it often decides to improve its organization and control of these marketing functions.

HOSTILITY TOWARD MARKETING

For all these reasons, companies sooner or later are forced to improve their marketing capacity. Yet marketing is rarely greeted with open arms. Many financial and manufacturing executives see marketing as glorified "hucksterism" and as a threat to their power and status. Some marketers contribute to this by their aggressiveness and overclaiming of the results that stem from marketing.

The nature of marketing's threatening quality is illustrated in Figure 1-1. Initially, the sales/marketing function is seen as one of several *equally* important business functions in a check-and-balance relationship (Fig. 1-1A). A dearth of demand then leads marketers to argue that their function is somewhat more important than the others (Fig. 1-1B). A few marketing enthusiasts go further and say marketing is the major function of the enterprise, for without customers, there would be no company. They put marketing at the center with other business functions serving as support functions (Fig. 1-1C). This view incenses the other managers, who do not want to think of themselves as working for marketing. Enlightened marketers clarify the issue by putting the customer rather than marketing at the center of the company (Fig. 1-1D). They argue for a *customer orientation* in which all functions work together to sense, serve, and satisfy the customer. Finally, some marketers say that marketing still needs to command a central position in the firm if customers' needs are to be correctly interpreted and efficiently satisfied (Fig. 1-1E).

The marketer's argument for the concept of the corporation shown in Fig. 1–1E is summarized as follows:

1. The assets of the firm have little value without the existence of customers.
2. The key task of the firm is therefore to create and hold customers.
3. Customers are attracted through promises and held through satisfaction.
4. Marketing's task is to define an appropriate promise to the customer and to insure the delivery of satisfaction.
5. The actual satisfaction delivered to the customer is affected by the performance of the other departments.
6. Marketing needs influence or control over these other departments if customers are to be satisfied.

[11] Paul Gibson, "Procter & Gamble: It's Got a Little List," *Forbes*, March 20, 1978, p. 34.

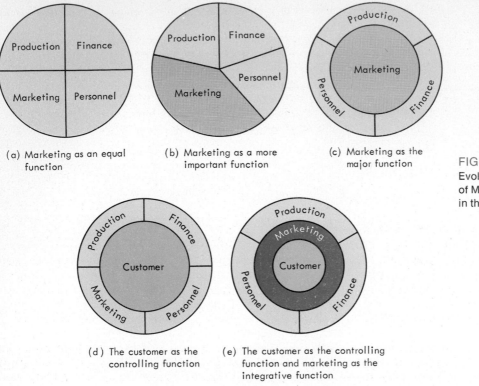

(a) Marketing as an equal function

(b) Marketing as a more important function

(c) Marketing as the major function

(d) The customer as the controlling function

(e) The customer as the controlling function and marketing as the integrative function

FIGURE 1–1
Evolving Views
of Marketing's Role
in the Company

Consider the following situation. The Moonrise Company (name disguised) is a manufacturer of high-quality packaged sliced meats—bacon, ham, bologna, and salami. The company's products sell in U.S. supermarkets at a premium price to match their premium quality. The vice president of marketing sees the Moonrise name as making a promise to the customer that the products are of consistently high quality. Yet from time to time, the manufacturing people fail to exercise adequate quality control; for example, some fatty bacon will be packaged instead of being discarded. Some consumers will find that they have paid a premium price for poor-quality bacon. The company's implicit promise to the customer has been broken. The resulting dissatisfaction can lead to customer loss. Marketing wants the power to insure that this does not happen by asking for some influence or control over manufacturing.

Customer satisfaction can be hurt in other ways. Poor production scheduling might result in late deliveries to the trade and out-of-stock conditions facing the customer. Poor research in the research and development (R&D) department may lead to new products that fail to satisfy real customer needs. Inadequte funds allocated to marketing may prevent the development of improved packaging. The interests of different departments often come into conflict.[12] Marketing's continuous effort to keep every department's attention riveted on producing customer satisfaction interferes with the felt autonomy of

[12] For a discussion of conflicts between marketing and other departments, see chap. 22, pp. 592–96.

these departments. It is no wonder that the other departments react with some hostility to marketing for trying to take center stage in the firm.

Not only is marketing an issue in industries where it is well established but it is a hot issue in industries that are on the brink of marketing. In the law, accounting, and medical professions, a few practitioners have advocated liberalizing the professions' canons of ethics to permit more explicit marketing of professional services. For example, lawyers have already won the right to advertise, and that is causing considerable consternation among many lawyers who regard marketing as unprofessional and unbecoming. Marketing is a growing issue in college and hospital circles, as these institutions struggle to find enough clients for their services. Those colleges and hospitals that have established marketing positions face the animosity of professors and doctors who consider marketing of their service to be degrading. In the newspaper industry, the hostility of old-liners is shown by one newspaper editor who wrote a diatribe entitled "Beware the 'Market' Thinkers."[13] This editor warned newspapers not to let marketers in because they do not understand the function of newspapers, which is to print news. Marketing is not the solution, he feels, to the national decline in newspaper readership. Marketers would corrupt all that is good about today's newspapers.

LAW OF SLOW LEARNING

In spite of resistance in many quarters, most companies eventually allow some marketing to enter their hallowed doors. Marketing is not allowed to enter full blown, ready to work its magic. Marketing is allowed to enter in highly constrained forms so as not to provoke too much opposition. The company adds a single advertising manager or a marketing research manager who can hardly cause any trouble. It does not hire a vice president of marketing to bring in a full marketing orientation. It takes years for a company to arrive at a mature understanding of marketing. Even with determination and a clear understanding of marketing, it may take the firm five to ten years to build a well-functioning marketing organization.

In the typical company, marketing enlightenment grows slowly and tends to pass through five distinct stages. The stages are described below in the context of the banking industry.

Before the mid-1950s, banks had no understanding or regard for marketing. Banks were supplying needed services. They did not have to make a case for checking accounts, savings, loans, or safe-deposit boxes. The bank building was created in the image of a Greek temple calculated to impress the public with the bank's importance and solidity. The interior was austere, and the tellers rarely smiled. One lending officer arranged his office so that a prospective borrower would sit across from his massive desk on a lower chair than his own. The office window was located behind the officer's back and the sun would pour in on the hapless customer as he or she tried to explain why he or she needed a loan. This was the bank's posture before the age of marketing.

---

[13] William H. Hornby, "Beware the 'Market' Thinkers," *The Quill*, 1976, pp. 14 ff. However, see William A. Mindak, "Do Newspaper Publishers Suffer from 'Marketing Myopia'?" *Journalism Quarterly*, summer 1965, pp. 433–42.

Marketing Is Advertising, Sales Promotion, and Publicity

Marketing came into banks in the late 1950s, not in the form of the "marketing concept" but in the form of the "advertising and promotion concept." Banks and other financial institutions were experiencing increased competition for savings. A few financial institutions decided to adopt the marketing tools of the soap companies. They established budgets for advertising and sales promotion and managed to attract many new customers. Their competitors were forced into adopting the same measures and scurried out to hire advertising agencies and promotion experts.

Marketing Is Smiling and a Friendly Atmosphere

The banks that first introduced modern advertising and promotion soon found their advantage cancelled by the rush of imitators. They also learned another lesson: Attracting people to a bank is easy; converting them to loyal customers is hard. These banks began to formulate a larger concept of marketing, that of trying to please the customer. Bankers had to learn to smile. The tellers had to be retrained. The bars had to be taken off the tellers' windows. The interior of the banks had to be redesigned to produce a warm, friendly atmosphere. Even the outside Greek-temple architecture had to be changed.

The first banks to implement this change began to outperform their competitors in attracting and holding new customers. However, their competitors quickly figured out what was happening and rushed into programs of institutionalizing thoroughgoing friendliness. Soon all banks became so friendly that it was impossible for a customer to find an unfriendly bank. Friendliness became so widespread that it lost its potency as a determinant factor in bank choice.

Marketing Is Innovation

Banks had to search for a new basis for differential advantage. Bankers who read Professor Levitt's article "Marketing Myopia"[14] began to realize that marketing transcends advertising and friendliness, although those are important ingredients. Banks are not narrowly in the savings business: They are in the business of meeting the varied and changing financial needs of customers. These banks began to think in terms of continuous innovation of new and valued customer services, such as credit cards, Christmas savings plans, and automatic bank loans. Bank of America, for example, today offers over 350 financial products to customers.

A successful innovation provides the innovative bank with a competitive lead. However, financial services are easily copied and advantages are short-lived. But, if the same bank invests in continuous innovation, it should stay ahead of the other banks in its area.

Marketing Is Positioning

What happens when all banks advertise, smile, and innovate? Clearly they begin to look alike. They are forced to find a new basis for distinction. They begin to realize that no bank can be the best bank for all customers. No bank can offer all products. A bank must choose. It must examine its opportunities and "take a position" in the market.

Positioning goes beyond image making. The image-making bank seeks to cultivate an image in the customer's mind as a large, friendly, or efficient bank. It often develops a symbol, such as a lion (Harris Bank in Chicago) or kangaroo (Continental Bank in Chicago) to dramatize its personality in a distinctive way. Yet the customer may see the competing banks as basically alike, except for the chosen symbols. Positioning is an attempt to distinguish the bank from its competitors along real dimensions in order to be the preferred bank to certain segments of the market. Positioning aims to help customers know the real differences between competing banks so that they can match themselves to the bank that can be of most value to them.

[14] Theodore Levitt, "Marketing Myopia," *Harvard Business Review*, September–October 1965, pp. 26–44, 173–81.

There is a still higher concept of bank marketing that represents the ultimate essence of modern marketing. The issue is whether the bank has installed effective systems for market analysis, planning, and control. One large bank, which had achieved sophistication in advertising, friendliness, innovation, and positioning, nevertheless lacked good systems of marketing planning and control. Each new fiscal year, commercial loan officers submitted their volume goal, usually a figure 10 percent higher than the previous year's goal. They also requested a budget increase of 10 percent. No rationale or plans accompanied these submissions. Top management was satisfied with its officers who achieved their goals. One loan officer, judged to be a good performer, retired and was replaced by a younger man, who proceeded to increase the loan volume 50 percent the following year! The bank painfully learned that it had failed to measure the potentials of its various markets, to require marketing plans, to set quotas, and to develop appropriate reward systems.

Thus, financial institutions demonstrate a law of slow learning with regard to grasping the revolutionary character of marketing. This pattern is repeated as marketing enters each new industry. The interesting question is whether organizations must go through these stages to learn their marketing or whether they can come to it more quickly. The truth is that each stage is so revolutionary in its potential not only for business growth but also for internal disruption that perhaps institutions are wise in coming to terms with marketing one step at a time. As each stage is installed and proves itself, it makes company management more receptive to further advances in marketing thought and practice.

LAW OF FAST FORGETTING

Even after marketing is installed in an organization and matures through the various stages, management must fight a strong tendency to forget basic marketing principles. Management tends to forget marketing principles in the wake of success. For example, a number of major American companies entered European markets in the 1950s and 1960s expecting to achieve high success with their sophisticated products and marketing capabilities. A number of them failed, and a major reason is they forgot the marketing maxim: Know your market and know how to satisfy it. American companies came into these markets with their current products and advertising programs instead of building them up on the basis of what the market needed. General Mills went into the British market with its Betty Crocker cake mixes only to have to withdraw a short time later. Angel cake and devil's food cake sounded too exotic for British housewives. And many housewives felt that such professional-looking cakes as those pictured on the Betty Crocker packages must be hard to make. American marketers failed to appreciate the major cultural variations between and even within European countries and the need to start where the consumers are, not where their products are. Sorenson noted:

> In the United States, the marketing concept appears to be well into the mature phase of its own life cycle. It is increasingly being questioned, criticized, and—in some instances—ignored or discarded. By contrast, the marketing concept in Europe is alive and vigorous and just entering the rapid growth stage of its life cycle.[15]

[15] Ralph Z. Sorenson II, "U.S. Marketers Can Learn from European Innovators," *Harvard Business Review*, September–October 1972, p. 97.

There is a tendency in successful firms toward marketing regression—going back to an earlier stage of marketing thinking, for instance, seeing marketing primarily as sales and promotion. A good illustration is the case of a management consulting firm that was founded with the objective of achieving sustained long-term growth.[16] The firm's management developed a long-range plan based on the application of the following marketing principles:

1. Marketing was recognized as a company-wide activity with clearly defined areas of responsibility. Staff men and supervisors were expected to work on expanding services to existing clients; officers were expected to develop new clients and to close sales leads opened by the staff.

2. There was a carefully planned and vigorous program for building referral sources. Each officer belonged to several clubs and associations. Bank contacts were pursued systematically as a source of leads. Officers were encouraged to fill speaking engagements or to write articles.

3. Frequent meetings were held to coordinate and plan new business development activities. Training sessions were conducted to improve new business development skills.

4. A public relations consultant was retained to obtain favorable newspaper and trade paper publicity. Seminars were held from time to time on important management techniques.

5. Every effort was made to motivate new business development activity. Staff men were paid bonuses for successful leads. Ability to generate new business was made a significant element in promotion to supervisor and the major element in promotion to officer. Officers' compensation was based almost entirely on the volume and rate of growth of the client assignments under their supervision.

Within ten years, this program produced outstanding results. Fee billings had risen to over $4 million a year from offices located in six major cities. However, this represented a high point from which the firm began a decline, at first slowly and then precipitously. As the fortunes of the company declined, the organization fell into disarray. All the branch offices were closed. Several officers resigned to establish their own consulting firms.

The reversal of the company's fortunes was not the result of new factors or conditions in the marketplace. Rather the company paid a deferred penalty for long-term overemphasis on selling to the detriment of marketing. Having committed itself to a rapid growth goal, it neglected other things, specifically:

1. The original objective was for a sustained rate of growth of over 15 percent a year. This rate was achieved, but the effort involved did not leave sufficient time for the acquisition, training, and development of the professional staff. The firm was developing business at a rate somewhat faster than it was developing the capacity to handle it.

2. This problem was exacerbated by the effects of the emphasis placed on new-business development and the methods that were adopted to motivate it. Staff men perceived that high awards were given for business development but not necessarily for professional excellence. A number of staff men of great professional promise, but with little interest in selling, left the firm to join competitors. The multiplier effect of these resignations increased the difficulty of coordinating staff development with growth.

[16] This description is taken from a letter from a well-known management consultant, who prefers anonymity.

3. In view of the fact that officers were selected primarily for their ability to develop new business, they occasionally lacked the technical background to supervise properly the assignments handled by their own staff, who were more likely to have been selected on the basis of proven professional skills. The difference in compensation between officers and staff consultants was substantial, giving rise to poor morale, increasing the problem of turnover, and making it impossible to give proper supervision to complex and important assignments.

4. The high financial rewards for new-business development led to savage competition and infighting between company officers and contributed to an unhealthy atmosphere throughout the firm.

Thus a firm can overemphasize the job of selling to the detriment of really serving the customers' interests. An intense passion for volume and growth can ultimately hurt quality and long-run profitability. Companies have to constantly remind themselves that the name of the business game is not short-term sales but long-run profitability. And long-run profitability is attained not through hard selling but through sound customer-oriented marketing, which produces value and long-run buyer satisfaction.

THE HIGHER PURPOSE OF MARKETING

This brings us to the final question in this chapter. What is the higher purpose of marketing? What should an enlightened marketer try to accomplish?

This question is raised because managers sometimes lose sight of their ultimate goals and settle for short-term gains of dubious benefit to themselves and others. When they lose a sense of higher purpose, their work becomes unsatisfying and their attitude cynical.

Different goals have been proposed to guide the marketing practitioner. The most common view is that the marketer's goal is to maximize the market's *consumption* of whatever the company is producing. In this view, the marketer is a technician who engineers sales gains. Marketing success means selling more and more gum, cars, and ice cream bars as if the consumer were a huge consumption machine that must constantly be stuffed with goods and services. Even if consumers don't want this much consumption, it is good for the economy and creates jobs. Yet Adam Smith observed that hunger is limited by the size of the human stomach. More generally, people will eventually run out of time to consume all that they could buy. They may rebel against overeating and overdressing, and start thinking "enough is enough" or even "less is more." Frederick Pohl wrote a science-fiction short story, "The Midas Touch," in which factories are completely automated and the goods roll out continuously and people consume as much as they can in order not to be buried under the goods. In the story, ordinary people are given high consumption quotas, while the elite are excused from having to consume so much. Furthermore, the elite are given the few jobs that are still left to do, so that they don't have to face the bleakness of no work.

A sounder goal for the marketer is to aim to maximize *consumer satisfaction*. The marketer's task is to track changing consumer wants and influence the company to adjust its mix of goods and services to those that are needed. The marketer makes sure that the company continues to produce value for the target customer markets.

Even consumer satisfaction, however, is not a complete goal for the marketer. The act of creating "goods" to satisfy human desires also creates some "bads" in the process. Every car that is produced satisfies a transportation need and at the same time contributes to the level of pollution in society. The economist Kenneth Arrow noted that high gross national product also means high gross national pollution. The sensitive marketer has to take responsibility for the totality of outputs created by the business. First, the marketer is a member of the public and therefore victimizing himself to some extent. Second, the society has spawned consumerists, environmentalists, and other public-action groups, who make life difficult for those firms that are indifferent to the "bads" they create in the process of pursuing profits.

Ultimately, the enlightened marketer is really trying to contribute to the *quality of life*. The quality of life is a function of the quantity and need-satisfying quality of goods and services, the quality of the physical environment, and the quality of the cultural environment. Too often the firm rests its case on its ability to produce great quantities of goods and services and does not pay enough attention to its impact on the other components of life quality.

Profits will still be a major test of business success in serving society. However, as Drucker observes, profits are really a by-product of doing business well and not the moral aim of business. Business, like other institutions of society, prospers only by maintaining legitimacy in the eyes of consumers, employees, and the general public. Legitimacy is grounded in the institution's commitment to serve higher moral aims.

SUMMARY

Marketing—the management of exchange processes and relationships—is the cornerstone discipline of some of the most successful companies in America and a discipline of growing interest to companies and nonprofit organizations throughout the world. All organizations face the problem of how to increase value for target markets that are undergoing continuously changing needs and wants. Organizations must thoughtfully define their products, services, prices, communications, and distribution in a way that meets real buyer needs in a competitively viable way. That is the task of marketing.

Although selling is a very old subject, marketing is a relatively new subject. It represents a higher-order integration of many separate functions—selling, advertising, marketing research, new-product development, customer service, physical distribution—that impinge on customer needs and satisfaction. Many organizations at first resist marketing because it threatens vested interests within the organization and their own concepts of how to manage the organization effectively. Marketing gradually gets established, however, first as a promotion function, later as a customer service function, still later as an innovation function, then as a market positioning function, and ultimately as an analysis, planning, and control function. Few companies understand and install marketing in its full form when first considering it. Even after marketing is effectively implemented in an organization, there is a tendency for many managers to forget its main principles in the wake of success.

Marketing's task in the organization is not only to help it recognize business opportunities and serve the various publics but also to harness the organization's energy to enhance the quality of life in society.

1. There are several different approaches to the study of marketing. A *managerial* approach is one of them. What are some other possible approaches?

2. "Marketing is not simply the job of a group of people in the company who are responsible for selling the company's products. Every member of the firm should know how to function as a marketer." What does it mean for a company recruiter, for example, to function like a marketer?

3. A company president recently told the author: "I cannot see how marketing can be taught. The only way to learn marketing is to go out and try to sell something." How would you answer this?

4. The five stages through which many organizations pass as they develop their use of marketing were discussed in the context of the banking industry. Discuss them in the context of four-year private liberal arts colleges that are facing declining enrollment.

5. Do you think that the adoption of marketing by companies in developing nations will follow the same patterns as in the U.S.? Why?

6. What would a perfume company be doing differently in the way of marketing if its objective were to maximize sales? profits? consumer satisfaction? consumers' life styles? quality of life? In other words, how does the company's objective make a difference to its marketing practice?

7. What should the aim of marketing be in an affluent society? One prominent marketing educator said: "Herein lies a challenge for marketing: to justify and stimulate our age of consumption . . . to enjoy (the affluent life) without pangs of guilt." Would you defend this as an appropriate philosophy for the times?

8. "With the supermarkets as our temple and the singing commercial our litany, are we likely to fire the world with an irresistible vision of America's exalted purposes and inspiring way of life?" This statement by Adlai Stevenson suggests that business is too dominant and enshrined in American life. Do you agree?

Tasks and Philosophies of Marketing Management

Everyone lives by selling something.
ROBERT LOUIS STEVENSON

The purpose of this chapter is to describe how a marketer views social phenomena. A marketer thinks in a particular way, as does a psychologist, a sociologist, an economist, and a political scientist. The marketer is trained to think about a certain set of issues, concepts, and relationships. Obviously if a marketer and the other social scientists were all shown a supermarket, each would be interested in different aspects of it and interpret a supermarket's role in different ways.

We will look at the structure of marketing thought first in terms of *marketing,* then in terms of *marketing management,* and finally in terms of *marketing philosophies.*

MARKETING

Various definitions of marketing have appeared through time:

It has been described by one person or another as a business activity; as a group of related business activities; as a trade phenomenon; as a frame of mind; as a coordinative, integrative function in policy making; as a sense of business purpose; as an economic process; as a structure of institutions; as the process of exchanging or transferring ownership of products; as a process of concentration, equalization, and dispersion; as the creation of time, place, and possession utilities, as a process of demand and supply adjustment; and as many other things.[1]

All of these definitions provide useful but partial perspectives on the nature of marketing. We would like to propose a definition of marketing that is rooted in human behavior:

Marketing is human activity directed at satisfying needs and wants through exchange processes.

Human Needs and Wants

The starting point for the discipline of marketing lies in *human needs and wants.* Mankind needs food, air, water, clothing, and shelter to survive. Beyond this, people have a strong desire for recreation, education, and other services. They have strong preferences for particular versions of basic goods and services.

There is no doubt that people's needs and wants today are staggering. In one year, in the United States alone, Americans purchased 67 billion eggs, 250 million chickens, 5.5 million hair dryers, 133 billion domestic air travel passenger miles, and over 20 million lectures by college English professors. These consumer goods and services led to a derived demand for more fundamental products, such as 150 million tons of steel and 3.7 billion pounds of cotton. These are a few of the wants and needs that get expressed in a $1.3 trillion economy.

A useful distinction can be drawn between *needs, wants,* and *intentions,* although these words are used interchangeably in common speech. *A need is a state of felt deprivation of some generic satisfaction arising out of the human condition.* People require food, clothing, shelter, safety, belonging, esteem, and a few other things for survival. People actually need very little. These needs are not *created* by their society or by marketers; they exist in the very texture of human biology and the human condition.

Wants are desires for specific satisfiers of these ultimate needs. A person needs food and wants a steak, needs clothing and wants a Pierre Cardin suit, needs esteem and buys a Cadillac. While people's needs are few, their wants are many. Human wants are continually shaped and reshaped by social forces and institutions such as churches, schools, corporations, and families.

Intentions are decisions to acquire specific satisfiers under the given terms and conditions. Many persons want a Cadillac; only a few intend to buy one at today's prices.

These distinctions shed light on the frequent charge by marketing critics that "marketers create needs" or "marketers get people to buy things they don't need." Marketers do not create needs; needs preexist marketers. Marketers, along with other influentials in the society, influence wants. They suggest to consumers that a particular car would efficiently satisfy the person's need for esteem. Marketers do not create the need for esteem but try to point out how a particular good would satisfy that need. Marketers also try to influence persons' *intentions* to buy by making the product attractive, affordable, and easily available.

Products

The existence of human needs and wants gives rise to the concept of *products.* Our definition of product is very broad:

---

[1] Marketing staff of Ohio State University, "A Statement of Marketing Philosophy," *Journal of Marketing,* January 1965, p. 43.

A *product* is something that is viewed as capable of satisfying a need or want.

A product can be an *object, service, activity, person, place, organization,* or *idea.* Suppose a person feels depressed. What might the person do to get out of his or her depression? What products might meet the need to feel better? The person can turn on a television set (object); go to a movie (service); take up jogging (activity); see a therapist (person); travel to Hawaii (place); join a Lonely Hearts Club (organization); or adopt a different philosophy about life (idea). All of these things can be viewed as products available to the "feeling depressed." If the term *product* seems unnatural at times, we may substitute the term *resource* or *offer* or *satisfier* to describe that which may satisfy a need.

In the case of physical objects, it is important to distinguish between them and the services they represent. People do not buy physical objects for their own sake. A tube of lipstick is bought to supply a service: helping the person look better. A drill bit is bought to supply a service: making a needed hole. Every physical object is a means of packaging a service. The marketer's job is to sell the service packages built into physical products. The seller who becomes enamored of the physical features has a case of "marketing myopia." Fixated on the features, he loses sight of the function. He forgets that a physical object is a tool to solve a problem. People do not remain loyal to horses and carriages when the modern automobile meets their needs better.

Exchange The fact that people have needs and wants and the fact that there are products capable of satisfying them are necessary but not sufficient to define marketing. Marketing exists when people decide to satisfy needs and wants in a certain way that we shall call *exchange.* Exchange is one of four ways in which a person can obtain a product capable of satisfying a particular need.

The first option is *self-production.* A hungry person can relieve hunger through personal efforts at hunting, fishing, or fruit gathering. The person does not have to interact with anyone else. In this case there is no market and no marketing.

The second option is *coercion.* The hungry person can forcibly wrest food from another. No benefit is offered to the other party except the chance not to be harmed.

The third option is *supplication.* The hungry person can approach someone and beg for food. The supplicant has nothing tangible to offer except gratitude.

The fourth option is *exchange.* The hungry person can approach someone who has food and offer some resource in exchange, such as money, another good, or some service.

Marketing centers on that last approach to the acquisition of products to satisfy human needs and wants. Exchange assumes four conditions:

1. There are two parties.
2. Each party has something that could be of value to the other.
3. Each party is capable of communication and delivery.
4. Each party is free to accept or reject the offer.

If these conditions exist, there is a potential for exchange. Whether exchange actually takes place depends upon whether the two parties can find *terms of exchange* that will leave them both better off (or at least not worse off) than before the exchange. This is the sense in which exchange is described as a value-creating process; that is, exchange normally leaves both parties with a sense of having gained something of value.

Market The concept of exchange leads naturally into the concept of a market:

> A *market* is the set of all actual and potential buyers of a product.

An example will illustrate this concept. Suppose an artist spends three weeks creating a beautiful sculpture. He has in mind a particular price. The question he faces is whether there is anyone who will exchange this amount of money for the sculpture. If there is at least one such person, we can say there is a market. The *size of the market* will vary with the price. The artist may ask for so high a price that there is no market for his sculpture. As he brings the price down, normally the market size increases because more people can afford the sculpture. The size of the market depends upon the number of persons who have (1) an interest in the object, (2) the necessary resources, and (3) a willingness to offer the resources to obtain it. These three things make up the *level of demand*.

Wherever there is a potential for trade, there is a market. The term "market" is often used in conjunction with some qualifying term that describes a *human need* or *product type* or *demographic group* or *geographical location*. An example of a *need market* is the relaxation market, which exists because people are willing to exchange money for lessons on yoga, transcendental meditation, and disco dancing. An example of a *product market* is the shoe market, so defined because people are willing to exchange money for objects called shoes. An example of a *demographic market* is the youth market, so defined because young people possess purchasing power that they are willing to use for such products as education, bikinis, motorcycles, and stereophonic equipment. An example of a *geographic market* is the French market, so defined because French citizens are a locus of potential transactions for a wide variety of goods and services.

The concept of a market also covers exchanges of resources not necessarily involving money. The political candidate offers promises of good government to a *voter market* in exchange for their votes. The lobbyist offers services to a *legislative market* in exchange for votes for the lobbyist's cause. A university cultivates the *mass-media market* when it wines and dines editors in exchange for more publicity. A museum cultivates the *donor market* when it offers special privileges to contributors in exchange for their financial support.

Marketing The concept of markets finally brings us full circle to the concept of marketing. *Marketing* means working with *markets*, which in turn means attempting to actualize *potential exchanges* for the purpose of *satisfying human needs and wants*. Thus we return to our definition of *marketing* as *human activity directed at satisfying needs and wants through exchange processes*.

MARKETING MANAGEMENT

Coping with exchange processes calls for a considerable amount of work and skill. Persons become fairly adept at buying to meet their household needs. Occasionally, they also undertake selling—selling their car, selling personal services.

21

Organizations are more professional in handling exchange processes. They must attract resources from one set of markets, convert them into useful products, and trade them in another set of markets. *Nations* also plan and manage exchange relations with others. They search for beneficial trade relations and exchanges with other nations. In this book we will take the perspective primarily of *organizational marketing* rather than that of personal or national marketing.

Our position is that *marketing management* takes place when at least one party to a potential exchange gives thought to objectives and means of achieving desired responses from other parties. Our formal definition of marketing management is:

> *Marketing management* is the analysis, planning, implementation, and control of programs designed to create, build, and maintain mutually beneficial exchanges and relationships with target markets for the purpose of achieving organizational objectives. It relies on a disciplined analysis of the needs, wants, perceptions, and preferences of target and intermediary markets as the basis for effective product design, pricing, communication, and distribution.

Marketing management can occur in an organization in connection with any of its markets. Consider an automobile manufacturer. The vice president of personnel deals in the *labor market;* the vice president of purchasing, the *raw materials market;* and the vice president of finance, the *money market.* They have to set objectives and develop strategies for producing satisfactory results in these markets. Traditionally, however, these executives have not been called marketers or trained in marketing. Instead, marketing management is historically identified with tasks and personnel dealing with the *customer market.* We shall follow this convention, although what we shall say about marketing concepts and principles applies to all markets.

Marketing work in the customer market is carried out by sales managers, sales representatives, advertising and promotion managers, marketing researchers, customer service managers, product managers, market managers, and the marketing vice president. Each of these job positions goes along with well-defined missions and responsibilities. Many of these job positions center around the management of particular marketing *resources,* such as advertising, sales force, or marketing research. On the other hand, product managers, market managers, and the marketing vice president manage *programs.* Their job is to analyze, plan, and implement programs that will produce a desired level of transactions with specified target markets.

Marketing-Management Tasks

The popular image of the marketing manager is someone whose task is primarily to stimulate demand for the company's products. However, this is too limited a view of the range of marketing tasks carried out by marketing managers. *Marketing management has the task of regulating the level, timing, and character of demand in a way that will help the organization achieve its objectives.* Simply put, marketing management is demand management.

The organization forms an idea of a *desired level of transactions* with a market. At any time, the *actual demand level* may be below, equal to, or above the *desired demand level.* This leads to the eight distinguishable demand states listed in Table 2–1. The marketing task and the formal name of each task is shown next to each demand state.[2]

TABLE 2–1
The Basic Marketing Tasks

DEMAND STATE	MARKETING TASK	FORMAL NAME
I. Negative demand	Reverse demand	Conversional marketing
II. No demand	Create demand	Stimulational marketing
III. Latent demand	Develop demand	Developmental marketing
IV. Faltering demand	Revitalize demand	Remarketing
V. Irregular demand	Synchronize demand	Synchromarketing
VI. Full demand	Maintain demand	Maintenance marketing
VII. Overfull demand	Reduce demand	Demarketing
VIII. Unwholesome demand	Destroy demand	Countermarketing

Conversional marketing   Conversional marketing grows out of the state of negative demand. *Negative demand is a state in which all or most of the important segments of the potential market dislike the product or service and in fact might conceivably pay a price to avoid it.*

Negative demand, far from being a rare condition, applies to many products and services. Vegetarians feel negative demand for meats of all kinds. Numerous Americans feel negative demand for kidneys and sweetbreads. People have a negative demand for vaccinations, dental work, vasectomies, and gall bladder operations. Many travelers have a negative demand for air travel; others have a negative demand for rail travel. Places such as the North Pole and the desert wastelands are in negative demand by tourists. Atheism, ex-convicts, military service, and even work are in negative demand by certain groups.

The challenge of negative demand to marketing management, especially in the face of a positive supply, is to develop a plan that will cause demand to rise from negative to positive and eventually equal the positive supply level. We call this marketing task *conversional marketing.* Conversional marketing is one of the two most difficult tasks a marketer might face (the other is countermarketing). The marketer must discover whether the market resists the product because of beliefs, values, emotions, or costs and take appropriate measures. When the product is considered good for consumers (e.g., auto safety belts), the conversional marketer is a hero; when the product is considered bad (e.g., junk food), the conversional marketer is a villain.

Stimulational marketing   There is a whole range of products and services for which there is no demand. Instead of having negative or positive feelings toward the offer, people are indifferent or uninterested. *No demand is a state in which*

---

[2] This discussion is drawn from the author's "The Major Tasks of Marketing Management," *Journal of Marketing,* October 1973, pp. 42–49.

*all or important segments of a potential market are uninterested in or indifferent
to a particular offer.*

Three different categories of offers are characterized by no demand. First,
there are those familiar objects that are perceived as having no value. Examples
would be urban junk, such as Coke bottles, old barbed wire, and political buttons
right after an election. Second, there are those familiar objects that are recognized to have value but not in the particular market. Examples would include
boats in areas not near any water, snowmobiles in areas where it never snows,
and burglar alarms in areas where there is no crime. Third, there are those unfamiliar objects that are innovated and face a situation of no demand because the
relevant market has no knowledge of the object. Examples would include trin-
kets of all kinds that people might buy if exposed to them but would not normally think about.

The task of transforming no demand into positive demand is called *stimulational marketing.* Stimulational marketing is a tough task because the marketer
faces a market that does not have a felt want for the offer. He can proceed in
three ways. The first is to try to connect the product or service with some existing need in the marketplace. Thus antique dealers can attempt to stimulate interest in old barbed wire on the part of those who have a general need to collect
things. The second is to alter the environment so that the offer becomes valued
in that environment. Thus sellers of motorboats can attempt to stimulate interest
in boats in a lakeless community by building an artificial lake. The third is to distribute information or the object itself in more places in the hope that its pervasive presence leads to desire and purchase.

Developmental marketing   Developmental marketing is associated with a state
known as latent demand. *A state of latent demand exists when a substantial
number of people share a strong need for something that does not exist in the
form of an actual product or service.* The latent demand represents an opportunity for the marketing innovator to develop the product or service that people
have been wanting.

Examples of products and services in latent demand abound. Many cigarette smokers would like a good-tasting cigarette that does not contain nicotine
and tars damaging to health. Such a product breakthrough would be an instant
success, just as the first filter-tip cigarette won a sizable share of the market.
Many people would like a car that promised substantially more safety and substantially less pollution than existing cars. There is a strong latent demand for
fast city roads, efficient trains, uncrowded national parks, unpolluted major
cities, safe streets, and good television programs.

The process of effectively transforming latent demand into actual demand
is that of *developmental marketing.* The marketer must invest in marketing research and product development to bring about an offer that promises to satisfy
the latent demand.

Remarketing   All kinds of objects, services, activities, places, organizations, and
ideas eventually experience *faltering demand. Faltering demand is a state in
which the demand for a product or service is less than it used to be and where
further decline is expected in the absence of remedial efforts to revise the target
market, offer, and/or marketing effort.*

For example, railway travel has been a service in steady decline for a number of years, and it is badly in need of imaginative remarketing. Many churches have seen their membership thin out in the face of competition from secular recreations and activities. The downtown areas of many large cities are in need of remarketing. Many popular entertainers and political candidates lose their following and badly need remarketing.

The challenge of faltering demand is revitalization, and the marketing task involved is *remarketing*. Remarketing is based on the premise that it is possible in many cases to start a new life cycle for a declining product or service. *Remarketing is the search for new propositions for relating the offer to its potential markets.*

Synchromarketing An organization might be satisfied with the average level of demand but quite dissatisfied with its temporal pattern. Some seasons are marked by demand surging far beyond the supply capacity of the organization, and other seasons are marked by a wasteful underutilization of the organization's supply capacity. *Irregular demand is a state in which the current timing pattern of demand is marked by seasonal or volatile fluctuations that depart from the timing pattern of supply.*

Many examples of irregular demand can be cited. In mass transit much of the equipment is idle during the off-hours and in insufficient supply during the peak hours. Hotels in Miami Beach are insufficiently booked during the summer and overbooked in the winter. Hospital operating facilities are overbooked at the beginning of the week and underutilized toward the end of the week to meet physician preferences.

The marketing task of trying to resolve irregular demand is called *synchromarketing* because the effort is to bring the movements of demand and supply into better synchronization. Many marketing steps can be taken to alter the pattern of demand. For example, a museum that is undervisited on weekdays and overvisited on weekends could (a) shift its special events to weekdays instead of weekends, (b) advertise only its weekday programs, (c) charge a higher admission price during the weekends. In some cases a pattern of demand can be readily reshaped through simple changes in incentives or promotion; in other cases the reshaping may require years of patient effort to alter habits and desires.

Maintenance marketing The most desirable situation that a marketer faces is that of *full demand. Full demand is a state in which the current level and timing of demand is equal to the desired level and timing of demand.* Various products and services achieve this state from time to time. However, it is not a time for resting on one's laurels and doing perfunctory marketing. Market demand is subject to two erosive forces. One force is changing needs and tastes in the marketplace. The demand for barber services, as well as the demand for mass magazines and college educations, has undergone an unexpected decline because of changing market preferences. The other force is active competition. When a product is doing well, competitors quickly move in and attempt to attract away some of the demand.

The task of the marketer facing full demand is *maintenance marketing*. Maintenance marketing calls for maintaining efficiency in the carrying out of day-to-day marketing activities and eternal vigilance in spotting new forces that threaten to erode demand. The maintenance marketer is primarily concerned with tactical issues such as keeping the price right, keeping the sales force and dealers motivated, and keeping tight control over costs.

Demarketing   Sometimes the demand for a product or service begins to outpace the supply substantially. That is known as *overfull demand, a state in which demand exceeds the level at which the marketer feels able or motivated to supply it.*

The problem may be due to *temporary shortages,* as when producers suddenly find themselves facing an unexpected surge in demand or unexpected interruptions of supply. Or the problem may be due to *chronic overpopularity.* For example, the state of Oregon felt that too many people were moving to Oregon and spoiling its natural environment; and the city of San Francisco felt that too many motorists were using the Golden Gate bridge and weakening its structure.

The task of reducing overfull demand is called *demarketing. Demarketing deals with attempts to discourage customers in general or a certain class of customers in particular on either a temporary or a permanent basis.* Demarketing calls for marketing in reverse. Instead of encouraging customers, it calls for the art of discouraging them. Prices may be raised and product quality, service, promotion, and convenience may be reduced. Demarketers must have thick skins because they are not going to be popular with certain groups.[3]

Countermarketing   There are many products or services for which the demand may be judged unwholesome from the viewpoint of the consumer's welfare, the public's welfare, or the supplier's welfare. *Unwholesome demand is a state in which any demand is felt to be excessive because of undesirable qualities associated with the offer.* Classic examples of unselling efforts have revolved around the so-called vice products: alcohol, cigarettes, and hard drugs.

The task of trying to destroy the demand for something is called *countermarketing,* or *unselling.* Whereas demarketing tries to reduce the demand without impugning the product itself, countermarketing is an attempt to designate the product as intrinsically unwholesome. The offer may be the organization's own product, which it wishes to phase out, a competitor's product, or a third party's product, which is regarded as socially undesirable. Efforts by organized groups to countermarket undesirable social ideas or practices, or to promote desirable social ideas or practices, are called *social marketing.*[4]

MARKETING-MANAGEMENT PHILOSOPHIES

We have described marketing management as the conscious effort to achieve desired exchange outcomes with target markets. Now the question arises, What is the philosophy that guides these marketing efforts? What is the relative weight given to serving the interests of the *organization,* the *customers,* and *society?*

---

[3] See Philip Kotler and Sidney J. Levy, "Demarketing, Yes, Demarketing," *Harvard Business Review,* November–December 1971, pp. 74–80.

[4] See Philip Kotler and Gerald Zaltman, "Social Marketing: An Approach to Planned Social Change," *Journal of Marketing,* July 1971, pp. 3–12.

Very often these conflict. It is desirable that marketing activities be carried out under a clear concept of responsive and responsible marketing.

There are five alternative concepts under which business and other organizations can conduct their marketing activity.

The Production Concept

The production concept is one of the oldest concepts guiding sellers:

> The *production concept* is a management orientation that assumes that consumers will favor those products which are available and affordable, and that therefore the major task of management is to pursue improved production and distribution efficiency.

The implicit premises of the production concept are:

1. Consumers are primarily interested in product availability and low price.
2. Consumers know the prices of the competing brands.
3. Consumers do not see or attach much importance to nonprice differences within the product class.
4. The organization's task is to keep improving production and distribution efficiency and lowering costs as the key to attracting and holding customers.

The production concept is an appropriate philosophy of management in two types of situations. The first is where the demand for a product exceeds supply. Here consumers are ready to buy any versions of the product they can find. Thus companies in developing nations that are able to sell all they produce put their energy into improving production. The second situation is where the product's cost is high and has to be brought down to expand the market. Texas Instruments provides a contemporary example of the production concept:[5]

> Texas Instruments, the Dallas-based electronics firm, is the leading American exponent of the "get-out-production, cut-the-price" philosophy that Henry Ford pioneered in the early 1900s in connection with developing the market for automobiles. Ford put all of his talent into perfecting the mass production of automobiles to bring down their costs so that Americans could afford them. Texas Instruments puts all of its efforts in building production volume and improving technology in order to bring down costs. It uses its lower costs to cut prices and expand the market size. It goes after and usually achieves the dominant position in its markets. It has become number one in pocket calculators and is about to do the same with digital watches, having recently introduced a $10 model, and is hoping to bring down the price in the early 1980s to somewhere around $5. To Texas Instruments, marketing means one thing: bringing down the price to buyers. This orientation is also found in many Japanese companies and makes Texas Instruments well prepared to compete with them in world markets.[5]

Service and nonprofit organizations also follow the production concept when they focus their main energy on achieving work efficiency. Many medical and dental practices are organized on assembly line principles, as are some gov-

[5] "Texas Instruments Shows U.S. Business How to Survive in the 1980s," *Business Week*, September 18, 1978, pp. 66ff.

ernment agencies, such as unemployment offices and license bureaus. While this type of management results in the handling of many cases per hour, it is open to the charge of impersonality and consumer insensitivity.

The Product Concept

The product concept is another venerable concept guiding sellers.

> The *product concept* is a management orientation that assumes that consumers will favor those products that offer the most quality for the price, and therefore the organization should devote its energy to improving product quality.

The implicit premises of the product concept are:

1. Consumers buy products rather than solutions to needs.
2. Consumers are primarily interested in product quality.
3. Consumers know the quality and feature differences of the competing brands.
4. Consumers choose among competing brands on the basis of obtaining the most quality for their money.
5. The organization's task is to keep improving product quality as the key to attracting and holding customers.

The best-known example of the product concept is the manufacturer who built a better mousetrap.[6] He followed Emerson's advice: "If a man . . . makes a better mousetrap . . . the world will beat a path to his door." But to his surprise, he found few customers panting at his door. People do not automatically learn about new and improved products, believe that they are really superior, or show a willingness to pay a higher price. The inventor of a better mousetrap will get nowhere unless he or she takes positive steps to design, package, and price the new product attractively, place it into convenient distribution channels, bring it to the attention of persons concerned with rodent problems, and convince them that it has superior qualities. He should even have considered whether people want mousetraps in the first place as opposed to other solutions that could have been developed to meet this problem.

Companies can be found in all fields that tend to operate on a product concept. Railroad management was so sure that it had a superior form of transportation that it underserved the customers and overlooked the emerging challenge of the airlines, buses, trucks, and automobiles. In another vein, a manufacturer of office files complained that his files should be selling better because they are the best in the world. "They can be dropped from a four-story building and not be damaged." "Yes," agreed his sales manager, "but our customers aren't planning to use this feature." Too often product-oriented manufacturers fall in love with their products and think of marketing as simply proving to customers they are the best of their kind. An example is provided by the Elgin National Watch Company:[7]

---

[6] See "So We Made a Better Mousetrap," *The President's Forum*, Fall 1962, pp. 26–27.

[7] The full case is described in Ralph Westfall and Harper W. Boyd, Jr., *Cases in Marketing Management* (Homewood, Ill.: Richard D. Irwin, 1961), pp. 16–24.

> Since its founding in 1864, the Elgin National Watch Company had enjoyed a reputation as one of America's finest watchmakers. Elgin placed its major emphasis on maintaining a superior product and merchandising it through a large network of leading jewelry and department stores. Its sales rose continuously until 1958, and thereafter its sales and market share began to slip. What happened to undermine Elgin's dominant position?
>
> Essentially, Elgin's management was so enamored with fine, traditionally styled watches that it didn't notice the major changes taking place in the consumer watch market. With regard to *customers,* many of them were losing interest in the idea that a watch needed superior timekeeping accuracy, had to carry a prestigious name, and last a lifetime. They expected a watch to tell time, look attractive, and not cost too much. Consumers had growing desires for convenience (self-winding watches), durability (waterproof and shockproof watches), and economy (pin-lever watches). With regard to *channels,* an increasing number of watches were being sold through mass-distribution outlets and discount stores. This suggested that many Americans wanted to avoid the higher markups of the local jeweler, and also that buying watches had impulse characteristics that could be exploited by increased store exposure, with resulting increased sales. With regard to *competitors,* many had added lower-priced watches to their line and had begun to sell them through mass-distribution channels. Elgin's problem was that it had riveted its attention to a set of products instead of interpreting and serving a changing set of wants.

Nonprofit organizations frequently exhibit a product orientation. Opera companies assume that the public will want the standard fare of Mozart, Verdi, and Puccini year after year. Colleges assume that high school graduates will continue to want their product. Churches, police departments, and the post office feel that they are offering the public the right product and that the public should be grateful. This concentration on the purity and immutability of the product eventually gets these organizations into deep trouble, as many are finding out. These organizations too often are looking in a mirror when they should be looking out of the window.

The Selling Concept

The selling concept (also called the sales concept) is another hallowed way in which producers have sought to guide their exchange activity.

> The *selling concept* is a management orientation that assumes that consumers will either not buy or not buy enough of the organization's products unless the organization makes a substantial effort to stimulate their interest in its products.

The implicit premises of the selling concept are:

1. Consumers have a normal tendency to resist buying most things that are not essential.
2. Consumers can be induced to buy more through various sales-stimulating devices.
3. The organization's task is to organize a strong sales-oriented department as the key to attracting and holding customers.

Companies practicing the selling concept typically assume their goods are "sold, not bought." For example, insurance agents hold that people do not feel a strong need for insurance and do not beat a path to their door; therefore it is necessary to aggressively search out potential customers and hard-sell them on the benefits of insurance. The same philosophy pervades the thinking of encyclopedia and bible companies, land developers, and home repair contractors. Auto dealers often are prime practitioners of the selling concept:

> From the moment the customer walks into the showroom, the auto salesman will engage in "psyching him out," exaggerating, baiting, and occasionally lying. The new model is described as an excellent car. If the customer likes the floor model, he may be told that there is another customer about to buy it and that he should decide as soon as possible. If the customer balks at the price (which is artificially high to begin with), the salesman offers to talk to the manager to get a special concession. The customer waits ten minutes and the salesman returns with "the boss doesn't like it but I got him to agree." The aim is to "work up the customer" to buy then and there.[8]

Obviously, there are great risks in practicing the selling concept, especially in its hard-driving form where customer satisfaction is considered secondary to getting the sale. This practice will spoil the market for this seller in that eventually there will be no customers who trust him. For the selling concept to work for an extended period of time, the following circumstances are required:

1. Many of the customers come in knowing that the dealers are hard sellers and feel they can handle the situation.
2. Customers who are dissatisfied soon forget their dissatisfaction.
3. Dissatisfied customers do not talk very much to other customers.
4. Dissatisfied customers probably will not complain to consumer organizations.
5. There are a great number of potential customers out there; the company does not have to depend upon repeat business.

Although we have used business organizations to illustrate the selling concept, it is frequently practiced by nonprofit organizations as well. A perfect example is the political party seeking votes for its candidate. Having chosen a candidate on whatever grounds, it must vigorously sell this candidate to the voters as a fantastic person for the job.[9] The candidate and his or her supporters stomp through voting precincts from early morning to late evening shaking hands, kissing babies, meeting power brokers, making breezy speeches. Countless dollars are spent on radio and television advertising, posters, and mailings. Any flaws in the candidate are shielded from the public because the aim is to get the sale, not worry about postpurchase satisfaction. After the election, the new official continues to take a sales-oriented view toward the citizens. There is little research into what the public wants and a lot of selling to get the public to accept policies that the politician or party wants.

[8] See Irving J. Rein, *Rudy's Red Wagon: Communication Strategies in Contemporary Society* (Glenview, Ill.: Scott, Foresman & Company, 1972).

[9] See Joseph McGinness, *The Selling of the President* (New York: Trident Press, 1969).

The Marketing Concept

The marketing concept is a more recent idea in the history of exchange relations.[10]

> The *marketing concept* is a management orientation that holds that the key task of the organization is to determine the needs and wants of target markets and to adapt the organization to delivering the desired satisfactions more effectively and efficiently than its competitors.

In short, the marketing concept says "find wants and fill them" rather than "create products and sell them." This orientation is reflected in various contemporary ads: "Have it your way" (Burger King); "You're the boss" (United Airlines); and "No dissatisfied customers" (Ford).

The underlying premises of the marketing concept are:

1. Consumers can be grouped into different market segments depending on their needs and wants.
2. The consumers in any market segment will favor the offer of that organization which comes closest to satisfying their particular needs and wants.
3. The organization's task is to research and choose target markets and develop effective offers and marketing programs as the key to attracting and holding customers.

The selling concept and the marketing concept are frequently confused by the public and many business people. Levitt draws the following contrast between these two orientations:

> Selling focuses on the needs of the seller; marketing on the needs of the buyer. Selling is preoccupied with the seller's need to convert his product into cash; marketing with the idea of satisfying the needs of the customer by means of the product and the whole cluster of things associated with creating, delivering and finally consuming it.[11]

The marketing concept replaces and reverses the logic of the selling concept. The two concepts are contrasted in Figure 2–1. The selling concept starts with the firm's existing products and considers the task as one of using selling and promotion to stimulate a profitable volume of sales. The marketing concept starts with the firm's target customers and their needs and wants; it plans a coordinated set of products and programs to serve their needs and wants; and it derives profits through creating customer satisfaction. In essence, the *marketing concept* is a *customer needs and wants orientation* backed by *integrated market-*

---

[10] See John B. McKitterick, "What Is the Marketing Management Concept?" *The Frontiers of Marketing Thought and Action* (Chicago: American Marketing Association, 1957), pp. 71–82; and Fred J. Borch, "The Marketing Philosophy as a Way of Business Life," *The Marketing Concept: Its Meaning to Management*, Marketing Series, no. 99 (New York: American Management Association, 1957), pp. 3–5. Also see the statement by a former president of Pillsbury: Robert J. Keith, "The Marketing Revolution," *Journal of Marketing*, January 1960, pp. 35–38.

[11] Theodore Levitt, "Marketing Myopia," *Harvard Business Review*, July–August 1960, pp. 45–56.

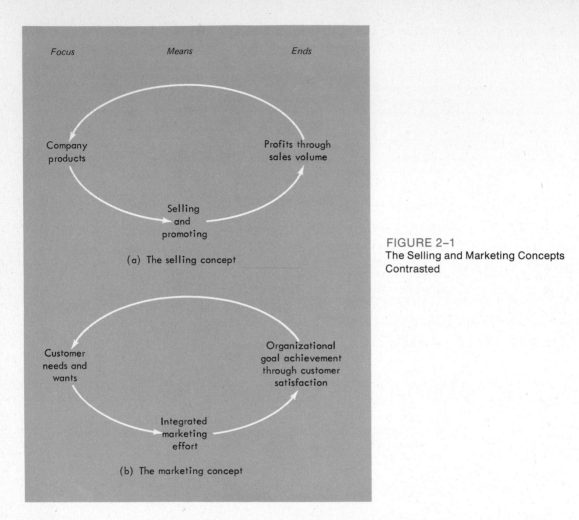

Focus   Means   Ends

Company products — Selling and promoting — Profits through sales volume

(a) The selling concept

Customer needs and wants — Integrated marketing effort — Organizational goal achievement through customer satisfaction

(b) The marketing concept

FIGURE 2–1
The Selling and Marketing Concepts Contrasted

ing effort aimed at generating *customer satisfaction* as the key to satisfying *organizational goals.* Drucker makes the contrast even more extreme:

> Indeed, selling and marketing are antithetical rather than synonymous or even complementary. There will always, one can assume, be need for some selling. *But the aim of marketing is to make selling superfluous.* The aim of marketing is to know and understand the customer so well that the product or service fits him and sells itself. Ideally, marketing should result in a customer who is ready to buy. All that should be needed then is to make the product or service available, i.e., logistics rather than salesmanship, and statistical distribution rather than promotion. [Italics added.] [12]

The marketing concept is the company's commitment to the time-honored concept in economic theory known as *consumer sovereignty.* The determination

[12] Peter F. Drucker, *Management: Tasks, Responsibilities, Practices* (New York: Harper & Row, 1973), pp. 64–65.

of what is to be produced should not be in the hands of the companies or in the hands of government but in the hands of consumers. The companies produce what the consumers want, and in this way maximize consumer welfare and earn their profits.

Among the prime practitioners of the marketing concept is McDonald's Corporation, the fast-food hamburger retailer.[13]

> In its short, twenty-year existence, McDonald's has served Americans and citizens of several other countries over 27 billion hamburgers! Today it commands a 20 percent share of the fast-food market, far ahead of its closest rivals, Kentucky Fried Chicken (8.4 percent) and Burger King (5.3 percent). Credit for this leading position belongs to a thoroughgoing marketing orientation. McDonald's knows how to serve people well and adapt to changing needs and wants.
>
> Before McDonald's, Americans could get hamburgers in restaurants or diners, but not without problems. In many places, the hamburgers were poor in quality, service was slow, decor was poor, help was uneven, conditions were unclean, and the atmosphere noisy. McDonald's was formulated as an alternative, where the customer could walk into a spotlessly clean outlet, be greeted by a friendly and efficient order-taker, receive a good-tasting hamburger less than a minute after placing the order, with the chance to eat it there or take it out. There were no jukeboxes or telephones to create a teenage hangout, and in fact, McDonald's became a family affair, particularly appealing to the children.
>
> As times changed, so did McDonald's. The sit-down sections were expanded in size, the decor improved, a very successful breakfast menu featuring Egg McMuffin was added, and new outlets were opened in high-traffic parts of the city. McDonald's was clearly being managed to evolve with changing customer needs and profitable opportunities.
>
> In addition, McDonald's management knows how to efficiently design and operate a complex service operation. It chooses its locations carefully, selects highly qualified franchise operators, gives them complete management training and assistance, supports them with a high-quality national advertising and sales promotion program, monitors product and service quality through continuous customer surveys, and puts great energy into improving the technology of hamburger production to simplify operations, bring down costs, and speed up service.

A marketing orientation is also relevant to nonprofit organizations. Most nonprofit organizations start out as product oriented. When they begin to suffer declines in support or membership, they resort to selling tactics. Thus many colleges facing declining enrollments are now investing heavily in advertising and recruitment activities. But these selling steps turn out to be only stopgap measures. These organizations begin to realize the need to define their target markets more carefully; research their needs, wants, and values; modernize their products and programs; and communicate more effectively. Such organizations turn from selling to marketing.

The Societal Marketing Concept

In recent years people have begun to raise a number of questions about the marketing concept. One of the major questions is whether the marketing concept is really being practiced by American business firms, or only given lip service. The marketing concept has such a nice-sounding rhetoric when used by businessmen

[13] See "The Burger That Conquered the Country," *Time*, September 17, 1973, p. 84.

in their speeches. They may even mean what they say. But there is a great deal to do between the utterance and the deed. Establishing the marketing concept in an organization is an extremely difficult task, and it takes considerable planning, persuasion, education, and reorganization.[14] Consequently, a great number of companies really do not practice the marketing concept even when they espouse it. Drucker considers *consumerism* to be evidence of this:

> That after twenty years of marketing rhetoric consumerism could become a powerful popular movement proves that not much marketing has been practiced. Consumerism is the "shame of marketing."[15]

There is a second, more disturbing doubt raised about the marketing concept, one that questions its validity. Some marketers have raised the question of whether the marketing concept is an appropriate organizational goal in an age of environmental deterioration, resource shortages, explosive population growth, worldwide inflation, and neglected social services.[16] The question is whether the firm that does an excellent job of sensing, serving, and satisfying individual consumer wants is necessarily acting in the best long-run interests of consumers and society. The marketing concept sidesteps the conflict between consumer wants, consumer interests, and long-run societal welfare.

As a concrete instance, consider once again McDonald's. It is doing an excellent job of meeting the wants of the American people for quick, inexpensive, tasty food in attractive surroundings. But is it really serving their long-run interests? Two recent criticisms that have been leveled against it by consumer and environmental groups are that:

1. McDonald's serves tasty but not necessarily nutritious food. The hamburgers have a lot of fat in them. McDonald's promotes fries and pies, two products that are dear to American taste but are high in starch and fat.
2. McDonald's uses up a great amount of paper in providing its food. The hamburgers are first wrapped in tissue paper and then placed in paper boxes, presumably to keep them warm. This results in substantial paper wastage and cost to the consumer.

Thus in the effort of a company to serve consumers' wants, questions can be raised about the uncovered social costs. The same thing occurs in many other instances:

1. The American auto industry has traditionally catered to the American demand for large automobiles, but meeting this desire results in high fuel consumption, heavy pollution, more fatal accidents to those in small cars, and higher auto purchase and repair costs.
2. The soft-drink industry has catered to the American demand for convenience by

---

[14] See Edward McKay, *The Marketing Mystique* (New York: American Management Association, 1972), pp. 22–30.

[15] Drucker, *Management*, p. 64.

[16] Laurence P. Feldman, "Societal Adaptation: A New Challenge for Marketing," *Journal of Marketing*, July 1971, pp. 54–60; and Martin L. Bell and C. William Emery, "The Faltering Marketing Concept," *Journal of Marketing*, October 1971, pp. 37–42.

increasing the share of one-way disposable bottles. The one-way bottle presents a great waste of resources in that approximately seventeen containers are necessary where one two-way bottle makes seventeen trips before it can no longer be used; many one-way bottles are not biodegradable; and these bottles often are a littering element.

3. The detergent industry has catered to the American passion for whiter clothes by offering a product that at the same time pollutes rivers and streams, killing fish and injuring the recreational possibilities.

These situations have led in recent years to the call for a new concept to revise or replace the marketing concept. Among the proposals are "the human concept," "the intelligent consumption concept," and "the ecological imperative concept,"[17] all of which get at different aspects of the same problem. We would like to propose "the societal marketing concept" as an answer to the dilemmas in the simple marketing concept. Our definition of societal marketing concept is:

> The *societal marketing concept* is a management orientation that holds that the key task of the organization is to determine the needs and wants of target markets and to adapt the organization to delivering the desired satisfactions more effectively and efficiently than its competitors in a way that preserves or enhances the consumers' and society's well being.

The underlying premises of the societal marketing concept are:

1. Consumers' wants do not always coincide with their long-run interests or society's long-run interests.
2. Consumers will increasingly favor organizations which show a concern with meeting their wants, long-run interests, and society's long-run interests.
3. The organization's task is to serve target markets in a way that produces not only want satisfaction but long-run individual and social benefit as the key to attracting and holding customers.

The societal marketing concept differs from the simple marketing concept by adding two considerations. First, it calls upon the marketer to concentrate on the buyers' needs and interests as well as on their wants. People have needs for which they have no defined solutions. Thus, consumers would like to find tasty food that is low in calories. Industrial buyers would like to find better machinery that will lower their production costs. The societal marketer will sense these needs and seek solutions. The solutions may amount to new products that the consumer never dreamed of. In this sense, the societal marketer is more attuned to the buyers' unexpressed needs than overexpressed wants. Consider the following case.[18]

[17] Leslie M. Dawson, "The Human Concept: New Philosophy for Business," *Business Horizons*, December 1969, pp. 29–38; James T. Rothe and Lissa Benson, "Intelligent Consumption: An Attractive Alternative to the Marketing Concept," *MSU Business Topics*, Winter 1974, pp. 29–34; and George Fisk, "Criteria for a Theory of Responsible Consumption," *Journal of Marketing*, April 1973, pp. 24–31.

[18] See Theodore Levitt, *The Marketing Mode: Pathways to Corporate Growth* (New York: McGraw-Hill Book Company, 1969), pp. 7–8.

American Airlines, in the effort to expand its air freight business, undertook a search for companies that would logically derive the most benefit from incorporating air freight into their physical distribution system. One such prospect was Raytheon. Raytheon executives had not expressed a want for air freight services. They told American Airlines, however, that they were always ready to save money and that if American could prove that they could save money through air freight, Raytheon would reorganize its physical distribution system and use air freight. American Airlines proceeded to work out the details of warehouse location, production scheduling, inventory control, and data transmission. They advanced a proposal for reorganizing Raytheon's physical distribution system that was so persuasive it was accepted by Raytheon. Thus, American Airlines started with Raytheon's need to save money and created a solution that the customer ended up wanting.

The other consideration added in the societal marketing concept is the emphasis on "long-run consumer and societal well being." It calls for a shift of the organization's perspective to include more marketing participants and longer-lasting effects. Societal marketing calls for including four considerations in marketing decision making: *consumer needs and wants, consumer interests, company interests,* and *society's interests.*

The major question facing companies is how societal marketing will affect their profitability. Companies cannot be expected to absorb losses or lower profits in the pursuit of societal marketing. Yet there have been cases where companies have actually increased their profits through practicing the societal marketing concept (see Chapter 27, p. 694). To the extent that societal marketing appears profitable, companies can be expected to give it serious consideration.

SUMMARY

Marketing has its origins in the fact that man is a creature of needs and wants. Needs and wants create a state of discomfort in persons, which is resolved through acquiring products to satisfy these needs and wants. These products are obtainable in several ways: self-production, coercion, supplication, and exchange. Most human society works on the principle of exchange, which means that people become specialists in the production of particular products and trade them for the other things they need. A market is an arena for potential exchanges—there are need markets, product markets, demographic markets, and geographic markets. Marketing encompasses all those activities that represent working through markets, that is, trying to actualize potential exchanges.

Marketing management is the conscious effort to achieve desired exchange outcomes with target markets. The marketer's basic skill lies in regulating the level, timing, and character of demand for a product, service, organization, place, person, or idea. The marketer faces up to eight different types of demand situations. If demand is negative, it must be reversed (conversional marketing); if nonexistent, it must be created (stimulational marketing); if latent, it must be developed (developmental marketing); if faltering, it must be revitalized (remarketing); if irregular, it must be synchronized (synchromarketing); if full, it must be maintained (maintenance marketing); if overfull, it must be reduced (demarketing); and if unwholesome, it must be destroyed (countermarketing).

Five alternative philosophies can guide organizations in carrying out their exchange activity. The production concept assumes that consumers will readily respond to products that are available and affordable and therefore that management's major task is to improve production efficiency and bring down prices. The product concept assumes that consumers will respond favorably to good products that are reasonably priced, and therefore little marketing effort is required. The selling concept assumes that consumers will normally not buy enough of the company's products unless they are reached with a substantial selling and promotion effort. The marketing concept holds that the main task of the company is to determine what a chosen set of customers' needs, wants, and preferences are and to adapt the company to delivering the desired satisfactions. The societal marketing concept holds that the main task of the company is to generate customer satisfaction and long-run consumer and societal well being as the key to satisfying organizational goals and responsibilities.

QUESTIONS AND PROBLEMS

1. Exchange is one of several ways of acquiring things. Propose some hypotheses explaining how trade or exchange may have begun.

2. The term *market* has many different usages. What does market mean to a stockbroker, produce merchant, sales manager, economist, and marketer?

3. Is there a contradiction between marketing something to people that is negatively demanded and practicing the marketing concept?

4. In the face of a long-term energy shortage, many public utilities have sought to reduce their customers' use of electricity. Propose a demarketing plan that will bring down the level of demand and help utilities avoid "brownouts."

5. Is the purpose of the marketing concept to maximize the customers' satisfaction or to maximize the company's long-run profitability?

6. Do you think the railroad passenger business is doomed? Why or why not? Could the passenger business be remarketed and made profitable through adoption of the marketing concept? Give illustrations.

7. Airlines seem to practice the marketing concept. They show a concern for passenger satisfaction, as exemplified by an attentive crew, complimentary flight meals, and other amenities. Would you agree that they deserve a high rating for their marketing orientation?

8. Do you think the marketing concept should provide the major orientation for every company? Could you cite companies which do not particularly need this orientation? Which companies need it most?

9. McDonald's faces two alternatives with respect to adopting the societal marketing concept. It can argue that its present practices are sound and in the public's interest. Or it can make some adjustments that will bring it closer to the societal marketing concept. Develop each possibility.

10. "Marketing is the science of actualizing the buying potentials of a market for a specific product." Does this definition reflect a product, selling, or marketing concept?

11. Coca-Cola has been accused of not practicing the societal marketing concept. Identify some aspects of the product that might be criticized.

The Marketing System

3

No substantial part of the universe is so simple that it can be grasped and controlled without abstraction. Abstraction consists in replacing the part of the universe under consideration by a model of similar but simple structure. Models . . . are thus a central necessity of scientific procedure.
ARTURO ROSENBLUETH and NORBERT WIENER

A marketer is someone skilled in knowing how to analyze and improve the ability of an organization to survive and grow in a complex and changing environment of markets and publics. This means that marketers must have a set of concepts and tools that enables them to grasp the complexity of the organization's environment and opportunities.

The two major tools are marketing system analysis and marketing process analysis. *Marketing system analysis* deals with identifying the major institutional components in an organization's environment that interact to produce results in the marketplace. *Marketing process analysis* consists of a set of logical steps to plan the organization's optimal adaptation to the marketplace of opportunities. These two forms of analysis handle the *structural* and *functional* aspects, respectively, of marketing phenomena. Marketing systems analysis is treated in this chapter, and marketing process analysis is treated in Chapter 4.

Marketing systems analysis consists of three levels of analysis of increasing scope and complexity. The first, *exchange system analysis*, deals with analyzing simple two-or-more person exchanges in a form that depicts what the individual parties are seeking through exchange. The second, *organizational marketing analysis*, deals with analyzing the major institutions and publics in the environment of the organization that affect its performance in the marketplace. The third, *macroenvironment analysis*, deals with analyzing the totality of interacting institutions in society, including the economic system, legal system, political system, and cultural system. This chapter will deal with exchange system analysis and organizational marketing analysis, and Chapter 5 will take up macroenvironment analysis.

EXCHANGE SYSTEM ANALYSIS

The core idea underlying marketing is that of exchange. The potential for exchange exists when two or more parties each possess something-of-value, which they might conceivably trade. The something-of-value could be *goods, services, money,* or *goodwill.* If the potential exchange is actualized, we say that a transaction takes place. A transaction signifies an agreement between two or more parties on the use, ownership, or transfer of resources. A transaction is the basic unit of exchange. Trillions of transactions take place each year.

In the simplest exchange situation, there are two parties. If one party is more actively seeking an exchange than the other, we call the first party a *marketer* and the second party a *prospect. A marketer is someone seeking a resource from someone else and willing to offer something-of-value in exchange.* The marketer is seeking a response from the other party in the form of a sale of what the marketer wants to sell or in the form of a purchase of what the marketer wants to buy. The marketer, in other words, can be a seller or a buyer.[1] In the event that both parties are actively seeking an exchange, we say that both of them are marketers and call the situation one of bilateral marketing.

A simple exchange system can be mapped by showing the two actors and the typical exchange media that flow between them. Figure 3–1 shows five familiar exchange situations. The most familiar is the commercial transaction—a seller offers a good or service to a buyer in exchange for money. The second is the employment transaction—an employer offers wages and fringe benefits to an employee in exchange for the employee's productive services (made up of time, energy, and skill). The third is the civic transaction—a police force, for example, offers protective services to citizens in exchange for their taxes and cooperation. The fourth is a religious transaction—a church offers religious services to members in exchange for their contributions of money and time. Finally, the fifth is a charity transaction—a charity organization offers gratitude and a feeling of well being to donors in return for contributions of money and time.

Figure 3–1 shows only the basic resources being exchanged by the two parties. A marketer interested in actualizing a potential transaction will make a more careful analysis of what the other party wants and what the marketer might offer in return. Suppose the Caterpillar Company, a leading manufacturer of earth-moving equipment, is interested in increasing its sales to target prospects, mainly construction companies. It researches the benefits that a typical construction company may be seeking in buying earth-moving equipment.

---

[1] This point is elaborated upon in Philip Kotler and Sidney J. Levy, "Buying Is Marketing, Too," *Journal of Marketing,* January 1973, pp. 54–59.

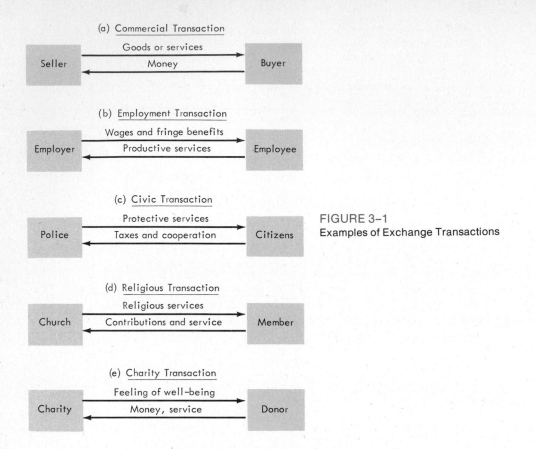

(a) Commercial Transaction

Seller →(Goods or services) Buyer
Seller ←(Money) Buyer

(b) Employment Transaction

Employer →(Wages and fringe benefits) Employee
Employer ←(Productive services) Employee

(c) Civic Transaction

Police →(Protective services) Citizens
Police ←(Taxes and cooperation) Citizens

FIGURE 3–1
Examples of Exchange Transactions

(d) Religious Transaction

Church →(Religious services) Member
Church ←(Contributions and service) Member

(e) Charity Transaction

Charity →(Feeling of well–being) Donor
Charity ←(Money, service) Donor

Those benefits are listed at the top of the exchange map in Figure 3–2. The prospect wants high-quality equipment, a fair price, on-time delivery, good financing, and good service. This is the *want list* (or *wish list*) of the buyer. The wants are not all equally important and may vary from buyer to buyer. One of Caterpillar's tasks is to find out the importance of these different wants of the buyer.[2] At the same time, Caterpillar as the marketer has a want list, as shown below the Caterpillar arrow in Figure 3–2. Caterpillar wants a good price for the equipment, on-time payment, and good word of mouth. If there is a sufficient match or overlap in the want lists, there is a basis for a transaction. Caterpillar's task is, then, to formulate an *offer* (also called a *benefit bundle* or *value package*) designed to motivate the construction company to buy the Caterpillar equipment. The construction company might in turn make a counteroffer. The process of trying to find mutually agreeable terms is called *negotiation*. Negotiation either ends in mutually acceptable terms of exchange or a decision not to transact.

Although we have been dealing with two-party exchange systems, we can extend the analysis to three-or-more-party exchange systems. Suppose a YMCA camp is trying to attract more campers for the coming summer season. The deci-

---

[2] See chap. 6, pp. 157–64 for further elaboration.

Caterpillar
(marketer)

1. High-quality, durable equipment
2. Fair price for the value
3. On-time delivery of equipment
4. Good financing terms
5. Good after-service and parts

Construction co.
(prospect)

1. Good price for equipment
2. On-time payment
3. Good word of mouth

FIGURE 3–2
Two-Party Exchange Map
Showing Want Lists of Both Parties

sion to go to a summer camp is jointly made by the child and parents. If either objects, the child is not likely to go. Therefore a YMCA camp director must develop a good understanding of what children and parents each want from summer camp. The analysis is shown in Figure 3–3. The parents want the camp to be a safe place and to provide fun and an opportunity to meet nice children. The parents want the child to learn good values, show good behavior, and be happy. The child wants the camp to be fun and have good counselors and good food. The child wants the parents' love and pampering. Against these want lists, the YMCA wants a fee, satisfaction, and good word of mouth from the parents and good behavior, satisfaction, and social learning from the child. The camp director's challenge is to formulate a camp experience that will jointly satisfy the wishes of the two markets and of the camp. Since other camps are also competing for the same family's patronage, the YMCA camp director must develop a distinctive value package that meets the needs of its target prospects better than competitors.

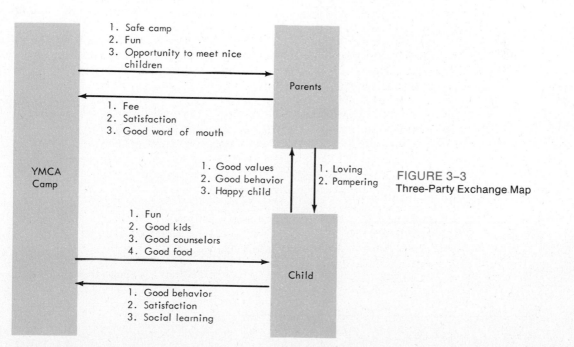

YMCA Camp

1. Safe camp
2. Fun
3. Opportunity to meet nice children

Parents

1. Fee
2. Satisfaction
3. Good word of mouth

1. Good values
2. Good behavior
3. Happy child

1. Loving
2. Pampering

FIGURE 3–3
Three-Party Exchange Map

1. Fun
2. Good kids
3. Good counselors
4. Good food

Child

1. Good behavior
2. Satisfaction
3. Social learning

Exchange analysis, as we have formulated it, is based on the assumption that, basically, people behave to maximize their self-interest. Marketers have found that the postulate of self-seeking behavior is the most useful one for understanding the actual behavior of parties in a market transaction. That people are motivated by self-interest is a long-standing philosophical postulate going back to Jeremy Bentham, Adam Smith, and even earlier to Greek philosophers such as the hedonists. Acting out of self-interest does not necessarily mean acting selfishly. Acting selfishly implies the pursuit of self-gratification at the expense of others. Acting out of self-interest can include a concern for the interests of others (called enlightened self-interest), since the welfare of others can have an impact on one's self-interest. The self-interest postulate asks us to look at each potential exchange situation and identify what each party might be seeking.

To take an extreme case, consider a donor who gives some money to a charity. On the surface, this looks like a one-way transfer of value rather than a transaction. It is reasonable to assume, however, that the donor expects something in return. The donor expects the gift to be used productively and might also expect a show of gratitude. If the charity organization appears irresponsible or ungrateful, the donor is not likely to give next year. Even an anonymous donor of a large gift gets something back for giving. The reward may be purely the private pleasure of being able to give a large gift without requiring acknowledgment. Thus even extreme altruism can be interpreted in terms of what the giver is getting or expecting. Interpreting human behavior from the perspective of self-interest provides the marketer with guidelines for developing effective value packages.

ORGANIZATIONAL MARKETING ANALYSIS

The exchanges that take place between two or more parties occur in a larger framework known as the organizational marketing system.

> An *organizational marketing system* is an organization and the set of significant interacting institutions and forces in the organization's environment that affect its ability to serve its markets.

The simplest marketing system consists of a single organization serving a single market with no intermediaries, suppliers, or other parties involved. This system is shown in Figure 3–4. The organization and its market are connected by four

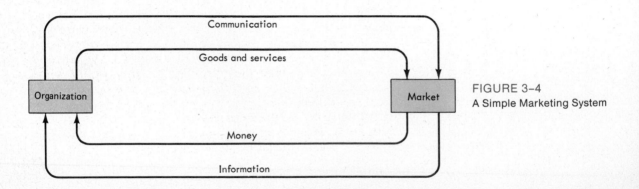

FIGURE 3–4
A Simple Marketing System

flows. The organization dispatches (1) goods and services and (2) communications to the market; in return it receives (3) money and (4) information. The inner loop shows an exchange of money for goods; the outer loop shows an exchange of information.

In reality, organizational marketing systems have many more components. We can distinguish five levels of successively larger environments in which the organization operates. These environments are shown in Figure 3–5 and described in the following sections, starting with the organization itself.

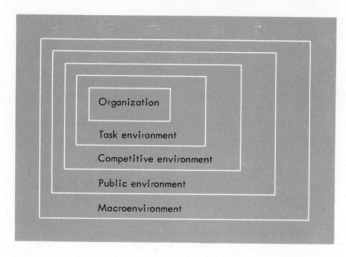

FIGURE 3–5
The Components of an Organizational Marketing System

ORGANIZATION ENVIRONMENT

The first thing to notice is that the organization itself contains a number of components that will affect its ability to perform in the marketplace. An organization—whether a company, college, or church—can be viewed as a resource conversion machine that takes inputs from the outside world, converts them into useful products and services, and makes them available to others as outputs. To accomplish this, the organization must carry on a number of functions, such as research and development, engineering, purchasing, manufacturing, financing, and marketing.

Let us focus on marketing, which is typically organized as a department. Assume that the organization sells many products to many end users in many geographical areas. This means that the marketing part of the organization must attend to *marketing functions* (e.g., field sales, advertising, marketing research, and customer service), *organization products, customer end-users,* and *geographical markets.* The design of an effective marketing department is itself a major challenge.[3] In addition, we must recognize that the other departments of the organization constitute an environment for the marketing department. If the marketing department wants to open a new geographical market, it must present a case to top management and the financial vice president, in particular, for support. If the marketing department wants useful new products, it must influence the work of the research and development department.

[3] See chap. 22.

An organization, however, is not just an economic machine. It has a culture, that is, the major participants share a set of attitudes toward what they want to accomplish and what they think is important. The organizational culture may be favorable or inimical to the marketing department. These are the facts of life, and they constitute an organizational environment that affects the marketing performance of the company.

TASK ENVIRONMENT

The organization operates in a task environment that consists of those basic institutions that cooperate to create marketing value for a marketplace. The task environment consists of the company and the three major institutions shown in Figure 3–6, namely, *suppliers, marketing intermediaries,* and the *market.* The four constitute a *total marketing channel* for meeting a particular set of customer needs. The channel begins with heterogeneous raw materials found in nature, which are converted by successive processes into an assortment of final products that bring form, place, time, and possession utility to final buyers.

FIGURE 3–6
The Task-Marketing System of an Organization

Suppliers
The organization, in order to produce value for the marketplace, must acquire a number of inputs needed in the production process from outside suppliers. For example, the Talon Company, the largest American producer of zippers, must obtain textiles, aluminum strip, brass strip, steel, dye, and other supplies in order to produce zippers. More generally, the main classes of inputs needed by sellers are labor, equipment, materials, fuel and energy, money, and information.

The company's task is to determine the optimal input mix for the given output mix that it wants to produce. The optimal input mix is influenced by the prices and availabilities of the various input goods. The company may decide to produce some of its own needed inputs and buy the rest from outside suppliers. The company's purchasing executive is responsible for buying the needed inputs at the best possible prices. This executive will check suppliers for the quality of their goods, prices, delivery reliability, warranties, credit terms, and miscellaneous services. For the more important inputs, the executive will negotiate contracts with multiple sources of supply to assure a sufficient supply and to be able to compare and watchdog prices.

The marketing department has a direct interest in the efficiency of the company's purchase of inputs. Before developing plans to increase sales, the marketing executive will check with the purchasing executive to make sure that the necessary materials can be obtained at the planned prices for producing the planned output, with the financial officer to make sure that the company has the necessary working capital, and with the personnel officer to make sure that the company has adequate manpower to produce the planned output.

The real "marketing" mettle of a purchasing department is tested during periods of shortages of needed inputs. During 1974, companies could not get enough plastic, fuel, paper, aluminum, copper, textiles, or glass. The purchasing manager had to scramble for additional suppliers, offer higher prices, and accept fewer services. The company's president had to make a personal appeal to the supplier for special consideration. Essentially, purchasing found that it had to "market" the company to suppliers.

The marketing executive is a direct purchaser of certain services to support the marketing effort, such as advertising, marketing research, sales training, and marketing consulting. In going outside, the marketing executive evaluates different advertising agencies, marketing research firms, sales-training consultants, and marketing consultants. The executive has to decide which services to purchase outside and which to produce inside by adding specialists to the staff.

Marketing Intermediaries

Marketing intermediaries are institutions that facilitate the distribution of the company's outputs to the final markets. For example, the Talon Company uses manufacturers' reps, wholesalers, jobbers, and retailers to sell its zippers to final markets. More generally, there are three main types of marketing intermediaries and many variants of each.[4] *Merchant middlemen* are business units—such as wholesalers and retailers—that buy, take title to, and resell merchandise (often called resellers). *Agent middlemen* are business units—such as brokers and sales reps—that negotiate purchases or sales but do not take title to merchandise. *Facilitators* are business units—such as transportation companies, warehouses, and banks—that assist in the performance of distribution but neither take title to goods nor negotiate purchases or sales.

The company that is seeking distribution for its output must either use established marketing intermediaries or set up its own. A company normally chooses established intermediaries because they have the experience and economies of scale for efficiently reaching the target markets. The company has to consider the cost of using these intermediaries against their sales performance, reliability, and cooperativeness. When the company finds existing intermediaries to be inadequate or unavailable, it may be forced to establish its own routes to the market. *Direct marketing* is the best example, in which the company seeks to reach the final market with its own sales force or by direct mail or telephone solicitation.

Marketing intermediaries perform one or more of several functions for the company. Among them are *research, promotion, contact, matching, negotiation, physical distribution, financing,* and *risk taking.*[5] The company that decides to sell through marketing intermediaries will look for those institutions that most efficiently perform the needed channel functions.

Markets

The final component of the company's task environment is the market itself. We have been referring to "the market" as a single entity although in fact the company usually sells to several markets. We can distinguish between *industrial markets* and *consumer markets.* Industrial markets buy for the sake of manufacture or resale, whereas consumer markets buy for the sake of consumption. For example, the Talon Company sells zippers to manufacturers, tailor shops, and consumers. Each of these markets in turn can be divided into submarkets called

[4] See chap. 16, p. 420.
[5] See chap. 16, p. 419.

market segments. Thus the manufacturers' market to which Talon sells zippers can be divided into manufacturers of clothing, of upholstery, of luggage, of automobiles, and of closet accessories. Similar breakdowns of the tailor market and the consumer market could be identified.

A company must decide whether it wants to sell to one, two, or all the market segments making up the larger market. Smaller companies tend to specialize in one or a few market segments and pick them carefully. A sound choice is a segment that the company has the resources to serve well and for which it can create a distinctive product.

Large companies serve several markets and market segments. They are wise if they formulate different marketing programs to meet the needs of the various served markets rather than trying to serve all the markets with the same marketing program. The latter is dangerous in that the company will lose share in those markets where competitors have tailored a superior marketing program. An example is the sale of ketchup to various markets. For example, the Heinz Company sells ketchup to such markets as food retailers, restaurants, industrial companies, colleges, hospitals, and prisons. Were it to sell one brand of ketchup to all these markets at the same price, it would have uneven success. The prison market wants to buy a cheap ketchup, not the expensive Heinz brand. To win a share of this market, Heinz has to formulate and offer a cheaper ketchup product for this market.

We might consider at this point how a map of a *total marketing channel* would look for an actual company, such as Heinz. Figure 3–7 presents a simplified version of how Heinz serves one of its final markets, namely, food retailers. Heinz acquires its raw materials from food producers and other inputs from other suppliers. These goods are warehoused by the suppliers and shipped to Heinz's plants as needed. The Heinz Company uses food brokers to contact wholesalers of several types: cooperatives, voluntaries, independents, and jobbers. Heinz ships its products to regional warehouses and from there, to wholesalers. The wholesalers in turn sell and ship Heinz products to such food retailers as discount supermarkets, convenience stores, independent supermarkets, and chain supermarkets. The retailers in turn sell the Heinz products to consumers.

The total marketing channel map is oversimplified to permit easy reading. The oversimplifications include the following:

1. The map shows only product flows and omits flows of title, payment, information, and promotion.[6]
2. The map omits the activities of other institutions in the task environment, such as auction markets, advertising agencies, and financial intermediaries.
3. Heinz sells and ships directly to large national chain supermarkets, but this bypass of brokers and wholesalers is not shown.

Nevertheless, Figure 3–7 gives the flavor of a company's marketing system at the level of the task environment.

[6] See chap. 16, pp. 414–16.

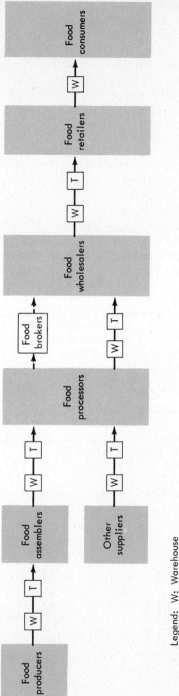

Legend: W: Warehouse
T: Transportation carrier
→ : Flow of product

FIGURE 3-7
Heinz Task-Marketing System

An organization rarely stands alone in its effort to serve a given market. Its efforts to build an efficient task-marketing system to serve the market are matched by similar efforts on the part of others. The organization, in fact, operates within a rich environment of competitors. These competitors have to be identified, monitored, and outmaneuvered to gain and maintain the loyalty of the market.

The competitive environment consists not only of other companies but also of more basic things. The best way for a company to grasp its competition is to take the viewpoint of a buyer. What does a buyer think about in the process of arriving at the answer to a question that might result in the purchase of something? Suppose a consumer has been feeling tired and asks, "How can I get more physical exercise?" (See Figure 3–8.) Several possibilities come to mind, including bicycling, jogging, weight lifting, yoga, and using exercise machines. The possibilities make up the set of *generic competitors*. If bicycling turns out to arouse the most interest, the consumer next thinks about what type of bicycle to purchase. This leads to a set of *product-form competitors*, such as three-speed, five-speed, or ten-speed bikes. The consumer might decide on a ten-speed. The consumer might then consider which brand to buy and recall a set of *enterprise competitors*. Further things should be noted:

1. The consumer will normally be aware of less than the *total set* of existing brands, and what he or she is aware of is called the *awareness set*. Even fewer brands will be seriously considered (the *consideration set*). Only a few brands will remain in the final running (the *choice set*).

2. The consumer may restrict shopping to a few favorite retailers who can be called the *merchant competitors*.

3. This picture of bicycle competition was formed out of a consumer's interest in physical exercise. If the consumer had raised the question, "How can I find another means of getting to work?" or the question, "What can I do with my leisure time?" different sets of generic competitors would have emerged. Thus a bicycle competes with other sets of generic competitors, depending on the consumer's need.

The company's enterprise competitors are typically the competitors it watches most closely. The enterprise competitors will differ in the quality of

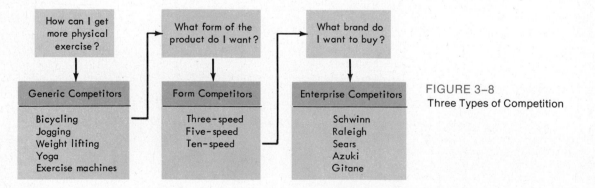

FIGURE 3–8
Three Types of Competition

their product, features, prices, service, and other factors. The company competes most closely with those enterprises occupying a similar position or niche in *product/market space.*[7] The company must therefore identify and monitor most closely those competitors who are seen to be closest to itself in the consumers' minds.

As an example, consider a gasoline marketer such as Shell, operating its stations in the Washington, D.C., market. A score of other gasoline marketers operate in this area, not all of equal competitive standing. Table 3–1 classifies these gasoline marketers according to their size and price policy in the marketplace. Shell is a major brander, in fact a market leader, and most of its competition is *intratype competition.* Its major marketing effort is spent in competing against the other market leaders, important majors, and minor majors. There is also some *intertype competition* between the major branders and price discounters. Furthermore, the price discounters are busy competing against each other. Thus, Shell competes differentially against a whole set of enterprise competitors. The market, given the range of choice, distributes itself among the enterprises according to their preference.

Our basic observation about the task and competitive environments can now be summarized. A company, in trying to successfully serve a set of customers, must keep four basic dimensions in mind, which can be called the four C's of market positioning. It must consider the nature of the *Customers, Channels, Competition,* and its own characteristics as a *Company.* Successful marketing is a matter of achieving an effective alignment of the company with customers, channels, and competitors.

TABLE 3–1
Classification of Gasoline Marketers in the Washington, D.C., Area

I. *Major branders:* large, vertically integrated oil companies emphasizing many stations, strong advertising, strong service, nongasoline products (tires, batteries, and accessories), and minor repairs.
   A. *Market leaders:* relatively large numbers of stations, good market acceptance, large market share. Examples: Exxon, Amoco, and Shell.
   B. *Important majors:* thinner market representation, weaker market acceptance, average market share. Examples: Sun, Gulf, Texaco, and Mobil.
   C. *Minor majors:* relatively few stations, poor market acceptance, small market share. Examples: Chevron, Citgo, Arco, and Phillips.
II. *Price discounters:* small, nonvertically integrated oil companies emphasizing low price, little service, few other products, long hours.
   A. *Deep discounters:* lowest prices, least service. Example: Poor Boy.
   B. *Limited-service operators:* low price, limited service. Example: Scot.
   C. *Stamp and premium givers:* below normal prices plus giveaways. Example: Star.

SOURCE: Assembled from information in Fred C. Allvine and James M. Patterson, *Competition, Ltd: The Marketing of Gasoline* (Bloomington: Indiana University Press, 1972).

---

[7] See chap. 7, pp. 84–85.

PUBLIC ENVIRONMENT

Not only does an organization have to contend with competitors in seeking to satisfy a target market but it must also acknowledge a large set of publics that take an interest, whether welcome or not, in its methods of doing business. Because the actions of the organization affect the interest of other groups, these groups become significant publics to the organization. We shall define a public in the following way:

> A *public* is any group that has an actual or potential interest or impact on an organization's ability to achieve its objectives.

The main publics of an organization are shown in Figure 3–9.

A public can facilitate or impede the ability of an organization to accomplish its goals. For example, a regulatory government agency, such as the Federal Trade Commission, typically constrains the actions of companies with respect to pricing, advertising, product design, and selling methods. Yet this short-term inhibition may in the long run enhance a company's ability to serve its markets. The regulations prevent predatory tactics by competitors, help to build consumer trust, and lead to better products. The media, too, can turn out to be a benign, neutral, or negative force in the company's fortunes. Good press can increase sales and bad press can substantially hurt sales. In general, a company can view its publics in three ways. A *reciprocal public* is one that the company is interested in and that is interested in the company (e.g., stockholders). A *sought public* is one that the company is interested in but that does not take a strong interest in the company (e.g., the press in regard to good news coverage). An *unwelcome public* is one that the company shuns but that insists on taking an interest in the company (e.g., a citizen-action group).

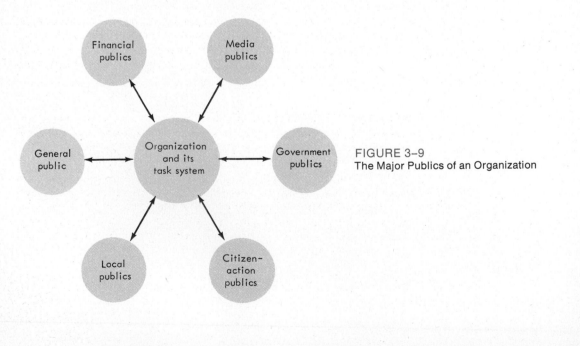

FIGURE 3–9
The Major Publics of an Organization

Since publics can substantially influence an organization's fortunes, the wise organization takes concrete steps to manage successful relations with its key publics, rather than sit back and wait. Most organizations establish public relations departments to plan constructive relations with various publics. These departments monitor the attitudes of the organization's publics and distribute information and communications to build goodwill. When negative publicity breaks out, these departments act as trouble shooters. In the best departments, there is an emphasis on counseling top management to adopt positive programs and to eliminate questionable practices so that negative publicity does not arise in the first place.

It would be a mistake for an organization to leave public relations entirely in the hands of the public relations department. All the employees of the organization are involved in public relations, from the chief officer who meets the general public to the financial vice president who addresses the financial community to the field sales representative who calls on customers.

We would propose that public relations should be conceived of as a broad marketing operation rather than a narrow communication operation.[8] A public is a group from which an organization wants some response, such as goodwill, favorable mentions, or donations of time or money. The organization must ask what that public is seeking that it could satisfy. It then plans a benefit package that is designed to build goodwill. We will take this point of view in describing the major publics surrounding an organization.

Financial Publics

Financial publics include all the groups who take an interest in, and might influence, the company's ability to obtain funds. Banks, investment houses, stock brokerage firms, and stockholders are the major financial publics. Management tries to cultivate the goodwill of these groups by issuing annual reports, answering financial questions, and satisfying the financial community that its house is in order.

Nonprofit organizations, such as universities, museums, and churches must mount a major marketing campaign every year to "sell" financial and donor markets on supporting them generously. This is often a greater marketing challenge than the problem of attracting and satisfying final customers with their services.

Media Publics

Media publics include mass and trade media companies that carry news, features, and editorial opinion: specifically, newspapers, magazines, and radio and television stations. Companies are acutely sensitive to the role played by the press in affecting their capacity to achieve their marketing objectives.

The company has two concerns. The first is how much coverage the press gives to the company's activities and products. Companies are hungry for news attention and free publicity, which substitute for paid advertising that the company would have to buy to build the same level of awareness in the marketplace.

The second issue is what the press says about the company's activities and

---

[8] The interrelations between marketing and public relations are examined in Philip Kotler and William Mindak, "Marketing and Public Relations: Partners or Rivals," *Journal of Marketing*, October 1978, pp. 13–20.

products. There is nothing more valuable to a company than favorable publicity, nor more damaging than unfavorable publicity. When the Mazda automobile (with the Wankel engine) was first introduced in the United States, it received extensive and favorable press coverage as a car with high performance and pollution control. This coverage boosted U.S. sales considerably. After the gasoline shortage erupted, the Environmental Protection Agency published the tested mileages of different automobiles and cited the Mazda as giving only about ten miles per gallon. This publicity caused a collapse of sales that completely upset Mazda's planned export level and marketing program.

Getting more and better coverage from the press calls for understanding what the press is really interested in and giving them what they want. The effective press relations manager knows most of the editors in the major media and systematically cultivates a mutually beneficial relation with them. The manager does not approach the press with threats or supplications but offers instead interesting news items, informational material, and quick access to top management. In return, the media reporters are more likely to give the company fair coverage.

Government Publics

Management is increasingly finding it necessary to take government developments into account when they formulate marketing plans and policies. In the past, companies were relatively free to set their marketing-mix variables—product features, packaging, price, advertising, sales promotion—at any level; they had to worry only about their consumers and competitors. In recent years, there has been a major and probably irreversible trend toward more government regulation and intervention in these marketing decisions. Manufacturers of drugs, toys, automobiles, appliances, and food items must carefully consider product safety and ecology in designing their products. Company pricing came under price controls for a while and might return at any time. Companies have to be careful about "truth in advertising" or face a suit by the Federal Trade Commission.

Companies have responded in three ways to growing government regulation. The first is to increase the company's *legal staff* to advise marketing managers as to what they can and cannot do. An understaffed legal department might seriously delay the company in making important decisions on advertising messages, price changes, and packaging moves. The second is to establish a *government relations department* or enlarge an existing department. Government relations managers must know the various agencies at the local, state, and federal levels as well as the key legislators. They must anticipate unfavorable developments, visit the right people, express the company's interests, and rally support. Lobbying is essentially company marketing in the arena of the legislative market. Lobbyists must know how to segment the legislative market; they must analyze legislators' needs and motives; they must know how a bill is passed, defeated, and influenced; and they must make personal calls and presentations. The third company response is to join with other companies in *trade associations* to lobby for the common interests of their industry.

Citizen-Action Publics

A company's marketing decisions are increasingly being affected by consumer organizations, environmental groups, minority organizations, neighborhood associations, and other vocal public-interest groups.

One morning not long ago a major Philadelphia bank found thirty senior citizens at its door demanding to talk to the bank's president. They called themselves the Gray Panthers and presented the bank's president with a list of ten nonnegotiable demands for citizens over sixty-five, including free checking, free safety-deposit boxes, and reduced interest rates. The bank president did his best to handle the situation diplomatically and in the end offered a few "senior citizen bank privileges." This kind of citizen action is becoming more frequent and is facing all organizations, from business firms to universities to churches.

Companies would be foolish to attack or ignore demands of public-interest groups. Progressive companies have made three responses. First, they are training their decision makers to introduce social criteria into their decision making, to strike a better balance between the needs of consumers, citizens, and stockholders. Second, they have established public-affairs departments to stay in touch with these groups to learn their interests and to express the companies' goals and activities to these groups. Third, these companies hold conferences with other companies to search for judicious ways to deal with these groups. Some companies have staked out a leadership role by identifying their interests with these groups and playing the role of leader and model company in furthering worthwhile social causes.

Local Publics

Every organization is physically located in one or more areas and comes into contact with local publics, such as neighborhood residents, community organizations, and local public officials. These groups will take an active or passive interest in the activities of the organization. The residents surrounding a hospital usually get concerned about ambulance sirens, parking congestion, and other things that go with running a hospital. Community groups are interested in the organization's employment policies, and the possibilities of its making donations to worthwhile local causes.

Organizations usually appoint a community relations officer whose job is to keep close to the community, attend meetings, answer questions, and make contributions to worthwhile causes. Smart organizations do not wait for local issues to erupt. They make investments in their community to help it run well and to build up a bank of company goodwill in case it is needed.

General Public

The company is ultimately concerned with the attitude of the general public toward its products and activities. The general public does not act in an organized way toward the company, as interest groups do. But the members of the general public carry around images of the company's standing as a corporate citizen and these images affect their patronage.

The company undertakes several activities to improve its public image. The company lends its officers to community fund drives and makes substantial contributions to charities. It sets up systems to respond to consumer grievances. It resorts to institutional advertising to describe what it is doing in the social field. In recent years the telephone company has run a campaign on "How to Save on Long-Distance Calls," the electrical utilities have run a campaign on "How to Conserve Electricity," and the Ford Motor Company has distributed tens of thousands of booklets on "How to Purchase a Car." These steps are designed to help the public become more intelligent buyers and users of the company's products.

MACROENVIRONMENT

The organization, its connected task institutions, competitors, and publics, all operate in a larger environment of macroforces and institutions that shape opportunities and pose threats to the successful functioning of the organization. These forces make up the "uncontrollables" to which organizations must adapt through judicious choice of the "controllable" factors, such as the markets they elect to serve and their marketing programs.

The major macroforces are six in number: demography, economics, natural resources, technology, law and politics, and culture. We mention these forces here to complete our modeling of the hierarchy of environments that affect a company's performance. They will be discussed in detail in Chapter 5 when we begin to look at marketing opportunities.

AN EXAMPLE OF A COMPANY MARKETING SYSTEM

The first task of a marketer in dealing with any marketing system is to depict the structure and components of that system. We shall illustrate by mapping the marketing system of a leading manufacturer of a popular soft-centered, chocolate-covered candy bar.[9] Instead of repeating the diagrams that have already been covered, we introduce some new mapping forms.

Figure 3–10 shows the major components and flows in the candy company marketing system. The diagram is divided into six elements.

1. The *environment* or, more precisely, those forces in the environment that affect candy demand and supply, such as population growth, per capita income, attitudes toward candy, and raw material availability and cost.
2. The *company and competitors' marketing strategies.*
3. The major *marketing decision variables* in this market—product characteristics, price, sales force, physical distribution and service, and advertising and sales promotion.
4. The major *marketing channels* that the company uses for this product.
5. The *buyer behavior model*, which shows customer response to the activities of the manufacturers and the distribution channels as well as to the environment.
6. The total *industry sales, company sales, and company costs.*

The various arrows show key flows in the marketing system. Flow 5, for example, would refer to a detailed diagram and description showing types of product characteristics decisions, the inputs that influence each of these decisions, and the sources of data for each of the inputs.

Let us select one element in Figure 3–10, the *company marketing strategy* box, and list on the right side of this box all the major marketing decisions made by the company (see Figure 3–11). There are two major types of decisions, trade decisions and consumer decisions. To influence the trade, the company uses the wholesale price, trade allowances, credit policy, and delivery policy. To influence consumers, the company uses product characteristics, packaging characteristics, retail price, consumer deals, and consumer advertising.

[9] This section is adapted from the author's "Corporate Models: Better Marketing Plans," *Harvard Business Review,* July–August 1970, pp. 135–49.

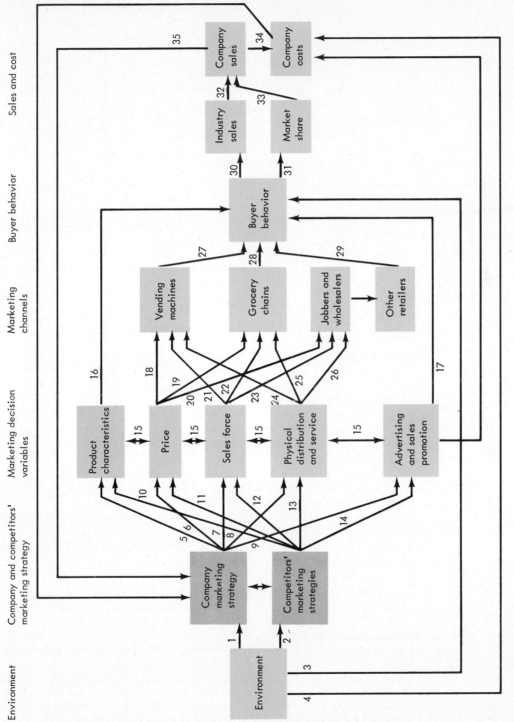

Environment   Company and competitors' marketing strategy   Marketing decision variables   Marketing channels   Buyer behavior   Sales and cost

FIGURE 3–10
Comprehensive Marketing System Map: Candy Company

55

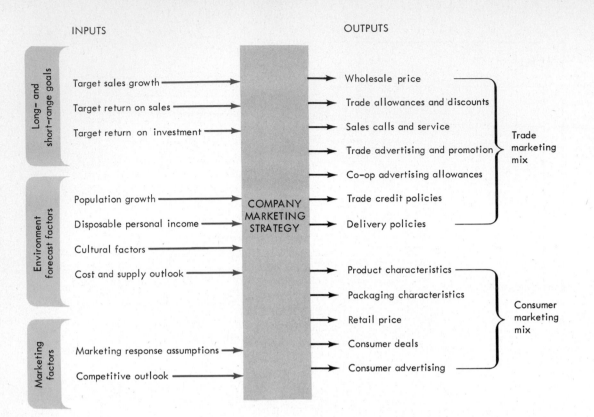

INPUTS
OUTPUTS

Long- and short-range goals
- Target sales growth
- Target return on sales
- Target return on investment

Environment forecast factors
- Population growth
- Disposable personal income
- Cultural factors
- Cost and supply outlook

Marketing factors
- Marketing response assumptions
- Competitive outlook

COMPANY MARKETING STRATEGY

- Wholesale price
- Trade allowances and discounts
- Sales calls and service
- Trade advertising and promotion
- Co-op advertising allowances
- Trade credit policies
- Delivery policies

Trade marketing mix

- Product characteristics
- Packaging characteristics
- Retail price
- Consumer deals
- Consumer advertising

Consumer marketing mix

FIGURE 3–11
Input-Output Map of Company Marketing Decisions: Candy Company

The next step is to list the various inputs and influences on these decisions, which fall into one of three groups:

1. The company's long- and short-range goals for sales growth, return on sales, and return on investment.
2. Forecastable factors in the environment, such as population growth, disposable personal income, cultural factors, and the cost and supply outlook.
3. Assumptions about the sales effectiveness of different marketing instruments as well as expectations concerning competition.

Any input can be elaborated further. For example, it is possible to isolate four cultural factors that will have a significant effect on future candy consumption:

Weight consciousness—if there is any relaxation of the pressures in American society toward the idea that "thin is beautiful," that will lead to a substantial increase in the sales of candy.

Cavity consciousness—as better dentifrices are developed, people will worry less about the negative effects of sugar on their teeth, and that will reduce their inhibitions against eating candy; on the other hand, some companies will see cavity-consciousness as an opportunity to develop a tasty, sugarless candy.

Nutrition consciousness—if recent interest in the ill effects of refined sugar on the human metabolism continues to grow, an increasing proportion of nutritionally conscious people will steer away from candy.

Cigarette consumption—if people reduce their cigarette consumption, we can expect candy, gum, and other oral gratifiers to replace cigarettes.

We can now trace how the various outputs feed into other parts of the system. Consider the output described as the trade marketing mix. This output becomes input into each of the distribution channels—for example, the grocery-chain model (see Figure 3–12). The trade marketing mix becomes the "handle" that the manufacturer uses to influence the retailer to provide favorable shelf facings and location, special displays and promotions, advertising, and in-stock maintenance.

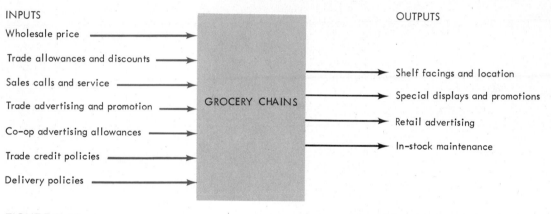

FIGURE 3–12
Input-Output Map of Grocery-Chain Decisions: Candy Company

The influence of the dealers' decisions on the final consumers is shown in Figure 3–13 along with influences coming from other parts of the marketing system. The various influences are classified into product and promotion factors (outputs coming from the company marketing decision model), distribution factors (outputs coming from the channels of distribution models), and environmental factors (outputs coming from the environmental model). These factors influence consumers' buying behavior to bring about a certain level of industry sales and brand-share sales of candy bars.

At some point it is necessary to estimate the quantitative relationships between various key elements. Figure 3–14 shows the estimated effect of chocolate weight percentage—a product characteristic—on candy bar sales. The company would like to keep this percentage down because chocolate is an expensive ingredient compared with the ingredients that make up the soft center. However, consumer tests reveal that as the chocolate content of the bar is reduced, the bar loses its appeal, and sales decline. The soft center begins to appear through the chocolate and leads consumers to feel that the bar is poorly made. Furthermore, their palates desire more chocolate to offset the soft center. When the layer of chocolate gets too thick (above 35 percent of the weight of the bar), consumer

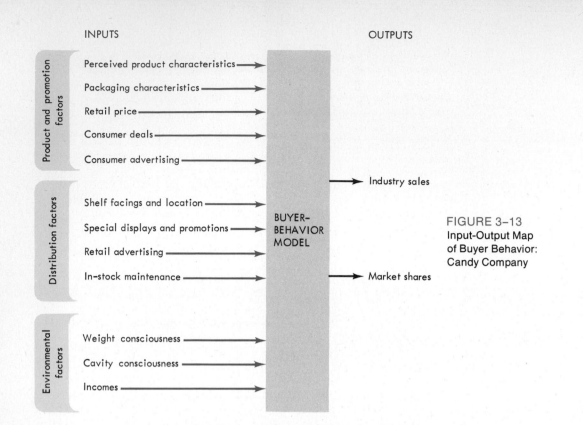

Product and promotion factors

Perceived product characteristics ⟶

Packaging characteristics ⟶

Retail price ⟶

Consumer deals ⟶

Consumer advertising ⟶

Distribution factors

Shelf facings and location ⟶

Special displays and promotions ⟶

Retail advertising ⟶

In-stock maintenance ⟶

Environmental factors

Weight consciousness ⟶

Cavity consciousness ⟶

Incomes ⟶

BUYER-BEHAVIOR MODEL

⟶ Industry sales

⟶ Market shares

FIGURE 3–13
Input-Output Map
of Buyer Behavior:
Candy Company

preference for the bar also falls. The consumers begin to think of it not as a soft-centered bar but as a chocolate bar with "some stuff in it." They compare this bar with pure chocolate bars, and it suffers by comparison. To the best of management's knowledge, sales have the curvilinear relationship to percentage chocolate weight that is shown in Figure 3–14.

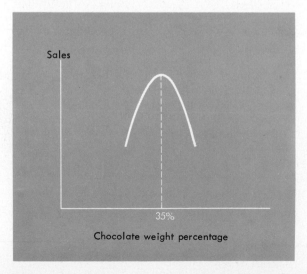

Sales

35%

Chocolate weight percentage

FIGURE 3–14
Functional Relationship Map:
Candy Company

Given this functional relationship, what is the optimum level of chocolate? If the company wishes to maximize sales, chocolate should constitute 35 percent of the candy bar's weight. However, since the company is primarily interested in maximizing profit, management needs the ingredient-cost functions, as well as the sales-response function, to determine the profit-maximizing amount of chocolate.

Other functional relationships should be studied—the relationship between the amount spent on advertising and the resulting sales, the number of sales representatives and the resulting sales, and so on. At some point, the various functional relationships must be put together into a model for analyzing the sales and profit consequences of a proposed marketing plan. A useful graphical-analytical device is shown in Figure 3–15.[10]

Quadrant 1 shows a relationship between population and the total sales of chocolate-covered, soft-centered candy bars. The functional relationship shows that sales tend to increase with population, but at a decreasing rate. The part of the curve describing candy consumption for stages where the American population was under 220 million persons is historically derived through least-squares regression analysis. The part of the curve showing sales for future sizes of the U.S. population is extrapolated and is influenced by anticipated cultural and economic trends. The curve indicates that a population of 220 million persons consumes approximately $105 million of soft-centered candy bars.

The second quadrant shows the relationship between total sales of soft-centered candy bars and company sales. When industry sales are $105 million, the company in question enjoys sales of $70 million—that is, a market share of approximately 67 percent. The part of the curve toward the lower level of industry sales is derived from historical information; the part toward the higher levels of sales is extrapolated on the assumption that there will be no dramatic changes in company and competitors' marketing efforts. Although the function is linear, it does not necessarily indicate that the company expects its market share to remain constant. This would be true only if the line started at the 0,0 origin of this quadrant (not shown). Actually the line indicates that the company expects its share of market to fall slightly as total sales increase. For example, when industry sales are $140 million, the expectation of company sales is $90 million, or an estimated market share of 61 percent as compared with 67 percent now.

The third quadrant shows the relationship between company sales and company profits. Again the company assumes that the relationship is basically linear. At the present time, profits are $7 million on company sales of approximately $70 million, or 10 percent. If company sales go up to $105 million, the company expects profits of approximately $10.2 million—that is, 9.7 percent.

This kind of graphical device, which assumes that all the underlying relationships have been combined and expressed in terms of three basic relationships, allows us to visualize the effect of a particular level of an environment factor and continued marketing program on company sales and profits. To this extent, it is a forecasting device. Its use extends beyond this, however, into marketing planning as well. Suppose, for example, that the company expects the

---

[10] This device was adapted to the candy company example and derives from a suggestion of Robert S. Weinberg, in "Multiple Factor Break-Even Analysis: The Applications of Operations-Research Techniques to a Basic Problem of Management Planning and Control," *Operations Research*, April 1956, pp. 152–86.

new antismoking campaign to have a big impact on candy bar sales, shifting the curve in the first quadrant higher (see Figure 3–15). Furthermore, suppose the company is considering intensifying its marketing effort to increase its market share even further. The anticipated effect of this on company market share can be seen by shifting the function in the second quadrant to the right, as shown in Figure 3–15. At the same time, the company's marketing costs increase and therefore shift the sales-profit curve to the right, as shown in the third quadrant of Figure 3–15. What is the net effect of this complicated set of shifts? The result is that, although sales have increased, profits have fallen. Apparently, the cost to the company of attaining a still higher market share exceeds the profits on the extra sales. The company would be wise not to intensify its marketing effort, at least according to the specific plan it is considering and its estimated effects.

FIGURE 3–15
Profit-Forecasting and Planning Map: Candy Company

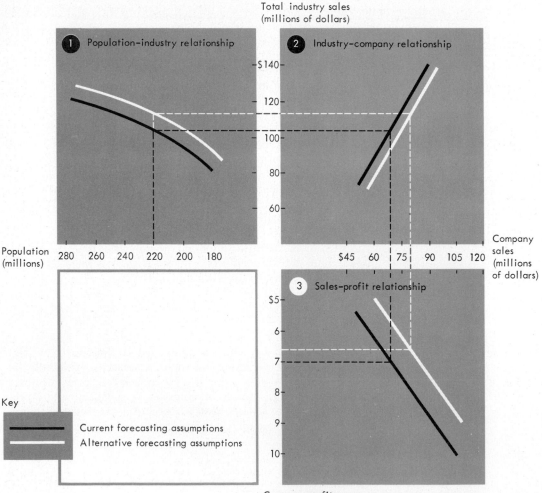

The four-quadrant model assists management in visualizing the impact of specific environmental assumptions and marketing plans on final sales and profits. It can be improved further by introducing more variables and representing their relationships in an overall mathematical model of the candy company's marketing system.

SUMMARY

A marketer is someone who is skilled in marketing system analysis and marketing process analysis. Marketing system analysis, the subject of this chapter, consists of three levels of analysis of increasing scope and complexity: exchange system analysis, organizational marketing analysis, and macroenvironment analysis.

An exchange system involves two or more parties each with something-of-value they might offer in trade. A transaction is the actualization of a potential exchange. The marketer who is seeking an exchange must understand the items making up the want list of the other party and formulate an offer that would be sufficient to motivate a transaction. Exchange maps, whether of two or more parties, assume each party to be pursuing its self-interest.

An organizational marketing system describes the organization and the set of significant interacting institutions and forces in the organization's environment that affect its ability to serve its markets. This system can be conceptualized on five levels. The first level involves the organization's internal environment and the factors and forces that facilitate or inhibit successful marketing action. The second level involves the task system, which consists of the basic institutions that cooperate to create marketing value for a marketplace: specifically the suppliers, organization, marketing intermediaries, and the final market. These four constitute a total marketing channel for meeting a particular set of customer needs. The third level involves the sets of competitors vying for the same market: generic competitors, product form competitors, and enterprise competitors. The fourth level consists of all the publics that have an actual or potential interest or impact on the organization's ability to achieve its objectives: financial publics, media publics, government publics, citizen-action publics, local publics, and the general public. The fifth level consists of the major macroenvironmental forces impinging on the organization: demography, economics, natural resources, technology, law and politics, and culture.

The various concepts of marketing systems analysis are illustrated for a major candy company that produces a candy bar for the mass market.

QUESTIONS AND PROBLEMS

1. Develop a comprehensive marketing system map of some company of your choice. Be sure to show the marketing mix elements and the channels of distribution.

2. Develop an input-output map for the advertising submodel in Figure 3–10.

3. Develop a functional relationship map which shows the relationship between (a) retail price and candy bar sales; (b) advertising and candy bar sales.

4. List as many specific marketing actions to stimulate sales as you can think of available to (a) supermarkets; (b) airlines.

5. Develop a diagram showing the major publics of a privately owned hospital.

6. Develop a three-party exchange map for a hospital's exchange system with the other two parties being the doctor and the patient.

7. "I hold strongly that marketing people should confine themselves to the marketing

field. I don't think most marketing oriented persons have the experience, aptitude, or approach for sound public relations." Do you agree?

8. The text distinguishes three types of competition: generic, product form, and enterprise. Illustrate the three types of competition for a firm in the photocopying machine industry.

9. Describe the marketing channel of a company of your choice.

The Strategic Management and Marketing Process

> *There are three types of companies. Those who make things happen. Those who watch things happen. Those who wonder what happened.*
>
> ANONYMOUS

The preceding chapter examined the structural components of organizational marketing systems but not their functioning. The task now is to show how organizations use the marketing process to convert unfulfilled market needs into profitable business opportunities.

A marketer's work starts long before the organization's products are produced and continues long after their sales are consummated. The professional marketer is involved in studying consumer needs and desires, developing product concepts aimed at satisfying unfulfilled needs, testing the validity of these product concepts, designing product features, developing packaging and a brand name, pricing the product to recover a reasonable return on investment, arranging for regional, national, and international distribution, creating effective marketing communications to let the public know about the product's availability, purchasing the most efficient media for the commercial messages, auditing sales, monitoring customer satisfaction, and revising marketing plans in the light of results. The marketer is a marketing researcher, inventor, psychologist, sociologist, economist, communicator, and lawyer all rolled into one.

There is a larger context for these specific activities, which we would like to consider in this chapter. Let us assume that we are dealing with a large *corporation* that has several *business divisions* and several *product lines* within each division. Marketing plays a role at each level, and we want to understand in what fashion. At the corporate level, marketing contributes perspectives and estimates to help top management decide on the corporation's mission, opportunities, growth strategy, and product portfolio. The policies set by corporate management then provide the context for strategy formulation in each of the business divisions by the divisional managers. Finally, the managers of each product and/or market within each division develop their marketing strategy within the context of the policies and constraints developed at the higher divisional and corporate levels.

We shall use the term *strategic management process* to describe the steps taken at the corporate and divisional levels to develop long-run master strategies for survival and growth. The term *strategic marketing process* will describe the steps taken at the product and/or market level to develop viable marketing positions and programs. The strategic marketing process takes place within the larger strategic management process of the corporation. We shall look first at the strategic management process and then the strategic marketing process.

STRATEGIC MANAGEMENT PROCESS

Many of today's major corporations got their start by coming out with the right products at the right time in a rapidly growing market. Many of their past decisions were made without the benefit of formal strategic thinking and planning. Wise, or lucky, management decisions carried these companies to where they stand today. However, management is recognizing that intuition alone is no longer enough for succeeding in today's environment. More and more companies are turning to formal planning systems to guide their course.

The early planning systems consisted of extrapolating current sales and environmental trends five or ten years out and basing plant and investment decisions on these numbers. Companies recognized the likely occurrence of cyclical and seasonal swings but basically assumed the dependability of the trends themselves. Within the last decade, however, the belief in a continuously growing economy gave way to the actuality of a highly discontinuous one. Companies experienced unexpected cost inflation, shortages of needed material, new technological breakthroughs, unwanted government regulations, high interest costs, aggressive international competition, and the end of the baby boom. As a result, management has come to believe that the only thing certain will be surprises and more surprises. The question becomes: How should a company carry on its planning in an "age of discontinuity" and "future shock"?

The answer of many companies is to switch from extrapolative planning to *strategic planning*. Strategic planning is based on the key concepts of *market evolution* and *strategic fit*. All markets undergo an evolutionary unfolding marked by changing customer needs, technologies, competitors, channels, and laws. The firm should be looking out of a "strategic window" watching these changes and assessing the requirements for continued success in each market.[1] There is only a limited period when the fit between the requirements of a particular market and the firm's competencies is at an optimum. At these times, the strategic window is

---

[1] See Derek F. Abell, "Strategic Windows," *Journal of Marketing,* July 1978, pp. 21–26.

open, and the firm should be investing in this market. In some subsequent period, the firm will find that the evolutionary path of this market is such that it can no longer be effective and efficient in serving this market. It should consider disinvesting and shifting its resources to areas of growing opportunity.

The increased pace of environmental change and rising cost of capital has shifted corporate power in recent years to strategic planners and financial vice presidents. They are calling the shots as to what businesses and products should be built, maintained, reduced, and terminated. Selective growth, rather than total product-line growth, is the key. Company marketers participate in the decision process by supplying estimates of market size and opportunity and presenting their views. Once business objectives are decided, marketing helps carry them out, even if they involve demarketing a product line or business. That is why strategic marketing must be seen today in the context of the strategic management process of the firm.

The strategic management process can be defined as *the managerial process of developing and maintaining a viable relationship between the organization and its environment through the development of corporate purpose, objectives and goals, growth strategies, and business portfolio plans for company-wide operations.* The major steps in this process are shown in Figure 4–1. The result is a strategic plan. We will look at how each component decision is made in terms of marketing inputs and implications.

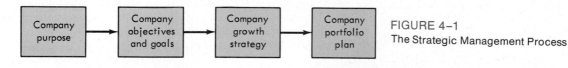

FIGURE 4–1
The Strategic Management Process

Company Purpose

An organization exists to accomplish something in the larger environment. Its specific purpose or mission is usually clear at the beginning.[2] Over time, however, one or more of the following things will happen. (1) The purpose becomes unclear as the organization grows and develops new products and markets. (2) The purpose remains clear but some managers lose their interest in the original purpose. (3) The purpose remains clear but loses its appropriateness to new conditions in the environment.

When management becomes aware that the organization is drifting, it is time to renew the search for purpose. The need is not simply to define a mission that helps management feel good or that serves public relations. A well-worked-out statement of purpose provides employees with a shared sense of opportunity, direction, significance, and achievement. An explicit purpose is an invisible hand, which guides widely scattered employees to work independently and yet collectively toward the realization of the organization's potentials.

In a large company that decides to take a fresh look at its purpose, the

[2] We shall use "purpose" and "mission" interchangeably. However, some authors distinguish the two. Steiner and Miner use "purpose" to describe the economic and ethical motivation of the business, e.g., "to strive for high product quality and corporate integrity." They use "mission" to describe the product and market domain of the firm, e.g., "to produce educational games for adults." See George A. Steiner and J. B. Miner, *Management Policy and Strategy: Text, Readings, and Cases* (Homewood, Ill.: Richard D. Irwin, 1977), p. 7.

people in top management bear the major responsibility. They may solicit ideas from stockholders, employees, customers, and distributors concerning the current and ideal character of the business. They will ask, "What is our business?" and "What should it be?"[3] These sound like simple questions but are among the most difficult ones the company will ever have to answer. A major company recently worked two years to forge a new and satisfactory statement of its purpose.

The purpose of the organization must take into account five key elements. The first is the *history* of the organization. Every organization has a history of aims, policies, and accomplishments. In reaching for a new purpose, the organization must honor the salient characteristics of its past history. It would not make sense for Harvard University, for example, to become a community college, even if such a move were a growth opportunity. The second consideration is the *current preferences* of the management and owners. Those who direct the company have their personal goals and predilections. If Sears's current management wants to serve higher-income consumers, this goal is going to influence the statement of corporate purpose. Third, *environmental considerations* influence the purpose of the organization. The environment defines the main opportunities and threats that must be realistically taken into account. The Girl Scouts of America would not get far in today's environment with the purpose "to prepare young girls for motherhood and wifely duties." Fourth, the organization's *resources* make certain missions possible and others not. Piedmont Airlines would be deluding itself if it adopted the mission to become the world's leading airline. Finally, the organization should base its choice of purpose on its *distinctive competences*. Although it may be able to accomplish many things, it should aim for that which it can do best. McDonald's could probably enter the solar energy business but that would not be making use of its main competence—providing low-cost food and fast service to large groups of customers.

More and more organizations are developing formal statements of corporate purpose that are shared with division heads, employees, and in many cases, customers and the public at large. Some of these statements, unfortunately, are very general and high minded and not very useful in corporate decision making. "We want to be the leading company of its kind producing the highest quality products with the widest distribution and service at the lowest possible prices." This sounds very good but fails to supply clear guidelines when tough business decisions need to be faced.

A number of characteristics should be embodied in a statement of purpose to make it maximally useful. The purpose should be stated in terms of accomplishing something *outside* of the organization. Statements such as "to make money" or "to become the market leader" fail to define a sufficient concept. Profits and leadership are the result of successful accomplishment of purpose rather than the purpose itself.

The statement of purpose should be *specific* as to the *business domain(s)* in which the organization will operate.[4] The business domain can be defined as a

[3] See Peter F. Drucker, *Management: Tasks, Responsibilities, Practices* (New York: Harper & Row, 1973), chap. 7.

[4] Exceptions are holding and investment companies, which operate over a wide range of business domains. They seek to make money wherever it can be made. A few companies, such as the 3M Company and Mobil, also seem ready to enter any business that shows promise of a substantial return.

product class, technological field, customer group, market need, or some combination. Companies have traditionally defined their business domain in product terms, such as "we are a computer manufacturer," or in technological terms, such as "we are a chemical processing company." An increasing number of companies have been moving in recent years to a customer-group definition of their business, such as "we help farmers increase their productivity," or a customer-need definition, such as "we are an entertainment company."

Some years ago, Levitt advanced the thesis that market definitions of a business are superior to product or technological definitions of a business.[5] His main argument is that products and technologies are transient, while basic market needs generally endure forever. A horse carriage company will go out of business as soon as the automobile is invented. But the same company, defined as a people-moving business, would switch from horse carriage manufacture to car manufacture. Levitt's widely read article, along with the economy's increasing uncertainty, encouraged many companies to shift their business domain definition from a product to a market focus. Several examples are given in Table 4–1.

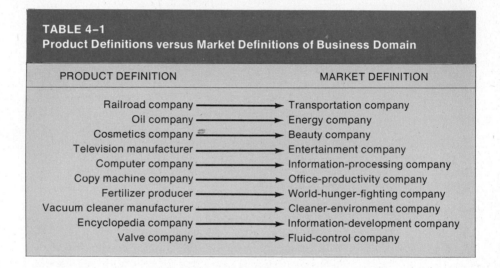

TABLE 4–1
Product Definitions versus Market Definitions of Business Domain

PRODUCT DEFINITION	MARKET DEFINITION
Railroad company	Transportation company
Oil company	Energy company
Cosmetics company	Beauty company
Television manufacturer	Entertainment company
Computer company	Information-processing company
Copy machine company	Office-productivity company
Fertilizer producer	World-hunger-fighting company
Vacuum cleaner manufacturer	Cleaner-environment company
Encyclopedia company	Information-development company
Valve company	Fluid-control company

Ansoff, however, has challenged some market-based definitions as being too broad to provide real direction:

> . . . the term "transportation business" fails to supply the common thread. First, the range of possible missions is very broad: intraurban, interurban, intracontinental, and intercontinental transportation; through the media of land, air, water, underwater; for moving passengers, and/or cargo. Second, the range of customers is wide: the individual, family, business firm, or government office. Third, the "product" varies: car, bus, train, ship, airplane, helicopter, taxi, truck. The number of practical combinations of the variables is large, and so is the number of common threads.[6]

[5] Theodore Levitt, "Marketing Myopia," *Harvard Business Review,* July–August 1960, pp. 45–56.

[6] H. Igor Ansoff, *Corporate Strategy* (New York: McGraw-Hill Book Company, 1965), p. 107.

In developing a market-based definition of a business, management should steer between being too narrow and too broad. A lead pencil manufacturer that believes it is in the business of making communication equipment is stating its mission too broadly. A useful approach is to move from the current product to successively higher levels of abstraction and then decide on the most realistic level of abstraction for the company to consider. Figure 4–2 shows two examples. A candy bar manufacturer can see itself operating in the broader candy market, the still broader snack market, or the still broader food market. A motorcycle manufacturer can see itself expanding to automobiles (motorized pleasure vehicles), trucks (motorized vehicles), or bikes (transportation vehicles). Each broadening step opens a vision of new opportunities but also may lead the company into unrealistic business ventures beyond its capabilities.[7]

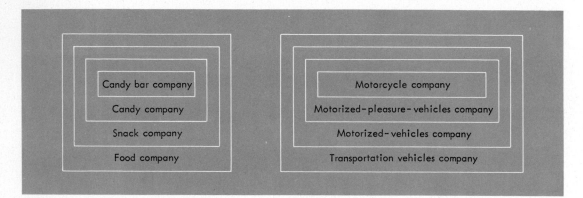

FIGURE 4–2
Successive Expansions of Business Domains

In its development of a definition of business domain, the company may want to specify up to four dimensions: customer need, customer group, product, and technology. Volkswagen, for example, may define its domain as "meeting the need for low-cost personal motorized transportation for low- to moderate-income consumers through providing small cars designed with the most fuel-efficient technology." The statement makes it clear that Volkswagen wants to serve the public's need for efficient cars and is not seeking to enter the large or expensive car market. On the other hand, this business domain would be too narrow for General Motors. However, it might not be too narrow for one of the business divisions of General Motors, and in fact, each division should carefully define its business domain.

Another useful characteristic of a corporate statement of purpose is that it

[7] The abstraction process is somewhat arbitrary. A yogurt producer can expand the domain as *yogurt → health food → health business* or as *yogurt → dessert → food business*. Much depends on what characteristic of a product is initially expanded.

is elevated and motivating in character. Employees would like to feel that their work is important and that they are making a contribution to people's lives. When the prosaic task of producing fertilizer is reshaped into the larger idea of improving agricultural productivity to feed the world's hungry, a new sense of purpose comes over the employees. When the task of selling vacuum cleaners is transformed into the larger idea of creating a cleaner and healthier environment, management is able to visualize a more exciting challenge.

Finally, a corporate statement of purpose should outline major policies that the company plans to honor in the pursuit of its mission. Policies describe the value system of the company: how employees are expected to deal with customers, suppliers, distributors, competition, and other actors and publics. Policies narrow the range of individual discretion, so that the company takes a consistent stand on important issues.

The company's mission, once settled upon, becomes the focus of its energy for the next ten or twenty years. Missions are not something to change every few years simply in response to environmental changes or new unrelated opportunities. On the other hand, sometimes a company has to reconsider its mission statement within a few years of its formulation because it no longer works or it does not define an optimal course for the company. The more rapid the pace of change in the environment, the more often companies will have to reexamine their basic statement of purpose.

Company Objectives and Goals

Management must translate the company's purpose into a set of specific objectives and goals that will support the realization of this purpose. The objectives indicate specific spheres of aim, activity, and accomplishment. The most common objectives of companies are *profitability*, *sales growth*, *market share improvement*, *risk diversification*, and *innovation*. These objectives may flow directly from the basic purpose or be considered as ancillary necessities for carrying out the basic purpose. To be useful, the organization's various objectives should be hierarchical, quantitative, realistic, and consistent.

Hierarchical   A company always pursues a large number of objectives. When possible, these objectives should be stated in a hierarchical fashion from the most important to the least important.[8] An excellent example of hierarchical objectives is provided by Interstate Telephone Company (name disguised).[9] The company has not been earning the allowed rate of 7.5 percent in recent years, giving various "stakeholders" a real cause for concern.[10] One of management's major objectives is to increase its return on investment to 7.5 percent. Starting from this objective, a whole hierarchy of further objectives can be derived, as shown in Figure 4–3.

There are only two ways to increase the return on investment: increase the

---

[8] Charles H. Granger, "The Hierarchy of Objectives," *Harvard Business Review*, May–June 1964, pp. 63–74.

[9] Leon Winer, "Are You Really Planning Your Marketing?" *Journal of Marketing*, January 1965, pp. 1–8.

[10] "Stakeholders" are stockholders and all the other parties who have a "stake" in the firm, such as bankers and managers.

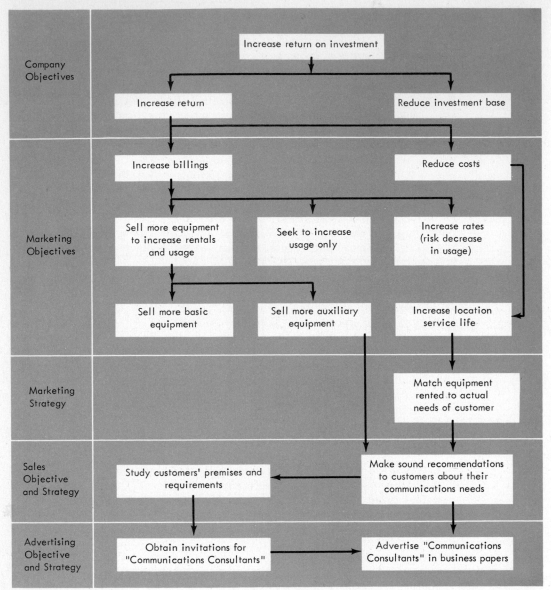

SOURCE: Adapted from Leon Winer, "Are You Really Planning Your Marketing?" *Journal of Marketing,* January 1965, pp. 1–8, here p. 3.

FIGURE 4–3
Hierarchy of Objectives for the Interstate Telephone Company

total return or reduce the investment base. The company is not about to do the latter. To increase its return, the company can strive to increase its billings or reduce its costs, or both. To increase its billings, the company can (1) sell more equipment to increase rentals and usage, (2) seek to increase usage of present equipment, and (3) increase its rates, providing this does not reduce customer usage and is allowed by the rate commission. As for reducing costs, this could be accomplished by increasing the service life of rented telephone equipment, which in turn suggests doing a better job of matching rented equipment to the actual needs of customers. To the extent that the company tries to increase its billings, subsidiary objectives must be set for sales force, advertising, and other elements of the marketing mix. For example, each sales district will be assigned a sales quota based on its potential. Each sales district quota in turn will be broken down and assigned to individual sales representatives. In this way a major objective of the company is ultimately translated into more specific objectives.

Quantitative   To the extent possible, objectives should be stated in quantitative terms. The objective "increase the return on investment" is not as satisfactory as "increase the return on investment to 7.5 percent," or even better, "increase the return on investment to 7.5 percent by the end of the second year." Analysts use the term *goals* to describe an objective that has been made highly specific with respect to *magnitude* and *time*. Turning the objectives into concrete goals facilitates the whole process of management planning and control.

Realistic   A company has to be careful in choosing target levels for its objectives. Not all levels will do. The levels should come out of an analysis of its opportunities and resources, not out of wishful thinking.

Consistent   A company's objectives are sometimes inconsistent, as when management says that it wants "to maximize sales and profits," or "achieve the greatest sales at the least cost," or "design the best possible product in the shortest possible time." These objectives are in a trade-off relationship. It is not possible to maximize sales and profits simultaneously. One can increase sales by lowering price, improving product quality, and increasing marketing effort, although these steps, beyond a point, are likely to reduce profit. Robert Weinberg has identified eight basic strategic trade-offs facing any firm:[11]

1. Short-term profits versus long-term growth
2. Profit margin versus competitive position
3. Direct sales effort versus market development effort
4. Penetration of existing markets versus the development of new markets
5. Related versus nonrelated new opportunities as a source of long-term growth
6. Profit versus nonprofit goals (that is, social responsibilities)
7. Growth versus stability
8. "Riskless" environment versus high-risk environment

A company has to determine the relative emphasis to give to these conflicting objectives, or else they will fail to serve as useful guidelines.

Company Growth Strategy

When an organization has clarified its purpose and objectives, it knows where it wants to go. The question is how best to get there. The company needs a "grand design" for achieving its objectives. That is called strategy. Strategy involves the choice of major directions for pursuing objectives and the allocation of support-

---

[11] Presented in a seminar, "Developing Management Strategies for Short-Term Profits and Long-Term Growth," sponsored by Advanced Management Research, Inc., Regency Hotel, New York City, September 29, 1969.

ing resources. Strategy is the company's concept of how to win the war. It should not be confused with tactics, which are derived activities designed to win battles.

Most companies have growth of sales and profits as one of their major objectives. They don't want to stand still. Lack of growth drains the company of new challenge, leads to the loss of its entrepreneurial managers, and exposes it to possible technological obsolescence. In wanting growth, companies need a growth strategy. They need to select from a whole set of possible investment directions those that are most likely to produce the desired growth. Consider the following case:

> Musicale Corporation (name disguised) is a leading phonograph records company, which along with other companies in the industry, faces some basic challenges. The costs and competition for top recording artists have been escalating. An alternative form of packaging music, tape cassettes, has been making rapid inroads. Channels of distribution have been shifting in favor of mass-merchandise outlets over small retailers. Larger promotion budgets are becoming necessary for launching new releases.
>
> Musicale has not sat idly by in the face of these challenges. It acquired a magnetic-tape-producing company and proceeded to market its music in cassette form with some success. Because its tape-manufacturing capacity exceeded its music-business needs, it formed a division to market magnetic tape to computer manufacturers and users. The company also tried its hand at manufacturing a complete line of phonographs under its own name; it later withdrew because their marketing required more resources than the company chose to invest. Still later Musicale entered the electronics business but withdrew in a few years.
>
> Although Musicale has been willing to venture away from the recording business, it has not done this with any great success. It did not show much patience with its new ventures because of their initial unprofitability. Its various ventures, while all loosely related to its major business, represented a set of ad hoc responses to fortuitous opportunities rather than the working out of a well-designed master plan for company growth. Musicale, sorely aware of its aimless growth history, is seeking a more systematic strategy for growth.

Alternative growth strategies can be generated for a company by mapping its marketing system and then moving to three levels of analysis. The first level identifies those opportunities available to the company in its current sphere of operations; we call them *intensive growth opportunities*. The second level identifies those opportunities available through integration with other parts of this marketing system; we call them *integrative growth opportunities*. The third level identifies those opportunities present completely outside the present marketing system; we call them *diversification growth opportunities*. Table 4–2 lists the specific possibilities latent in each of these broad opportunity classes.

Intensive growth   Intensive growth makes sense for a company if it has not fully exploited the opportunities latent in its current products and markets. Ansoff has proposed a useful classification of intensive-growth opportunities based on a *product/market expansion matrix*.[12] The matrix is shown in Figure 4–4 and the three major types of intensive growth opportunities are described as follows:

[12] H. Igor Ansoff, "Strategies for Diversification," *Harvard Business Review*, September–October 1957, pp. 113–24. The same matrix can be expanded into nine cells by adding modified products and modified markets. See S.C. Johnson and Conrad Jones, "How to Organize for New Products," *Harvard Business Review*, May–June 1957, pp. 49–62.

TABLE 4–2
Major Classes of Growth Opportunities

I. INTENSIVE GROWTH	II. INTEGRATIVE GROWTH	III. DIVERSIFICATION GROWTH
A. Market penetration	A. Backward integration	A. Concentric diversification
B. Market development	B. Forward integration	B. Horizontal diversification
C. Product development	C. Horizontal integration	C. Conglomerate diversification

FIGURE 4–4
Product/Market
Expansion Matrix

1. ***Market penetration.*** *Market penetration consists of the company's seeking increased sales for its current products in its current markets through more aggressive marketing effort.* There are three possibilities:

   a. The company can try to stimulate current customers to increase their *current rate of purchase.* This is a function of the *purchase frequency* times the *purchase amount.* Musicale can try to encourage customers to buy records more frequently and to buy more on each occasion. New releases, price promotion, advertising, publicity, and wider distribution aid in this effort. More basically, Musicale can think of opportunities to increase the *current rate of consumption,* which underlies the current rate of purchase. The consumption rate is a function of the *number of use occasions* times the *amount used per occasion.* If consumers start listening to their records on more occasions (say, early morning as well as evening) and listen to more records each time, they will buy more records.

   b. The company can increase its efforts to attract competitors' customers. To increase their market share, Musicale can develop bigger stars, record better performances, design more attractive record jackets, offer more attractive prices, use stronger advertising, and gain wider distribution.

   c. The company can increase its efforts to attract nonusers located in its current market areas. Such steps might be taken as exposing nonusers to more music, reducing the price of phonographs, and developing more publicity about music listening as a hobby.

2. ***Market development.*** *Market development consists of the company's seeking increased sales by taking its current products into new markets.* There are two possibilities:

   a. The company can open additional geographical markets through regional, national, or international expansion. The company is currently underrepresented in certain U.S. cities and is doing only an average job of participating in the growing international market.

b. The company can try to attract new market segments through developing product versions that appeal to these segments, entering other channels of distribution, or advertising in other media. The company, for example, is not well represented in the preteen segment of the market.

3. **Product development.** *Product development consists of the company's seeking increased sales by developing new or improved products for its current markets.* There are three possibilities:

a. The company can develop new product features or content through attempting to adapt, modify, magnify, minify, substitute, rearrange, reverse, or combine existing features.[13]

b. The company can create different-quality versions of the product.

c. The company can develop additional models and sizes. For example, Musicale might research and develop a new type of record that carries more sound track or better quality. It might produce all-plastic sheet records, such as those that are increasingly being inserted in magazines. It might produce new program content, such as a do-it-yourself series or a basic education series.

Integrative growth   Integrative growth makes sense for a company if the basic industry has a strong growth future and/or the company can increase its profitability, efficiency, or control by moving backward, forward, or horizontally within the industry. Figure 4–5 shows the task-marketing system for Musicale. Three integrative-growth possibilities are discussed below.

1. **Backward integration.** *Backward integration consists of a company's seeking ownership or increased control of its supply systems.* Musicale relies heavily on plastic-material producers and recording equipment manufacturers. Musicale might see an advantage in backward integration if any of these suppliers is enjoying high growth or profits, or if there is some uncertainty over the availability or cost of future supplies.

2. **Forward integration.** *Forward integration consists of a company's seeking ownership or increased control of its distribution systems.* Musicale might see an advantage in forward integration if any of these marketing intermediaries is enjoying high growth or profits, or if Musicale is not getting satisfactory service. It might also start a direct-mail-order record club to reduce its dependence on middlemen.

3. **Horizontal integration.** *Horizontal integration consists of a company's seeking ownership or increased control of some of its competitors.* Musicale has seen several new companies enjoy phenomenal growth in a short time, based on a sharp ability to spot new recording talent. These companies could be attractive targets for takeover and could provide Musicale with new management talent and some new stars. Musicale would have to be sure that the acquisitions would not be challenged by the government as "tending substantially to lessen competition."

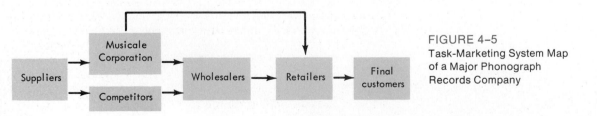

FIGURE 4–5
Task-Marketing System Map
of a Major Phonograph
Records Company

---

[13] See Alex F. Osborn, *Applied Imagination*, 3rd ed. (New York: Charles Scribner's Sons, 1963), pp. 286–87.

Diversification growth   Diversification growth makes sense for a company if the task-marketing system does not show much additional opportunity for growth or profit or if the opportunities outside of the present task-marketing system are superior. Diversification does not mean that the company will take up any opportunity that comes along. The company would attempt to identify fields that make use of its distinctive competences or help it overcome a particular problem. There are three broad types of diversification moves:

1. *Concentric diversification. Concentric diversification consists of the company's seeking to add new products that have technological and/or marketing synergies with the existing product line; these products normally will appeal to new classes of customers.* Musicale, for example, would search for other products that make use of its ability to work with plastics, sound recording, or artistically talented performers. One intriguing idea is for Musicale to go into other businesses with the talent under contract (such as name franchising) and manage other classes of talent (business executives, writers, and professors).

2. *Horizontal diversification. Horizontal diversification consists of the company's seeking to add new products that could appeal to its current customers though technologically unrelated to its current product line.* The products might appeal to the company's ultimate customers or its intermediate customers. For example, Musicale might publish a teenage magazine or make teenage clothing because of its great understanding of teenage tastes and life styles. Or it might manufacture other products that are carried by record retailers, such as phonographs or tape recorders. However, we saw that these horizontal diversification moves did not work out well for Musicale, primarily because the company did not have the competences to meet the success requirements in these businesses.

3. *Conglomerate diversification. Conglomerate diversification consists of the company's seeking to add new products for new classes of customers either because such a move promises to offset some deficiency or because it represents a great environmental opportunity; whichever the case, the new products have no relationship to the company's current technology, products, or markets.* Most companies experience seasonal or cyclical fluctuations, which are costly in terms of manpower, inventory carrying costs, or cash-flow management. Musicale has high sales in certain seasons, such as Christmas and Easter, and low sales during business recessions. These factors might lead it to look for business opportunities that have a different seasonal or cyclical pattern. Or companies like Musicale may be attracted to environmental opportunities, such as pollution control or health sciences, simply because they are very attractive. It might feel that it could acquire whatever competences were necessary to be successful in the new business. This optimism often proves, however, to be very naive.

Thus we see that a company can systematically identify growth opportunities through application of a marketing systems framework, looking first at current product-market opportunities, then at opportunities in other parts of the task-marketing system, and finally at relevant opportunities outside of the task system.

Company Portfolio Plan   Another major task of top management is the shaping of a business portfolio plan. At any point in time, a company consists of a portfolio of businesses (divisions, product lines, products, brands). This is true for nonprofit organizations as well as industrial companies. For example, a university consists of a number of schools, departments, and courses; and the YMCA consists of hotels, schools, summer camps, and recreational facilities. In the past, most organizations encouraged all their business units to grow by giving all of them a larger budget each year. All were held to increased sales and profit goals. The exceptions were seriously declining or troubled products. In recent years, organizations have moved to more selectivity because cash is scarce and opportunities differ greatly. Organizations now view themselves as managing a portfolio of businesses, and top management's job is to decide which businesses to build, maintain, phase down, and phase out. Thus a major company objective is to keep refreshing the company's portfolio of businesses by flushing out poor ones and adding promising new ones.

To carry out this objective, management first has to identify the *strategic business units* (SBUs) making up the company. An SBU has, ideally, the following characteristics:

1. It is a single business or collection of related businesses.
2. It has a distinct mission.
3. It has its own competitors.
4. It has a responsible manager.
5. It consists of one or more program units and functional units.
6. It can benefit from strategic planning.
7. It can be planned independently of the other businesses.

An SBU can, depending on the circumstances, be one or more company divisions, a product line within a division, or sometimes a single product.

The next step calls for management to classify all of the SBUs in a way that would reveal their resource-allocation merit. The two best-known classification schemes are those of the Boston Consulting Group and General Electric.

Boston Consulting Group approach   In this approach, pioneered by the Boston Consulting Group, the company classifies all of its SBUs in the *business portfolio matrix* (also called growth-share matrix) shown in Figure 4–6.[14] There are several things to notice.

1. The vertical axis, *market growth rate,* shows the annualized rate at which the various markets are growing in which each business unit is located. Market growth is arbitrarily divided into high and low growth by a 10 percent growth line.
2. The horizontal axis, *relative market share,* shows the market share for each SBU relative to the share of the industry's largest competitor. Thus a relative market share of .4 means that the company's SBU stands at 40 percent of the leader's share; and a relative market share of 2.0 means that the company's SBU is the leader and has twice the share of the next strongest company in the market. Relative market share gives more information about competitive standing than absolute market share; an absolute market share of 15 percent may or may not mean market leadership until we know the leader's share. The more that its SBUs have a relative market share greater than 1.5, the more the company is a leader in its various markets. The relative market share is drawn in log scale.

---

[14] For additional reading, see Charles W. Hofer and Dan Schendel, *Strategy Formulation: Analytical Concepts* (St. Paul, Minn.: West Publishing Company, 1978); George S. Day, "Diagnosing the Product Portfolio," *Journal of Marketing,* April 1977, pp. 29–38; and "Olin's Shift to Strategic Planning," *Business Week,* March 27, 1978, pp. 102–5.

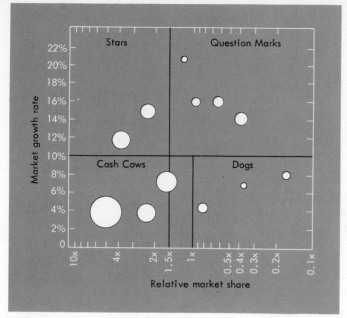

FIGURE 4–6
The BCG Business Portfolio Matrix

SOURCE: B. Hedley, "Strategy and the 'Business Portfolio'," *Long-Range Planning*, February 1977, p. 12.

3. The circles depict the growth-share standings of the company's various SBUs. The areas of the circles are proportional to the SBUs' dollar sales.

4. Each quadrant represents a distinct type of cash-flow situation, leading to the following classification of SBUs:

   • **Stars.** Stars are high-growth, high-share SBUs. They are often cash-using SBUs because cash is necessary to finance their rapid growth. Eventually their growth will slow down, and they will turn into cash cows and become major cash generators supporting other SBUs.

   • **Cash cows.** Cash cows are low-growth, high-share SBUs. They throw off a lot of cash that the company uses to meet its bills and support other SBUs that are cash using.

   • **Question marks.** Question marks (also called problem children or wildcats) are low-share SBUs in high-growth markets. They require a lot of cash to maintain their share, let alone increase their share. Management has to think hard about whether to spend more to build these question marks into leaders; if not, the question marks will have to be phased down or out.

   • **Dogs.** Dogs (also called cash traps) are low-growth, low-share SBUs. They may generate enough cash to maintain themselves but do not promise to be a large source of cash.

5. The higher an SBU's market share, the higher its cash-generating ability. That is because higher market shares appear to be accompanied by higher levels of profitability. On the other hand, the higher the market-growth rate, the higher the SBU's cash-using requirements in order for it to grow and maintain its share.

6. The distribution of the SBUs in the four quadrants of the business portfolio matrix suggests the company's current state of health and desirable future strategic directions. The company in Figure 4–6 is fortunate in having some large cash cows

to finance its question marks, stars, and dogs. The company should seriously consider some decisive actions concerning its dogs and question marks. The picture would be worse if the company discovered that it had no stars, or had too many dogs, or had only a few weak cash cows.

7. As time passes, SBUs will change their positions in the business portfolio matrix. Many SBUs start out as question marks, move into the star category if they succeed, later become cash cows as market growth falls, and finally turn into dogs toward the end of their life cycle. Companies must be willing to let go of their weakening cash cows and not treat them as sacred cows.

8. Management's job is to project a future matrix showing where each SBU is likely to be assuming no change in its strategy. By comparing the current and future matrices, management can identify the major strategic issues facing the firm. The task of strategic planning is then to determine what role should be assigned to each SBU in the interest of efficient resource allocation. Four basic strategies can be pursued.

- **Build.** A strategy aiming at an improved market position with the willingness to forego short-term earnings to achieve this goal. This strategy is particularly appropriate for question marks, whose share has to grow if they are to become stars.
- **Hold.** A strategy designed to preserve the market position of an SBU. This strategy is particularly appropriate for strong cash cows if they are to continue to yield a large, positive cash flow.
- **Harvest.** A strategy that aims at getting short-term increase in cash flow regardless of the long-term effect. This strategy is particularly appropriate for a weak cash cow whose future is dim and from which more cash flow is needed. It can also be used with question marks and dogs.
- **Divest.** A strategy that aims at selling or liquidating the business because resources can be used better elsewhere. This stragegy is particularly appropriate for dogs and for question marks that the company decides it cannot finance for growth.

General Electric approach   The appropriate objective to assign to an SBU cannot be determined solely on the basis of its position in the growth-share matrix. If additional factors are introduced, the growth-share matrix can be seen as a special case of a more fundamental portfolio classification system, one that General Electric (GE) has pioneered, called a *nine-cell strategic business screen* (see Figure 4–7). Several things should be noticed.

1. The vertical axis represents the *industry's attractiveness*, which is based on rating such factors as *market growth rate* (used earlier in the growth-share analysis), *market size, profit margin, competitive intensity, cyclicality, seasonality,* and *scale economies*. Each of these factors is given a certain weight, a procedure that results in classifying a particular industry as high, medium, or low in overall industry attractiveness.[15]

2. The horizontal axis represents the SBU's *business strength* or ability to compete in that industry. Each industry has certain success requirements, which must be matched by the SBU having the required competences. Business strength is a

[15] An example of the weighting of factors is described in a future evolution of the business screen developed by the Shell Company which they call the directional policy matrix. See S. J. Q. Robinson, R. E. Hichens, and D. P. Wade, "The Directional Policy Matrix—Tool for Strategic Planning," *Long-Range Planning*, June 1978, pp. 8–15; and D. E. Hussey, "Portfolio Analysis: Practical Experience with the Directional Policy Matrix," *Long-Range Planning*, August 1978, pp. 2–8.

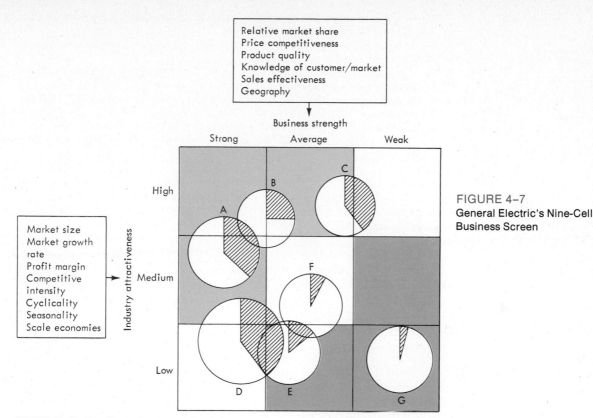

Relative market share
Price competitiveness
Product quality
Knowledge of customer/market
Sales effectiveness
Geography

Business strength

Strong   Average   Weak

Market size
Market growth
rate
Profit margin
Competitive
intensity
Cyclicality
Seasonality
Scale economies

Industry attractiveness

High

Medium

Low

FIGURE 4–7
**General Electric's Nine-Cell
Business Screen**

SOURCE: Modified from Charles W. Hofer and Dan Schendel, *Strategy Formulation: Analytical Concepts* (St. Paul, Minn.: West Publishing Co., 1978), p. 32.

weighted rating of such factors as the SBU's *relative market share* (used earlier in the growth-share analysis), *price competitiveness, product quality, knowledge of customer/market, sales effectiveness,* and *geography.*

3. The screen is divided into three zones, which are known as green, yellow, and red. The green zone consists of the three cells at the upper left (vertical lines) indicating those industries that are favorable in industry attractiveness and SBU business strength, suggesting that the company has the green light to "invest and grow." The yellow zone consists of the diagonal cells stretching from the lower left to upper right, indicating industries that are medium in overall attractiveness. The company usually decides to maintain the SBU's share rather than have it grow or reduce its share. The red zone consists of the three cells in the lower right (horizontal) indicating those industries that are low in overall attractiveness, and here the company gives serious consideration to harvesting or divesting.

4. The circles represent individual SBUs. The areas of the circles are proportional to the size of the industries in which the various businesses compete, while the pie slices within the circles represent each SBU's market share. Thus G represents an SBU with a very small market share in a fair-size industry that is not very attractive and in which the company has little business strength.

5. The management should also plot a business screen showing projected positions of the SBUs if there is no change in strategies. By comparing the current and projected business screens, management can identify the major strategic issues and

opportunities it faces. For example, this type of analysis led GE to sort its current mix of SBUs into five investment groups:[16]

a. *High-growth products deserving the highest investment support*—engineering plastics, medical systems, transportation
b. *Steady reinvestment products deserving high and steady investment*—major appliances, steam and gas turbines, lamps
c. *Support products deserving steady investment support*—meters, specialty transformers
d. *Selective pruning or rejuvenation products deserving reduced investment*
e. *Venture products deserving heavy R&D investment*—"10-ton aircraft engine," microwave ovens, man-made diamonds

Many companies first classify their business using the Boston Consulting Group approach and then go into greater detail with the General Electric approach. Decisions are made on each SBU as to whether it will be built, held, harvested, or divested. Managers of SBUs in the latter three groups are given the opportunity to take issue with the judgment by supplying market data showing an SBU's greater potential. However, once the decision is made, the manager has to carry it out. For marketers, this means that their task is not always to build sales volume. If a business is slated for harvesting, then the marketer has to develop an optimal harvesting marketing plan, which might call for reducing plant and equipment expenditure, reducing R&D investment, reducing product quality and services, reducing advertising and sales-force expenditures, and raising price.[17]

The other implication of portfolio planning is that company marketers bear the main burden for coming up with new ideas for products and businesses to replace those that are being eliminated from the company's portfolio. Finding sound new ideas and developing them successfully calls for a well-worked-out theory of the strategic marketing process, to which we now turn.

STRATEGIC MARKETING PROCESS

Here we will examine the *strategic marketing process*, which defines the larger context for carrying out the day-to-day marketing activities of the firm. The strategic marketing process is *a managerial process of analyzing market opportunities and choosing marketing positions, programs, and controls that create and support viable businesses that serve the company's purpose and objectives.* The specific steps in the strategic marketing process are shown in Figure 4–8 and discussed in the following paragraphs.

Market Opportunity Analysis

The strategic marketing process begins with the effort to develop an attractive set of opportunities for the firm. Although new opportunities can be generated anywhere in the company, the marketing department bears this as a major responsibility. Some firms are chronically short of good ideas; here the marketer's task is to generate new ones. Other firms feel they have too many opportunities; here the marketer's task is to assist in selecting among them. In general, market-

---

[16] "GE Growth Plans Outline by Jones," *Bridgeport Telegram,* November 8, 1974.

[17] For the art of harvesting, see Philip Kotler, "Harvesting Strategies for Weak Products," *Business Horizons,* August 1978, pp. 15–22.

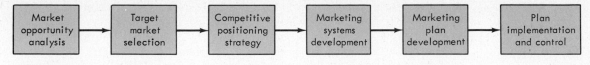

FIGURE 4–8
The Strategic Marketing Process

ers make a major contribution in generating, evaluating, and selecting attractive opportunities.

It is important to distinguish between *environmental opportunities* and *company opportunities*. There are countless environmental opportunities available in any economy as long as there are unsatisfied needs. Currently there are great opportunities to develop new sources of energy, new food products, improved agricultural methods, improved forms of transportation, new forms of leisure, and improved teaching technology. There are opportunities in refuse disposal, low-cost legal services, containerization, prefab housing, water purification, day-care centers, and biomedical instruments. But none of these necessarily represents opportunities for any specific company. Day-care centers are probably not an opportunity for U.S. Steel, nor are biomedical instruments an opportunity for Kentucky Fried Chicken.

The company should be concerned with relevant marketing opportunities. These are suggested by the purpose, objectives, growth strategies, and portfolio decisions of the company. We define a *company marketing opportunity* as follows:

> A *company marketing opportunity* is an attractive arena of relevant marketing action in which a particular company is likely to enjoy a differential advantage.

An opportunity is attractive if it is consistent with the company's purpose and likely to advance the company's objectives. The question is whether the company can bring more to this environmental opportunity than its potential competitors can. We make the following assumptions:

1. Every environmental opportunity has specific *success requirements*.
2. Each company has *distinctive competences*, that is, things that it can do especially well.
3. A company is likely to enjoy a *differential advantage* in an area of environmental opportunity if its distinctive competences match the success requirements of the environmental opportunity better than its potential competition.

Suppose General Motors, General Electric, and Sears all become interested at the same time in developing and marketing an electric car. Which firm would enjoy the greatest differential advantage? First we consider the success requirements. The success requirements would include (1) having good relations with suppliers of metal, rubber, plastic, glass, and other materials needed to produce an automobile, (2) having skill at mass production and mass assembly of complicated pieces of equipment, (3) having a strong distribution capacity to store, show, and deliver automobiles to the public, and (4) having the confidence of buyers that the company is able to produce and service a good auto product. Now General Motors has distinctive competences in all four of these areas. General Electric has distinctive competences in (1) supply and (2) production but not in (3) distribution or (4) automobile reputation. It does have great know-how in electrical technology. Sears's major distinctive competence is its extensive retailing system, but it would have to acquire the other competences. All said, General Motors would enjoy a major differential advantage in the production and marketing of electric cars.

The set of marketing opportunities available to a company at a particular time can be called the *company opportunity set.* The marketer's main technical contribution is to evaluate the *sales potential* of each opportunity. Who would buy the product? How much would they pay? What would be the optimal features? How many would buy? Where are they located? Who will the competition be? What distribution channels would be needed? These and other questions would be researched to estimate the sales potential. Financial and manufacturing executives would add their estimates of costs for a final evaluation of each opportunity.

Target Market Selection

Each market opportunity that looks good would have to be analyzed more closely from the point of view of how to enter that market. Each market is filled with many more customer groups and customer needs than one company can possibly serve, or serve in a superior fashion. The task calls for *market segmentation,* that is, breaking the total market into logical market segments (also called submarkets) that differ in their requirements, buying habits, or other critical characteristics. Once a useful segmentation approach is developed, the company can consider what part of the market it wants to serve.

A useful approach to segmentation is to develop a *product/market grid.* Possible products (or customer needs) can be shown in the rows and market segments (or customer groups) in the columns. Consider the following situation. A large equipment manufacturer has reviewed a set of opportunities and finds the idea of entering the boating industry to be attractive in terms of sales potential and company fit. The marketing vice president undertakes to examine in depth the product/market structure of the boating industry. The result is shown in Figure 4–9. The product/market consists of three distinguishable types of boats (shown in the rows) and three distinguishable customer markets (shown in the columns). The marketing vice president now proceeds to estimate, for each of the nine segments, the degree of market attractiveness and the company's degree of business strength, using the factors cited earlier on page 78. Suppose the segment that looks best is the "small lake speedboat" segment that is shaded in Figure 4–9.

Even this market segment may be larger than the company can serve, in which case *subsegmentation* is warranted. Figure 4–10 shows a subsegmentation of the "small lake speedboat" segment by geographical areas and family incomes. Suppose the company reviews each subsegment and decides that its best opportunity lies in designing and selling speedboats to families with incomes from $20,000 to $35,000 who live near small lakes in the Midwest. The company has now arrived at a clear idea of its *target market.*

This target market may constitute the total ambition of the company or may be viewed as a launching pad for later invasions of the larger market. In

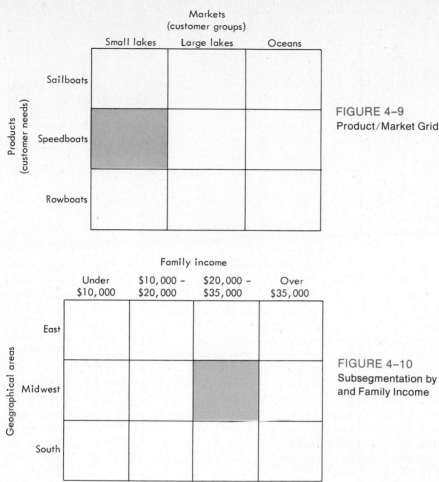

FIGURE 4–9
Product/Market Grid

FIGURE 4–10
Subsegmentation by Geographical Areas
and Family Income

fact, companies have been observed to entertain one of five *market-coverage strategies*, shown in Figure 4–11. In the first, called *product/market concentration*, a company niches itself in one part of the market. Usually smaller companies choose this pattern of market coverage. In the second, *product specialization*, a company decides to produce a full line of speedboats for all customer groups. In the third, *market specialization*, a company decides to make a full line of boats that serve the sundry needs of boaters on small lakes. In the fourth, *selective specialization*, a company enters multiple niches that have no relation to each other except that each provides an individually attractive opportunity. This pattern is usually the end result of an opportunistic acquisition program. The last strategy, *full coverage*, is typically undertaken by larger companies that seek market leadership. In general, a company might initially enter the most attractive market segment and spread out systematically as opportunities arise.

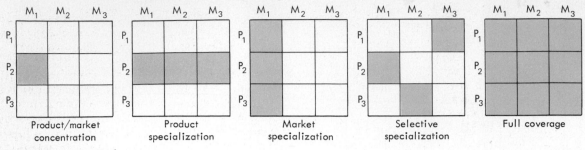

P = Product   M = Market

SOURCE: Adapted from Derek F. Abell, *Defining the Business: The Starting Point of Strategic Planning* (Englewood Cliffs, N.J.: Prentice-Hall, Inc., 1980), Chapter 8.

FIGURE 4–11
Five Patterns of Market Coverage

Competitive Positioning

The third step in the strategic marketing process is called *competitive positioning* and requires the firm to develop *a general idea of what kind of offer to make to the target market in relation to competitors' offers.*[18] Recall that the boat company decided to produce speedboats for medium-income people living near small lakes. The company should now make an effort to learn what competitors are offering to customers in this market and what customers really want. On the basis of the findings, the company is ready to choose a competitive positioning.

Suppose the company learns that boat buyers look at boat size and boat complexity as two product attributes of interest. The company can ask prospective customers and dealers where they perceive competitors' boats to be located along these dimensions, and the results can be plotted in the *product space map* shown in Figure 4–12. Competitor A is seen as producing large/complex boats, B, medium-size/medium-complex boats, C, medium-size/simple boats, and D, small/simple boats.[19] The areas of the circles are proportional to the competitors' sales.

Given these competitor positions, what position should the new manufacturer seek? The company has two basic choices. One is to take a position next to one of the existing competitors and fight for the customers who want that type of boat. The company might choose to do this if it feels that (1) it can build a better boat of this type, (2) the market buying this kind of boat is large enough for two competitors, (3) it has more resources than the existing competitor, and/or (4) this position is the most consistent with the company's reputation and competence.

The other choice is to develop a boat that is not currently offered to this

[18] Other terms that will be used interchangeably with competitive positioning are *market positioning* and *product positioning*. Market positioning suggests defining where the company and competitors stand in relation to market needs or attributes within the target market. Product positioning suggests defining where existing products of the company and/or competitors stand in terms of product attributes.

[19] These maps must be interpreted with care. Not all customers share the same perceptions. The map shows the average perception. Attention should also be paid to the scatter of perceptions. See chap. 13, pp. 322–23.

market, such as a small complex boat (see empty northwest quadrant of Figure 4–12). The company would gain instant leadership in this part of the market since competitors are not offering this type of boat. But before making this decision, the company has to be sure that (1) it is technically feasible to build a small complex speedboat, (2) it is economically feasible to build a small complex speedboat at the planned price level, and (3) there are a sufficient number of buyers who would prefer a small complex speedboat to any other kind. If the answers are all positive, the firm has discovered a "hole" in the market and should quickly move to fill it.

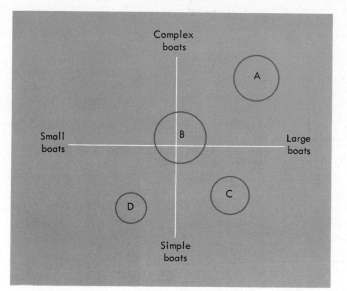

FIGURE 4–12
A Product Space Map Showing
Perceived Offers of Four Competitors

Suppose, however, the company decides there is more profit potential and less risk in building a large complex boat to compete with competitor A. In this case, the company would study A's boat and other aspects of A's offer, seeking a way to differentiate its offer in the eyes of potential buyers. Instead of competitive positioning through product-feature differentiation, it might seek competitive positioning through price/quality differentiation. In this case, the company faces the nine options shown in Figure 4–13. If competitor A, for example, is producing an average-quality boat and charging an average price, the new company could consider introducing a high-quality boat selling at a higher price (called a premium strategy). Or it can give careful consideration to one of the other strategies in Figure 4–13.

Two further factors affect the decision on target market and competitive position. The first is how the firm will acquire the resources to enter the boating industry. The company can proceed through acquisition, internal development, or collaboration with other companies.

Acquisition of an existing product or company is the easiest and quickest way to enter a new market. Acquisition obviates the costly and time-consuming process of attempting to build up internally the knowledge, resources, and reputation necessary to become an effective participant in that part of the market. The following conditions would favor acquisition:

1. The acquiring company has very little knowledge of the industry.
2. There is a strong advantage in entering the new market as soon as possible.
3. The company would face several barriers to entry through internal development, such as patents, substantial economies of scale, closed or difficult-to-enter channels of distribution, costly advertising requirements, or lack of raw materials or other supplies.

		Price		
		High	Medium	Low
Product quality	High	1. Premium strategy	2. Penetration strategy	3. Superbargain strategy
	Medium	4. Overpricing strategy	5. Average-quality strategy	6. Bargain strategy
	Low	7. Hit-and-run strategy	8. Shoddy-goods strategy	9. Cheap-goods strategy

FIGURE 4–13
Nine Competitive Positioning Strategies on Price/Quality

Some companies prefer to achieve most of their growth through *internal development*. They may feel that true leadership is achieved by innovation. They may feel that acquiring a company will raise the brows of antitrust people. They may feel that acquirable companies are not very good or are asking for too much. Or there may be no companies to acquire.

Entry into a new market or market segment may also be accomplished by *collaboration* with others to jointly exploit the new opportunity. A major advantage is that the risk is shared, and therefore reduced, for each of the participating companies. Another advantage may be that each company brings specific skills or resources, the lack of which makes it impossible for either company to venture by itself. In the best joint-venturing combinations, there is not only complementarity but synergy.

In addition to mode of entry, there is the question of timing. Just because a company has spotted a good opportunity does not mean it should immediately move in. It may lose by moving in too soon or too late. Is the nation headed for recession or prosperity? Is the major competitor back-ordered or hungry for business? These and other questions must be considered in determining the best moment to strike.

Marketing Systems Development

Once the company has chosen a target market and defined its competitive position, it is ready to undertake *marketing systems development. Marketing systems development is the task of developing a marketing organization, information system, planning system, and control system that promises to accomplish the company's objectives in the target market.*

Returning to our illustration, the company must establish a new SBU to take responsibility for the boating venture. The first step should be a marketing department, consisting of a divisional vice president of marketing, a sales force, and one or more staff members handling marketing research, promotion, customer service, and marketing planning. The size of the marketing organization will be small initially but will grow over time.

The SBU will need an information system to process inquiries and orders, gather marketing intelligence, forecast market and sales potential, survey buyers and dealers, and analyze sales and profits results. The information will have to be current, accurate, relevant, and comprehensive if the company is going to outperform competitors in meeting customer needs. The SBU will need a planning system that will lead to the annual development of goals, strategies, and tactics and their review and approval by higher levels of management. The overall sales goals will have to be broken down into quotas for sales territories and individual salespersons. The marketing budget will have to be allocated to various marketing-mix elements and territories.

Finally, the SBU will need to establish a system of controls to monitor performance, detect problems, improve efficiency, and take corrective actions when needed. The controls will have to address major questions, such as whether the business unit is going after the right market with the right marketing mix, as well as smaller questions, such as whether the sales force is using its time optimally and whether the advertising money is being spent efficiently.

Marketing Plan Development

The key to the SBUs success will lie in the quality of the long-range and annual marketing plans developed for the target market. A marketing plan is a written document that spells out the goals, strategies, and tactics that will be used to gain and maintain the competitive position and results that the company is seeking. The major elements of a marketing plan are as follows:

Situation analysis   A marketing plan begins with a summary of recent performance followed by a presentation of trends and issues connected with the macroenvironment, competitors, customers, suppliers, distributors, and other parties. Major problems and opportunities are laid out, and strategic alternatives are posed and evaluated.

Marketing objectives and goals   This section states the major marketing objectives for the coming period and translates them into goals that are achievable and measurable. The overall sales goal is allocated to the sales units of the company, such as sales regions, sales districts, and finally individual salespersons. In this form the goals are called sales quotas and are based on the past performance and estimated potential facing each of these units.

Marketing strategy, action program, and budget. To achieve the marketing objectives and goals, the SBU must develop a sound marketing strategy and action program. Rough strategic ideas were presumably established earlier in the competitive positioning decision. In the marketing-planning stage, the actual marketing strategy must be worked out in detail. We will define a marketing strategy as follows:

> *Marketing strategy* is a set of objectives, policies, and rules that guides over time the firm's marketing effort—its level, mix, and allocation—partly independently and partly in response to changing environmental and competitive conditions.

Here we will look more closely at the three elements of marketing strategy: marketing expenditure level, marketing mix, and marketing allocation.

MARKETING EXPENDITURE LEVEL   Management has to make a decision on what scale of marketing effort will be needed to achieve its goals. Companies typically establish their marketing budget at some conventional percentage of the sales goal. For example, a perfume company might set its marketing budget at about 35 percent of sales and a fertilizer company at 15 percent of sales. Companies entering a new market are especially interested in learning what the marketing *budget-to-sales ratio* is in the typical company. A particular company may spend more than the normal ratio in the hope of achieving a higher market share. Ultimately, the company should analyze the marketing work that has to be done to attain a given sales volume or market share and then price this work; the result is the required marketing budget.

MARKETING MIX   The company has to decide how to allocate the total marketing budget for a product to the various marketing-mix elements. Marketing mix is one of the key concepts in modern marketing theory.

> *Marketing mix* is the set of controllable variables and their levels that the firm uses to influence the target market.

Any variable under the control of the firm that can influence the level of customer response is a marketing-mix variable. Commodity firms usually assume that their marketing mix is narrow, consisting primarily of price and service. Other firms see dozens of controllable elements that might affect customer response. Various attempts have been made to develop a list of basic marketing variables. McCarthy popularized a four-factor classification called the four *P*s: *product, place, promotion,* and *price.*[20] A list of the particular marketing variables under each *P* is provided in Table 4–3.

[20] E. Jerome McCarthy, *Basic Marketing: A Managerial Approach,* 6th ed. (Homewood, Ill.: Richard D. Irwin, 1978), p. 39 (1st ed., 1960). Two alternative classifications are worth noting. Frey proposed that all marketing-decision variables could be divided into two factors: (1) *the offering* (product, packaging, brand, price, and service), and (2) *methods and tools* (distribution channels, personal selling, advertising, sales promotion, and publicity). See Albert W. Frey, *Advertising,* 3rd ed. (New York: Ronald Press, 1961), p. 30. Lazer and Kelley proposed a three-factor classification: (1) *goods and service mix,* (2) *distribution mix,* and (3) *communications mix.* See William Lazer and Eugene J. Kelley, *Managerial Marketing: Perspectives and Viewpoints,* rev. ed. (Homewood, Ill.: Richard D. Irwin, 1962), p. 413.

TABLE 4–3
Elaboration of the "Four Ps"

PRODUCT	PLACE	PROMOTION	PRICE
Quality	Channels	Advertising	List price
Features	Coverage	Personal selling	Discounts
Options	Locations	Sales promotion	Allowances
Style	Inventory	Publicity	Payment period
Brand name	Transport		Credit terms
Packaging			
Sizes			
Services			
Warranties			
Returns			

The company's marketing mix at time t for a particular product can be conveniently represented by the vector:

$$(P, A, D, E)_t$$

where:

P = price
A = promotion (advertising)
D = place (distribution)
E = product (product-effectiveness rating, with 1.00 = average)

If the firm decides to produce a boat priced at \$3,000, supporting it with advertising expenditures of \$20,000 per month and distribution expenditures of \$30,000 per month, and the product's quality is rated at 1.20, the company's marketing mix at time t is:

$$(\$3,000, \$20,000, \$30,000, 1.20)_t$$

One can readily see that a marketing mix is selected from a great number of possibilities. If the product's price is constrained to lie between \$3,000 and \$4,000 (to the nearest \$100), its advertising and its distribution expenditures are constrained to lie between \$10,000 and \$50,000 (to the nearest \$10,000) each, and its product quality can take on one of two values, then 550 (11 x 5 x 5 x 2) marketing-mix combinations are possible.

It should also be recognized that marketing-decision variables are not all adjustable in the short run. The firm can typically change its price, increase the size of its sales force, and raise its advertising expenditures in the short run. It can only develop new products and modify its marketing channels in the long run. Thus, the firm typically makes fewer period-to-period marketing-mix changes in the short run than the number of marketing-mix variables suggest.

Marketing staff members will have different opinions on how incremental marketing funds should be used. The sales manager would like to hire another salesperson; the advertising manager would like to buy another ad; the product manager would like to improve product quality or packaging; and the marketing research manager would like to carry out a deeper study of the market. In principle, the decision should be based on estimates of the net marginal revenue produced by alternative marketing investments. In practice, much debate will occur over the estimates of the net marginal revenues.

MARKETING ALLOCATION   In addition to determining the level and mix of marketing effort, management must determine how to allocate marketing resources among its products, customer segments, and sales areas. Typically, the company allocates a higher proportion of its marketing resources to those entities that are larger and/or have more unrealized market potential. In other words, it is looking for the highest return when allocating marketing funds to different uses.

We can represent a distinct allocation in the following way: Suppose management sets a price of $3,000, a monthly advertising budget of $5,000, a monthly distribution budget of $10,000, and a product quality of 1.00 for product i selling to customer type j in area k at time t. This is represented by the vector:

$$(\$3,000, \$5,000, \$10,000, 1.00)_{i,j,k,t}$$

Plan Implementation and Control

A plan is nothing "unless it *degenerates into work.*"[21] The goals and tasks must be assigned to specific persons to accomplish within specific time periods. Those responsible must accept them and be motivated to achieve them. Implementation requires good and continuous communication up and down the management ladder as well as across.

Control requires that each manager knows what to watch. The district sales manager examines the sales volumes and expenses of each sales representative against individual quotas and budgets. The manager gets on the phone and asks questions of the sales representatives who are lagging behind. The approach is constructive rather than critical, trying to pinpoint the trouble and determine how it can be corrected. In the meantime the regional sales manager scans the actual sales of this district sales manager and the other district sales managers, getting on the phone when noting deviations from quotas. The president of the company watches total sales and calls in the sales vice president when the sales are off.

This aspect of control is called *annual-plan control*. Management also exercises *profitability control* by examining the profitability of its various products, markets, territories, and marketing channels. It exercises *efficiency control* by looking for ways to improve the impact of its marketing expenditures. Finally, there is the major issue of *strategic control*, that is, the question of whether the company's products, resources, and objectives are properly matched to the right markets. In times of rapid change, a company's marketing strategy rapidly becomes obsolete. A marketing auditor might be called in to evaluate the question of strategic control.

[21] Drucker, *op. cit.*, p. 128.

SUMMARY

Management is the entrepreneurial agent that interprets market needs and translates them into meaningful products and services. To do so, management goes through a strategic management process and a strategic marketing process. The strategic management process consists of the steps taken at the corporate and divisional levels to develop long-run strategies for survival and growth. This process provides the context for the strategic marketing process, which consists of the steps taken at the product and market level to develop viable marketing positions and programs.

The strategic management process consists of defining the company's purpose, objectives, growth strategies, and portfolio plans. A clear statement of company purpose provides employees with a shared sense of opportunity, direction, significance, and achievement. It should define the company's business domain, preferably in market-oriented terms.

Strategic management then calls for developing a set of objectives, such as growth in sales and market share, profitability, and innovation to support the company purpose. These objectives should be hierarchical, quantitative, realistic, and consistent.

To achieve growth, the company must identify market opportunities where it would enjoy a differential advantage over competitors. The company can generate relevant opportunities by considering intensive growth opportunities within its present product-market scope (such as market penetration, market development, and product development), then considering integrative growth opportunities within its task-marketing system (such as backward, forward, and horizontal integration), and finally considering diversification growth opportunities outside of its task-marketing system (such as concentric, horizontal, and conglomerate diversification).

Finally, strategic management must define, for each strategic business unit (SBU) in the company's portfolio, whether that SBU will be built, maintained, harvested, or terminated.

Within this context, the strategic marketing process can be enacted. The first task consists of generating, evaluating, and recommending market opportunities. For any sound opportunity, the next step is to examine the product/market structure and identify the best target market. The third step is to decide on the best competitive position for the company within that target market, as well as the best mode of entry and timing. The fourth step calls for designing a marketing organization, information system, planning system, and control system to operate within that market. The fifth step calls for developing long-range and annual marketing plans that specify sales goals, marketing expenditures, marketing mix, and marketing allocation. The final step calls for implementing and controlling the marketing plan so that the marketing objectives are achieved. In addition to annual-plan control, management must carry out profitability, efficiency, and strategic control.

QUESTIONS AND PROBLEMS

1. Develop a market-oriented definition of the business domain of computer equipment manufacturers.

2. An automotive parts manufacturer produces three products: mufflers, filters, and silencers. The company is seeking new growth opportunities. Develop a product-market matrix showing some potential expansion opportunities for this manufacturer.

91

3. What is the major distinctive competence of (a) Sears; (b) Polaroid Company; (c) Procter & Gamble; (d) Ford Foundation?

4. Develop some propositions of the form "if . . . then" indicating whether a company should pursue an intensive, integrative, or diversification strategy.

5. Develop expansions of the business domains for each of the following types of organizations: (a) ballpoint pen company; (b) wristwatch manufacturer; (c) local swimming pool.

6. What kind of diversification growth strategy is illustrated by: (a) General Foods' acquisition of Burger Chef, a fast-food service chain; (b) Philip Morris' acquisition of Miller Brewing Company; (c) Mobil Oil's acquisition of Montgomery Ward?

7. The Kraftco Corporation states that it is seeking to provide a *quality* product that will *maximize customer satisfaction*, provide an *adequate return*, and increase the company's total *market share*. Is this a helpful statement of objectives that will help resolve major marketing issues facing the company?

8. A local high school has operated a night school program with only marginal success for several years. Due to a recent tax referendum, the school board has decided it must either significantly increase night school enrollments or cancel the entire program. Suggest a statement of purpose for the night school program and a hierarchy of objectives based upon the intention to increase enrollments.

9. Develop a list of specific growth strategies (in each of the opportunity categories under intensive, integrative, and diversification growth) for a medium-sized stapler manufacturing company.

10. An industrial equipment company consists of five strategic business units (SBUs), as shown below. Using the Boston Consulting Group portfolio analysis, determine whether the company is in a healthy condition. What future strategies should it consider?

SBU	DOLLAR SALES (IN MILLIONS)	NUMBER OF COMPETITORS	DOLLAR SALES OF THE TOP 3 (IN MILLIONS)	MARKET GROWTH RATE
A	.5	8	.7, .7, .5	15%
B	1.6	22	1.6, 1.6, 1.0	18%
C	1.8	14	1.8, 1.2, 1.0	7%
D	3.2	5	3.2, .8, .7	4%
E	.5	10	2.5, 1.8, 1.7	4%

Analyzing Marketing Opportunities

2

THE MARKETING ENVIRONMENT

> *We are all continually faced with a series of great opportunities brilliantly disguised as insoluble problems.*
> JOHN W. GARDNER

Marketing planning begins with the analysis of marketing opportunities. The job of spotting and evaluating marketing opportunities breaks down into a logical sequence of questions:

1. What are the main environmental trends, opportunities, and threats facing the industry and the firm? *(Environmental analysis)*
2. What are the major operating characteristics of each basic type of market? *(Market analysis)*
3. How do buyers buy in this market? *(Buyer behavior analysis)*
4. What are the major segments making up this market? *(Market segmentation analysis)*
5. What is the current and future size of this market? *(Demand measurement and forecasting)*

This chapter takes up environmental analysis, and the following four chapters will deal with the remaining topics.

Modern marketing theory holds that the key to an organization's success is the ability to make timely and appropriate adaptations to a complex and ever-changing environment. *The marketing environment is the totality of forces and institutions that are external and potentially relevant to the firm.* We saw in

Chapter 3 that the marketing environment surrounding a firm consists of four levels: (1) the *task environment,* consisting of the institutions that help the organization carry out its major task, such as suppliers, distributors, and final buyers; (2) the *competitive environment,* consisting of the institutions that compete with the organization for customers and scarce resources; (3) the *public environment,* consisting of institutions that watch or regulate the activities of the organization, and (4) the *macroenvironment,* consisting of the major societal forces that shape the character of business opportunities and threats. This chapter will examine the major trends in the macroenvironment that affect marketing, leaving the more immediate environments of the organization to be analyzed elsewhere. The major components of the macroenvironment are demography, economics, natural resources, technology, politics, and culture.

ORGANIZATION / ENVIRONMENT ADAPTATION

A major fact about the macroenvironment is that it does not stand still. The decade of the 1970s, for example, was marked in different periods by shortages, runaway inflation, and high unemployment. It was also marked by various movements, such as consumerism, environmentalism, and women's liberation.

No firm can afford to ignore the changing times. An organization's performance in the marketplace is a matter of the degree of alignment between the *organization's environmental opportunities, objectives, marketing strategy, organizational structure,* and *management systems.* In the ideal case,

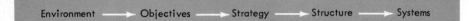

This says that the organization first studies the environment in which it is operating and specifically the opportunities and threats in this environment. It then develops a set of objectives describing what it wants to achieve in this environment. Then it formulates a corporate strategy that promises to achieve the corporate objectives. It then builds an organizational structure that is capable of carrying out the corporate strategy. Finally, it designs various systems of analysis, planning, and control to support the effective implementation of the strategy by the organization.

In practice, various things happen to prevent this ideal from being realized. The main problem is that these various components alter at different rates, resulting in a lack of optimal alignment. A typical situation is:

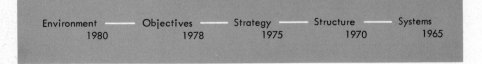

This says that the company is operating in a 1980 environment but with objectives that were set in 1978 for the environment at that time. Its strategy lags even more, having been the strategy that was successful in 1975. Its organizational structure is not even geared to supporting its strategy, having been designed almost ten years earlier in a quite different environment. Finally, its systems were developed many years ago and have not been adjusted to the new conditions.

Too often, in fact, organizations are run in a reverse (and perverse) way of thinking:

Structure and Systems ⟶ Objectives and Strategy ⟶ Environment

The organization believes that its structure and systems are sound because they worked during the firm's most successful years. Using these, it chooses objectives and strategies that are manageable under the present systems and structure. Then it scans the environment to find the opportunities that are best suited to its objectives and strategy.

> An example would be a hospital that primarily serves tuberculosis patients. Its organization, staffing, and systems are maximally adapted to providing health care to this type of patient. As a result, it sets its objectives in terms of attracting a certain number of tubercular patients and its strategy as one of appealing to patients who are self-paying and want quality care. Then it searches the environment broadly for this type of patient. The irony is, however, there are fewer such patients around thanks to various miracle drugs.

This is an example of bureaucratic thinking at its worst. The organization has set up a very *efficient* machine, but not an effective machine. Peter Drucker made the observation long ago that it is more important to do the *right thing* than to do *things right.*

The main problem is that the environment is the fastest changing element in the picture. Progressive companies are not even satisfied to bring the various elements into alignment in the current year. Instead, a company like IBM or Xerox will attempt to forecast what their business environment will be like in (say) 1985. Given this 1985 environmental forecast, they will set objectives that describe where they want to be in 1985. They will then formulate a strategy that will deliver these objectives by 1985. They will begin to alter the organization and its systems so that these will support the new strategy, rather than act as a drag on its fulfillment. This forward-looking thinking is summarized below:

Environment ⟶ Objectives ⟶ Strategy ⟶ Structure ⟶ Systems
1985   1985   1985   1985   1985

Environmental Change

A successful organization is one that has found a useful niche within the larger environment where it produces and receives value. The part of the environment it occupies is called its *habitat*. The various institutions and forces that support the organization in its habitat constitute its *ecosystem*.

> The auto industry is central to a vast *business ecosystem* consisting of rubber, glass, and steel plants, petroleum refineries, gasoline stations, superhighways, the economy of Detroit, and the incomes of millions of people.

As long as the institutions and forces in the ecosystem remain in balance, the ecosystem will persist from year to year without major change.

We can distinguish between the degrees of stability of an environment. The first is a *stable environment*, in which the major forces of economics, technology, law, and culture remain stable from year to year. The second is a *slowly evolving environment*, in which smooth and fairly predictable changes take place. The individual firm survives in this type of environment to the extent that it foresees change *and* takes intelligent steps to adapt. The third is a *turbulent environment*, in which major and unpredictable changes occur often.[1]

> Sudden changes in fuel availability, auto technology, or safety legislation can threaten auto manufacturers and the character of the auto ecosystem itself. Suppose a company develops an efficient electric automobile. The petroleum industry and the familiar gas station would be threatened with near extinction. Used car dealers would panic. Industries selling major consumer durables such as boats, small planes, and kitchen appliances would see their sales slow down. Such a major innovation, through its "creative destruction" of the present ecosystem, would pose a tremendous threat to many and a tremendous opportunity to others.

There is increasing evidence that more and more firms are finding themselves operating in turbulent environments. In his *Future Shock*, Toffler documents how key technological, economic, and social forces show an "accelerative thrust." One study shows that the average span between introduction and peak production of appliances introduced in the United States before 1920 was thirty-four years; for a group of appliances that appeared between 1939 and 1959, the span was only eight years. Many products that have appeared since 1959 have had even shorter spans.[2] Other forces, such as consumer life styles and government legislation, also show an accelerative thrust.

The firm operating in a turbulent environment has three tasks: (1) systematically scanning its environment, (2) identifying environmental threats and opportunities, and (3) making intelligent adaptations to the changing environment.

Environmental Scanning

The more energy a firm devotes to broad environmental scanning, the greater its capacity to survive. Environmental scanning calls for identifying the major environmental areas of interest to management, assigning responsibility for each area, and developing efficient systems for collecting and disseminating the information.

[1] For a useful discussion of types of environment and their implications, see F. E. Emery and E. L. Trist, "The Causal Texture of Organizational Environments," *Human Relations*, February 1965, pp. 21–32.

[2] See Alvin Toffler, *Future Shock* (New York: Bantam Books, 1970), p. 28.

> An automobile company will have a high interest in monitoring congressional thinking, among other things. It will hire one or more intelligence officers, locate them in a Washington office, and give them a budget for initiating and maintaining contacts with knowledgeable people. These officers will assemble information and relay the highlights to the company decision makers for whom they are relevant.

Opportunity and Threat Analysis

Within the large amount of information flowing into the firm, management must be able to spot the *environmental forces* that have the greatest import for future marketing strategy. They can be classified as either threats or opportunities facing the firm. We define an *environmental threat* as follows:

> An *environmental threat* is a challenge posed by an unfavorable trend or specific disturbance in the environment that would lead, in the absence of purposeful marketing action, to the stagnation or demise of a company, product, or brand.

A major threat is one that (1) would cause substantial damage to profits if it became a reality and (2) has a moderate to high probability of occurring. No company is free of such threats, and every manager should be able to identify several such threats.

> An automobile executive would readily identify the following threats: (1) successful development of an efficient electric car by a competitor, (2) growing preference for foreign-made cars by American consumers, (3) growing preference for mass transportation or for bicycles and motorcycles, and (4) a sudden and lasting fuel shortage.

A business facing several major threats is highly vulnerable. Its management should prepare contingency plans and give serious thought to diversification moves.

We define a *company marketing opportunity* as follows:

> A *company marketing opportunity* is an attractive arena of relevant marketing action in which a particular company is likely to enjoy a differential advantage.

A major company marketing opportunity is one that (1) has a high dollar potential for the firm and (2) a moderate-to-high probability that the firm would have success with it.

> Among the major marketing opportunities facing an auto company are: (1) developing an extremely fuel efficient small car, (2) developing a successful electric car, or (3) developing a successful mass-transportation vehicle.

To the extent that there are strong opportunities facing that business, we simply say that the business faces high opportunity.

An important exercise for the management of any company is to periodically identify the major threats and opportunities facing the company and each of its business units (divisions, product lines, and products). This is best done when management is preparing its annual or long-range marketing plans. Each threat and opportunity is assigned a number and then evaluated according to its probable level of impact and occurrence. The threats and opportunities can then be plotted in the threat and opportunity matrices shown in Figure 5–1.

The threat matrix shows seven identifiable threats. Management should give the greatest attention to threats 1 and 2 because they would have a high impact on the company and have a high probability of occurrence. Threat 3 can also substantially hurt the company but it has a low probability of occurrence; and threat 4 would not hurt much but is highly likely to occur. Management can safely ignore minor threats 5, 6, and 7.

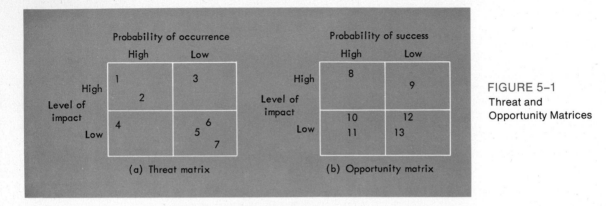

FIGURE 5–1
Threat and
Opportunity Matrices

The opportunity matrix shows six identifiable opportunities. The best is opportunity 8 which would have a high positive impact if the company is successful at developing this opportunity, and the company is highly likely to be successful. Opportunity 9 is an attractive opportunity but the company may not have the resources or competence to succeed in this opportunity. Opportunities 10 and 11 are minor in their impact although easy to carry off successfully. Opportunities 12 and 13 can be ignored.

Considering the two matrices together, this business unit faces two major threats and one major opportunity. This makes it a somewhat speculative business: it is high on opportunity and high on risk. In fact, four outcomes are possible with this analysis. They are shown in the opportunity-threat matrix in Figure 5–2. An *ideal business* is one which is high in major opportunities and low or devoid of major threats. A *speculative business* is high in both major op-

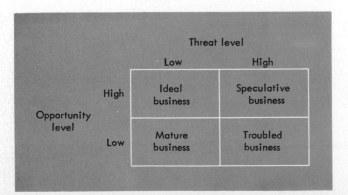

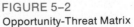

FIGURE 5–2
Opportunity-Threat Matrix

portunities and threats. A *mature business* is low in major opportunities and threats. Finally, a *troubled business* is low in opportunities and high in threats.

Each business unit can seek to better its situation by moving toward its major opportunities and away from its major threats. With respect to opportunities, the firm must carefully appraise their quality. There is a whole profession of "futurologists" who conjure up wonderful products and services the public needs. Levitt has cautioned business men to judge opportunities carefully:

> There can be a need, but no market; or a market, but no customer; or a customer, but no salesman. For instance, there is a great need for massive pollution control, but not really a market at present. And there is a market for new technology in education, but no customer really large enough to buy the products. Market forecasters who fail to understand these concepts have made spectacular miscalculations about the apparent opportunities in these and other fields, such as housing and leisure products.[3]

Even in pursuing a marketing opportunity, the firm can control its level of risk taking. The firm might make a *token investment* in marketing research and R&D just to keep up, without getting sidetracked from its main business. Or it might make a *moderate investment* in the hope of becoming one of the leaders. Or it might make a *substantial investment* in the hope of becoming the leader, although this may involve great risk to its present business.

In facing a major threat, the firm has three modes of adaptation available:

1. *Opposition.* The firm can try to fight, restrain, or reverse the unfavorable development. Opposition may be used to "buy" the time needed to make more fundamental adjustments.
2. *Modification.* The firm can try to improve its environmental fit through changing its customer mix or marketing mix.
3. *Relocation.* The firm can decide to shift to another market in which it can produce more value.

The key implication for company marketing strategy in a turbulent environment is that the company must invest more to keep abreast of significant social changes and be prepared to adapt faster than before. It must not stick to the tried-and-true after this has become dysfunctional. It must not become a bundle of obsolete responses. It must be prepared to adapt creatively to the changing environment.

ENVIRONMENTAL FORECASTING

We saw that the key to organizational survival and growth is the firm's ability to adapt its strategies and organization to a rapidly changing environment. This puts a big burden on the firm of correctly anticipating the character of the future environment. The price can be enormous when a mistake is made. For example, Montgomery Ward lost its leadership in the chain-store retailing field after the Second World War because its chairman, Sewell Avery, bet on a stag-

[3] Theodore Levitt, "The New Markets—Think Before You Leap," *Harvard Business Review*, May–June 1969, pp. 53–67, especially pp. 53–54.

nant economy, while its major competitor, Sears, bet on an expanding economy. Major investments in products, markets, and marketing channels ride on the management's strategic judgments about the future environment. That is why a growing number of companies are getting into formal *environmental forecasting*.

Strategic planning has to begin with an environmental forecast that identifies the most important and likely developments for several years to come. Since any long-run forecast is tentative, the environmental forecast has to be revised at least once each year to bring in new factors.

No one disputes that environmental forecasting is still more art than science. While there has been some progress in the methodologies for forecasting economic and technological developments, there has been little progress in the reliable forecasting of political and cultural developments. These latter factors interact so much with the former factors that forecasts can be much in error. Some people even question the whole exercise of long-range forecasting. Our position, however, is that long-range forecasting contributes greatly to the identification of opportunities and the assessment of risks.

How do firms develop their forecasts? Large firms usually operate planning departments that are responsible for developing long-run forecasts of key environmental factors affecting their markets. General Electric, for example, has a large staff of forecasters, who conduct numerous studies of domestic and worldwide forces that are affecting its operations in various parts of the world. It makes its forecasts available to various divisions and also sells certain forecasts to other firms. Few firms, of course, can afford to do their own forecasting at this level of intensity and must find other ways to obtain sound forecasts.

These firms can buy forecasts from several types of suppliers. *Marketing research firms* can be hired to develop a forecast for a particular market through interviewing customers, distributors, and other knowledgeable parties. *Specialized forecasting firms* will produce long-range forecasts of particular macroenvironmental components, such as the economy, the population, natural resources, or technology. Finally, there are *futurist research firms* that produce total future scenarios that are rich in speculation and creative ideas. Among the latter are the Hudson Institute, the Futures Group, and the Institute for the Future.

A variety of methodologies are used in producing long-range forecasts, the following being the key ones.[4]

1. *Expert opinion.* Here knowledgeable people are selected and asked to assign importance and probability rating to various possible future developments. The most refined version, the Delphi method, puts experts through several rounds of event assessment, where they keep refining their assumptions and judgments.

2. *Trend extrapolation.* Here researchers fit best-fitting curves (linear, quadratic, or S-shaped growth curves) through past time series to serve as a basis for extrapolation. This method can be very unreliable in that new developments can completely alter the expected direction of movement.

3. *Trend correlation.* Here researchers correlate various time series in the hope of identifying leading and lagging relationships that can be used for forecasting.

4. *Dynamic modeling.* Here researchers build sets of equations that attempt to de-

[4] James R. Bright and Milton E. F. Schoeman, *A Guide to Practical Technological Forecasting* (Englewood Cliffs, N. J.: Prentice-Hall, 1973).

scribe the underlying system. The coefficients in the equations are fitted through statistical means. Econometric models of more than three hundred equations, for example, are used to forecast changes in the U.S. economy.

5. *Cross-impact analysis.* Here researchers identify a set of key trends (those high in importance and/or probability). The question is then put: "If event A occurs, what will be the impact on all other trends?" The results are then used to build sets of "domino chains," with one event triggering others.

6. *Multiple scenarios.* Here researchers build pictures of alternative futures, each internally consistent and with a certain probability of happening. The major purpose of the scenarios is to stimulate contingency planning.

7. *Demand/hazard forecasting.* Here researchers identify major events that would affect the firm greatly. Each event is rated for its *convergence* with several major trends taking place in society. It is also rated for its *appeal* to each major public in the society. The higher the event's convergence and appeal, the higher its probability of occurring. The highest scoring events are then researched further.

Having considered the nature of environmental threats and opportunities, we will now examine the major components of the marketing environment: demography, economy, natural resources, technology, politics, and culture. These environmental forces exercise a greater impact on the company than the company exercises on them. They constitute the "uncontrollables" to which companies adapt through setting the "controllable" factors, namely the firm's selection of target markets and marketing mixes. We want to examine the main trends in each component and the implications of these trends for marketing strategy.

DEMOGRAPHIC ENVIRONMENT

The first environmental fact of interest to marketers is *population* because people make up markets. Marketers are keenly interested in the size of the world's population—geographical distribution; density; mobility trends; age distribution; birth, marriage, and death rates; and racial, ethnic, and religious structure. We shall review here the major demographic trends and indicate the implications for marketing planning.

Worldwide Explosive Population Growth

Perhaps the major fact about the world population is its "explosive" growth:

In 1650 the population numbered about 0.5 billion, and it was growing at a rate of approximately 0.3 percent per year. That corresponds to a doubling time of nearly 250 years. In 1970 the population totaled 3.6 billion and the rate of growth was 2.1 percent per year. The doubling time at this growth rate is 33 years. Thus, not only has the population been growing exponentially, but the rate of growth has also been growing.[5]

The world population explosion has been a major concern of many governments and groups throughout the world. Two factors underlie this concern. The

[5] Donella H. Meadows, Dennis L. Meadows, Jorgen Randers, and William W. Behrens III, *The Limits to Growth* (New York: New American Library, 1972), p. 41.

first is the possible finiteness of the earth's resources to support this much human life, particularly at levels of living that represent the aspiration of most people. The famous eighteenth-century economist, Thomas Malthus, was concerned in his time about the population explosion. He saw the population growing at a geometric rate, while the world's food supply grew at an arithmetic rate. To him, this spelled unavoidable disaster for mankind. If mankind could not regulate its own rate of growth, then natural and other forces such as famine, disease, and war would intervene to keep population down to the available food supply. The Malthusian specter has been resurrected many times since—most recently in the tour de force called *The Limits to Growth*.[6] This book presents an impressive array of evidence that unchecked population growth and consumption must eventually result in insufficient food supply, depletion of key minerals, over-crowdedness, pollution, and an overall deterioration in the quality of life. One of its strong recommendations is the worldwide *social marketing* of birth control and family planning.[7]

The second cause for concern is that the rate of population growth is not equal everywhere but is highest in the countries and communities that can least afford it. In many developing nations the death rate has been falling as a result of modern medical advances, while the birthrate has remained fairly stable. For these countries to feed, clothe, and educate the children and also provide a rising standard of living for the population is out of the question. Furthermore, the poor families have the most children, and this reinforces the cycle of poverty.

The rate of increase of the world's population has great importance for business. A growing population means growing human needs. It means growing markets, if there is sufficient purchasing power. On the other hand, if the growing population presses too hard against the available food supply and resources, costs will shoot up and possibly profit margins will be depressed.

Slowdown in U.S. Birthrate

In contrast to many countries experiencing a rapid increase in population, the U.S. is undergoing a population slowdown. The U.S. population stood at 216.8 million on July 1, 1977.[8] The birthrate dipped below the "replacement rate" of 2.0 children per family to a record low of 1.8 in 1977. The preschool population declined 11.2 percent between 1970 and 1977. Among the factors contributing to smaller families are (1) desire to improve personal living standards, (2) increasing desire of women to work and enjoy more life outside of the home, (3) improved technology and knowledge of birth control, and (4) increasing concern about the future of civilization on this planet.

The declining birthrate is a threat to some industries, a boon to others. It has produced anxiety attacks in the board rooms of companies involved in children's toys, clothes, furniture, and food. The Gerber Company for years advertised, "Babies are our business—our *only* business," but quietly dropped this slogan a few years ago. It has responded to the shrinking market by trying to introduce baby food in other countries of the world where the birthrate is still

---

[6] Ibid.

[7] See Eduardo L. Roberto, "Social Marketing Strategies for Diffusing the Adoption of Family Planning," *Social Science Quarterly*, June 1972, pp. 33–51.

[8] Most of the statistical data in this chapter, unless otherwise indicated, are found in the *Statistical Abstract of the United States* (Washington, D.C.: Government Printing Office, 1977).

high.[9] Johnson & Johnson has responded by trying to interest grownups in using their baby powder and baby hair shampoo. Abbott Laboratories has added a geriatric food line to complement its line of infant formulas.

Other industries have benefited from the declining birthrate. With fewer children, young couples have more time and income to spend on travel, eating out, and adult recreation, thus contributing to a boom in these industries.

Aging of U.S. Population

Recent generations have benefited from a substantial decline in the death rate thanks to the miracles of modern medicine and greater education in preventative health care. Average life expectancy is now 72.5 years and may reach 74 years by the year 2000. This, coupled with the declining birthrate, has meant an aging of the U.S. population. The median age at the time of the country's founding was 16; now it is about 30; and it should reach 35 by the year 2000.[10]

Different age groups, of course, will grow at different rates. The age group 14 to 24 will shrink about 4 percent in absolute numbers during the coming decade, resulting in a possible weakening in influence of America's youth culture. The decline forebodes sagging sales for motorcycles, baseball and football equipment, denim clothing, records, *Playboy*-type magazines, and other goods for the youth market. It means enrollment declines in American colleges, which are already experiencing overcapacity and having to think about attracting new groups to the campus, such as homemakers and retired people.

Meanwhile the age group 25 to 44 will have the largest spurt in growth, something on the order of 35 percent by 1990. Marketers who sell to this group—furniture makers, vacation planners, tennis and ski equipment manufacturers—have to watch trends in this group's social patterns carefully, particularly such phenomena as falling marriage and rising divorce rates, deferred childbearing, and the two-wage-earning household.

The age group 45 to 64 will shrink slightly until the second half of the 1980s, when it will enter a period of rapid growth. This is the "empty-nester" group, whose children leave home and who find themselves with increased time and income on their hands. This group is a major market for eating out, travel, expensive clothes, and golf and other recreations.

The over-65 group will show the second largest rate of growth in the years ahead, increasing by at least 23 million Americans and perhaps as many as 32 million by the year 2000. This expected increase foretells a burgeoning demand for retirement homes and communities, campers, quieter forms of recreation (fishing, golf), single-portion food packaging, and medical goods and services (medicine, eyeglasses, canes, hearing aids, and convalescent homes). This group also means more conservative politics, demands for new rights by senior citizens to protect their standard of living, and a slowing down in the adoption of new cultural ideas.

The Changing American Family

The American ideal of the two-children, two-car suburban family—which provided great marketing opportunity in the post-World War II period—has been losing some of its luster. There will be fewer families forming (and surviving), and they will show a different orientation. Here are the major forces at work:

[9] See "Gerber: 'Selling More to the Same Mothers Is Our Objective Now'," *Business Week*, October 16, 1978.

[10] See "The Graying of America," *Newsweek*, February 28, 1977, pp. 50–65.

1. *Later marriage.* While 96 percent of all Americans will marry, the average age of first marriage has been rising over the years and now stands at 23.8 years for males and 21.3 years for females. This will slow down the sales of engagement and wedding rings, bridal outfits, and life insurance.

2. *Fewer children.* Couples with no children under 18 now make up 47 percent of all families. The newly married are also delaying childbearing longer. Of those families that have children, the mean number is 1.8, down from 3.5 in 1955.

3. *Higher divorce rate.* America has the world's highest divorce rate, with about 38 percent of marriages ending in divorce. This has created over a million single-parent families and the need for additional housing units. About 79 percent remarry, leading to the phenomenon of the "blended" family. Currently about 72.2 percent of adult males are married and 66.2 percent of adult females.

4. *More working wives.* Today more than 40 percent of all married women with school-age children hold some kind of job. There is less stigma attached to working (in fact, often a stigma is attached to being "just a housewife"), a greater number of job opportunities, and new freedom resulting from birth-control acceptance. These working women constitute a market for better clothing, day nursery services, home cleaning services, and more frozen dinners. The growing number of working women means less viewing of television soap operas and reading of the traditional women's magazines. In families where both husband and wife work, the woman's salary represents 40 percent of the household income and influences the purchase of higher-quality goods and services. Marketers of such things as tires, automobiles, insurance, and travel service have found it necessary to change their advertising messages and media selections so as to reach the increasingly significant working women's market.[11]

The Rise of Nonfamily Households

An important development is the rapid rise in the number of *nonfamily households.* They take several forms, each constituting a different market segment with special needs:

1. *Single-adult households.* Many young adults leave home earlier and move into their own apartments. In addition, many divorced and widowed people live alone. Altogether, more than 15.5 million people live alone. They account for 21 percent of all the households. The SSWD group (single, separated, widowed, divorced) need smaller apartments; inexpensive and smaller appliances, furniture, and furnishings; and food that is packaged in smaller sizes. Their car preferences are different in that they buy half of all Mustangs and other small specialty cars, and only 8 percent of the large cars.[12] Singles are a market for various services that supply opportunities for singles to meet each other, such as singles bars, tours, and cruises.

2. *Two-person cohabitant households.* There may be as many as 3 to 6 million unmarried people living together today, primarily heterosexual couples but homosexual couples as well. Since their arrangements are more temporary, they are a market for inexpensive or rental furniture and furnishings.

3. *Group households.* Fewer in number, group households can nevertheless be found, consisting of three or more persons of the same or opposite sex sharing ex-

[11] See Ellen Graham, "Advertisers Take Aim at a Neglected Market: The Working Woman," *Wall Street Journal,* July 5, 1977, p. 1.

[12] See June Kronholz, "A Living-Alone Trend Affects Housing, Cars, and Other Industries," *Wall Street Journal,* November 16, 1977, p. 1.

penses by living together. This pattern is frequently found among college students and also among certain secular and religious groups who live in communes.

Marketers have to pay attention to the special needs and buying habits of these nonfamily households, which are growing more rapidly in number than family households.

Geographical Shifts in Population

Americans are a mobile people, with approximately one out of five, or 42 million Americans, moving each year. Among the major mobility trends are:

1. *Movement of people to the Sunbelt states.* Over the next ten years, the West's population will grow 17 percent and the South's population will grow 14 percent. Major cities in the North, on the other hand, have been losing population between 1970–1975 (New York, 4.7 percent; Pittsburgh, 4.1 percent; Jersey City, 5.8 percent; and Newark, 3.2 percent). These regional population shifts are of special interest to marketers because of marked differences in regional spending patterns and consumer behavior. Consumers in the West, for example, spend relatively less on food and relatively more on automobiles than their counterparts in the Northeast. The exodus to the Sunbelt will lessen the demand for warm clothing and home heating equipment and increase the demand for air conditioning.

2. *Movement from rural to urban areas.* This movement has been going on for over a century. In 1880 approximately 70 percent of the nation's population lived in rural areas; now approximately 70 percent live in urban areas. Cities are characterized by a faster pace of living, more commuting, typically higher incomes, and a greater variety of goods and services than the small towns and rural areas that dot America. The largest cities, such as New York, Chicago, and San Francisco, account for most of the sales of expensive furs, perfumes, luggage, and works of art, and they still boast most of what there is of opera, ballet, and other forms of "high culture." Recently, there has been a slight shift of population back to rural areas on the part of some people who have grown tired of the big city.

3. *Movement from the city to the suburbs.* Many persons have moved far away from their places of work, owing largely to the development of automobiles, major highways, and rapid rail and bus transit. Cities have become surrounded by suburbs, and these suburbs in turn by "exurbs." The U.S. Census Bureau has created a separate population classification for sprawling urban concentrations, called Standard Metropolitan Statistical Areas (SMSA).[13] Over 63 percent of the nation's entire population (and 95 percent of the nation's urban population) are estimated to live in the 212 recognized Standard Metropolitan Statistical Areas, and it is the SMSAs rather than the cities proper that constitute the primary market focus of firms.

Firms normally distinguish between the city and the suburban segments of the metropolitan areas. About 60 percent of the total metropolitan population now live in suburbs. Suburban areas are frequently marked by a style of living different from that in the cities. Suburbs tend to be characterized by casual, outdoor living, greater neighbor interaction, higher incomes, and younger families. Suburban dwellers are the source of much of the demand for station wagons, home workshop equipment, garden furniture, lawn and gardening tools and supplies, and outdoor cooking equipment. Retailers have recognized the importance of

---

[13] An SMSA consists of the counties of an integrated economic area with a large volume of daily travel and communication between a central city of at least fifty thousand inhabitants and the outlying parts of the area.

convenience and have brought their goods out to the suburbs through the development of branch department stores and suburban shopping centers.

At the same time, marketers should recognize a recent counter movement back to the central city, especially in cities where urban renewal has been successful. Young adults as well as older families whose children have grown up are attracted by the superior cultural and recreational opportunities and less interested in suburban commuting and gardening. This means strong opportunities for new high-rise apartment construction and new retail outlets within the central city.

A Better-
Educated
Populace

The number of Americans who have attended or graduated from college will reach 44 million by 1985, or 19 percent of the population. This will present both opportunities and challenges to marketers. A greater white-collar and educated work force will mean increased affluence and demand for quality products, books, upscale magazines, and travel. It will also mean a decline in television viewing because educated consumers tend to watch less than the population at large.

The demographic trends stated above are highly reliable for the short and intermediate run. There is little excuse for a company to be suddenly surprised by a demographic development. The alert firm will have plenty of advance notice and can start searching for new-product lines and more attractive markets when it reads the writing on the wall.

ECONOMIC ENVIRONMENT

Markets require not only people but purchasing power. Total purchasing power is a function of current income, prices, savings, and credit availability. The main economic trends that have implications for marketers are described below.

Slowdown in
Real-Income
Growth

American per capita income stood in 1976 at $6,393 and median household income stood at $12,686. Although per capita income keeps rising in money terms, there has been little or no growth in real terms for the last several years, in contrast to the 1950s and 1960s when real incomes grew substantially and ushered in a period of great affluence and optimism. Real per capita income growth has been hurt by (1) an inflation rate exceeding the money-income growth rate, (2) the hovering of unemployment between 6 and 8 percent, and (3) the increase in the tax burden, which has reduced the disposable-income level. Although mitigated somewhat by the rise in two-income families, most Americans have turned to more cautious buying both in regard to product categories and brands chosen. A survey by *Better Homes and Gardens* indicated that 72 percent of the respondents were buying more store brands to save money.[14] Many companies have introduced economy versions of their products and have turned to price appeals in their advertising messages. As for durable goods purchases, some consumers have postponed their purchase, while others have decided to buy out of fear that

[14] Reported in *Grey Matter*, "Private Brands Seek Growth in Faltering Economy," June 1974, p. 1.

prices will be 10 percent higher next year. Many consumers feel that the elements of the good life—a large home, two cars, foreign travel, and private higher education—are now beyond their reach.

Marketers have to pay attention to income differences as well as to average income trends. Income distribution in the U.S. is still pronouncedly skewed. At the top are *wealthy consumers* whose expenditure patterns have not been affected by current events and who are a major market for luxury goods (Rolls Royces starting at $49,000) and services (around-the-world cruises starting at $10,000). There is a comfortable *upper middle class,* who must exercise some expenditure restraint but are able to afford expensive clothes, minor antiques, and a small boat or second home. The *working class* must stick closer to the basics of food, clothing, and shelter, husband their resources, and try hard to save. Finally, there is the *underclass* (persons on welfare and retirees), who have to carefully count their pennies when making purchases of even the most basic kind.

Income levels and growth rates also vary regionally. They are affected by the level of local economic activity and employment, the rate of in- and out-migration, and union wage scales. Marketers have to take geographical income differences into account in planning their marketing effort.

Continued Inflationary Pressure

Although the double-digit inflation of the early seventies has been brought under control, inflation continues to push up the prices of homes, furniture, medical care, and food at rates that many consumers find disheartening. The inflationary pressure is fed by (1) hikes in the price of oil and other natural resources due to real scarcity or cartel price fixing, (2) the lack of competition in certain sectors of the economy, (3) the demands of labor unions for wage increases that exceed productivity gains, (4) the unfavorable balance of foreign trade, which shrinks the value of the dollar and pushes up the prices of foreign goods, (5) rising interest rates that push up costs in an effort to reduce demand, (6) the high expenditures on public services and on nonproductive capital investment, and (7) a psychology of inflationary expectation, which in turn feeds the inflation. Inflation leads consumers to search for opportunities to save money, including buying cheaper brands in larger, economy sizes, buying from less-expensive retail outlets, performing more of their own services, and bartering services with others.

Changing Savings and Debt Pattern

Consumer expenditures are influenced not only by income but also by consumer savings and debt patterns. Eighty-four percent of American spending units hold some liquid assets, the median amount being $800. Americans hold their savings in the form of bank savings accounts, bonds and stocks, real estate, insurance, and other assets. In many cases, the inflation rate has reduced the purchasing power of these savings, but still they constitute a gigantic reservoir of purchasing power to supplement income and are a major source of financing major durable purchases.

Consumers can also expand their purchases through borrowing. In fact, consumer credit has been a major contributor to the rapid growth of the American economy, enabling people to buy more than their incomes and savings permitted, thus creating more jobs and still more income and more demand. In 1978, outstanding consumer credit (including home mortgages) stood at $1 trillion, or $4,600 for every man, woman, and child in America. The cost of credit, however, is also high (with interest rates around 10 percent), and consumers are paying around 21¢ of every dollar they earn to pay off existing debts. This retards the further growth of housing and other durable-goods markets that are heavily dependent on credit.

Changing
Consumer-
Expenditure
Patterns

As people's incomes change, marketers can expect pronounced shifts in the relative demand for different categories of goods and services. The particular types of shifts were stated as early as 1857 by the German statistician Ernst Engel, who compared the budgets of individual working-class families. Engel observed that while rising family income tended to be accompanied by increased spending in all categories, *the percentage spent on food tended to decline, the percentage spent on housing and household operations tended to remain constant, and the percentage spent on other categories (clothing, transportation, recreation, health, and education) and savings tended to increase.* These "laws" have been generally validated in subsequent budget studies. At the same time, a company involved in a particular product category will want to look more closely at how expenditures on this product category varies with income. In the case of food, for example, a higher income, while it may not lead to buying more food, may lead to buying higher-quality food, thus causing food expenditures to remain constant for a while. But in general, as incomes rise, people will spend a higher proportion of their incomes on major durables, luxury goods, and services.

NATURAL ENVIRONMENT

The 1960s produced a growing public concern over whether the natural environment was being irreparably damaged by the industrial activities of modern nations. Kenneth Boulding pointed out that the planet earth was like a spaceship in danger of running out of fuel if it failed to recycle its materials. The Meadows, in *The Limits to Growth,* raised concern about the adequacy of future natural resources to sustain economic growth. Rachel Carson, in *The Silent Spring,* pointed out the environmental damage to water, earth, and air caused by industrial activity of certain kinds. These cries led to the formation of various watchdog groups, such as the Sierra Club and Friends of the Earth, as well as concerned legislators who have proposed various measures to regulate the impact of industrial activity on the natural environment.

Marketers should be aware of the challenges and opportunities created by four particular trends in the natural environment.

Impending
Shortages of
Certain Raw
Materials

The earth's materials fall into three groups: the infinite, the finite renewable, and the finite nonrenewable. *Infinite resources,* such as water and air, pose no immediate problem, although some groups argue that there is too high a level of pollution. Environmental groups lobbied for the banning of aerosol cans because of their potential damage to the ozone layer of air; and they have fought against the pollution of lakes and streams, Lake Erie, for one, by unregulated industrial wastes.

Finite renewable resources, such as forests and food, pose no immediate problem, but perhaps there is one in the long run. Companies in the forestry business are now required to reforest timberlands in order to protect the soil and to insure a sufficient level of wood supply to meet future demand. Food supply can be a major problem in that the amount of arable land is relatively fixed and urban areas are constantly expanding to absorb farmland.

Finite nonrenewable resources, such as oil, coal, and various minerals, do pose a serious problem.

> ... it would appear at present that the quantities of platinum, gold, zinc, and lead are not sufficient to meet demands ... silver, tin, and uranium may be in short supply even at higher prices by the turn of the century. By the year 2050, several more minerals may be exhausted if the current rate of consumption continues.[15]

The marketing implications are many. Firms that rely on these minerals face substantial cost increases, even if the materials remain available. They may not find it easy to pass on these cost increases. There is a need to search for substitute minerals. Firms engaged in research and development and exploration have an incredible opportunity to develop valuable new sources and materials.

Increased Cost of Energy

One finite nonrenewable resource, oil, has created the most serious problem for future economic growth. Much of contemporary economic and political history has been shaped by oil politics. The major industrial economies of the world are heavily dependent on oil resources and until substitute forms of energy can be developed on a practical basis, oil will continue to dominate the world political and economic picture. The shortage of oil and its price manipulation have created a frantic search for alternative forms of energy. Coal is once again popular, and companies are searching for practical schemes to harness solar, nuclear, wind, and other forms of energy. In the solar energy field alone, hundreds of firms are putting out first-generation products to harness solar energy for heating homes and other uses.[16] Other firms are searching for ways to make a practical electric automobile, with a prize going to the winners amounting to billions.

Increased Levels of Pollution

Some portion of modern industrial activity will inevitably damage the quality of the natural environment. One has only to think of the disposal of chemical and nuclear wastes, the dangerous mercury levels in the ocean, the quantity of chemical pollutants in the soil and food supply, and the littering of the environment with nonbiodegradable bottles, plastics, and other packaging materials. The public concern constitutes a marketing opportunity in two ways. First, it creates a large market for pollution-control solutions such as scrubbers and recycling centers. Second, it creates a major marketing opportunity for finding alternative ways to produce and package goods that do not cause environmental damage. Many marketers have become interested in using social marketing to find new solutions and influence consumers and business firms to be more ecology minded.[17]

---

[15] *First Annual Report of the Council on Environmental Quality* (Washington, D.C.: Government Printing Office, 1970), p. 158.

[16] See "The Coming Boom in Solar Energy," *Business Week,* October 9, 1978, pp. 88–104.

[17] See Karl E. Henion II, *Ecological Marketing* (Columbus, Ohio: Grid, 1976).

Increasing
Government
Intervention in
Natural Resource
Management

The growing concern with the deteriorating quality of the natural environment has led government to take an active role in regulating and enforcing conservation and pollution-control behavior. The responsibility is dispersed and is in the hands of many federal, state, and local agencies, each attempting to monitor environmentally damaging actions. Ironically, the effort to protect the environment often runs counter to the attempt to increase employment and economic growth, as for example, when business is forced to buy expensive pollution-cleanup equipment instead of investing in capital producing goods. From time to time, conservation politics takes a back seat to economic-growth politics. Marketing management must be alert to regulatory developments and the opportunities that open up with the effort to protect the natural environment.

TECHNOLOGICAL ENVIRONMENT

The most dramatic force shaping human destiny is technology. Technology has released such wonders as penicillin, open-heart surgery, and the birth-control pill. It has released such horrors as the hydrogen bomb, nerve gas, and the submachine gun. It has released such mixed blessings as the automobile, television sets, and white bread. Depending upon whether one is more enthralled with the wonders or the horrors determines one's attitude toward technology.

Every new technology may potentially spawn a major industry. One only has to think of transistors, xerography, computers, and antibiotics. These industries not only create but destroy. Transistors hurt the vacuum-tube industry and xerography hurt the carbon-paper business. The auto hurt the railroads and television hurt the movies. Schumpeter saw technology as a force for "creative destruction." Every enterprise must watch what is new in the environment, for this might eventually destroy it. If it has the imagination, the new might save it. It is discouraging that most phonograph companies did not enter the radio field, wagon manufacturers did not enter the automobile business, and steam locomotive companies did not enter the diesel locomotive business.

The growth rate of the economy is intimately tied to how many *major* new technologies will be discovered in the coming years. Unfortunately, technological discoveries do not arise evenly through time—the railroad industry created a lot of investment, and then there was a dearth until the auto industry emerged; later radio created a lot of investment, and then there was a dearth until television appeared. In the absence of major innovations that open up great markets and opportunities, an economy can stagnate. Some scientists do not foresee further promising innovations of the magnitude of the invention of the automobile or television. Others see an unlimited number of important innovations on the horizon.

In the meantime there are sure to be small innovations filling the gaps. Freeze-dried coffee probably made no one happier and antiperspirant deodorants probably made no one wiser, but they meet certain daily needs in an improved manner.

New technology creates some major long-run consequences that are not always foreseeable at the time. The contraceptive pill, for example, led to smaller families, more working wives, and larger discretionary incomes resulting in higher expenditures on vacation travel, among other things. Little did the airlines foresee that the pill would increase their traffic. The pill also led to a larger average size in brassieres, something the women's lingerie industry has missed entirely.

Here are some of the main trends in technology that the marketer should watch.

Accelerating Pace of Technological Change

Most of the technological products we take for granted today were not present even one hundred years ago. Abraham Lincoln did not know of automobiles, airplanes, phonographs, radio, or the electric light. Woodrow Wilson did not know of television, aerosol cans, home freezers, automatic dishwashers, room air conditioners, antibiotics, or electronic computers. Franklin Delano Roosevelt did not know of xerography, synthetic detergents, tape recorders, birth-control pills, or earth satellites. And John Kennedy did not know of freeze-dried coffee, fuel injection engines, or laser technology. As much as 20 percent of our products and brands were not around a decade earlier.

Toffler sees an *accelerative thrust* in the invention, exploitation, and diffusion of new technologies.[18] More ideas are being worked on; the time lag between idea and successful implementation is falling rapidly; and the time between introduction and peak production is shortening considerably. He sees technology as feeding on itself. As someone observed, 90 percent of all scientists who ever lived are now alive.

Unlimited Innovational Opportunities

There seems to be no dearth of ideas for needed new products and services, only an inability to bring them into a technical or commercially successful form. Among the most important things researchers are working on are cancer cures, chemical control of mental illness, aging postponers, electric cars, desalinization of sea water, home computer systems, butler robots, and nonfattening foods. Researchers are also working on a host of other innovations, including small flying cars, lightweight single-person rocket belts, commercial space shuttles, space colonies, and human cloning.[19]

An astute student of the technological scene, James R. Bright, stated that the strongest technological developments are occurring in transportation, energy, life-extension research, new materials, instrumentation, mechanization of physical activities, and mechanization of intellectual activities. His detailed description of the specific types and means of advance, as well as the results, constitutes an excellent guide to new opportunities.[20]

High R&D Budgets

One of the fastest-growing budgets in this generation has been the nation's research and development budget. In 1928, R&D expenditures totaled less than $100 million. By 1953, the figure had grown fifty times larger, to $5 billion, and

[18] Toffler, *Future Shock*, pp. 25–30.

[19] For a long list of possible innovations, see Dennis Gabor, *Innovations: Scientific, Technological, and Social* (London: Oxford University Press, 1970).

[20] James R. Bright, "Opportunity and Threat in Technological Change," *Harvard Business Review*, November–December 1963, pp. 76–86.

by 1976, R&D stood at over $37 billion, or almost 2.3 percent of gross national product (GNP).

The federal government is the largest supplier of R&D funds, and industry is the largest user. Almost 90 percent of the funds go to applied R&D. The remainder is spent on basic research, almost half of which takes place in colleges and universities.

The five industries spending the most on R&D (in billions of dollars) are aircraft and missiles ($5.7), electrical equipment and communication ($5.5), chemicals and allied products ($2.6), machinery ($2.6) and motor vehicles and other transportation ($2.3). These five industries account for 54 percent of total R&D expenditures and boast such research-minded firms as Du Pont, General Electric, Minnesota Mining & Manufacturing, Pfizer, Searle, and Texas Instruments. The least R&D spending is found in such industries as lumber, wood products, furniture, textiles, apparel, and paper and allied products. Industries at the top range spend between 5 and 10 percent of their sales dollars for R&D expenditures, and those in the lowest range spend less than 1 percent of their sales dollar.

Most of today's research is carried out by scientific teams working in research laboratories rather than by lone independent inventors of the breed of Thomas Edison, Samuel Morse, or Alexander Graham Bell. Managing scientific personnel poses major challenges. They are professionals who resent too much cost control. They are more interested in solving scientific problems than in coming up with marketable products. Yet companies are making some progress in impressing a stronger marketing orientation on their scientific personnel.[21]

Concentration on Minor Improvements Rather than on Major Discoveries

Tight money in recent years has led many companies to concentrate more on pursuing minor product improvements than gambling on major innovations. In the past, such companies as Du Pont, Bell Laboratories, and Pfizer would invest heavily to make major breakthroughs and were successful in many cases. Even these companies seem to be pursuing more modest goals today. Most companies are content to put their money into such things as improving antiperspirant deodorants, restyling automobiles, and developing new soft-drink flavors. Some part of every R&D budget is spent simply to match or copy competitors' products rather than in striving to surpass them.

Increased Regulation of Technological Change

Technological change is encountering more regulation and opposition than ever before. As products get more complex, the public needs assurance of their safety. Government agencies have responded by expanding their powers to investigate and ban new products that might be directly harmful or have questionable side effects. Thus the federal Food and Drug Administration has issued elaborate regulations governing the scientific testing of new drugs, resulting in (1) much higher research costs, (2) lengthening of the time span between idea and introduction from five to about nine years, and (3) the driving of much drug research to other parts of the world where regulations are less stringent. Safety

[21] See chap. 22, p. 594.

and health regulations have substantially increased in other areas, such as food, automobiles, clothing, electrical appliances, and construction. Marketers must know these regulations and take them seriously when proposing, developing, and launching new products. Many companies have had the experience of spending millions to develop a new product only to have a government agency pronounce it unsafe and force its withdrawal from the market.

Technological change is also meeting opposition from those who see large-scale technology as destroying many of the values they cherish.[22] They see technology as threatening to destroy nature, privacy, simplicity, and even humankind. They have adopted Schumacher's philosophy in *Small Is Beautiful*,[23] and have replaced cars with bicycles, synthetic food with organic food, and fancy clothes with denim clothes. They have opposed the construction of new nuclear plants, high-rise buildings, and recreational facilities where they believe these threaten to destroy existing ecological balances. They have clamored for official groups to perform *technological assessment* on new technologies before permitting those technologies to be commercialized in this society.

Marketers must understand the technological environment and the nuances of technology. They must be able to envision how technology can be connected up with human needs. They must work closely with R&D people to encourage more market-oriented research. They must be alert to possible negative aspects of any innovation that might harm the users and bring about distrust and opposition.

POLITICAL ENVIRONMENT

Developments in the political environment are increasingly affecting decisions on the marketing of goods and services. The political system is a broad term covering the forms and institutions by which a nation is governed. It consists of an interacting set of *laws, government agencies,* and *pressure groups* that influence and constrain the conduct of various organizations and individuals in the society.

Here we will examine the main political trends and their implications for marketing management.

Increasing Amount of Legislation Regulating Business

In the United States and several other countries, the basic political model is that of *liberal democracy.* Consumers and business firms are free to pursue their self-interest except where this pursuit is clearly harmful to others or to the larger society. Government is to play a minor role, limiting itself to those activities that cannot be carried on by other groups, namely (1) war and defense, (2) public works (roads, public monuments), (3) public services (fire, police, schools, justice), and (4) regulation to maintain competition and protect public health. Over the years, the government sector has steadily increased its power, until it is now

---

[22] Theodore Roszak, *The Making of a Counter Culture: Reflections on the Technocratic Society and Its Youthful Opposition* (Garden City, N.Y.: Anchor Books, Doubleday & Company, 1969).

[23] E.F. Schumacher, *Small Is Beautiful* (New York: Harper & Row, 1973).

the major employer in the United States, accounting for 19 percent of the non-agricultural labor force and spending approximately 21 percent of the gross national product. Its growth has been abetted by the demands of pressure groups to receive favors or protection, rather than by a belief that government ought to be the major employer in the economy. While many nations have gone over to a socialist model of society with government owning and operating major industries, U.S. citizens prefer to view government as a regulator, not an initiator of economic activity.

Legislation affecting business has increased steadily over the years, partly in reaction to the growing complexity of technology and business practices. The legislation seeks to accomplish any of three purposes. *The first is to protect companies from each other.* Business executives all praise competition in the abstract but try to neutralize it when it touches them. If threatened, they show their teeth:[24]

> ReaLemon Foods, a subsidiary of Borden, held approximately 90 percent of the reconstituted lemon juice market until 1970. Fearing antitrust action, ReaLemon began to allow companies on the West Coast and in the Chicago area to make inroads. By 1972, however, a Chicago competitor, Golden Crown Citrus Corporation, had captured a share that ReaLemon considered too large. ReaLemon went on the offensive and in 1974, the Federal Trade Commission filed a complaint charging ReaLemon with predatory pricing and sales tactics.

So laws are passed to define and prevent unfair competition. These laws are enforced by the Federal Trade Commission and the Antitrust Division of the attorney general's office. Sometimes, unfortunately, the laws end up protecting the inefficient rather than promoting the efficient. Some students of business regulation go so far as to charge that "judges and the Federal Trade Commission have remade the law into a body of rules of which a large portion impair competition and the ability of the economy to operate efficiently."[25] But, by and large, regulations are needed to keep executives fearful about overstepping the line in trying to neutralize or harm competitors. It is hard to imagine that the economy would be more efficient if competition were not supervised by some regulatory agencies.

The second purpose of government regulation is to protect consumers from business firms. A few firms are ready to adulterate their products, mislead through their advertising, deceive through their packaging, and bait through their prices. Unfair consumer practices must be defined and agencies established to protect consumers. Many business executives see purple with each new consumer law, and yet a few have said that "consumerism may be the best thing that has happened . . . in the past 20 years."[26]

---

[24] Dennis D. Fisher, "ReaLemon Sales Tactics Hit," *Chicago Sun-Times*, July 4, 1974.

[25] See Yale Brozen, "Antitrust Out of Hand," *The Conference Board Record*, March 1974, pp. 14–19.

[26] Leo Greenland, "Advertisers Must Stop Conning Consumers," *Harvard Business Review*, July–August 1974, p. 18.

The third purpose of government regulation is to protect the larger interests of society against unbridled business behavior. Gross national product might be rising, and yet the quality of life might be deteriorating. Most firms are not charged with the social costs of their production or products. Their prices are artificially low and their sales artificially high until agencies such as the Environmental Protection Agency shift the social costs back to these firms and their customers. As the environment continues to deteriorate, new laws and their enforcement will continue or increase. Business executives have to watch these developments in planning their products and marketing systems.

The marketing executive cannot plan intelligently without a good working knowledge of the major laws and regulations that exist to protect competition, consumers, and the larger interests of society. The laws are numerous; only the key ones can be listed here. Table 5–1 lists the main federal laws that concern marketing executives. They should know these federal laws and particularly the evolving courts' interpretations.[27] And they should know the state and local laws that affect their local marketing activity.

In addition to these laws, new bills to regulate business are proposed in Congress each year, but very few of them are passed or passed in the intended form. Lobbying activity tends to compromise bills until they are only a shadow of the original proposal. For example, many consumerists hold that the Fair Packaging and Labeling Act (1966) failed to do the job of improving consumer information and protection in the area of packaging.[28] What is sorely lacking in the whole area of business legislation is a mechanism for formally evaluating the full effects of the law's enforcement upon companies and consumers, so that learning could take place on how to formulate more effective legislation, which fulfills its purpose.[29]

Several countries have gone further than the United States in the passage of strong consumerist legislation. Norway has banned several forms of sales promotion, such as trading stamps, contests, and premiums, as being inappropriate or "unfair" instruments for the sellers to use in promoting their products. The Philippines requires food processors selling national brands to also market low-price brands so that low-income consumers will find economy brands on the market. In India food companies need special approval to launch brands that duplicate what already exists on the market, such as another cola drink or brand of rice. These and other legislative developments have not surfaced prominently in the United States, but they suggest how far regulations might be pushed to constrain marketing practice.

[27] See chap. 27, pp. 701–5 for a further discussion of legal constraints on marketing decisions. For recent cases, see G. David Hughes, "Antitrust Caveat for the Marketing Planner," *Harvard Business Review*, March–April 1978, pp. 40 ff.; and Ray O. Werner, "The 'New' Supreme Court and the Marketing Environment 1975–1977," *Journal of Marketing*, April 1978, pp. 56–62.

[28] See Laurence P. Feldman, *Consumer Protection: Problems and Prospects* (St. Paul, Minn.: West Publishing Co., 1976), pp. 278–79.

[29] See Louis W. Stern, Robert Dewar, Allan R. Drebin, Lynn W. Phillips, and Brian Sternthal, *The Evaluation of Consumer Protection Laws: The Case of the Fair Credit Reporting Act* (Cambridge, Mass.: Marketing Science Institute, 1977).

TABLE 5-1
Milestone U.S. Legislation Affecting Marketing

Sherman Antitrust Act (1890)

Prohibited (a) "monopolies or attempts to monopolize" and (b) "contracts, combinations, or conspiracies in restraint of trade" in interstate and foreign commerce.

Federal Food and Drug Act (1906)

Forbade the manufacture, sale, or transport of adulterated or fraudulently labeled foods and drugs in interstate commerce. Supplanted by the Food, Drug, and Cosmetic Act, 1938; amended by Food Additives Amendment in 1958 and the Kefauver-Harris Amendment in 1962. The 1962 amendments dealt with pretesting of drugs for safety and effectiveness and labeling of drugs by generic names.

Meat Inspection Act (1906)

Provided for the enforcement of sanitary regulations in meat-packing establishments, and for federal inspection of all companies selling meats in interstate commerce.

Federal Trade Commission Act (1914)

Established the commission, a body of specialists with broad powers to investigate and to issue cease and desist orders to enforce Section 5, which declared that "unfair methods of competition in commerce are unlawful." (Amended by Wheeler-Lea Act, 1938, which added the phrase "and unfair or deceptive acts or practices.")

Clayton Act (1914)

Supplemented the Sherman Act by prohibiting certain specific practices (certain types of price discrimination, tying clauses and exclusive dealing, intercorporate stockholdings, and interlocking directorates) "where the effect . . . may be to substantially lessen competition or tend to create a monopoly in any line of commerce." Provided that corporate officials who violate the law could be held individually responsible; exempted labor and agricultural organizations from its provisions.

Robinson-Patman Act (1936)

Amended the Clayton Act. Added the phrase "to injure, destroy, or prevent competition." Defined price discrimination as unlawful (subject to certain defenses) and provided the FTC with the right to establish limits on quantity discounts, to forbid brokerage allowances except to independent brokers, and to prohibit promotional allowances or the furnishing of services or facilities except where made available to all "on proportionately equal terms."

Miller-Tydings Act (1937)

Amended the Sherman Act to exempt interstate fair-trade (price fixing) agreements from antitrust prosecution. (The McGuire Act, 1952, reinstated the legality of the nonsigner clause.)

Antimerger Act (1950)

Amended Section 7 of the Clayton Act by broadening the power to prevent intercorporate acquisitions where the acquisition may have a substantially adverse effect on competition.

Automobile Information Disclosure Act (1958)

Prohibited car dealers from inflating the factory price of new cars.

National Traffic and Safety Act (1966)

Provided for the creation of compulsory safety standards for automobiles and tires.

Fair Packaging and Labeling Act (1966)

Provided for the regulation of the packaging and labeling of consumer goods. Required manufacturers to state what package contains, who made it, and how much it contains. Permitted industries' voluntary adoption of uniform packaging standards.

Child Protection Act (1966)

Banned sale of hazardous toys and articles. Amended in 1969 to include articles that pose electrical, mechanical, or thermal hazards.

Federal Cigarette Labeling and Advertising Act (1967)

Required that cigarette packages contain the statement, ''Warning: The Surgeon General Has Determined That Cigarette Smoking Is Dangerous to Your Health.''

Consumer Credit Protection Act (1968)

Required lenders to state the true costs of a credit transaction, outlawed the use of actual or threatened violence in collecting loans, and restricted the amount of garnishments. Established a National Commission on Consumer Finance.

National Environmental Policy Act (1969)

Established a national policy on the environment and provided for the establishment of the Council on Environmental Quality. The Environmental Protection Agency was established by ''Reorganization Plan No. 3 of 1970.''

Consumer Product Safety Act (1972)

Established the Consumer Product Safety Commission and authorized it to set safety standards for consumer products as well as to exact penalties for failure to uphold the standards.

Magnuson-Moss Warranty/FTC Improvement Act (1975)

Authorized the FTC to determine rules concerning consumer warranties and provided for consumer access to means of redress, such as the ''class action'' suit. Also expanded FTC regulatory powers over unfair or deceptive acts or practices.

Other Laws

Many other federal laws affect business competition and regulate practices found in specific industries. A multitude of state and local laws also regulate competition and specific practices within each state and legally designated locality.

The real issue raised by business legislation is where the point is reached when the costs of regulation exceed the benefits of regulation. The laws are not always administered fairly by those responsible for enforcing them. They may hurt many legitimate business firms and discourage new investment and market entry. They may increase consumer costs much more than consumer protection. Whereas each new law may have a legitimate rationale, their totality may have the effect of sapping initiative and slowing down economic growth.

More Vigorous Government-Agency Enforcement

Government agencies, like other human organizations, seek to grow in power and influence. Their mandate is to carry out the law. They have to find cases and win them to demonstrate the agency's usefulness and need for larger budgets. Their self-interest drives them to take an adversarial position toward business. In addition, some of the persons attracted to regulatory agencies start out with an antibusiness attitude.

The adversarial and costly nature of business regulation is well illustrated in the long-drawn-out suit by the Federal Trade Commission (FTC) against the four leading ready-to-eat breakfast cereal companies, Kellogg, General Mills, General Foods, and Quaker Oats.[30] In 1972, the Federal Trade Commission charged these firms with practicing a *shared monopoly*. This is a new, untested legal concept, which if upheld in the courts, would allow the FTC to attack other oligopolistic industries, such as automobiles, steel, and oil. The charge was that the Big Four of this industry (1) do not compete on a price basis, (2) enjoy monopoly level profits, and (3) make it tough for other firms to enter this industry because of their large advertising budgets and their grip on shelf space through their brand proliferation. While the Big Four were not charged with any explicit price conspiracy, it was suggested that they had tacitly agreed to compete not on price but on promotion. Since the case began in 1972, the FTC staff working on the case has turned over several times, and both sides have spent millions of dollars prosecuting and defending the case, with very little progress. Recently, a court ordered the FTC to release Quaker Oats from the suit on the grounds that its market share (10 percent) was too small to be charged with shared monopoly—a move that came after Quaker Oats had spent millions of dollars defending itself. Cases like this tend to go on even after the original issues vanish, simply because the sides will fight to the end. Business firms complain that they are the ultimate victims because government agencies (1) do not have to show a profit and (2) are less accountable to others for their actions.

Growth of Public-Interest Groups

The third major political development is the rapid growth in recent years of public-interest groups dedicated to lobbying for increased consumer protection and business regulation. The most successful of these groups is Ralph Nader's *Public Citizen*, which acts as watchdog for consumers' interests. Nader, more than any other single individual, lifted consumerism into a major social force,[31] first with his successful attack on auto safety (culminating in the passage of the National Traffic and Motor Vehicle Safety Act of 1962), and then through fur-

---

[30] See "Too Many Cereals for the FTC," *Business Week*, March 20, 1978, pp. 166, 171.

[31] Many other factors contributed to the emergence of consumerism as a major force. See Philip Kotler, "What Consumerism Means to Marketers," *Harvard Business Review*, May–June 1972, pp. 48–57.

ther investigations into meat processing (resulting in the Wholesome Meat Act of 1967), truth-in-lending, auto repairs, insurance and X-ray equipment. In addition to Nader's, there are hundreds of other consumer-interest groups—private and governmental—operating on the national, state, and local levels. There are also various other groups that affect marketing decision making—groups seeking to protect the environment (Sierra Club, Environmental Defense) or to advance the rights of women, blacks, senior citizens, and so on. The eight major public-interest groups have attracted collectively more members and funds than the two national political parties! They represent a new and dynamic form of political representation.[32]

What are the main consumer issues that consumer-interest groups are pressing before legislators and the public? They are:

1. *More and better consumer information.* Consumer advocates want companies to supply consumers with more and better information about the things consumers buy. Among the proposals: (a) Food packagers should be required to put more information on their packaging, such as a fuller description of the ingredients and even the nutritional levels. (b) Appliance manufacturers should write their warranties in clearer English so that buyers are not surprised later to learn that certain things are not covered. (c) Banks should be required to state their interest rates in standard terms so that consumers can compare interest rates at different institutions. (d) Advertisers should be prevented from creating advertisements that mislead or deceive consumers about a product's qualities.

2. *More and better consumer protection.* Consumer advocates feel that government agencies should be given larger budgets for testing products for their safety and health levels and for prosecuting offenders. They feel that automobiles are not safe enough, our food contains too many chemical additives, and many drugs have damaging side effects that outweigh their benefits.

3. *More and better consumer education.* Consumer advocates feel that American consumers do not receive enough education on how to judge values in goods and services and how to interpret marketing communications. For example, Swedish children receive consumer-education training throughout their public schooling, in contrast to the U.S. where one course may be offered on a required or elective basis. Furthermore, Swedish media (broadcast and print) carry much more news about consumer affairs, including a weekly show where the host demonstrates some poorly made products and takes calls from consumers who complain about specific products.

Consumerism is a powerful force that marketing must reckon with. Rather than seeing it as a threat to the marketer's "freedom to act," it should be viewed as an opportunity to do a better job of sensing, serving, and satisfying consumer needs. Peter Drucker called consumerism "the shame of marketing," implying that if marketers were serving consumers as well as they should be, consumerism wouldn't exist.[33] Companies should strive to incorporate consumerist considerations in the design and marketing of their products, as a further step in the implementation of the marketing concept.

[32] See Milton Kotler, "New Life for American Politics," *The Nation*, October 30, 1976, pp. 429–31.

[33] Peter F. Drucker, "The Shame of Marketing," *Marketing/Communications*, August 1969, pp. 60–64.

Another key component of the macroenvironment is the cultural system. People grow up in a particular society that shapes their basic beliefs, values, and norms. They absorb, almost unconsciously, a world view that defines their relationship to themselves, others, institutions, society at large, nature, and the cosmos. The following things are important to understand about culture as it affects marketing decision making.

Core Cultural Values Have High Persistence

People in a given society hold many beliefs and values, not all of which are equally important. Those that are most central to people can be called their core beliefs and values.

The set of core beliefs and values in a society has a high degree of persistence. For example, most Americans believe in work, getting married, giving to charity, and being honest. These beliefs shape and color more specific attitudes and behaviors found in everyday life. Core beliefs and values are passed on from parents to children and are reinforced by the major institutions of society—schools, churches, businesses, and government.

People also hold secondary beliefs and values that are more open to change in the wake of new social forces. Believing in the institution of marriage is a core belief; believing that people ought to get married early is a secondary belief. When students of culture debate about whether cultural change is slow or fast in this society, they often fail to distinguish between core and secondary beliefs and values.

Marketers who would like to change core beliefs and values would be wise not to try. Suppose a women's clothing designer wanted to sell women on the idea of going topless. That designer would be attacking a core value held by both men and women. The same designer, however, might have success in selling women on wearing shorter skirts or lower necklines because these styles do less violence to their core beliefs.

Each Culture Consists of Subcultures

A society is made up of people who share the same core beliefs and values. Yet there are always certain groups of deviants, such as criminals or anarchists. Furthermore, there can be much variation in the secondary beliefs and values that people hold, giving rise to *subcultures*. For example, immigrants, the super-rich, and the intelligentsia, because they have had different life experiences and face different issues, will exhibit somewhat different systems of beliefs and values. Those will be reflected in different patterns of consumer wants and behavior.

One also finds intergenerational differences in culture stemming from differences in life experiences. In a modern American family, the grandparents are conservative in their tastes and careful in their expenditures; the parents work and play hard and purchase many things on credit; their eighteen-year-old son might show little interest in either work or consumption. Recently a ten-year-old boy was told by his mother to behave more like his fourteen-year-old brother, to which he retorted: "Mom, he's from a different generation."

A clear expression of different secondary patterns of belief and behavior is seen in *life-style groups*. A life-style group is one whose members share similar *attitudes, interests, and opinions.* The persons making up a life-style group are similar in what they like, want, and do. One study distinguished eight male life-style groups and reported on the percentages in the population: (1) *quiet family men* (8 percent); (2) *traditionalists* (16 percent); (3) *discontented men* (13 percent); (4) *ethical highbrows* (14 percent); (5) *pleasure-oriented men* (9 percent); (6) *achievers* (11 percent); (7) *he-men* (19 percent); and (8) *sophisticated men* (10 percent).[34] Another study distinguished five female life-style groups and reported their percentages in the sample: (1) *homemakers* (35 percent); (2) *matriarchs* (10 percent); (3) *variety women* (17 percent): (4) *Cinderellas* (13 percent); and (5) *glamour women* (23 percent).[35] The researchers found that the various life-style groups had somewhat different product, brand, and media preferences. Thus life style becomes a useful segmentation variable for certain types of markets.

Secondary Cultural Values Undergo Shifts Through Time

Although core cultural values are fairly persistent, there are always small shifts taking place through time that are worth monitoring. In the early 1960s, a small group of young people, particularly in New York and San Francisco, were developing a "hippie" life style. They drew widespread media coverage, and this led other young people to adopt this life style or some of its component attitudes toward life, work, and relationships. Elsewhere, certain cultural heroes emerged, such as the late Elvis Presley and the Beatles, whose music and styles had a major impact on young people's hairstyles, clothing, and sexual norms. Others were affected by new magazines such as *Playboy,* or films such as *Easy Rider* and *The Graduate.* The changing ideas of the young began to spill over to their parents, leading to changes in some of their attitudes and behavior.

The measurement and forecasting of cultural change is still highly speculative. Some major corporations, marketing research firms, and futures research firms put out reports from time to time that summarize cultural trends. One of the best known of these is the Monitor series put out by the marketing research firm of Yankelovich. Monitor tracks 41 different cultural values, such as "antibigness," "mysticism," "living for today," "away from possessions," and "sensuousness," describing the percentage who share the attitude as well as the percentage who are antitrend. For example, the percentage of people who place a strong value on physical fitness and well being has been going up steadily over the years (35 percent currently), with the main support group being people under thirty, especially young women, the upscale consumers, and people living in the West. About 16 percent of the population, however, is antitrend.

A distinction should be drawn between the *dominant value system* and *trends in the value system.* Most people in this society see themselves as "happy, home loving, clean, and square" (the dominant value system), and there is a slight trend toward less conventional behavior (e.g., open marriage, cohabitation).[36] But the less conventional behavior is never practiced by more than a small percentage of the population, despite the distorted coverage of the news media. Thus major producers will want to cater to dominant value groups, and minor producers might see less conventional groups as a market-niche opportunity.

Here we will attempt to summarize the major values and value shifts that

[34] Quoted in William D. Wells, "Psychographics: A Critical Review," *Journal of Marketing Research*, May 1975, pp. 196–213, found on p. 201.

[35] Daniel W. Greeno, Montrose S. Sommers, and Jerome B. Kernan, "Personality and Implicit Behavior Patterns," *Journal of Marketing Research*, February 1973, pp. 63–69, found on p. 65.

[36] William D. Wells, "It's a Wyeth, Not a Warhol, World," *Harvard Business Review*, January–February 1970, pp. 26–32.

characterize people's relationships to themselves, others, institutions, society, nature, and the cosmos.

People's relationship to themselves People vary in how much emphasis they put on gratifying their own needs versus serving others. The doctrine of primarily serving one's own needs is called self-fulfillment. More people are concerned with self-fulfillment today, seeking to do the things they want to do rather than follow convention or please other people. They are attaching more importance to *instant gratification* in the *here-and-now* rather than delayed gratification in the future. They want to enjoy all that life offers rather than make sacrifices for parents, family, or even friends. Some are *pleasure seekers,* wanting to have fun, change, and escape from the humdrum. Others are pursuing *self-realization,* by joining therapeutic or religious groups. A Yankelovich study has shown that self-fulfillment has become a guiding principle in a growing number of families. The study reported that 43 percent of the parents in a large sample are "new breed" rather than "traditionalist" and stress "freedom over authority, self-fulfillment over material success, and duty to self over duty to others—including their own children." [37]

The marketing implications of this trend toward self-fulfillment are many. People seek self-expression through the product, brand, and service choices they make. They are more willing to buy their "dream cars," take "dream vacations," and "dress more elegantly." People will spend more time in the wilderness, in health activities (jogging, tennis, yoga), in introspection, in arts and crafts. The lesiure industry (camping, boating, arts and crafts, sports) has a good growth outlook as a result of this search for self-fulfillment.

People's relationship to others People choose to live their lives with different degrees of sociability, from the hermit who completely avoids others to the gregarious person who feels happy and alive only in the company of others. One trend seems to be a desire for more *open and easy relationships* with others. Relationships in the past, whether with parents, teachers, employers, or friends, were more structured and formal. Today people are seeking more spontaneous and natural interactions with others. They want to be able to say things on their mind without causing offense ("tell it like it is") and to listen more empathically. They are against the charade of phoniness that drove Holden Caulfield mad in J. D. Salinger's *Catcher in the Rye.*

For marketers, this means several things. People may prefer such products as furniture to be more casual and less formal and pretentious. They may want packaging to provide more complete and honest information. They may want advertising messages to be straighter. They may want salespersons to be more honest and open in their dealings.

People's relationship to institutions People vary in how they feel about the major institutions in their lives, such as corporations, government agencies, trade unions, universities, and hospitals. Most people accept these institutions, although there are always groups that are highly critical of particular institutions, whether business, government, labor, or others. By and large, people are ready to work in the major institutions and rely on them to carry out society's work.

---

[37] "Family: New Breed v. the Old," *Time,* May 2, 1977, p. 76.

There is at present a trend toward a *decline in institutional loyalty*. People are inclined to give a little less to these institutions and trust them a little less. The work ethic has been gradually eroding. Instead of the old ethic of "living to work," an increasing number of people are "working to live." They put in their time in order to make the money to enjoy "what really counts." Pride in doing the job well and in giving all one has to the institution seems to be waning.

The marketing implications of this decline in institutional loyalty are several. Companies will be challenged to find new ways to build the loyalty of their work force. Many see the answer in programs of *job enrichment*, to make the work more interesting; *job enlargement*, which will give employees more responsibility; and *incentive pay*, which will give a larger reward to the more-productive employees. Companies will also be challenged to find new ways to build consumer confidence in themselves and their products. They will have to review their advertising communications to make sure that their messages don't raise the question, Can you trust this company? They will have to review their various interactions with the public to make sure that they are coming across as good guys. More companies are turning to *social audits*[38] and to enlightened *public relations*[39] to maintain a positive relationship with their publics.

People's relationship to society People vary in their attitudes toward the society in which they live, from patriots who defend it, to reformers who want to change it, to discontents who want to leave it. There is a trend toward declining patriotism and stronger criticism and cynicism as to where the country is going. Recently, the concept of *life ways* has been used for classifying people's relationships to the society in which they live. People fall into one of six *life-way* groups:

1. *Makers.* Makers are those who make the system go. They are the leaders and the up-and-comers. They are much involved in worldly affairs, generally prosperous and ambitious. They are found in the professions and include the managers and proprietors of business.
2. *Preservers.* Preservers are people who are at ease with the familiar and proud of tradition. They are a powerful force in promoting stability, solidity, and examination before embracing the new and different.
3. *Takers.* Takers take what they can from the system. They live in the interstices of the work world, finding their pleasures outside the realm of making things go. They are attracted to bureaucracies and tenured posts.
4. *Changers.* Changers tend to be answer-havers; they commonly wish to change things to conform with their views. They are the critics, protestors, radicals, libbers, advocates, and complainers—and a significant segment of the doers. Their focus is chiefly outward.
5. *Seekers.* Seekers are the ones who search for a better grasp, a deeper understanding, a richer experience, a universal view. The pathways of their seeking and the rewards sought tend to be internal. They are often the originators and promulgators of new ideas.

[38] See Raymond A. Bauer and Dan H. Fenn, Jr., "What Is a Corporate Social Audit?" *Harvard Business Review*, January–February, 1973, pp. 37–48.

[39] Leonard L. Berry and James S. Hensel, "Public Relations: Opportunities in the New Society," *Arizona Business*, August–September 1973, pp. 14–21.

6. *Escapers.* Escapers have a drive to escape, to get away from it all. Escape takes many forms from dropping out to addiction to mental illness to mysticism.[40]

These types are found in all societies, and over time the relative size of the groups changes. Mitchell sees American society drifting toward a greater ratio of takers to makers, which does not argue well for future economic growth. He also sees an increasing ratio of escapers to changers, which means that society will grow more conservative and self-indulgent.

Marketers can view life-way groups as market segments with specific symbolic and material needs. Makers are high achievers who collect success symbols, such as elegant homes, expensive automobiles, and fine clothes, whereas changers live more austerely, drive smaller cars and wear simpler clothes. Escapers go in for motorcycles, chic clothes, surfing, and disco. In general, the consumption patterns of individuals will reflect to some extent their orientation toward society at large.

People's relationship to nature   People vary in their relation to nature, some feeling subjugated by it, others feeling in harmony with it, and still others seeking mastery over it. One of the major long-term trends in Western society has been humankind's growing mastery over nature through technology. People can turn on a heater when cold and an air conditioner when warm; they can buy food when hungry and get stomach relief when they overeat. Along with this has been an attitude that nature is bountiful and that it is all right to wrest nature's riches. More recently, there has been a growing awareness of nature's fragility and a desire to preserve its magnificence. People are becoming aware that nature can be destroyed or spoiled by human activities. People are showing a growing interest in achieving a harmonious relationship with nature rather than exploiting it.

Consumers are showing increasing participation in such activities as camping, hiking, boating, and fishing. Business is responding by producing a large assortment of hiking boots, tenting equipment, and other gear for nature enthusiasts. Various retail stores have emerged specializing in back-to-nature equipment. Tour operators are packaging more tours to wilderness areas in Alaska and northern Finland. Food producers have found growing markets for "natural" products such as 100 percent "natural" cereal, ice cream with no artificial flavor or color, and health foods, while construction material companies have found growing markets for wood, stone, and other natural materials. Marketing communicators are using beautiful natural backgrounds in advertising many of their products. Industrial companies have found growing markets for products related to conservation and pollution control.

People's relationship to the cosmos   People vary in their belief system about the origin of the universe and their place in it. Americans by and large are monotheistic, although their religious convictions and practices have been waning through the years. Church attendance has been falling steadily, with the exception of certain evangelical movements (e.g., Crusade for Christ) reaching out to bring people back into organized religion. Some of the religious impulse has not been lost but translated into a growing interest in Eastern religions, mys-

---

[40] Arnold Mitchell, private communication.

ticism, and the occult with more Americans than ever studying yoga, zen, and transcendental meditation. What has been changing is the grip of conventional religion and morality on the lives of people.

The marketing implications are several. As people lose their religious orientation, they increase their efforts to enjoy their one life on earth as fully as possible. Their interest grows in earthly possessions and experience. Secularization and materialism go hand in hand. "Enjoy yourself" becomes the dominant theme, and people gravitate to those goods and services that offer them fun and pleasure in this life. In the meantime, religious institutions face a continuing decline in membership and support and turn to marketers for help in reworking their appeals to compete against the secular attractions of modern society.

In summary, cultural values are showing the following long-run trends:

Other-centeredness	→ Self-fulfillment
Postponed gratification	→ Immediate gratification
Hard work	→ The easy life
Formal relationships	→ Informal, open relationships
Religious orientation	→ Secular orientation

Marketers should recognize that each trend is subject to exceptions. A long perspective on cultural change shows that much cultural change follows a model of long-term pendulum swings rather than one-way movements. Every force seems to breed a counterforce, and in many cases, the counterforce eventually becomes dominant.

SUMMARY

Those who plan and manage products operate within a complex and rapidly changing marketing environment, which the firm must continuously monitor and adapt to if it is to survive and prosper. The marketing environment has several layers: the task environment, the competitive environment, the public environment, and the macroenvironment. In this chapter we are concerned with the macroenvironment. The firm and its macroenvironment make up an ecosystem; disturbances in this ecosystem may spell profound threats or new opportunities for the firm. The alert firm will set up formal systems for identifying, appraising, and responding to the various opportunities and threats in its environment.

The marketing macroenvironment of the firm can be factored into six components: the demographic, economic, natural, technological, political, and cultural environments. The demographic environment is characterized by a worldwide explosive population growth, a slowdown in the U.S. birthrate, and aging of the U.S. population, a changing American family, the rise of nonfamily households, geographical shifts in population, and a better-educated populace. The economic environment shows a slowdown in real-income growth, continued inflationary pressure, changing savings and debt patterns, and changing consumption-expenditure patterns. The natural environment is marked by impending shortages of certain raw materials, increased cost of energy, increased levels of pollution, and increasing government intervention in natural resource management. The technological environment exhibits an accelerating pace of technological change, unlimited innovational opportunities, high R&D budgets, concentration on minor improvements rather than major discoveries, and increased regulation of technological change. The political environment shows an increasing amount of legislation regulating business, more vigorous government-agency enforcement, and the growth of public-interest groups. Finally, the cultural environment shows long-run trends toward self-fulfillment, immediate gratification, the easy life, informal and open relationships, and a more secular orientation.

**QUESTIONS
AND
PROBLEMS**

1. Many companies have defined the food industry as a major area of opportunity. Cite some trends and opportunities that characterize the food industry's future.

2. Describe the threats facing: (a) home diaper delivery services; and (b) night clubs.

3. Name two major threats and two major opportunities facing each of the following industries: (a) automobiles; (b) beer; (c) steel.

4. Indicate some of the ecological consequences of television on dating, automobile demand, eating habits, and housing.

5. Would you support or not support each of the following new legislative proposals (give your reasoning): (a) a bill to require companies in concentrated industries to go through federal hearings before each price boost; (b) a bill to allow auto makers to prevent dealers from selling outside their territories; (c) a bill to require manufacturers to grant wholesalers a bigger discount than they give to large retail chains; (d) a bill to protect independent retailers from price competition by a manufacturer who does retailing of his own?

6. Do you agree that the cultural trends cited in this chapter are taking place? Does it follow that firms should move with majority values?

7. A medium-sized candy bar company has experienced a serious decline in its market share in recent years, primarily because of the growing appeal of granola bars and other health food snacks. List different responses the company can make to this change in its environment.

8. What demographic trends are sure to affect Walt Disney Productions and how can it respond to these trends?

9. How can a company keep track of the technological trends that may affect it?

CONSUMER MARKETS AND BUYING BEHAVIOR

> *There is an old saying in Spain: To be a bullfighter, you must first learn to be a bull.*
> ANONYMOUS

The preceding chapter described the role of major *macroenvironmental forces* in creating broad opportunities as well as threats for the company. We are now ready to move to an understanding of *markets*, which are the starting point for all marketing planning and action. In this chapter, we will examine the nature of *consumer markets*. In the next chapter, we will examine *organizational markets*—specifically producer, reseller, and government markets.

We will first consider the general concept of a market, before turning to the consumer market.

THE CONCEPT OF A MARKET

What is a "market"? The term *market* has acquired many usages over the years.

1. One of the earliest usages is that a market is a *physical place* where buyers and sellers gather to exchange goods and services. Medieval towns had market squares where sellers brought their goods and buyers shopped for goods. Most American cities at one time had well-known sections called markets where owners of goods set up carts and buyers came from all over the city to look for bargains. Today, transactions occur all over the city in what are called shopping areas rather than markets.

129

2. To an economist, a market describes all the buyers and sellers involved in actual or potential transactions over some good or service. Thus the soft-drink market consists of major sellers, such as Coca-Cola, Pepsi-Cola, and Seven-Up, and all the consumers who buy soft drinks. The economist is interested in describing and evaluating the *structure, conduct,* and *performance* of the market. Market structure describes the number and size distribution of buyers and sellers, the degree of product differentiation, and entry barriers. Market conduct describes how firms set their policies on product development, pricing, selling, and advertising. Market performance describes the level of efficiency and innovation of a firm's operation and the major results achieved in sales and profits.

3. To a marketer, a market is *the set of all individuals and organizations who are actual or potential buyers of a product or service.* Thus the marketer limits market to mean the buyer side of the economist's definition of a market; the seller side is called the industry or competition. The marketer wants to know several things about the market, such as its size, purchasing power, needs, and preferences.

We will adopt the last definition of a market. The definition hinges on the definition of a buyer. *A buyer is anyone who might conceivably buy a given product.* This means someone (a person or organization) who (1) might have a latent interest in the product and (2) the means to acquire it. A buyer is someone who is potentially "willing and able to buy." Let us apply this to the market for microwave ovens. The market consists of both households and firms (such as restaurants). Focusing on households, we recognize that not all households will be in the market. Some consumers have no interest: their kitchens are too small; they feel these machines are too complex; they fear that they are dangerous. And among interested consumers, many are unwilling to pay $400 or more for one of these appliances.

This means that the size of a market at a given time is a function of existing parameters such as consumer beliefs and product prices. A seller can expand the size of a market by recognizing its dependence on these parameters. A manufacturer of microwave ovens can wage an educational campaign to convince consumers that microwave ovens are safe. Or the manufacturer might lower its prices below $400, which will expand the number of consumers who can afford it.

Whether there is a market for something is highlighted in the story of an American shoe company that sent a salesman to a large South Seas island to see if there was a market for shoes. He came back disappointed and said, "The people don't wear shoes; there is no market." The chief executive, however, decided to double check and he sent his ace salesman to the island. The day after arriving, the salesman wired back, "The people don't wear shoes; there is a tremendous market." The first salesman thought that a market consists of the current users of a product; the second salesman thought a market consists of everyone with two feet whose interest in shoes might be developed. The true market lies somewhere between these two extremes.

The job of a marketer is to know the market. To understand a specific market, one needs first a working knowledge of the operating characteristics of four generic types of markets: *consumer market, producer market, reseller market,* and *government market.* These markets are essentially distinguished on the basis of *the buyers' role and motives* rather than the characteristics of the purchased product. Consumers are individuals and households buying for personal use; producers are individuals and organizations buying for the purpose of producing; resellers are individuals and organizations buying for the purpose of reselling; and governments are governmental units buying for the purpose of carrying out governmental functions.

Because markets are complex, we need a common framework for grasping a market's operating characteristics. The marketer can develop a good understanding of any market by asking the following questions, which can be called the six *O*s of a market:[1]

1. Who is in the market?—*Occupants*
2. What does the market buy?—*Objects*
3. When does the market buy?—*Occasions*
4. Who is involved in the buying?—*Organization*
5. Why does the market buy?—*Objectives*
6. How does the market buy?—*Operations*

Just as in the alphabet the letter *O* precedes the letter *P*, the six *O*s of a market should be grasped before one contemplates the four *P*s of the marketing mix (see Figure 6–1). For example, the fact that price and service are the most important marketing variables in selling steel, while advertising and sales promotion are the most important variables in selling soap, derives from the substantial differences in these markets regarding the six *O*s.

We will now examine the consumer market in terms of the six *O*s.

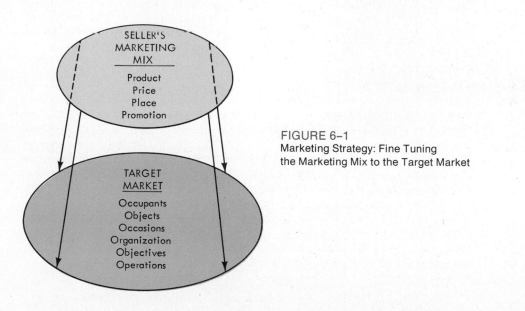

FIGURE 6–1
Marketing Strategy: Fine Tuning
the Marketing Mix to the Target Market

[1] Two other possible questions are, Where is the market? (outposts) and Where does the market buy? (outlets). The first will be treated in the next section (Who Is in the Consumer Market?), and the second will be treated in chap. 16.

WHO IS IN THE CONSUMER MARKET?

The consumer market consists of *all the individuals and households who buy or acquire goods and services for personal consumption*. We will use the American consumer market as an illustration of how a consumer market can be described. In 1976, the American consumer market consisted of 216.5 million persons who annually consume about $1.1 trillion worth of products and service—the equivalent of $5,080 worth for every man, woman, and child. Each year this market grows by another 1.5 million persons and another $100 billion, representing one of the most lucrative consumer markets in the world.[2]

Consumers vary tremendously in their ages, incomes, educational levels, mobility patterns, and tastes. Marketers have found it worthwhile to distinguish different groups and develop products and services tailored to their particular needs. If a market segment is large enough, some companies may set up special marketing programs to serve this market. Consider, for example, the black market:

> Comprising an important group in the United States are the 25 million blacks with a spending power of $60 billion. Blacks are especially good consumers—out of proportion to their numbers—of such products as soft drinks, clothing, and canned luncheon meats, making special marketing effort desirable on the part of manufacturers of those products. Furthermore, the rise in black "class consciousness" suggests the desirability of applying more differentiated marketing effort in terms of selling appeals, ad copy, ad media, and packaging.

Profitable marketing requires observing not only who the consumers are but also where they live. The 216 million Americans are scattered unevenly over an area of 3.6 million square miles. The major trends, as described in Chapter 5, are (1) movement of people to the Sunbelt states, (2) movement from rural to urban areas, and (3) movement from the city to the suburbs. Each of these has important implications for the formulation and location of marketing effort.

WHAT DO CONSUMERS BUY?

Available to the 216.5 million American consumers is a variety of products and services that until recently no one ever dreamed was possible. Today's consumer confronts an average of 6,800 grocery products in the modern supermarket. Each week that passes sees manufacturers trying to place 150 to 250 new products on the grocery shelves. The modern department store and mail-order catalog offer products in the tens of thousands.

Our interest is in finding some basis for classifying the vast number of consumer products. Two different classification schemes will be considered.

Durable Goods, Nondurable Goods, and Services

Three categories of goods can be distinguished on the basis of their rate of consumption and tangibility:[3]

[2] Major statistics on the consumer and other markets are taken from the *Statistical Abstract of the United States, 1977.*

[3] The definitions are taken from *Marketing Definitions: A Glossary of Marketing Terms*, compiled by the Committee on Definitions of the American Marketing Association, Ralph S. Alexander, chairman (Chicago: American Marketing Association, 1960).

Nondurable goods *Tangible goods which normally are consumed in one or a few uses* (examples: meat, soap). Since these goods are consumed fast and purchased frequently, they are likely to be made available in many locations, command a small margin, and develop strong brand loyalty.

Durable goods *Tangible goods which normally survive many uses* (examples: refrigerators, clothing). Durable products are likely to need more personal selling and service, command a higher margin, and require more seller guarantees.

Services *Activities, benefits, or satisfactions which are offered for sale* (examples: haircuts, repairs). Consumer services have the characteristics of being intangible, perishable, variable, and personal. As a result, they are likely to require more quality control, supplier credibility, and continuous availability.

Convenience Goods, Shopping Goods, and Specialty Goods

Goods can also be classified into three groups on the basis of consumer shopping habits:[4]

Convenience goods *Those consumers' goods which the customer usually purchases frequently, immediately, and with the minimum of effort in comparison and buying* (examples: tobacco products, soap, newspapers). Convenience goods can be further subdivided into *impulse goods* (for which the consumer puts forth no search effort) and *staple goods*.

Shopping goods *Those consumers' goods which the customer, in the process of selection and purchase, characteristically compares on such bases as suitability, quality, price, and style* (examples: furniture, dress goods, used automobiles, and major appliances). The consumer is likely to shop in a number of retail outlets to learn about the available goods and find the right item.

Specialty goods *Those consumers' goods with unique characteristics and/or brand identification for which a significant group of buyers are habitually willing to make a special purchasing effort* (examples: specific brands and types of fancy goods, hi-fi components, photographic equipment, and men's suits). Specialty goods do not involve shopping effort (since the consumer knows what he or she wants) but only shopping time to reach the outlets that carry these goods.[5]

WHEN DO CONSUMERS BUY?

The occasions for consumer buying can be analyzed along several dimensions. Whether consumers purchase a product frequently depends upon the rate of their consumption of the product. For example, households with young children

---

[4] *Marketing Definitions.*

[5] For further readings on the classification of goods, see Richard H. Holton, "The Distinction Between Convenience Goods, Shopping Goods, and Specialty Goods," *Journal of Marketing,* July 1958, pp. 53–56; Louis P. Bucklin, "Retail Strategy and the Classification of Consumer Goods," *Journal of Marketing,* January 1963, pp. 50–55; Leo V. Aspinwall, "The Characteristics of Goods Theory," in *Managerial Marketing: Perspectives and Viewpoints,* rev. ed., ed. William Lazer and Eugene J. Kelley (Homewood, Ill.: Richard D. Irwin, 1962), pp. 633–43; and Gordon E. Miracle, "Product Characteristics and Marketing Strategy," *Journal of Marketing,* January 1965, pp. 18–24.

consume milk at a much faster rate than childless households. Marketing strategy for such items is often based on segmenting the market into buyers with different consumption rates, that is, heavy, medium, and light users.

The purchase rate is also influenced by seasonal factors. Religious and secular holidays that entail entertaining and/or gift giving are eagerly anticipated by many industries as the time in which the highest percentage of the year's sales will be made. Seasonal fluctuations in the weather conditions affect the demand for swimsuits, snowmobiles, resort vacations, and air conditioners. Strong seasonal fluctuations in consumer purchasing can make cash flow and inventory management very difficult for businesses, and many try to counteract their effects by offering off-season discounts or sales.

Consumers also vary as to the time during the day or week they are most likely to make their purchases. The recent influx of women into the labor force with the consequent increase in men's participation in shopping has meant that an increased amount of shopping is done before or after work hours or on weekends. Stores of all kinds have extended their regular hours. Public transportation companies, restaurants, and museums have tried to minimize the effects of daily and weekly fluctuations in demand by offering discounts to users in off-peak hours.

Finally, economic conditions affect consumer purchase timing, particularly for durable or shopping and specialty goods. When the economic outlook is poor, consumers tend to postpone major purchases, although some will "buy now before it's too late."

WHO PARTICIPATES IN THE CONSUMER BUYING DECISION?

A key task facing a company is to determine who is the *customer* or *decision-making unit* for its product or service. For some products and services, the answer is relatively simple. For example, men are normally the decision-making unit for pipe tobacco, and women are the decision-making unit for pantyhose. On the other hand, the decision-making unit for a family automobile or vacation is likely to consist of husband, wife, and older children. In these cases the marketer must identify the roles and respective influence of the various family members in order to design the right product features and appeals.

There are five different roles that persons can play in a buying decision:

1. *Initiator.* The initiator is the person who first suggests or thinks of the idea of buying the particular product.
2. *Influencer.* An influencer is a person who explicitly or implicitly carries some influence on the final decision.
3. *Decider.* The decider is a person who ultimately determines any part or the whole of the buying decision: whether to buy, what to buy, how to buy, when to buy, or where to buy.
4. *Buyer.* The buyer is the person who makes the actual purchase.
5. *User.* The user is the person(s) who consumes or uses the product or service.

For example, in the decision to buy a new automobile, the suggestion might have come from the oldest child. Each member of the family may exert some influence on the decision or some component part, and even neighbors may have some influence. The husband and wife may make the final decision and act as the purchasing unit. The wife may be the prime user of the car.

The marketer's task is to study the roles played by different participants in each stage of the buying decision and the criteria that each typically applies in his or her role. For example, we noted that husbands and wives jointly participate in the family's decision to buy a new automobile. It would be helpful to know the roles played by husbands and wives in the different decision areas.

> Davis found that the decision of "when to buy an automobile" was influenced primarily by the husband in 68 percent of the cases, primarily by the wife in 3 percent of the cases, and equally in 29 percent of the cases.[6] On the other hand, the decision of "what color automobile to buy" was influenced primarily by the husband in 25 percent of the cases, by the wife in 25 percent of the cases, and equally in 50 percent of the cases.

An auto company would take these factors into account in designing a family car and promoting it.

Marketers have researched various family characteristics that might provide a clue to the relative influence of different family members in the purchase process. One characteristic is the *locus of family authority*. Herbst has observed four types of families: (1) *autonomic,* where an equal number of separate decisions is made by each partner; (2) *husband-dominance,* the husband dominates; (3) *wife-dominance,* the wife dominates; and (4) *syncratic,* where most decisions are made jointly.[7] All types of families may be found at any time, although the relative proportions may be changing over time. With rising education and income, families are moving away from a husband-dominance model toward a syncratic model, and this has important implications for marketers in their prospect targeting.

WHAT ARE CONSUMERS SEEKING?

The consumer market buys products and services to satisfy a variety of needs—physiological, social, psychological, and spiritual. Economists say that consumers are *utility maximizers,* that is, they will use their limited resources to acquire a bundle of goods that will put them on the highest utility curve.

In considering a particular good, the consumer will see it as a bundle of attributes. Thus a toothpaste offers a combination of dental protection, taste, and breath-freshening. Each brand of toothpaste will combine these attributes in different proportions. Furthermore, the individual consumer will place different values on these various attributes reflecting what he or she is seeking. Thus each brand offers the customer a certain total utility at a certain price. The consumer will choose the brand that maximizes the *value-to-cost* ratio.

---

[6] Harry L. Davis, "Dimensions of Marital Roles in Consumer Decision-Making," *Journal of Marketing Research,* May 1970, pp. 168–77.

[7] P. G. Herbst, "Conceptual Framework for Studying the Family," in *Social Structure and Personality in a City,* ed. O. A. Oeser and S. B. Hammond (London: Routledge & Kegan Paul Ltd., 1954), chap. 10.

This economic interpretation of consumer motivation is formally correct but lacks the rich explanations and insights of behavioral analysis. We will present a behavioral interpretation of motivation later in this chapter.

HOW DO CONSUMERS BUY?

We now come to a key task facing marketers, that of trying to understand how consumers buy. For example, camera manufacturers would like to know how consumers end up deciding to buy cameras in the first place and particular brands of cameras in the second place. Colleges would like to know how high school students decide to attend college in the first place and how they end up in particular colleges in the second place. What are the buyers' decision-making processes that lead to particular buying decisions?

The task of understanding consumer buying behavior is enormously complex, and whole books have been written on the topic.[8] Here we will attempt to present the main concepts and findings. We will present them in the course of answering four questions:

1. What are the major factors influencing the consumers' buying decisions? *(Buying influences)*
2. What is the role played by the type of buying situation? *(Buying situation)*
3. What subdecisions are involved in the buying decision? *(Buying decision)*
4. What is the buying process through which the buyer passes? *(Buying process)*

Major Factors Influencing Consumer Buying Behavior

If we were to analyze any specific consumer purchase, say a purchase of a Nikon camera by a Betty Smith, we would be able to identify a multitude of factors that played some role in influencing Betty Smith to end up buying that particular camera. These factors could be sorted into four major groups, those associated with the *buyer*, with the *product*, with the *seller*, or with the *situation* (see Figure 6–2). The various factors associated with each major component are described on p. 137.

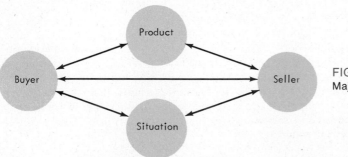

FIGURE 6–2
Major Factors Affecting the Buying Process

[8] See John A. Howard and Jagdish N. Sheth, *The Theory of Buyer Behavior* (New York: John Wiley & Sons, 1969); Francesco M. Nicosia, *Consumer Decision Processes* (Englewood Cliffs, N. J.: Prentice-Hall, 1966); and James F. Engel, Roger D. Blackwell, and David T. Kollat, *Consumer Behavior*, 3rd ed. (New York: Holt, Rinehart and Winston, 1978).

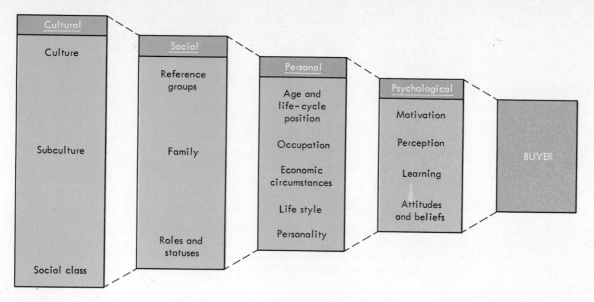

FIGURE 6–3
Buyer Characteristics Influencing Consumer Buying Behavior

1. **Buyer characteristics.** We would first need to know several things about Betty Smith to understand how she came to buy a Nikon camera. We would want to understand *cultural, social, personal,* and *psychological* factors that operate in her life (see Figure 6–3). Cultural factors include the *culture* from which she comes, her *subculture* identifications, and her *social* class. Social factors include the influence of other people in her life, particularly her *reference groups, family,* and *roles and statuses.* Personal characteristics include her *age and life-cycle position, occupation, economic circumstances, life style,* and *personality.* Finally, psychological characteristics include her *motivation, perceptions, attitudes and beliefs,* and *learning.* We will shortly examine these buyer characteristics in more detail.

2. **Product characteristics.** Various characteristics of the product will influence the buying decision. Betty Smith will pay attention to the Nikon's features, styling, quality, price, and backup services in making her decision. The marketer has control over these product attributes and can design them in a way to maximize the product's appeal to the target market.

3. **Seller characteristics.** Characteristics of the seller will influence the buying outcome. In this case, Betty Smith will form an opinion about the manufacturer, Nikon, and the retail outlet, say the ABC Camera Company. Betty will have a certain image of Nikon's reliability and service as a manufacturer. Betty will also form an impression of the retailer's knowledgeability, friendliness, and service. Thus the manufacturer and the retailer will want to consider the seller characteristics that affect Betty's decision as to whether she buys the camera.

4. **Situational characteristics.** Various situational factors also influence the buying decision. One such factor is the *time pressure* felt by Betty Smith to make a decision: under great time pressure, she might make the decision with less information, relying more on the salesperson than she would if she had more time to investigate. Other factors include the time of the year, weather, chance meetings with friends who have opinions about cameras, and the current economic outlook.

All four components of the buying situation—buyer, product, seller, and situation—interact to produce the buying outcome. We shall have much to say about the product, the seller, and the situation throughout the book. Here we will concentrate on the buyer's characteristics. We want to understand more deeply how the buyer's cultural, social, personal, and psychological characteristics influence the buying outcome.

Cultural characteristics   The broadest influence on the buyer is the buyer's cultural characteristics, particularly the buyer's culture, subcultures, and social-class identifications. We shall look at the role played by each of these.

CULTURE   Culture is the most fundamental determinant of a person's wants and behavior. Whereas the behavior of lower creatures is largely governed by instinct, human behavior is largely learned. The new baby as it grows up in a society will learn a basic set of values, perceptions, preferences, and behaviors, through a process of socialization involving the family and other key institutions.

Betty Smith's knowledge and interest in cameras are a function of being raised in a modern society where camera technolgy as well as a whole set of consumer learnings and values have developed. Betty is able to consider a camera because she knows what cameras are, because she knows how to read instructions on how to operate cameras, and because her society has accepted the idea that women use cameras. In another culture, say a remote backward tribe in central Australia, a camera would mean nothing to the tribespeople. It would simply be a curiosity. International marketers know that cultures are at different stages of development and interest with respect to buying cameras and other objects, and they have to consider this in choosing target markets and preparing marketing programs.

SUBCULTURES   Each culture contains smaller groups or subcultures, and each of these provides more specific identification and socialization for its members. Four types of subcultures can be distinguished. *Nationality groups* such as the Irish, Polish, Italians, and Puerto Ricans are found within large communities and exhibit distinct ethnic tastes and proclivities. *Religious groups* such as the Catholics, Mormons, Presbyterians, and Jews represent subcultures with specific cultural preferences and taboos. *Racial groups* such as the blacks and Orientals have distinct cultural styles and attitudes. *Geographical areas* such as the Deep South, California, and New England are distinct subcultures with characteristic life styles.

Betty Smith's interest in various goods obviously will be influenced by her nationality, religion, race, and geographical background. Most likely her food preferences will be similarly influenced and also her clothing choices, recreations, and career aspirations. Her subculture identifications may or may not have played a prominent role on her wanting to buy a camera and choosing a Nikon. We can imagine that various subcultures attach different meanings to picture taking, and her interest could have been influenced by the meaning photography has in her subculture.

SOCIAL CLASS   Virtually all human societies exhibit social stratification. Stratification may take the form of a caste system where the members of different castes are reared for certain roles and cannot change their caste membership. More frequently, stratification takes the form of social classes (see Table 6–1). *Social classes are relatively homogeneous and enduring divisions in a*

TABLE 6–1
Characteristics of Six Major American Social Classes

1. *Upper uppers* (less than 1 percent). Upper uppers are the social elite who live on inherited wealth and have a well-known family background. They give large sums to charity, run the debutante balls, maintain more than one home, and send their children to the finest schools. They are a market for expensive jewelry, antiques, homes, and vacations. While small as a group, they serve as a reference group for others to the extent that their consumption decisions trickle down and are imitated by the other social classes.

2. *Lower uppers* (about 2 percent). Lower uppers are persons who have earned high income or wealth through exceptional ability in the professions or business. They usually come from the middle class. They tend to be active in social and civic affairs and seek to buy the symbols of status for themselves and their children, such as expensive homes, schools, yachts, swimming pools, and automobiles. They include the *nouveaux riches,* whose pattern of conspicuous consumption is designed to impress those below them. The ambition of lower uppers is to be accepted in the upper-upper stratum, which is more likely to be achieved by their children than themselves.

3. *Upper middles* (12 percent). Upper middles are concerned with "career." They have attained positions as lawyers, physicians, scientists, and college professors. They believe in education and want their children to develop professional or administrative skills so that they do not drop into a lower stratum. This class likes to deal in ideas and "high culture." They are the quality market for good homes, clothes, furniture, and appliances. They seek to run a gracious home entertaining friends and clients.

4. *Lower middles* (30 percent). Lower middles are concerned with "respectability." They exhibit conscientious work habits and adhere to culturally defined norms and standards, including going to church and obeying the law. The home is important, and lower middles like to keep it neat and "pretty." They buy conventional home furnishings and do a lot of their own work around the home. The lower-middle-class wife spends a lot of time shopping for the family looking for buys. Although "white collars" make up a large part of this group, so do "gray collars" (mailmen, firemen) and "aristocrat blue collars" (plumbers, factory foremen).

5. *Upper lowers* (35 percent). Upper lowers lead a day-to-day existence of unchanging activities. They live in small houses and apartments in dull areas of the city. The men work at manual jobs and have only a moderate education. The working-class wife spends most of her time in the house cooking, cleaning, and caring for her children. She sees being the mother of her children as her main vocation, and she has little time for organizations and social activity.

6. *Lower lowers* (20 percent). Lower lowers are at the bottom of society and considered by the other classes as slum dwellers or "riffraff." Some lower lowers try to rise above their class but often fall back and ultimately stop trying. They tend to be poorly educated. They often reject middle-class standards of morality and behavior. They buy more impulsively. They often do not evaluate quality, and they pay too much for products and buy on credit. They are a large market for food, television sets, and used automobiles.

SOURCE: From *Consumer Behavior*, 3rd ed. by James F. Engel, Roger D. Blackwell, and David T. Kollat. Copyright © 1978 by The Dryden Press. Reprinted and adapted by permission of Holt, Rinehart and Winston.

society that are hierarchically ordered and whose members share similar values, interests, and behavior.

Social classes have several characteristics: (1) persons within a given social class tend to behave more alike; (2) persons are ranked as occupying inferior or superior positions according to their social class; (3) social class is not indicated by any single variable but is measured as a weighted function of one's occupation, income, wealth, education, value orientation, and so on; and (4) social class is continuous rather than discrete, with individuals able to move into a higher social class or drop into a lower one.

Social classes show distinct product-form and brand preferences in such areas as clothing, home furnishings, leisure activity, and automobiles. For example, Betty Smith's interest in an expensive and complex camera is more likely if she comes from an upper-middle-class background than from a lower-lower-class background. We can imagine that she attended an elite women's college in the East where she majored in writing and film making, and this experience led her to want to become a professional photographer. Even the retail stores that Betty patronizes for cameras and other goods may be heavily influenced by her social-class background.

Social characteristics   The next group of factors affecting the buying outcome relates to people in the buyer's life and the impact they have on his or her buying behavior. We call these social factors, and they include reference groups, family, and the roles and statuses of the buyer.

REFERENCE GROUPS   Reference groups are all those groups that influence a person's attitudes, opinions, and values. Some are *primary groups* (also called face-to-face groups), such as family, close friends, neighbors, and fellow workers, and others are *secondary groups*, such as fraternal organizations and professional associations. People are also influenced by groups they are not members of, called *aspirational groups*. Sports heroes and movie stars are typical members of these groups.

A person is significantly influenced by his or her reference groups in at least three ways. These reference groups expose the person to possible new behaviors and life styles. They also influence the person's attitudes and self-concept because the person normally desires to "fit in." And they create pressures for conformity that may affect the person's actual product and brand choices.

A company would like to know whether a consumer's decisions to purchase its product and brand are importantly influenced by reference groups, and if so, which reference groups. In the case of some products, such as soap and canned peaches, the buyer normally makes choices without any reference-group influence. Betty Smith's friends are not a factor in her decision to buy soap or in her brand choice. To the extent that product or brand choice is not subject to reference-group influence, the seller's marketing communications should stress the product's attributes, price, and quality, or other differential advantages.

There are other products where reference-group influence tends to be a strong factor in product and/or brand choice.[9] Reference-group influence tends to be strong when the product is visible and conspicuous to other people whom the buyer respects. Betty Smith's decision to buy a camera and her brand choice may be strongly influenced by some of her reference groups. Members of a pho-

[9] Bourne found that reference-group influence is strong for both product and brand choice in the case of cars and cigarettes; strong in product choice but weak in brand choice for air conditioners, instant coffee, and TV; strong in brand choice but weak in product choice for clothing, furniture, and toilet soap; and weak in both in soap, canned peaches, and radios. Francis S. Bourne, *Group Influence in Marketing and Public Relations*, Foundation for Research on Human Behavior (Ann Arbor, Mich.: The Foundation, 1956).

tography club that she belongs to may have a strong influence on her decision to buy a better camera and on the brand she chooses. At the same time, another reference group, such as her girl friends, probably had no influence on either decision. The more cohesive the reference group, the more effective its communication process, and the higher the person esteems it, the more influential it will be in shaping the person's product and brand choices.

If the company senses a high influence coming from certain reference groups, its task is to figure out how to reach the group's opinion leaders. At one time, sellers thought that *opinion leaders* were primarily community social leaders whom the mass market imitated because of "snob appeal." Today, it is recognized that opinion leaders are found in all strata of society and that a particular person may be an opinion leader in certain product areas and an opinion follower in other areas. The marketer then tries to reach the opinion leaders by identifying certain personal characteristics associated with opinion leadership, determining the newspapers and magazines read by opinion leaders, and developing messages that are likely to be picked up by opinion leaders.

FAMILY   Of all the face-to-face groups, a person's family undoubtedly plays the largest and most enduring role in influencing his or her attitudes, opinions, and values. From the family the person acquires a mental set not only toward religion, politics, and economics but also toward personal ambition, self-worth, and love. Even if the buyer no longer interacts very much with his or her family, the family's influence on the unconscious behavior of the buyer can be strong.

In the case of Betty Smith buying a camera, her family may or may not be an influence. They may state their opinions; they may support her career goal; they may loan or refuse to loan her money. They can make a difference in her behavior. With respect to the other products that she buys, the potential role of family members as coinfluencers should always be considered by the marketer.

ROLES AND STATUSES   A person participates in many groups throughout life—family, other reference groups, organizations, and institutions. The person will have a certain position in each group that can be defined in terms of *role* and *status*. For example, with her parents Betty Smith plays the role of *daughter;* in her family she plays the role of *wife;* in her part-time job she plays the role of *artist*. A role consists of a set of activities that the person is supposed to perform according to the definition and expectations of the individual and the persons around him or her.

Each role has a status attached to it, which reflects the general esteem accorded to that role in society or in the eyes of the immediate group. The role of Supreme Court Justice has extremely high status in this society; the role of artist has a lower status. Betty's interest in becoming an independent professional photographer is partly for self-fulfillment and partly to raise her status in society.

A person's roles and statuses influence not only general behavior but also buying behavior. Betty Smith's role within her own family as wife means that she will probably take responsibility for certain purchases for the family. Although the role of wives is changing, women still make the majority of buying decisions in connection with such household items as laundry supplies, food, paper products, and health-care products. Betty Smith's role as photographer means that she will be buying camera, film, developing paper, chemicals, an enlarger, and so on. If she aspires to be a high-status photographer, this aspiration will influence the type of equipment she will want to own and operate.

Personal characteristics   A buyer's decisions are also influenced by personal outward characteristics, notably the buyer's age and life cycle, occupation, economic circumstances, life style, and personality. We shall examine these personal characteristics below.

AGE AND LIFE CYCLE   There is no question that the goods and services that people buy change over their lifetime. While people eat throughout their lives, the type of food changes from baby food in the early years to most foods in the growing and mature years to a more restricted list in the later years because of special diets and food taboos. People's taste in clothes, furniture, and recreation is also age-related.

The concept of *family life cycle* has been developed to help identify possible changing wants, attitudes, and values as people grow older. Seven stages of the family life cycle have been distinguished:

1. *The bachelor stage:* Young, single people
2. *Newly married couples:* Young, no children
3. *The full nest I:* Young married couples with youngest child under six
4. *The full nest II:* Young married couples with youngest child six or over
5. *The full nest III:* Older married couples with dependent children
6. *The empty nest:* Older married couples with no children living with them
7. *The solitary survivors:* Older single people

Each life-cycle group has certain distinguishable needs and interests. The full nest I group is very much in the market for washers and dryers, TVs, baby food, and toys, whereas the full nest III group is in the market for nonessential appliances, boats, dental services, and magazines. The patterns of buying task specialization, authority, and relative influence vary for different life-cycle groups.

Some recent work has attempted to identify *psychological life stages*. Adults will experience certain *passages* or *transitions*.[10] Thus Betty Smith may move from being a satisfied housewife to a stage in which she is an unsatisfied one searching for new ways to fulfill herself. This may have contributed to her current strong interest in photography. Clearly, marketers ought to pay more attention to the changing needs of adults for goods and services that might be associated with adult passages.

OCCUPATION   A person's occupation will lead to certain needs and wants for goods and services. A blue-collar worker will buy workclothes, workshoes, lunch boxes, and bowling recreation. His or her company president will buy expensive cashmere jackets or ultra-suede dresses, air travel, country club membership, and a large sailboat. Betty Smith's interest in being a photographer will lead her to buy a whole range of photographic equipment and supplies as long as she remains in this occupation. In general, marketers can study whether certain occupational groups will have an above-average interest in their products and services. Or they can even choose to specialize in producing the particular products and services needed by a particular occupational group.

ECONOMIC CIRCUMSTANCES   People's economic circumstances will greatly affect the goods and services they consider and buy. Their circumstances consist

---

[10] Gail Sheehy, *Passages: Predictable Crises in Adult Life* (New York: E. P. Dutton & Co., 1974); and Daniel J. Levinson, *Seasons of a Man's Life* (New York: Alfred Knopf, 1978).

of their *income* (its level, stability, and time pattern), *savings and assets* (including the percentage that is liquid), *borrowing power,* and *attitude toward spending versus saving.* Thus Betty Smith can consider buying an expensive Nikon only if she has enough income, savings, or borrowing power and places more importance on spending now than on saving. Marketers of various income-sensitive goods and services pay continuous attention to trends in personal income, savings, and interest rates. If economic indicators indicate a worsening economic climate, they can take positive steps to redesign, reposition, and reprice their product, reduce their production and inventories, and do other things to protect their financial solvency.

LIFE STYLE   Another personal characteristic affecting buying behavior is the style of life that people choose to lead. People coming from the same subculture, social class, and even occupational group can choose to lead quite different life styles. Betty Smith, for example, can choose to be a solid homemaker, a career woman, or a "glamour woman." As it turns out, she plays several roles, and her way of reconciling them becomes her life style. Her wish to be a professional photographer has further life-style implications—she might be away from home more, stay out late at night, and enter somewhat marginal situations to take pictures.

Marketers believe that a person's product and brand choices are a key indicator of his or her life style. The following person is very real to us as a result of knowing his consumer preferences:

> He's a bachelor . . . lives in one of those modern high-rise apartments and the rooms are brightly colored. He has modern, expensive furniture, but not Danish modern. He buys his clothes at Brooks Brothers. He owns a good hi-fi. He skis. He has a sailboat. He eats Limburger and any other prestige cheese with his beer. He likes and cooks a lot of steak and would have filet mignon for company. His liquor cabinet has Jack Daniels bourbon, Beefeater gin, and a good Scotch.[11]

The implications of the life-style concept are well stated by Levy:

> Marketing is a process of providing customers with parts of a potential mosaic from which they, as artists of their own life styles, can pick and choose to develop the composition that for the time seems the best. The marketer who thinks about his products in this way will seek to understand their potential settings and relationships to other parts of consumer life styles, and thereby to increase the number of ways they fit meaningfully into the pattern.[12]

PERSONALITY   Another characteristic influencing the person's buying behavior is personality. Personality describes the organization of the individual's distinguishing character traits, attitudes, and habits. Each person has a distinct personality marked by such traits as their degree of extroversion versus introversion; impulsiveness versus deliberateness; creativity versus conventionality; and activeness versus passiveness. Suppose Betty Smith is extroverted,

---

[11] Sidney J. Levy, "Symbolism and Life Style," in *Toward Scientific Marketing,* ed. Stephen A. Greyser (Chicago: American Marketing Association, 1964), pp. 140–50.

[12] Harper W. Boyd, Jr., and Sidney J. Levy, *Promotion: A Behavioral View* (Englewood Cliffs, N. J.: Prentice-Hall, 1967), p. 38.

impulsive, creative, and active. This explains to some extent her interest in photography. It also implies that she will be active in searching for a camera, talking to people, asking them questions, and buying when it feels right.

Marketers of various products search for potential personality traits that their target market might show. For example, a beer company might discover that heavy beer drinkers are more outgoing, aggressive, and dogmatic. It might decide to develop a brand image for its beer that will appeal to that type of person. The likely step is to feature a real person in the ad who has these traits, so that heavy beer drinkers can identify and feel that this is their brand. While personality variables have not shown up that strongly in all product areas, some companies have been able to use personality segmentation to advantage.[13]

Many marketers use a related idea, that of a person's *self-concept*. Self-concept describes the way we see ourselves and think others see us. The theory holds that people generally choose products and brands that match their self-concept. Therefore the marketer tries to develop a brand concept that matches the target market's self-concept. This has worked with mixed success, however. Some of the problem stems from the fact that people have at least two types of self-concepts: their *actual self-concept* (the way a person really sees herself), and their *ideal self-concept* (the way a person would like to see herself). Thus it is not clear whether people like a product that is made for how they actually see themselves or for how they would like to see themselves.

Psychological characteristics A person's buying choices are also influenced by four major psychological processes—motivation, perception, learning, and beliefs and attitudes. We shall explore the role of these psychological processes in the following paragraphs.

MOTIVATION We saw that Betty Smith became interested in buying a camera. Why? What is she really seeking? What needs is she trying to satisfy?

A person will recognize himself or herself as having all kinds of needs at any point in time. Some needs are *biogenic,* so called because they arise from physiological states of tension such as might be caused by the need for food, drink, sex, and bodily comfort. Other needs are *psychogenic,* so called because they arise from psychological states of tension, such as the need for recognition, response, or variety of experience. Most of these needs, whether latent or recognized, do not necessarily move or motivate the person to act at a given point in time. A need must be aroused to a sufficient level of intensity for it to serve as a motive. A *motive* (or drive) is a stimulated need that is sufficiently pressing to direct the person toward the goal of satisfying the need. When the need is satisfied, the person's tension is discharged, and the person returns to a state of equilibrium.

Psychologists have offered various theories of human motivation. Two of the most popular are Maslow's and Freud's.

MASLOW'S THEORY OF MOTIVATION Maslow's theory of motivation is based on the following premises:[14]

1. A person will have many needs.

---

[13] See chap. 8, pp. 201–2.

[14] Abraham H. Maslow, *Motivation and Personality* (New York: Harper & Row, 1954).

2. These needs will vary in importance (or potency level) and therefore can be ranked in a hierarchy.
3. The person will seek to satisfy the most important need first.
4. When the person succeeds in satisfying an important need, it will cease being a motivator for the time being.
5. The person will then turn his or her attention to the next important need.

According to Maslow, the needs, in order of their importance, are *physiological needs, safety needs, social needs, esteem needs*, and *self-actualization needs*. They are defined in Table 6–2.

What light does Maslow's theory throw on Betty Smith's interest in buying a camera? We can surmise that Betty has well satisfied her physiological, safety, and social needs, and therefore they are not motivators of her interest in cameras. We can consider the possibility that her camera interest grows out of a strong need she has for more esteem from others, a need that would come to a person who has been a homemaker for a long time. It may well be, however, that Betty is not even motivated by a need for self-esteem in that she feels quite secure about herself and her roles. Then we would surmise that her camera interest is aroused by a higher level of need, that of self-actualization. She wants to actualize her potential as a creative person and express herself through photography.

TABLE 6–2
Maslow's Hierarchy of Needs

PHYSICAL

1. *Physiological*—the fundamentals of survival, including hunger and thirst.
2. *Safety*—concern over physical survival, ordinary prudence, which might be overlooked in striving to satisfy hunger or thirst.

SOCIAL

3. *Belongingness and love*—striving to be accepted by intimate members of one's family and to be an important person to them. This striving could also include others to whom the person feels close.
4. *Esteem and status*—striving to achieve a high standing relative to others, including desire for mastery, reputation, and prestige.

SELF

5. *Self-actualization*—a desire to develop a personal system of values leading to self-realization.

FREUD'S THEORY OF MOTIVATION Freud asserts that people are not likely to be conscious of the real motives guiding their behavior because these motives have been shaped in early childhood and are often repressed from their own consciousness. Only through special methods of probing can their motives really be discovered and understood.

According to Freud, a child enters the world with instinctual drives and tries to gratify them through blatant means such as grabbing or crying. Very quickly and painfully the child becomes aware that instant need gratification is not possible. Repeated frustration leads the child to perfect more subtle means for gratification.

The child's psyche grows more complex as the child grows older. A part, the id, remains the reservoir of strong drives and urges. Another part, the ego, becomes the child's conscious center for planning to obtain satisfactions. A third part, the superego, causes the instinctive drives to be channeled into socially approved outlets to avoid the pain of guilt or shame.

The guilt or shame a person feels about some urges, especially sexual urges, leads to their repression. Through such defense mechanisms as rationalization and sublimation, these urges are denied or transmuted into socially acceptable behavior. Yet these urges are never eliminated or under perfect control; they emerge in dreams, in slips of the tongue, in neurotic and obsessional behavior, or ultimately in mental breakdowns when the ego can no longer maintain the delicate balance between the impulsive power of the id and the oppressive power of the superego.

A person's behavior, therefore, is never simple. His or her motivational wellsprings are not obvious to a casual observer or deeply understood by the person. If Betty is about to purchase an expensive camera, she may describe her motive to wanting a hobby or career. At a deeper level, she may be purchasing the camera to impress others with her talent. At a still deeper level, she may be buying the camera to feel young and independent again.

An important marketing implication of Freudian motivation theory is that buyers are motivated by *psychological* as well as *functional* product concerns. When Betty looks at cameras, she will not only process the functional information about the camera's performance but also react emotionally and intellectually to various other cues. The camera's shape, size, weight, material, color, and case are all capable of triggering deep emotions. A rugged-looking camera can arouse Betty's feelings about being independent, feelings that she either can handle or will want to avoid. Thus the manufacturer, in designing the product, should be aware of the role of visual and tactile elements in triggering deeper emotions that can stimulate or inhibit purchase.

The leading exponent of Freudian motivation theory in marketing is Ernest Dichter who for over two decades has been interpreting buying situations and product choices in terms of underlying unconscious motives. Dichter calls his approach *motivational research*. It consists of in-depth interviews with a few dozen target buyers designed to uncover deeper motives that the product has triggered in them. Various "projective techniques" are used to throw the ego off guard—techniques such as word association, sentence completion, picture interpretation, and role playing.

Motivation researchers have produced some interesting and occasionally bizarre hypotheses about what may be in the buyer's mind regarding certain purchases. They have suggested that:

Some businessmen don't fly because of a fear of posthumous guilt—if they crashed, their wives would think them stupid for not taking trains.

Men want their cigars to be odoriferous in order to prove their masculinity.

Women prefer vegetable shortening to animal fats because the latter arouse a sense of guilt over killing animals.

Men who wear suspenders are reacting to an unresolved castration complex.

A woman is very serious when baking a cake because she is going through the symbolic act of giving birth. She is averse to cake mixes that involve no labor because the easy life evokes a sense of guilt.

PERCEPTION   A motivated person is ready to act. How the motivated person decides to act is influenced by his or her perception of the situation. Two people in the same motivated state and objective situation may act quite differently because they perceive the situation differently. Betty Smith might see a fast-talking camera salesperson as pushy, insincere, and aggressive. Another camera buyer might see the same salesperson as intelligent, helpful, and articulate.

Why do people have different perceptions of the same situation? We start with the notion that all of us apprehend a stimulus object through *sensations*, that is, flows of information through one or more of our five senses: sight, hearing, smell, touch, and taste. However, each of us attends, organizes, and interprets this sensory information in an individual way. In fact, perception can be defined as "the process by which an individual selects, organizes, and interprets information inputs to create a meaningful picture of the world."[15] Perception depends not only on (1) the character of the physical stimuli but also on (2) the relation of the stimuli to the surrounding field (the gestalt idea) and on (3) conditions within the individual.

The following three mechanisms explain why people can have quite different perceptions of the same stimulus object or situation: selective exposure, selective distortion, and selective retention.

SELECTIVE EXPOSURE   People are exposed to a tremendous number of stimuli every moment of their lives. Consider the stimuli that come from various forms of advertising—people may be exposed to over 1,500 ads a day. It is impossible for a person to attend to all of the stimuli. Most of the stimuli will be screened out. The real challenge is to explain which stimuli people will notice. People will be selectively exposed to certain stimuli.

1. People are more likely to notice stimuli that bear on a current felt need of theirs. Betty Smith will notice all kinds of ads about cameras because she is motivated to buy one but will probably not notice ads about stereophonic equipment.

2. People are more likely to notice stimuli that they anticipate. Betty Smith is more likely to notice cameras in the camera store than a line of radios also carried by the store because she did not expect to see radios in the store.

3. People are more likely to notice stimuli whose change level is large in relation to the normal size of the stimuli. Betty Smith is more likely to notice an ad offering $100 off the list price of a Nikon than one offering $5 off the list price of a Nikon.[16]

[15] Bernard Berelson and Gary A. Steiner, *Human Behavior: An Inventory of Scientific Findings* (New York: Harcourt Brace Jovanovich, 1964), p. 88.

[16] This relationship is known as Weber's Law and is one of the main laws in psychophysics. See Steuart Henderson Britt, *Psychological Principles of Marketing and Consumer Behavior* (Lexington, Mass.: Lexington Books, 1978), p. 133.

Selective exposure means that marketers have to work especially hard to gain the attention of consumers in the marketplace. Their messages will be lost on most people who are not in the market for the product. Even people who are in the market may not notice a message unless it stands out from the surrounding sea of stimuli. Ads that are larger in size, or use four-color where most ads are black and white, or are novel and provide contrast are more likely to be noticed.

SELECTIVE DISTORTION   Even stimuli that consumers note do not necessarily come across in the intended way. Each person has an organized mind set and attempts to fit incoming stimuli into preexisting modes of thinking. Selective distortion is the name given to the tendency of people to twist information into personal meanings. Thus Betty Smith may hear the salesperson mention some good and bad points about a competing camera brand. Since she already has a strong leaning toward Nikon, she is likely to distort the points she hears in order to conclude that Nikon is the better camera. People tend to interpret information in a way that will be consonant rather than dissonant with their preconceptions.

SELECTIVE RETENTION   People will forget much that they learn. They will tend to retain information that supports their attitudes and beliefs. Because of selective retention, Betty is likely to remember good points mentioned about the Nikon and forget good points mentioned about competing cameras. She remembers Nikon's good points because she "rehearses" them more whenever she thinks about her decision to buy a camera.

These three perceptual factors—selective exposure, distortion, and retention—mean that marketers have to work hard to break through very strong perceptual filters. This explains why marketers have to buy so much message repetition, and why they place such an emphasis on message simplicity and clarity.

LEARNING   When people act, they experience direct and indirect effects which influence their future behavior. Learning is the name given to changes in an individual's behavior arising from experience. Most behavior is learned. The exception is behavior based on instinctive responses, growth, or temporary physiological states of the organism such as hunger or fatigue.

Learning theorists hold that a person's learning is produced through the interplay of drives, stimuli, cues, responses, and reinforcement.

We have seen that Betty Smith has a drive toward self-actualization. A *drive* is defined as a strong internal stimulus impelling action. Her drive becomes a *motive* when it is directed toward a particular drive-reducing *stimulus object*, in this case a camera. Betty's response to the idea of buying a camera is conditioned by the surrounding configuration of cues. *Cues* are minor stimuli that determine when, where, and how the person responds. Her husband's opinion on buying a camera, the economic outlook, and the season of the year are all cues that may affect her *response* to the impulse to buy a camera.

Suppose Betty buys the camera. If the experience is *rewarding*, the probability is that she will use the camera more and more. Her response to cameras will be reinforced.

Later on, Betty may also want to buy a tape recorder and may experience cues similar to those she encountered when she bought a camera. If she responds in the same way to these cues and buys the tape recorder, and is satisfied, this reinforces her response to similar stimuli and drives in the future. We say that she *generalizes* her response to similar stimuli.

A countertendency to generalization is *discrimination*. When Betty has the opportunity to use two similar cameras on a trial basis and finds one more rewarding, her ability to discriminate between fairly similar cue configurations in the future improves. Discrimination means she has learned to recognize differences in sets of stimuli and can adjust her responses accordingly.

The practical import of learning theory for marketers is that they can build up demand for a product by associating it with strong drives, providing motivating cue configurations and providing positive reinforcement. A new company can enter the market by appealing to the same drives that competitors do and providing similar cue configurations because buyers are more likely to transfer loyalty to similar brands than to dissimilar brands (generalization). Or it may aim its brand to appeal to a different set of strong drives and offer cue inducements to switch.

BELIEFS AND ATTITUDES   Through the learning process, people acquire their beliefs and attitudes. These in turn influence their behavior.

A *belief* is a *descriptive thought that a person holds about something*. Betty Smith may believe that a Nikon takes great pictures, stands up well under rugged usage, and costs $550. These beliefs may be based on real knowledge, opinion, or faith. They may or may not carry any emotional charge. For example, Betty Smith's belief that a Nikon is black in color may or may not matter to her decision.

Manufacturers, of course, are very much interested in the beliefs that people carry in their heads about their products and services. These beliefs make up product and brand images, and people's behavior will be partly a function of their beliefs. If some of the beliefs are wrong and inhibit purchase, the manufacturer will want to launch a campaign to correct these wrong beliefs.

An *attitude* describes a person's *enduring favorable or unfavorable cognitive evaluations, emotional feelings, and action tendencies toward some object or idea.*[17] People carry attitudes toward almost everything: religion, politics, clothes, music, food, and so on. Attitudes put them into a frame of mind of liking or disliking things, moving toward or moving away from them. Thus Betty Smith may hold such attitudes as "buy the best," "the Japanese make the best products in the world," and "creativity and self-expression are among the most important things in life." The Nikon camera is therefore salient to Betty because it fits well into her preexisting attitudes. A company would benefit greatly from researching the various attitudes people have that might bear on their product.

Attitudes function in people's lives to enable them to have a fairly consistent behavior toward similar classes of objects. They do not have to interpret and react to everything in a fresh way. Attitudes economize in energy and thought. For this very reason, attitudes are very hard to change. A person's various attitudes have settled into some consistency and to change one may require painful adjustments in many other attitudes.

Thus a company is well advised to try to fit its products into existing attitudes rather than to try to change people's attitudes. There are exceptions, of course, where the greater cost of trying to change attitudes might pay off.

---

[17] See David Krech, Richard S. Crutchfield, and Egerton L. Ballachey, *Individual in Society* (New York: McGraw-Hill Book Company, 1962), chap. 2.

Honda entered the U.S. motorcycle market facing a major decision. It could either sell its motorcycles to a small market of people already interested in motorcycles or try to increase the number of people who would be interested in motorcycles. The latter would be more expensive because many people carried negative attitudes toward motorcycles and motorcycle riders. They associated motorcyclists with negative elements such as knives, black leather jackets, and crime. Honda took the second course and launched a major campaign based on the theme "You meet the nicest people on a Honda." Their campaign worked, and many people adopted a new attitude toward motorcycling.

We are now in a position to appreciate the incredible complexity involved in the act of someone's buying something. The person's choice is the result of the complex interplay of cultural, social, personal, and psychological factors. Many of these factors are beyond the influence of the marketer. However, they are useful in identifying those buyers who might be more interested in the product than others. Other factors are subject to marketer influence and clue the marketer on how to develop the product, and decide on price, place, and promotion elements for optimum impact on the marketplace.

Major Types of Buying Situations

The complexity of buyer behavior will of course vary with the type of purchase. There are great differences between buying toothpaste, a tennis racquet, an expensive camera, and a new car. Howard has suggested that consumer buying can be viewed as problem-solving activity and has distingushed three classes of buying situations.[18]

Routinized response behavior   The simplest type of buying behavior occurs in the purchase of low-cost, frequently purchased items. The buyers are well acquainted with the product class, are aware of the major brands and their attributes, and have a fairly well-defined preference order among the brands. They do not always buy the same brand because the choice can be influenced by stockouts, special terms, and a wish for variety. But, in general, buyers' operations are routinized, and they are not likely to give much thought, search, or time to the purchase. The goods in this class are often called *low-involvement goods.*

The marketer's task in this situation is twofold. With respect to current customers, the brand should provide positive reinforcement. Its quality, stock level, and value must be maintained. With respect to noncustomers, the marketer must break normal buying routines by cues that call attention to the brand and its value in relation to the buyers' preferred brands. These cues include new features or benefits, point-of-purchase displays, price specials, and premiums.

Limited problem solving   Buying is more complex when buyers confront an unfamiliar brand in a familiar product class. It requires information before making a purchase choice. For example, persons thinking about buying a new tennis racket may hear about an unfamiliar oversized brand called the Prince. They may ask questions and look at ads to learn more about the new brand concept before choosing. This is described as limited problem solving because buyers are

---

[18] Howard and Sheth, *Theory of Buyer Behavior*, pp. 27–28.

fully aware of the product class and the qualities they want but are not familiar with all the brands and their features.

The marketer recognizes that consumers are trying to reduce risk through information gathering. The marketer must design a communication program that will increase the buyer's brand comprehension and confidence.

Extensive problem solving Buying reaches its greatest complexity when buyers face an unfamiliar product class and do not know the criteria to use. For example, a man may decide to buy a citizen band transceiver for the first time. He has heard brand names such as Cobra, Panasonic, and Midland but lacks clear brand concepts. He does not even know what product-class attributes to consider in choosing a good citizen band transceiver. He is in a state of extensive problem solving.

The marketer of products in this class must understand the information-gathering and evaluation activities of prospective buyers. The marketer's task is to facilitate the buyer's learning of the attributes of the product class, their relative importance, and the high standing of the brand on the more important attributes.

Major Subdecisions Involved in the Buying Decision

Whatever the type of buying situation, the buying decision is really a collection of decisions. Figure 6–4 illustrates nine decisions that a consumer may make on the way to concluding a particular transaction. Consider again Betty Smith. The process started with Betty feeling a need for some new activity. She tries to clarify the nature of her need and decides that she needs some new form of self-expression *(need-class decision)*. She considers various alternatives and decides

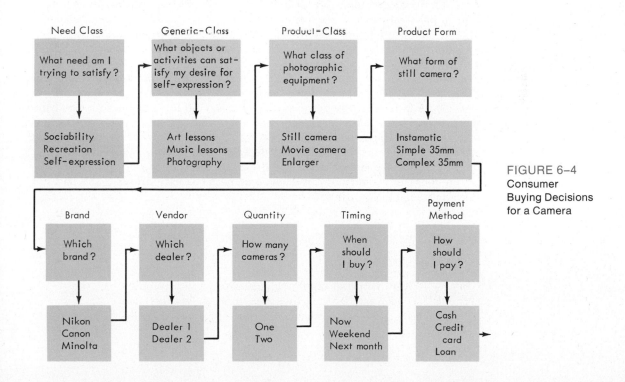

FIGURE 6–4
Consumer
Buying Decisions
for a Camera

Need Class
What need am I trying to satisfy?
Sociability
Recreation
Self-expression

Generic-Class
What objects or activities can satisfy my desire for self-expression?
Art lessons
Music lessons
Photography

Product-Class
What class of photographic equipment?
Still camera
Movie camera
Enlarger

Product Form
What form of still camera?
Instamatic
Simple 35mm
Complex 35mm

Brand
Which brand?
Nikon
Canon
Minolta

Vendor
Which dealer?
Dealer 1
Dealer 2

Quantity
How many cameras?
One
Two

Timing
When should I buy?
Now
Weekend
Next month

Payment Method
How should I pay?
Cash
Credit card
Loan

that photography would satisfy her need *(generic-class decision)*. In considering the different classes of photographic equipment, she concludes a camera would be the answer *(product-class decision)*. She decides that a complex 35 mm camera would be best *(product-form decision)*. Among the brands she recalls, Nikon gives her the most confidence *(brand decision)*. She thinks that she will go to dealer 2, who is said to run the best camera shop for professional photographers *(vendor decision)*. She also thought of suggesting that her girlfriend buy a camera and take up photography but dropped the idea *(quantity decision)*. She thinks that she will buy the camera on the weekend *(timing decision)*. And finally, she will pay for it using her credit card *(payment-method decision)*.

Several things should be noted. The model suggests that the buyer behaves in a conscious and rational way in making buying decisions. This exaggerates the degree of deliberateness in the buying behavior of many consumers, who often go and buy a camera without much prior thought. In the case of everyday products such as soap and cigarettes, the decision detail would be even more compressed. On the other hand, the model allows the marketer to imagine the full decision structure on the chance that it will provide useful insight into the consumer's problem-solving behavior that can suggest effective marketing strategies.

In the second place, the number and nature of the decisions will vary for different buying situations. Suppose Betty Smith also decides to apply to graduate school and to major in film making. In this case, the college represents both the brand and vendor. The quantity decision has to be reinterpreted to mean whether she would go full- or part-time to school. Betty also chose a particular department in which to major, and this decision has to be interpreted as a product form.

Third, the consumer probably will not make all the decisions in the order shown. Betty may first notice a friend enjoying a new camera (product-class decision), then consider alternatives to photography (generic-class decision), then consider how she would pay for a camera (payment-method decision) and who would accept her credit card (vendor decision). While Figure 6–4 shows a logical movement from major to minor decisions, consumers may not make them in this order.

The top row of boxes in Figure 6–4 takes the form of questions and the lower row of boxes takes the form of sets of alternative solutions or, more technically, *evoked sets*.[19] *An evoked set is the set of alternatives that the buyer would actually consider at that stage of the decision process.* Marketers have a strong interest in the size and content of the evoked set at each decision point. The Nikon company would not have sold a camera to Betty Smith if she had not moved through the *decision chain:*

Self-expression ⟶ Photography ⟶ Cameras

[19] Howard and Sheth, *Theory of Buyer Behavior*, p. 26.

Thus in selling cameras, the Nikon Company could gain from promoting the value of self-expression and the role of cameras in photographic self-expression. If Betty had followed a different chain, neither Nikon nor any other camera manufacturer would have had a sale.

Given that Betty got interested in a camera, Nikon needed to be one of the brands included in her brand-evoked set. If Betty had not heard of Nikon, Nikon would not have made the sale. The purpose of Nikon's advertising budget is to make sure that Nikon appears in almost every expensive-camera buyer's brand-evoked set. The purpose of Nikon's retail strategy is to make sure Nikon is widely carried and favorably promoted by dealers even if Nikon was not initially in the brand-evoked set of the buyer. Ideally, Nikon would like to be the only brand in the buyer's evoked set. The fact is, however, that a buyer will usually consider two or more brands of a shopping good. Nikon would find it useful to know how many brands of cameras the average buyer considers and the particular brands. They define Nikon's competition.

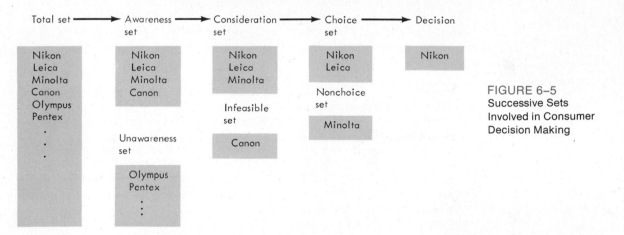

FIGURE 6–5
Successive Sets
Involved in Consumer
Decision Making

The notion of an evoked set can be refined further by recognizing that the buyer moves through a succession of sets on the way to a purchase decision.[20] Let us continue to stay at the level of the brand-evoked set. The various sets are shown in Figure 6–5. The *total set* represents all the brands of cameras that are available to this consumer (i.e., sold in the local area), whether or not the buyer knows about them. The total set can be divided into the consumer's *awareness set* (those brands that she recalls), and the *unawareness set*. Of the brands that Betty recalls, only some of them meet her buying criteria, and they constitute her *consideration* (or evoked) *set*; the others are relegated to an *infeasible set*. As she gets information or gives thought to these brands, a few of the brands remain strong choices and constitute her *choice set*, the others being relegated to a *nonchoice set*. She carefully evaluates the brands in the choice set and then makes her final decision, in this case choosing a Nikon camera.

[20] See Chem L. Narayana and Rom J. Markin, "Consumer Behavior and Product Performance: An Alternative Conceptualization," *Journal of Marketing*, October 1975, pp. 1–6.

The company's task is to work hard to get its brand included in the buyer's awareness set and to remain in the successive consideration and choice sets. The marketer must research the other brands that are likely to be included and the criteria used by the buyer as she moves to successively smaller sets in making her decision.

Major Stages in the Buying Process

The final step in attempting to understand how consumers buy is to map the actual stages they pass through to reach their buying decision. Each stage suggests certain things that marketers can do to facilitate or influence the consumer's decision making.

To map these stages, a sample of consumers can be asked to describe when they first felt a desire for the product, how they gathered information, what problems they tried to resolve, how they made their final choice, and how they felt afterwards.

Consumers, of course, vary in the way they buy any given object. In buying an automobile, for example, some consumers will spend a great deal of time seeking information and making comparisons; others will go straight to a dealer showroom, look at the cars, point to one, negotiate a price, and sign a contract. Thus consumers can be segmented in terms of *buying styles*, for instance, deliberate buyers versus impulsive buyers, and different marketing strategies directed at each segment.

How can marketers identify the typical stages in the buying process for any given product? They can introspect about their own behavior, although this is of limited usefulness *(introspective method)*. They can interview a small sample of recent purchasers, asking them to recall the events leading to the purchase of the product *(retrospective method)*. They can find some consumers who are contemplating buying the product and ask them to think out loud about how they would go through the buying process *(prospective method)*. Or they can ask a group of consumers to describe the ideal way for people to go about buying the product *(prescriptive method)*. Each method results in a *consumer-generated report* of the steps in the buying process.

An example of a consumer report of a car-buying decision is shown in Table 6–3. The buyer is a married male who first got the idea when he saw a neighbor's new car. He then developed reasons for possibly purchasing one. A few days later he saw an ad for a Ford. Two weeks later he stopped in a Ford showroom just to browse. He liked the car and the salesman, found that he could afford financing it, and purchased it. He picked it up a few days later and drove away. The car did not satisfy him completely, but an ad for a competitive brand made him feel that he had still bought the best make. He was annoyed a few days later when his salesman did not seem very cooperative in answering some questions.

The marketer should collect a number of consumer reports and attempt to identify one or more typical buying processes for that product. Some analysts have employed graph theory to summarize an individual or group's decision process in buying a product.[21] Figure 6–6 shows a graph version of several of the elements that appeared in the consumer-generated report in Table 6–3. The

---

[21] See James R. Bettman, "The Structure of Consumer Choice Processes," *Journal of Marketing Research*, November 1971, pp. 465–71.

154

TABLE 6–3
Consumer-Generated Report of a Purchase Decision

3/17   My neighbor just bought a new car. He says he likes it.
It would be nice to buy a new car.
My present car is getting ready to fall apart.
New cars are safer.

3/19   There's an ad for a new Ford. It looks nice.

4/2   I don't have any plans this evening. I'll go over to the Ford showroom.
The cars are nice, especially that deluxe model with air conditioning.
Here comes a salesman.
He's very helpful. I'm pleased that he is not trying to pressure me.
I don't think I can afford the car.
How much would it cost a month to finance?
I can afford it.
My wife has been nagging me for a new car. I'll buy it.

4/5   The car is ready.
I wish I had driven it before buying. It seems a little stiff.
It is hard to get in and out.

4/6   There's the new Chevy advertised. It doesn't look as good as my car.

4/8   My other neighbor wants to buy a car. I told him the good and bad points about the Ford.

4/11   I phoned the auto salesman for some information. He wasn't helpful. He told me to call the service department.

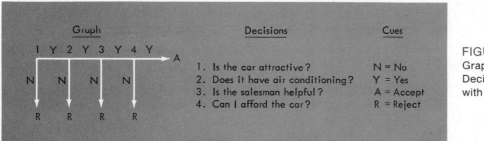

FIGURE 6–6
Graph of
Decision Process
with Four Cues

consumer experienced four cues, each having the capacity to lead him to accept or reject the car. The fact that he bought the car was the result of all four cues being positive.

Based on examining many consumer reports of the buying process, "Stage" models of the buying process have been conceptualized by consumer-behavior specialists. We will use the model shown in Figure 6–7, which shows the consumer as passing through five stages: *need arousal, information search, evaluation behavior, purchase decision,* and *postpurchase feelings.* This model emphasizes that the buying process starts long before the actual purchase and has consequences long after the purchase. It encourages the marketer to focus on the buying process rather than the purchase decision.

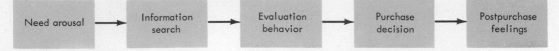

FIGURE 6-7
Five-Stage Model of the Buying Process

Need arousal   The buying process starts with need arousal. A need can be activated through internal or external stimuli. In the first case, one of the person's normal needs—hunger, thirst, sex—rises to a threshold level and becomes a drive. The person has learned how to cope with this drive from previous experience and is motivated toward a class of objects that he or she knows will satisfy this drive.

Or a need can be aroused by an external stimulus, or *triggering cue*. A woman passes a bakery and the sight of freshly baked bread stimulates her appetite; she admires a neighbor's new car; or she watches a television commercial for a Jamaican vacation.

The marketing significance of the need arousal stage is twofold. First, the marketer must understand the drives that might actually or potentially connect to the product class and brand. An auto marketer recognizes that cars satisfy a need for mobility; cars also can satisfy the need for status, power, excitement. To the extent that a car can satisfy several drives simultaneously, it becomes a more intensely wanted object.

Second, the concept of need arousal helps the marketer recognize that need levels for the product fluctuate over time and are triggered by different cues. The marketer can arrange cues to conform better to the natural rhythms and timing of need arousal.

Information search   If an aroused need is intense and a well-defined gratification object is near at hand, the person is likely to gratify the need right then. The hungry person who sees a candy bar will probably buy it and consume it immediately. In more cases, however, an aroused need is not gratified immediately. The need enters the memory's register as an item for future gratification.

Depending on the intensity of the stored need, the need produces one of two states in the individual. The first state is called *heightened attention*. The individual becomes alert to information bearing on the need and its gratification. Betty Smith may not search actively for information on cameras but is simply more receptive. She pays more attention to camera ads, cameras she sees being used, and remarks made about cameras by friends.

Under conditions of more intense need, the individual enters a state of active *information search*. The amount of information sought depends upon whether the person is facing limited problem solving or extensive problem solving. In the latter case, the person needs more information about the key attributes of the product class, about the qualities of the various brands, and about the outlets at which they are available.

Of key interest to the marketer are the various information sources that the consumer will turn to and the relative influence they will have on choice behavior. *Consumer-information sources* fall into four groups:

1. *Personal sources* (family, friends, neighbors, acquaintances)
2. *Commercial sources* (advertising, salesmen, dealers, packaging, displays)
3. *Public sources* (mass media, consumer rating organizations)
4. *Experiential sources* (handling, examining, using the product)

The relative influence of these information sources varies with the product category and the consumer's personal characteristics. Generally speaking, the consumer receives the most information exposure about a product from commercial sources, that is, marketer-dominated sources. On the other hand, the most effective exposures tend to come from personal sources. Each type of source may perform a somewhat different function in influencing the buying decision. Commercial information normally performs an *informing* function, and personal sources perform a *legitimizing* or an *evaluation* function. For example, physicians normally learn of new drugs from commercial sources but turn to other doctors for evaluation information.

The marketer will find it worthwhile to study the consumers' information sources whenever (1) a substantial percentage of the target market engages in overt search and (2) the target market shows some stable patterns of using the respective information sources. Identifying the information sources and their respective roles and importance calls for interviewing consumers and asking them how they happened to hear about the product, what sources of information they turned to, and what influence each source of information had. The marketer can use the findings to plan commercial communications and stimulate favorable word of mouth.

Evaluation behavior The incoming information helps the consumer clarify and evaluate the alternatives. The marketer needs to know how the consumer processes the incoming information to arrive at product judgments. Unfortunately, there is not a simple and single evaluation process used by all consumers, or even by one consumer in all buying situations. There are alternative processes, and recent research has been directed to studying them. Most current models of the consumer evaluation process are *cognitively oriented*—that is, they see the consumer as forming product judgments largely on a conscious and rational basis.

Certain basic concepts help in understanding consumer evaluation processes. The first concept is that of *product attributes*. The consumer sees products as multiattribute objects. A particular product is perceived in terms of where it stands on a set of attributes that are relevant to that product class. The attributes of normal interest to buyers in some familiar product classes are:

Beer: Smooth taste, alcohol content, bitterness, calorie content, price
Aspirin: Speed of relief, reliability, side effects, price
Tires: Tread life, safety, ride quality, price
Air travel: Departure time, speed, aircraft, preflight service, inflight service, price
Cameras: Picture sharpness, speed, closeup distance, size, ruggedness, price

While the above attributes are of normal interest, individual consumers will vary as to which they consider relevant. The market for a product can often be segmented according to the attributes that have primary interest to different buyers.

Second, the consumer is likely to attach different *importance weights* to the relevant attributes. A distinction can be drawn between *attribute importance* and *attribute salience*.[22] Salient attributes are those that come to the consumer's mind when asked about the attributes that will be considered. The marketer must not conclude that these are necessarily the most important attributes. Some of them may be salient because the consumer has just been exposed to a commercial message mentioning them or has had a problem involving them; hence these attributes are "top of the mind." Furthermore, in the class of nonsalient attributes may be some that the consumer has forgotten but whose importance would be recognized when they are mentioned. We shall be more concerned with attribute importance than attribute salience.

Third, the consumer is likely to develop a set of *brand beliefs*—beliefs about where each brand stands on each attribute. The set of beliefs held about a particular brand is known as the *brand image.* The consumer's beliefs or perceptions may be at variance with the true attributes due to the consumer's particular experience and the effect of selective perception, selective distortion, and selective retention.

Fourth, the consumer is assumed to have a *utility function* for each attribute.[23] The utility function describes how the consumer expects product satisfaction to vary with alternative levels of each attribute. For example, Mr. Smith may expect his satisfaction from a car to increase linearly with gas economy; to peak with an intermediate-size car as opposed to a subcompact or a very large car; to be higher for a red car than a green car. If we combine the attribute levels where the utilities are highest, they make up Mr. Smith's ideal car. This should not be confused with his fantasy car, but rather, it is the car he would most like to obtain if it were available and affordable.

Fifth, the consumer arrives at an attitude (judgment, preference) toward the brand alternatives through some *evaluation procedure.* Starting with an evoked set, the consumer compares products using some procedure and emerges with an order of preferences.

Consumers have been found to apply various evaluation procedures to make a choice among multiattribute objects.[24] Alternative evaluation procedures will be described using the following illustration.

[22] James H. Myers and Mark I. Alpert, "Semantic Confusion in Attitude Research: Salience vs. Importance vs. Determinance," in *Advances in Consumer Research,* vol. IV, proceedings of the Seventh Annual Conference of the Association of Consumer Research, October 1976, pp. 106–10.

[23] Some progress has been made in attempting to measure individual and market utility functions. One method, *conjoint analysis,* requires consumers to rank alternative product descriptions in order of their preferences. The data are then analyzed to reconstruct the implicit utility functions for the separate attributes. See Paul E. Green and Yoram Wind, "New Ways to Measure Consumers' Judgments," *Harvard Business Review,* July–August 1975, pp. 107–17. Another method, *tradeoff analysis,* presents consumers with matrices showing two attributes at a time, with different levels of each attribute, and asks them to enter numbers in each cell showing the most preferred to the least preferred combinations of attribute levels. See Richard M. Johnson, "Trade-Off Analysis of Consumer Values," *Journal of Marketing Research,* May 1974, pp. 121–27. For a comparison of these to direct utility assessment methods, see John R. Hauser and Glen L. Urban, "Assessment of Attribute Importance and Consumer Utility Functions," *Journal of Consumer Research,* March 1979.

[24] See Paul E. Green and Yoram Wind, *Multiattribute Decisions in Marketing: A Measurement Approach* (Hinsdale, Ill.: Dryden Press, 1973), chap. 2.

TABLE 6–4
A Buyer's Brand Beliefs about Alternative Brands

	CAR	PRICE	GAS MILEAGE (MILES/GAL)	CAR LENGTH (INCHES)	STYLE*	HANDLING*
			PRODUCT-CLASS ATTRIBUTES			
Evoked set	1	$6,000	10	220	10	10
	2	5,000	16	190	9	10
	3	4,000	14	210	5	6
	4	3,500	20	180	4	9

*A score of 10 represents the highest rating.

Mr. Smith wants to buy a new car and has seen ads and visited some dealer showrooms. His current information about the buying situation is summarized in Table 6–4. He is interested in the four brands shown in the rows (i.e., the evoked set) and the five product-class attributes shown in the columns. The cell numbers describe his brand beliefs. He perceives the first three attributes in terms of real numbers (although his perceptions may not be accurate). The last two attributes reflect his subjective ratings on a scale of 1 to 10.

Which car will Mr. Smith buy? Much depends upon his utility function for the various attributes. We will assume that Smith prefers a low price to a higher price, more gas mileage to less gas mileage, a car length of 180 inches, more style to less style, and better handling to poorer handling. The utility function can be further specified as to its actual shape, but we will assume linearity. Mr. Smith's choice is still not determinant. In fact, at least seven alternative models can explain how consumers form a preference ordering of objects.

DOMINANCE MODEL   Suppose one car was priced lowest, gave the highest mileage, and had the ideal length and the highest-rated style and handling. This car would be the buyer's choice. No car in the evoked set has this clear superiority. Dominance can be used, however, to remove a car that is inferior in all respects to some other car in the set. We can imagine a brand that the consumer dropped from consideration because it was exactly like brand 4 in the first four attributes and its handling was inferior. Dominance is used by consumers to reduce the number of brand alternatives in the evoked set.

CONJUNCTIVE MODEL   Mr. Smith can try to sort the cars into two classes, acceptable and unacceptable, and drop those in the latter class from consideration. He could establish minimum attribute levels that acceptable cars must possess. He might consider only cars costing less than $5,500, giving gas mileage of more than fifteen miles per gallon, not longer than 195 inches, and with a rated style of at least 4 and a handling of at least 6. These cutoffs eliminate brands 1 and 3 from further consideration. Conjunctive evaluation in the extreme could eliminate all brands. A consumer might not purchase any car because no brand meets his minimal requirements. Note that conjunctive evaluation does not pay attention to how high an attribute level is as long as it exceeds the minimum. A high level of one attribute does not compensate for a below-minimum level of another attribute. Conjunctive evaluation is non-compensatory.

DISJUNCTIVE MODEL   Mr. Smith might decide to consider only cars that exceed specified levels on one or a few attributes, regardless of their standing on the other attributes. Mr. Smith might decide that he will consider only cars that have superior styling (≥ 9) or handling (≥ 9). According to the evoked set in Table 6–4, Mr. Smith is left with cars 1, 2, and 4 as choices. The model is non-compensatory in that high scores on other variables have no bearing on keeping them in the acceptable set.

LEXICOGRAPHIC MODEL   Another noncompensatory process occurs if Mr. Smith arranges the attributes in order of importance and compares the brands on the first important attribute. If one brand is superior on the most important attribute, it becomes his choice. If two or more brands are tied on this attribute, Mr. Smith considers the second most important attribute; he continues this until one brand remains. Suppose Mr. Smith "prioritizes" the attributes in the following order: handling, style, gas mileage, car length, and cost. He looks at handling and finds cars 1 and 2 to be superior and equal to each other. He eliminates cars 3 and 4 from further consideration. Then he considers style and finds car 1 to be superior to car 2. At this point he has determined that car 1 is the preferred automobile.

EXPECTANCY-VALUE MODEL   Another evaluation model says that Mr. Smith forms an attitude toward each brand that is based on the importance weights he assigns to the brand attributes times his brand beliefs. This "expectancy-value" model takes the following form:[25]

$$A_{jk} = \sum_{i=1}^{n} W_{ik} B_{ijk} \qquad (6\text{--}1)$$

where:

A_{jk} = consumer k's attitude score for brand j
W_{ik} = the importance weight assigned by consumer k to attribute i
B_{ijk} = consumer k's belief as to the amount of attribute i offered by brand j
n = the number of attributes important in the selection of a given brand

To illustrate, suppose Mr. Smith feels that only two attributes, style and handling, are important to him in the selection of a car (the other three attributes have a zero weight). Furthermore, he feels that style is three times as important as handling. We would predict his attitude toward the four cars shown in Table 6–4 to be: $A_1 = 40[=3(10) + 1(10)]$; $A_2 = 37[=3(9) + 1(10)]$; $A_3 = 21[=3(5) + 1(6)]$; and $A_4 = 21[=3(4) + 1(9)]$. Note that although cars 3 and 4 differ greatly in their style and handling, they emerge with the same level of overall attractiveness ($= 21$) because of compensatory attributes.

IDEAL-PRODUCT MODEL   One of the most interesting models is the ideal-product model (also called ideal-point model), which holds that consumers have

---

[25] The model also goes under other names (linear compensatory model, multiattribute attitude model). For an excellent review of this model, see William L. Wilkie and Edgar A. Pessemier, "Issues in Marketing's Use of Multi-Attribute Attitude Models," *Journal of Marketing Research*, November 1973, pp. 428–41.

or can form an image of the ideal product they want. An ideal product embodies the ideal combination of attributes for that consumer. The closer that existing products come to the consumer's ideal product, the more attractive they will be.

A consumer's concept of the ideal product is influenced by the *consumer's goal* and *self-concept,* among other things. If the consumer's goal in buying a car is cheap transportation, then the consumer will look for a car with such characteristics as low price, low operating costs, few options, and high durability. This goal may be further supported by the consumer's self-concept such as being a practical, plain person. A major premise is that consumers choose goods that express or enhance their self-concept. Every product includes symbolic content that communicates something to others about the consumer. The consumer will select products whose symbolic content is congruent with his or her self-concept.

To use the ideal-product model, the marketer would interview a sample of buyers and ask them to describe the characteristics of their ideal product in that product class. The marketer will obtain three classes of response. Some consumers will have clear pictures of their ideal product. Other consumers will mention two or more ideal products that would satisfy them equally. The remaining consumers will have trouble defining an ideal product and would find a wide range of product versions or brands equally acceptable.

Suppose Mr. Smith, who is buying a car, reports that his ideal car would be 180 inches in length and would average 15 miles per gallon. (He knows that more fuel economy would give him less power, and so he is satisfied with 15 miles per gallon.) Suppose these are the only two attributes of interest. Formula (6–1) can be modified to read:

$$D_{jk} = \sum_{i=1}^{n} W_{ik}|B_{ijk} - I_{ik}| \qquad (6-2)$$

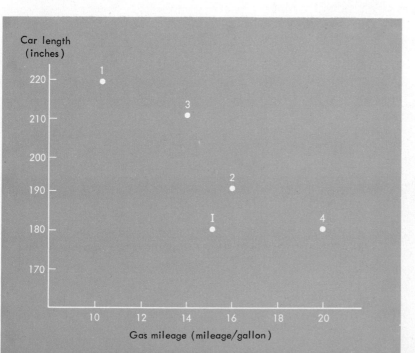

FIGURE 6–8
Brand Space Map Showing the Consumer's Perceptions of Four Brands and Ideal Brand *(I)*

where D_{jk} is consumer k's *dissatisfaction* score with brand j, and I_{ik} is consumer k's *ideal level* of attribute i. Other terms remain the same. The lower the D, the more favorable consumer k's attitude toward brand j. For example, if there were a brand whose attributes were all at the ideal levels, the term $|B_{ijk} - I_{jk}|$ would disappear, and the dissatisfaction would be zero.

The ideal-product model is illustrated in Figure 6–8, which shows the consumer's perceptions of four brands as well as his ideal brand (I). Cars closer to Mr. Smith's ideal product will be preferred more. Car 2 comes out best.

DETERMINANT-ATTRIBUTE MODEL   Several of the previous models employed the notion of *attribute importance* as being influential in brand choice. But in many buying situations, some attributes that consumers state are highly important to them do not seem to function strongly in their brand choice. For example, many consumers rate auto safety as highly important in buying a car. Yet they normally do not shop around and investigate the safety level of differ-

FIGURE 6–9
Determinant-Attribute Model

| | Dealer | Dealer Attributes | | | | Dealer preference (I)[d] | Dealer preference (D)[e] |
		Good service	Convenience	Honesty	Friendliness		
Evoked set	1	20	20	50	30	27	301.0
	2	40	20	20	30	29	295.2
	3	20	20	10	10	17	142.6
	4	10	20	10	20	14	103.6
	5	10	20	10	10	13	93.6
Importance (I)[a]		.40	.30	.20	.10		
Variability (V)[b]		12.25	00.00	17.32	10.00		
Determinance (D)[c]		4.90	0.00	3.46	1.00		

[a] The attribute importance weights are assigned by the consumer and must add up to 1.
[b] The variability is measured by the standard deviation of the numbers in each column.
[c] The determinance is found by multiplying each importance weight by the corresponding standard deviation. A determinance score of 0 indicates a nondeterminant attribute; and the greater the determinance score, the more determinant the attribute.
[d] Dealer preference according to the importance weights is found by multiplying each dealer's attribute scores by the corresponding importance weights.
[e] Dealer preference according to the determinance scores is found by multiplying each dealer's attribute scores by the corresponding determinance scores.

ent cars. Although safety is important, the consumers largely believe that most cars are "safe enough." Cars that appear unsafe are not considered, and the safety levels of the remaining cars are not important. The irony is that competitors normally match each other on the important attributes, and therefore the less important attributes tend to be more determinant.[26]

To illustrate determinance, suppose that Mr. Smith wants to decide on the dealer from whom to purchase the car. Figure 6–9 shows five dealers in his evoked set and four attributes. He rates good service as most important (= .40), convenience next (= .30), then honesty (= .20), and finally friendliness (= .10). Figure 6–9 also shows his beliefs about where each dealer stands on each of these attributes. Note that the beliefs in each column are represented by scores that add up to 100.

Which dealer will Mr. Smith prefer? If we use the importance weights, we will predict that he will prefer dealer 2 (see the column scores in the next-to-last column). However, notice that the attributes differ in their variability among the dealers. For example, all five dealers are equally convenient. The model calls for measuring the variability of each attribute (using the standard deviation). The determinance of an attribute is then the product of its importance times its variability. Figure 6–9 shows, for example, that convenience is a nondeterminant attribute and has no influence over the outcome. The final step is to multiply the determinance scores by the dealer-attribute levels. The results are shown in the last column, and we can predict that this consumer will end up choosing dealer 1, not dealer 2.

MARKETING IMPLICATIONS   The preceding models indicate that buyers can form their product preferences in several different ways. A particular buyer, on a particular buying occasion, facing a particular product class, might be a conjunctive buyer, an expectancy-value buyer, or some other type of buyer. The same buyer may behave as a conjunctive buyer for large-ticket purchases and a disjunctive buyer for small-ticket items. Or the same buyer, in buying a large-ticket item, may behave first like a conjunctive buyer to eliminate many alternatives and then make a final choice as an expectancy-value buyer. When we realize that a market is made up of many buyers, it seems almost hopeless to assess the nature of buying behavior in that market.

Yet marketers can gain useful insights by interviewing a sample of buyers to find out how they form their evaluations in that product class. The marketer might find that the majority of consumers in that market use one particular evaluation procedure. In such a case, the marketer can consider the most effective ways to make his brand salient to consumers who are using that evaluation procedure.

For example, suppose the marketer discovers that most of the buyers form their preferences by comparing actual brands to their ideal products. Furthermore, suppose that there is a large market segment that has the same ideal product as Mr. Smith (see Figure 6–8). Suppose the marketer sells brand 4, which is less appealing to this market segment than brand 2. What can the marketer of brand 4 do to improve sales to this market segment?

[26] See James H. Myers and Mark I. Alpert, "Determinant Buying Attitudes: Meaning and Measurement," *Journal of Marketing*, October 1968, pp. 13–20.

The ideal-product model suggests at least seven alternative strategies. They are:[27]

1. *Developing a new brand.* The marketer could introduce a second brand that is closer to this segment's ideal brand.

2. *Modifying the existing brand.* The marketer could alter the attributes of the existing brand to bring it closer to this segment's ideal brand. This is called *real brand repositioning.*

3. *Altering beliefs about the company's brand.* The marketer could try to alter consumers' perceptions of where the company's brand actually stands on key attributes. The marketer may find that the market thinks its car is too long and may undertake a communication campaign to shift the market's perceptions of the company's brand closer to the ideal product. This is called *psychological brand repositioning.*

4. *Altering beliefs about the competitors' brands.* The marketer could try to alter consumers' perceptions of where a leading competitor's brand stands on different attributes. Thus the marketer may, through comparison advertising, represent car 2 as being much longer than its own car 4. This is called *competitive depositioning.*

5. *Altering the attribute-importance weights.* The marketer could try to persuade consumers to attach more importance to those attributes that the company brand happens to excel in. Thus the manufacturer of car 4 may promote the importance of gas mileage to consumers who may not have attached enough importance to it.

6. *Calling attention to neglected attributes.* The marketer could try to convince consumers to pay attention to an attribute that they are normally unaware of or indifferent to.

7. *Shifting the ideal product.* The marketer could try to persuade consumers to change their ideal levels for one or more attributes.

Purchase decision   The evaluation stage leads the consumer to form a ranked set of preferences among the alternative objects in his or her evoked set. Normally, a consumer will buy the object he or she likes most. But there are a number of additional links between his or her evaluation behavior and the purchase decision. They are shown in Figure 6–10.

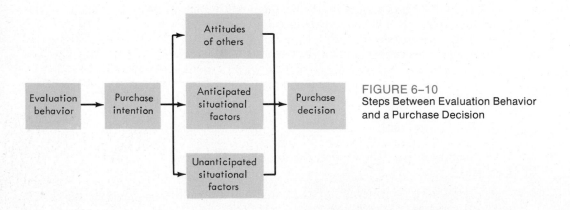

FIGURE 6–10
Steps Between Evaluation Behavior
and a Purchase Decision

---

[27] For further discussion, see Harper W. Boyd, Jr., Michael L. Ray, and Edward C. Strong, "An Attitudinal Framework for Advertising Strategy," *Journal of Marketing*, April 1972, pp. 27–33.

The consumer's evaluations will lead to an intention to purchase one of the objects. At that point, three additional factors intervene.[28]

The first is the *attitude of others*. Suppose a man prefers a Cadillac but his wife thinks a Cadillac is pretentious. His overall favorable attitude toward the Cadillac is consequently reduced. The extent to which the attitude of others will reduce a favorable attitude depends upon two things: (1) the intensity of the other person's negative attitude, and (2) the consumer's motivation to comply with the other person's wishes.[29] The more intense the other person's negativism, and the closer the other person is to the consumer, the more the consumer will revise downward his purchase intention.

Purchase intention is also influenced by *anticipated situational factors*. The consumer forms a purchase intention on the basis of such factors as expected family income, the expected total cost of the product, and the expected benefits of the product.

When the consumer is about to act, *unanticipated situational factors* may intervene to prevent her or him from carrying out the purchase intention. The buyer may not be able to negotiate desirable terms. He or she may not like the looks or manner of the salesperson or the way business is carried on in the showroom. There may be a sudden loss of nerve and worry about his or her income situation. Marketers believe that unanticipated factors in the *critical contact situation* can have a great influence on the final decision.

Thus preferences and even purchase intentions are not completely reliable predictors of actual buying behavior. They give direction to purchase behavior but fail to include a number of additional factors that may intervene.

The decision of an individual to modify, postpone, or avoid a purchase decision is heavily influenced by *perceived risk*. Marketers have devoted a lot of effort to understand buying behavior as *risk taking*.[30] Consumers cannot be certain about the performance and psychosocial consequences of their purchase decision. This uncertainty produces anxiety. The amount of perceived risk varies with the amount of money at stake, the amount of attribute uncertainty, and the amount of consumer self-confidence. A consumer develops certain routines for reducing risk, such as decision avoidance, information gathering from friends, and preference for national brand names and warranties. The marketer must understand the factors that provoke a feeling of risk in the consumer and attempt to provide information and support that will help reduce this risk.

Postpurchase feelings   After buying and trying the product, the consumer will experience some level of satisfaction or dissatisfaction. If asked, she or he may report being very satisfied, somewhat satisfied, somewhat dissatisfied, or very dissatisfied. What determines the level of postpurchase satisfaction? The major theory holds that a consumer's satisfaction is a function of her or his *expectations (E)*

[28] See Jagdish N. Sheth, "An Investigation of Relationships among Evaluative Beliefs, Affect, Behavioral Intention, and Behavior," in *Consumer Behavior: Theory and Application,* ed. John V. Farley, John A. Howard, and L. Winston Ring (Boston: Allyn & Bacon, 1974), pp. 89–114.

[29] See Martin Fishbein, "Attitude and Prediction of Behavior," in *Readings in Attitude Theory and Measurement,* ed. Martin Fishbein (New York: John Wiley & Sons, 1967), pp. 477–92.

[30] See Raymond A. Bauer, "Consumer Behavior as Risk Taking" in *Risk Taking and Information Handling in Consumer Behavior,* ed. Donald F. Cox (Boston: Division of Research, Harvard Business School, 1967); and James W. Taylor, "The Role of Risk in Consumer Behavior," *Journal of Marketing,* April 1974, pp. 54–60.

and the product's *perceived performance (P)*, that is, $S = f(E, P)$.[31] If the product matches up to expectations, the consumer is satisfied; if it exceeds them, she or he is highly satisfied; if it falls short, the consumer is dissatisfied.

Consumers form their expectations on the basis of messages and claims sent out by the seller and other communication sources. If the seller makes exaggerated claims for the product, the consumer experiences *disconfirmed expectations,* which lead to dissatisfaction. The amount of dissatisfaction depends on the size of the difference between expectations and performance. Different psychological theories have been advanced suggesting that consumers may either magnify or diminish the importance of the differences between expectations and performance.[32] *Contrast theory* says that the amount of dissatisfaction will be larger than the performance gap. *Cognitive dissonance theory* says that the amount of dissatisfaction will be less because the consumer will try to reduce the dissonance by imputing higher performance.

The smart seller will make claims for a product that are congruent with its quality so that the buyer experiences satisfaction. Some sellers even understate performance levels so that consumers will experience higher-than-expected satisfaction with the product.

Thus we see that brand experience has an important effect on subsequent brand preference. If the purchased brand fails to deliver the expected satisfaction to the buyer, the buyer will revise downward his or her attitude toward the brand and may even eliminate it from his or her evoked set. On the other hand, a satisfying experience will tend to strengthen the buyer's brand preference.

The reinforcement effect of past brand choices on subsequent brand preferences has been described in a brand learning model developed by Kuehn.[33] This model postulates the existence of a pair of "learning operators" that explicitly alter current brand purchase probabilities on the basis of the last brand choice. The basic device is illustrated in Figure 6–11. The horizontal axis represents the probability of choosing brand *j* in period *t*, and the vertical axis represents the probability of choosing brand *j* in period *t* + 1. The figure contains a positively sloped 45-degree line as a norm. The figure also contains two positively sloped lines called the purchase and rejection operators. These operators show how the probability of purchasing brand *j* is modified from period *t* to period *t* + 1, depending on whether or not brand *j* was just purchased.

For example, suppose the probability of a person's purchasing brand *j* this period is .60. Suppose it is actually what he or she buys. The probability that the person will buy brand *j* again, assuming that he or she is satisfied, is found by running a dotted line up from the horizontal axis at .60 to the purchase-operator line (because brand *j* was purchased) and going across the vertical axis and reading the new probability. In this illustration, the new probability is .78. If the buyer had not purchased *j*, the dotted line from .60 would have been run up only to the rejection operator and read on the vertical axis. The probability of that person's buying *j* next time would have fallen from .60 to .31.

[31] See John E. Swan and Linda Jones Combs, "Product Performance and Consumer Satisfaction: A New Concept," *Journal of Marketing Research*, April 1976, pp. 25–33.

[32] See Rolph E. Anderson, "Consumer Dissatisfaction: The Effect of Disconfirmed Expectancy on Perceived Product Performance," *Journal of Marketing Research*, February 1973, pp. 38–44.

[33] Alfred A. Kuehn, "Consumer Brand Choice—A Learning Process?" in *Quantitative Techniques in Marketing Analysis,* eds. R. E. Frank, A. A. Kuehn, and W. F. Massy (Homewood, Ill.: Richard D. Irwin, 1962), pp. 390–403.

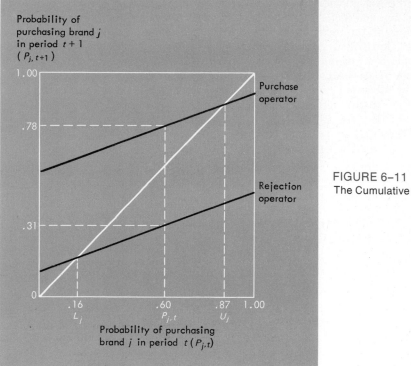

Probability of purchasing brand *j* in period *t* + 1 ($P_{j, t+1}$)

1.00

Purchase operator

.78

FIGURE 6–11
The Cumulative Learning Model

Rejection operator

.31

0

.16   .60   .87   1.00
L_j $P_{j, t}$ U_j

Probability of purchasing brand *j* in period *t* ($P_{j.t}$)

SOURCE: Kuehn, p. 391

If the consumer continues buying brand *j*, the probability of buying brand *j* approaches .87 in the limit. This upper limit, given by the intersection of the purchase-operator and the 45-degree line, represents a phenomenon known as *incomplete habit formation*. No matter how much brand *j* is bought, some probability still remains that the consumer may buy another brand. On the other hand, if the consumer does not buy brand *j* for a long time, the probability of his buying this brand falls continuously but never to zero. This is the phenomenon of *incomplete habit extinction*. There is always some positive probability that a consumer may buy a previously neglected brand.

The model has been fitted for some consumer staples (such as beer, coffee, frozen orange juice) and has found some limited empirical support. For example, Kuehn found that the probability of rebuying Snow Crop frozen orange juice was .33 with one past (last) purchase of this brand and .806 with four past purchases of this brand.

Brand purchase probabilities are less likely to be strengthened when consumers buy an expensive product. In the case of a car, the consumer finds attractive and unattractive qualities in each brand. Presumably the brand with the most attractive qualities is selected, but this does not resolve doubts about the unattractive qualities of the chosen brand or the attractive qualities of the rejected brands. The purchaser may subsequently hear information that reflects badly on the brand, for instance, that the brand will be discontinued or that the brand could have been purchased for less. Negative feelings can also arise through finding the brand's performance disappointing.

Postpurchase cognitive dissonance is common among purchasers of homes, automobiles, and major appliances. Cognitive dissonance means there is a lack of harmony in the buyer's various cognitions about purchased product and the foregone alternatives. According to Festinger, "The magnitude of postdecision dissonance is an increasing function of the general importance of the decision and of the relative attractiveness of the unchosen alternatives."[34] The dissonant consumer will seek to reduce the dissonance because of a drive in the human organism "to establish internal harmony, consistency, or congruity among his opinion, knowledge, and values."[35] Consumers will resort to one of two courses of action. They may try to reduce the dissonance by *removing* the product, returning it for a credit where that is possible, or selling it to someone else. Or they may try to reduce the dissonance by *confirming* the product, seeking information that might confirm its high value.

Marketers try to help buyers feel good about their purchase choice. A disappointed buyer may not only stop buying but also bad-mouth the product to others. The main step is to direct supportive communications to recent buyers. Auto manufacturers build assurances into the information brochures that accompany the product. They also run ads featuring recent purchasers showing satisfaction with their choice.

SUMMARY

Markets have to be understood before marketing can be planned. A market is the set of all individuals and organizations who are actual or potential buyers of a product or service. To understand a market, we ask six questions: Who is in the market? (occupants); What do they buy? (objects); When do they buy? (occasions); Who does the buying? (organization); Why do they buy? (objectives); and How do they buy? (operations). Answering these six Os of a market is a prerequisite to making decisions on the four Ps of marketing strategy.

We can distinguish between consumer markets and organizational markets (producers, resellers, government). This chapter examined the six Os of consumer markets.

The consumer market is the ultimate market for which economic activities are organized. It consists of the whole population, and it is important for the marketer to research age distribution, family formation, incomes, educational levels, mobility patterns, and tastes. The consumer market buys objects that can be classified according to their tangibility (durables, nondurables, and services) and according to how the consumers go about buying them (convenience, shopping, and specialty goods). The timing of consumer purchases is influenced by family size, seasonal factors, and economic conditions. The purchase decision is influenced by various parties playing various roles (initiator, influencer, decider, buyer, and user). In the family, which is the major purchasing organization for consumers, there is some buying task specialization, with the wife normally buying most of the household's goods, and other members buying or influencing the purchase of other things.

The objectives of consumers are to satisfy a variety of needs—phys-

[34] Leon Festinger, *A Theory of Cognitive Dissonance* (Stanford, Calif.: Stanford University Press, 1957), p. 262.

[35] Ibid., p. 260.

iological, safety, belongingness, status, and self-actualization. The consumer is not always fully conscious of the needs that are driving his or her behavior.

The buying situation itself can vary from one of routinized response behavior to limited problem solving to extensive problem solving. Buying is not a single act but a multicomponent decision on the need class, generic class, product class, product form, brand, vendor, quantity, timing, and method of payment. With each decision component, the buyer starts with an initial evoked set that gets narrowed down. The buyer goes through a process consisting of need arousal, information search, evaluation behavior, purchase decision, and postpurchase feelings. At each decision stage, characteristics of the buyer, product, seller, and selling situation interact to influence the buying outcome.

QUESTIONS AND PROBLEMS

1. Purchasing furniture is an uneasy experience for most families, one involving high perceived risk. Recommend a marketing approach that will help meet the buyer's concerns.

2. Recall some recent important purchase you made and construct a consumer buying protocol of what took place.

3. A grooming aid company has just developed a cologne product available in towelettes, that is, flat miniature packages with presoaked cloth that are handy to carry around and open when needed. Develop a map showing the structure of purchase decisions facing a buyer and the decision route he must follow to end up purchasing the new product and becoming a loyal customer.

4. Jim Beam, a brand of whisky, is advertised "Coffee, Tea, or Beam." What is the advertiser trying to accomplish?

5. A friend of yours is planning to buy a new car. He has a preference for foreign makes and his choice has narrowed down to Volkswagen, Opel, and Volvo. He is looking for three things in a car: economy, quality, and roominess, and he values them at .5, .3, and .2, respectively. He would rate Volkswagen as standing at .8, .8, and .2 on the three attributes; Opel, .3, .5, and .9; and Volvo, .5, .8, and .7. Predict the cars he is most likely to buy and least likely to buy if he evaluates cars according to the expectancy value model.

6. "A person will tend to buy the brand in the product class whose image is most congruent with his self-image." Is a person's self-image a highly reliable prediction of his brand choice?

7. Develop a map showing the structure of purchase decisions as they may be made by potential buyers of paint. Indicate how a paint company such as DuPont can determine points at which advertising might favorably affect DuPont's share of the market.

8. Name some attitudes that you or others have expressed about prunes. Suggest some strategies and appeals that might overcome negative attitudes toward prunes.

9. A homebuilder is planning to design homes for "empty-nesters." Can this life-cycle group be further segmented? What kind of home design features fit the needs of empty nesters?

10. Describe the consumer market for briefcases, using the framework developed in this chapter.

ORGANIZATIONAL MARKETS AND BUYING BEHAVIOR

7

> *Companies don't make purchases; they establish relationships.*
> CHARLES S. GOODMAN

The needs and wants of consumers lead to the phenomenon of consumer markets described in the preceding chapter. In turn, those who supply consumer markets with goods and services are themselves in need of goods and services to run their business. These organizations—producers, resellers, and governments—therefore make up vast organizational markets that buy a multitude of things such as equipment, raw material, labor, and other services. Various organizations emerge to sell goods and services to these organizational buyers. A great many organizations sell exclusively to other organizations and never come in contact with consumer buyers.

Selling to organizations introduces several considerations not found in consumer marketing:

1. Organizations do not buy for personal consumption or utility but to obtain goods and services that will be used in further production, reselling, or servicing.

2. More persons normally get involved in organizational buying, especially for major items, than in consumer buying. The decision makers usually have different organizational responsibilities and apply different criteria to the purchase decision.

3. The organization imposes policies, constraints, and requirements that must be heeded by its buyers.

4. The buying instruments, such as requests for quotations, proposals, and purchase contracts, add another dimension not found in consumer buying.

Companies that sell such industrial products as steel, computers, and nuclear power plants need to understand organizational buying behavior. Webster and Wind define organizational buying as "the decision-making process by which formal organizations establish the need for purchased products and services, and identify, evaluate, and choose among alternative brands and suppliers."[1] No two companies buy in the same way. Yet the seller hopes to spot enough uniformities in organizational buying behavior to contribute to improved marketing-mix planning.

In this chapter, we shall examine each of three generic organizational markets—producers, resellers, and government units—in terms of the six Os framework developed in the preceding chapter: occupants, objects, occasions, organization, objectives, and operations.

THE PRODUCER MARKET

Who Is in the Producer Market?

The producer market (also called the industrial or business market) consists of all individuals and organizations who acquire goods and services that enter into the production of other products or services that are sold, rented, or supplied to others. The major types of industries making up the producer market are (1) agriculture, forestry, and fisheries; (2) mining; (3) manufacturing; (4) construction; (5) transportation; (6) communication; (7) public utilities; (8) banking, finance, and insurance; and (9) services. There are over 14 million different industrial units and each is a market for specific types of goods and services. They employ over 87 million workers, generate an annual national income of over $1 trillion, and constitute a buying market for the goods of most firms.

More dollars are involved in sales to industrial buyers than to consumers! To bring a simple pair of shoes into existence, hide dealers (mainly meat packers) must sell the hides to tanners, who sell the leather to shoe manufacturers, who sell the shoes to wholesalers, who in turn sell the shoes to retailers. Each party in the chain of production and distribution pays more than the previous party. The transactions based on one pair of finished shoes selling for $30 may have been $4 (hide dealer to tanner), $5 (tanner to shoe manufacturer), $20 (shoe manufacturer to wholesaler), and $24 (wholesaler to retailer), making a total of $53, whereas the transaction to the consumer involved but $30. More industrial marketing goes on than consumer marketing, although many people have the opposite impression.

Within the producer market, customers tend to be larger and fewer than in consumer markets. But even here, great variations are found. First, the number of industrial firms making up the market varies from one (monopsony), to few (oligopsony), to many. A French carburetor manufacturer has no choice but to sell to state-owned Renault; whereas an American carburetor manufacturer can sell to General Motors, Ford, Chrysler, and American Motors. Second, the size distribution of firms varies. We can distinguish between producer markets made up of only large firms, or a few large and many small firms, or only small firms. The seller's strategic problem is whether to sell to all firms or to concentrate on a few large firms or to concentrate on the many small firms.

[1] Frederick E. Webster, Jr. and Yoram Wind, *Organizational Buying Behavior* (Englewood Cliffs, N.J.: Prentice-Hall, 1972), p. 2.

Compared to ultimate consumers, producers tend to be concentrated geographically. The seven states of New York, California, Pennsylvania, Illinois, Ohio, New Jersey, and Michigan contain within their borders over half of the nation's manufacturing firms. Particular manufacturing industries, such as petroleum, rubber, and steel, show even greater geographic concentration. Most agricultural output comes from a relatively small number of states, and specific commodities, such as tobacco and citrus fruit, are grown in even fewer states. All of this geographical concentration of producers helps to reduce the costs of selling to them. Industrial marketers will want to watch any pronounced tendencies toward or away from further geographic concentration.

What Do Producers Buy?

The producer market buys a vast variety of products and services. An industrial-goods classification scheme would help us understand the varying marketing practices in the producer market. It is not particularly appropriate to base goods classification on the *shopping habits of the producers*, as we did in consumer-goods classification, because producers do not shop in the same sense. More often suppliers seek them out. Industrial goods are more usefully classified in terms of *how they enter the production process and their relative costliness*. These considerations determine who in the industrial firm buys (organization) and how they buy (operations). Using these principles, industrial goods fall into the three broad classes shown in Table 7–1.

TABLE 7–1
Goods Classification in the Industrial Market

I. *Goods entering the product completely—materials and parts*
  A. Raw materials
    1. Farm products (examples: wheat, cotton, livestock, fruits and vegetables)
    2. Natural products (examples: fish, lumber, crude petroleum, iron ore)
  B. Manufactured materials and parts
    1. Component materials (examples: steel, cement, wire, textiles)
    2. Component parts (examples: small motors, tires, castings)
II. *Goods entering the product partly—capital items*
  A. Installations
    1. Buildings and land rights (examples: factories, offices)
    2. Fixed equipment (examples: generators, drill presses, computers, elevators)
  B. Accessory equipment
    1. Portable or light factory equipment and tools (examples: hand tools, lift trucks)
    2. Office equipment (examples: typewriters, desks)
III. *Goods not entering the product—supplies and services*
  A. Supplies
    1. Operating supplies (examples: lubricants, coal, typing paper, pencils)
    2. Maintenance and repair items (examples: paint, nails, brooms)
  B. Business services
    1. Maintenance and repair services (examples: window cleaning, typewriter repair)
    2. Business advisory services (examples: legal, management consulting, advertising)

Each type of industrial good, as a result of its physical characteristics and use pattern in production, has acquired particular patterns of marketing effort and mix. Here are two examples:

Steel. Steel serves as an important component material in a large part of the industrial market, especially in durable-goods manufacture and construction. There are different grades and alloys of steel, but within any category most steel is identical. Therefore steel is basically a commodity, and the major product variables that count are (1) consistency of quality and (2) extent of the steelmaker's product line. The buyer's main concern is price, and a seller who offers his product for even a fraction of a cent less has the best chance of getting the order. The price reduction can come off the basic price or indirectly through volume discounts, freight absorption allowances, or more generous credit terms. Therefore these instruments figure importantly in steel marketing.

Because most sellers offer similar terms, competition also takes place on a nonprice front. An important variable is the seller's delivery reliability, because the buyer's production operation is geared to the continual delivery of steel or its emergency ordering. The steel seller who is located nearest to the buyer, or who reliably meets promised delivery dates, has a comparative advantage. Company salesmen cannot make much of a difference if their company's price or delivery reliability is not right, but can make a contribution by making contacts and being in the right place at the right time. Advertising plays only a small role, usually taking the form of either corporate-image advertising or new-product advertising to promote a new steel alloy. In this kind of business it is hard for a company to discover a marketing angle that helps it substantially increase its market share without competitors' being able to retaliate effectively with the same or an offsetting tactic.

Electric forklift trucks. The marketing mix for forklift trucks differs from that for steel because the trucks can be engineered in many variations to perform different tasks. The buyer seeks a truck that meets certain desiderata of size, lifting capacity, operating cost, features, and price. The seller's product-design capability is an important factor in getting business. A higher price can be charged for trucks with better performance or extra features. Some buyers are willing to pay more for such factors as the seller's reputation, extra styling, or comfort.

Another important marketing variable is the seller's backup for the purchase—particularly delivery times, parts availability, and service. Some of these things are in the hands of channel middlemen through whom the manufacturer sells. Advertising in trade journals plays a useful role in creating buyer awareness and interest in the company's product line. The promotional budget also goes into specification sheets, catalogs, training films, trade shows, and sales-force contests.

When Do Producers Buy?

A number of factors affect the frequency with which industrial goods and services are purchased. First, the characteristics of the product, such as its perishability, costliness, and bulk, affect how often it will be ordered or received. Thus a steel company will take almost continuous or daily delivery of iron ore as needed in its operations; it might order office supplies only monthly or quarterly; and it might purchase new furnaces once every few years.

Second, the inventory policies of the buyer will influence purchase frequency. Buyers can affect cost savings by ordering high volumes of regularly needed materials infrequently; they get volume discounts and engage in less paperwork. On the other hand, the company ties up more of its resources in inventory, thus incurring opportunity costs and risking some product obsolescence or spoilage. The industrial marketer has to take the industrial buyer's inventory policies into account in shaping offers and timing the sales calls.

Third, industrial purchase frequency is affected by the economic outlook. When the economic outlook is poor, companies will postpone purchases. They will carry minimum inventory levels and postpone larger capital investments. They have neither the funds nor the incentive to invest until they see improved economic conditions on the horizon. Industrial marketers find it harder to market their goods and services if they do not offer special terms, such as discounts and return privileges, to reluctant buyers. The buyers simply do not want to tie up their money. Their demand for goods and services is not *primary* but *derived* from the demand level for other goods into which their goods enter.

Who Participates in the Producer Buying Decision?

Who does the buying of the hundreds of billions of dollars of products and services needed by the industrial market? Buying organizations vary tremendously, from small firms with one or a few people in the purchasing function to huge corporations with large purchasing departments headed by a vice president of purchasing. In some cases the buyers make the entire decision as to product specifications and supplier, in other cases they are responsible for supplier choice only, and in still other cases they make neither decision but simply place the order. They typically make the decisions regarding smaller items and carry out the wishes of others regarding major capital items.

The challenge to the industrial marketer is to make a careful assessment of each customer's buying organization, roles, and influences and then determine the optimal marketing approach to that organization. Every industrial seller in approaching a prospective buying organization must try to answer three questions:

1. Who are the decision participants?
2. What is each member's relative influence in the decision?
3. What are each member's evaluation criteria and how does he or she rate each prospective supplier on those criteria?

Webster and Wind call the decision-making unit of a buying organization the *buying center,* defined as "all those individuals and groups who participate in the purchasing decision-making process, who share some common goals and the risks arising from the decisions."[2]

The buying center includes all members of the organization who play any of five roles in the purchase decision process:[3]

1. *Users.* Users are the members of the organization who will use the product or service. In many cases, the users initiate the buying project and play an important role in defining the purchase specifications.
2. *Influencers.* Influencers are those members of the organization who directly or indirectly influence the buying decision. They often help define specifications and also provide information for evaluating alternatives. Technical personnel are particularly important as influencers.
3. *Buyers.* Buyers are organizational members with formal authority for selecting the supplier and arranging the terms of purchase. Buyers may help shape product

[2] Ibid., p. 6.

[3] Ibid., pp. 78–80.

specifications, but they play their major role in selecting vendors and negotiating within the purchase constraints. In more complex purchases, high-level officers of the company might participate in the negotiations.

4. **Deciders.** Deciders are organizational members who have either formal or informal power to select the final suppliers. In the routine buying of standard items, the buyers are often the deciders. In more complex buying, the officers of the company are often the deciders.

5. **Gatekeepers.** Gatekeepers are members of the organization who control the flow of information to others. For example, purchasing agents often have authority to prevent salespersons from seeing users or deciders. Other gatekeepers include technical personnel and even switchboard operators. The main impact of gatekeepers comes from their ability to control the inflow of information on buying alternatives.

Within any organization, the buying center will vary in size and composition for different classes of products. More *decision participants* will be involved in buying a computer, for example, than in buying paper clips. The challenge to the industrial marketer is to figure out the major decision participants for any given type of purchase.

The well-known *How Industry Buys/1970*[4] study identified eight management groups that might get involved in the purchasing process: (1) overall corporate policy and planning, (2) operations and administration, (3) design and development engineering, (4) production engineering, (5) research, (6) finance, (7) sales, and (8) purchasing.

After identifying the decision participants, the industrial marketer has to figure out the participation level and influence of each participant in each stage of the buying process. The *How Industry Buys/1970* survey, for example, provides this kind of information. Consider the role, for example, of purchasing departments in the buying of industrial equipment. Purchasing departments rarely initiate the project; in about 10 percent of the companies, they participate in determining the kind of equipment, and in 46 percent of the cases, they participate in selecting the supplier.[5] An industrial salesperson, therefore, does not have to seek out the purchasing agent at the beginning of an effort to interest a company in a major piece of equipment. The salesperson should instead seek out production engineers because they are responsible for initiating purchase projects in 42 percent of the cases.

The salesperson must also recognize that each decision participant is likely to bring a different set of evaluation criteria to apply to the purchase decision. Consider the following:

> The production manager of the buying organization may view a new component under consideration in terms of its effects on assembly cost and reliability of supply. Quality control may be concerned with the uncertainties introduced by the proposed change itself. Purchasing personnel are concerned with relative costs and the risks associated with shifting to a supplier whose performance is unknown. The sales manager is concerned with the effect of modification on the attractiveness and suitability of the changed end product for his customers and thus the effect of the specification change on sales. Customer service is concerned with expected breakdown rates, possible misuse by customer personnel, the costs of

---

[4] Published by *Scientific American*, 1970.

[5] Ibid., p. 7.

adding new items to the repair parts inventories and of additional training of maintenance, repair, and service personnel. Thus each possible buying influence employs his own criteria in evaluating the worth of the salesman's offer.[6]

The practical implication is that the industrial marketer must learn the relevant criteria of each decision participant in order to communicate effectively about the product's merits.

Since a buying center may include several persons (it is estimated that buying centers vary from three to twelve persons), the industrial marketer may not have the time or resources to reach them all or may not have access to all of them. Smaller companies try to figure out who the key buying influences are and concentrate their limited advertising and personal selling resources on them. Larger companies go for *multilevel in-depth selling* to reach as many decision participants as possible. Then salespeople "live" with the customer when it is a major account with recurrent sales.

Industrial marketers must periodically review their assumptions on the roles and influence of different decision participants. For example, for years Kodak's strategy for selling X-ray film to hospitals was to sell through lab technicians. The company did not notice that the decision was being made increasingly by professional administrators. As its sales declined, it finally grasped the change in buying practices and hurriedly changed its marketing strategy.

What Are Producers Seeking?

Industrial buyers are not buying goods and services for personal consumption or utility. They buy things for any of the following motives: (1) to make money, (2) to reduce operating costs, (3) to satisfy a social or legal obligation. A steel company will add another furnace if it sees a chance to make more money. It will computerize its accounting system if this will reduce the costs of doing business. It will add pollution-control equipment to satisfy legal requirements.

The main tradeoff faced by industrial buyers is between cost and quality. Some industrial buyers are partial to the best goods they can get, and others will buy the lowest-cost goods providing that these meet minimum standards. Often the producer can segment the market by identifying groups with different quality/cost preferences. An example is the transistor market:

> The market for transistors consists of three submarkets: military, industrial, and commercial. The buyer behavior differences among these three markets can be analyzed clearly.
>
> The military buyer attaches utmost importance to the producer's quality standards and the adequacy of his plant facilities. Only after these two considerations have been realized does price become a factor.
>
> Quality is also of great importance to industrial customers such as computer manufacturers, for their products are used by industrial manufacturers like themselves. Loyalties can be established in this segment through high quality and good service. Price itself is not a critical matter unless it becomes completely out of line.
>
> Commercial buyers, such as pocket-radio manufacturers, are in the most competitive user market and consequently buy their components completely on price and delivery. No loyalty to suppliers exists, and quality requirements are usually minimal.
>
> Because of these differences, marketing strategies have to be varied. In order

[6] See Charles S. Goodman, *Management of the Personal Selling Function* (New York: Holt, Rinehart and Winston, 1971), p. 204.

to sell transistors in the military market, firms must make a considerable investment in R&D, use salesmen who know military buying procedures, and specialize in limited-line products. In order to sell in the industrial market, firms must make a modest investment in R&D, use sales people who have technical knowledge concerning the product, and offer a broad line. In order to sell to the commercial market, firms need little or no R&D effort, use high-pressure sales people who are relatively nontechnical, and offer the most common lines that can be mass-produced.

Some buyers have a lot of latitude in selecting a quality/cost level of goods to buy. Consider the *institutional market:*

The institutional market consists of institutions that make purchases in order to provide goods and services to those they care for and are responsible for. Schools, hospitals, nursing homes, and prisons are prime examples of institutional buyers. They are generally characterized by low budgets and captive clienteles. A hospital purchasing agent has to decide on the quality of food to buy for the patients. The buying objective is not profit since the food is provided free to the patients. The basic objective is not cost minimization either, because patients served poor food in a hospital will complain to others and hurt the hospital's reputation. The hospital purchasing agent has to find institutional-food vendors whose quality meets a certain minimum standard and yet whose prices are low. Many food vendors set up a separate division to sell to institutional buyers because of their special buying needs and characteristics.

Over the years, company purchasing executives have been improving their purchasing skills and tools. The competency of buyers is a function of their degree of knowledge, analytical capacity, and negotiating ability. Buyers need to be fully informed about competing vendors, products, and terms. They have to be good at applying formal cost-evaluation models. When buying a computer, they have to know how much value to place on different attributes, such as calculation speed and information capacity. When evaluating the replacement of a generator, they have to know how to use payout-period and rate-of-return analysis. When considering different ways in which some function can be performed, they have to know value analysis.

Value analysis, which General Electric developed in 1948, is *an approach to cost reduction in which components are carefully studied to determine if they can be redesigned or standardized or made by cheaper methods of production.* The purchasing agent who is a value analyst will carefully examine the high-cost components in a given product—usually 20 percent of the parts will comprise about 80 percent of the costs. The examination proceeds through five steps:

1. Analyze a part's function to determine whether a standardized shelf item could be used.
2. See whether a nonstandardized part could be slightly redesigned into a standardized part. If so, competitive bidding could be solicited, and this generally leads to lower prices.
3. See whether two or more parts could be combined into one.
4. See whether cheaper substitute materials could be used. If so, there may be savings not only in the materials but also in the costs of molds and dies.
5. Contact suppliers and discuss whether certain parts could be made for less by improvements in tooling, by grouping similar work, or by increasing quantities.

Finally, the industrial buyer must have the knack of getting the vendors to compete for the business and have the negotiating skill to win the most favorable terms. ... A good example of a cagey buyer is [the] vice president in charge of purchasing for Rheingold's big New York brewery. ... Using the leverage of hundreds of millions of cans a year, like many other buyers, he takes punitive action when one company slips in quality or fails to deliver. "At one point American started talking about a price rise," he recalls, "Continental kept its mouth shut. ... American never did put the price rise into effect, buy anyway, I punished them for talking about it." For a three-month period he cut the percentage of cans he bought from American.[7]

Most descriptions of industrial buyers portray them as rational, hard-nosed persons seeking to secure the best terms for their company. Other studies emphasize personal motives and influences in the industrial buyer's world. A study of buyers in ten large companies concluded:

> Corporate decision makers remain human after they enter the office. They respond to "image"; they buy from companies to which they feel "close"; they favor suppliers who show them respect and personal considerations, and who do extra things for them; they "over-react" to real or imagined slights, tending to reject companies which fail to respond to such items as reader service cards bound into magazines, or which delay in submitting requested bids. ... Advertising and promotional materials are key factors in establishing a "good image." Good image qualities are said to include being "well known," being considered "big" or a "leader in the field," and having a reputation for providing good service.[8]

In truth, industrial buyers respond to both rational and subjective factors. Where there is substantial similarity in what suppliers offer in the way of products, price, and service, industrial buyers have little basis for rational choice. Since they can meet organizational goals with any one of a number of suppliers, buyers can bring in personal factors. On the other hand, where competing products differ substantially, industrial buyers are more accountable for their choice and pay more attention to objective factors. Short-run personal gain becomes less motivating than the long-run gain that comes from serving their organization well.

How Do Producers Buy?

How do industrial buyers carry out their buying operations? We want to consider the following four questions: (1) What factors influence the industrial buyer's decisions? (2) What are the major types of buying situations in industrial buying? (3) What are the major decisions made by industrial buyers? and (4) What are the major stages in the industrial buying process?

Factors influencing industrial buying decisions   Many theories have been advanced to explain how industrial buyers make their purchase decisions. Webster and Wind classify them into task- and nontask-oriented models.[9]

Task models view the organization as behaving in the manner of a rational

[7] Walter Guzzardi, Jr., "The Fight for 9/10 of a Cent," *Fortune*, April 1961, p. 152.

[8] The study was conducted by Motivational Programmers, Inc., a marketing research firm, and was reported in "Who Makes the Purchasing Decision?" *Marketing Insights*, October 31, 1966, pp. 16–18.

[9] "Who Makes the Purchasing Decision?" pp. 13–20.

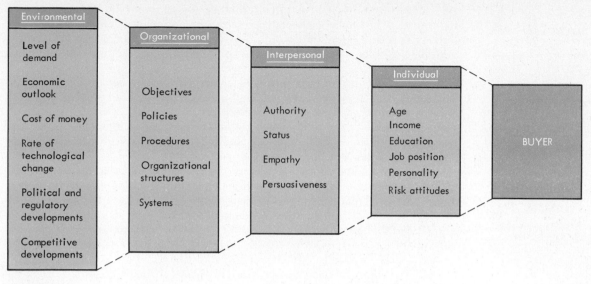

FIGURE 7–1
Major Factors Influencing Industrial Buying Behavior

buyer pursuing economic objectives in an efficient way. The organization is seen as making its decision in favor of the supplier with the minimum price, or the lowest total cost, or who buys things from the company in return (i.e., reciprocity), or who is the most ready to accommodate. Task models imply that industrial marketers should offer strong economic values to the buyer.

Nontask models emphasize the role of personal motives in the buying process, such as buyers who respond to personal favors (self-aggrandizement), or to attention (ego enhancement), or to personal-risk containment (risk avoiders). These nontask models suggest that industrial marketers should concentrate on the human and social factors in the buying situation and that they could overcome offer deficiencies by being more manipulative of emotional and interpersonal factors.

Webster and Wind see these factors as partial determinants in the total picture and prefer to classify all influences into four main groups: environmental, organizational, interpersonal, and individual [10] (see Figure 7–1).

Environmental factors are factors outside of the organization, such as are found in the macroenvironment, the public environment, and the marketing channel environment. Buying decisions are influenced by the level of primary demand, economic outlook, the cost of money, the rate of technological change, political and regulatory developments, and competitive developments. These environmental influences are normally beyond the control of both buyer and seller and have to be taken as given in the situation.

Organizational factors are another set of influences on the buying process. Each company spells out objectives, policies, procedures, structures, and systems to guide the buying process. Buying decisions are affected by the company's systems of reward, authority, status, and communication.

[10] Ibid.

Interpersonal factors constitute another important set of forces in the buying process. The buying center involves the interaction of several persons of different status, authority, empathy, and persuasiveness in the company. It is very hard for the seller to know in advance how interpersonal factors work in a particular company.

Individual factors constitute still another important set of determinants. The issue here is how the individual decision participants form their perceptions of and preferences for product characteristics and supplier offers. Furthermore, there is the issue of the role of such factors as the person's age, income, education, professional identification, personality, and attitudes toward risk in influencing his or her buying behavior.

Some of the most interesting work is going on in the area of trying to determine the relative importance of different attributes of the seller and the offer in creating preference among individual buyers. Cardozo and Cagley explored the role of four attributes in influencing the selection of suppliers and bids.[11] They found that a company that (1) is "in," (2) has a well-known name, (3) provides more information about its offer, and (4) stresses low-price appeals as a bidder will be unusually effective with professional buyers in large organizations. If the company lacks one or more of these attributes, it should direct its selling efforts to other participants in the buying center or to smaller organizations.

Lehmann and O'Shaughnessy undertook to research the relative importance of seventeen attributes in influencing purchase decisions: reputation, financing, flexibility, past experience, technical service, confidence in salesmen, convenience in ordering, reliability data on product, price, technical specifications, ease of use, preference of user, training offered, training required, delivery reliability, maintenance, and sales service.[12] They found that the relative importance of each attribute varied with the type of buying situation. For *routine-order products*, they found that delivery reliability and price were highly important, along with reputation of suppliers and experience with them. For *procedural-problem products*, such as a dry copying machine, the three most important attributes were technical service offered, flexibility of supplier, and product reliability. Finally, for *political-problem products*, those that stir rivalries in the organization, the most important attributes were price, reputation, product reliability, service reliability, and supplier flexibility.

Major types of buying situations   Organizational buying behavior varies with the type of buying situation. Some buying situations are highly routinized and programmed, and others are new tasks. Robinson et al. distinguish among three types of buying situations, which they call *buyclasses*.[13]

THE STRAIGHT REBUY   The straight rebuy describes the simplest buying situation—the company reorders something without any modifications. It is usually handled on a routine basis by the purchasing department. The company

---

[11] Richard N. Cardozo and James W. Cagley, "Experimental Study of Industrial Buyer Behavior," *Journal of Marketing Research*, August 1971, pp. 329–34.

[12] See Donald R. Lehmann and John O'Shaughnessy, "Difference in Attribute Importance for Different Industrial Products," *Journal of Marketing*, April 1974, pp. 36–42.

[13] Patrick J. Robinson, Charles W. Faris, and Yoram Wind, *Industrial Buying and Creative Marketing* (Boston: Allyn and Bacon, 1967).

chooses from suppliers already on its "list," giving much weight to its past buying experience with the various suppliers. The "in" suppliers make an effort to keep up product and service quality. They often propose automatic reordering systems so that the purchasing agent will save time on reordering from them. The "out" suppliers attempt to offer something new or create some dissatisfaction so that the buyer will reconsider the buying assumptions. Out suppliers will attempt to get their foot in the door with a small order and then try to enlarge their purchase share over time.

THE MODIFIED REBUY   The modified rebuy describes a situation in which the buyer is seeking to modify product specifications, prices, other terms, or suppliers in connection with something the company purchases. Somehow, the company thinks it can do better. The modified rebuy usually expands the number of decision participants. The in suppliers get nervous and have to put their best foot forward to protect the account. The out suppliers see it as an opportunity to make a better offer to gain some new business.

NEW TASK   A company faces a new task when it is considering buying a product or service for the first time. The greater the cost and/or risk, the larger the number of decision participants, and the greater their information seeking. The new-task situation is the marketer's greatest opportunity and challenge. The marketer must plan to reach as many key buying influences as possible and provide information and assistance in helping them resolve their problem, hoping, of course, that it will be in favor of his product. Because of the complicated selling involved in the new task, many companies use a specialized sales force, called a *missionary sales force*, to carry out this task.

New-task buying passes through several stages, each with its own requirements and challenges to the marketer. Ozanne and Churchill have applied an innovation diffusion perspective to the new task, identifying the stages as *awareness, interest, evaluation, trial,* and *adoption.*[14] They found that information sources varied in effectiveness at each stage. Mass media were most important during the initial awareness stage, whereas salespersons had their greatest impact at the interest stage. Technical sources were the most important during the evaluation stage. These findings provide clues to the new-task marketer as to efficient communications to use at different stages of the buying process.

Major types of buying decisions   The number of decisions involved in a particular buying project varies with the type of buying situation, the fewest being in the case of a straight rebuy and the most numerous in the new-task situation. In the new-task situation, the buying center will have to determine: (1) product specifications, (2) price limits, (3) delivery terms and times, (4) service terms, (5) payment terms, (6) order quantities, (7) acceptable suppliers, and (8) the selected supplier. Different decision participants will influence each decision, and the order in which the decisions will be made will vary.

The marketer's task is to anticipate the full range of decisions facing the buyer and offer an attractive and convenient total solution if possible. Suppose, for example, that a company wants to build a fertilizer plant. At one extreme, the company can make all the separate decisions and hire its own architects, en-

---

[14] Urban B. Ozanne and Gilbert A. Churchill, Jr., "Adoption Research: Information Sources in the Industrial Purchase Decision," *Proceedings,* Fall Conference (Chicago: American Marketing Association, 1968).

gineers, contractors, legal staff, and so on. At the other extreme, the company can hire one company that will put together the whole package. The second is called a *turnkey operation* because all the buyer has to do is turn the key when the plant is ready to start operating. The underlying idea is that the marketer should try to sell a system, not just a single component, because buyers find this more convenient and attractive. *Systems selling* is a key industrial-marketing strategy for winning and holding accounts.[15]

Major steps in industrial buying   The industrial marketer needs to grasp how the organizational buying process is carried out. The buying process consists of eight stages called *buyphases*.[16] They are (1) need recognition, (2) need definition, (3) need description, (4) seller identification, (5) proposal solicitation, (6) proposal evaluation and selection, (7) ordering procedure, and (8) performance review. The eight buyphases are listed in the rows of Figure 7–2 along with the three types of buyclasses. The model is called the *buygrid* framework.

All of the buyphases operate in new-task buying, whereas some are compressed or absent in the more straight rebuy situations. Each phase successively narrows the number of alternatives, indicating that sellers have to get into the act as early as possible.

BUYPHASES	BUYCLASSES		
	NEW TASK	MODIFIED REBUY	STRAIGHT REBUY
1. Anticipation or recognition of a problem (need) and a general solution			
2. Determination of characteristics and quantity of needed item			
3. Description of characteristics and quantity of needed item			
4. Search for and qualification of potential sources			
5. Acquisition and analysis of proposals			
6. Evaluation of proposals and selection of supplier(s)			
7. Selection of an order routine			
8. Performance feedback and evaluation			

FIGURE 7–2
The Buygrid Analytic Framework for Industrial Buying Situations

SOURCE: Redrawn from Patrick J. Robinson, Charles W. Faris, and Yoram Wind, *Industrial Buying and Creative Marketing* (Boston: Allyn & Bacon, 1967), p. 14.

[15] See chap. 14, footnote 1, p. 353.

[16] Robinson et al., *Industrial Buying*.

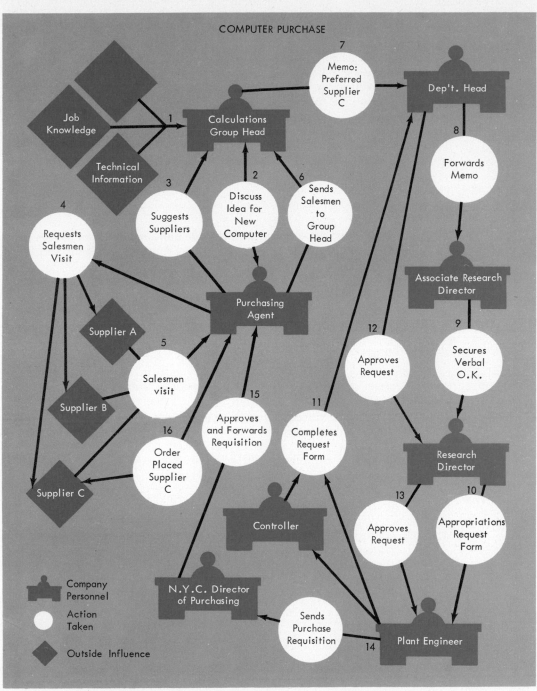

COMPUTER PURCHASE

SOURCE: "Who Makes the Purchasing Decision?" *Marketing Insights.* October 31, 1966, p. 18.

FIGURE 7–3
Map of Company Events in the Purchase of a Computer

The actual sequence of buying steps should be studied by the marketer. Each buying situation involves a flow of work. This *buyflow* should be mapped when possible as a guide to developing effective marketing strategies. Mapping the buyflow is especially worthwhile with large prospective customers or when several customers can be identified who have similar buying operations. An example of a buyflow map for a computer purchase is shown in Figure 7–3. The map shows that eight different company employees (represented by desk symbols) were involved in this buying decision process at one time or another. Three suppliers also were involved, as well as other outside influences (shown in diamond-shaped figures). Finally, fifteen different events (shown as circles) fed up to the placing of the order ultimately with supplier C.

THE RESELLER MARKET

Who Is in the Reseller Market?

The reseller market consists of *all individuals and organizations who acquire goods for the purpose of reselling or renting them to others at a profit.* Instead of producing form utility, the reseller market produces time, place, and possession utility. The reseller market includes over 276,000 wholesaling firms employing 4,216,000 persons, and 1,665,000 retailing firms employing 11,961,000 persons; both sectors account for over 16 percent of the national income. Resellers are more dispersed geographically than producers but more concentrated than consumers.

What Do Resellers Buy?

Resellers purchase (1) goods for resale and (2) goods and services for conducting their operations. The latter are bought by resellers in their role as "producers," so we shall confine the discussion here to the goods they purchase for resale.

Resellers handle a vast variety of products for resale, indeed everything produced except the few classes of goods that producers choose to sell direct to final customers. The excluded class includes heavy or complex machinery, customized products, and products sold on a direct-mail or a door-to-door basis. With these exceptions, most products are sold to the final buyer through one or more selling intermediaries.

Each reseller faces the problem of determining its unique *assortment*—the combination of products and services that it will offer to the marketplace. The wholesaler or retailer can choose one of four assortment strategies:

1. *Exclusive assortment:* representing the line of only one manufacturer
2. *Deep assortment:* representing a given homogeneous product family in depth, drawing on many producers' outputs
3. *Broad assortment:* representing a wide range of product lines that still fall within the natural coverage of the reseller's type of business
4. *Scrambled assortment:* representing many unrelated product families

Thus a camera store can decide to sell only Kodak cameras (exclusive assortment), many brands of cameras (deep assortment), cameras, tape recorders, radios, and stereophonic equipment (broad assortment), or the last plus stoves and refrigerators (scrambled assortment). The assortment the reseller ultimately chooses will influence its customer mix, marketing mix, and supplier mix.

When Do Resellers Buy?

Resellers order goods according to their current stock level and anticipated demand level. Their ordering practice is influenced by two opposite forces. By placing large orders infrequently, they keep down their order-placement costs and may obtain good discounts. By placing small orders frequently, they keep down their inventory carrying costs. Resellers analyze the relative costs and make decisions on ordering points for replacing stock. Producers have to be aware of the inventory systems used by resellers in developing their marketing strategies.

Who Participates in the Reseller Buying Process?

Who does the deciding and buying for wholesale and retail organizations? In the smaller firms, the merchandise selection and buying functions may be carried out by persons who also carry out several other functions in the firm. In the larger firms, buying is a specialist function and often a full-time job. It is carried on in different ways by department stores, supermarkets, drug wholesalers, and so on, and differences can even be found within each type of distributive enterprise.

Much of the flavor of reseller buying practices can be sensed by examining the particular case of supermarket chains and the respective roles played by corporate-headquarter buyers, storewide buying committees, and the individual store managers. In the corporate headquarters of a supermarket chain specialist buyers will be found (sometimes called merchandise managers) for different product lines carried by the supermarket. These buyers have the responsibility for developing brand assortments and listening to presentations by salespersons offering new brands. In some chains these buyers have great latitude with respect to accepting or rejecting new items. In many chains, however, their latitude is limited to screening "obvious rejects" (and sometimes "obvious accepts"); otherwise they must bring the new-item proposals to the chain's buying committee at one of the weekly meetings.

There is some evidence that buying committees serve a "checking" function rather than an actual decision-making function. Borden found that the buyer's recommendation is highly important and influential in the committee decision.[17] The buyer decides what to communicate to the committee, thus exerting considerable influence on the decision. Buying committees exert some important indirect effects on product evaluations and decisions. By serving as a buffer between buyers and salespersons, committees provide buyers with an excuse for rejecting a seller's proposition.

Even if an item is accepted by a chain-store buying committee, it will not necessarily appear in a large number of the chain's outlets. According to one supermarket-chain executive: "No matter what the sales representatives sell or buyers buy, the person who has the greatest influence on the final sale of the new item is the store manager." In the nation's chain and independent supermarkets, two-thirds of the new items accepted at the warehouse are ordered on the individual store manager's own decision, and only one-third represent forced distribution.[18]

[17] Neil H. Borden, Jr., *Acceptance of New Food Products by Supermarkets* (Boston: Division of Research, Graduate School of Business Administration, Harvard University, 1968).

[18] Robert W. Mueller and Franklin H. Graf, "New Items in the Food Industry, Their Problems and Opportunities," a special report to the Annual Convention of the Supermarket Institute, Cleveland, Ohio, May 20, 1968, p. 2.

185

This picture of the reseller organization's buying procedure for new items points to the formidable problem faced by the producers of new items. Industry offers the nation's supermarkets between 150 and 250 new items each week, of which store space does not permit more than 10 percent to be accepted.

Several studies have attempted to rank the major criteria used by buyers, buying committees, and store managers. A. C. Nielsen Company carried out a study in which store managers were asked to rank on a three-point scale the importance of different elements in influencing their decision to accept a new item.[19] The final ranking showed:

Evidence of consumer acceptance	2.5
Advertising/promotion	2.2
Introductory terms and allowances	2.0
Why item was developed	1.9
Merchandising recommendations	1.8

The first three items are reported to be the most important criteria in other studies also.[20] They suggest that sellers stand the best chance when they can report strong evidence of consumer acceptance, present a well-designed and extensive introductory advertising and sales promotion plan, and provide incentives to the retailer.

These respective roles of chain buyers, chain buying committees, and store managers characterize, with some variation, the buying organizations of other distributive enterprises. Large department stores or chains rely on buyers for merchandise lines, and usually they have a lot of authority and latitude. They may report to buying committees. The buyers are aided by assistant buyers, who carry out a preliminary search as well as clerical tasks involved in ordering. The buyers may perform other functions such as demand forecasting, stock control, and merchandising. Individual store managers or their staff usually have some freedom with respect to which goods to order as well as which to display prominently.

What Are Resellers Seeking?

Resellers, like producers, are in business to make a profit. They must be adept at buying goods "cheap" and selling them "dear." This means they must know the various sources of supply, be able to negotiate, and be able to set services, prices, and promotional expenditures at levels that will generate a high level of revenue in relation to the costs of doing business. Buyers must master principles of demand forecasting, merchandise selection, stock control, space allocation, and display, not to mention the careful management of money and personnel resources. They must learn to measure return on a profit-per-cubic-foot basis

[19] Ibid., p. 5.

[20] "Merchandising New Items at Retail: The Payoff at Point of Purchase," *Progressive Grocer,* June 1968; also Borden, *New Food Products,* p. 203. Also see David B. Montgomery, *New Product Distribution: An Analysis of Supermarket Buyer Decisions* (Cambridge, Mass.: Marketing Science Institute, March 1973). Montgomery found the two most important variables to be company reputation and the perceived newness of the product.

rather than on a product-by-product basis.[21] In many retail lines the profit margin on sales is so low (for example, 1 to 2 percent in supermarkets) that a sudden decline in demand will drive profits into the red. Those who complain about middlemen profits overlook the enormous work and risk that must be borne by middlemen in their effort to create assortments that meet the wants and needs of final buyers.

Resellers tend to develop different buying styles to carry out their work. Dickinson has distinguished the following buyer types:

1. *Loyal buyer.* This type remains loyal to a resource, or group of resources, year after year, for reasons other than that he obtains the best deal.

2. *Opportunistic buyer.* This type selects mainly from a preselected list of those vendors who will further his long-term interests. Within his preselected list, he will pursue the best arrangement possible.

3. *Best-deal buyer.* This type looks for and selects the best deal available to him in the market at a given point in time.

4. *Creative buyer.* This type tries not to accept the marketing mixes offered by any of the vendors. He attempts to sell his offers to the market. This may or may not involve a change in the physical product.

5. *Advertising buyer.* This type attempts primarily to obtain advertising moneys; advertising moneys must be a part of every deal and are the prime target of each negotiation.

6. *The chiseler.* This type of buyer constantly negotiates extra concessions in price at the time of the offering. He tends to accept the vendor offer carrying the greatest discount from the price he feels that other accounts might pay.

7. *Nuts-and-bolts buyer.* This buyer selects merchandise that is the best constructed, assuming that the merchandise policies of the vendor are acceptable within a very broad range. He is more interested in the thread count than in the number that will sell.[22]

How Do Resellers Buy?

Resellers are influenced by the same set of factors—environmental, organizational, interpersonal, and individual—that were shown in Figure 7–1 as influencing producers.

The specific buying operations vary with the type of buying situation. Three situations can be distinguished.

The *new-item situation* describes the case where the reseller has been offered a new item. The new-item situation differs from the new-task situation faced by producers in that the former is a "yes-no" opportunity presented to the buyer while the latter means that the buyer is confronted with a new problem arising in the manufacturing process and must initiate research and evaluation of solutions and vendors.

The *best-vendor situation* faces the reseller who knows what is needed but must determine the best supplier. It occurs (1) when the reseller can carry only a subset of the available brands offered because of space constraints or (2) when

[21] See Robert D. Buzzell, *Product Profitability Measurement and Merchandising Decisions* (Boston: Harvard University Press, 1965).

[22] Roger A. Dickinson, *Buyer Decision Making* (Berkeley, Calif.: Institute of Business and Economic Research, 1967), pp. 14–17.

the reseller wants to sponsor a private brand and is seeking a willing and qualified producer. Resellers such as Sears and the A&P sell a substantial number of items under their own names; therefore much of their buying operation consists of vendor selection.

The *better-terms situation* arises when the reseller wants to obtain a better set of terms from current suppliers. The buyer is not eager to change the supplier but does want more advantageous treatment. Legally sellers are prevented, under the Robinson-Patman Act, from giving different terms to different resellers in the same reseller class unless these reflect corresponding cost differences, distress sales, or a few other special conditions. Nevertheless, individual resellers and classes of resellers (discounters, mass merchandisers) do press their suppliers for preferential treatment, and this treatment can take many forms, such as more supplier services, easier credit terms, and higher volume discounts.

Buying procedures in all three situations can be expected to grow more sophisticated over time, as better-trained persons are hired for these jobs, receive more extensive data with which to work, and learn how to use more analytical methods. Major changes in purchasing operations are being made possible by advances in computers and telecommunications. Computers are finding increased application in keeping current inventory figures, computing economic order quantities, preparing purchasing orders, developing requests for vendor quotations or expediting of orders, and generating printouts of dollars spent on vendors and products. Through telecommunications, the buyer can feed prepunched cards describing items and quantities needed into a transmitter that is linked to the supplier's receiving equipment. The supplier's equipment prepares cards or tapes, which become the input for mechanized preparation of shipping tickets, invoices, and other documents. Many resellers are going over to stockless purchasing of certain items, which means that the supplier inventories the items and supplies them to the buyer on short notice.

THE GOVERNMENT MARKET

Who Is in the
Government
Market?

The government market consists of federal, state, and local *governmental units that purchase or rent goods for carrying out the main functions of government.* In 1976, governmental units purchased $366 billion of products and services, or 21 percent of the gross national product, making it the nation's largest customer. The federal government accounts for approximately 60 percent of the total spent by government at all levels.

Although substantial government purchasing takes place in Washington, D.C., in state capitals, and in other major cities, it takes place in every county and village as well. The federal government operates an elaborate set of geographically dispersed buying information offices. Local products and services may be bought by local government offices, army posts, and so on. As one example, the naval complex at Hampton Roads, Virginia, paid local Virginia firms $500,000 in one year just for ice cream.

What Do
Government
Units Buy?

What else does government buy, besides ice cream? Practically everything. Governmental agencies buy bombers, sculpture, chalkboards, furniture, toiletries, clothing, materials-handling equipment, fire engines, mobile equipment, and fuel. In 1975, all government spent approximately $95 billion for education, $87 billion for defense, $39 billion for public welfare, $35 billion for health and hospitals, $23 billion for highways, $16 billion for natural resources, and smaller sums for postal service, space research, and housing and urban renewal. The mix of expenditures varied considerably with the particular type of governmental unit, with defense looming large in the federal budget (34 percent) and education looming large in the state and local budgets (38 percent). No matter how one feels about government marketing, it represents a tremendous market for any producer or reseller.

When Do Government Units Buy?

The factors determining when government buying occurs are the same as those for the previous markets. This is because there is a wide variety of government buyers who function essentially as industrial, reseller, or consumer buyers, even though the duration of the purchase process may be much longer.

Who Participates in the Government Buying Process?

Who in the government does the buying of the $366 billion of goods and services? Government buying organizations are found on the federal, state, and local levels. The federal level is the largest, and its buying units can be subclassified into the civilian and military sectors. The *federal civilian buying* establishment consists of seven categories: departments (e.g., Commerce), administration (e.g., General Services Administration), agencies (e.g., Federal Aviation Agency), boards (e.g., Railroad Retirement Board), commissions (e.g., Federal Communications Commission), the executive office (e.g., Bureau of the Budget), and miscellaneous (e.g., Tennessee Valley Authority). "No single federal agency contracts for all the government's requirements and no single buyer in any agency purchases all that agency's needs for any single item of supplies, equipment, or services."[23] Many agencies control a substantial percentage of their own buying, particularly of industrial products and specialized equipment. At the same time, the General Services Administration plays a main role in attempting to centralize the procurement of the items most commonly used by the civilian section (office furniture and equipment, vehicles, fuels, and so on) and to promote standardized buying procedures for the other agencies. It acts in the capacity of a wholesaler on its own account and as a reseller and an agent middleman for other government agencies.

Federal military buying is carried out by the Defense Department largely through the Defense Supply Agency and the three military departments of the Army, Navy, and Air Force. The Defense Supply Agency was set up in 1961 to procure and distribute supplies used in common by all military services in an effort to reduce costly duplication (thus it is the equivalent of the General Services Administration in the military sector). It operates six supply centers, which specialize in construction, electronics, fuel, personnel support, industrial, and general supplies. The trend has been toward "single managers" for major product classifications. Each individual service branch procures equipment and supplies in line with its own mission; for example, the Army Department operates special branches for acquiring its own material, vehicles, medical supplies and services, and weaponry.

State and local buying agencies include school districts, highway departments, hospitals, housing agencies, and many others.

---

[23] Stanley E. Cohen, "Looking in the U.S. Government Market," *Industrial Marketing*, September 1964, pp. 129–38.

Government buying is premised on a different fundamental objective than is found in the other sectors of the economy. Government does not pursue a personal consumption or a profit-making standard; rather it buys a level and mix of products and services that it or the voters establish as necessary or desirable for the maintenance of the society.

Government purchasing of specific goods and services largely follows the objective of *minimizing taxpayer cost.* Government buyers are supposed to buy from the lowest-cost bidders providing that their goods meet the stated specifications. Increasingly, however, the buyers will relax low-cost purchasing rules in the pursuit of other objectives, such as favoring depressed business firms or areas, small business firms, and business firms that do not practice racial, sex, or age discrimination.

Government buying practices appear complex to the uninitiated supplier because of the many agencies and procedures that characterize the government market. Yet most of the system can be mastered in a short time, and the government is generally helpful in diffusing information about its buying needs and procedures. In fact, government is often as anxious to attract new suppliers as the suppliers are to find customers. For example, the Small Business Administration publishes a useful booklet, *U.S. Government Purchasing, Specifications and Sales Directory,* listing thousands of items most frequently purchased by government and cross-referenced by the agencies most frequently using them. The Government Printing Office publishes *Commerce Business Daily,* which lists current proposed defense procurements estimated to exceed $10,000 and civilian agency procurements expected to exceed $5,000, as well as information about recent contract awards that can provide leads to subcontracting markets. The General Services Administration operates Business Service Centers in several major cities, whose staffs are set up to provide a complete education on the way GSA and other agencies buy and the steps that the supplier should follow. Various trade magazines and associations provide information on how to reach schools, hospitals, highway departments, and other government agencies.

Government buying procedures can be classified into two major types: the *open bid* and the *negotiated contract.* In both cases the emphasis is on competitive procurement. Open-bid buying means that the government procuring office invites bids from qualified suppliers for carefully described items, generally awarding a contract to the lowest bidder. Specifically, the interested supplier fills out an application requesting to be placed on the bidders' list. The supplier receives mailings of "invitations for bids," which carefully specify the item and quantity needed. The specifications include a description of the materials, dimensions, quality, reliability, and packing and crating requirements, as well as the terms of the contract that will be awarded to the successful bidder. The supplier firm must carefully consider whether it can meet the specifications and if it likes the terms. For commodities and standard items, such as fuel or school supplies, the specifications are not a hurdle. However, specifications may constitute a hurdle for nonstandard items, although the government unit is barred from issuing such narrow specifications that only one existing seller can meet them. Furthermore, the government procurement office is usually—but not always—required to award the contract to the lowest bidder on a winner-take-all basis. In some cases allowance can be made for the supplier's superior product or reputation for completing contracts. A more recent development is to ask for bids, particularly on equipment, to cover life-cycle maintenance as well as initial price. The award will go to the firm submitting the lowest life-cycle bid. This practice was started by the Defense Department in recognition of the fact that it might spend up to ten times the original purchase price to own and operate the equipment.

In negotiated-contract buying, the agency works with one or a few companies and directly negotiates a contract with one of them covering the project and terms. This occurs primarily in connection with complex projects, often involving major research and development cost and risk and/or where there is little effective competition. Contracts can have countless variations, such as *cost-plus pricing*, *fixed-pricing*, and *fixed price-and-incentive* (the supplier earns more if costs are reduced). Contract performance is open to review and renegotiation if the supplier's profits appear excessive.

Government contracts won by large companies give rise to substantial subcontracting opportunities, as much as 50 percent, for small companies. Thus government purchasing activity in turn creates derived demand in the producer market. Subcontracting firms going after this business, however, must be willing to place performance bonds with the prime contractor, thereby assuming some of the risk.

By and large, companies that have served the government have not manifested much of a marketing orientation—for a number of reasons. Total government spending is determined by elected officials rather than by marketing effort to develop this market. The government's procurement policies have emphasized price, leading the suppliers to invest all their effort in a technological orientation to bring their costs down. Where the product's characteristics are carefully specified, product differentiation is not a marketing factor. Nor are advertising and personal selling of much consequence in winning bids on an open-bid basis.

More companies are now establishing marketing departments to guide government-directed marketing. There is greater effort to coordinate bids and prepare them more scientifically, to propose projects to meet government needs rather than just to respond to government initiatives, to gather competitive intelligence, and to prepare better communication programs to describe the company's competence.

SUMMARY

The organizational market consists of all organizations that buy goods for purposes of further production or resale or distribution to others. Organizations are a market for raw and manufactured materials and parts, installations and accessory equipment, and supplies and services.

Producer organizations buy goods and services for the purpose of increasing sales, cutting costs, or meeting social and legal requirements. Compared to households, they show more skill in buying, are larger and more concentrated geographically, and are more influenced by the level of economic activity. In producer buying, more people are likely to participate; and they operate under a more specific set of policies and procedures. Their buying decisions are influenced by environmental, organizational, interpersonal, and individual factors. The decision-making unit of a buying organization, the buying center, consists of individuals who play any of five roles: users, influencers, buyers, deciders, and gatekeepers. Their involvement and behavior depend on the buying situation, whether a straight rebuy, modified rebuy, or new task. The number and type of buying decisions also vary with the type of buying situation, being the most complex in the new-task situation. The buying process itself consists of up to eight stages, called buyphases.

The reseller market consists of individuals and organizations who acquire and resell goods produced by others. Producers must apply modern marketing concepts and techniques in approaching resellers, because their buying organizations, needs, styles, and operations vary considerably.

The government market is a vast one that annually purchases $366 billion of products and services—for the pursuit of defense, education, public welfare, and other public needs. Government buying practices are highly specialized and specified, with open bidding and/or negotiated contracts characterizing most of the buying.

QUESTIONS AND PROBLEMS

1. Describe some of the major characteristics of commercial services firms (finance, insurance, and real estate) as a market for goods and services.

2. There are several important institutional markets: hospitals, educational institutions, welfare organizations, and the like. Discuss the characteristic buying needs and buying organization for, say, educational institutions.

3. Are industrial buyers more "rational" than household buyers?

4. The location of buying authority in a company will vary with the level of the *product's complexity* and with the level of the *commercial investment*. Given two levels (low, high) for each variable, predict who will make the buying decision in each of the four possible cases.

5. What types of assortment strategies are used by the following types of firms: (a) bicycle shop, (b) sports shop, (c) pawn shop, (d) Salvation Army Store, and (e) discount store.

6. Cessna Aircraft Company is interested in expanding its sales of small aircraft to business firms. Its marketing research analyst decides to study the buying process using the paradigm: (a) need arousal; (b) information search; (c) evaluation behavior; (d) purchase decision; and (e) postpurchase feelings. List factors under each that affect the potential industrial buyer of a private aircraft.

7. A home decorating service is confronted with the following paint mixing machines having the indicated attributes:

EVOKED SET	PRICE	NUMBER OF SPEEDS	SIZE (IN OUNCES)	NOISE LEVEL*
1	$30	10	32	3
2	$22	7	30	4
3	$25	5	48	5
4	$22	5	30	4

* A score of 5 represents the least noise.

Which machine(s) would this company prefer if its decision making could be explained by: (a) a dominance model; (b) a conjunctive model which used cut-off points of less than $28, at least 5 speeds and 32 ounces, and a quietness level equal to or greater than 4; (c) a disjunctive model based upon criteria of at least 8 speeds or at least 48 ounces; and (d) a lexicographic model with an importance ordering of least cost, size, speeds, and noise. (See chapter 7 for discussion of these models).

Market Segmentation and Targeting

Never follow the crowd.
BERNARD M. BARUCH

An organization that decides to operate in some market—whether consumer, industrial, reseller, or government—recognizes that it normally cannot serve all the customers in that market. The customers are too numerous, widely scattered, or heterogeneous in their buying requirements or buying practices to be effectively and superiorly served by one organization. Some competitors will be in a better position to effectively serve particular customer segments of that market. The firm, instead of competing everywhere, sometimes against superior odds, should identify those parts of the market that are the most attractive and that it could serve the most effectively. This calls for two steps. The first is *market segmentation*, the act of subdividing a market into distinct and meaningful subsets of customers who might merit separate marketing programming and effort. The second is *target marketing*, the act of evaluating, selecting, and concentrating on those market segments that the company can serve most effectively. This chapter will deal with the major concepts and tools for market segmentation and targeting.

MARKET SEGMENTATION

Market segmentation represents an important recent advance in marketing thinking and strategy. In earlier years many business firms saw the key to profits to be in the development of a single brand that was mass produced, mass dis-

194

tributed, and mass communicated. This would lead to the lowest costs and prices and create the largest potential market. The firm would not recognize variations and would try to get everyone in the market to want what it produced.

As competition intensified, prices dropped and sellers' earnings declined. Sellers did not have much control over price because of the similarity of their products. At this stage, some sellers began to recognize the potential value of *product differentiation*—that is, the introduction of differential features, quality, style, or image in their brands as a basis for commanding a premium. This led to a proliferation of sizes, models, options, and other characteristics. It is important to recognize, however, that the product variations were not based on an analysis of natural market segments.

Market segmentation, the most recent idea for guiding marketing strategy, starts not with distinguishing product possibilities, but rather with distinguishing customer groups and needs. *Market segmentation is the subdividing of a market into distinct subsets of customers, where any subset may conceivably be selected as a target market to be reached with a distinct marketing mix.* The power of this concept is that in an age of intense competition for the mass market, individual sellers may prosper through developing offers for specific market segments whose needs are imperfectly satisfied by the mass-market offerings.

Nature of Market Segmentation

Markets consist of customers, and customers are likely to differ in one or more respects. They may differ in size, resources, geographical location, product requirements, buying attitudes, or buying practices. Any of these variables can make a difference in customer attractiveness or in company capability to effectively serve that customer. Any of these variables can be used to segment a market. Any market with two or more buyers is capable of being segmented.

Figure 8–1A shows a market consisting of six buyers before it is segmented. The maximum number of segments that a market can contain is the total number of buyers making up that market. Each buyer is potentially a separate market because of unique needs and desires. Ideally, a seller might study each buyer in order to tailor the best marketing program to that buyer's needs. Where there are only a few major customers, this is done to some extent. For example, the

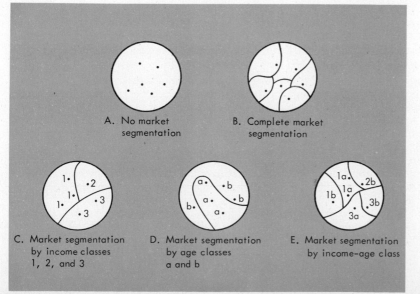

A. No market
segmentation

B. Complete market
segmentation

FIGURE 8–1

Different Approaches
to Market Segmentation

C. Market segmentation
by income classes
1, 2, and 3

D. Market segmentation
by age classes
a and b

E. Market segmentation
by income-age class

major airframe producers such as Boeing and Douglas face only a few buyers and treat them as separate markets. This ultimate degree of market segmentation is illustrated in Figure 8–1B.

Most sellers will not find it worthwhile to customize their product to satisfy each buyer's specific wants. Instead, the seller identifies broad classes of buyers who differ in their product requirements and/or marketing susceptibilities. For example, the seller may discover that income groups differ in their product requirements and marketing susceptibilities. In Figure 8–1C a number (1, 2, or 3) is used to identify each buyer's income class. Lines are drawn around buyers in the same income class. Segmentation by income class results in three segments, the most numerous one being income class 1 in the illustration.

On the other hand, the seller may find pronounced differences in buyer behavior between younger and older buyers. In Figure 8–1D the same individuals are shown, but a letter (a or b) is used to indicate the buyer's age class. Segmentation of the market by age class results in two segments, both equally numerous.

It may turn out that income and age both count heavily in differentiating the buyer's behavior toward the product. The seller may find it desirable to partition the market according to those joint characteristics. In terms of the illustration, the market can be broken into the following six segments: 1a, 1b, 2a, 2b, 3a, and 3b. Figure 8–1E shows that segment 1a contains two buyers, segment 2a contains no buyers (a null segment), and each of the other segments contains one buyer. In general, as the market is segmented on the basis of a larger set of joint characteristics, the seller achieves finer precision but at the price of multiplying the number of segments and thinning out the populations in the segments. If the seller segmented the market using all conceivable characteristics, the market would again look like Figure 8–1B, where each buyer would be a separate segment.

Patterns of Market Segmentation

In the preceding illustration, the market was segmented by income and age, resulting in different *demographic segments*. Suppose that, instead, buyers are asked how much they want of each of two product attributes (say *sweetness* and *creaminess* in the case of an ice cream). This results in identifying different *preference segments* in the market. Three different patterns can emerge.

1. *Homogeneous preferences.* Figure 8–2 reveals a market where all the consumers have roughly the same preference. The market shows no *natural segments,* at least as far as the two attributes are concerned. We would predict that existing brands would be similar and located in the center of the preferences.

2. *Diffused preferences.* At the other extreme, consumer preferences may be scattered fairly evenly throughout the space with no concentration (Figure 8–2B). Consumers simply differ a great deal in what they want from the product. If one brand exists in the market, it is likely to be positioned in the center because it would appeal to the most people. A brand in the center minimizes the sum of total consumer dissatisfaction. A competitor coming into the market could locate next to the first brand and engage in an all-out battle for market share. This is the typical situation in a political market where the two candidates both go middle-of-the-road to gain the greatest following. The other choice is for the competitor to locate in some corner to gain the loyalty of a customer group that is not satisfied with the center brand. If there are several brands in the market, they are likely to eventually position themselves fairly evenly throughout the space and show real differences to match consumer preference differences.

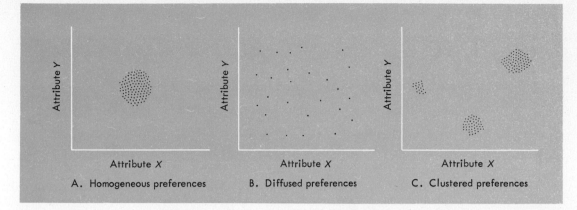

FIGURE 8–2
Basic Market-Preference Patterns

3. ***Clustered preferences.*** An intermediate possibility is the appearance of distinct preference clusters (Figure 8–2C). They may be called *natural market segments.* The first firm to enter this market has three options. (1) It might position itself in the center hoping to appeal to all the groups (undifferentiated marketing). (2) It might position itself in the largest market segment (concentrated marketing). (3) It might develop several brands, each positioned in a different segment (differentiated marketing). Clearly, if it developed only one brand, competition would come in and introduce brands in the other segments.

Market Segmentation Procedure

We have seen that market segments can be arrived at by applying a succession of variables to subdivide the market. As an illustration: An airline is interested in attracting nonflyers (segmentation variable: *user status*). Nonflyers consist of those who fear flying, those who are indifferent, and those who are positive toward flying (segmentation variable: *attitude*). Among those who feel positive are people with higher incomes and who have the ability to afford flying (segmentation variable: *income*). The airline may decide to target those higher-income persons who are positive about flying but simply have not been sufficiently motivated to travel by air.

How does the seller know which variables to apply in succession to the market? The answer is by interviewing a sample of consumers and attempting to discover the *hierarchy of variables* that these consumers use on their way to a purchase decision. Consider the purchase of an automobile. Figure 8–3A shows a few of the variables that buyers might consider in choosing a car. Years ago, many car buyers were primarily brand loyal and would first decide the brand they wanted and then on the car form. Thus buyer 1 in Figure 8–3A decided on a Chevrolet and then a station wagon. When most of the buyers buy this way, we call it a *brand-form market.* On the other hand, buyer 2 decided that he wanted a high-performance car, then an intermediate-size car, then a four-door, and finally a Cadillac. If most car buyers buy this way, we call it a *need-size-form-brand market.* In this kind of market, most of the brands do not compete against each other. The competitive brands are only those that satisfy the need-size-form prerequisites. The Hendry Corporation of New York has built a suc-

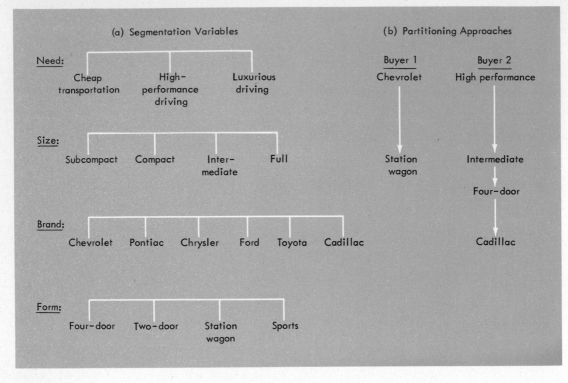

FIGURE 8–3
Market Partitioning

cessful brand-forecasting system based on examining how buyers buy and the character of the primary partitioning variables. They call this system *market partitioning theory* and have helped a number of companies understand their market segments and major competitors.[1]

Bases for Segmenting Consumer Markets

As we have seen, market segmentation involves the creative search for the most useful segmentation variables. The most market-oriented variables are *customers' product requirements* and *customers' responses to marketing stimuli*. These variables (called *bases of segmentation*) are often associated with other variables such as buyer demographics and media habits (called *market descriptors*). Some segmenters, in fact, go right to these later variables first because good data exist and the segments are more definable.

In this section, we will review the major geographic, demographic, psychographic, and behavioristic variables used in segmenting consumer markets. They are shown in Table 8–1. Then we will briefly review the major segmentation variables used in industrial market segmentation.

[1] See Manohar U. Kalwani and Donald G. Morrison, "A Parsimonious Description of the Hendry System," *Management Science*, January 1977, pp. 467–77.

TABLE 8–1
Major Segmentation Variables for Consumer Markets

VARIABLES	TYPICAL BREAKDOWNS
Geographic	
Region	Pacific, Mountain, West North Central, West South Central, East North Central, East South Central, South Atlantic, Middle Atlantic, New England
County size	A, B, C, D
City or SMSA size	Under 5,000, 5,000–19,999, 20,000–49,999, 50,000–99,999, 100,000–249,999, 250,000–499,999, 500,000–999,999, 1,000,000–3,999,999, 4,000,000 or over
Density	Urban, suburban, rural
Climate	Northern, southern
Demographic	
Age	Under 6, 6–11, 12–19, 20–34, 35–49, 50–64, 65 +
Sex	Male, female
Family size	1–2, 3–4, 5 +
Family life cycle	Young, single; young, married, no children; young, married, youngest child under six; young, married, youngest child six or over; older, married, with children; older, married, no children under 18; older, single; other
Income	Under $3,000, $3,000–$5,000, $5,000–$7,000, $7,000–$10,000, $10,000–$15,000, $15,000–$25,000, $25,000 and over
Occupation	Professional and technical; managers, officials and proprietors; clerical, sales; craftsmen, foremen; operatives; farmers; retired; students; housewives; unemployed
Education	Grade school or less; some high school; graduated high school; some college; graduated college
Religion	Catholic, Protestant, Jewish, other
Race	White, black, oriental
Nationality	American, British, French, German, Scandinavian, Italian, Latin American, Middle Eastern, Japanese
Social class	Lower-lower, upper-lower, lower-middle, upper-middle, lower-upper, upper-upper
Psychographic	
Life style	Straights, swingers, longhairs
Personality	Compulsive, gregarious, authoritarian, ambitious
Behavioristic	
Purchase occasion	Regular occasion, special occasion
Benefits sought	Economy, convenience, prestige
User status	Nonuser, exuser, potential user, first-time user, regular user
Usage rate	Light user, medium user, heavy user
Loyalty status	None, medium, strong, absolute
Readiness stage	Unaware, aware, informed, interested, desirous, intending to buy
Marketing-factor sensitivity	Quality, price, service, advertising, sales promotion

Geographic segmentation In geographic segmentation, the market is divided into different locations—nations, states, counties, cities, or neighborhoods. The organization recognizes that market potentials and costs vary with market location. It determines those geographical markets that it could serve best. Thus the Coors Brewery until recently primarily served Denver and the surrounding area because its plant and supplies were concentrated there.

Demographic segmentation In demographic segmentation, the market is subdivided into different parts on the basis of demographic variables—age, sex, family size, income, occupation, education, family life cycle, religion, nationality. Demographic variables have long been the most popular bases for distinguishing significant groupings in the market place. One reason is that consumer wants or usage rates are often highly associated with demographic variables; another is that demographic variables are easier to measure than most other types of variables.

For example, a furniture company may be interested in segmenting its market. Suppose that the company's marketing research reveals three important demographic variables: age of head of household, size of family, and level of income. Figure 8–4 shows a joint segmentation of the market according to these variables. Each variable is subdivided into the number of levels deemed useful for analysis; the result is 36(4 x 3 x 3) distinct segments. Every family belongs to one of these 36 segments. Having conceptualized the market in this way, management can proceed to determine the profit potential of each segment. This involves estimating for each segment the number of families, the average purchase rate, and the extent of competition. These pieces of information can be combined to estimate the value of each segment.

A company must be careful in its use of demographics because their influence on consumer buying potential does not always operate in the expected direction. For example, the Ford Motor Company used buyers' age in developing its target market for its Mustang automobile; the car was designed to appeal to young people who wanted an inexpensive sporty automobile. Ford found, to its surprise, that the car was being purchased by all age groups. It then realized that its target market was not the chronologically young but those who were psychologically young.

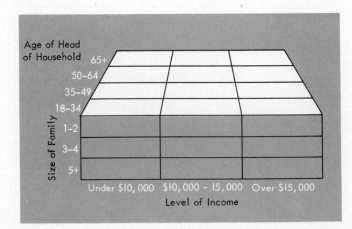

FIGURE 8–4
Segmentation of the Furniture Market
by Three Demographic Variables

Income is another demographic variable that can be deceptive. One would think that working-class families would buy Chevrolets and managerial-class families would buy Cadillacs. Yet many Chevrolets are bought by middle-income people (often as a second car), and some Cadillacs are bought by working-class families (such as high-paid plumbers and carpenters). Members of the working class were among the first purchasers of expensive color television sets; it was cheaper for them to buy these sets than go out to movies and restaurants. Coleman suggested that a distinction should be drawn between the "underprivileged" segments and the "overprivileged" segments of each social class.[2] The cheapest, most economic cars are not bought by the really poor, but rather by "those who think of themselves as poor relative to their status aspirations and to their needs for a certain level of clothing, furniture, and housing, which they could not afford if they bought a more expensive car." On the other hand, medium-priced and expensive cars tend to be purchased by the over-privileged segments of each social class.

Psychographic segmentation   In psychographic segmentation, buyers are divided into different groups on the basis of life style or personality differences. People within the same demographic group can exhibit very different psychographic profiles.

LIFE STYLE   Life style refers to the distinctive mode of orientation an individual or a group has toward consumption, work, and play. Such terms as hippies, swingers, straights, and jet-setters are all descriptive of different life styles. Marketers are increasingly being drawn to life style segmentation.[3] They are targeting versions of their products to life style groups and studying new-product opportunities arising out of life style analysis. Volkswagen, for example, is introducing life-styled automobiles: there will be a car for "the good citizen" emphasizing economy, safety, and ecology; and a car for the "car freak" emphasizing handling, maneuverability, and sportiness. Manufacturers of women's clothing have followed Du Pont's advice to design different clothes for the "plain woman," the "fashionable woman," and the "manly woman." Cigarette companies develop brands for the "defiant smoker," the "casual smoker," and the "careful smoker." Companies making cosmetics, alcoholic beverages, and furniture are seeing increasing opportunities in life style segmentation. At the same time, some companies have not found this variable to always work; for example, Nestlé introduced a special brand of decaffeinated coffee for "late nighters" and it failed.

PERSONALITY   Marketers have used personality variables to segment the market. They try to endow their products with *brand personalities* (brand image, brand concept) designed to appeal to corresponding *consumer personalities* (self-images, self-concepts). In the late fifties, Fords and Chevrolets were promoted as having different personalities. Ford buyers were thought to be "independent, impulsive, masculine, alert to change, and self-confident, while Chevrolet owners are conservative, thrifty, prestige-conscious, less masculine, and seeking to

---

[2] Richard P. Coleman, "The Significance of Social Stratification in Selling," in *Marketing: A Maturing Discipline,* ed. Martin L. Bell (Chicago: American Marketing Association, 1961), pp. 171–84.

[3] See Mark Hanan, *Life-Styled Marketing* (New York: American Management Association, 1972).

avoid extremes."[4] Evans investigated whether this was true by subjecting Ford and Chevrolet owners to the Edwards Personal Preference test, which measured needs for achievement, dominance, change, aggression, and so on. Except for a slightly higher score on dominance, Ford owners did not score significantly differently from Chevrolet owners, and Evans concluded that "the distributions of scores for all needs overlap to such an extent that [personality] discrimination is virtually impossible." Work subsequent to Evans on a wide variety of products and brands has occasionally turned up personality differences but more often has not. Westfall found some evidence of personality differences between the owners of convertibles and nonconvertibles, the former appearing to be more active, impulsive, and sociable.[5] Gottlieb found compulsive people to be heavier users of aspirin.[6] Tucker and Painter found some statistically significant but weak personality correlations for nine products in their study.[7]

Behavioristic segmentation   In behavioristic segmentation, buyers are divided into different groups on the basis of their knowledge, attitude, use, or response to the actual product or its attributes. Many marketers believe that behavioristic variables are the key starting point in identifying market segments.

PURCHASE OCCASION   Buyers may be distinguished on the basis of the occasion that gives rise to their purchasing the product. For example, the flying public includes people traveling on business, vacation, or family affairs. Those who are making long distance telephone calls may be conducting business or making personal calls.

BENEFITS SOUGHT   Buyers are drawn to products through different buying motives. In the case of toothpaste, various customers seek decay prevention, bright teeth, good taste, or low price. An attempt is made to determine the demographic or psychographic characteristics associated with each benefit segment. Haley has characterized those seeking decay prevention as worriers, bright teeth as sociables, good taste as sensories, and low price as independents.[8]

Further characteristics of each group may be found, such as that consumers concerned with decay prevention have larger families and those interested in bright teeth are often tobacco users or single people. Media habits may even vary with each group. The company can choose the benefit it wants to emphasize, create a product that delivers it, and direct a message to the group seeking that benefit.

Choosing a benefit group to market to has some difficulties. First, it is usually difficult to estimate the size of different benefit groups in the total population. It depends on the ease with which persons can cite one benefit as domi-

[4] Quoted in Franklin B. Evans, "Psychological and Objective Factors in the Prediction of Brand Choice; Ford versus Chevrolet," *Journal of Business*, October 1959, pp. 340–69.

[5] Ralph Westfall, "Psychological Factors in Predicting Product Choice," *Journal of Marketing*, April 1962, pp. 34–40.

[6] Maurice J. Gottlieb, "Segmentation by Personality Types," in *Advancing Marketing Efficiency*, ed. Lynn H. Stockman (Chicago: American Marketing Association, 1959), p. 154.

[7] W. T. Tucker and John J. Painter, "Personality and Product Use," *Journal of Applied Psychology*, October 1961, pp. 325–29.

[8] Russell J. Haley, "Benefit Segmentation: A Decision-Oriented Research Tool," *Journal of Marketing*, July 1968, pp. 30–35.

nating their interest in the product. Yankelovich found that people could do this with watches: as of 1962, "approximately 23 percent of the buyers bought [watches] for lowest price, another 46 percent bought for durability and general product quality, and 31 percent bought watches as symbols of some important occasion."[9] Second, the cited benefit might cover up something deeper; favoring the lowest-price watch may be a form of "sensibility snobbery." Finally, some buyers are interested in a particular benefit bundle rather than in a single benefit; this means the marketers may have to segment by benefit-bundle groups.[10]

USER STATUS   Many markets can be segmented into nonusers, exusers, potential users, first-time users, and regular users of a product. High-market-share companies such as Kodak (in the film market) are particularly interested in going after potential users, whereas a small film competitor will concentrate on trying to attract regular users to its brand. Potential users and regular users require different kinds of communication and marketing efforts. In the social marketing area, agencies such as antidrug agencies pay close attention to user status. They direct most of their effort at young people who might be potential users and try to immunize them against an interest in hard drugs. They sponsor rehabilitation programs to help regular users who want to quit their habit. They utilize exusers to lend credibility to various programs.

USAGE RATE   Many markets can be segmented into light-, medium-, and heavy-user groups of the product (called volume segmentation). Heavy users may constitute only a small percentage of the numerical size of the market but a major percentage of the unit volume consumed. For example, 50 percent of the beer drinkers account for 88 percent of beer consumption.[11] Naturally, beer companies will want to go after the "heavy half" of the market because every heavy drinker drinking their brand is worth several light drinkers. Unfortunately, when all the companies go after the same heavy drinkers, their campaigns look alike and cancel each other.

The hope is that the heavy users of a product have certain common demographics, personal characteristics, and media habits. One research company found that the "frequent beer drinker" earns less than $10,000 a year, is married (with two and a half children), and has simple manly tastes. He likes TV and he likes to watch sports.[12] Profiles like this are obviously helpful to the marketer in developing pricing, message, and media strategies.

In the area of social marketing campaigns, agencies often face a heavy-user dilemma. The heavy users are often the most resistant to the selling proposition. A family-planning agency, for example, would normally target its marketing effort to those families who would have the most children; but these families are also the most resistant to birth-control messages. The National Safety Council should target its marketing effort primarily to the unsafe drivers; but these drivers are also the most resistant to safe-driving appeals. The agencies

[9] See Daniel Yankelovich, "New Criteria for Market Segmentation," *Harvard Business Review*, March–April 1964, pp. 83–90, here p. 85.

[10] See Paul E. Green, Yoram Wind, and Arun K. Jain, "Benefit Bundle Analysis," *Journal of Advertising Research*, April 1972, pp. 31–36.

[11] See Dik Warren Twedt, "How Important to Marketing Strategy Is the 'Heavy User'?" *Journal of Marketing*, January 1964, pp. 71–72.

[12] See Norton Garfinkle, "A Marketing Approach to Media Selection," *Journal of Advertising Research*, December 1963, pp. 7–14.

must consider whether to use their limited budget to go after a few heavy users who are highly resistant or many light users who are less resistant.

LOYALTY STATUS   Loyalty status describes the amount of loyalty that users have to a particular object. The amount of loyalty can range from zero to absolute. We find buyers who are absolutely loyal to a brand (such as Budweiser beer), to an organization (such as the Republican party), to a place (such as New England), and so on.

Companies try to identify the characteristics of their hard-core loyals so that they can target their market effort to similar people in the population. Frank found some brand-loyal customers in the consumer-staples category but concluded that they "were not identifiable by socioeconomic or personality characteristics, did not have different average demand levels from nonloyal customers, and did not differ in sensitivity to promotion."[13] In this case, brand loyalty did not appear to be a useful basis for market segmentation.

Furthermore, the concept of brand loyalty has some ambiguities. What may appear to be brand loyalty may be explainable in other ways. Suppose a shopper purchased brand B on the last seven shopping occasions. The purchase pattern BBBBBBB would seem to reflect intrinsic preference for the product but may really reflect *habit, indifference, a lower price,* or the *nonavailability of substitutes.* The pattern BBBBAAA for another shopper would seem to indicate a switch in loyalty but may only reflect the fact that the store dropped brand B, or that she switched stores, or that she switched to brand A because of a price promotion. Marked brand continuity in brand-purchase sequences is not necessarily evidence that individual brand loyalty exists or is strong.

STAGES OF READINESS   At any point of time, there is a distribution of people in various stages of readiness toward buying the product. Some members of the potential market are unaware of the product; some are aware; some are informed; some are interested; some are desirous; and some intend to buy. The particular distribution of people over stages of readiness makes a big difference in designing the marketing program. Suppose a health agency wants to attract women to take an annual Pap test to detect cervical cancer. At the beginning, most of the potential market is unaware of the concept. The marketing effort should go into high-reach advertising and publicity using a simple message. If successful, more of the market will be aware of the Pap test and the advertising should be changed to dramatizing the benefits of taking an annual examination and the risks of not taking it, so as to move more people into a stage of desire. Facilities should also be readied for handling the large number of women who may be motivated to take the examination. In general, the marketing program must be adjusted to the changing distribution of readiness.

MARKETING FACTORS   Markets can often be segmented into groups responsive to different marketing factors such as price and price deals, product quality, and service. This information can help the company in allocating its marketing resources.[14] The marketing variables are usually proxies for particular benefits sought by buyers. A company that specializes in a certain marketing factor will

[13] Ronald E. Frank, "Is Brand Loyalty a Useful Basis for Market Segmentation?" *Journal of Advertising Research*, June 1967, pp. 27–33, here pp. 27–28.

[14] This approach is investigated in Henry J. Claycamp and William F. Massy, "A Theory of Market Segmentation," *Journal of Marketing Research*, November 1968, pp. 388–94. Also see Ronald Frank, William Massy, and Yoram Wind, *Market Segmentation* (Englewood Cliffs, N.J.: Prentice-Hall, 1972), part IV.

build up hard-core loyals seeking that factor or benefit. Thus Avon, which sells cosmetics on a door-to-door basis, appeals to women who like personal attention and service.

Bases for Segmenting Industrial Markets

Industrial markets can also be effectively segmented, although Wind and Cardozo observed that "industrial marketers typically fail to employ market segmentation as a foundation for planning and control of marketing programs."[15] In their study they proposed a two-stage approach to industrial market segmentation. The first stage calls for identifying *macrosegments* through the use of such characteristics as (1) end-use market, (2) product application, (3) customer size, (4) usage rate, (5) geographical location, and (6) organization structure. The second stage calls for dividing each selected macrosegment into *microsegments* through the use of such characteristics as (1) position in authority, (2) personal characteristics, (3) perceived product importance, (4) attitudes toward vendor, (5) buying decision criteria, and (6) stage in buying process.

As an example of industrial market segmentation, consider the following:

An aluminum company wants to select some market segments on which to focus its offers and market effort.[16] The first stage is macrosegmentation—determining which end-use market the company can best serve: automobiles, residential, or beverage containers. This can be called a horizontal product/market choice. Suppose the company decides that it can best serve the residential-housing market. The second step is to determine the best vertical level at which to enter the residential-housing market: semifinished material, building components, or end products. Suppose the company decides to enter the building-components market. The third step is to determine the best customer size to serve. Suppose the company decides to focus on large customers.

The second stage of analysis calls for forming microsegments within this macrosegment. For example, the company might discover that large customers fall into three groups—according to whether they buy on price, service, or quality. If the aluminum company has a high service profile, the company will probably decide to concentrate on the service-motivated microsegment of the market.

Requirements for Effective Segmentation

Clearly, there are many ways to segment a given market. Not all resulting segments are meaningful from a marketing point of view. The market for table salt, for example, could be subdivided into blond and brunet customers. But hair color is not relevant to the purchase of salt. Buyers of table salt are fairly homogeneous with respect to the relevant buying variables. In fact, if all salt buyers wanted to buy the same amount of salt each month, believed all salt was the same, and wanted to pay the same price, this market would be minimally segmentable from a marketing point of view.

To be useful, market segments must exhibit the following characteristics:

The first is *measurability*, the degree to which the size and purchasing power of the resulting segments can be measured. Certain segmentation variables are hard to measure. An illustration would be the size of the segments of

---

[15] Yoram Wind and Richard Cardozo, "Industrial Market Segmentation," *Industrial Marketing Management*, vol. 3, 1974, pp. 153–66.

[16] See E. Raymond Corey, "Key Options in Market Selection and Product Planning," *Harvard Business Review*, September–October 1975, pp. 119–28.

automobile buyers who are primarily motivated by automobile styling or by performance.

The second is *accessibility*, the degree to which the resulting segments can be effectively reached and served. It would be helpful if advertising could be directed mainly to the segment of opinion leaders, but their media habits are not always distinct from those of opinion followers.

The third is *substantiality*, the degree to which the resulting segments are large and/or profitable enough to be worth considering for separate marketing attention. A segment should be the smallest unit for which it is practical to tailor a separate marketing program. Segmental marketing is expensive, as we shall see shortly. It would not pay, for example, for an automobile manufacturer to develop special cars for midgets.

Benefits of Segmentation

The main conclusion from this discussion is that markets are made up of segments that are not all equally attractive to any one company. Given limited resources, a company should try to identify those market segments that it can best serve in terms of segment preferences, patterns of competition, and company strengths. The company can shape its marketing mix to be maximally effective in the chosen target market segments. Market segmentation offers companies at least three benefits.

First, *sellers are in a better position to spot and compare market opportunities.* They can examine the needs of each segment in the light of the current competitive offerings and determine the extent of current satisfaction. Segments with relatively low levels of satisfaction from current offerings may represent excellent market opportunities.

Second, *sellers can make finer adjustments of their product and marketing appeals.* Instead of one marketing program aimed to draw in all potential buyers (the "shotgun" approach), sellers can create separate marketing programs aimed to meet the needs of different buyers (the "rifle" approach).

Third, *sellers can develop marketing programs and budgets based on a clearer idea of the response characteristics of specific market segments.* They can allocate funds to the different segments in line with their likely levels of purchase response.

TARGET MARKETING

Market segmentation reveals the extent of market heterogeneity and the opportunities facing the firm from target marketing. This still leaves the firm a choice among three broad strategies for responding to the revealed market structure.

1. The firm might decide to go after the largest part of the market with one offer and marketing mix, trying to attract as many customers as possible. We call this *undifferentiated marketing.*
2. The firm might decide to go after a narrow market segment and develop the ideal offer and marketing mix. We call this *concentrated marketing.*
3. The firm might decide to go after several market segments, developing an effective offer and marketing mix for each. We call this *differentiated marketing.*

Here we will describe the rationale and merits of each of these strategies.

Undifferentiated Marketing

In undifferentiated marketing, the firm chooses not to recognize the different market segments making up the market. It treats the market as an aggregate, focusing on what is common in the needs of people rather than on what is different. It tries to design a product and a marketing program that appeal to the broadest number of buyers. It relies on mass channels, mass advertising media, and universal themes. It aims to endow the product with a superior image in people's minds, whether or not this image is based on any real difference.[17] An excellent example of undifferentiated marketing is the Coca-Cola Company's earlier production of only one drink in one bottle size in one taste to suit all.

Undifferentiated marketing is primarily defended on the grounds of cost economies. It is thought to be "the marketing counterpart to standardization and mass production in manufacturing."[18] The fact that the product line is kept narrow minimizes production, inventory, and transportation costs. The undifferentiated advertising program enables the firm to enjoy media discounts through large usage. The absence of segmental marketing research and planning lowers the costs of marketing research and product management. On the whole, undifferentiated marketing results in keeping down several costs of doing business.

Nevertheless, an increasing number of marketers have expressed strong doubts about the optimality of this strategy. Gardner and Levy, for example, admit that "some brands have very skillfully built up reputations of being suitable for a wide variety of people" but add:

> In most areas audience groupings will differ, if only because there are deviants who refuse to consume the same way other people do. . . . It is not easy for a brand to appeal to stable lower middle-class people and at the same time to be interesting to sophisticated, intellectual upper middle-class buyers. . . . It is rarely possible for a product or brand to be all things to all people.[19]

The firm practicing undifferentiated marketing typically develops a product and marketing program aimed at the largest segment of the market. When several firms in the industry do this, the result is hypercompetition for the largest segment(s) and undersatisfaction of the smaller ones. Thus the American auto industry for a long time produced only large automobiles, while foreign firms capitalized on the smaller segments. The "majority fallacy," as the American firms' policy has been called by Kuehn and Day, describes the fact that the larger segments may be less profitable because they attract disproportionately heavy competition.[20] The recognition of this fallacy has led many firms to reevaluate the opportunities latent in the smaller segments of the market.

Differentiated Marketing

Under differentiated marketing, a firm decides to operate in two or more segments of the market but designs separate product and/or marketing programs

[17] This strategy has also gone under other names, such as "product differentiation" or "market aggregation." See Wendell R. Smith, "Product Differentiation and Market Segmentation as Alternative Marketing Strategies," *Journal of Marketing*, July 1956, pp. 3–8; and Alan A. Roberts, "Applying the Strategy of Market Segmentation," *Business Horizons*, fall 1961, pp. 65–72.

[18] Smith, "Product Differentiation," p. 4.

[19] Burleigh Gardner and Sidney Levy, "The Product and the Brand," *Harvard Business Review*, March–April 1955, p. 37.

[20] Alfred A. Kuehn and Ralph L. Day, "Strategy of Product Quality," *Harvard Business Review*, November–December 1962, pp. 101–2.

for each. Thus General Motors tries to produce a car for every "purse, purpose, and personality." By offering product and marketing variations, it hopes to attain higher sales and a deeper position within each market segment. It hopes that a deep position in several segments will strengthen the customers' overall identification of the company with the product field. Furthermore, it hopes for greater loyalty and repeat purchasing, because the firm's offerings have been bent to the customer's desire rather than the other way around.

In recent years an increasing number of firms have moved toward a strategy of differentiated marketing. This is reflected in trends toward multiple product offerings and multiple trade channels and media. Coca-Cola now produces different drinks for different tastes; and International Harvester produces light, medium, and heavy trucks for different market segments.

The net effect of differentiated marketing is to create more total sales than undifferentiated marketing does. "It is ordinarily demonstrable that total sales may be increased with a more diversified product line sold through more diversified channels."[21] However, it also tends to be true that differentiated marketing increases the costs of doing business. The following costs are likely to be higher:

Product modification costs. Modifying a product to meet different market segment requirements usually involves some R&D, engineering, and/or special tooling costs.

Production costs. Generally speaking, it is more expensive to produce m units each of n differentiated products than mn units of one product. This is especially true the longer the production setup time for each product and the smaller the sales volume of each product. On the other hand, if each model is sold in sufficiently large volume, the higher costs of setup time may be quite small per unit.

Administrative costs. Under differentiated marketing, the company has to develop separate marketing plans for the separate segments of the market. This requires extra marketing research, forecasting, sales analysis, promotion, planning, and channel management.

Inventory costs. It is generally more costly to manage inventories of differentiated products than an inventory of only one product. The extra costs arise because more records must be kept and more auditing must be done. Furthermore, each product must be carried at a level that reflects basic demand plus a safety factor to cover unexpected variations in demand. The sum of the safety stocks for several products will exceed the safety stock required for one product. Thus carrying differentiated products leads to increased inventory costs.

Promotion costs. Differentiated marketing involves trying to reach different segments of the market through advertising media most appropriate to each case. This leads to lower usage rates of individual media and the consequent forfeiture of quantity discounts. Furthermore, since each segment may require separate creative advertising planning, promotion costs are increased.

Since differentiated marketing leads to higher sales and higher costs, nothing can be said a priori regarding the optimality of this strategy. Some firms are finding, in fact, that they have overdifferentiated their market offers. They would like to manage fewer brands, with each appealing to a broader customer

---

[21] Roberts, "Marketing Segmentation," p. 66.

group—reverse line extension or broadening the base. They seek a larger volume for each brand. Johnson and Johnson, for example, managed to attract adults to use its baby shampoo. Blue Nun was launched as a white wine equally good for meat and fish courses.

Concentrated Marketing

Both differentiated marketing and undifferentiated marketing imply that the firm goes after the whole market. Many firms see a third possibility, however, one that is especially appealing when the company's resources are limited. Instead of going after a small share of a large market, the firm goes after a large share of one or a few submarkets. Put another way, instead of spreading itself thin in many parts of the market, it concentrates its forces to gain a good market position in a few areas.

Many examples of concentrated marketing can be cited. Volkswagen has concentrated on the small-car market; Bobbie Brooks, on women's junior sportswear; Gerber, on the baby market; Richard D. Irwin, on the economics and business texts market. Through concentrated marketing the firm achieves a strong market position in the particular segments it serves, owing to its greater knowledge of the segments' needs and the special reputation it acquires. Furthermore, it enjoys many operating economies because of specialization in production, distribution, and promotion. If the segment of the market is well chosen, the firm can earn high rates of return on its investment.

At the same time, concentrated marketing involves higher than normal risks. The particular market segment can suddenly turn sour; for example, when young women suddenly stopped buying sportswear and turned to knit dresses one year, it caused Bobbie Brooks's earnings to go deeply into the red. Or a competitor may decide to enter the same segment. For these reasons, many companies prefer to diversify in several market segments.

Selecting a Target Marketing Strategy

Particular characteristics of the seller, the product, or the market serve to constrain and narrow the actual choice of a target marketing strategy.[22]

The first factor is *company resources*. Where the firm's resources are too limited to permit complete coverage of the market, its only realistic choice is concentrated marketing.

The second factor is *product homogeneity*. Undifferentiated marketing is more suited for homogeneous products such as grapefruit or steel. Products that are subject to great variation, such as cameras and automobiles, are more naturally suited to differentiation or concentration.

The third factor is *product stage in the life cycle*. When a firm introduces a new product into the marketplace it usually finds it practical to introduce one or, at the most, a few product versions. The firm's interest is to develop primary demand, and undifferentiated marketing seems the suitable strategy; or it might concentrate on a particular segment. In the mature stage of the product life cycle, firms tend to pursue a strategy of differentiated marketing.

The fourth factor is *market homogeneity*. If buyers have the same tastes, buy the same amounts per period, and react in the same way to marketing stimuli, a strategy of undifferentiated marketing is appropriate.

[22] R. William Kotrba, "The Strategy Selection Chart," *Journal of Marketing*, July 1966, pp. 22–25.

The fifth factor is *competitive marketing strategies.* When competitors are practicing active segmentation, it is hard for a firm to compete through undifferentiated marketing. Conversely, when competitors are practicing undifferentiated marketing, a firm can gain by practicing active segmentation if some of the other factors favor it.

Evaluating the Worth of Different Target Markets

The problem facing all firms that segment their market is how to estimate the value of operating in each of the segments. The firm that pursues differentiated marketing must know this in order to allocate its marketing effort over the various segments. The firm that pursues concentrated marketing must know this in order to decide which segments offer the best opportunities.

A useful analytical approach is illustrated in Figure 8–5.[23] The market is one for the mechanical line of a steel-fabricating company. Stage 1 shows a segmentation of this market, using as two variables the customer-prospect mix and the product-service mix. The customer-prospect mix consists of contractors in the electrical, general, and plumbing line, respectively. The product-service mix consists of three products sold to these contractors: pipe hangers, concrete inserts, and electrical supports. Nine cells result from this joint segmentation of the market. Each cell represents a distinct submarket, or product-market segment. A dollar figure is placed in each cell, representing the company's sales in that submarket.

Relative company sales in the nine submarkets provide no indication of their relative profit potential as segments. The latter depends upon market demand, company costs, and competitive trends in each submarket. Stages 2 and 3 show how a particular product submarket, the general-contractor market for concrete inserts, can be analyzed in depth.

Stage 2 appraises present and future sales in the selected submarket. The vertical axis accommodates estimates of industry sales, company sales, and company market share. The horizontal axis is used to project future sales in these categories and market share. The company sold in this submarket last year $200,000 worth of goods, or one-fourth of total estimated industry sales. Looking ahead, the company expects industry sales in this submarket to rise by 6 percent and its own sales to rise by 15 percent.

Stage 3 probes deeper into the marketing thinking behind the sales forecasts of Stage 2. The horizontal axis shows the promotional mix that the company is using or plans to use to stimulate the sales of concrete inserts to general contractors. The vertical axis shows the distribution mix that the company is using or plans to use to move concrete inserts into the hands of general contractors. The actual promotion-distribution mix could be detailed by placing budget figures (funds and men) in the relevant cells. The company will use all three types of distribution and rely mainly on personal selling and field service for stimulating sales to general contractors.

By carrying out this analysis, the seller is led to think systematically about each segment as a distinct opportunity. The analysis of the profit potential of each segment will help the seller decide on the appropriate target markets to serve.

[23] See William J. Crissy and Frank H. Mossman, "Matrix Models for Marketing Planning: An Update and Expansion," *MSU Business Topics,* autumn 1977, pp. 17–26.

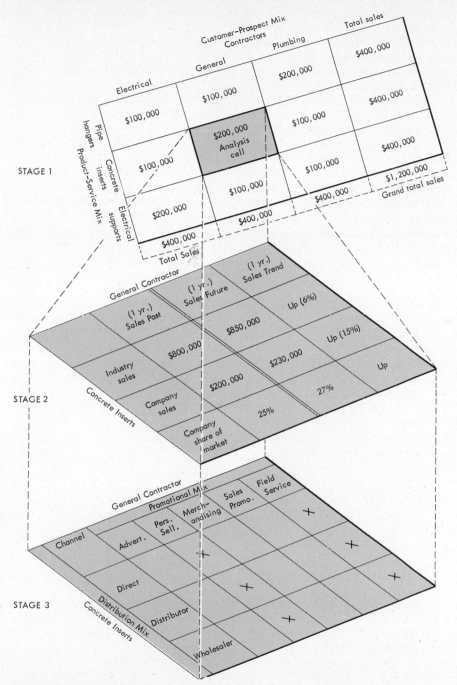

STAGE 1

STAGE 2

STAGE 3

SOURCE: From an unpublished paper by Rhett W. Butler, Northwestern University, 1964.

FIGURE 8–5
Analyzing the Worth of Different Market Segments for Steel-Fabricated Products

SUMMARY

Market segmentation is the subdividing of a market into distinct subsets of customers, where any subset may conceivably be selected as a market target to be reached with a distinct marketing mix. The opportunities present in a market increase when the marketer recognizes that it is made up of customer groups with varying preferences, not all of whom are likely to be receiving complete satisfaction from the current offerings of sellers.

Markets can be segmented on geographic, demographic, psychographic, and behavioristic variables. To be ultimately useful, the segments should be measureable, accessible, and substantial.

Firms have adopted different targeting strategies toward market segments, either ignoring the differences (undifferentiated marketing), developing a variety of products and marketing programs to meet different needs (differentiated marketing), or going after only a few segments (concentrated marketing). No particular strategy is superior in all circumstances. Much depends on company resources, product homogeneity, product stage in the life cycle, market homogeneity, and competitive marketing strategies. The firm must analyze the worth of the different market segments as a prelude to selecting its target markets.

QUESTIONS AND PROBLEMS

1. Market segments can be developed by cross-classifying different variables deemed to be important in the market. What are the problems that arise in trying to cross-classify more than a few variables?

2. Suggest a useful way to segment the markets for each of the following products: (a) household detergents; (b) animal feeds; (c) household coffee; (d) automobile tires.

3. A camera manufacturer is interested in developing a benefit segmentation of the camera market. Could you suggest some major benefit segments?

4. One critic has suggested that most segmentation is unnecessary. Buyers want variety and they switch around. The firm should produce various products, and it will catch those people who switch. Do you agree?

5. The Quaker Oats Company produces a dry breakfast cereal called Life. Life's brand manager is interested in ranking different market target groups for the cereal. The groups are to be formed by using age of housewife, family size, and size of city. Propose a list of market target groups ranging from extremely important to extremely unimportant.

6. A shaving cream manufacturer is planning to introduce a new aftershave lotion. Research indicates that light blue is the favored color by a strong margin. Does it follow that light blue should be adopted?

7. There are certain product markets where brand loyalty is weak and cannot be used as a segmentation variable. What are the characteristics of produce markets where brand loyalty is weak?

8. It is claimed that some markets are oversegmented, that is, the market segments are too small to be served profitably. Some companies are beginning to think of "desegmentation," that is, putting out fewer products, each designed to satisfy a larger group. How would you view this development?

9. A firm that manufactures wristwatches recognizes that it is basically in the time measurement business. It would like to segment the time measurement market in order to find new opportunities for expansion. Develop a segmentation of this market.

212

Market Measurement and Forecasting

Marketing planning requires the conversion of the various qualitative understandings of a market into quantitative estimates of specific demand by product, territory, and type of customer. Furthermore, estimates must be made of the future course of market demand. These tasks are called *demand measurement* and *demand forecasting*, respectively. Demand estimates are essential in carrying out three important management functions—the *analysis* of market opportunities, the *planning* of marketing effort, and the *control* of marketing performance.

MAJOR CONCEPTS IN DEMAND MEASUREMENT

Demand measurement describes the activity of developing quantitative estimates of demand. Figure 9–1 shows *ninety* different types of demand measurement! Demand can be measured for six different *product levels* (product item, product form, product line, company sales, industry sales, national sales), five different *space levels* (customer, territory, region, U.S.A., world), and three different *time levels* (short-range, medium-range, and long-range).

Each type of demand measurement serves a specific purpose. Thus a company might make a short-range forecast of the total demand for a particular

213

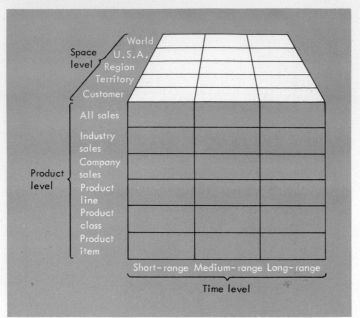

FIGURE 9–1
Ninety Types of Demand Measurement (6 x 5 x 3)

product item to provide a basis for ordering raw materials, planning production, and scheduling short-run financing. Or it might make a long-range forecast of regional demand for its major product line to provide a basis for considering market expansion.

The field of demand measurement is filled with a confusing number of terms. Company executives talk of forecasts, predictions, potentials, estimates, projections, goals, targets, quotas, and budgets. Many of these terms are redundant. The major concepts in demand measurement are *market demand* and *company demand*. Within each, we distinguish between a *demand function*, a *potential*, and a *forecast*.

Market Demand In evaluating marketing opportunities, the first step is to estimate total market demand. It is not a simple concept, however, as the following definition makes clear:

> *Market demand* for a *product* is the *total volume* that would be *bought* by a defined *customer group* in a defined *geographical area* in a defined *time period* in a defined *marketing environment* under a defined *marketing program*.

There are eight elements in this definition.

PRODUCT Market demand measurement requires a careful definition of the scope of the product class. A company that manufactures tin cans has to define whether its market is all metal-can users or all container users. It depends on how the company views its opportunities for penetrating adjacent markets.

TOTAL VOLUME Market demand can be measured in terms of physical volume, dollar volume, or relative volume. The U.S. market demand for automobiles may be described as 10 million cars or $60 billion. The market demand for

214

automobiles in Greater Chicago can be expressed as 3 percent of the nation's total demand.

BOUGHT   In measuring market demand, it is important to define whether "bought" means the volume ordered, shipped, paid for, received, or consumed. For example, a forecast of new housing for the next year usually means the number of units that will be ordered, not completed (called housing starts).

CUSTOMER GROUP   Market demand may be measured for the whole market or for any segment(s). Thus a steel producer may estimate the volume to be bought separately by the construction industry and by the transportation industry.

GEOGRAPHICAL AREA   Market demand should be measured with reference to well-defined geographical boundaries. A forecast of next year's passenger automobile sales will vary depending upon whether the boundaries are limited to the United States or include Canada and/or Mexico.

TIME PERIOD   Market demand should be measured with reference to a stated period of time. One can talk about the market demand for the next calendar year, for the coming five years, or for the year 2000 A.D. The longer the forecasting interval, the more tenuous the forecast. Every forecast is based on a set of assumptions about environmental and marketing conditions, and the chance that some of these assumptions will not be fulfilled increases with the length of the forecast period.

MARKETING ENVIRONMENT   Market demand is affected by a host of uncontrollable factors. Every forecast of demand should explicitly list the assumptions made about the demographic, economic, technological, political, and cultural environment. Demographic and economic forecasting are well developed, technological forecasting is coming into its own, but political and cultural forecasting are still in their infancy.[1] Much interest in the whole subject of predicting future environments is being stimulated by futurists such as Kahn and Weiner.[2] At the same time, Levitt has cautioned: "The easiest kind of expert to be is the specialist who predicts the future. It takes only two things: imagination and a good command of the active verb."[3]

MARKETING PROGRAM   Market demand is also affected by controllable factors, particularly marketing programs developed by the sellers. Demand in most markets will show some elasticity with respect to industry price, promotion, product improvements, and distribution effort. Thus a market demand forecast requires assumptions about future industry prices, product features, and marketing expenditures. We shall use the term *marketing effort* to describe the sum of the company's demand-stimulating activities. Marketing effort has four dimensions that make a difference in its impact: (1) *marketing expenditure level*, the total expenditures spent on marketing, (2) *marketing mix*, the amounts and types of marketing tools the company is using at a particular time, (3) *marketing allocation*, the company's division of its marketing effort over different customer groups and sales territories, and (4) *marketing effectiveness*, the efficiency with which the company employs its marketing funds.

[1] For a discussion of environmental forecasting methods, see chap. 5, pp. 101–3.

[2] Herman Kahn and Anthony J. Weiner, *The Year 2000* (New York: Macmillan Company, 1967).

[3] Theodore Levitt, "The New Markets—Think before You Leap," *Harvard Business Review*, May–June 1969, pp. 53–68, here p. 53.

The most important thing to realize about market demand is that it is not a single number, but a function. For this reason it is also called the *market demand function* or *market response function.* The functional nature of market demand is shown in Figure 9–2A. Market demand is shown on the vertical axis, industry marketing effort on the horizontal axis. The market demand function is shown as

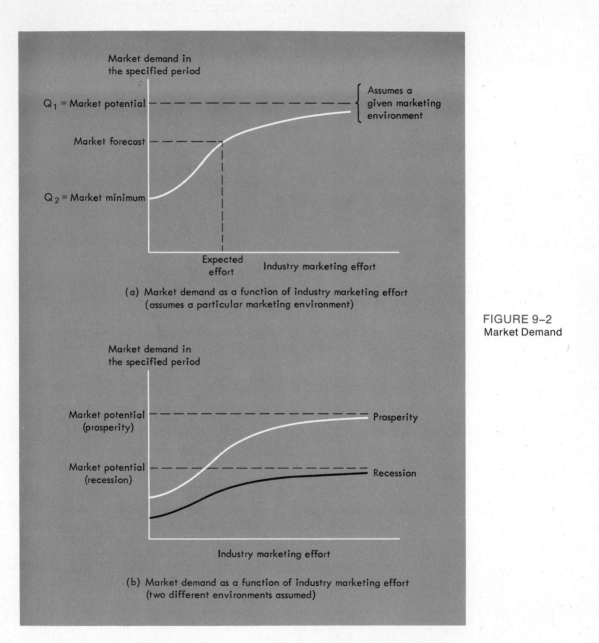

(a) Market demand as a function of industry marketing effort (assumes a particular marketing environment)

FIGURE 9–2
Market Demand

(b) Market demand as a function of industry marketing effort (two different environments assumed)

a curve that rises with higher levels of industry marketing effort. The curve is defined for a given marketing environment.

The shape of the curve has to be determined for each market. The curve in the illustration has the familiar **S** shape, suggesting that market demand shows first increasing, then diminishing, sales response to increased industry marketing effort. Some base sales, the *market minimum*, would take place without any demand-stimulating marketing expenditures by the industry. Positive marketing expenditures will yield increasing, then decreasing, returns. Still higher marketing expenditures would not stimulate much further demand, thus suggesting an upper limit to market demand, called the *market potential*.

The distance between the market minimum and the market potential shows the overall *marketing sensitivity of demand* in that industry. We can think of two extreme types of markets, the *expansible* and the *nonexpansible*. The expansible market, epitomized by markets for new products, is quite affected in its total size by the level of marketing expenditures. In terms of Figure 9–2A the distance between Q_1 and Q_2 is relatively large. The nonexpansible market, epitomized by cigarettes or steel, is not much affected by the level of marketing expenditures; the distance between Q_1 and Q_2 is relatively small. The firm selling in a nonexpansible market can take the market's size (the level of *primary demand*) for granted and concentrate its marketing resources on getting a desired market share (the level of *selective demand*).

It is important to emphasize that the *market demand function* is *not* a picture of market demand *over time*. Rather, the curve shows alternative current forecasts of market demand associated with alternative possible levels of industry marketing effort in the current period.

Market Forecast

Only one of the many possible levels of industry marketing effort will actually occur. The market demand corresponding to the expected effort is called the *market forecast*. The market forecast shows the expected level of market demand for the expected level of industry marketing effort and the given environment.

Market Potential

The market forecast shows the expected market demand, not the highest possible market demand. For the latter, we have to visualize the level of market demand for a very "high" level of industry marketing effort, where further increases in marketing effort would have little effect in stimulating further demand. *Market potential is the limit approached by market demand as industry marketing effort goes to infinity, for a given environment.*

The phrase "for a given environment" is crucial in the concept of market potential. Consider the market potential for automobiles in a period of recession versus a period of prosperity. The market potential is higher during prosperity. In other words, market demand is income-elastic. The dependence of market potential on the environment is illustrated in Figure 9–2B. Thus the analyst distinguishes between the position of the market demand function and movement along it. The sellers cannot do anything about the position of the market demand function; this is the result of a given marketing environment. The sellers influence their particular location on the function, however, in deciding how much to spend on marketing.

Company Demand

We are now ready to define company demand. *Company demand is the company's share of market demand.* In symbols:

$$Q_i = s_i Q \qquad (9\text{--}1)$$

where:

Q_i = company i's demand
s_i = company i's market share
Q = total market demand

Company demand, like market demand, is a function—called the *company demand function* or *sales response function*—and is subject to all the determinants of market demand *plus whatever influences company market share.*

But what influences company market share? The most popular theory is that the *market shares* of various competitors will be proportional to their *marketing-effort shares.* This normal expectation can be called *the fundamental theorem of market-share determination* and is expressed:

$$s_i = \frac{M_i}{\Sigma M_i} \qquad (9\text{--}2)$$

where:

M_i = company i's marketing effort.

For example, consider the simple case where two identical firms are selling the same product but spending different amounts on marketing: $60,000 and $40,000 respectively. Using equation (9–2), company one's market share is predicted to be 60 percent:

$$s_1 = \frac{\$60{,}000}{\$60{,}000 + \$40{,}000} = .60$$

If company one is not enjoying a .60 market share, additional factors must be brought in. Suppose the companies also differ in the *effectiveness* with which they spend marketing dollars. Then equation (9–2) can be revised to read:

$$s_i = \frac{\alpha_i M_i}{\Sigma \alpha_i M_i} \qquad (9\text{--}3)$$

where:

α_i = marketing effectiveness of a dollar spent by company i (with α = 1.00 for average effectiveness)
$\alpha_i M_i$ = company i's effective marketing effort

Suppose that company one spends its marketing funds less effectively than company two, with α_1 = .90 and α_2 = 1.20. Then company one's market share would be forecast to be 53 percent:

$$s_1 = \frac{.90(\$60{,}000)}{.90(\$60{,}000) + 1.20(\$40{,}000)} \cong .53$$

Equation (9–3) assumes a strict proportionality between market share and effective effort share. Yet if there are grounds for expecting diminishing returns as one firm's effective effort increases relative to the industry's effective effort, equation (9–3) should be modified to reflect this. One way to reflect diminishing returns is through the use of a marketing-effort elasticity exponent that is less than unity:

$$s_i = \frac{(\alpha_i M_i)^{em_i}}{\Sigma(\alpha_i M_i)^{em_i}}, \qquad \text{where } 0 < em_i < 1 \tag{9–4}$$

where:

em_i = elasticity of market share with respect to company i's effective marketing effort.

Assume that the marketing-effort elasticity is .8 for all companies. As a result, company one's market share would be

$$s_1 = \frac{[(.90)(\$60{,}000)]^{.8}}{[(.90)(\$60{,}000)]^{.8} + [(1.20)(\$40{,}000)]^{.8}} \cong .50$$

Thus company one's estimated market share is revised to take into account diminishing returns. Although company one is spending 60 percent of the marketing funds in the industry, its market share is only 50 percent, because of both a lower spending efficiency than its competition *and* diminishing returns.

A further improvement in the formulation of market-share determination can be introduced by breaking up each company's marketing effort into its major components and separately expressing the effectiveness and elasticity of each type of marketing effort. The equation becomes:

$$s_{it} = \frac{R_{it}^{eRi} P_{it}^{-ePi}(a_{it}A_{it})^{eAi}(d_{it}D_{it})^{eDi}}{\Sigma[R_{it}^{eRi} P_{it}^{-ePi}(a_{it}A_{it})^{eAi}(d_{it}D_{it})^{eDi}]} \tag{9–5}$$

where:

s_{it} = company i's estimated market share at time t
R_{it} = quality rating of company i's product in year t
P_{it} = price of company i's product in year t
A_{it} = advertising and promotion costs of company i in year t
D_{it} = distribution and sales-force costs of company i in year t
a_{it} = advertising-effectiveness index for company i at time t
d_{it} = distribution-effectiveness index for company i at time t
$\left.\begin{matrix} eRi, ePi \\ eAi, eDi \end{matrix}\right\}$ = elasticities of quality, price, advertising, and distribution, respectively, of company i.

Thus equation (9–5) is a flexible way to take account of four major influences on a company's market share: *marketing expenditures, marketing mix, marketing effectiveness,* and *marketing elasticity.* Although this would seem to be a great deal, the expression could be further refined (we shall not do so here) to take into account (1) *marketing allocation to territories,* (2) *carry-over effects of past marketing expenditures,* and (3) *synergistic effects of marketing decision variables.*[4]

Company Forecast

Company demand describes estimated company sales at alternative levels of company marketing effort. It remains for management to choose one of the levels.[5] The chosen level of marketing effort implies a particular level of sales, which may be called the company sales forecast:

> The *company sales forecast* is the expected level of company sales based on a chosen marketing plan and assumed marketing environment.

The company sales forecast is represented graphically in the same way as the market forecast was in Figure 9–2A; substitute company sales for the vertical axis and company marketing effort for the horizontal axis.

Too often the sequential relationship between the company forecast and the company marketing plan is confused. One frequently hears that the company should plan its marketing effort on the basis of its sales forecast. The forecast-to-plan sequence is valid if "forecast" means an estimate of national economic activity or if company demand is minimally expansible. The sequence is not valid, however, where market demand is expansible, nor where "forecast" means an estimate of company sales. The company sales forecast does not establish a basis for deciding on the amount and composition of marketing effort; quite the contrary, it is the *result* of an assumed blueprint for marketing action. The sales forecast must be viewed as a dependent variable that is affected, among other things, by the planned marketing activity of the firm.

Two other concepts are worth mentioning in relation to the company forecast.

> A *sales quota* is the sales goal set for a product line, company division, or sales representative. It is primarily a managerial device for defining and stimulating sales effort.

The sales quota set by management is arrived at through a joint consideration of the company forecast and the psychology of stimulating its achievement. The latter consideration generally leads to setting sales quotas that total to a slightly higher figure than the estimated sales forecast.

The other concept is a *sales budget.*

> A *sales budget* is a conservative estimate of the expected volume of sales and is used primarily for making current purchasing, production, and cash-flow decisions.

[4] For further development, see the author's *Marketing Decision Making: A Model-Building Approach* (New York: Holt, Rinehart and Winston, 1971). Also see David E. Bell, Ralph L. Keeney, and John D. C. Little, "A Market Share Theorem," *Journal of Marketing Research,* May 1975, pp. 136–41.

[5] The theory of choosing the best level of marketing effort is described in chap. 10, pp. 251–70.

The sales budget is arrived at through a joint consideration of the sales forecast and of the need to avoid excessive investment in case the forecast is not realized. The latter consideration generally leads to setting a sales budget slightly lower than the company forecast.

Company Potential

Company sales potential is *the limit approached by company demand as company marketing effort increases relative to competitors*. The absolute limit of company demand is, of course, the market potential. The two would be equal if the company achieved 100 percent of the market—that is, if the company became a monopolist. In most cases, company sales potential is less than market potential, even when company marketing expenditures increase considerably over those of competitors. The reason is that each competitor has a hard core of loyal buyers who are not very responsive to other companies' efforts to woo them away.

METHODS OF ESTIMATING CURRENT DEMAND

We are now ready to consider practical methods of estimating current demand. There are two types of current demand estimates in which a seller might be interested: *total market potential* and *territorial potential*. Total market potential is of interest whenever a seller is facing a decision to introduce a new product or drop an existing one. The seller wants to know whether the market is large enough to justify the company's participation.

Total Market Potential

Total market potential is the maximum amount of sales (in units or dollars) that might be available to all the firms in an industry during a given period under a given level of industry marketing effort and given environmental conditions. A common way to estimate it is as follows:

$$Q = n \times q \times p \qquad (9\text{–}6)$$

where:

Q = total market potential
n = number of buyers in the specific product/market under the given assumptions
q = quantity purchased by an average buyer
p = price of an average unit

Thus if there could be 121,000,000 buyers of books each year, and the average book buyer buys 3 books a year, and the average price is $4, then the total market potential for books is approximately $1,452,000,000 (= 121,000,000 × 3 × $4).

The most difficult component to estimate in (9–6) is n, the number of buyers in the specific product/market. One can always start with the total population in the nation, say 216,000,000 people. This can be called the *suspect pool*. The next step is to introduce criteria to eliminate groups that obviously would not buy the product. Let us assume that illiterate people, children under twelve, and persons with poor eyesight do not buy books, and they constitute 20 percent of the population. Then only 80 percent of the population, or 172,800,000

221

people, would be in the *prospect pool*. We might do further research and conclude that persons of low income and low education do not read books, and they are over 30 percent of the prospect pool. Eliminating them, we arrive at a *hot prospect pool* of approximately 121,000,000 for book buying. We would now use this as the number of potential buyers in formula (9–6) for calculating total market potential.

A variation on formula (9–6) is known as the *chain ratio method*. It is based on the notion that it may be easier to estimate the separate components of a magnitude than the magnitude directly.[6] Suppose a brewery is interested in estimating the market potential for a new dietetic beer. An estimate can be made by the following calculation:[7]

$$
\left. \begin{array}{c} \text{Demand} \\ \text{for the} \\ \text{new} \\ \text{dietetic} \\ \text{beer} \end{array} \right\} = \left\{ \begin{array}{l} \text{Population} \times \text{ personal discretionary income per capita } \times \\ \text{average percentage of discretionary income spent on food } \times \text{average percentage of amount spent on food that is spent on beverages } \times \text{ average percentage of amount spent on beverages that is spent on alcoholic beverages } \times \text{ average percentage of amount spent on alcoholic beverages that is spent on beer } \times \text{ expected percentage of amount spent on beer that will be spent on dietetic beer.} \end{array} \right.
$$

Once the total market potential is estimated, it should be compared with the current market size. *Current market size* is the actual volume (in units or dollars) that is currently being purchased. Current market size is always smaller than the total market potential. It is important to estimate what percentage current market size is of the total market potential. In Figure 9–3, A and B show current market size as a high percentage of total market potential, which means that most of the people who could buy the product are buying it. C and D, however, show current market size at one-half of total market potential, a situation often typical of new-product markets.

The remaining factor is the company's current market share. A and C in Figure 9–3 show the company with a small market share, while B and D show the company with a large market share. The company has a choice in each case whether to go after its competitors' customers or after the untapped market potential. In case D, the company already has a large market share and its best growth opportunity is to go after the untapped market potential. In case C, however, the company could go after either its competitors' customers or the untapped market potential.

Here we must introduce another concept, that of the served market. *A company's served market are all those buyers for whom the company's product is available, accessible, and attractive.* If the company in C distributes its product in only one part of the country and if its price would not appeal to many of its competitors' customers, then the company could not penetrate its competition very much. It has a low share of the current market but a high share of its served

---

[6] J. Scott Armstrong, William B. Denniston, Jr., and Matt M. Gordon, "The Use of the Decomposition Principle in Making Judgments," *Organizational Behavior and Human Performance*, vol. 14, 1975, pp. 257–63.

[7] See Russell L. Ackoff, *A Concept of Corporate Planning* (New York: Wiley-Interscience, 1970), pp. 36–37.

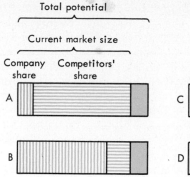

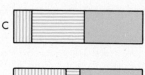

FIGURE 9–3
Total Potential, Current Market Size,
and Company Share

market. Its best course is to go after the untapped potential in its served market rather than after its competitors' customers.

Territorial Potentials All companies are concerned with (1) selecting the markets to sell in, (2) allocating their marketing budget optimally among these markets, and (3) evaluating their performance in the different markets. The basis for these decisions lies in competent estimation of the market potential of different territories. Two major methods are available. The first, or *market-buildup method*, is used primarily by industrial-goods firms. The second, or *index-of-buying-power method*, is used mainly by consumer-goods firms.

Market-buildup method The market-buildup method calls for identifying all the potential buyers for the product in each market and adding up the estimated potential purchases of each. The market-buildup method is straightforward if one has available a list of all potential buyers *and* a good estimate of what each will buy. Unfortunately one, if not both, is usually lacking.

Consider the market-measurement problem faced by a machine tool company. Suppose it wants to estimate territorial market potentials for one of its machines, a medium-size wood lathe. Let us focus on one of the markets, the Greater Boston area.

The first step is to identify all potential buyers of lathes in the Boston area. Household buyers can be excluded because the lathe is too large for home-workshop purchase. The lathe is of no purchase interest to many other types of buyers, such as hospitals, retailers, and farmers. The market for this lathe is found primarily in manufacturing establishments. Even here, the lathe is of interest only to manufacturing establishments that have to shape or ream wood as part of their operation.

The company could go through a directory of all manufacturing establishments in the Greater Boston area and list those that might do woodworking. Then it might estimate the number of lathes each might purchase, based on some ratio of the number of lathes per thousand employees or the number of lathes per $1 million of sales. This would be an arduous task, especially considering that the task would have to be repeated for every other market.

A more efficient method of estimating territorial market potentials makes use of the Standard Industrial Classification System (S.I.C.). The system was developed by the federal government in connection with taking its Census of

Manufacturers. The classification is based on the *product produced* or *operation performed*. The S.I.C. System classifies all manufacturing into twenty major industry groups, each having a two-digit code. Thus, #25 is Furniture and Fixtures and #35 is Machinery, except electrical. Each major industry group is further subdivided into about 150 industry groups designated by a three-digit code (#251 is household furniture and #252 is office furniture). Each industry is further subdivided into approximately 450 product categories designated by a four-digit code (#2521 is wood office furniture and #2522 is metal office furniture).

For each four-digit S.I.C. number, the Census of Manufacturers provides the number of establishments subclassified by location, number of employees, annual sales, and net worth.

To use the S.I.C. System, the lathe manufacturer first must determine the four-digit S.I.C. codes that represent products whose manufacture is likely to require lathe machines. For example, lathes will be used by manufacturers in S.I.C. #2511 (wood household furniture), #2521 (wood office furniture), and so on. To get a full picture of all four-digit S.I.C. industries that might use lathes, the company can use three methods. (1) It can look at past sales and determine the S.I.C. codes of the past customers. (2) It can go through the S.I.C. manual and check off all the four-digit industries that in its judgment would have an interest in lathes. (3) It can mail questionnaires to a wide range of companies to inquire about their interest in wood lathes.

Once the company identifies the S.I.C. groups relevant to its product, its next step is to determine an appropriate base for estimating the likely number of lathes that will be used in each industry. Suppose customer industry sales are the most appropriate base. For example, in S.I.C. #2511, ten lathes may be used for every $1 million worth of sales; in S.I.C. #2521, five lathes for every $1 million sales. Once the company is able to establish the rate of lathe ownership relative to the customer industry's sales (or number of employees, net worth, or whatever), it can turn to the Census of Manufacturers' data and compute the market potential.

Table 9–1 shows a hypothetical computation for the Boston area involving two S.I.C. codes. In #2511 (wood household furniture) there are six estab-

---

TABLE 9–1
Market-Buildup Method Using S.I.C. Codes
(Hypothetical Lathe Manufacturer—Boston Area)

	1	2	3	4
			POTENTIAL NUMBER OF LATHE SALES	MARKET
	ANNUAL SALES	NUMBER OF	PER $1 MILLION	POTENTIAL
S.I.C.	(IN MILLIONS $)	ESTABLISHMENTS	CUSTOMER SALES	$(1 \times 2 \times 3)$
2511	$1	6	10	60
	5	2	10	100
2521	1	3	5	15
	5	1	5	25
				200

lishments with annual sales of $1 million and two establishments with annual sales of $5 million. Furthermore, it is estimated that ten lathes can be sold in this S.I.C. code per every $1 million customer sales. Since there are six establishments with annual sales of $1 million, they account for $6 million of sales, which is a potential of 60 lathes (6 × 10). The other figures in the table are similarly computed. When the estimated sales for each S.I.C. code are added up, it appears that there is a market potential for 200 lathes in the Greater Boston area.

In a similar way, the company can estimate the market potential for other territories in the country. Suppose the market potentials for all the markets sum up to 2,000 lathes. In this case the company concludes that the Boston market contains 10 percent of the total market potential. Without further qualification, this might warrant the company's allocating 10 percent of its marketing effort (sales force, advertising, and so on) to the Boston market. In practice, the lathe manufacturer should determine additional things about each market, such as the extent of market saturation, the number of competitors, the market growth rate, and the average age of the equipment in use, before actually deciding on the amount of resources to allocate to each market.

If the company decides to sell lathes in Boston, it needs a system for identifying the best prospect companies. In the old days, sales reps called on companies door to door; this was called bird-dogging or smokestacking. This method is far too costly today. The answer is to get a list of all the companies in Boston, qualify them by some criteria, and then use direct mail or phone calls to identify the better prospects. The lathe manufacturer can use *Dun's Market Identifiers*, which lists twenty-seven key facts for over 3,250,000 establishments in the U.S. and Canada in manufacturing, wholesaling, retailing, transportation, communications, public utilities, agriculture, mining, and services.[8] The files can be screened for S.I.C. lines of business, company size (annual sales volume, number of employees, and net worth), and location by states, counties, cities, or ZIP code. The lathe manufacturer would buy a printout (and mailing labels) of all those companies in the Boston area that were in the high prospect S.I.C. lines of business and over a certain size.

Index-of-buying-power method   Consumer companies also face the problem of estimating territorial market potentials. Because their final customers are typically so numerous, they cannot list every potential customer and estimate its buying requirements. Nor is there such a thing as a Standard Household Classification that classifies households by types and provides the number of households of each type in each location. Therefore, the company that sells to households has to resort to a different solution.

The method most commonly used is a straightforward *index method*. Suppose the company is a drug manufacturer. It might assume that the market potential for drugs is directly related to a single factor, such as population. For example, if the state of Virginia has 2.28 percent of the U.S. population, the company might readily assume that Virginia would be a market for 2.28 percent of total drugs sold.

A single factor, however, is rarely a complete indicator of sales opportunity. Obviously, regional drug sales are also influenced by such factors as per

[8] *Dun's Market Identifiers (DMI)*, Dun & Bradstreet, New York, 1978.

capita income and the number of physicians per, say, ten thousand people. This leads to the desirability of developing a multiple-factor index, each factor being assigned a specific weight in the index.

One of the best-known, general-purpose, multiple-factor indices of area demand is the "Annual Survey of Buying Power" published by *Sales and Marketing Management*.[9] The index is designed to reflect the relative buying power in the different regions, states, and metropolitan areas of the nation. *Sales and Marketing Management*'s index of the relative buying power of an area is given by

$$B_i = .5y_i + .3r_i + .2p_i \qquad (9\text{--}7)$$

where:

B_i = percentage of total national buying power found in area i
y_i = percentage of national disposable personal income originating in area i
r_i = percentage of national retail sales in area i
p_i = percentage of national population located in area i

For example, suppose Virginia has 2.00 percent of the U.S. disposable personal income, 1.96 percent of U.S. retail sales, and 2.28 percent of U.S. population. The buying-power index for Virginia would be:

$$.5(2.00) + .3(1.96) + .2(2.28) = 2.04$$

That is, 2.04 percent of the nation's drug sales might be expected to take place in Virginia. *Sales and Marketing Management* holds that these weights reflect market potential for many consumer goods that are neither low-priced staples nor high-valued luxury goods. The weights, however, vary in their appropriateness for different products. A company can use multiple regression to find the weights that work best for estimating market potential for its products.

It should be understood that area market-potential estimates reflect relative industry opportunities rather than relative company opportunities. The company would adjust the market-potential estimates by factors left out of the index. It would want to consider such additional factors as its brand share, number and type of competitors, sales-force strength, physical-distribution system, local promotional costs, and local market idiosyncrasies.

Many companies will compute some specific additional indices for the various areas as a guide to allocating marketing resources. Suppose the company is reviewing the eight cities listed in Table 9–2. The first three columns show the percentage of total U.S. population, category sales, and brand A sales, respectively, in these eight cities. Column 4 shows the *category development index*, which is the ratio of consumption intensity to population intensity. Seattle, for example, has a category development index of 221 because it accounts for 2.71

[9] For a helpful exposition on using this survey and three other surveys published by *Sales and Marketing Management*, see "Putting the Four to Work," *Sales Management*, October 28, 1974, pp. 13 ff.

TABLE 9–2
Indices of Category Development, Brand Development, and Market Opportunity

TERRITORY	PERCENT OF TOTAL U.S. POPULATION (1)	PERCENT OF TOTAL SALES OF PRODUCT CATEGORY (2)	PERCENT OF TOTAL SALES OF BRAND A (3)	CATEGORY DEVELOP-MENT INDEX (4) = (2 ÷ 1)	BRAND DEVELOP-MENT INDEX (5) = (3 ÷ 1)	MARKET OPPORTUNITY INDEX (6) = (4 ÷ 5)
Seattle	1.23	2.71	3.09	221	252	.88
Portland	1.02	2.17	2.48	212	242	.88
Los Angeles	5.54	10.41	6.74	188	122	1.54
Boston	2.18	3.85	3.49	177	160	1.11
San Francisco	3.66	6.41	7.22	175	198	.88
Toledo	.79	.81	.97	102	123	.83
Albuquerque	.79	.81	1.13	102	143	.71
Baltimore	2.67	3.00	3.12	113	117	.97

percent of the nation's consumption of this category while it has only 1.23 percent of the nation's population. Column 5 shows the *brand development index*, which is the ratio of brand consumption intensity to population intensity. For Seattle, the brand development index is 252 because Seattle consumes 3.09 percent of this brand and has only 1.23 percent of the nation's population. Column 6 shows the *market opportunity index*, which is the ratio of category development to brand development. This ratio is .88 for Seattle, indicating that the company's brand is more developed in Seattle than in other cities. Seattle is therefore an area of low (incremental) opportunity in that the company brand is highly developed in Seattle. In Los Angeles, on the other hand, the market opportunity index stands at 1.54, indicating a high opportunity in that the company's brand is relatively underdeveloped. Companies do not necessarily put all of their money in the high market-opportunity areas. Procter & Gamble, for example, uses an allocation of resouces such that 50 percent of the advertising budget for Tide is devoted to those geographic areas where the brand is weak (i.e., high-opportunity areas) and 50 percent to areas where the brand is strong.

After the company has decided on the amount of effort it wants to put into each territory, it can refine its allocations down to smaller units such as *census tracts* or *ZIP-code centers*. Census tracts are small areas about the size of city neighborhoods, and ZIP-code centers (which were designed by the U.S. Post Office Department) are larger areas, often the size of small towns. Information on population size, median family income, and other characteristics is available for each type of unit. Marketers have found these data extremely useful in identifying high potential retail areas within large cities or buying mailing lists for direct mail.[10]

[10] See Bob Stone, *Successful Direct Marketing Methods* (Chicago: Crain Books, 1975), pp. 57–63.

227

We are now ready to examine the problem of forecasting the future demand for a product. Very few products or services lend themselves to easy forecasting. The few cases generally involve a product whose absolute level or trend is fairly constant and where competitive relations are nonexistent (public utilities) or stable (pure oligopolies). In the vast majority of markets, market demand and especially company demand are not stable from one year to the next, and good forecasting becomes a key factor in company success. Poor forecasting can lead to overly large inventories, costly price markdowns, or lost sales because the product is out of stock. The more unstable the demand, the more critical is forecast accuracy, and the more elaborate is forecasting procedure.

Forecasting methods range from the crude to the highly sophisticated. Many technical aspects fall in the province of experts. Yet there are compelling reasons why marketing managers should be familiar with the major alternative forecasting methods. This familiarity is necessary in order to understand the limitations of the current methods as well as whether better methods are available. Furthermore, forecasting is influenced by marketing planning, requiring a continuous dialogue between marketing managers and company forecasters. This dialogue is aided considerably when marketing managers understand the basic forecasting techniques.

Six major methods of forecasting demand are discussed below.[11] The proliferation of forecasting methods should not be surprising, given the diversity of products, the variations in the availability, reliability, and types of information, and the variety of forecast objectives. Although six methods are discussed, there are actually only three information bases for building a forecast. The investigator can build the forecast on the basis of *what people say, what people do,* or *what people have done.*

The first basis—*what people say*—involves systematic determination of the opinions of buyers or of those close to them, such as salesmen or outside experts. It encompasses three methods: (1) surveys of buyer intentions, (2) composites of sales-force opinions, and (3) expert opinion. Building a forecast on *what people do* involves another method: (4) putting the product to a market test to provide indications of future buyer response. The final basis—*what people have done*—involves analyzing, with mathematical and statistical tools, records of past buying behavior, using either (5) time-series analysis or (6) statistical demand analysis.

Surveys of Buyer Intentions

Forecasting is essentially the art of anticipating what buyers are likely to do under a given set of conditions. This immediately suggests that a most useful source of information would be the buyers themselves. Ideally, a list of all potential buyers would be drawn up; each buyer would be approached, preferably on a face-to-face basis, and asked how much the company would buy of the stated product in the defined future time period under stated conditions. The buyers would also be asked to state what proportion of the total requirements would be

---

[11] For other classifications and discussions of forecasting methods, see *Forecasting Sales,* National Industrial Conference Board, Business Policy Study No. 106, 1963; Harry Deane Wolfe, *Business Forecasting Methods* (New York: Holt, Rinehart and Winston, 1966); and John C. Chambers, Satinder K. Mullick, and Donald D. Smith, "How to Choose the Right Forecasting Technique," *Harvard Business Review,* July–August 1971, pp. 45–74.

bought from the particular firm, or at least what factors would influence supplier choice. With this information, the firm would have an ideal basis for forecasting its sales.

Unfortunately, this method has a number of limitations in practice. Let us accept for the moment that the buyers could be identified and could and would convey valid information about their intentions. Would the value of this information be worth the cost of gathering it? In the case of consumer convenience goods, such as soda beverages, it would be prohibitively expensive to pay a personal call on every buyer. This objection is answered in part by taking a probability sample of consumers. The cost can also be reduced by substituting telephone or mail interviewing for personal interviewing.

Would the buyers freely report their intentions? In many situations buyers would not confide their buying intentions. A Defense Department official would not reveal how many atomic weapons will be purchased.

The value of this method would depend ultimately on the extent to which the buyers had clearly formulated intentions and then carried them out. The two areas where buyer-intention surveys have proved to be of some value are major consumer durable goods and industrial goods.

In regard to *major consumer durables,* such as automobiles, new housing, furniture, and appliances, several sampling services regularly produce reports on consumer buying intentions.[12] They ask some form of the question whether the consumer intends to buy within a stated period each of several different durables. In the past the question was usually worded:

Do you intend to buy an automobile within the next six months?
Yes _____   No _____   Don't know _____

While the proportion of automobile buyers tended to be higher for those reporting a purchase intention than for those who had not, the forecasting performance was far from satisfactory. It was believed that two problems were associated with the simple intention-to-buy (0, 1) scale: (1) some consumers who said they didn't intend to buy had a finite, though small, probability of buying, and (2) the "don't know" category had too many responses. Juster suggested the use of a *purchase-probability scale,* such as

---

.00	.10	.20	.30	.40	.50	.60	.70	.80	.90	1.00
No chance	Very slight possibility	Slight possibility	Some possibility	Fair possibility	Fairly good possibility	Good possibility	Probably	Very probably	Almost sure	Certain

---

[12] The consumer pollsters include the Survey Research Center at the University of Michigan, Sindlinger & Company of Norwood, Pa., The Conference Board, Inc., and the Commercial Credit Corporation. For a discussion, see "How Good Are Consumer Pollsters?" *Business Week,* November 9, 1969, pp. 108–10.

Juster showed, on the basis of a random sampling of 800 households, that the purchase-probability approach accounted for approximately twice the actual purchase variance for automobiles as the intention-to-buy approach.[13] In addition to this improvement of the basic question, the various surveys also inquire into the consumer's present and future personal finances, and expectations about the economy. The various bits of information are combined into a *consumer sentiment measure* (Survey Research Center) or a *consumer confidence measure* (Sindlinger). Consumer durable-goods producers subscribe to these indices in the hope of learning in advance of major shifts in consumer buying intentions so that they can adjust their production and marketing plans accordingly. These surveys of consumer buying intentions have proved useful, though not completely accurate, for short-range consumer-durable sales forecasting.

In the realm of *industrial buying*, intention surveys regarding plant, equipment, and materials have been carried out by various agencies. The two best-known capital-expenditures surveys are the one conducted by the U.S. Department of Commerce in collaboration with the Securities and Exchange Commission and the one conducted annually in the late fall by McGraw-Hill through its publication *Business Week*. Most of the estimates have been within a 10 percent error band of the actual outcomes. This is a good record, considering that the business investment component of national income is highly variable.

Various industrial firms find it useful to carry on their own survey of customer buying intentions:[14]

> National Lead's marketing research personnel periodically visit a carefully selected sample of 100 companies and interview the manufacturer's technical research director, sales manager, and purchasing director, in that order. The technical research director is asked about the rate of incorporation of titanium in the manufacturer's various products; the sales manager is questioned about the sales outlook for the company's products that incorporate titanium; and the purchasing director is queried about the total amount of titanium his company plans to purchase in relation to past purchases. On the basis of these interviews and supplementary information, National's marketing research department estimates the market demand for titanium and prepares a "most favorable" forecast and a "least favorable" forecast. There are also indirect benefits. National Lead's analysts learn of new developments and modes of thinking that would not be apparent through published information. Their visits also promote National's image as a company that is concerned about buyers' needs. Another advantage of this method is that it yields subestimates for various industries and territories in the process of building an aggregate estimate.

In summary, the appropriateness of the buyer-intentions survey method increases to the extent that (1) the buyers are few, (2) the cost of effectively reaching them is small, (3) they have clear intentions, (4) they follow out their original intentions, and (5) they are willing to disclose their intentions. As a result, it is of value for industrial products, for consumer durables, for product purchases where advanced planning is required, and for new products where past data do not exist.

[13] F. Thomas Juster, *Consumer Buying Intentions and Purchase Probability, An Experiment in Survey Design*, National Bureau of Economic Research, Occasional Paper No. 99 (New York: Columbia University Press, 1966).

[14] Adapted from *Forecasting Sales*, pp. 31–32.

Composite of Sales-Force Opinion

Where it is impractical to make direct buyer inquiries, the company may decide to ask its sales representatives for estimates. An example is the Pennwalt Corporation:

> In August, the field sales personnel are provided with tabulating cards to prepare their sales forecasts for the coming year. Individual cards are prepared for each product sold to each major customer, showing the quantity shipped to the customer in the previous six months. Each card also provides space in which the field salesmen post their forecasts for the coming year. Additional tab cards are also supplied for those customers who were not sold in the current six-month period but who were customers in the prior year; and finally, blank cards are provided for submitting forecasts of sales to new customers. Salesmen fill in their forecasts (on the basis of current prices) using their own informed judgment; in some divisions, they are also in a position to substantiate their forecasts by obtaining purchase estimates from their customers.[15]

Few companies use their sales force's estimates without some adjustments. In the first place, sales representatives are biased observers. They may be congenitally pessimistic or optimistic, or they may go to one extreme or another because of a recent sales setback or success. Furthermore, they are often unaware of larger economic developments and of marketing plans of their company that will influence future sales in their territory. They may understate demand so that the company will set a low sales quota.[16] They may not have the time or concern to prepare careful estimates.

In the light of these contaminating factors, why are sales-force estimates used at all? There is the possibility that the over-and-under errors may cancel out, leaving a good aggregate forecast. Or a consistent bias in the forecast of individual sales representatives may be recognized and an adjustment made in each before aggregating the individual sales forecasts.

The company may supply certain aids or incentives to the sales force to encourage better estimating. The sales representatives may receive a record of their past forecasts compared with their actual sales, and also a set of company assumptions on the business outlook. Some companies will summarize individual forecasting records and distribute them to the sales force. A tendency for sales representatives to produce ultraconservative estimates to keep down their sales quota can be countered by basing territorial advertising and promotional expenditures on each sales representative's estimate.

Assuming these biasing tendencies can be countered, a number of benefits can be gained by involving the sales force in forecasting. Being closest to the customers, sales representatives may have more knowledge or better insight into developing trends than any other single group. This is especially likely where the product is fairly technical and subject to a changing technology. Second, because of their participation in the forecasting process, the sales representatives may have greater confidence in the derived sales quotas, and this confidence may increase their incentive to achieve those quotas. Finally, a grass-roots forecasting procedure results in estimates broken down by product, territory, customer, and sales representative.

[15] Ibid., p. 25.

[16] However, see Jacob Gonik, "Tie Salesmen's Bonuses to Their Forecasts," *Harvard Business Review*, May–June 1978, pp. 116–23.

In summary, the appropriateness of the composite-of-sales-force opinion method increases to the extent that the sales representatives (1) are likely to be the most knowledgeable source of information, (2) are cooperative, (3) are unbiased or can be corrected in their biases, and (4) will derive some benefits from participating in the procedure.

Expert Opinion

Another method of forecasting involves tapping the opinion of well-informed persons other than buyers or company sales representatives, such as distributors or outside experts.

The automobile companies gather estimates of sales directly from their dealers. These estimates are subject to the same strengths and weaknesses as sales-force estimates: the dealers may not give the necessary attention to careful estimating; their perspective concerning future business conditions may be too narrow; and they may supply biased estimates to gain some immediate advantage.

Firms also resort to outside experts for estimates of future demand. A firm may use or buy general economic forecasts or special industry forecasts prepared outside of the firm. Or a firm may invite a group of experts to estimate the probability of a development, such as a new technology or a change in business conditions.

There are at least three ways to gather the judgments of a group of experts. They may meet as a committee and come up with a group estimate *(group discussion method)*. They may supply their separate estimates to a project leader who merges them into a single estimate *(pooled individual estimates method)*. They may supply individual estimates and assumptions that are reviewed by the project leader, revised, and followed by a second round of individual estimation, a third round, and so forth, until the assumptions and estimates converge *(Delphi method)*. The third method is becoming increasingly popular for developing market and technological forecasts.[17]

An interesting variant of the expert-opinion method has been used by Lockheed Aircraft Corporation.[18] A group of Lockheed executives pose as different major customers. In a hardheaded way, they evaluate Lockheed's offer in relation to competitors' offers. A decision on what and where to buy is made for each customer. The purchases from Lockheed are totaled and reconciled with an independent statistical forecast to become Lockheed's sales forecast.

The use of expert opinion has the following advantages: (1) forecasts can be made relatively quickly and inexpensively, (2) different points of view are brought out and balanced in the process, and (3) there may be no alternative if basic data are sparse or lacking. The main disadvantages are: (1) opinions are generally less satisfactory than hard facts, (2) responsibility is dispersed, and good and bad estimates are given equal weight, and (3) the method usually is more reliable for aggregate forecasting than for developing reliable breakdowns by territory, customer group, or product.

[17] See Norman Dalkey and Olaf Helmer, "An Experimental Application of the Delphi Method to the Use of Experts," *Management Science*, April 1963, pp. 458–67. Also see Roger J. Best, "An Experiment in Delphi Estimation in Marketing Decision Making," *Journal of Marketing Research*, November 1974, pp. 447–52.

[18] See, for example, Gerald A. Busch, "Prudent Manager Forecasting," *Harvard Business Review*, May–June 1961, pp. 57–64.

Market-Test Method

The usefulness of opinions, whether those of buyers, sales representatives, or other experts, depends upon the cost, availability, and reliability of this type of information. In cases where buyers do not plan their purchases carefully or are very erratic in carrying out their intentions or where experts are not very good guessers, a more direct market test of likely behavior is desirable. A direct market test is especially desirable in forecasting the sales of a new product or the likely sales of an established product in a new channel of distribution or territory. Where a short-run forecast of likely buyer response is desired, a small-scale market test is usually an ideal answer.[19]

Time-Series Analysis

As an alternative to costly surveys or market tests, some firms prepare their forecasts on the basis of a statistical-mathematical analysis of past data. The underlying logic is that past data are an expression of enduring causal relations that can be uncovered through quantitative analysis. They can be used to predict future sales. Thus forecasting becomes an exercise in adroit backcasting.

A time series of past sales of a product can be analyzed into four major temporal components.

The first component, *trend* (*T*), is the result of basic developments in population, capital formation, and technology. It is found by fitting a straight or gradually curved line through the time-series data. If the trend turns out to be statistically significant, then it becomes central in the preparation of a long-range forecast.

The second component, *cycle* (*C*), is seen in the wavelike movement of sales. Properly speaking, a cycle exists when the time series shows an undulation of a fairly constant amplitude and periodicity. Few if any business series exhibit pure cyclical behavior in this sense. Some, such as housing construction, hog sales, and pig-iron sales, exhibit approximate cyclical behavior. Many sales series are affected by swings in the level of general economic activity, which tends to be somewhat periodic. Isolation of the cyclical component can be useful in intermediate-range forecasting.[20]

The third component, *season* (*S*), refers to a consistent pattern of sales movements within the year. Although "season" suggests a distinct quarterly pattern induced by changes in the weather, it is used more broadly to describe any recurrent hourly, weekly, monthly, or quarterly sales pattern. The seasonal component may be related to weather factors, holidays, and/or trade customs. The seasonal pattern provides the investigator with a norm for forecasting short-range sales.

The fourth component, *erratic events* (*E*), includes strikes, blizzards, fads, riots, fires, war scares, price wars, and other disturbances. These erratic components have the effect of obscuring the more systematic components, and the problem becomes one of starting with the original "noisy" time series and separating the underlying systematic forces from the erratic.

Classical time-series analysis involves procedures for decomposing the original sales series (*Y*) into the components, *T*, *C*, *S*, and *E*. According to one model, these components interact linearly—that is, $Y = T + C + S + E$; ac-

[19] Market testing is discussed in chap. 13, pp. 334–40.

[20] The most careful methodology for isolating and studying cyclical movements is that developed by the National Bureau of Economic Research. Arthur F. Burns and Wesley C. Mitchell, *Measuring Business Cycles* (New York: National Bureau of Economic Research, 1946).

cording to another model, they interact multiplicatively—that is, $Y = T \times C \times S \times E$. The multiplicative model makes the more realistic assumption that the seasonal and cyclical effects are proportional to the trend level of sales. T is stated in absolute values, and C, S, and E are stated as percentages.

This is not the place to describe the methodology for decomposing a time series. The procedures are outlined in elementary business statistics textbooks.[21] The main caution is to avoid mechanical extrapolation. The forecast is not simply a matter of putting together systematic components but rather a creative and further act in itself. The systematic forces underlying past sales may not remain unchanged. Any one of the three components can take on a different form starting tomorrow; the past trend can be altered by the appearance of a competitive product; the cyclical pattern can be altered by new countercyclical government policies; the seasonal pattern can be altered by new counterseasonal company policies. A mechanical extrapolation ignores marketing plans, the effect of which has to be built into the final forecast. The impact of possible erratic forces can be conveyed by preparing an optimistic, pessimistic, and most likely forecast. The size of the forecast error band conveys to management a sense of how much confidence it can repose in the most likely forecast.

For a company with hundreds of items in its product line that wants to produce efficient and economical short-run forecasts, a newer time-series technique called *exponential smoothing* is available. In its simplest form, exponential smoothing requires only three pieces of information: this period's actual sales, Q_t; this period's smoothed sales, $\bar{Q}_t$; and a smoothing parameter, a. The sales forecast for next period's sales is given by

$$\bar{Q}_{t+1} = aQ_t + (1-a)\bar{Q}_t \tag{9-8}$$

where:

$\bar{Q}_{t+1}$ = sales forecast for next period
a = the smoothing constant, where $0 \leq a \leq 1$
Q_t = current sales
$\bar{Q}_t$ = smoothed sales

Suppose the smoothing constant is .4, current sales are $50,000, and smoothed sales are $40,000. Then the sales forecast is

$$\bar{Q}_{t+1} = .4(\$50,000) + .6(\$40,000) = \$44,000$$

In other words, the sales forecast is always between (or at an extreme of) current sales and smoothed sales. The relative influence of current and smoothed sales depends on the smoothing constant, here .4. Thus the sales forecast "tracks" actual sales.

For each of its products, the company determines an initial level of smoothed sales and a smoothing constant. The initial level of smoothed sales can

[21] See Ya-Lun Chou, *Statistical Analysis with Business and Economic Applications*, 2nd ed. (New York: Holt, Rinehart and Winston, 1975), chap. 2. For computer programs, see Julius Shiskin, *Electronic Computers and Business Indicators* (New York: National Bureau of Economic Research, 1957). For an application, see Robert L. McLaughlin, "The Breakthrough in Sales Forecasting," *Journal of Marketing*, April 1963, pp. 46–54.

be simply average sales for the last few periods. The smoothing constant, on the other hand, is derived by trial-and-error testing of different smoothing constants between zero and one to find the one that produces the best fit of past sales. The method can be refined to reflect seasonal and trend factors by adding two more constants.[22]

Statistical Demand Analysis

Time-series analysis treats past and future sales as a function of time, rather than of any real demand factors. Its main use is in markets where the underlying demand factors remain stable over time. Where this is not the case, it is much more desirable to try to discover the direct relationship between sales and real demand factors.

Numerous real factors, of course, affect the sales of any product. Statistical demand analysis is an attempt not to derive a complete set of factors but rather to discover the most important factors in the hope that they will explain a significant amount of the variations in sales. The factors most commonly analyzed are prices, income, population, and promotion.

The procedure consists of expressing sales (Y) as a dependent variable and trying to explain sales variation as a result of variation in a number of independent demand variables $X_1, X_2, \ldots, X_n$; that is,

$$Y = f(X_1, X_2, \ldots, X_n) \tag{9-9}$$

For example, Palda found that the following demand equation gave a fairly good fit to the historical sales of Lydia Pinkham's Vegetable Compound between the years 1908 and 1960:

$$Y = -3649 + .665X_1 + 1180 \log X_2 + 774X_3 + 32X_4 - 2.83X_5 \tag{9-10}$$

where:

Y = yearly sales in thousands of dollars
X_1 = yearly sales (lagged one year) in thousands of dollars
X_2 = yearly advertising expenditures in thousands of dollars
X_3 = a dummy variable, taking on the value 1 between 1908 and 1925 and 0 from 1926 on
X_4 = year (1908 = 0, 1909 = 1, and so on)
X_5 = disposable personal income in billions of current dollars[23]

The five independent variables on the right helped account for 94 percent of the yearly variation in the sale of Lydia Pinkham's Vegetable Compound between 1908 and 1960. To use it as a sales-forecasting equation for 1961, it would be necessary to insert figures for the five independent variables. Sales in 1960 should be put in X_1, the log of the company's planned advertising expenditures for 1961 should be put in X_2, 0 should be put in X_3, the numbered year corre-

[22] See Robert G. Brown, *Smoothing Forecasting, and Prediction of Discrete Time Series* (Englewood Cliffs, N.J.: Prentice-Hall, 1963). For another interesting method, the *Box-Jenkins method*, see Box-Jenkins, *Time Series Analyses, Forecasting and Control* (San Francisco: Holden-Day, 1970).

[23] Kristian S. Palda, *The Measurement of Cumulative Advertising Effects* (Englewood Cliffs, N.J.: Prentice-Hall, 1964), pp. 67-68.

sponding to 1961 should be put in X_4, and estimated 1961 disposable personal income should be put in X_5. The result of multiplying these numbers by the respective coefficients and summing them gives a sales forecast (Y) for 1961.

Basically, demand equations are derived by trying to fit the "best" equation to historical or cross-sectional data. The coefficients of the equation are estimated according to the *least squares* criterion. According to this criterion, the best equation is one that *minimizes the sum of the squared deviations of the actual from the predicted observations.* The equation can be derived through the use of standard formulas. The closer the fit, the more useful the equation, all other things being equal.

With the advent of high-speed computers, statistical demand analysis is becoming an increasingly popular approach to forecasting. The user, however, should be wary of five problems that might diminish the validity or usefulness of any statistical demand equation: (1) too few observations, (2) too much correlation among the independent variables, (3) violation of normal distribution assumptions, (4) two-way causation, and (5) emergence of new factors not accounted for.[24]

SUMMARY

No firm can conduct its business successfully without trying to measure the actual size of markets, present and future. Quantitative measurements are essential for the analysis of market opportunity, the planning of marketing programs, and the control of marketing effort. The firm may make many measures of demand, varying in the level of product aggregation, the time dimension, and the space dimension. In all its studies, however, the company should be clear about its demand measurement concepts, particularly the distinction between market demand and company demand, and the corollary concepts of forecasts and potentials.

Current demand may be estimated for the market as a whole or for various territories. In the latter case, the market-buildup method is commonly used for industrial goods and the index of buying power is commonly used for consumer goods.

For estimating future demand, the company may use one or any combination of at least six different forecasting methods: surveys of buyer intentions, sales-force estimates, expert opinions, market tests, time-series analysis, or statistical demand analysis. These methods vary in their appropriateness with the purpose of the forecast, the type of product, and the availability and reliability of data.[25]

**QUESTIONS
AND
PROBLEMS**

1. Two forecasters working for the same automobile manufacturer arrived at substantially different estimates of next year's demand. Does this variance imply that forecasting is largely guesswork?

2. A manufacturer of printing equipment makes estimates of sales by first asking the district sales managers for district forecasts. Describe how these initial forecasts may be refined at higher company levels to arrive at a final companywide forecast.

---

[24] For further discussion, see the author's *Marketing Decision Making: A Model-Building Approach* (New York: Holt, Rinehart and Winston, 1971), pp. 596–602.

[25] For further reading on contemporary methods of demand analysis, see G. David Hughes, *Demand Analysis for Marketing Decisions* (Homewood, Ill.: Richard D. Irwin, 1973).

3. A beverage company wants to use multiple regression to determine what factors explain state-to-state variations in the consumption of soft drinks. (a) What independent variables should be tested? (b) If the fitted regression equation "explains" most of the state-to-state variation in sales, does it follow that it is a good device for indicating relative market potential by state?

4. A manufacturer of women's hair products (home permanents, hair rinses, shampoos, etc.) wanted to determine the relative market potential for its products in each county of the United States. What three or four factors are most likely to belong in a weighted index of potential?

5. A marketing researcher sought a multiple regression equation to explain past sales in an industry. Good industry data on the dependent and independent variables only went back five years. He fitted the following equation:

$$Y = 5,241 + 31X_1 + 12X_2 + 50X_3$$

where:

Y = yearly sales in thousands of dollars
X_1 = U.S. disposable personal income in billions of dollars
X_2 = U.S. population in millions of households
X_3 = time, in years (1960 = 0)

He was pleased to find that this equation accounted for 98 percent of the yearly variations in industry sales. List any reservations you would have about using this equation in forecasting future industry sales.

6. A chemical company wants to estimate the demand for sulphur next year. One of the many uses of sulphur is the manufacture of sulphuric acid, one of whose end uses is its application in polishing new cars. Automaker C is a customer of this manufacturer. Suggest the ratios that have to be linked to go from automaker C's new car production to its impact on the company's sulphur sales.

7. Suppose a company's past sales are: 10, 12, 15, 12, 11, 13, 18, 20. The company forecaster uses an exponential smoothing equation with $a = .4$ and initial $\bar{Q}_t = 10$. Estimate the exponentially smoothed sales that would have been predicted for the third period on.

8. An automotive manufacturer is attempting to develop a sales forecast for next year. The company forecaster has estimated demand for six different environment-strategy combinations:

	SALES FORECASTS		
	HIGH MARKETING BUDGET	MEDIUM MARKETING BUDGET	LOW MARKETING BUDGET
Recession	15	12	10
Normal	20	16	14

He believes that there is a .20 probability of recession and an .80 probability of normal times. He also believes the probabilities of a high, medium, and low company marketing budget are .30, .50, and .20, respectively. How might he arrive at a single point forecast? What assumptions are being made?

9. A motorboat company based in Washington state is considering opening up additional retail outlets in several counties on the Columbia River and Puget Sound. Using

market opportunity indexes, recommend in which counties the outlets should be located.

COUNTY	POPULATION	SALES OF MOTORBOATS (IN DOLLARS)	SALES OF COMPANY'S BOATS (IN DOLLARS)
Clark	161,300	2,800,000	186,200
Klickitat	13,400	140,000	38,000
Cowlitz	72,000	455,000	72,000
Snohomish	261,700	2,835,000	361,000
Pacific	16,200	1,750,000	836,000
Skagit	56,200	2,310,000	155,800
Total in State	3,583,400	35,000,000	3,800,000

Planning Marketing Strategy

3

Marketing Planning

Plans are nothing; planning is everything.
DWIGHT D. EISENHOWER

We are now ready to examine how an organization can efficiently develop plans and strategies for serving its markets. No organization will thrive simply through reacting to each new development as it occurs. Taking ad hoc initiatives will only result in inconsistent actions and uncontrolled expenditures, leaving the organization vulnerable to more-forward-planning competitors. Each organization must take a planned approach to the marketplace.

The four chapters in Part III will deal with the larger issues in planning, to be followed by several chapters in Part IV dealing with the individual elements of the marketing mix. This chapter examines the nature and role of marketing planning as a key element in effective marketing. Chapter 11 analyzes specific marketing strategies that are used by market leaders, aggressors, followers, and nichers. Chapter 12 discusses the tailoring of marketing strategies to the different stages of the life cycle through which a product passes. Finally, Chapter 13 deals with the company's need to find and successfully launch new products and services to replace those approaching the end of their product life cycle.

Many questions arise in connection with marketing planning. What are the stages through which business- and marketing-planning systems evolve? What is the nature and content of a marketing plan? What is the theory of effective marketing planning? We shall address each of these questions in this chapter.

EVOLUTION OF BUSINESS PLANNING

Business planning is a relatively new development in the corporate world. Businesses appear to pass through four stages on their way to sophisticated planning. Various companies today can be found in each of these stages.

Unplanned Stage

When businesses first get started, their managers are so busy hunting for funds, customers, equipment, and materials that they have no time for planning. Management is totally engrossed in the day-to-day operations required for survival. There is no planning staff and little time to plan.

Budgeting-system Stage

Eventually management recognizes the need to develop and install a budgeting system to facilitate orderly financing of company growth. An estimate is made by management of total sales for the coming year and the expected costs and cash flows associated with this sales level. Each departmental manager prepares a budget for carrying out the department's work for the coming year. These budgets are essentially financial and do not require the thought that goes into real business planning. Budgets are not to be confused with plans.

Annual-planning Stage

Management eventually turns to planning, usually annual planning. To carry this out, management adopts one of three basic approaches. The first is *top-down planning*, so called because top management sets *goals* and *plans* for all the lower levels of management. This model is taken from military organizations where the generals prepare the plans and the troops carry them out. In commercial organizations it goes along with a Theory X view of employees—that they dislike work and responsibility and prefer to be directed.[1]

The second system is *bottom-up planning*, so called because the various units of the organization prepare their own goals and plans, based on the best they think they can do, and send them to upper management for approval. This style is based on Theory Y thinking about human nature—that employees like work and responsibility and are more creative and committed if they participate in the planning and running of the enterprise.

Most companies use a third system known as *goals-down–plans-up planning*. Here top management takes a broad look at the company's opportunities and requirements and sets corporate goals for the year. The various units of the company are responsible for developing plans designed to help the company reach these goals. These plans, when approved by top management, become the official annual plan. A typical example is afforded by the Celanese Company:

> The annual planning process starts in late August, with top management receiving marketing research reports and sending out a guidance letter stating overall volume and profit goals. During September and October, product planning managers develop overall marketing plans in consultation with the field sales manager and the marketing vice president. In the middle of October, the marketing vice president reviews and approves the plans and submits them to the president for final approval. In the meantime, the field sales manager works with his regional sales managers and salesmen to develop field sales plans. Finally, in the fourth week in October, the controller prepares an operating budget; it goes, in early

[1] Douglas McGregor, *The Human Side of Enterprise* (New York: McGraw-Hill Book Company, 1960).

November, to top management for final approval. Thus, three months after the planning process started, a completed plan and budget are ready to be put into operation.[2]

Annual-planning systems may take several years before they work successfully. Initially, several of the executives will resist having to draft plans for their operations. Their resistance is based on: (1) not wanting to commit themselves in advance to goals and strategies in a rapidly changing environment; (2) resenting the time-consuming nature of preparing plans when they can be doing "more important" things; and (3) thinking of planning as something to satisfy higher levels of management rather than seeing it as a personal tool for improving business performance. Therefore top management must give thought to an effective strategy for introducing a planning culture into the organization. Management needs a plan for planning and a plan for selling employees on the benefits of planning.

The prime requisite is that the president be sold on planning. The president will then see to it that the senior officers carry out their planning responsibilities. The officers should be encouraged to discuss the pros and cons of formal planning. The following arguments can be presented in favor of planning:

Encourages systematic thinking ahead by management.

Leads to a better coordination of company efforts.

Leads to the development of performance standards for control.

Causes the company to sharpen its guiding objectives and policies.

Results in better preparedness for sudden developments.

Brings about a more vivid sense in the participating executives of their interacting responsibilities.[3]

To facilitate the acceptance of planning, a planning officer should be hired. The planning officer meets with various executives to get their ideas about a planning system, designs a planning methodology, and tests it further with various executives until it seems ready to launch. After the design and calendar for planning is approved, this officer assists the executives in gathering information and writing their plans. The initial plans should be short and practical. Over the years, desirable elaborations will be added in phase with the executives' readiness to engage in more-sophisticated planning.

Strategic-planning Stage

In this stage, the planning system of the company takes on several elaborations in an effort to improve its overall effectiveness.

The major change is the addition of *long-range planning*. Management realizes that annual plans make sense only in the context of a long-range plan. In fact, the long-range plan should come first, and the annual plan should be a detailed version of the first year of the long-range plan. For example, managers at American Hospital Supply Company prepare a strategic five-year plan early in the year and an annual operating plan later in the year. The five-year plan is re-

[2] *The Development of Marketing Objectives and Plans: A Symposium* (New York: Conference Board, 1963), p. 38.

[3] See Melville C. Branch, *The Corporate Planning Process* (New York: American Management Association, 1962), pp. 48–49.

worked each year (called *rolling planning*) because the environment changes rapidly and requires an annual review of the long-run planning assumptions. The choice of five years for a planning horizon is somewhat arbitrary. Brand managers at the Henkel Company of Germany annually prepare a three-year plan. Executives at Xerox prepare intermediate and long-range plans as well as annual plans. A Xerox executive described Xerox as being on a continuous planning basis, by which he meant that some plan is being written or revised every day of the year.

A further development is that the various plans begin to take on a more *strategic character*. When a company first turns to planning, the planning documents are very simple: they are long on statistics and specific tactical actions and short on strategy. One often looks in vain for a clear statement of strategy. In more-advanced planning systems, the plan formats are constructed so as to require a section on strategy.

As the company gains experience with planning, an effort is made to *standardize the plan formats* so that higher management can make more valid comparisons among similar units. It is important that the plans written for different comparable units, such as divisions, product lines, products, or brands, follow the same or a similar format to permit intelligent comparison by higher management.

As the planning culture takes hold in the company, further improvements are introduced. Managers receive more training in the use of *financial analysis* and are required to justify their recommendations not in sales volume terms but in terms of contribution margin, cash flow, and rate of return on manageable assets. *Computer programs* are developed to help product managers examine the impact of alternative marketing plans and environmental assumptions on sales and profit. The managers are eventually asked to develop *contingency plans* in addition to main plans, showing how they would respond to unexpected but critical developments. These and other developments mark the emergence of a true strategic-planning culture in the firm.

THE NATURE OF A MARKETING PLAN

As a company's planning system evolves, there is increasing talk of "marketing planning and marketing plans." Unfortunately, no common usage attaches to these terms. Companies that are highly market oriented sometimes use the term "marketing plan" synonymously with the overall business plan; perhaps a better title would be "market-oriented business plan." In other companies, "marketing plan" is used to describe the section within the larger business plan that deals specifically with marketing issues and strategies, in contrast to the financial and manufacturing sections of the same plan. In still other companies, it is used to describe a special marketing document for attaining some marketing goal, such as a successful new-product launch or an orderly development of a new market.

Because of these varying usages, the term "marketing plan" may not be as useful as a more specific designation of the particular type of plan being discussed. There are at least eight different plans that require marketing input:

1. *Corporate plan.* The corporate plan describes the overall business plan for the corporation. It might be an annual, intermediate, or long-range plan. The corpo-

rate plan deals with company missions, growth strategies, portfolio decisions, investment decisions, and current objectives and goals. It does not contain details on the activities of individual business units.

2. **Divisional plan.** The divisional plan is similar to the corporate plan and describes the division's plan for growth and profitability. It describes marketing, financial, manufacturing, and personnel strategies and may use a short, intermediate, or long-run planning horizon. In some cases, the divisional plan is the sum of all the separate plans prepared within the division.

3. **Product-line plan.** A product-line plan describes objectives, goals, strategies, and tactics for a specific product line. Each product-line manager prepares this plan.

4. **Product plan.** A product plan describes objectives, goals, strategies and tactics for a particular product or product category. Each product manager prepares this plan.

5. **Brand plan.** A brand plan describes objectives, goals, strategies, and tactics for a specific brand within the product category. Each brand manager prepares a brand plan.

6. **Market plan.** A market plan is a plan for developing and serving a particular market. If the organization has market managers as well as product managers, the market managers would prepare these plans.

7. **Product/market plan.** A product/market plan is a plan for marketing a particular product or product line of the company in a particular industrial or geographical market. An example would be a plan by a bank to market its lending services to the real estate industry.

8. **Functional plan.** A functional plan is a plan for one of the major functions, such as marketing, manufacturing, manpower, finance, or research and development. It also describes plans for subfunctions within a major function, such as, in the case of marketing, an advertising plan, a sales promotion plan, a sales-force plan, and a marketing research plan.

As noted earlier, most of these plans have a marketing component. In fact, the marketing component not only is essential but usually takes priority in the plan's development. Planning often starts with the question, How great a sales volume can we hope to obtain at a profit? This step is answered by marketing analysis and the development of a marketing plan. After this plan is approved, the nonmarketing executives start working on their manufacturing, financial, and personnel plans to support the marketing plan. Thus the marketing plan is a foundation for the planning of the other activities of the company.

THE COMPONENTS OF A MARKETING PLAN

How does a marketing plan look? A review of the planning formats used by various companies quickly reveals great variations in the topics included and in the sequence of topics addressed by the planner. Each company develops a format that reflects the planning capability of its executives, their tolerance for short or long plans, and the special topics that must be emphasized in that industry.

In spite of the variation, however, certain basic topics should find their way into every plan. We shall focus on product or brand plans in our discussion. A product or brand plan should contain the following sections: *executive summary, situation analysis, objectives and goals, strategy statement, action programs, budgets,* and *controls.*

Executive Summary   The plan should open with a one- or two-page summary of the main facts and recommendations contained within the plan. Here is an abbreviated example:

> The 1981 Marketing Plan seeks to generate significant increases in corporate sales and profits, in comparison to the previous year's achievements. The sales target is set at $80,000,000, which represents a planned 20 percent sales gain in comparison to last year. This increase is deemed to be attainable because of the improved economic, competitive, and distribution picture. The operating margin is forecast at $8,000,000, which represents a 25 percent increase in comparison with last year. To achieve these goals, the sales promotion budget will amount to $1,600,000, which amounts to 2 percent of projected sales. The advertising budget will amount to $2,400,000, which represents 3 percent of projected sales. . . . [More detail follows.]

The purpose of the executive summary is to permit higher management to grasp quickly the major thrust of each plan and then read further in search of the information that is most critical in evaluating the plan. To facilitate this, a table of contents should follow the executive summary.

Situation Analysis   The first major section of the plan is the *situation analysis* (also called "current situation" or "where we stand"). In this section, the manager describes the major features of the situation facing his or her operation that must be addressed by the subsequent objectives, strategies, and actions. The situation-analysis section itself can be usefully divided into four sections—background, normal forecast, opportunities and threats, and strengths and weaknesses—to encourage a systematic situation appraisal by the manager.

Background   This section usually starts with a summary of key sales and profit data for the last several years. An example of five years of past data is shown in Table 10–1.[4]
Row 1 shows that the market volume is growing at 200,000 units a year. Row 2 shows that the company's brand rose from a 6 percent share to a fairly stable 10 percent share. Row 3 shows that the product's price of $2 has been increasing recently. Row 4 shows that variable cost per unit originally declined but has been increasing recently. Row 5 shows that the gross contribution margin per unit—the difference between price (row 3) and unit variable cost (row 4)—first increased and then decreased in the most recent year. Rows 6 and 7 show sales volume in both units and dollars, and row 8 shows the total gross contribution margin. Row 9 shows a stable and then rising level of overhead. Row 10 shows net contribution margin, that is, gross contribution margin less overhead. Rows 11 and 12 show advertising and distribution expenses, respectively. Finally, row 13 shows net operating profit after marketing expenses. The picture is one of growing sales, with profits, however, growing at a slower rate. These data should be followed by a description of noteworthy facts and trends about the market, distributors, and competitors. The market description should include the definition of the served market, major market segments, market size and trends, and buyer behavior. The distribution section should describe the major features and trends occurring in distribution. In the case of competitors, their

---

[4] For another example, see the case, "Concorn Kitchens," in Harper W. Boyd, Jr., and Robert T. Davis, *Marketing Management Casebook* (Homewood, Ill.: Richard D. Irwin, 1971), pp. 125–36.

TABLE 10–1
Historical Product Data

VARIABLE	COLUMNS	1975	1976	1977	1978	1979
1. Market—total units		1,000,000	1,200,000	1,400,000	1,600,000	1,800,000
2. Share		.06	.08	.10	.10	.10
3. Price per unit $		2.00	2.00	2.00	2.20	2.40
4. Variable cost per unit $		1.20	1.10	1.10	1.30	1.55
5. Gross contribution margin per unit $	(3 − 4)	.80	.90	.90	.90	.85
6. Sales volume in units	(1 × 2)	60,000	96,000	140,000	160,000	180,000
7. Sales $	(3 × 6)	120,000	192,000	280,000	352,000	432,000
8. Gross contribution margin $	(5 × 6)	48,000	86,400	126,000	144,000	153,000
9. Overhead $		20,000	20,000	20,000	30,000	30,000
10. Net contribution margin $	(8 − 9)	28,000	66,400	106,000	114,000	123,000
11. Advertising $		8,000	12,000	15,000	18,000	20,000
12. Distribution $		4,000	8,000	15,000	15,000	20,000
13. Net operating profit $	(10 − 11 − 12)	16,000	46,400	76,000	81,000	83,000

market shares, strategies, and strengths and weaknesses should be described. Some of the factors explaining the most recent sales and profit results should be presented.

Normal forecast   The background should be followed by a forecast of market size and company sales under "normal conditions," that is, assuming no major changes in the *marketing environment* or *marketing strategies*. This forecast could be obtained in a number of ways. The simplest method is straightforward extrapolation of past growth rates of market size and company sales. For example, the market volume in Table 10–1 for the coming year can be forecast at 2,000,000 units, on the assumption that the 200,000 annual increase continues. Market share can be assumed to stay at 10 percent. Prices can be expected to rise by, say, twenty cents. Another method is to forecast the economy and other major variables affecting sales and then use a regression equation to forecast sales. Still another method is to gather sales-force estimates of what they expect to sell next year. Most companies use more than one method and take some average of the estimates.

The forecast would have to be revised if quite different environmental conditions are expected or strategies are planned. If the forecast does not satisfy higher management, the product or brand manager would have to consider new strategies, hoping to find one that promises a higher level of sales and profits.

Opportunities and threats   The normal forecast section should be followed by a section in which the manager identifies the main opportunities and threats facing the business unit. Usually the manager is aware of a number of these but should be challenged to put them into words. Higher management can review this list and raise questions about factors that are listed or missing. At year end, higher management can review the earlier list of opportunities and threats and see how many of them materialized and what actions were taken.

Table 10–2(A) shows the opportunities and threats listed by a product-line manager in charge of a company's line of television sets. The opportunities and threats describe *outside* factors facing the business unit. They are written so as to suggest some possible actions that might be warranted. The manager may be asked to list the opportunities and threats in order of importance, as an indicator of which deserve the most attention and planning.

TABLE 10–2(A)
Major Opportunities and Threats in the Television Business

Opportunities
1. There is a growing market for life-size home television. We should give thought to entering this market and attempting to establish leadership.
2. Our dealer coverage in the South is thin, although consumer preference for our brand is high.
3. The federal government is getting ready to slap a quota on foreign television sets.

Threats
1. Many consumers are shifting to lower-price brands. We may have to lower prices on our existing line or introduce some new lower-cost models.
2. The cost of cabinet wood is expected to jump 15 percent in the coming year. We may have to find new, substitute exterior materials.
3. The federal government may pass a more stringent product-safety law. This would necessitate some product redesign.

TABLE 10–2(B)
Strengths and Weaknesses of the Television Company

Strengths
1. Ninety-five percent of consumers know our brand. This awareness level is the highest in the industry.
2. Forty percent of consumers believe our brand to be the most reliable one in the industry. No one brand comes close to this.
3. Our dealers are the best trained in the industry in terms of knowledge and salesmanship.

Weaknesses
1. Our brand is considered high in price relative to other brands, and it loses the price-conscious buyer. Pricing strategy should be reevaluated.
2. The quality of the picture is no longer the best in the industry. We need to invest more in research and development.
3. Our advertising campaign is not particularly creative or exciting. We may want to consider switching advertising agencies.

Strengths and weaknesses   In this section of the plan the manager lists the main internal strengths and weaknesses of the business unit (see Table 10–2(B)). The list of strengths has implications for strategy formulation, while the list of weaknesses has implications for investments to correct weaknesses. Higher management can raise important questions about the business units based on the manager's list of strengths and weaknesses.

Objectives and Goals

The situation analysis points out where the business stands and where it might go. The next task now is to develop a statement about where the business should go. Management has to set specific objectives and goals that will be accepted by higher management.

Higher management typically defines overall goals for the coming period for the corporation as a whole. The top management of an electronics firm may state that they want the company to achieve (1) a 15 percent growth in sales volume, (2) a pretax profit of 20 percent on sales, and (3) a pretax profit of 25 percent on investment. Within this context, each business-unit manager develops goals that will support the corporate goals. Those business units that are in a good market situation will be expected to adopt even more ambitious goals than the corporate goals. Those in difficult markets will adopt more modest goals. Top management wants to "stretch" each business unit to its maximum potential level.

Assume that the managers of the television product line in this company see the key need to be that of increasing the profitability of the line. Suppose the line's current return on investment (ROI) is 10 percent, and higher management wants the television line to yield 15 percent. That can be accomplished by (1) increasing the sales revenue, (2) decreasing the cost (or not increasing it by as much as the higher sales revenue), and (3) decreasing the investment (or not increasing it by as much as the increase in profit). Any or all of these can be adopted as objectives for the coming period.

The objectives the manager decides to emphasize can be turned into goals, that is, given magnitudes and target dates. The manager might propose the following goals for attaining a 15 percent ROI in the television line: (1) attain a 12 percent increase in sales revenue for the coming year, (2) increase the expense budget by 8 percent for the coming year, and (3) hold the investment level constant for the coming year.

Strategy Statement

In this section of the plan, the manager formulates an overall strategy that will achieve the stated goals. To overcome the tendency toward tunnel vision, the manager should be requested to list some alternative marketing strategies. Unfortunately, many managers tend to avoid thinking deeply about alternative strategies. According to a study reported by Ames:

> In one company when each planner was asked by top management to outline alternative strategies . . . the request drew a complete blank. The planners were so locked into their accustomed way of thinking about their markets that they could not conceive of a different approach that made any commercial sense at all.[5]

[5] B. Charles Ames, "Marketing Planning for Industrial Products," *Harvard Business Review,* September–October 1968, p. 103.

A marketing strategy is not a collection of specific actions but rather a statement that indicates where major efforts should be directed in order to attain the goals. The strategy is made up of elements that can be generated by a further analysis of each objective.

For example, the objective "increase the sales revenue" can be broken down into three subobjectives. Sales revenue can be increased by (1) increasing the average price on all units, (2) increasing the overall sales volume, and (3) managing to sell more of the higher-price units. Each of these points can be examined further. For example, the overall sales volume can be increased by (1) increasing market growth and (2) increasing market share. In turn, increased market growth can come about by convincing people (1) to own more television sets per household and/or (2) to replace their old sets more frequently. By going down the path of each objective and its constituents, the manager will be able to identify in a systematic manner the major strategy opportunities facing the product line. Presumably the manager will choose the strategy that promises to produce the best results. The manager should state the basic strategy as clearly and succinctly as possible. For example:

Our basic strategy for producing higher profit will be to lengthen the product line by adding some lower-price units at the lower end and some expensive units at the high end. The average price of the existing brands will be raised moderately. A new advertising campaign will be developed to further build the perceived superiority of our brand in the consumers' minds, with much emphasis on the higher-price units. New dealerships will be opened in our weaker areas. Dealers will receive a new high-impact training program.

In developing the strategy, the manager will want to discuss it with others whose cooperation will make the difference between failure and success. He or she will see the purchasing and manufacturing people to make sure that they are able to buy enough material and produce enough goods to meet the planned sales volume levels, the sales manager to make sure of obtaining the planned sales-force support, and important dealers to make sure that they will cooperate.

Action Program

The strategy statement represents the broad outline of how the manager hopes to accomplish the stated goals. The broad outline must be filled in with specific actions (also called tactics). A useful approach is to take each strategy element and make it someone's responsibility. For example, improving the advertising campaign might be assigned to Jane Jones, advertising manager. Jones should then proceed to list the various actions required to carry out the strategy, such as inviting proposals for competing advertising agencies, selecting the best agency, approving the final copy, and approving the media plan. Each activity is assigned to someone in the advertising department along with a completion date. This format would be repeated for each strategy element.

The overall action plan may take the form of a matrix, with the twelve months (or fifty-two weeks) of the year serving as columns and various marketing activities serving as rows. Dates can be entered when various activities or expenditures will be started, reviewed, and completed. This action plan is subject to change during the year as new problems and opportunities arise, but it serves as a general implementation framework for tactics.

Budgets The goals, strategies, and planned actions allow the manager to formulate a supporting budget statement for the operation. The budget statement is essentially a projected profit-and-loss statement.[6] On the revenue side, it shows the forecasted number of units that would be sold and the average net realized price. On the expense side, it shows the costs of production, physical distribution, and marketing, broken into finer categories. The difference, or projected profit, is shown. In some companies, managers prepare alternative budgets for high and low levels of realized sales. Management reviews the budget and either approves or asks for modifications. Once approved, the budget is the basis for material procurement, production scheduling, manpower planning, and marketing operations.

Controls The last section of the plan deals with the controls that will be applied to monitor the plan's progress. Normally the budget is spelled out for each month or quarter. This means that higher management can review the results each period and spot those businesses that are not attaining their goals. Managers of lagging businesses are asked to cite the new factors in the picture and the actions they are taking to improve plan fulfillment. Higher management usually resists lowering the sales and profit goals and instead recommends shifts or reductions of certain expenditures.

Some control sections require the manager to identify major contingencies and to state what steps would be taken in the event of each contingency. A contingency plan is not a complete plan but rather an outline of some steps that the manager would consider. The purpose of a contingency plan is to encourage the manager to face up to the most important challenges that might occur and to give prior thought to response strategies.

THE THEORY OF EFFECTIVE MARKETING RESOURCE ALLOCATION

We are now ready to examine more closely the task of developing an optimal marketing plan. Effective marketing planning calls for finding the relationships between different levels, types, and allocations of marketing resources and the corresponding impact on sales and profits. An effective marketing manager will utilize these relationships in preparing marketing plans. Assume that John Smith is a product manager at a large company and is preparing his annual plan. He has data on the product's recent history, the economic outlook, competitors' strategies, plant capacity, forecasted raw material costs, and other important variables. He has given some preliminary thought to the situation analysis, objectives and goals, and marketing strategy, and is at the point of trying to develop specific budget numbers. *With what budget item(s) should he start?* Should he start by estimating sales? Costs? Profits? At least three approaches are used by product managers in practice.

Profit and Sales Equations Before describing these approaches, we will introduce two tools—a *profit equation* and a *sales equation*. These equations can be used for the double purpose of sales planning and profit planning.

[6] For an example, see chap. 24, p. 640.

The profit equation The profit equation is developed in the following way. Profits (Z) by definition are equal to the product's revenue (R) less its costs (C):

$$Z = R - C \tag{10-1}$$

Revenue is equal to the product's net price (P') times its unit sales (Q):

$$R = P'Q \tag{10-2}$$

But the product's net price (P') is equal to its list price (P) less any allowance per unit (k) representing freight allowances, commissions, and discounts:

$$P' = P - k \tag{10-3}$$

The product's costs can be conveniently classified into unit variable non-marketing costs (c), fixed costs (F), and marketing costs (M):

$$C = cQ + F + M \tag{10-4}$$

Substituting equations (10–2), (10–3), and (10–4) into (10–1) and simplifying,

$$Z = [(P - k) - c]Q - F - M \tag{10-5}$$

where:

Z = total profits
P = list price
k = allowance per unit (such as freight allowances, commissions, discounts)
c = production and distribution variable cost (such as labor costs, delivery costs)
Q = number of units sold
F = fixed costs (such as salaries, rent, electricity)
M = discretionary marketing costs

The expression $[(P - k) - c]$ is the *gross contribution margin per unit*—the amount the company realizes on the average unit after deducting allowances and the variable costs of producing and distributing the average unit. The expression $[(P - k) - c]Q$ is the *gross contribution margin*—the net revenue available to cover the fixed costs, profits, and discretionary marketing expenditures.

The sales equation In order to use the profit equation for planning purposes, the product manager will need to develop an understanding of the determinants of sales volume (Q). The relation of sales volume to its determinants is specified in a sales equation (also called the *sales volume equation*, or *sales response function*):

$$Q = f(X_1, X_2 \ldots, X_n, Y_1, Y_2, \ldots, Y_m) \tag{10-6}$$

where:

$(X_1, X_2, \ldots, X_n)$ = sales variables under the control of the firm
$(Y_1, Y_2, \ldots, Y_m)$ = sales variables not under the control of the firm

Let us look at the Y variables first. They include such things as the cost-of-living index, the population size of the target market, and the market's average purchasing power. As these variables change, so does the buying rate of the target market. The manager has no influence over the Y variables but needs to estimate them and base the forecast partly on them. We shall assume that the manager has estimated the Y variables and their effect on sales volume, which is conveyed by:

$$Q = f(X_1, X_2, \ldots, X_n / Y_1, Y_2, \ldots, Y_m) \qquad (10\text{-}7)$$

which says that sales volume is a function of the X variables, for given levels of the Y variables.

The X variables are the variables that the manager can use to influence the sales level. The X variables include the list price (P), allowances (k), variable cost (C) (to the extent that high variable costs reflect improved product quality, delivery time, and customer service), and marketing expenditures (M). Thus sales, as a function of the manager's controllable variables, is described by:

$$Q = f(P, k, c, M) \qquad (10\text{-}8)$$

We can make one additional refinement. The marketing budget, M, can be spent in several ways, such as advertising (A), sales promotion (S), sales force (D), and marketing research (R).

The sales equation (or *marketing-mix equation*) (10–8) can be related as follows:

$$Q = f(P, k, c, A, S, D, R) \qquad (10\text{-}9)$$

where the elements in the parentheses represent the marketing mix elements.

Approaches to Developing Marketing Plans

We now are ready to contrast three approaches—sales volume planning, target profit planning, and profit-optimization planning—used by product managers to develop their plans.

Sales volume planning In this system, the product manager is told the target sales volume for the coming year. Higher management sets the sales goal on the basis of the economic outlook, the competitive picture, and the desire to run the plant at or near capacity. Sales volume planning is typically found in capital-intensive industries such as steel, autos, and chemicals where the task is to keep the equipment operating as much as possible and find ways to sell all of the output. The product manager may not even have much to say about the price that will be charged. In a few cases, the product manager will not even propose the marketing budget necessary to do the job, in that top management will develop a budget based on a conventional percentage of marketing expenditures to planned sales. The manager's main discretion comes in dividing the marketing budget among various elements of the marketing mix, such as advertising, sales promotion, and marketing research. He or she also determines or proposes how to allocate these expenditures among the different geographical and end-use markets for the product.

This system is also found in some consumer-packaged-goods companies. At Procter & Gamble, the brand manager is often given the sales volume goal, the product price, and the marketing budget, and his job is to produce and develop a plan (largely a promotion plan) for spending the budget in a way that will attain the planned sales. He usually does not even know the true profit being earned by the company on his own brand.

Target profit planning   In many companies, the product manager is responsible for proposing a marketing plan that promises to deliver a stated target level of profits. In some cases, the target profit level is set by higher management and it is the product manager's job to build a plan to achieve this level of profits. In other cases, the product manager proposes a target profit level that he or she believes will satisfy higher management, given the corporation's overall profit goal and the expected capacity of the product to contribute to profits.

Table 10–3 provides a realistic, though hypothetical, illustration of how a product manager at the Heinz Company makes up a marketing budget for the coming year. Heinz product managers are profit oriented rather than sales volume oriented in their marketing planning.

Let us assume that the product is ketchup. We will limit this illustration to the household market. The product manager first estimates the total market for ketchup for the coming year. An estimate can be formed by applying the recent growth rate of the market (6 percent) to this year's market size (23,600,000 cases). This forecasts a market size of 25,000,000 cases for next year. The product manager then forecasts Heinz's sales based on assuming the continuation of

---

TABLE 10–3
A Target Profit-Oriented Product Plan

1. *Forecast of total market* This year's total market (23,600,000 cases) × recent growth rate (6%)	25,000,000 cases
2. *Forecast of market share*	.28
3. *Forecast of sales volume* (2 × 3)	7,000,000 cases
4. *Price per case to distributor*	$4.45 per case
5. *Estimate of sales revenue* (3 × 4)	$31,150,000
6. *Estimate of variable costs* Tomatoes and spices ($.50) + bottles and caps ($1.00) + labor ($1.10) + physical distribution ($.15)	$2.75 per case
7. *Estimate of contribution margin to cover fixed costs, profits, and marketing* ([4–6] 3)	$11,900,000
8. *Estimate of fixed costs* Fixed charge $1.00 per case × 7 million cases	$7,000,000
9. *Estimate of contribution margin to cover profits and marketing* (7–8)	$4,900,000
10. *Estimate of target profit*	$1,900,000
11. *Amount available for marketing* (9–10)	$3,000,000
12. *Split of the marketing budget* Advertising Sales promotion Marketing research	$2,000,000 $ 900,000 $ 100,000

its past market share of 28 percent. Thus Heinz's sales *(Q)* are forecasted to be 7,000,000 cases.

Next, the product manager sets a distributor price of $4.45 per case *(P)* for next year based on such factors as this year's price, expected rises in cost, and expected competitors' prices. For simplicity, assume that there are no allowances *(k = 0)*. Then the planned sales revenue *(PQ)* will be $31,150,000.

The product manager then estimates next year's variable costs at $2.75 per case. This means that the contribution margin to cover fixed costs, profit, and marketing is $11,900,000. Suppose the company charges this brand with a fixed cost *(F)* of $1.00 a case, or $7,000,000. This leaves a contribution margin to cover profits and marketing of $4,900,000.

At this step, the product manager brings in the target profit goal. Suppose a profit level of $1,900,000 will satisfy higher management. It is usually some increase, say 5 to 10 percent, over this year's profit. He then subtracts the target profit from what remains of the contribution margin to learn that $3,000,000 is available for marketing. To summarize:

$$[(P - k) - c]Q - F - Z = M \qquad (10\text{--}10)$$

$$[(\$4.45 - 0) - \$2.75]\,7{,}000{,}000 - \$7{,}000{,}000 - \$1{,}900{,}000 = \$3{,}000{,}000$$

Thus, the marketing budget is not determined on independent grounds but rather as a residual amount coming out of a budget-planning process. The marketing budget is established, in effect, as the amount the company can "afford." This method is nothing other than an elaboration of the first of Joel Dean's four methods of setting the advertising budgeting, which he dubbed the affordable method.[7]

The product manager accepts this as the necessary or desirable marketing budget if it appears reasonable in relation to last year's marketing budget and the new sales target. If it appears inadequate to produce the desired level of sales, he may do one of a number of things. He may reduce the profit goal. He may try to negotiate for lower fixed charges to his operations. He may consider raising next year's price by more than the initial planned increase. Or he may press manufacturing to find a way to reduce or keep down the unit costs of producing his product.

The last step involves the product manager in splitting the marketing budget into its mix elements, such as advertising, sales promotion, and marketing research. (We will assume that the sales force will remain fixed in size and is part of fixed cost.) The split is normally based on the previous year's split and on how competitors are using their marketing budgets. Table 10–3 shows two-thirds of the money going for advertising, almost a third for sales promotion, and the remainder for marketing research.

Against this method of developing the marketing budget, several criticisms can be leveled. In the first place, the manager estimated sales before he estimated the marketing budget, which is justified only on the inadmissible assumption that the level of marketing expenditures does not affect sales! This assumption is inadmissible. If it were true, marketing expenditures either should not be budgeted or should be kept very low. Second, this approach calls upon

[7] See chap. 19, p. 498.

the product manager to find a "satisficing" plan, not an optimizing one. That is, the manager seeks the price and budget that will achieve a satisfactory profit level rather than maximize profits. Third, the manager set next year's price largely on the basis of covering expected cost increases rather than by considering price jointly with other marketing-mix variables. Markup pricing is normally not a logically defensible pricing method. Finally, the allocation of the marketing budget to the marketing-mix elements seems highly arbitrary.

Profit-optimization planning Profit optimization requires that the manager give explicit recognition to the relationship between sales volume and the various elements of the marketing budget as represented in the *sales equation*. We shall use the term *sales response function* to describe the relationship between sales volume and a particular element of the marketing mix. Specifically, *the sales response function forecasts the likely sales volume during a specified time period associated with different possible levels of a marketing-mix element, holding constant the other marketing-mix elements.* It should not be thought of as describing a relationship over time between the two variables. To the extent that managers have a good feel for the relevant sales response functions, they are in a position to formulate more effective marketing plans.

What are the possible shapes of sales response functions? Figure 10–1 shows some major possibilities. Part A shows the well-known relationship between price and sales volume, known as the Law of Demand. The relationship states that more sales will occur, other things being equal, at lower prices. The illustration shows a curvilinear relationship, although linear and other relationships are possible.

Figure 10–1B shows four possible shapes for the relationship between sales volume and the level of marketing expenditures. Marketing expenditure function (A) is the least plausible: it states that sales volume is not affected by the level of marketing expenditures. It would mean that the number of customers and their purchasing rates are not affected by sales calls, advertising, sales pro-

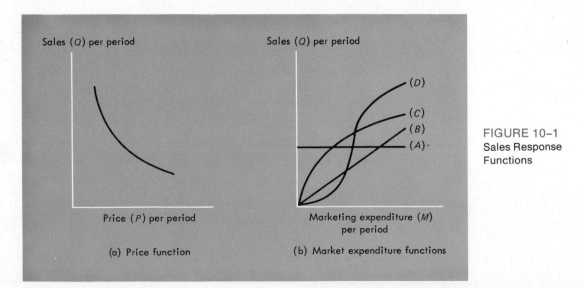

Sales (Q) per period

Sales (Q) per period

(D)
(C)
(B)
(A)·

Price (P) per period

Marketing expenditure (M) per period

(a) Price function

(b) Market expenditure functions

FIGURE 10–1
Sales Response
Functions

motion, or marketing research. Marketing expenditure function *(B)* states that sales volume grows linearly with the level of marketing expenditure. That is, $Q = a + bM$ where *a* is the intercept and *b* the slope, both to be estimated. In the illustration, the intercept is 0 but this is inaccurate if some sales would take place even in the absence of marketing expenditures.

Marketing expenditure function *(C)* is a concave function showing sales volume increasing throughout at a decreasing rate.[8] It is a plausible description of sales response to alternative-size sales forces. The rationale is as follows: If a field sales force consisted of one sales representative, that representative would call on the best prospects, and hence the marginal rate of sales response would be highest. A second sales rep would call on the next best prospects, and the marginal rate of sales response would be somewhat less. Successively hired sales reps would call on successively less responsive prospects, and this accounts for the continuously diminishing rate of sales increase.

Marketing expenditure function *(D)* is an S-shaped function showing sales volume initially increasing at an increasing rate and then increasing at a decreasing rate.[9] It is a plausible description of sales response to different levels of advertising expenditure.[10] The rationale is as follows: Small advertising budgets do not buy enough advertising to create more than minimal brand awareness. Larger budgets can produce high brand awareness, interest, and preference, all of which might lead to purchase response if the price and other things are right. Very large budgets, however, may not produce much additional response because the target market is already highly familiar with the brand.

The occurrence of eventually diminishing return to increases in marketing expenditures as shown in marketing expenditure functions *(C)* and *(D)* is plausible for a number of reasons. First of all, there tends to be an upper limit to the total potential demand for any particular product. The easier sales prospects are sold first; the more recalcitrant sales prospects remain. As the upper limit is approached, it becomes increasingly expensive to stimulate further sales. In the second place, as a company steps up its marketing effort, its competitors are likely to do the same, with the net result that each company experiences increasing sales resistance. In the third place, if sales were to increase at an increasing rate throughout, natural monopolies would result. A single firm would tend to take over in each industry because of the greater level of its marketing effort. Yet this is contrary to what we observe in industry.

How can a marketing manager estimate the sales response functions that apply to his business? Essentially, three methods are available. The first is the *statistical method,* where the manager gathers data on past sales and levels of marketing-mix variables and estimates the sales equation through standard statistical estimation procedures. Several researchers have done this with varying degrees of success, the success being related to the quantity and quality of avail-

---

[8] Mathematically, this concave function can be represented by a log function of the form $Q = a \log M$, a power function of the form $Q = aM^b$ (where $0 < b < 1$), or a modified exponential function of the form $Q = \overline{Q}(1 - e^{-aM})$. See Philip Kotler, *Marketing Decision Making: A Model Building Approach* (New York: Holt, Rinehart and Winston, 1971).

[9] Mathematically, this S-shaped function can be represented by a Gompertz function of the form $Q = \overline{Q}b^{cM}$ or a logistic function of the form $Q = \overline{Q}/1 + e^{-(a+bM)}$. See Kotler, *Marketing Decision Making.*

[10] However, see chap. 19, pp. 500–501.

able data and the seeming stability of the underlying relationships.[11] The second is the *experimental method*, which calls for deliberately varying the marketing expenditure and mix levels in matched samples of geographical or other units and noting the resulting sales volume.[12] The experimental method produces the most reliable results but is not used extensively enough because of its complex requirements, high cost, and inordinate level of management resistance. The third is the *judgmental method*, where experts are asked to estimate the needed magnitudes. This method requires a careful selection of the experts and a defined procedure for gathering and combining their estimates, such as the Delphi method.[13] The judgmental method is often the only feasible one, and under many circumstances it can be quite useful. We believe that getting informed estimates from experts is better than making no estimates at all.

In estimating sales response functions, some cautions have to be observed. The sales response function assumes that other variables remain constant over the range of the function. Thus the company's price and competitors' prices and marketing mix are assumed to remain unchanged, no matter what the company spends on marketing. Since this *ceteris paribus* condition is unrealistic, the sales response function would have to be modified to reflect competitors' probable responses. The sales response function also assumes a certain level of company efficiency in the expenditure of the marketing dollars. If the expenditure efficiency rises or falls, the sales response function would have to be modified accordingly. Also, the sales response function would have to be modified to reflect the delayed impacts of expenditures on sales beyond one year. These and other characteristics of sales response functions are spelled out in more detail elsewhere.[14]

Once the sales response functions are estimated, how are they used in profit optimization? Graphically, we must introduce some further curves to find the point of optimal marketing expenditure. The analysis is shown in Figure 10–2. The sales response function shown here is S-shaped, although the same analysis applies to any form. First the manager subtracts all nonmarketing costs from the *sales response function* to derive the *gross profit curve*. Next, marketing expenditures are drawn in such a way that a dollar on one axis is projected as a dollar on the other axis. This amounts to a 45-degree line when the axes are scaled in identical dollar intervals. The *marketing expenditures curve* is then subtracted from the *gross profit curve* to derive the *net profit curve*. The net profit curve shows positive net profits with marketing expenditures between M_L and M_U, which could be defined as the rational range of marketing expenditure. The net profit curve reaches a maximum at M. Therefore the marketing expenditure that would maximize net profit is $\$M$.

The graphical solution can alternatively be carried out in algebraic terms;

[11] For examples of fitted sales response functions, see Doyle L. Weiss, "Determinants of Market Share," *Journal of Marketing Research*, August 1968, pp. 290–95; Donald E. Sexton, Jr., "Estimating Marketing Policy Effects on Sales of a Frequently Purchased Product," *Journal of Marketing Research*, August 1970, pp. 338–47; and Jean-Jacques Lambin, "A Computer On-Line Marketing Mix Model," *Journal of Marketing Research*, May 1972, pp. 119–26.

[12] See Russell Ackoff and James R. Emshoff, "Advertising Research at Anheuser-Busch," *Sloan Management Review*, winter 1975, pp. 1–15.

[13] See the author's "A Guide to Gathering Expert Estimates," *Business Horizons*, October 1970, pp. 79–87.

[14] See the author's *Marketing Decision Making*.

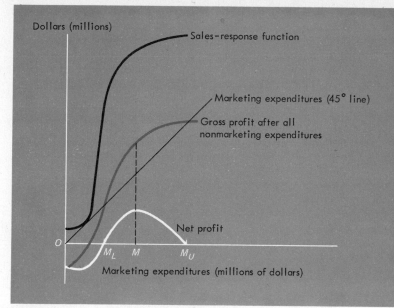

Dollars (millions)

Sales–response function

Marketing expenditures (45° line)

Gross profit after all
nonmarketing expenditures

Net profit

O

M_L M M_U

Marketing expenditures (millions of dollars)

FIGURE 10–2
Relationship Between Sales
Volume, Marketing Expenditures,
and Profits

indeed it has to be if the sales volume is a function of more than one marketing-mix variable. Here we will present a numerical example of how this is done.

A numerical example   Ms. Jones, a product manager, has been selling her product for some years using a low-price, low-promotion strategy. The current price is $16, and $10,000 is being spent on advertising and another $10,000 on sales promotion. Sales are around 12,000 units and profits around $14,000. Higher management considers this unimpressive. Ms. Jones is anxious to find a better strategy to increase profits.

Her first step is to generate a set of alternative marketing-mix strategies. She generates the eight strategies shown in the first three columns of Table 10–4

TABLE 10–4
Marketing Mixes and Estimated Sales

MARKETING MIX NO.	PRICE (P)	ADVERTISING (A)	PROMOTION (S)	SALES (Q)
1.	$16	$10,000	$10,000	12,400
2.	16	10,000	50,000	18,500
3.	16	50,000	10,000	15,100
4.	16	50,000	50,000	22,600
5.	24	10,000	10,000	5,500
6.	24	10,000	50,000	8,200
7.	24	50,000	10,000	6,700
8.	24	50,000	50,000	10,000

(the first strategy is the current one). They were formed by assuming a high and a low level of each of three marketing variables and elaborating all the combinations ($2^3 = 8$).

Her next step is to estimate the likely sales that would be attained with each alternative mix. She feels that the needed estimates are unlikely to be forthcoming through fitting past historical data or through conducting marketing-mix experiments. She decides to ask the sales manager for his estimates since he has shown an uncanny ability to be on target. Suppose he provides the sales estimates shown in the last column of Table 10–4.

The final step calls for determining which marketing mix maximizes profits, assuming the sales estimates are reliable. This calls for introducing a profit equation and inserting the different marketing mixes into this equation to see which maximizes profits.

Suppose fixed costs, F, are \$38,000; unit variable costs, c, are \$10; and the contemplated allowance off list price, k, is \$0. Then profit equation (10–5) reads:

$$Z = (P - 10)Q - 38,000 - A - S \qquad (10\text{–}11)$$

Profits are shown to be a function of the chosen price and the advertising and sales promotion budgets.

At this point the manager can introduce each marketing mix and estimated sales level (from Table 10–4) into this equation. The resulting profits are #1(\$16,400), #2(\$13,000), #3(−\$7,400), #4(−\$2,400), #5(\$19,000), #6(\$16,800), #7(−4,200), and #8(\$2,000). Marketing mix #5, calling for a price of \$24, advertising of \$10,000, and promotion of \$10,000, promises to yield the highest profits (\$19,000).

There is one more step the product manager can take. Some marketing mix not shown might yield a still higher profit. To check on this possibility, the product manager can fit a sales equation to the data shown in Table 10–4. The sales estimates in the table can be viewed as a sample from a larger universe of expert judgments concerning the sales equation $Q = f\ (P,A,S)$. A plausible mathematical form for the sales equation is the multiple exponential:

$$Q = bP^pA^aS^s \qquad (10\text{–}12)$$

where:

b = a scale factor
p,a,s = price, advertising, and promotion elasticity, respectively

Using least-squares regression estimation (not shown), the manager finds the fitted sales equation to be:

$$Q = 100,000P^{-2}A^{1/8}S^{1/4} \qquad (10\text{–}13)$$

This fits the sales estimates in Table 10–4 extremely well. Price has an elasticity of −2, that is, a 1 percent reduction in price, other things being equal, tends to increase unit sales by 2 percent. Advertising has an elasticity of ⅛, and promotion has an elasticity of ¼. The coefficient 100,000 is a scale factor that translates the dollar magnitudes into sales volume in units.

The product manager now substitutes this sales equation into the Q term in profit equation (10–11). This yields, when simplified:

$$Z = 100,000\, A^{1/8} S^{1/4}[P^{-1} - 10P^{-2}] - 38,000 - A - S \qquad (10\text{–}14)$$

Profits are strictly a function of the chosen marketing mix. The manager can insert any marketing mix (including those not shown in Table 10–4) and derive an estimate of profits. To find the profit-maximizing marketing mix, she applies standard calculus.[15] The optimal marketing mix (P,A,S) is ($20, $12,947, $25,894). Twice as much is spent on promotion as on advertising because its elasticity is twice as great. The product manager would forecast a sales volume of 10,358 units and profits of $26,735. While other marketing mixes can produce higher sales, no other marketing mix can produce higher profits. Using this equation, the product manager has solved not only the optimum marketing mix but also the optimum marketing budget $(A + S = \$38,841)$.

Having examined the procedure for identifying the profit-optimizing marketing mix, let us return to the Heinz example in Table 10–3. We saw that the Heinz product manager arrived at a marketing plan involving a price of $4.45, an advertising budget of $2,000,000, a sales promotion budget of $900,000, and a marketing research budget of $100,000. Instead of stopping at this point, he should develop some alternative marketing-mix strategies and attempt to forecast the probable sales volume associated with each strategy. He could do a financial analysis to find out which strategy promises the highest profit level. Or he could fit a sales equation to the estimates to capture the implied elasticities. The sales equation could then be incorporated into the profit equation, and the latter could be maximized to find the best marketing mix and expenditure.

To facilitate profit-optimization planning, some companies have designed computer programs for use by marketing managers to identify and assess the impact of alternative marketing plans on profits and sales. The marketing manager goes to a computer terminal, types in a request for the particular program, and then proceeds to build and test a marketing expenditure plan. One well-known computer program consists of four subprograms.[16] First the marketing manager requests the computer to retrieve and display the major statistics on the product for the last several years. This material is called the *historical base* and is similar to Table 10–1. He then instructs the computer to produce a *straightforward projection* of the major statistics for the next several years, using extrapolation. He then modifies any projections based on his own knowledge, and the result is called the *profit-and-loss planning base*. This shows a normal "extrapolated" level of marketing expenditures, price, and sales, and the resulting profits. If the projected profits are satisfactory, the marketing manager can stop here. However, a fourth subprogram called a *marketing plan simulator* is available for trying out alternative marketing plans and estimating their sales and profits. The simulator incorporates an estimated sales equation. The marketing manager tests alternative marketing plans until he finds a highly satisfactory one.

[15] The derivation is shown in the appendix of the author's "Marketing Mix Decisions for New Products," *Journal of Marketing Research*, February 1964, pp. 43–49.

[16] See Boyd and Davis, *Marketing Management Casebook*, pp. 125–36.

Long-run profit projection   Computer programs have also been designed to help marketing managers build and test long-run strategies for the development of a product or market. For example, the marketing manager may be asked to forecast, for a given product, the expected costs, prices, sales, profits, cash flow, and return on investment for the next several years as an indication of whether the particular product business should be built, maintained, harvested, or terminated. Table 10–5 shows the printout from one such computer program for a ready-to-eat cereal product.

The first line shows that this projection is for a seven-year planning horizon. Details then appear on the undepreciated value of plant and equipment devoted to this product, current opportunity cost, working capital, and expected terminal salvage value.

The rest of the printout shows the expected or planned year-to-year levels of important variables that ultimately affect the internal rate of return. Column 1 shows the retail price per unit, which is expected to rise from $.58 to $.70 in the course of seven years. Column 2 shows that the retail margin for this product (18 percent) is not expected to change. Column 3 shows the resulting wholesale prices. Since this company will sell direct to the retailers, there is no wholesale margin (column 4), and the factory price (column 5) is the same as the wholesale price.

Column 6 shows estimated variable manufacturing costs, and they too are expected to rise over the period, from a present level of $.19 to $.23 in 1982. The ratio of variable manufacturing costs to factory prices is shown in column 7, followed by the planned ratio of variable marketing costs to factory prices (column 8). Subtracting variable manufacturing and marketing costs per unit from the price, the result is the contribution to fixed costs and profits, which is shown in dollar and percentage form in columns 9 and 10 respectively.

The next step calls for estimating fixed manufacturing costs and fixed marketing costs over the next seven years, which are shown in columns 11 and 12. The symbol $E + 06$ is computer printout shorthand and means that the reader should move the decimal place, in the associated number, six places to the right. Thus $\$1.028E + 06$ means $1,028,000. Columns 13 and 14 show the anticipated investments in plant, equipment, and building over the next seven years, and column 15 shows the estimated total depreciation expense.

We now arrive at the estimated sales and profits. Columns 16 and 17 show management's estimates of sales (in percentage and in unit terms, respectively) over the next seven years. The figures indicate that management expects company sales (in units) to rise at the rate of about 10 percent a year, on the basis of its planned levels of marketing expenditures. Column 18 presents management's estimates of industry sales for the next seven years.

The figures in column 19, market share, are derived by dividing estimated company sales (column 17) by estimated industry sales (column 18). We see that management expects market share to grow from 2.6 percent to 3.8 percent over a seven-year period. Column 20 expresses total marketing expenditures (columns 8 and 12) as a percent of sales, and this percentage is expected to fall. Examining this more closely, we see that management expects sales to rise faster than marketing expenditures; hence it is assuming an increase in marketing productivity.

Columns 21 and 22 are a derivation of the implied yearly profits after taxes in percentage and dollar terms. The computer program uses the following formula to calculate dollar profits after taxes:

TABLE 10–5
Sample Printout from Computer System

```
                    TIME HORIZON = 7                        YEARS

        REMAINING UNDEPR. P&E INVEST. AT BEGIN. YR. 1 = 900000    DOLLARS
        REMAINING NO. OF YEARS OF P&E DEPRECIATION    = 3         YEARS
        REMAINING UNDEP. BLDG. INVEST. AT BEGIN. YR. 1 = 210000   DOLLARS
        REMAINING NO. OF YEARS OF BLDG. DEPRECIATION  = 21        YEARS

        DEPRECIATION HORIZON FOR P&E INVESTMENTS      = 10        YEARS
        DEPRECIATION HORIZON FOR BLDG. INVESTMENTS    = 30        YEARS

        OPPORTUNITY COST (AT BEGINNING OF PERIOD)     = 2.E+06    DOLLARS
                           WORKING CAPITAL            = 13        PCNT SALES
                SALVAGE VALUE (AT END OF PERIOD)      = 10        X EARNINGS
```

	1	2	3	4
YEAR	RET.PRICE ($)	RET.MAR.(PCNT)	WHOLE.PRICE($)	WHOLE.MAR.(PCNT)
1981	.577	18	.473	0
1982	.602	18	.494	0
1983	.621	18	.509	0
1984	.639	18	.524	0
1985	.659	18	.54	0
1986	.675	18	.554	0
1987	.698	18	.572	0

	5	6	7	8
	FACTORY	VARIABLE MAN.	VARIABLE MAN.	VARIABLE MKTG
YEAR	PRICE($)	COST($)	COST(PCNT)	COST(PCNT)
1981	.473	.191	40.4	5
1982	.494	.196	39.7	5
1983	.509	.202	39.7	5
1984	.524	.208	39.7	5
1985	.54	.214	39.6	5
1986	.554	.221	39.9	5
1987	.572	.227	39.7	5

	9	10	11	12
	CONTRIB. TO FIXED COSTS AND PROFIT		FIXED MAN.	FIXED MKTG.
YEAR	($)	(PCNT)	COST($)	COST($)
1981	.258	54.6	915000	4.25E+06
1982	.273	55.3	971000	4.9E+06
1983	.282	55.3	1.028E+06	5.5E+06
1904	.29	55.3	1.31E+06	5.75E+06
1985	.299	55.4	1.386E+06	6.25E+06
1906	.305	55.1	1.471E+06	6.85E+06
1987	.317	55.3	1.824E+06	7.6E+06

	13	14	15
YEAR	P&E INVEST.	BLDG. INVEST.	DEPREC. EXPENSE
1980	850000	0	
1981	0	0	395000
1982	0	0	395000
1983	850000	1.E+06	395000
1984	0	0	213333
1985	0	0	213333
1986	850000	1.E+06	213333
1987	0	0	331666

	16	17	18	19
	INDEX OF	COMPANY	INDUSTRY	MARKET
YEAR	COMPANY SALES	SLS(UNITS)	SLS(UNITS)	SHARE
1981	1	3.E+07	1.166E+09	2.6
1982	1.1	3.3E+07	1.182E+09	2.8
1983	1.2	3.6E+07	1.198E+09	3
1984	1.3	3.9E+07	1.215E+09	3.2
1985	1.4	4.2E+07	1.23E+09	3.4
1986	1.5	4.5E+07	1.247E+09	3.6
1987	1.6	4.8E+07	1.265E+09	3.8

	20	21	22	23
YEAR	MKTG. EXP. (PCNT SLS)	P.A.T. (PCNT SLS)	P.A.T.($)	CSH FLOW(A.T.)
1980				-2.85E+06
1981	34.9	7.7	1.097245E+06	-353001
1982	35.1	8.4	1.370807E+06	1.493337E+06
1983	35	8.8	1.610162E+06	-110272
1984	33.1	9.9	2.014062E+06	1.953967E+06
1985	32.5	10.4	2.361914E+06	2.281351E+06
1986	32.5	10.4	2.591395E+06	667228
1987	32.7	9.9	2.723974E+06	2.722089E+06

```
        CALCULATED INTERNAL RATE OF RETURN (AFTER TAXES) = 45        PCNT
```

SOURCE: Case material of the Harvard University Graduate School of Business Administration, prepared by Professors Derek Abell and Ralph Sultan, used by permission.

$$Z = (1 - t)(mQ - F - D) \qquad (10\text{-}15)$$

where:

Z = profits after taxes
t = tax rate
m = contribution margin to fixed costs and profit
Q = sales in units
F = fixed manufacturing and marketing costs
D = depreciation

For example, the profits after taxes for 1981 are

$$(1 - .4967)[(\$.258)(30,000,000) - \$5,165,000 - \$395,000] = \$1,097,245$$

Column 23 shows the results of the conversion of *profits after taxes* to *cash flow after taxes*. The formula for cash flow is

$$L = Z + D - W - I \qquad (10\text{-}16)$$

where:

L = cash flow after taxes
Z = profits after taxes
D = depreciation
W = working capital in dollars (that is, working capital as a percent of sales, times wholesale price, times sales in units)
I = new investment expenditure

For example, the cash flow after taxes for 1981 is

$$\$1,097,245 + \$395,000 - [.13(\$.473)(30,000,000)] - 0 = -\$353,001$$

The computer now calculates the internal rate of return implicit in the cash flow in column 23. This is found by taking the opportunity cost at the beginning of the period and searching for the interest rate that would discount the future cash flows so that the sum of the discounted cash flows is equal to the initial opportunity cost; this rate turns out to be 45 percent.

Thus computer programs enable the product manager to estimate the financial consequences implied by a particular strategy, environment, and set of costs. The manager can easily calculate the impact on profit of any alterations in the data or assumptions.

Optimal marketing mix   The theory of profit optimization leads to finding the optimal marketing expenditure level. Now we want to examine the issue of finding the optimal marketing mix. Clearly, the elements of the mix are somewhat substitutable for each other. A company that is seeking increased sales can think of achieving them by lowering the price, or increasing the sales force, advertising budget, or promotion budget. The issue is, What changes in an element, or what combination of elements, would produce the optimal response?

Let us assume that a product manager has identified advertising and promotion dollars as the two major elements of the marketing budget. In principle, there are an infinite number of combinations of spending on these two items. This is shown in Figure 10–3A. If there are no constraints on the levels of advertising and promotion, then every point in the A-S plane shown in Figure 10–3A is a possible marketing mix. An arbitrary line drawn from the origin, called a *constant-mix line,* shows the set of all marketing mixes where the two tools are in a fixed ratio but where the budget varies. Another arbitrary line, called a *constant-budget line,* shows a set of varying mixes that would be affordable with a fixed marketing budget.

Associated with every possible marketing mix is a resulting sales level. Three sales levels are shown in Figure 10–3A. The marketing mix (A_1S_2)—calling for a small budget and a rough equality between advertising and promotion—is expected to produce sales of Q_1. The marketing mix (A_2S_1) involves the same budget with more expenditure on advertising than on promotion; this is expected to produce slightly higher sales, Q_2. The mix (A_3S_3) calls for a larger budget but a relatively equal splitting between advertising and promotion, and with a sales estimate of Q_3. Given these and many other possible marketing mixes, the marketer's job is to find the sales equation that predicts the Qs.

For a given marketing budget, the money should be divided among the various marketing tools in a way that gives the same marginal profit on the marginal dollar spent on each tool. A geometrical version of the solution is shown in Figure 10–3B. Here we are looking down at the A-S plane shown in Figure 10–3A. A constant-budget line is shown, indicating all the alternative marketing mixes that could be achieved with this budget. The curved lines are called *iso-sales curves.* An iso-sales curve shows the different mixes of advertising and personal selling that would produce a given level of sales. It is a projection into the A-S plane of the set of points resulting from horizontal slicing of the sales function shown in Figure 10–3A at a given level of sales. Figure 10–3B shows iso-sales curves for three different sales levels: 75, 100, and 150 units. Given the budget line, it is not possible to attain sales of more than 100 units. The optimum marketing mix is shown at the point of tangency between the budget line and the last-touching iso-sales curve above it. Consequently, the marketing mix $(A°S°)$, which calls for somewhat more advertising than promotion, is the sales-maximizing (and in this case profit-maximizing) marketing mix.

This analysis could be generalized to more than two marketing tools. Dorfman and Steiner proved that the marketing mix of price, promotion, and product quality would be optimized when the following side conditions were met:[17]

$$
\begin{array}{c}
\text{Price elasticity} \\
\text{of demand}
\end{array}
=
\begin{array}{c}
\text{Marginal value product} \\
\text{of promotion}
\end{array}
=
\begin{array}{c}
\text{Quality elasticity of demand} \\
\text{times price markup over} \\
\text{average cost of production}
\end{array}
$$

Ferber and Verdoorn stated the rule more intuitively:

> In an optimum position the additional sales obtained by a small increase in unit costs are the same for all nonprice instruments and at the same time equal to additional sales accompanying a corresponding decrease in unit prices.[18]

[17] Robert Dorfman and Peter O. Steiner, "Optimal Advertising and Optimal Quality," *American Economic Review,* December 1954, pp. 826–36.

[18] Robert Ferber and P. J. Verdoorn, *Research Methods in Economics and Business* (New York: Macmillan Company, 1962), p. 535.

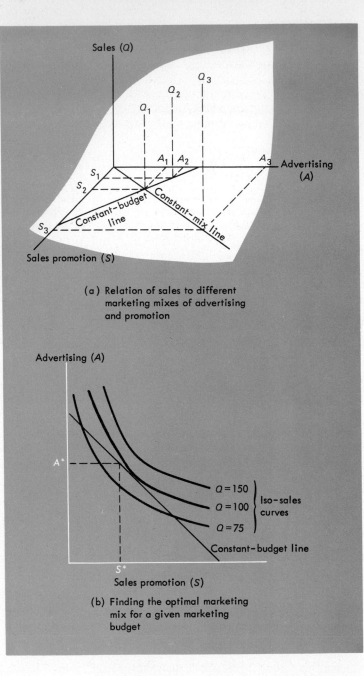

(a) Relation of sales to different marketing mixes of advertising and promotion

(b) Finding the optimal marketing mix for a given marketing budget

FIGURE 10–3
The Sales Function Associated with Two
Marketing-Mix Elements

Optimal marketing allocation   A final issue facing the marketing planner is to optimally allocate a given marketing budget to the various *target markets* (TMs). The TMs could be different sales territories, customer groups, or other market segments. With a given marketing budget and mix, it may be possible to increase sales and profits by shifting funds among different markets.

Most marketing managers allocate their marketing budget to the various TMs on the basis of some percentage to actual or expected sales. Consider the following example:

> The marketing manager at the Guardian Oil Company (name disguised) estimates total gasoline sales volume (which combines regular and premium gasoline) and adds premium sales volume back to this figure to yield "profit gallons" (thus giving double weight to premium gasoline sales). The manager then takes the ratio of the advertising budget to the profit gallons to establish a figure for advertising dollars per profit gallon. This is called the prime multiplier. Each market receives an advertising budget equal to its previous year's profit gallons sold multiplied by the prime multiplier. Thus the advertising budget is allocated largely on the basis of last year's company sales in the territory.[19]

Unfortunately, size rules for allocating funds lead to inefficient allocations. They confuse "average" and "marginal" sales response. Figure 10–4A illustrates the difference between the two and makes it clear that there is no reason to assume they are correlated. The two dots in the figure show current marketing expenditures and company sales in two *TMs*. The company spends $3,000 on marketing in both *TMs*. Company sales are $40,000 in *TM* 1 and $20,000 in *TM* 2. The average sales response to a dollar of marketing effort is thus greater in *TM* 1 than in *TM* 2; it is $\frac{40}{3}$ as opposed to $\frac{20}{3}$, respectively. It might therefore seem desirable to shift funds out of *TM* 2 into *TM* 1 where the average response is greater. Yet the real issue is one of the marginal response. The marginal response is represented by the *slope* of the sales function through the points. A higher slope has been drawn for *TM* 2 than for *TM* 1. The respective slopes show that another $1,000 of marketing expenditure would produce a $10,000 sales increase in *TM* 2 and only a $2,000 sales increase in *TM* 1. Clearly, marginal response, not average response, should guide the allocation of marketing funds.

Marginal response is indicated along the sales response function for each territory. We will assume that a company is able to estimate *TM* sales response functions. Suppose the sales response functions for two *TMs* are those shown in Figure 10–4B. The company wishes to allocate a budget of B dollars between the two *TM*'s to maximize profits. When costs are identical for the two *TMs*, then the allocation that will maximize profits is the one that will maximize sales. The funds are optimally allocated when (1) they exhaust the budget and (2) the marginal sales response is the same in both *TMs*. Geometrically, this means that the slopes of the tangents to the two sales response functions at the optimal allocations will be equal. Figure 10–4B shows that a budget of $6 million would be allocated in the amounts of approximately $4.6 million to *TM* 1 and $1.4 million to *TM* 2 to produce maximum sales of approximately $180 million. The marginal sales response would be the same in both *TMs*.

[19] Donald C. Marschner, "Theory versus Practice in Allocating Advertising Money," *Journal of Business*, July 1967, pp. 286–302.

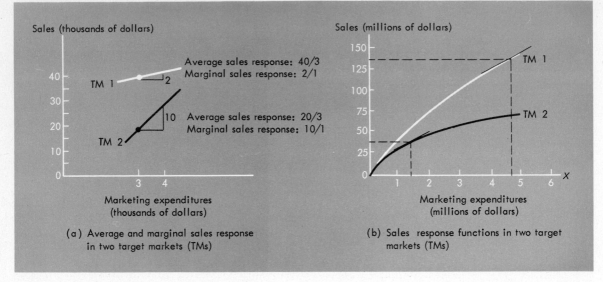

FIGURE 10-4

Sales Response Functions in Two Target Markets (TMs)

The principle of allocating funds to TMs to equalize the marginal response is used in the planning technique called *zero-based budgeting*.[20] The manager of each TM is asked to formulate a marketing plan and estimate the resulting sales for (say) three levels of marketing expenditure, such as 67 percent of the normal level, the normal level, and 133 percent of the normal level. An example is shown in Table 10–6, outlining what the Heinz marketing manager would do with each budget level and his estimate of sales. A sales response function can be fitted through these estimates for each TM. Then higher management reviews these functions and gives serious consideration to shifting funds from TMs with low marginal responses to TMs with higher marginal responses. Thus higher management at Heinz will consider whether it would be worthwhile withdrawing $1 million from the Heinz budget of $3 million (and losing 2 million case sales) or adding $1 million to gain another million in case sales. This depends on how productive the money would be in other parts of the business.

The result of measuring the shape of a sales response function can lead to substantial shifts in marketing strategy by a company. A major oil company had been locating its service stations in every major U.S. city.[21] In many markets, it operated only a small percentage of the total stations. Company management began to question whether this situation was wise. It decided to estimate how the company's city market share varied with its percentage share of marketing expenditures in each city (as measured by the share of outlets). A curve was fitted through observations of the share of outlets and share of markets in differ-

[20] See Paul J. Stonich, *Zero-Base Planning and Budgeting: Improved Cost Control and Resource Allocation* (Homewood, Ill.: Dow Jones-Irwin, 1977).

[21] See John J. Cardwell, "Marketing and Management Science—A Marriage on the Rocks?" *California Management Review*, summer 1968, pp. 3–12.

TABLE 10–6
Illustration of Zero-based Marketing Budgeting

BUDGET (M)	MARKETING PLAN	SALES FORECAST (Q)
$2,000,000	Try to maintain sales and market share in the short term by concentrating sales effort on largest chain stores, advertising only on TV, sponsoring two promotions a year, and carrying on only limited marketing research.	5,000,000 cases
$3,000,000	Implement a coordinated effort to expand market share by contacting 80 percent of all retailers, adding magazine advertising, adding point-of-purchase displays, and sponsoring three promotions during the year.	7,000,000 cases
$4,000,000	Seek to expand market size and share by adding two new product sizes, enlarging the sales force, increasing marketing research, and expanding the advertising budget.	8,000,000 cases

ent cities in its system. The resulting curve was S-shaped (see Figure 10–5). This meant that having a low percentage of stations in a city yielded an even lower percentage of market volume. The practical implication was clear: the company should either withdraw from its weak markets or build them up to, say, having

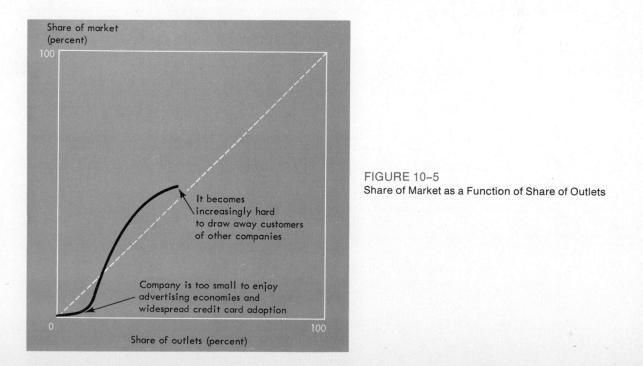

FIGURE 10–5
Share of Market as a Function of Share of Outlets

at least 15 percent of the competitive outlets. Instead of an allocation strategy of locating a few outlets in each of many cities, the oil company should set up a greater number of outlets in a more limited number of cities.

SUMMARY

Marketing planning is one of the key expressions of the modern marketing concept. Systems of formal company planning in general have been slow to evolve, with companies going first through an unplanned stage, then a budgeting-system stage, an annual-planning stage, and finally a strategic-planning stage. Even the term marketing plan has several usages. It turns out that marketing input is necessary in the formulation of various company plans, including the corporate plan, divisional plans, product-line plans, product plans, brand plans, market plans, product/market plans, and functional plans. The contents of marketing plans vary from company to company, but at a minimum should contain an executive summary, situation analysis, objectives and goals, strategy statement, action program, budgets, and controls.

In order to plan effectively, marketing managers must understand the key relationships between marketing expenditures of various types and their sales and profit consequences. These relationships are captured in a profit equation and a sales equation. Both equations can be used in any of three types of planning found in today's companies. Sales volume planning calls for developing a marketing plan to sell a target sales volume. Target profit planning calls for developing a marketing plan to achieve a target profit level. Finally, profit-optimization planning calls for finding the profit-maximizing plan. The latter involves methods of determining the optimal marketing expenditure level, marketing mix, and marketing allocation.

QUESTIONS AND PROBLEMS

1. What kinds of suboptimizing practices often take place in (a) setting sales targets; (b) setting departmental budgets?

2. A marketing decision maker evaluates two alternative marketing strategies and estimates their expected rates of return to be 8 percent and 12 percent, respectively. Which strategy should be chosen if this decision is to be made many times? Which strategy should be chosen if this decision is to be made only once?

3. Suppose the quantity sold (Q) of an item depends upon the price charged (P), the level of advertising expenditure (A), and the level of distribution expenditure (D). Develop a sales response equation (a) where the marginal effect of each marketing variable is uninfluenced by the level of the other marketing variables; (b) where the marginal effect of each marketing variable is influenced by the level of the other variables.

4. A firm is trying to decide how much quality to build into a new machine tool. Illustrate diagrammatically the logic of determining the optimal quality level.

5. How many different marketing mixes could be formulated given a dozen marketing activities that could each be performed at five different levels?

6. Suggest four improvements in the computer program shown in Table 10–5 for projecting sales and profits.

7. Suggest some equation forms that might be used to represent (a) a sales response function when sales increase at a decreasing rate with marketing expenditures; (b) a sales response function where sales increase at an increasing and then decreasing rate.

8. The product manager in charge of a well-established dry breakfast cereal has the following margin and expense statement:

Net Sales	100%
Manufacturing and shipping costs	
Fixed	12.9
Variable	39.6
Total	52.5
All other expenses (excluding advertising and merchandising expenses)	
Distribution and delivery expenses	5.4
Administrative and general expenses	4.0
Salesmen's expenses	3.5
Market research	.5
Total	13.4
Available for advertising and merchandising and profit	34.1

Name several ways the product manager can try to increase profit.

COMPETITIVE MARKETING STRATEGY

Success is a product of unremitting attention to purpose.
BENJAMIN DISRAELI

Top management today is putting increased pressure on marketing executives to think more strategically. And marketing executives are responding by spelling out their strategy in clearer terms in their plans. They are providing better rationales for favoring one strategy over another.

What do we mean by a marketing strategy? We will use the following definition:

> A *marketing strategy* is a consistent, appropriate, and feasible set of principles through which a particular company hopes to achieve its long-run customer and profit objectives in a particular competitive environment.

A company's marketing strategy will have to take several factors into account, including: (1) the company's competitive size and position in the market; (2) the company's resources, objectives, and policies; (3) the competitors' marketing strategies; (4) the target market's buying behavior; (5) the stage of the product life cycle; and (6) the character of the economy. Many of these factors are reviewed in other chapters of the book.

In this chapter, we will focus on the first factor, namely, the dependence of marketing strategy on the company's size and position in the market. Let us imagine a market that has the competitive structure shown in Figure 11–1.

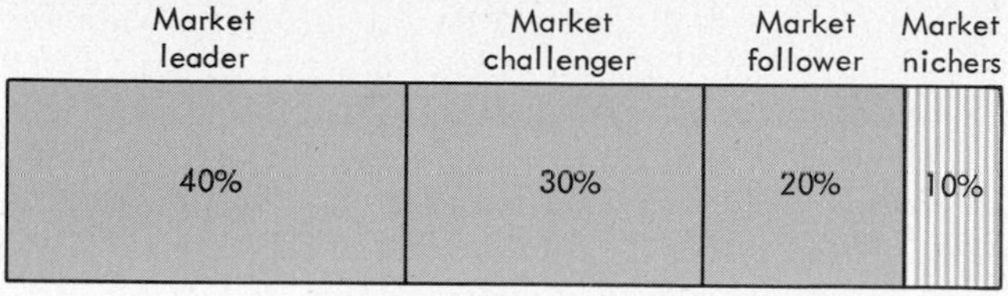

Market leader	Market challenger	Market follower	Market nichers
40%	30%	20%	10%

FIGURE 11–1
Hypothetical Market Structure

Forty percent of the market is in the hands of a *market leader,* the firm with the largest market share. Another 30 percent of the market is in the hands of a *market challenger,* a runner-up firm that is actively trying to expand its share using highly aggressive tactics. Another 20 percent is in the hands of a *market follower,* another runner-up firm that seeks to maintain its market share and not rock the boat. The remaining 10 percent is in the hands of several small firms called *market nichers,* which serve small market segments that they hope will not attract the interest of the larger firms.

We will examine and illustrate the various strategies that are used by market leaders, challengers, followers, and nichers.

MARKET-LEADER STRATEGIES

Almost every industry contains one firm that is acknowledged to be the market leader. This firm has the largest market share in the relevant product market. It usually leads the other firms in price changes, new-product introductions, distribution coverage, and promotional intensity. The leader may or may not be admired or respected, but other firms will acknowledge its dominance. The leader is an orientation point for competitors, a company to either challenge, imitate, or avoid. Some of the best-known market leaders are General Motors (autos), Kodak (photography), U.S. Steel (steel), IBM (computers), Xerox (copying), Procter & Gamble (consumer packaged goods), Caterpillar (earth-moving equipment), Coca-Cola (soft drinks), Sears (retailing), McDonald's (fast food), and Gillette (razor blades).

Unless a dominant firm enjoys a legal monopoly, its life is not altogether easy. It must maintain a constant vigilance. Other firms keep challenging its strengths or trying to take advantage of its weaknesses. The market leader can easily miss a turn in the road and plunge into second place. A product innovation may come along and make the leader's product obsolete (e.g., *Life* magazine was displaced by television). The leader might spend conservatively, expecting hard times, while a challenger spends liberally, expecting a buoyant economy (Montgomery Ward's loss of its retail dominance to Sears after World War II). The dominant firm might grow to look old-fashioned against new and peppier rivals (*Playboy* magazine falling to second place in newsstand circulation after *Penthouse*). The dominant firm may grow sloppy in its costs and find its profits slipping (Food Fair's decline, resulting from poor cost control).

A dominant firm's objective is to remain number one. This objective breaks down into three subobjectives. The first is to find ways to make the total market grow larger. The second is to protect the current market share through good offensive and defensive strategies. The third is to expand the current market share further.

273

Expanding the Total Market The dominant firm usually stands to gain the most from any increases in market size. If Americans decide to buy ten million cars instead of eight million, General Motors stands to gain the most because they sell one out of every two cars in the U.S. To the extent that General Motors can convince Americans to own two or three cars per family or replace their cars more often, they will benefit. In fact, dominant firms can attempt to expand the total market in three ways.

New users The first way is to attract *new users* to the product class. Every product class has the potential of attracting buyers who are currently unaware of the product or resisting it because of its price or failure to supply certain features or take certain forms. A manufacturer can search for new users among three groups. For example, a perfume manufacturer can try to convince women who do not use perfume to use perfume *(market-penetration strategy)*, or convince men to start using perfume *(new-market strategy)*, or sell perfume in other countries *(geographical-expansion strategy)*.

One of the modern success stories in developing a new class of users is that of Johnson & Johnson's baby shampoo, the leading brand of baby shampoo. The company became concerned with the future sales growth of this product when the birthrate started to slow down. Their marketers noticed that other members of the family occasionally used the baby shampoo and liked it for their own hair. Management decided to launch an advertising campaign to create adult preference for the baby shampoo. In a short time, Johnson & Johnson baby shampoo became the leading brand in the total shampoo market.

In another case, the Boeing Corporation faced a sharp decline in orders for B-747 jumbo jets when the airlines felt they had acquired enough aircraft to serve the existing level of demand. Boeing concluded that the key to more B-747 sales was to help the airlines attract more people to flying. They analyzed potential flying segments and concluded that the working class did not do much flying, although the cost was within their reach. Boeing encouraged the airlines and the travel industry to create charter travel packages that could be sold to unions, churches, and lodges to get their members to fly. This strategy had proven very successful in Europe and seemed like a natural way to expand the size of the American flying market.

New uses Another way to expand a market is to discover and promote new uses for the product. For example, the average American eats a dry breakfast cereal three mornings a week. Manufacturers would gain if they could convince people to eat breakfast cereal on other occasions during the day. Some cereals are specifically promoted for their tastiness as snacks, to increase their use frequency.

Du Pont's nylon provides a classic story of new-use expansion. Every time nylon seemed to enter a mature stage of its life cycle, some important new use was discovered. Nylon was first used as a synthetic fiber for parachutes; then as a major material in women's stockings; later, a major material in women's blouses and men's shirts; still later, it entered automobile tires, seat upholstery, and carpeting.[1] Each new use started the product on a new life cycle. Credit goes to the

[1] See Theodore Levitt, "Exploit the Product Life Cycle," *Harvard Business Review*, November–December 1965, pp. 81–94. The original study is reported in Jordan P. Yale, "The Strategy of Nylon's Growth," *Modern Textiles Magazine*, February 1964, pp. 32, 49. By permission.

continuous research and development program conducted by Du Pon
cover new uses.

In even more cases, the credit goes to users rather than the company
discovering new uses. Vaseline petroleum jelly started out as a simple mach
lubricant, and over the years users have reported all kinds of new uses for the
product, including use as a skin ointment, a healing agent, and a hair dressing.

Arm & Hammer, a manufacturer of baking soda, had a product on its
hands whose sales were on a plateau for 125 years. Baking soda had hundreds of
uses but no single important use. The company discovered some consumers were
using it as a refrigerator deodorant. It decided to mount a heavy advertising and
publicity campaign focusing on this single use and succeeded in the first year of
promotion in getting half of the homes in America to place an open box of baking soda in their refrigerator.

In these cases, the company's task is to do a good job of monitoring consumer usages through periodic inquiries and surveys. This is as true for industrial
products as consumer products. Von Hippel, who has studied how ideas for new
industrial products originate, claims that most of the ideas come from users
rather than company research-and-development laboratories.[2] This makes *marketing research* an important contributor to company growth and profits.

More usage   A third market-expansion strategy is to convince people to *use
more of the product per use occasion.* If a cereal manufacturer can convince consumers of the benefits of eating a full bowl of cereal instead of half a bowl, total
sales will increase. Procter & Gamble advises that its Head and Shoulders shampoo is more effective in reducing dandruff with two applications instead of one.

A very creative example of a company stimulating higher usage per occasion is the Michelin Tire Company (French). The company was seeking ways to
encourage French car owners to drive their cars more miles per year—thus leading to more tire replacement. They conceived the idea of rating restaurants
throughout France on a three-star system and publishing the results in a guide-
book. Many of the best restaurants were reported in the south of France, leading
many Parisians to consider making weekend excursions to the south of France.

**Protecting Market
Share**   In addition to expanding the total market size, the dominant firm must be eter-
nally vigilant in protecting its current market share. Challenger firms are constantly stalking the market leader looking for possible weaknesses. Fuji attacks
Kodak; Avis attacks Hertz; Bic attacks Gillette; *Penthouse* attacks *Playboy.* The
plight of a number-one firm, such as Procter & Gamble, is aptly described
below.

> Colgate can pick and choose where it wants to hit the giant; the giant, by con-
> trast, must defend itself everywhere. It's not unlike the situation in guerilla war-
> fare, where the guerillas, with a lot less to defend, can concentrate their forces on
> one or two points and take a heavy toll. This is what Colgate has been doing:
> attacking first one P&G strong point, then another, hoping to keep P&G off
> balance.[3]

[2] See Eric von Hippel, *A Customer-Active Paradigm for Industrial Product Idea Generation,*
unpublished working paper, Sloan School of Management, MIT, Cambridge, Mass., May 1977.

[3] "Colgate vs. P&G," *Forbes,* February 1, 1966, pp. 27–28.

Dominant firms cannot be expected to sit idly by as smaller firms nibble away at them. Some years ago, Chrysler's share of automobile sales started to rise from 12 percent to 18 percent, following the appointment at Chrysler of a new top management team, the restyling of their line of cars, and the intensive grooming of dealers. At this point, one rival marketing executive was overheard to say, "If they (Chrysler) go to 20 percent, it will be over our dead bodies. We've still got some leverage."[4] Thus the Big Two (General Motors and Ford) have an idea of a proper maximum share for the third largest firm in the industry, and they will initiate a counteroffensive when this share is approached.

What can the market leader do to discipline an upstart firm? From a military point of view, they can try "brinkmanship," "massive retaliation," "limited warfare," "graduated response," "diplomacy of violence," "threat systems," and so on. From a business point of view, they can practice one of four broad strategies:

1. *Innovation strategy.* A strategy of innovation is the most constructive from the point of view of the firm and the society. It means that the dominant firm refuses to be content with the way things are and leads the industry in new-product ideas, customer services, means of distribution, and cost-cutting discoveries. By continuously creating new customer values, the dominant firm takes the best course possible to discourage competitors. It is applying the military "principle of the offensive": the commander must exercise initiative, set the pace, and exploit enemy weaknesses. It makes use of the principle that the best defense is a good offense.

2. *Fortification strategy.* A strategy of fortification is also a positive approach to maintaining leadership. The dominant firm keeps its prices reasonable in relation to the perceived value of its offer and competitors' offers. It produces its brand in a variety of sizes and forms so as to cover the varying preferences of the market instead of letting competitors get a foothold. It creates additional brands to fortify its hold on shelf space and dealers' efforts.

3. *Confrontation strategy.* Often the dominant firm will face an extremely aggressive challenger whose actions demand a quick and direct response. The dominant firm can wage a *promotional war,* engaging in massive promotional expenditures that the aggressor cannot match. The promotional increases can take the form of more or better deals to the trade if that leads the trade to stock up and push the dominant firm's brand. The dominant firm may engage in a *price war,* being careful, however, to avoid the charge of *predatory pricing.*[5] A large pharmaceutical company uses the threat of a price war whenever another firm is considering entering its markets. The dominant firm leaks information to the press that it is contemplating a price reduction. The word reaches the potential competitor, who gets frightened and withdraws.

4. *Harassment strategy.* The dominant firm will sometimes resort to a *harassment strategy.* It might go to major suppliers and threaten to reduce its purchases if the latter supply the upstart firm. Or it might put pressure on distributors not to carry the competitor's product. Or their salesmen might bad-mouth the competitors. Or it might try to hire away the better executives of an aggressive firm. When a dominant firm is bent on taming or destroying a competitor, there is very little it is not capable of, except as it is constrained by its own policies and the threat of triple-damage suits by the aggrieved competitor.

[4] "If the Big Three's a Crowd, Blame Chrysler," *Newsweek,* May 20, 1968, p. 84.

[5] See Ralph Cassady, Jr., "The Price Skirmish—A Distinctive Pattern of Competitive Behavior," *California Management Review,* winter 1964, pp. 11–16.

The dominant firm can often restrain its competitors through legal devices. It might push legislation that would be more unfavorable to the competitors than to itself. A common example is that of the Sunday blue laws banning business on Sunday, which established merchants' support because these laws retard the growth of the discount house. These and other laws have been used at various times by dominant interests in the drug, hardware, and grocery business to prevent the growth of pesky new channels of distribution.[6]

A harassment strategy is apt to be used by dominant firms that have grown sluggish, inefficient, or overly content. Their expenses rise rapidly; their aspirations do not keep up with the available resources, and the firm gets soft. This condition becomes a strong attractor of competitors, and the dominant firm is thrown back to confrontation or harassment tactics to defend its position.

The principles of protecting market leadership are admirably illustrated by companies such as Procter & Gamble, Caterpillar, IBM, General Motors, and Hertz, all of whom have shown a remarkable ability to protect their market shares against repeated attacks by very able challengers. Their viability is not based on doing one thing well but rather on doing everything right. They don't leave themselves exposed in any respect. We shall examine the cases of Procter & Gamble and Caterpillar.

Procter & Gamble P&G is considered to be the nation's most skillful marketer of consumer packaged goods. It enjoys market leadership in virtually every market in which it sells. It has the leading toothpaste (Crest), the leading disposable diaper (Pampers), the leading laundry detergent (Tide), and the leading anti-dandruff shampoo (Head and Shoulders). Its market leadership rests on several principles:

1. *Product innovation.* P&G is a practitioner of product innovation that relies heavily on benefit segmentation. It enters markets by introducing a new product with a new benefit rather than launching a me-too product backed by heavy advertising. For example, P&G spent ten years researching and developing the first effective anticavity toothpaste, Crest. It spent several years researching the first effective over-the-counter antidandruff shampoo, Head and Shoulders. The company thoroughly tests its new products with consumers, and only when real preference is indicated does it proceed with launching them in the national market.

2. *Quality strategy.* P&G designs its products with higher-than-average quality. Furthermore, the company makes a continuous effort to improve the product quality over the product's life. When they announce "new and improved," they mean it. This is in contrast to many companies that, after establishing the quality level, rarely improve it, and to some companies that deliberately reduce the quality in an effort to squeeze out more profit.

3. *Product flanking.* P&G makes a practice of producing each of its brands in several sizes and forms to satisfy varying preferences in the marketplace. This practice also gives its brands more total shelf space and prevents competitors from spotting uncovered needs in the market.

4. *Multibrand strategy.* P&G is the originator and master practitioner of the art of launching several brands in the same product category. For example, it produces ten brands of laundry detergent, each positioned somewhat differently in the consumers' mind. The trick is to design brands that compete against specific

---

[6] See Joseph C. Palamountain, Jr., *The Politics of Distribution* (Cambridge, Mass.: Harvard University Press, 1955).

competitors' brands rather than each other. Each brand manager runs the brand independently of the other brand managers but knows he or she is competing for resources and results. Having several brands on the shelf, the company "locks up" shelf space and gains more clout with distributors.

5. **Brand-extension strategy.** P&G will often exploit its good brand names by introducing new products under the same brand name. For example, the Ivory brand has been extended from a soap to also include liquid soap and a detergent. Launching a new product under a well-known brand name gives it more recognition and credibility with much less advertising outlay.

6. **Heavy advertising.** P&G is the nation's largest consumer-packaged-goods advertiser, spending over $460 million per year. It never stints on spending money to create strong consumer awareness and preference.

7. **Aggressive sales force.** P&G has a top-flight field sales force, which is very effective in gaining shelf space and retailer cooperation in point-of-purchase displays and promotions.

8. **Effective sales promotion.** P&G has a sales promotion department that stands ready to advise brand managers on the most effective promotions to achieve particular objectives. The department collects the results of different types of consumer and trade deals and develops an expert sense of their effectiveness under varying circumstances. At the same time, P&G prefers to minimize the use of sales promotion, preferring to rely on the long-term buildup of consumer preference through advertising.

9. **Competitive toughness.** P&G carries a big stick when it comes to constraining aggressors. P&G is willing to spend large sums of money to outpromote new competitive brands and prevent them from getting a foothold in the market.

10. **Manufacturing efficiency.** P&G's reputation as a great marketing company should not obscure its greatness as a manufacturing company. The company spends large sums of money developing and improving production operations to keep its costs among the lowest in the industry.

11. **Brand-management system.** Some fifty years ago P&G originated the brand-management system in which one executive is totally responsible for the development of each brand. The system has been copied by many competitors, but frequently without the success that P&G has achieved through perfecting its system over a number of years.

Thus we see that P&G's market leadership strategy is not based on doing one thing well but on a successful orchestration of all the factors that count in market leadership.

Caterpillar Since the 1940s, Caterpillar has enjoyed the dominant position in the construction equipment industry. Its tractors, crawlers, and loaders, painted in familiar yellow, are a common sight at any construction area and account for 50 percent of the world's sales of heavy construction equipment. Caterpillar has managed to retain leadership in spite of charging a premium price for its equipment and being challenged by a number of able competitors, including John Deere, Massey-Ferguson, International Harvester, and J.I. Case. Several principles combine to explain their success:

1. **Premium-product quality.** Caterpillar produces high-quality equipment known for its reliability. Reliability is a major consideration in the purchase of heavy industrial equipment. It is said that Caterpillar designs its equipment with a heavier gauge of steel than necessary, to convince buyers of its superior quality.

2. ***Extensive-and-efficient-dealership system.*** Caterpillar maintains the largest number of independent construction-equipment dealers in the industry. Its 260 dealers are located throughout the world and carry a complete line of Caterpillar equipment. Caterpillar dealers can focus all of their attention on Caterpillar equipment without needing to carry other lines. Competitors' dealers, on the other hand, normally lack a full line and have to carry complementary, noncompeting lines. Caterpillar is in a position to enfranchise the finest dealers (a new dealership costs the franchisee $5,000,000) and spends the most money in training, servicing, and motivating them.

3. ***Superior service.*** Caterpillar has built a worldwide parts and service system that is second to none in the industry. Caterpillar can deliver replacement parts and service anywhere in the world within a few hours of equipment breakdown. This degree of service is very hard for competitors to match without a substantial investment. Any competitor duplicating the service level would only neutralize Caterpillar's advantage rather than gaining any net advantage.

4. ***Superior parts management.*** Thirty percent of Caterpillar's sales volume and over 50 percent of its profits come from the sale of replacement parts. Caterpillar has developed a superior parts-management system to keep margins high in this end of the business.

5. ***Premium price.*** Caterpillar is able to charge a price premium of 10 to 20 percent on comparable equipment because of the extra value perceived by buyers.

6. ***Full-line strategy.*** Caterpillar produces a full line of construction equipment to enable buyers to do one-stop buying.

7. ***Good financing.*** Caterpillar arranges generous financial terms to customers buying its equipment. This is important because of the large sums of money involved.

**Expanding
Market Share**

Market leaders can also try to grow through further expansion of their market share. The well-publicized Profit Impact of Market Strategies (PIMS) studies indicate that *profitability* (measured by pretax ROI) rises with *market share.*[7] The empirical relationship is shown in Figure 11–2A.[8]

> According to a PIMS report, "The average ROI for businesses with under 10 percent market share was about 9 percent. . . . On the average, a difference of 10 percentage points in market share is accompanied by a difference of about 5 points in pretax ROI." The PIMS study shows that businesses with market shares above 40 percent earn an average ROI of 30 percent, or three times that of those with shares under 10 percent.

These findings have been taken by many major firms to mean that they should not only strive for market dominance but also try to push their market share higher. This is a sound pursuit for dominant marketers whose market share is less than (say) 50 percent. But for dominant marketers with a share of over 50 percent—such as General Motors, Eastman Kodak, IBM, Campbell's, Gillette, Coca-Cola, Kellogg, and Caterpillar—market share expansion may be both ex-

---

[7] Sidney Schoeffler, Robert D. Buzzell, and Donald F. Heany, "Impact of Strategic Planning on Profit Performance," *Harvard Business Review*, March–April 1974, pp. 137–45; and Robert D. Buzzell, Bradley T. Gale, and Ralph G. M. Sultan, "Market Share—A Key to Profitability," *Harvard Business Review*, January–February 1975, pp. 97–106.

[8] See Buzzell et al., "Market Share," pp. 97, 100. The results, however, should be interpreted cautiously because (1) the data came from a limited number of industries and (2) there was some variance around the main line of relationship.

pensive and risky. They might be better off spending their time building up market size rather than market share.

The first reason for self-restraint has to do with the possibility of provoking antitrust action. Jealous competitors and antitrust legislators are likely to cry "monopolization" if the dominant firm makes further inroads on market share. Each company has to assess the shape of the antitrust probability function it faces. The hypothetical function in Figure 11–2B indicates that the firm feels the antitrust risk rises after it achieves a 25 percent market share and becomes almost a certainty at a 75 percent market share. This rise in the risk would cut down the attractiveness of pushing market share gains too far.

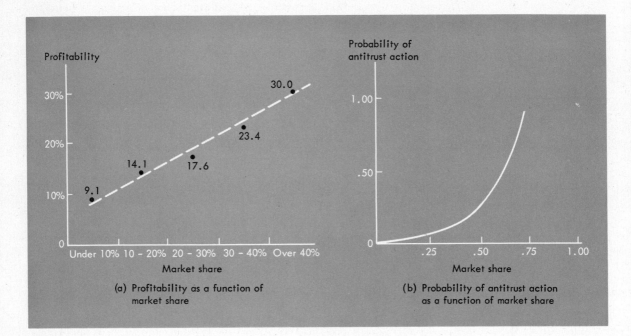

FIGURE 11–2
Market Share Functions

The second reason is economic. The cost of making further gains in market share after a large share has been achieved may rise fast and reduce the profit margin. A company that has (say) 60 percent of the market must recognize that the "holdout" customers and distributors may be holding out because of negative attitudes toward the company, loyalty to competitive suppliers, unique needs that cannot be met by the leader, or the desire to deal with smaller suppliers. Furthermore, the competitors are likely to fight harder to defend their diminishing market share. The cost of legal work, public relations, and lobbying rises with market share. After a certain point, profitability may stabilize or decline with further market share gain. This, combined with the risk of antitrust action, may caution the leader to stabilize rather than expand the existing market share. In fact, some dominant marketers may even consider reducing their share to reduce their risk, and there are techniques for doing this.[9]

MARKET-CHALLENGER STRATEGIES

The firms that occupy second, third, and fourth place in an industry can be called runner-up or trailing firms. They may be quite large in their own right although smaller than the leader. Examples include Colgate, Ford, Montgomery Ward, Avis, Westinghouse, Schlitz, and Pepsi-Cola. These runner-up firms can adopt one of two postures. They can decide to attack the leaders and others in a grab for further market share (market challengers). Or they can be content to play ball and not rock the boat (market followers). We shall examine the strategies of market challengers in this section.[10]

Market challengers can attempt to gain market share in three ways. The first is through a *direct-attack strategy* (also called head-on strategy) in which a challenger tries to best the market leader through sheer doggedness and fight. For years, Colgate launched direct attacks on Procter & Gamble but without much success.[11] The second way is through a *backdoor strategy* (also called end-run or blindside) in which the challenger runs *around* the dominant firm rather than *into* it. Timex gained its leadership in the low-price watch market by selling its watches through mass-merchandise outlets rather than through conventional jewelry stores that were "locked up" by the major watch manufacturers. The third way is through a *guppy strategy* of attacking smaller competitors rather than the market leader. Many major beer companies owe their growth not to taking share away from the leader or each other but to the gobbling up of smaller regional and local beer companies in the process of competition.

Basically the market challenger has to decide whether to aggress against the leader, other runner-ups, or smaller firms, based on discovered weaknesses. It then builds a strategy to take advantage of the weakness. Yet challengers are found from time to time going after competitors with nothing more than a strong determination to win. Recently the second-place razor blade manufacturer in Brazil decided to go after Gillette, the market leader. Management was asked if they were offering the consumer a better blade. "No," was the reply. "A lower price?" "No." "A better package?" "No." "A cleverer advertising campaign?" "No." "Better allowances to the trade?" "No." "Then how do you expect to take share away from Gillette?" they were asked. "Will power," was the reply. Needless to say, their offensive failed.[12]

[9] See Paul E. Bloom and Philip Kotler, "Strategies for High Market-Share Companies," *Harvard Business Review*, November–December 1975, pp. 63–72.

[10] For additional reading, see C. David Fogg, "Planning Gains in Market Share," *Journal of Marketing*, July 1974, pp. 30–38; and Bernard Catry and Michel Chevalier, "Market Share Strategy and the Product Life Cycle," *Journal of Marketing*, October 1974, pp. 29–34.

[11] "How to Be Happy Though No. Two," *Forbes*, July 15, 1976, pp. 36, 38.

[12] Also see William E. Fruham, Jr., "Pyrrhic Victories in Fights for Market Share," *Harvard Business Review*, September–October 1972, pp. 100–107.

In fact, several strategies are available to the market challenger who is seeking an advantage vis-à-vis competition. They are described here.

1. *Price-discount strategy.* A major attack strategy for challengers is to offer buyers a product of comparable quality to the leader's at a lower price. (See Figure 4–13, p. 86. Leader in cell 1, challenger in cell 2.) The Fuji Corporation used this strategy to attack Kodak's preeminence in the photographic-paper field. Its paper is of comparable quality and is priced 10 percent lower than Kodak's. Kodak chose not to lower its price, with the result that Fuji made strong gains in market share. Bristol-Meyers adopted a price-discount strategy in launching its new-type aspirin called Datril against Johnson & Johnson's leading brand, Tylenol.[13] It budgeted a heavy advertising campaign to announce its lower price and to convince consumers that all the new-type aspirins are identical. Tylenol, however, countered by lowering its price and Bristol-Meyers's brand never achieved the expected market share. Texas Instruments is perhaps the prime practitioner of price cutting. It will enter a market by offering a comparable-quality product that is progressively lowered in price to gain market share and lower costs. Texas Instruments is willing to forego profits in the first few years in order to gain unchallenged market leadership. They did this with transistors and hand calculators and now seem bent on doing it in the low-price watch market.[14]

For a price-discount strategy to work, three assumptions must be fulfilled. First, the challenger must be able to convince buyers that its product and service are of comparable quality to the leader's. Second, the buyers must be sensitive to the price difference and feel comfortable about turning their back on existing suppliers. Third, the market leader must stubbornly stick to its price in spite of the competitor's attack.

2. *Cheaper-goods strategy.* Another strategy to gain market position is to offer the market an average- or low-quality product at a much lower price. (See Figure 4–13, p. 86. Leader in cell 1, challenger in cell 5 or 9.) This works when there is a sufficient segment of price-conscious buyers. Firms that get established through this strategy, however, are vulnerable to attack by "cheaper-goods" firms whose prices are even lower. In defense, they try to upgrade their quality gradually to the level of the market leader or slightly less.

3. *Prestige-goods strategy.* A market challenger can attempt to get around the market leader by launching a higher-quality product and charging a higher price. (See Figure 4–13, p. 86. Leader in cell 1, challenger goes to northwest of cell 1.) Mercedes gained on Cadillac in the American market by offering the American public a car that was of even higher quality and higher priced. Some attackers, after gaining market acceptance for their premier products, later roll out lower-price products.

4. *Product-proliferation strategy.* The challenger can go after the leader by launching a large number of product variants. Hunt went after Heinz's leadership in the ketchup market by creating several new ketchup flavors and bottle sizes, in contrast to Heinz's reliance on one flavor of ketchup, sold in a limited number of bottle sizes. The success of this strategy depends upon the new product's managing to attract and hold customers and the failure of the leader to react fast enough with its own product variants.

5. *Product-innovation strategy.* The challenger may pursue the path of product innovation to attack the leader's position. Polaroid and Xerox are two examples of companies whose success is based on continuously introducing outstanding in-

[13] See "A Painful Headache for Bristol-Myers?" *Business Week,* October 6, 1975, pp. 78–80.

[14] See "The Great Digital Watch Shake-Out," *Business Week,* May 2, 1977, pp. 78–80.

novations in the camera and copying fields, respectively. Miller recently took over second place in the beer industry because of its successful development of a light beer and its introduction of "pony-sized" bottles for light-beer drinkers. In many ways, the public gains most from challenger strategies oriented toward product innovation.

6. *Improved-services strategy.* The challenger may attack the leader by finding ways to offer new services or better service. IBM achieved its success in the computer market by recognizing that customers were more interested in the quality of the software and the service than in the hardware. Avis's famous attack on Hertz, "We're only second. We try harder," was based on promising and delivering cleaner cars and faster service than Hertz.

7. *Distribution-innovation strategy.* A challenger should examine the possibility of expanding its market share by developing a new channel of distribution. Avon became one of the largest and most profitable cosmetics companies by perfecting the ancient method of door-to-door selling instead of battling other cosmetic firms in conventional store outlets. U.S. Time Company decided to sell its low-price Timex watches through mass merchandise channels, thus bypassing the jewelry stores.

8. *Manufacturing-cost-reduction strategy.* Some companies see the key to building market share as lying in achieving lower manufacturing costs than their competitors'. The lower manufacturing costs can be achieved by more efficient purchase of materials, lower labor costs, and more modern production equipment. A company can use its lower costs to price more aggressively to gain market share. This strategy has been the key to the successful Japanese invasion of various world markets. A company like Texas Instruments reverses the process by first lowering its prices aggressively, then winning market share, and then finding its costs falling through the "experience curve."[15] As it captures more volume, its costs continue to fall, thus providing a basis for further price cutting or profit taking.

9. *Intensive advertising promotion.* Some challengers seek to gain on the leader by increasing the quantity and/or quality of their advertising and promotion. When Hunt went after Heinz in the ketchup market, it built its annual spending level to $6.4 million as against Heinz's $3.4 million. Miller Beer has similarly been outspending Budweiser in its attempt to achieve first place in the U.S. beer market. Substantial promotional spending, however, is usually not a sensible strategy unless the challenger's product or advertising message exhibits some superiority over competition.

A challenger rarely succeeds in improving its market share by relying on only one strategy element. Its success depends on designing a total strategy that will improve its position over time. This is shown in the following examples.

Pepsi-Cola and Coca-Cola Before the Second World War, Coca-Cola dominated the American soft-drink industry. There was really no second-place firm worth mentioning. "Pepsi raised hardly a flicker of recognition in Coke's consciousness."[16] Pepsi-Cola was a newer drink that cost less to manufacture and whose taste was generally thought to be less satisfying than Coke's. Its major

[15] The experience curve describes the rate at which costs fall as a function of accumulated production experience. See "Selling Business a Theory of Economics," *Business Week*, September 8, 1973, pp. 86–88.

[16] Alvin Toffler, "The Competition that Refreshes," *Fortune*, May 1961. Also see "Pepsi Takes on the Champ," *Business Week*, June 12, 1978, pp. 88–97.

selling point was that it offered more drink for the same price. Pepsi exploited this difference by advertising, "Twice as much for a nickel, too." Its bottle was plain, and it carried a paper label that often got dirty in transit, thereby adding to the general impression that it was a second-class soft drink.

During the Second World War, Pepsi and Coke both enjoyed increased sales as they followed the flag around the world. After the war ended, Pepsi's sales started to fall relative to Coke's. A number of factors contributed to Pepsi's problems, including its poor image, poor taste, poor packaging, and poor quality control. Furthermore, Pepsi had to raise its prices to cover increased costs, and this made it less of a bargain than before. Morale was quite low at Pepsi toward the end of the 1940s.

At this point, Alfred N. Steele came to the presidency of Pepsi-Cola with a great reputation for merchandising. He and his staff recognized that the main hope lay in transforming Pepsi from a cheap imitation of Coke into a first-class soft drink. They recognized that this turnaround would take several years. They conceived of a *grand offensive* against Coke that would take place in two phases. In the first phase, which lasted from 1950 to 1955, the following steps were taken: First, the taste of Pepsi was improved. Second, the bottle and other corporate symbols were redesigned and unified. Third, the advertising campaign was redesigned to upgrade Pepsi's image. Fourth, Steele decided to concentrate on hitting the take-home market, which Coke had relatively neglected. Finally Steele singled out twenty-five cities for a special push for market share.

By 1955, all of Pepsi's major weaknesses had been overcome, sales had climbed substantially, and Steele was ready for the next phase. The second phase consisted of mounting a direct attack on Coke's "on-premise" market, particularly the vending-machine and cold-bottle segments, which were growing fast. Another decision was to introduce new size bottles that offered convenience to customers in the take-home and cold-bottle markets. Finally, Pepsi offered to finance any of its bottlers who were willing to buy and install Pepsi vending machines. These various steps, running from 1955 to 1960, again led to considerable sales growth for Pepsi. Within one decade, Pepsi's sales had grown fourfold.

Yamaha versus Honda In the early 1960s, Honda had established itself as the number one motorcycle brand in the United States. Its lightweight machines with their great eye appeal, the slogan, "You Meet the Nicest People on a Honda," and an aggressive sales organization and distribution network all combined to greatly expand the market for motorcycles. Yamaha, another Japanese manufacturer, decided to enter the market against Honda. Its first step was to study the leader's major weaknesses, which included several dealers who had grown rich and lazy, abrupt management changes, discouragement of franchise-seeking dealers, and a neglect of promoting the mechanical aspects of their motorcycles. Yamaha offered franchises to the best of the Honda-rejected franchisees and built an enthusiastic sales team to train and motivate their dealers. They improved their motorcycle to the point that they could claim and demonstrate its mechanical superiority. They spent liberally on advertising and sales promotion programs to build buyer awareness and dealer enthusiasm. When motorcycle safety became a big issue, they designed superior safety features and advertised extensively. The sum of these strategies propelled Yamaha into a clear second position in an industry of over fifty manufacturers.

MARKET-FOLLOWER STRATEGIES

Not all runner-up companies choose to challenge the market leader. The effort to draw away the leader's customers is never taken lightly by the leader. If the challenger's lure is lower prices, improved service, additional product variants, the leader can match these all in sufficient time to defuse the attack. The leader probably has more staying power in an all-out battle. A hard fight might leave both firms worse off, and this means the challenger has to think twice before attacking. Unless the challenger is able to launch a preemptive strike—through a substantial product innovation or distribution breakthrough—he often settles in favor of following rather than attacking the leader.

Patterns of "conscious parallelism" are quite common in homogeneous product industries of high-capital intensity, such as steel, fertilizers, and chemicals. The opportunities for product differentiation and image differentiation are low; service quality is often comparable; price sensitivity runs high. Price wars can erupt at any time. The mood in these industries is against short-run grabs for market share, because that strategy only provokes retaliation. Most firms decide against stealing each other's customers. Instead they present similar offers and values to buyers, usually by copying the leader. Market shares tend to remain highly stable.

This is not to say that market followers are without strategics. A market follower must be clear on how it is going to hold on to current customers and win a fair share of new ones. Each follower must work a set of target markets to which it can bring distinctive advantages—location, services, financing. It must be ready to enter new markets that are opening up. The company must keep its manufacturing costs low and its product quality and services high. Followship is not the same as passivity or being a carbon copy of the leader. The follower has to define its own path to growth, but decides to do this in a way that does not create intense competitive retaliation.

Market followers, although they have lower market shares than the leader, may be as profitable or even more profitable. A recent study reported that numerous companies with less than half the market share of the leader had a five-year average return on equity that surpassed the industry median.[17] Burroughs (computers), Crown Cork & Seal (metal containers), and Union Camp Corporation (paper) were among the successful market followers. The keys to their success were conscious market segmentation and concentration, effective research and development, profit emphasis rather than market share emphasis, and strong top management.

MARKET-NICHER STRATEGIES

Almost every industry includes a number of minor firms that operate in some part of the market and try to avoid clashing with the majors. These smaller firms attempt to find and occupy market niches that they can serve effectively through specialization and that the majors are likely to overlook or ignore.

[17] R. G. Hamermesh, M. J. Anderson, Jr., and J. E. Harris, "Strategies for Low Market Share Businesses," *Harvard Business Review*, May–June 1978, pp. 95–102.

These firms are variously called market nichers, market specialists, threshold firms, or foothold firms. Market niching is of interest not only to small companies but also to smaller divisions of larger companies that are not able to achieve major standing in that industry.

The salvation of these firms is to find one or more market niches that are safe and profitable. An ideal market niche would have the following characteristics:

1. The niche is of sufficient size and purchasing power to be profitable.
2. The niche has growth potential.
3. The niche has been bypassed or neglected by major competitors.
4. The firm has superior competencies to serve the niche effectively.
5. The firm can defend its position against an attacking major because of the goodwill it has built up.

The key idea in nichemanship is specialization. The firm has to identify a viable form of specialization along market, customer, product, or marketing-mix lines. At least ten specialist roles are open to a market nicher.

1. *End-use specialist.* This firm decides to specialize in serving one type of end-use customer. For example, a law firm can decide to specialize in the criminal, civil, or business law markets.
2. *Vertical-level specialist.* This firm specializes at some vertical level of the production-distribution cycle. For example, a copper firm may concentrate on the production of raw copper, copper components, or finished copper products.
3. *Customer-size specialist.* This firm concentrates on selling to either small-, medium-, or large-size customers. Many nichers specialize in serving small customers because they are neglected by the majors.
4. *Specific-customer specialist.* This firm limits its selling to one or a few major customers. Many firms sell their entire output to a single company such as Sears or General Motors.
5. *Geographic specialist.* This firm focuses on the needs of a certain locality, region, or area of the world.
6. *Product or product-line specialist.* This firm produces only one product line or product. Within the laboratory equipment industry are firms that produce only microscopes, or even more narrowly, only lenses for microscopes.
7. *Product-feature specialist.* This firm specializes in producing a certain type of product or product feature. Rent-a-Junk, for example, is a California car rental agency that rents only "beat-up" cars.
8. *Job-shop specialist.* This firm stands ready to make customized products as ordered by the customer.
9. *Quality/price specialist.* This firm chooses to operate at the low or high end of the market. For example, Hewlett-Packard specializes in the high-quality, high-price end of the hand-calculator market.
10. *Service specialist.* This firm offers or excels in one or more services not readily available from other firms. An example would be a bank that takes loan requests over the phone or dispatches an officer to deliver the money at the client's home or office.

Thus we see that small firms have many opportunities to serve customers in profitable ways. Many small firms discover good niches through blind luck, although good opportunities can be detected and developed in a more systematic manner.

SUMMARY
Marketing strategy forms the heart of a marketing plan. Yet many marketing plans are vague on strategy, taking up most of the space with very specific tactics. A marketing strategy is a consistent, appropriate, and feasible set of principles through which a particular company hopes to achieve its long-run customer and profit objectives in a particular competitive environment.

A marketing strategy has to take several factors into account, a prime one being the company's position in the particular market, specifically whether it is a market leader, challenger, follower, or nicher.

A market leader has three problems, those of expanding the total market, protecting its market share, and expanding its market share. The market leader is usually extremely interested in expanding market size through looking for new users, new uses, and more usage. The leader also protects itself through strategies of innovation, fortification, confrontation, and occasionally harassment. The most sophisticated leaders cover themselves by doing everything right, leaving no openings for competitive attack. As for expanding their market share, leaders whose shares are already large will put less emphasis on that because it would increase the risk of antitrust action.

A market challenger is a firm that is seeking to aggressively expand its market share by attacking the leader, other runner-up firms, or smaller firms in the industry. Among the most common challenger strategies are price discounts, cheaper goods, prestige goods, product proliferation, product innovation, improved services, distribution innovation, manufacturing cost reduction, and intensive advertising.

A market follower is a runner-up firm that chooses not to rock the boat, usually out of fear that it stands to lose more than it might gain in the process. The follower is not without a strategy, however, and seeks to use its particular competences to participate actively in the growth of the market. Some followers enjoy a higher rate of return on equity than the leaders in their industry.

A market nicher is a smaller firm that chooses to operate in some part of the market that is specialized and not likely to attract the larger firms. Market nichers often become specialists in some end-use, vertical level, customer size, specific customer, geographic area, product or product line, product feature, or service.

QUESTIONS AND PROBLEMS
1. Many people have noted a similarity between business strategy and military strategy. There are the gasoline "price wars," the "border clashes" and "skirmishes" of the major computer manufacturers, the "escalating arms budgets" of the soap companies, "guerilla warfare" by Purex against the soap giants, the "sabotaging" of and "spying" on test markets by competitors, and so on. Without denying the usefulness of military insights and principles, name some limitations of the analogy between business and military competition.

2. Comment on the following statements made about the appropriate marketing strategy of smaller firms: (a) "The smaller firm should concentrate on pulling away the larger firm's customers, while the larger firm should concentrate on stimulating new customers to enter the market." (b) "Larger firms should pioneer new products and the smaller ones stick to copying them."

3. What information about each major competitor should a company regularly gather?

4. It might appear that Caterpillar has no vulnerabilities. However, this is not true. Name some potential threats to Caterpillar.

5. What are some of the marketing principles that General Motors has used to maintain its four decades of leadership in the U.S. auto industry?

6. Briefly critique the following marketing strategy statement: "The company will develop the best product and the best service at the lowest price."

7. The major producer of dance shoes is interested in expanding the total market for its ballet shoes. These are flat-soled slippers which are different from the pointed shoes used for toe dancing. Suggest ways they can do so.

8. Identify the specialist roles assumed by the following firms: (a) Kenmore; (b) Coors Beer; (c) Rolls Royce; (d) Mom and Pop grocery with home delivery.

Product Life-Cycle Strategy

This is one of the saddest days of my life, a sad one for me, for our employees, officers, and directors; indeed, it is sad for the American public. Apparently, there is just not the need for our product in today's scheme of living.
MARTIN ACKERMAN, President of *The Saturday Evening Post*

We are now ready to examine the role played by product life cycle and market evolution in the formulation of marketing strategy. A product's marketing strategy needs periodical revision during its passage through the life cycle. The first part of the chapter will examine the concept of product life cycle and consider appropriate strategies during the stages of introduction, growth, maturity, and decline. The second part will examine how markets as a whole evolve under the impetus of innovation and competition.

THE CONCEPT OF PRODUCT LIFE CYCLE

A product's sales position and profitability can be expected to change over time. The product life cycle is an attempt to recognize *distinct stages* in the *sales history* of the product. Corresponding to these stages are distinct opportunities and problems with respect to marketing strategy and profit potential. By identifying the stage that a product is in, or may be headed toward, companies can formulate better marketing plans.[1]

[1] For some excellent articles on product life cycle, see Robert D. Buzzell, "Competitive Behavior and Product Life Cycles," in *New Ideas for Successful Marketing*, ed. John S. Wright and

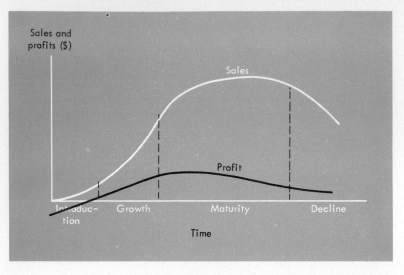

FIGURE 12–1
Sales and Profit Life Cycles

Most discussions of product life cycle (PLC) portray the sales history of a typical product as following the form of an S-shaped sales curve as illustrated in Figure 12–1. This curve is typically divided into four stages known as *introduction, growth, maturity,* and *decline*.[2] *Introduction* is a period of slow growth as the product is introduced in the market. The profit curve in Figure 12–1 shows profits as almost nonexistent in this stage because of the heavy expenses of product introduction. *Growth* is a period of rapid market acceptance and substantial profit improvement. *Maturity* is a period of a slowdown in sales growth because the product has achieved acceptance by most of the potential buyers. Profits peak in this period and start to decline because of increased marketing outlays (not shown) to sustain the product's position against competition. Finally, *decline* is the period when sales continue a strong downward drift and profits erode toward the zero point.

The designation of where each stage begins and ends is somewhat arbitrary. Usually the stages are based on where the rate of sales growth or decline tends to become pronounced. Polli and Cook proposed an operational measure based on a normal distribution of percentage changes in real sales from year to year.[3]

Not all products pass through the idealized S-shaped product life cycle

Jac L. Goldstucker (Chicago: American Marketing Association, 1966), pp. 46–68; William E. Cox, Jr., "Product Life Cycles as Marketing Models," *Journal of Business,* October 1967, pp. 375–84; Theodore Levitt, "Exploit the Product Life Cycle," *Harvard Business Review,* November–December 1965, pp. 81–94; Rolando Polli and Victor Cook, "Validity of the Product Life Cycle," *Journal of Business,* October 1969, pp. 385–400; and Thomas A. Staudt and Donald A. Taylor, *A Managerial Introduction to Marketing* (Englewood Cliffs, N.J.: Prentice-Hall, 1970), chap. 10.

[2] Some authors distinguish additional stages. *Maturity* describes a stage of sales growth slowdown and *saturation* a stage of flat sales after sales have peaked. A stage of *petrification* follows *decline* if sales again stabilize at some low but positive level. See George C. Michael, "Product Petrification: A New Stage in the Life Cycle Theory," *California Management Review,* fall 1971, pp. 88–91.

[3] Polli and Cook, "Product Life Cycle."

shown in Figure 12–1. Some products show a rapid growth from the very beginning, thus skipping the slow sales start implied by the introductory stage. Other products, instead of going through a rapid-growth stage, go directly from introduction to maturity. Some products move from maturity to a second period of rapid growth. Cox studied the product life cycles of 754 ethical-drug products and found six different product life-cycle patterns.[4] The most typical form was a "cycle-recycle" pattern (see Figure 12–2A). Cox explained the second "hump" in sales as being caused by a traditional promotional push in the decline stage. Some investigators have reported a "scalloped" life-cycle pattern (see Figure 12–2B), which represents a succession of life cycles for this product based on the discovery of new-product characteristics, new usages, or new markets. Often the more anomalous life-cycle patterns are really temporal sequences of the normal life-cycle pattern.

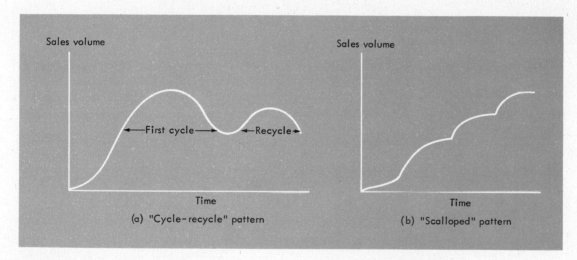

FIGURE 12–2
Some Anomalous Product Life-Cycle Patterns

Studies by Buzzell of grocery food products and Polli and Cook of various consumer nondurables showed the PLC concept to hold up well for many product categories. Those planning to use this concept must investigate the extent to which the PLC concept holds up for products in their industry. They will learn whether the normal sequence of stages is followed and the average duration of each stage. Cox found that a typical ethical drug that followed the normal PLC cycle spanned an introductory period of one month, a growth stage of six months, a maturity stage of fifteen months, and a decline stage that exceeded the sum of the previous three stages—mainly because of the reluctance of manufacturers to drop drugs from their catalogs. These lengths must be reviewed periodically. It appears that increasing competition is leading to a shortening of PLCs over time, which means that products make profits for shorter periods.

[4] Cox, "Product Life Cycles."

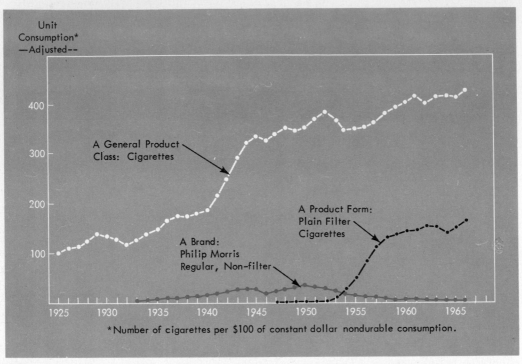

Unit Consumption* —Adjusted--

A General Product Class: Cigarettes

A Product Form: Plain Filter Cigarettes

A Brand: Philip Morris Regular, Non-filter

*Number of cigarettes per $100 of constant dollar nondurable consumption.

SOURCE: Rolando Polli and Victor Cook, "Validity of the Product Life Cycle," *Journal of Business*, October 1969, p. 389.

FIGURE 12–3

PLCs for a Product Class, Product Form, and Brand

The PLC concept should be defined with respect to whether the product is a product class (cigarettes), a product form (plain filter cigarettes), or a brand (Philip Morris regular nonfilter). (See Figure 12–3.) The PLC concept has a different degree of applicability in these three cases. Product classes have the longest life histories, longer than particular product forms, and certainly longer than most brands. The sales of many product classes can be expected to continue in the mature stage for an indefinite duration since they are highly related to population (cars, perfume, refrigerators, and steel). Product forms, on the other hand, tend to exhibit the standard PLC histories more faithfully than do product classes. Product forms such as the dial telephone and cream deodorants seem to pass through a regular history of introduction, rapid growth, maturity, and decline. As for brands, a brand's sales history can be erratic because changing competitive strategies and tactics can produce substantial ups and downs in sales and market shares, even to the extent of causing a mature brand to suddenly exhibit another period of rapid growth.

Fad and Fashion Life Cycles

There are two special categories of new-product life cycles that should be distinguished from the others: fads and fashions. *Fads* are practices or interests that come quickly into being, are adopted with great zeal, peak early, and decline very fast. Their acceptance cycle is short, and they tend to attract only a limited following. Fads often have a bizarre or capricious aspect, as when people start buying "pet rocks" or "streak" (run naked). Fads appeal to people who are searching for excitement or who want a way to distinguish themselves from others or have something to talk about to others. Fads do not survive because they normally do not satisfy a strong need, or at least do not satisfy it well. It is difficult to predict whether something will only be a fad, and if so, how long it will last—a few days, weeks, or months. The amount of media attention it receives, along with other factors, will influence its duration.

Fashions, in contrast, are interests that tend to grow slowly, remain popular for a while, and decline slowly. Fashion life cycles come closer to resembling the normal product life cycle. There are fashion styles in cars (long and low look), women's clothing (mini-skirt), and men's haircuts (long hair). Some fashions are classic and last a long time, such as a man's dark blue business suit and a woman's basic black dress.

The length of a fashion cycle is hard to predict in advance. Wasson believes that fashions come to an end because they represent an inherent purchase compromise such that the consumer starts looking for missing attributes after a while.[5] For example, as automobiles get shorter, they get less comfortable, and then a growing number of buyers start wanting longer cars. Furthermore, too many consumers adopt the fashion, thus turning others away. Reynolds suggests that the length of a particular fashion cycle depends on the extent to which the fashion meets a genuine need, is consistent with other trends in the society, as well as societal norms and values, and does not meet technological limits as it develops.[6] Robinson, however, sees fashions as living out inexorable cycles regardless of economic, functional, or technological changes in society.[7]

We have described the PLC concept without offering any underlying explanation in market terms. Support for it lies in the theory of the diffusion and adoption of innovations (see pp. 342–46). When a new product appears, steps must be taken by the company to stimulate awareness, interest, trial, and purchase. This takes time, and in the introductory stage only a few persons ("innovators") will buy it. If the product is satisfying, larger numbers of buyers ("early adopters") are drawn in. The entry of competitors into the market speeds up the adoption process by increasing the market's awareness and by exerting a downward pressure on prices. More buyers come in ("early majority") as the product is legitimized. Eventually the rate of growth decreases as the proportion of potential new buyers approaches zero. Sales become steady at the replacement purchase rate. Eventually they decline as new-product classes, forms, and brands appear and divert the interest of the buyers from the existing product. Thus the product life cycle is closely related to normal developments that can be expected in the diffusion and adoption of any new product.

The PLC concept is useful mainly as a framework for developing effective marketing strategies in different stages of the product life cycle. We now turn to the major stages and consider the appropriate marketing strategies.

[5] Chester R. Wasson, "How Predictable Are Fashion and Other Product Life Cycles?" *Journal of Marketing*, July 1968, pp. 36–43.

[6] William H. Reynolds, "Cars and Clothing: Understanding Fashion Trends," *Journal of Marketing*, July 1968, pp. 44–49.

[7] Dwight E. Robinson, "Style Changes: Cyclical, Inexorable, and Foreseeable," *Harvard Business Review*, November–December 1975, pp. 121–31.

INTRODUCTION STAGE

The introduction stage starts when the new product is first made available for general purchase in the marketplace. Prior to introduction, the product has been under a long period of development, which might have included some test marketing in a few cities but not a full-scale launching. The actual introduction of the product in one or more markets takes time, and sales growth is apt to be slow. Such well-known products as instant coffee, frozen orange juice, and powdered coffee creamers lingered for many years before they entered a stage of rapid growth. Buzzell identified four causes for the slow growth of many processed-food products:

1. Delays in the expansion of production capacity
2. Technical problems (working out the bugs)
3. Delays in making the product available to customers, especially in obtaining adequate distribution through retail outlets
4. Customer reluctance to change established behavior patterns[8]

In the case of expensive new products, sales growth is retarded by additional factors such as:

5. Small number of buyers who are attuned to innovations
6. High cost of the product inhibits purchase

In the introductory stage, profits are negative or low because of the low sales and heavy distribution and promotion expenses. Much money is needed to attract distributors and "fill the pipelines." Promotional expenditures are at their highest ratio to sales "because of the need for a high level of promotional effort to (1) inform potential consumers of the new and unknown product, (2) induce trial of the product, and (3) secure distribution in retail outlets."[9]

There are only a few competitors and they produce basic versions of the product, since the market is not ready for product refinements. The firms direct their selling effort to those buyers who are the readiest to buy, usually higher-income groups. Prices tend to be on the high side because "(1) costs are high due to relatively low output rates, (2) technological problems in production may have not yet been fully mastered, and (3) high margins are required to support the heavy promotional expenditures which are necessary to achieve growth."[10]

In launching a new product, marketing management can set a high or a low level for each marketing variable such as price, promotion, distribution, and product quality. Working only with price and promotion, management can choose one of the four strategies shown in Figure 12–4.

A *rapid-skimming strategy* consists of launching the new product with a high price and a high promotion level. The firm charges a high price in order to recover as much gross profit per unit as possible. It spends a lot on promotion to convince the market of the product's merits even at the high-price level. The high promotion serves to accelerate the rate of market penetration. This

[8] Buzzell, "Competitive Behavior," p. 51.

[9] Ibid, p. 51.

[10] Ibid, p. 52.

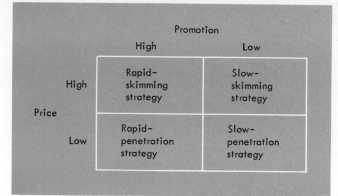

FIGURE 12–4
Four Introductory Marketing Strategies

strategy makes sense under the following assumptions: (1) a large part of the potential market is unaware of the product; (2) those who become aware of the product are eager to have it and are able to pay the asking price; (3) the firm faces potential competition and wants to build up brand preference.

A *slow-skimming strategy* consists of launching the new product with a high price and low promotion. The purpose of the high price is to recover as much gross profit per unit as possible; and the purpose of the low promotion is to keep marketing expenses down. This combination is expected to skim a lot of profit from the market. This strategy makes sense under the following assumptions: (1) the market is relatively limited in size; (2) most of the market is aware of the product; (3) those who want the product are prepared to pay a high price; and (4) there is little threat of potential competition.

A *rapid-penetration strategy* consists of launching the product with a low price and heavy promotion. This strategy promises to bring about the fastest rate of market penetration and the largest market share for the company. This strategy makes sense under the following assumptions: (1) the market is large in size; (2) the market is relatively unaware of the product; (3) most buyers are price sensitive; (4) there is strong potential competition; and (5) the company's unit manufacturing costs fall with the scale of production and accumulated manufacturing experience.

A *slow-penetration strategy* consists of launching the new product with a low price and low level of promotion. The low price will encourage the market's rapid acceptance of the product; at the same time, the company keeps its promotion costs down in order to realize more net profit. The company firmly believes that market demand is highly price-elastic but minimally promotion-elastic. This strategy makes sense if (1) the market is large; (2) the market is highly aware of the product; (3) the market is price sensitive; and (4) there is some potential competition.

GROWTH STAGE

If the new product satisfies the market, sales will start climbing substantially. The early innovators will continue their purchasing and a large number of conventional consumers will begin to follow their lead, especially if there is favorable word of mouth. New competitors will enter the market attracted by the opportunities for large-scale production and profit. They will introduce new features in the product and this will expand the market. The increase in the number of competitors leads to an increase in the number of distribution outlets, and factory sales jump just to fill the pipelines.

Prices tend to remain where they are or fall only slightly during this period, insofar as demand is managing to increase quite rapidly. Companies maintain their promotion expenditures at the same or at a slightly raised level to meet competition and continue educating the market. Sales rise much faster, causing a decline in the promotion-sales ratio.

Profit margins peak during this stage as promotion costs are spread over a larger volume, and unit manufacturing costs fall faster than price declines owing to the "experience-curve" effect. During this stage, the firm tries to sustain rapid market growth as long as possible. This is accomplished in several ways:

1. The firm undertakes to improve product quality and add new features and models.
2. It vigorously searches out new market segments to enter.
3. It keeps its eyes open to new distribution channels to gain additional product exposure.
4. It shifts some advertising copy from building product awareness to trying to bring about product acceptance and purchase.
5. It decides when the time is right to lower prices to attract the next layer of price-sensitive buyers into the market.

The firm that aggressively pursues any or all of these market-expanding strategies will increase its competitive position. But this comes at additional cost. The firm in the growth stage faces a tradeoff between high market share and high current profit. By spending a lot of money on product improvement, promotion, and distribution, it can capture a dominant position; but it forgoes maximum current profit in the hope, presumably, of making up for it in the next stage.

MATURITY STAGE

At some point a product's rate of sales growth will slow down, and the product will enter a stage of relative maturity. This stage normally lasts much longer than the previous stages, and it poses some of the most formidable challenges to marketing management. *Most products are in the maturity stage of the life cycle, and therefore most of marketing management deals with the mature product.*

The maturity stage can be divided into three phases. The first phase is called *growth maturity*. Here, the rate of sales growth starts to decline because of distribution saturation. There are no new distribution channels to fill, although some laggard buyers are continuing to enter the market. The second phase is *stable maturity*, when sales become level on a per capita basis because of market saturation. Most potential consumers have tried the product, and future sales are governed by the rate of population growth and replacement demand. The third phase is *decaying maturity*. The absolute level of sales now starts to decline as some of the customers move toward other products and substitutes.

The beginning of a slowdown in the rate of sales growth has the effect of producing overcapacity in the industry. This overcapacity leads to intensified competition. Competitors engage more frequently in markdowns and off-list pricing. There is a strong increase in promotional budgets, in the form of trade and consumer deals. Other firms increase their research and development budgets to find better versions of the product. These steps, to the extent that they do not stimulate adequate sales increases, mean some profit erosion. Some of the weaker competitors start dropping out. The industry eventually consists of a set of well-entrenched competitors whose basic orientation is toward gaining competitive advantage.

The product manager of a mature product should not be content to simply defend its current position. A good offense will provide the best defense of the product. Three basic strategies are available in this stage: market modification, product modification, and marketing-mix modification.

Market modification   The product manager first looks for opportunities to find new buyers for the product. There are several possibilities.

First the manager looks for *new markets and market segments* that have not yet tried the product. The key to the growth of air freight service, for example, is the constant search of the industry for new business markets to whom they can demonstrate the benefits of air freight over ground transportation.

Second, the manager looks at ways to stimulate *increased usage* among present customers. A common practice of food manufacturers, for example, is to list several recipes on their packages to broaden the consumers' uses of the product.

Third, the manager may want to consider *repositioning* the brand to achieve larger brand sales, although this will not affect total industry sales. For example, a manufacturer of a chocolate drink mix may find that its heavy users are mostly older people. This firm should give serious consideration to trying to reposition the drink in the youth market, which is experiencing faster growth.

Product modification   Managers also try to break out of a stagnant sales picture by initiating calculated changes in the product's characteristics that will attract new users and/or more usage from current users. The *product relaunch* can take several forms.

A strategy of *quality improvement* aims at increasing the functional performance of the product—such aspects as its durability, reliability, speed, and taste. A manufacturer can often make a real gain on competition by launching the "new and improved" automobile, television set, coffee, or cigarette. Grocery manufacturers often call this a "plus" launch and talk about a new additive or advertise the terms "stronger," "bigger," or "better." This strategy is effective to the extent that (1) the product is capable of quality improvement, (2) buyers believe the claims about improved quality, and (3) a sufficient number of buyers are highly responsive to improved quality.

A strategy of *feature improvement* aims at adding new features that expand the product's versatility, safety, or convenience. For example, the addition of power to hand lawn mowers increased the speed and ease of cutting grass. Manufacturers then worked on the problem of engineering better safety features. Some manufacturers have built in conversion features so that the lawn mower doubles as a snow plow. All of these feature improvements are distinguishable from quality improvements on the one hand and styling improvements on the other. Stewart outlines five advantages flowing from a strategy of feature improvement:

1. The development of new functional features is one of the most effective means of building a company image of progressiveness and leadership.

2. Functional features are an extremely flexible competitive tool because they can be adapted quickly, dropped quickly, and often can be made optional at very little expense.

3. Functional features allow the company to gain the intense preference of pre-selected market segments.

4. Functional features often bring the innovating company free publicity.

5. Functional features generate a great amount of sales-force and distributors' enthusiasm.[11]

The chief disadvantage is that feature improvements are highly imitable; unless there is a permanent gain from being first, the feature improvement may not pay.

A strategy of *style improvement* aims at increasing the aesthetic appeal of the product in contrast to its functional appeal. The periodic introduction of new car models amounts to style competition rather than quality or feature competition. In the case of packaged-food and household products, companies introduce color and texture variations and often put great emphasis on package restyling, treating the package as an extension of the product. The outstanding advantage of a style strategy is that each firm may achieve a unique market identity and secure some durable share of the market on the basis of that identification. Yet styling competition also brings a number of problems. First, it is difficult to predict whether people—and which people—will like a new style. Second, style changes usually mean discontinuing the old style, and the company risks losing some of the customers who liked the old style.

Marketing-mix modification   As a final category of mature-product strategy, the product manager should consider the possibility of stimulating sales through altering one or more elements of the marketing mix. One tactic is to cut *prices* in order to attract new triers and competitors' customers. Another is to develop a more effective *advertising* campaign that attracts consumers' attention and interest. A more direct way to attract other brand users is through aggressive promotion—trade deals, cents-off, gifts, and contests. The company can also consider moving into higher-volume *market channels,* particularly discount channels, if they are in a growth stage. The company can also offer new or improved service to the buyer as a patronage-building step.

The main problem with relying exclusively on marketing-mix modification is that these steps are highly imitable by competition, especially price reductions, additional services, and mass-distribution penetration. This means that the firm may not gain as much as expected, and, in fact, all firms may pay a price in the form of profit erosion.

[11] John B. Stewart, "Functional Features in Product Strategy," *Harvard Business Review,* March–April 1959, pp. 65–78.

Most product forms and brands eventually enter a stage of sustained sales decline. The decline may be slow, as in the case of oatmeal; or rapid, as in the case of the Edsel automobile. Sales may plunge to zero and the product may be withdrawn from the market, or sales may petrify at a low level and continue for many years at that level.

Sales decline for a number of reasons. Technical advances may give birth to new product classes and forms that become effective substitutes. Changes in fashion or tastes lead to buyer migration. The lower costs of imported products hurt the domestic producers. All of these have the effect of intensifying overcapacity and price competition, leading to a serious erosion of profits.

As sales and profits decline, a number of firms withdraw from the market in order to invest their resources in more-profitable areas. Those remaining in the industry tend to reduce the number of product offerings. They withdraw from smaller market segments and marginal trade channels. The promotion budget is reduced. The price may also be reduced to halt the decline in demand.

Unfortunately, most companies have not developed a well-thought-out policy for handling their aging products. Sentiment plays a role:

> But putting products to death—or letting them die—is a drab business, and often engenders much of the sadness of a final parting with old and tried friends. The portable, six-sided pretzel was the first product The Company ever made. Our line will no longer be our line without it.[12]

Logic also plays a role. Sometimes it is expected, or hoped, that product sales will improve when the economy improves. Sometimes the fault is thought to lie in the marketing program, and so the company makes plans to revise it. Management may feel that the solution lies in product modification. When none of these explanations works, a weak product may be retained because of its alleged contribution to the sales of the company's other products. The ultimate argument may be that its sales volume at least covers out-of-pocket costs, and the company may temporarily have no better way of keeping its fixed resources employed.

Unless strong retention reasons exist, carrying a weak product is very costly to the firm. The cost of sustaining a weak product is not just the amount of uncovered overhead and profit. No financial accounting can adequately convey all the hidden costs:

> The weak product tends to consume a disproportionate amount of management's time.
>
> It often requires frequent price and inventory adjustments.
>
> It generally involves short production runs in spite of expensive setup times.
>
> It requires both advertising and sales-force attention that might better be diverted to making the "healthy" products more profitable.
>
> Its very unfitness can cause customer misgivings and cast a shadow on the company's image.

[12] R. S. Alexander, "The Death and Burial of 'Sick' Products," *Journal of Marketing*, April 1964, p. 1.

The biggest cost imposed by carrying weak products may well lie in the future. By not being eliminated at the proper time, these products delay the aggressive search for replacement products; they create a lopsided product mix, long on "yesterday's breadwinners" and short on "tomorrow's breadwinners"; they depress current profitability and weaken the company's foothold on the future.

A company faces a number of tasks and decisions to insure the effective handling of its aging products.

Identifying the weak products   The first task is to establish a system that will identify those products that are in a declining stage. Six steps are involved:

1. A product-review committee is appointed with the responsibility for developing a system for periodically reviewing weak products in the company's mix. This committee includes representatives from marketing, manufacturing, and the controller's office.

2. This committee meets and develops a set of objectives and procedures for reviewing weak products.

3. The controller's office supplies data for each product showing trends in market size, market share, prices, costs, and profits.

4. This information is run against a computer program that identifies the most dubious products. The criteria include the number of years of sales decline, market-share trends, gross profit margin, and return on investment.

5. Products put on the dubious list are then reported to those managers responsible for them. The managers fill out diagnostic and prognostic rating forms showing where they think sales and profits on dubious products will go with no change in the current marketing program and with their recommended changes in the current program.

6. The product-review committee examines the product-rating form for each dubious product and makes a recommendation (a) to leave it alone, (b) to modify its marketing strategy, or (c) to drop it.[13]

Determining marketing strategies   In the face of declining sales, some firms will abandon the market earlier than others. The firms that remain enjoy a temporary increase in sales as they pick up the customers of the withdrawing firms. Thus any particular firm faces the issue of whether it should be the one to stay in the market until the end. For example, Procter & Gamble decided to remain in the declining liquid-soap business until the end and made good profits as the others withdrew.

If it decides to stay in the market, the firm faces further strategic choices. The firm could adopt a *continuation strategy*, in which case it continues its past marketing strategy: same market segments, channels, pricing, and promotion. The product simply continues to decline until at last it is dropped from the line. Or the firm could follow a *concentration strategy*, in which case it concentrates its resources only in the strongest markets and channels while phasing out its efforts elsewhere. Finally, it could follow a *harvesting strategy*, in which case it sharply reduces its expenses to increase its current profits, knowing this will accelerate the rate of sales decline and ultimate demise of the product. In some sit-

---

[13] This system is spelled out in detail in the author's "Phasing Out Weak Products," *Harvard Business Review*, March–April 1965, pp. 107–18. Also see Paul W. Hamelman and Edward M. Mazze, "Improving Product Abandonment Decisions," *Journal of Marketing*, April 1972, pp. 20–26.

uations the hard-core loyalty may remain strong enough to allow marketing the product at a greatly reduced level of promotion and at the old or even a higher price, either of which will mean good profits. An interesting example is afforded by Ipana toothpaste:

> Ipana toothpaste was marketed by Bristol-Myers until 1968, when it was abandoned in favor of promoting new brands. In early 1969, two Minnesota businessmen picked up the Ipana name, concocted a new formula but packaged the product in tubes similar to those used by the former marketer. With no promotion, the petrified demand for Ipana turned out to be $250,000 in the first seven months of operation.[14]

The drop decision   When a product has been singled out for elimination, the firm faces some further decisions. First, it has the option of selling or transferring the product to someone else or dropping it completely. Second, it has to decide whether the product should be dropped quickly or slowly. Third, it has to decide what level of parts inventory and service to maintain to cover existing units.

The key characteristics of each of the four stages of the product life cycle are summarized in Table 12–1. In addition, the table summarizes the type of responses typically made by business organizations in each stage.[15]

[14] "Abandoned Trademark Turns a Tidy Profit for Two Minnesotans," *Wall Street Journal*, October 27, 1969, p. 1.

[15] A more elaborate version of normative marketing responses for each stage of the PLC cycle is found in Chester R. Wasson, *Dynamic Competitive Strategy and Product Life Cycles* (Austin, Texas: Austin Press, 1978).

TABLE 12–1
Product Life Cycle: Characteristics and Responses

	INTRODUCTION	GROWTH	MATURITY	DECLINE
Characteristics				
Sales	Low	Fast growth	Slow growth	Decline
Profits	Negligible	Peak levels	Declining	Low or zero
Cash flow	Negative	Moderate	High	Low
Customers	Innovative	Mass market	Mass market	Laggards
Competitors	Few	Growing	Many rivals	Declining number
Responses				
Strategic focus	Expand market	Market penetration	Defend share	Productivity
Mktg. expenditures	High	High (declining %)	Falling	Low
Mktg. emphasis	Product awareness	Brand preference	Brand loyalty	Selective
Distribution	Patchy	Intensive	Intensive	Selective
Price	High	Lower	Lowest	Rising
Product	Basic	Improved	Differentiated	Rationalized

SOURCE: Peter Doyle, "The Realities of the Product Life Cycle," *Quarterly Review of Marketing,* summer 1976, pp. 1–6.

To date, the PLC concept has been the major concept used by marketers to interpret product and market dynamics. Its usefulness varies in different decision-making situations. As a *planning* tool, the PLC concept appears useful in characterizing the main marketing realities of each stage and indicating the major alternative marketing strategies available to the firm in each stage. As a *control* tool, the PLC concept allows the company to roughly gauge how well a product is doing in relation to successful and comparable products that were launched in the past. As a *forecasting* tool, the PLC concept may be of less usefulness because sales histories exhibit various patterns in practice, and the stages last for varying durations.

At the same time, PLC theory has its share of criticism. Critics have said that the life-cycle patterns are too variable, that it is difficult to know what stage the product really is in, and the company marketing actions can influence the course of the product life cycle. Dhalla and Yuspeh have argued that management action based on the PLC is actually harmful in many cases:

> Suppose a brand is acceptable to consumers but has a few bad years because of other factors—for instance, poor advertising, delisting by a major chain, or entry of a "me-too" competitive product backed by massive sampling. Instead of thinking in terms of corrective measures, management begins to feel that its brand has entered a declining stage. It therefore withdraws funds from the promotion budget to finance R&D on new items. The next year the brand does even worse, panic increases. . . . Clearly, the PLC is a *dependent* variable which is determined by marketing actions; it is not an *independent* variable to which companies should adapt their marketing programs.[16]

To this can be added another criticism, that PLC focuses on what is happening to a particular product rather than on what is happening in the overall market. It produces a product-oriented picture rather than a market-oriented picture. It needs to be complemented by a theory that analyzes the evolution of the market itself and the opportunities that are continually emerging.

THE CONCEPT OF MARKET EVOLUTION

Firms need a way to understand not only market statics but also market dynamics. Market statics addresses the question: What are the nature, size, and operations of a particular market? Market dynamics addresses the question: How do markets evolve through time? Firms need a way to anticipate the evolutionary path of a market as it is marked by new needs, competitors, technology, channels, and other developments.

Stages in Market Evolution

A market can be viewed as evolving through stages of market crystallization, expansion, fragmentation, reconsolidation, and termination. We shall describe and illustrate these stages below.

Market-crystallization stage Before a market materializes, it exists as a *latent market*. A *latent market* consists of people who share a similar need or want for

---

[16] Nariman K. Dhalla and Sonia Yuspeh, "Forget the Product Life Cycle Concept!" *Harvard Business Review*, January–February 1976, pp. 102–12, here p. 105.

something that does not yet exist. For example, people want a means of more rapid calculation than can be achieved by mental calculation or by using a paper and pencil. Until recently, this need was imperfectly satisfied through abacuses, slide rules, and large desk calculators.

Suppose John Smith, an entrepreneur, recognizes the latent interest of people in a more convenient and rapid means of calculation. Suppose he imagines a solution in the form of a small, hand-size electronic calculator. He works hard and succeeds in developing a workable prototype. Having solved the technical problem, this entrepreneur now must turn his attention to the marketing problem. He faces the problem of determining target markets, product attributes, price, distribution channels, and promotion for the initial version of this product. Here we will concentrate on only one of these problems, that of determining the product attributes. Suppose he has to decide on two product attributes: (1) *physical size* and (2) *number of arithmetic functions*. Being market oriented, the entrepreneur decides to interview a sample of potential buyers. They are asked to state their preference level for each attribute. Each person's preference, or ideal product, can be represented by a point (called ideal point) in a diagram showing the two attributes.

Suppose the resulting preferences are those shown in Figure 12–5A. Evidently target customers differ greatly in their design preferences. Some consumers want a simple four-function calculator (adding, subtracting, multiplying, and dividing) and others want more functions (calculating percentages, square roots, logs, and so forth). Some consumers want a small hand calculator and others want a large one. When buyer preferences are evenly scattered in a market, it is called a *diffused-preference market*.

The entrepreneur's problem is to design an optimal product for this market.[17] The entrepreneur faces three broad options.

1. He or she can locate the new product in one of the corners of the market *(a single-niche strategy);*
2. He or she can simultaneously launch two or more products to capture two or more parts of the market *(a multiple-niche strategy);*
3. He or she can locate the new product in the middle of the market *(a mass-market strategy).*

For small firms, a single-niche market strategy makes the most sense. A small firm has insufficient resources for capturing and holding the mass market. Larger firms would enter and clobber the small firm. Its best bet is to specialize the new product in size, number of functions, or some other attributes and capture a corner of the market that won't attract competitors for a long time. If it has adequate resources, it might design and introduce products in two or more niches.

If the firm is large, it makes sense to go after the mass market by designing a product that is "medium" in size and number of functions. A product in the center will minimize the sum of the distances of existing preferences from the product. An electronic hand calculator designed for the mass market will create the minimum total dissatisfaction.

[17] This problem is trivial if consumers' preferences turn out to be concentrated; the product will be located where the market is. If there are distinct clusters of preference, the entrepreneur can design a product for the largest cluster or for the cluster that the company can serve best.

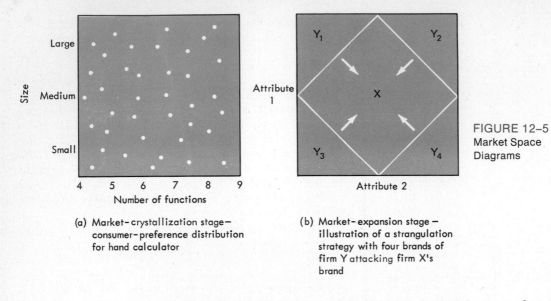

Size

Large

Medium

Small

4 5 6 7 8 9

Number of functions

(a) Market–crystallization stage—
consumer–preference distribution
for hand calculator

Attribute 1

Y_1 Y_2

X

Y_3 Y_4

Attribute 2

(b) Market–expansion stage —
illustration of a strangulation
strategy with four brands of
firm Y attacking firm X's
brand

FIGURE 12–5
Market Space
Diagrams

We will assume that the pioneer firm is large and desires to design a product for the mass market. It is subsequently launched and sales start to climb. We can say that the stage of *market crystallization* has begun.

Market-expansion stage   An interesting question now arises. Where will a second firm enter the market, assuming that the first firm has established itself in the center? This begins the *market-expansion stage*. The second firm has three broad options:

1. It can locate its brand in one of the corners (*a single-niche strategy*).
2. It can locate its brand next to the first competitor (*a mass-market strategy*).
3. It can launch two or more products in different unoccupied corners of the market space (*a multiple-niche strategy*).

If the second firm is small, it will want to avoid head-on competition with the pioneer. It will launch a product in one of the market corners. Thus Hewlett-Packard chose to produce an advanced and premium-priced hand calculator instead of battling it out with Bowmar, the pioneer, for control of the mass market.

If the second firm is large, it might choose to launch its brand in the center against the pioneer firm. The two firms can easily end up sharing the mass market almost equally. In political markets, the two major candidates will each go after the mass market because a candidate needs 50-plus percent to win.

A large second firm can alternatively try to implement a multiniche strategy. Procter & Gamble will occasionally enter a market containing a large entrenched competitor, and instead of launching a me-too product or single-segment product, it introduces a succession of products aimed at different segments. Each entry creates its own loyal following and takes some business away from the major competitor. Soon the major competitor is surrounded, its revenue is weakened, and it is in no position to launch a counteroffensive of new brands in outlying segments. P&G, in a moment of final triumph, then launches a brand against the major segment. This is called a strangulation strategy and is illustrated in Figure 12–5B.

Market-fragmentation stage Each successive firm that enters the market will go after some position, either locating next to a competitor or seeking to serve some new segment. A point is reached where the competitors now cover and serve all the major market segments. In fact, they go further and invade each other's segments, reducing everyone's profit levels in the process. The market splits into finer and finer fragments. This is called the *market-fragmentation stage*. There are a few uncovered segments whose needs are not met by existing products, but they are too small to be served economically. The market reaches maturity, with few new products emerging at this stage. This is illustrated in Figure 12–6A, with the letters representing different companies supplying various segments. Note that two segments are unserved.[18]

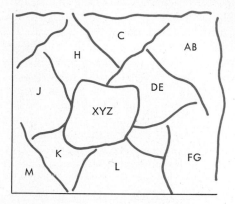

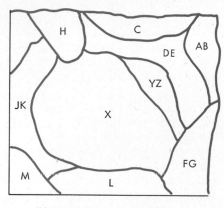

FIGURE 12–6
Market-Fragmentation
and Market-Reconsolidation
Stages

(a) Market-fragmentation stage

(b) Market-reconsolidation stage

Market-reconsolidation stage This, however, is not the end of the evolution of a market. The stage of fragmentation is often followed by a *market-reconsolidation stage*, caused by the development of a new attribute that has cogent market appeal. This happened in the toothpaste market, for example, when P&G introduced its new fluoride toothpaste, Crest, which effectively retarded dental decay. Suddenly other toothpaste brands that claimed whitening power, cleaning power, sex appeal, taste, or mouthwash effectiveness were pushed into the corners because consumers predominantly wanted a toothpaste that gave anticavity protection. P&G's Crest won a lion's share of the market, as shown by the X territory in Figure 12–6B.

But even a reconsolidated market is not the terminal stage in the evolution of a market. Other companies will copy the successful brand, and the market will eventually become fragmented again. Markets seem to swing between mar-

---

[18] The product space is drawn with two attributes for simplicity. In point of fact, more attributes come into being as the market evolves. The product space grows from a two-dimensional to an *n*-dimensional space, which unfortunately cannot be drawn.

ket fragmentation and market reconsolidation. The fragmentation is brought about by competition and the reconsolidation is brought about by innovation.

Market-termination stage   Termination of this "see-saw" process occurs when a radically new innovation destroys the old market. If an entrepreneur discovers a spray that is more effective than toothpaste, the discovery will eventually destroy the toothpaste market. This is called the *market-termination stage.* Thus a product form ends when a new form emerges that meets consumer needs in a superior way.

Dynamics of Attribute Competition

We have seen how markets move through the stages of *market crystallization, market expansion, market fragmentation, market reconsolidation,* and eventually *market termination.* In the long run, markets have a tendency to deteriorate in their value to the sellers because of free entry and competition. The process is temporarily reversed through *innovation,* that is, the development of new customer benefits. The evolution of markets is very much the history of various firms identifying new benefits to offer to the buyers.

We can illustrate this process with the example of paper towels. Formerly, homemakers used only cotton and linen dish cloths and towels in their kitchens. A paper company, looking for new markets, developed paper towels to compete with the cloth. This development crystallized a new market. Other paper manufacturers entered and expanded the market. Eventually, the number of brands proliferated and created market fragmentation. Overcapacity in the industry led the various manufacturers to search for new features. One manufacturer, hearing consumers complain that the paper towels were not sufficiently absorbent, introduced "superabsorbent" paper towels and regained a large market share. This stage of market reconsolidation did not last long because competitors soon came out with their version of superabsorbent paper towels. Soon the market was fragmented again. Then another manufacturer heard consumers express a wish for a "superstrength" paper towel, and proceeded to introduce one. It was soon copied by other manufacturers. Later another manufacturer introduced a lint-free paper towel, which was subsequently copied. Thus paper towels evolved from a simple product to one with various absorbencies, strengths, and applications. Market evolution was driven by the forces of innovation and competition.

Competition in a market produces a succession of product attributes. If a new attribute draws demand, then several competitors soon offer it, and it loses its determinance. To the extent that most banks are now "friendly," friendliness is no longer a basis for consumer choice among banks. To the extent that most airlines serve in-flight meals, meals are no longer a basis for air-carrier choice. This suggests the strategic importance of a company's maintaining leadership in the innovation of new attributes. Each new attribute, if successful, creates a differential advantage for the firm, leading to temporarily higher-than-average market share and profits. The market leader must learn to routinize innovation.

The crucial question is, Can a firm look ahead and anticipate the sequence of attributes that are likely to be high in demand and technologically feasible over time? How can the firm search for new attributes? There are four possible approaches.

The first approach employs an *empirical process* to identify new attributes. The company surveys consumers to find out what attributes consumers would like added to the product and the relative demand intensity for each. The firm also considers the cost of developing each new attribute and likely competitive initiatives and reactions. It then seizes on those attributes promising to generate the highest profit contribution.

The second approach sees attribute search as primarily the outcome of an *intuitive process*. Entrepreneurs, in particular, prefer to use their intuition to identify new attributes. They go into product development without using marketing research to confirm their hunches. Natural selection determines the winners and the losers. If a manufacturer spots an attribute that the market turns out to want, that manufacturer is considered smart, although from another perspective, he or she was only lucky. This theory offers no guidance as to how to foresee new valued attributes.

A third approach says that new attributes unfold through a *dialectical process*. Any valued attribute gets pushed to an extreme through the competitive process. Thus blue jeans started out as an inexpensive article of clothing and over time have become fashionable and more expensive. This unidirectional elaboration, however, contains the seeds of its own destruction. Eventually some manufacturer will discover a new cheap material and consumers will flock to buy it. The message of dialectical theory is that the same innovators should not try to march ahead of their competitors but rather should head in the opposite direction toward market segments that are suffering from neglect.

A fourth approach holds that new attributes emerge through a *needs-hierarchy process*. On this theory, we would predict that the first automobiles would provide basic transportation and be designed for safety. At a later time, automobiles would start appealing to social acceptance and status needs. Still later, automobiles would be designed to help people "fulfill" themselves. The innovator's task is to assess when the market is ready to satisfy the next-higher level of need.

The actual unfolding of new attributes in a market is more complex than any simple theories would suggest. We should not underestimate the influence of technological and societal processes in influencing the emergence of new attributes. For example, the strong consumer interest in compact-size television sets remained unmet until miniaturization technology was sufficiently advanced. Technological forecasting is one important approach to trying to anticipate the timing of future technological developments that will permit new attribute offers to consumers. The societal factor also plays a major role in shaping attribute evolution. Developments such as inflation, shortages, environmentalism, consumerism, and new life styles create consumer disequilibrium and lead consumers to reevaluate actual and potential product attributes. For example, inflation increases the desire for a smaller car, and car safety increases the desire for a heavier car. The innovator must use marketing research to gauge the values that consumers put on different attributes in order to determine the company's best move vis-à-vis competition.

SUMMARY

Every new product that is launched enters a product life cycle marked by a changing set of problems and opportunities. The sales history of the typical product is commonly thought to follow an S-shaped curve made up of four stages. The *introduction* stage is marked by slow growth and minimal profits as the product is pushed into distribution. The company has to decide during this stage between the four strategies of rapid skimming, slow skimming, rapid penetration, or slow penetration. If successful, the product enters a *growth* stage marked by rapid sales growth and increasing profits. During this stage, the company attempts to improve the product, enter new market segments and distribution channels, and reduce its prices slightly. There follows a *maturity* stage in which sales growth slows down and profits stabilize. The company seeks innovative strategies to renew sales growth, including market, product, and marketing-mix modification. Finally, the product enters a stage of *decline* in which little can be done to halt the deterioration of sales and profits. The company's task during this period is to identify the truly declining products, develop for each one a strategy of continuation, concentration, or milking, and finally phase out the product in a way that minimizes the hardship to company profits, employees, and customers.

Product life-cycle theory must be complemented by a theory of market dynamics that provides guidelines as to the structure of the total market and the kinds of new attributes to which the market is ready to respond. The general theory of market evolution holds that new markets *crystallize* with the recognition of an unsatisfied need or a way to better satisfy existing needs. The innovator usually designs a product for the mass market. Competitors start entering the market with similar or different products leading to *market expansion*. The market undergoes increasing *fragmentation* until some firm recognizes a new determinant attribute that *reconsolidates* the market into fewer and larger parts. This stage does not last because firms are always seeking differential advantage and their actions continue to break large markets into smaller markets. There is often a cycling back and forth between market reconsolidation based on innovation and fragmentation based on competition. The market may ultimately terminate upon the discovery of a superior new product form.

Companies must know how to anticipate specific attributes that the market may want. Profits go to those who are early in introducing new and valued benefits. The search for new attributes can be based on empirical work, intuition, dialectical reasoning, or needs-hierarchy reasoning.

The main role of market evolution theory is to shift the attention of marketers from specific product and brand evolution to the evolution of the overall market. Each product tells only a limited story about the opportunities and evolution of the market. Successful marketing comes through creative interpretation of the market's evolutionary potential.

**QUESTIONS
AND
PROBLEMS**

1. Beer is a product that appears to be in the mature stage of its life cycle. Can you suggest some steps that can be taken by the industry to boost sales?

2. "In fact, it is this writer's contention that once one has stated that products are 'born' and that most 'die,' most of the usefulness of the life cycle model has been exhausted. It is simply not a very rich model." Do you agree?

3. Develop a long-range plan for marketing a new line of electric can openers, indicating for each stage in the product's life cycle (introductory, growth, maturity, and decline) the major objective and the likely policy on price, quality, advertising, personal selling, and channels.

4. For each appliance, indicate in which stage of the product life cycle it is found: (a) refrigerators; (b) room air conditioners; (c) wringer-type washing machines; (d) compactors.

5. As a product passes through the successive stages of its product life cycle, both its rate of sales growth and its rate-of-return on investment change. Using these two variables as axes, develop a diagram showing the typical trajectory of these variables over the product life cycle.

6. Discuss the changes in the promotion level and mix in the different stages of the product life cycle.

7. Select a fad and a fashion and plot their product life-cycle patterns on one graph. How do they differ from each other?

8. What is the difference between a product life-cycle analysis of the product class "paper towels" and the market evolution analysis of them found in the chapter?

New-Product-Development Strategy

Nothing in this world is so powerful as an idea whose time has come.
VICTOR HUGO

The message of the product life cycle is that companies cannot rely on their current products to produce the target rate of sales and profit growth. As some of the company's products enter the decline stage, the company will have to take concrete steps to replace them. The "planning gap" between desired and expected sales growth can be filled by the company in only two basic ways: *acquisition* or *innovation*.

The acquisition route can take one of three forms. First, the company can pursue a *corporate-acquisition* program involving the search for smaller companies that have attractive product lines. Acquisition-minded companies, such as Beatrice Food and Litton Industries, have developed great experience in spotting and negotiating with companies for takeover. Second, the company can pursue a *patent-acquisition* program in which it buys the rights to new products from their original inventors or patent holders. Third, the company can make an effort to become a *licensee* in the manufacture of various products that it wants to produce. In all three cases, the company does not contribute to the development of new products but simply acquires the rights to produce existing ones.

The innovation route can take one of two basic forms. The company can pursue *internal innovation* by setting up and operating its own research and development department. Or it can pursue *contract innovation*, which involves hiring independent researchers or new-product-development agencies to attempt to develop specified products for the firm.

Many companies will combine several of these strategies for growth. General Mills, for example, tries to base its growth on a fifty-fifty mix of acquisition and innovation. Its management feels that the economics favor acquisition at times and innovation at other times, and they want to be skilled at both.

This chapter will focus on innovation as growth strategy, because of the heavy role that marketing plays in finding, developing, and launching successful new products. "New products" for our purposes will mean *products, product modifications,* and *brands* that the firm brings into existence through research and development effort conducted either inside or outside the firm. We will also be concerned with whether the consumer sees them as "new," although this will not be our primary criterion.

THE NEW-PRODUCT-DEVELOPMENT DILEMMA

Under modern conditions of competition, it is becoming increasingly risky not to innovate. Consumers and industrial customers want and expect a stream of new and improved products. Competition will certainly do its best to meet these desires. A program of managed innovation seems to be a necessity.

At the same time, innovation can also be very risky. Ford lost an estimated $350,000,000 on its ill-fated Edsel; and Du Pont lost an estimated $100,000,000 on its Corfam (synthetic leather). Xerox's venture into computers was a disaster; and the French Concorde aircraft probably will never recover its investment. A survey of 125 companies indicated that the median percentage of major new products and services whose performance fell short of expectations was 20 percent for industrial product manufacturers, around 18 percent for service industries, and approximately 40 percent for consumer-product manufacturers.[1] The last rate is particularly discouraging and very costly to the consumer-product manufacturers who miss the mark.

Looking ahead, successful new-product development may be even harder to achieve as time goes on. There are several reasons for this.

1. *Shortage of important new-product ideas.* Some technologists think there is a shortage of fundamentally new technologies—on the order of the automobile, television, computers, xerography, and wonder drugs. Although there are many minor new products emerging, the nation needs major innovations to avoid economic stagnation.

2. *Fragmented markets.* Keen competition is leading to increasingly fragmented markets. Companies have to aim new products at smaller market segments rather than the mass market. This means lower sales and profits, although the companies may maintain their positions longer.

3. *Growing social and governmental constraints.* New products increasingly have to satisfy public criteria in addition to promising reasonable profits. They must be designed with consideration given to consumer safety and ecological compatibility. Government requirements have slowed down the rate of innovation in

[1] David S. Hopkins and Earl L. Bailey, "New Product Pressures," *The Conference Board Record,* June 1971, pp. 16–24.

the drug industry and have considerably complicated product design and advertising decisions in such industries as industrial equipment, chemicals, automobiles, and toys.

4. *Costliness of new-product-development process.* A company typically has to develop a great number of new-product ideas in order to finish with a few good ones. Booz, Allen & Hamilton studied this question for fifty-one companies and summarized its findings in the form of a decay curve of new-product ideas. (See Figure 13–1.) Of every fifty-eight ideas, about twelve pass the initial screening test, which shows them to be compatible with company objectives and resources. Of these, some seven remain after a thorough evaluation of their profit potential. About three survive the product-development stage, two survive the test-marketing stage, and only one is commercially successful. Thus, about fifty-eight new ideas must be generated to find one good one. This one successful idea must be priced at a profitable enough level to cover all the money lost by the company in researching fifty-seven other ideas that failed.

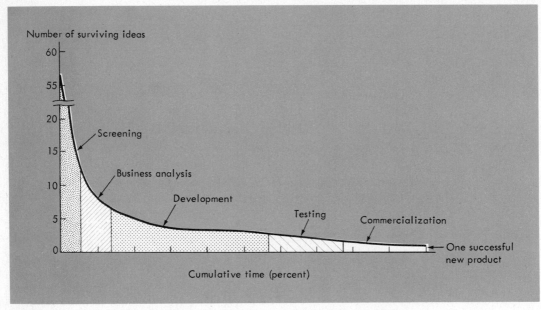

SOURCE: Redrawn from *Management of New Products,* 4th ed. (New York: Booz, Allen & Hamilton, 1968), p. 9.

FIGURE 13–1
Decay Curve of New-Product Ideas (Fifty-One Companies)

5. *Capital shortage.* The high cost of new-product development is no longer affordable by many companies because of the high cost of money. This is pushing many companies to favor product modification and imitation in preference to true innovation.

6. *Shorter life spans of successful products.* Even when a new product turns out to be a commercial success, rivals are so quick to follow suit that the new product is typically fated for only a short, happy life. The race to be first on the market sometimes assumes grotesque proportions. Alberto-Culver was so eager to beat a

new Procter & Gamble shampoo to the market that it developed a name and filmed a TV commercial before it had even developed its own product.

Thus management faces a dilemma; it should develop new products, yet the odds weigh heavily against their success. The answer must lie in conducting new-product development in a way that reduces the risk of failure. But what are the major causes of new-product failure? The most frequently cited causes are:

1. A high-level executive favors the idea and pushes it through in spite of the lack of supporting evidence.
2. Poor organizational systems for handling new-product ideas (poor criteria, poor procedures, poor coordination of departments).
3. Poor market-size measurement, forecasting, and market research.
4. Poor marketing planning, such as poor positioning, poor segmentation, under-budgeting, overpricing.
5. Lack of product distinctiveness or consumer benefit.
6. Poor product design.
7. Unexpectedly high product-development costs.
8. Unexpectedly intense competitive response.

The first two factors call for better organizational arrangements, and the last five factors call for improved techniques at each stage of the new-product-development process.

EFFECTIVE ORGANIZATIONAL ARRANGEMENTS

Top management must take the ultimate responsibility for the quality of the new-product-development work at the company. It cannot simply hire some new-product specialists and leave it to them to come up with useful new ideas. Effective new-product-development work must start with a clear definition by top management of its growth strategy, particularly in terms of the business domains and product categories in which it wants to do business. This will avoid lower management's working on ideas that top management won't ultimately buy. In one food company, the new-product manager spent thousands of dollars researching an exciting new snack idea only to hear the president say months later, "Drop it. We don't want to be in the snack business."

Top management should try to get quite specific about their criteria for new-product idea acceptance, especially in a large multidivisional company where all kinds of projects can bubble up as the favorites of specific managers. The Gould Corporation, for example, established the following acceptance criteria: (1) the product can be introduced within five years; (2) the product has a market potential of at least $50 million and a 15 percent growth rate; (3) the product will provide at least 30 percent return on sales and 40 percent on investment; and (4) the product will achieve technical or market leadership.

A major problem of top management is how much to budget for new-product development. Research and development is so uncertain in its outcomes that it is difficult to use normal investment criteria for budgeting. Some companies solve this problem by encouraging as many project proposals as possible

TABLE 13–1

Estimated Cost of Finding One Successful New Product (Starting with Sixty-four New Ideas)

STAGE	NUMBER OF IDEAS	PASS RATIO	COST PER PRODUCT IDEA	TOTAL COST
1. Idea screening	64	1:4	$ 1,000	$ 64,000
2. Concept test	16	1:2	20,000	320,000
3. Product development	8	1:2	200,000	1,600,000
4. Test marketing	4	1:2	500,000	2,000,000
5. National launch	2	1:2	5,000,000	10,000,000
			$5,721,000	$13,984,000

and financing as many as are promising. Other companies set their R&D budget by using a conventional percentage-to-sales figure, or by spending an amount comparable to competition. Still other companies develop a set of objectives with respect to how many successful new products they want, and work backwards to estimate the rough investment cost required.

Table 13–1 shows the worksheet for this last method. The manager of the new-products department reviewed the results of sixty-four recent new-product ideas processed in the company. Only one in four, or sixteen, ideas passed the idea-screening stage, and it cost the company an average of $1,000 per idea reviewed at this stage. Half of the surviving ideas, or eight, survived the concept-testing stage, at a cost of $20,000 each. Half of those, or four, survived the product-development stage, at a cost of $200,000 each. Half of those, or two, did well in the test market, at a cost of $500,000 each. When these two ideas were launched, at a cost of $5,000,000 each, only one was highly successful. Thus the one successful idea had cost the company $5,721,000 to develop. In the process, sixty-three other ideas fell by the wayside. Therefore the total cost for developing one successful new product was $13,984,000. Unless the company can find ways to improve the pass ratios and reduce the costs at each stage, it will have to budget nearly $14,000,000 for each successful new idea it hopes to find. If top management wants four successful new products over the next few years, it will have to budget $56,000,000 (= 4 × $14,000,000) for new-product development, and even more, to allow for inflation.

A key factor in effective new-product-development work is to establish workable organizational structures. Companies use five different organizational arrangements for handling the new-product development.[2]

1. *Product managers.* Many companies leave new-product development up to their product managers. In practice, this system has several faults. The product managers are usually too busy managing their product lines to give much thought to new products other than brand modification or extension; they also lack the specific skills and knowledge needed to successfully develop new products.

[2] See *Organization for New-Product Development* (New York: Conference Board, 1966); and David S. Hopkins, *Options in New-Product Organization* (New York: Conference Board, 1974).

2. **New-product managers.** General Foods and Johnson & Johnson have established positions of new-product managers who report to group product managers. This position adds professionalization to the new-product function; on the other hand, new-product managers tend to think in terms of product modifications and line extensions limited to their product market. The position often does not have sufficient authority or top-level support.

3. **New-product committees.** Most companies have a high-level management committee charged with reviewing new-product proposals. Consisting of representatives from marketing, manufacturing, finance, engineering, and other departments, its function is not development or coordination so much as the reviewing and approving of new-product plans.

4. **New-product departments.** Large companies often establish a new-product department headed by an executive who is given substantial authority and access to top management. This executive normally reports to the chief executive, or marketing vice president, or research and development vice president. The department's major responsibilities include generating and screening new ideas, directing and coordinating research and development work, and carrying out field testing and precommercialization work.

5. **New-product venture teams.** Dow, Westinghouse, Monsanto, and General Mills assign major new-product-development work to venture teams. A venture team is a group specifically brought together from various operating departments and charged with the responsibility of bringing a specific product to market or a specific new business into being.

We are now ready to look at the successive stages of the new-product-development process. Eight stages are involved: *idea generation, screening, concept development and testing, marketing strategy, business analysis, product development, market testing,* and *commercialization.*

IDEA GENERATION

The first stage in the new-product-development process is the generation of ideas. Firms vary in how they go about finding ideas. Some are very casual and simply keep their ears open to new possibilities. Others identify product categories in which to concentrate their search effort. The search effort is narrow gauged when they rely on one or a few sources for ideas; or broad gauged when they rely on many sources. Furthermore, ideas may be generated intuitively or through special techniques. Here we will examine the major sources and techniques for generating ideas.

Sources of New-Product Ideas

The major sources of new-product ideas are customers, scientists, competitors, company salesmen and dealers, and top management.

Customers The marketing concept suggests that customers' needs and wants are the logical starting point in the search for new-product ideas. Hippel has shown that a great number of ideas for new industrial products are user generated, which means companies must design better systems for spotting these ideas.[3] Companies can identify customers' needs and wants in several ways: (1) direct customer surveys, (2) projective tests, (3) focused group discussions, (4)

---

[3] Eric A. von Hippel, "Users as Innovators," *Technology Review,* January 1978, pp. 3–11.

suggestion systems and letters received from customers, and (5) perceptual and preference mapping of the current product space to discern new opportunities. Many idea hunters claim to find more ideas by asking customers to describe their *problems* with current products rather than by asking them for new-product ideas directly.

Scientists   Many companies hope to find new-product ideas through their scientific research programs. Basic laboratory research has yielded television and transistors, new forms of packaging, and synthetic fibers for clothing. Du Pont and Bell Laboratories are particularly noted for basic research, whereas most companies' R&D labs carry out applied research and often make only minor modifications of existing products.

Competitors   Companies must carefully watch the new-product-development work being done by their competitors. They can catch certain gleanings by listening to distributors, suppliers, and sales representatives as to what seems to be in the works. The sales of new products launched by their competitors should be monitored. The company should assess why they are bought and by whom. Many companies will buy the competitors' products, take them apart, and build a better one. Their growth strategy is one of product imitation and improvement rather than product origination.

Company sales representatives and dealers   Company sales representatives and dealers are a particularly good source of new-product ideas. They have firsthand exposure to customers' unsatisfied needs and complaints. They are often the first to learn of competitive developments. An increasing number of companies are training and rewarding their sales representatives and dealers for producing new ideas.

Top management   Top management is another major source of new-product ideas. Some company leaders, such as Edwin H. Land of Polaroid, take personal responsibility for driving forward technological innovation in their companies. This isn't always constructive, as when a top executive pushes through pet ideas that are insufficiently researched or supported by the available data.

Miscellaneous sources   Other sources of new-product ideas include inventors, patent attorneys, university and commercial laboratories, industrial consultants, advertising agencies, marketing research firms, and industrial publications.

Idea-Generating Techniques

Really good ideas come out of a combination of inspiration, perspiration, and techniques. A large number of "creativity" techniques have been developed over the years to help individuals and groups generate better ideas.

Attribute listing   This technique involves listing the major attributes of an existing object and then imagining ways to modify each attribute in the search for a new combination that will improve the object. Consider a screwdriver.[4] Its attributes are the following: a round, steel shank, a wooden handle, manually oper-

---

[4] See John E. Arnold, "Useful Creative Techniques," in *Source Book for Creative Thinking*, ed. Sidney J. Parnes and Harold F. Harding (New York: Charles Scribner's Sons, 1962), p. 255.

ated, and torque provided by twisting action. Now a group can be asked to propose possible corrections in each attribute to improve product performance or appeal. The round shank could be changed to a hexagonal shank so that a wrench could be applied to increase the torque; electric power could replace manual power; the torque could be produced by pushing. Osborn suggested that useful ideas can be stimulated by putting the following questions to an object or its attributes: put to other uses? adapt? modify? magnify? minify? substitute? rearrange? reverse? combine?[5]

Forced relationships   This technique relies upon listing several objects and then considering each object in relation to every other object. Suppose an office-equipment manufacturer is looking for a novel piece of office equipment.[6] Several objects are listed—a desk, bookcase, filing cabinet, chair. If these pieces are paired, certain ideas occur, for instance, a desk with a built-in bookcase, or a desk with a built-in filing cabinet.

Morphological analysis   This method consists of singling out the most important dimensions of a problem and then examining all the relationships among them. Suppose the problem is described as that of "getting something from one place to another via a powered vehicle."[7] The important dimensions are the type of vehicle to use (cart, chair, sling, bed); the medium in which the vehicle operates (air, water, oil, hard surface, rollers, rails); the power source (pressed air, internal combustion engine, electric motor, steam, magnetic fields, moving cables, moving belt). The next step is to let the imagination loose on every combination. A cart-type vehicle powered by an internal-combustion engine and moving over hard surfaces is the automobile. The hope is that some other combinations will turn out to be quite novel and appealing.[8]

Problem analysis   The preceding creativity techniques have in common an effort to imagine new products without going to the consumer for any input. Problem analysis, on the other hand, starts with the consumer. Consumers are asked to name problems associated with the use of a particular product or product category. Thus Bell & Howell might ask consumers about problems they have with their movie projectors. Each problem can be the source of a new idea. For example: "It is time consuming to rewind the film" suggests automatic rewinding. "The scene is too small to see on the screen" suggests zoom lens. "Some of the film is boring" suggests a fast-forward mechanism. Not all of these ideas, however, are worth developing. The problems have to be rated by their *seriousness, incidence,* and *cost of remedying* in order to choose the ones to work on.

The technique can be reversed and consumers can be given a list of problems and asked to suggest which products come to mind as having each prob-

[5] See Alex F. Osborn, *Applied Imagination*, 3rd ed. (New York: Charles Scribner's Sons, 1963), pp. 286–87.

[6] Ibid., pp. 213–14.

[7] Arnold, "Useful Creative Techniques," pp. 256–57.

[8] See Edward M. Tauber, "HIT: Heuristic Ideation Technique—A Systematic Procedure for New Product Search," *Journal of Marketing*, January 1972, pp. 58–70; and Charles L. Alford and Joseph Barry Mason, "Generating New Product Ideas," *Journal of Advertising Research*, December 1975, pp. 27–32.

lem.[9] Thus the question: "The package of _____ doesn't fit well on the shelf" might lead consumers to name dog foods and dry breakfast cereals. A food marketer might think of entering these markets with a different shape package.

Brainstorming Persons can also be stimulated to greater creativity through certain forms of organized group exercise. One well-known technique is *brainstorming*, whose principles were developed by Alex Osborn. A brainstorming session is held for the sole purpose of producing a lot of ideas. Generally the group size is limited to between six and ten. It is not a good idea to include too many experts in the group, because they tend to have a stereotyped way of looking at a problem. The problem should be made as specific as possible, and there should be no more than one problem. The sessions should last about an hour and may be held at almost any time of the day, although the morning is often the most effective time.

When the meeting takes place, the chairman starts with, "Remember now, we want as many ideas as possible—the wilder the better, and remember, no *evaluation*." The ideas start to flow, one idea sparks another, and within the hour over a hundred or more new ideas may find their way into the tape recorder. For the conference to be maximally effective, Osborn believes the following four rules must be observed:

1. *Criticism is ruled out.* Adverse judgment of ideas must be withheld until later.
2. *Freewheeling is welcomed.* The wilder the idea, the better; it is easier to tame down than to think up.
3. *Quantity is wanted.* The greater the number of ideas, the more the likelihood of useful ideas.
4. *Combination and improvement are sought.* In addition to contributing ideas of their own, participants should suggest how ideas of others can be joined into still another idea.[10]

Freewheeling brainstorming sessions are highly productive of new-product ideas. Within forty minutes, one group of twelve men and women produced 136 ideas.

Synectics William J. J. Gordon felt that the main weakness of the Osborn brainstorming session was that it produced solutions too quickly, before a sufficient number of perspectives had been developed. Gordon decided that instead of defining the problem specifically, he would define it so broadly that the group would have no inkling of the specific problem.

For instance, one of the problems was to design a vaporproof method of closing vaporproof suits worn by workers who handled high-powered fuels.[11] Gordon kept the specific problem a secret and sparked a discussion of the general notion of "closure," which led to images of different closure mechanisms, such as birds' nests, mouths, or thread. As a group exhausted the initial per-

[9] See Edward M. Tauber, "Discovering New Product Opportunities with Problem Inventory Analysis," *Journal of Marketing*, January 1975, pp. 67–70.

[10] Osborn, *Applied Imagination*, p. 156.

[11] John W. Lincoln, "Defining a Creativeness in People," in *Source Book for Creative Thinking*, Parnes and Harding, pp. 274–75.

spectives, Gordon would gradually interject facts that further defined the problem. Only when the group was close to a good solution would Gordon describe the exact nature of the problem. Then the group would start to refine the solution. These sessions would last a minimum of three hours, for Gordon believed that fatigue played an important role in unlocking ideas.

Gordon described five themes that guided these idea-conception conferences:

1. *Deferment.* Look first for viewpoints rather than solutions.
2. *Autonomy of object.* Let the problem take on a life of its own.
3. *Use of the commonplace.* Take advantage of the familiar as a springboard to the strange.
4. *Involvement/detachment.* Alternate between entering into the particulars of the problem and standing back from them, in order to see them as instances of a universal.
5. *Use of metaphor.* Let apparently irrelevant, accidental things suggest analogies which are sources of new viewponts.[12]

IDEA SCREENING

The purpose of idea generation is to create a number of good ideas. The main purpose of all the succeeding stages is to *reduce* the number of ideas. The first idea-pruning stage is screening.

In the screening stage, the company must seek to avoid two types of errors. A *DROP-error* occurs when the company dismisses an otherwise good idea because of a lack of vision of its potentialities. Some companies still shudder when they think of some of the ideas they dismissed:

> Xerox saw the novel promise of Chester Carlson's copying machine; IBM and Eastman Kodak did not see it at all. RCA was able to envision the innovative opportunity of radio; the Victor Talking Machine Company could not. Henry Ford recognized the promise of the automobile; yet only General Motors realized the need to segment the automobile market into price and performance categories, with a model for every classification, if the promise was to be fully achieved. Marshall Field understood the unique market development possibilities of installment buying; Endicott Johnson did not, calling it "the vilest system yet devised to create trouble." And so it has gone.[13]

If a company makes too many DROP-errors, its standards are obviously too conservative.

A *GO-error* occurs when the company lets a poor idea proceed to development and commercialization. We can distinguish at least three types of product failures that ensue. An *absolute product failure* loses money and its sales do not cover variable costs; a *partial product failure* loses money but its sales cover all the variable costs and some of the fixed costs; and a *relative product failure* yields a profit that is less than the company's normal rate of return.

[12] Ibid., p. 274.

[13] Mark Hanan, "Corporate Growth through Venture Management," *Harvard Business Review*, January–February 1969, p. 44.

The job of screening is to spot and drop poor ideas as early as possible. The rationale is that product-development costs rise substantially at each successive stage of the process. When products reach later stages, management often feels that so much has been invested in developing the product that it ought to be launched in the hope of recouping some of the investment. But this is letting good money chase bad money and the real solution is to not let poor product ideas get this far.

Product-Idea-Rating Devices

Most companies require their executives to write up each new-product idea on a standard form that can be reviewed by a new-product committee. At this stage, the ideas are rough, and the form simply requires a description of the product, the target market, competition, and some rough guesses as to market size, product price, development time and costs, manufacturing costs, and level of return.

Even if the idea looks good, the question arises whether the idea is appropriate for the particular company. Does it mesh well with the company's objectives, strategies, and resources? Table 13–2 shows a common type of rating form for this question. The first column lists factors required for successful launching of the product in the marketplace. In the next column, management allocates weights to these factors according to their importance. Thus management believes marketing competence will be very important (.20), and purchasing and supplies competence will be of minor importance (.05). The next task is to rate the company's degree of competence on each factor on a scale from .0 to 1.0. Here management feels that its marketing competence is very high (.9) and its location and facilities competence is low (.3). The final step is to multiply the

TABLE 13–2
Product-Idea-Rating Device

PRODUCT SUCCESS REQUIREMENTS	(A) RELATIVE WEIGHT	(B) COMPANY COMPETENCE LEVEL .0 .1 .2 .3 .4 .5 .6 .7 .8 .9 1.0	RATING (A × B)
Company personality and goodwill	.20	✓ (.6)	.120
Marketing	.20	✓ (.9)	.180
Research and development	.20	✓ (.7)	.140
Personnel	.15	✓ (.6)	.090
Finance	.10	✓ (.9)	.090
Production	.05	✓ (.8)	.040
Location and facilities	.05	✓ (.3)	.015
Purchasing and supplies	.05	✓ (.9)	.045
Total	1.00		.720*

* Rating scale: .00–.40 poor; .41–.75 fair; .76–1.00 good. Present minimum acceptance rate: .70.

SOURCE: Adapted with modifications from Barry M. Richman, "A Rating Scale for Product Innovation," *Business Horizons*, summer 1962, pp. 37–44.

relative importance of the success requirements by the corresponding levels of company competence to obtain a single overall rating of the company's fitness to carry this product successfully into the market. Thus, if marketing is an important success requirement, and this company is very good at marketing, this will increase the overall rating of the product idea. In the example, the product idea scored .72, which, in the company's experience, places it at the high end of the "fair idea" level.

This basic rating device is capable of additional refinements.[14] Whether it is advisable to introduce them is largely a matter of how much more would be gained. The checklist serves as a means of promoting systematic evaluation and discussion of the product idea among management—it is not designed to make the decision for them.

CONCEPT DEVELOPMENT AND TESTING

Those ideas that survive screening must undergo further development into fully mature product concepts. It is important to distinguish between a product idea, a product concept, and a product image. A *product idea* is a possible product, described in objective functional terms, that the company can see itself offering to the market. A *product concept* is a particular subjective consumer meaning that the company tries to build into the product idea. A *product image* is the particular subjective picture consumers actually acquire of the product.

Concept Development

Assume that a large food processor gets the idea to produce a powder that consumers could add to milk to increase the nutritional level and improve the taste. This is a product idea. Consumers, however, do not buy product ideas; they buy product concepts.

A product idea can be turned into a large number of alternative product concepts. First, the question can be asked, Who is to use this product? The powder can be aimed at infants, children, teenagers, young or middle-aged adults, senior citizens, or some combination. Second, What primary benefit should be built into this product? Taste, nutrition, refreshment, energy? Third, What is the primary occasion for this drink? Breakfast, midmorning, lunch, midafternoon, dinner, late evening? By asking these questions, a company can form many alternative product concepts. One is an *instant breakfast drink* aimed at adults who want a quick way to get nutrition at breakfast without preparing a breakfast. Another is a *health supplement* aimed at senior citizens as a nighttime beverage; still another is a *tasty snack drink* designed for children for midday refreshment.

The company must narrow down the choice to one of these concepts. Here it introduces criteria that it wants to achieve with this new product: good rate of return, high sales volume, rounding out of product line, utilization of idle capacity. The criteria could be listed as rows of a matrix, and the alternative product concepts as columns. In each cell a number between 1 and 10 can be placed to indicate how high that product concept stands on that criterion. Certain concepts will profile very poorly on the set of criteria: the market is not large

---

[14] See John T. O'Meara, Jr., "Selecting Profitable Products," *Harvard Business Review*, January–February 1961, pp. 83–89; and John S. Harris, "New Product Profile Chart," *Chemical and Engineering News*, April 1969, pp. 110–18.

enough, the concept is too novel, and so forth. More data are then collected on the remaining concepts until one is finally chosen as the core product concept.

Product and Brand Positioning

Once the core product concept is chosen, it defines the character of the product space in which the new product has to be positioned. An *instant breakfast drink* means that this product will compete against bacon and eggs, breakfast cereals, coffee and pastry, and other breakfast alternatives. A *tasty snack drink* means that this product will compete against soft drinks, fruit juices, and other tasty thirst quenchers. Thus the product concept, and not the product idea, defines the product's competition.

Assume that the instant breakfast drink concept is selected. Figure 13–2A is a *product-positioning map* showing where an instant breakfast drink stands in relation to other breakfast products, using the two dimensions of cost and preparation time. An instant breakfast drink stands in a distinct part of the market, offering the buyer low cost and quick preparation. Its nearest competitor is cold cereal; its most distant competitor is bacon and eggs. This should be kept in mind and utilized in communicating the concept to the market.

If the company is entering an existing product market, then it also has to develop a *brand-positioning map*. Suppose companies A, B, and C have already introduced brands of instant breakfast drinks, which are positioned as shown in Figure 13–2B. The company must decide on how much to charge and how calorific to make its drink, assuming these are salient attributes used by buyers. One possibility is to position the new brand in the medium-price, medium-calorie part of the market; another is to position it in the low-price, low-calorie end of

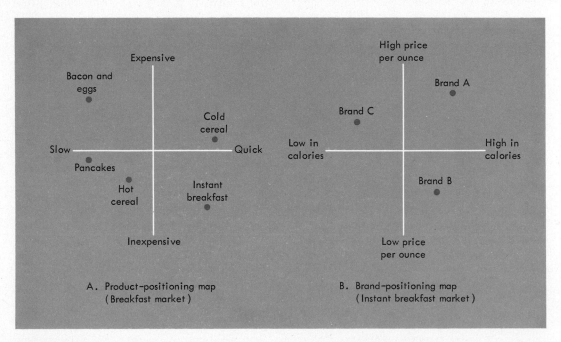

A. Product-positioning map
(Breakfast market)

B. Brand-positioning map
(Instant breakfast market)

FIGURE 13–2
Product and Brand Positioning

the market. Both would give the new brand distinctiveness, as opposed to positioning the brand right next to another brand and fighting intensely for share-of-market. This decision requires researching the size of alternative preference segments of the market.

Concept Testing Through these steps, the company hopes to arrive at a set of viable product or brand concepts. Concept testing calls for taking these concepts to a group of target consumers and getting their reactions. The concepts may be presented symbolically or physically. At this stage, usually a word and/or picture description suffices, although the reliability of a concept test increases, the more concrete and physical the stimulus. The consumers will be shown a word description of a concept, such as:

> A powdered product that is added to milk to make an instant breakfast that gives the person all the breakfast nutrition he or she needs, along with good taste and high convenience. The product would be offered in three flavors, chocolate, vanilla, strawberry, and would come in individual packets, six to a box, at 79¢ a box.

The consumer will be asked to react to each concept and its specific attributes. The concept test should include the following questions:

1. *Is the concept clear and easy to understand?* (Often the concept test reveals that people are not really grasping the concept.)
2. *Do you see some distinct benefits of this product over competing offerings?* (The respondents must recognize distinct benefits of this product over its near substitutes.)
3. *Do you find the concept and claims believable?* (The respondents may have strong doubts about the product claims, which the manufacturer will have to overcome.)
4. *Do you like this product better than its major competitors?* (The respondents report whether they really prefer this product.)
5. *Would you buy this product?* (The company must find out if there is a sufficient percentage of respondents with an actual intention to buy this product.)
6. *Would you replace your current product with this new product?* (The company must find out if the consumer envisions not only trying this product but also substituting it permanently for the current product.)
7. *Would this product meet a real need of yours?* (If consumers do not feel a real need for the product, they may buy it only once for curiosity.) [15]
8. *What improvements can you suggest in various attributes of the product?* (This enables the company to bring about further improvements in form, features, pricing, quality, and so on.)
9. *How frequently would you buy this product?* (This indicates whether the consumer sees it as an everyday product or a specialty product.)
10. *Who would use the product?* (This question helps the marketer define the user target.)
11. *What do you think the price of this product should be?* (This question helps the marketer know the consumer's value perception of the product.)

[15] For a good discussion, see Edward M. Tauber, "Reduce New Product Failures: Measure Needs as Well as Purchase Intention," *Journal of Marketing*, July 1973, pp. 61–64.

The consumers' responses will enable the company to know which concept has the strongest appeal. For example, question 5 goes after the consumer's *intention to buy* and usually reads: "Would you *definitely, probably, probably not, definitely not* buy this product?" Suppose 40 percent of the consumers said "definitely" and another 30 percent said "probably." Most companies have developed norms from past experience to judge how well these intention-to-buy results predict actual buying. One food manufacturer rejects any product idea that does not draw a definite intention-to-buy score above 50 percent. Another food manufacturer takes the "definite" score plus half of the "probable" score and wants the sum to exceed 50 percent.

More advanced methods of concept development and testing are coming into general usage. In the method known as *conjoint analysis*,[16] the researcher develops a set of concepts that share the same attributes but differ in their attribute levels. For example, one concept is an instant breakfast drink that claims nutrition as a benefit, comes in one flavor, and is 79¢; another concept claims refreshment as a benefit, comes in three flavors, and is 69¢; and so on. Each consumer is asked to rank all the concepts from the most preferred to the least preferred. Then the researcher takes the consumers' rankings and applies a mathematical program that estimates the market's utility function for the levels of each attribute. The researcher might discover, for example, that the claim of nutrition adds a great deal to consumer utility but additional flavors add very little. With the aid of these estimated attribute-utility functions, the researcher can go ahead to develop the optimal characteristics for the new brand.

We have focused on a particular example in describing concept development and testing. But the methodology applies to any product, service, or idea, such as an electric car, a new banking service, a new type of museum, or a new health plan. Too many companies think their job is done when they get a product idea. They do not mature it into a full concept and subject it to adequate concept testing. Later the product encounters all kinds of problems in the marketplace that would have been avoided if the company had done a good job of concept development and testing.

MARKETING STRATEGY DEVELOPMENT

The new-product developer will have to develop a preliminary concept of the marketing strategy for introducing this product into the market. The marketing strategy will be rough at this stage and will be refined in subsequent stages.

The marketing strategy statement consists of three parts. The first part describes the size, structure, and behavior of the target market, the intended positioning of the new product in this market, and the sales, market share, and profit goals being sought in the first few years. Thus for the instant breakfast drink the statement might read:

> The target market is families with children who are receptive to a new, convenient, nutritious, and inexpensive form of breakfast. The company's brand will be positioned at the higher-price, higher-quality end of the market. The company

[16] See chapter 6, footnote 23, p. 158. One of the most impressive models for product-concept development and positioning is Glen L. Urban, "Perceptor: A Model for Product Positioning," *Management Science*, April 1975, pp. 858–71.

will aim initially to sell 500,000 cases or 10 percent of the market, with a loss in the first year not exceeding $1.3 million dollars. The second year will aim for 700,000 cases or 14 percent of the market, with a planned profit of $2.2 million dollars.

The second part of the marketing strategy statement will outline the product's intended price, distribution strategy, and marketing budget for the first year. For the instant breakfast cereal, the statement might read:

The product will be offered in a chocolate flavor in individual packets of six to a box at a retail price of 79¢ a box. There will be forty-eight boxes per case and the case's price to distributors will be $24. For the first two months, dealers will be offered one case free for every four cases bought, plus cooperative advertising allowances. Free samples will be distributed door to door. Coupons with 10¢ off will be advertised in newspapers. The total sales promotion budget will be $2,900,000. An advertising budget of $6,000,000 will be split between national and local 50:50. Two-thirds will go into television and one third into newspapers. Advertising copy will emphasize the benefit concept of nutrition and convenience. The advertising-execution concept will revolve around a weak little boy who drinks instant breakfast and grows strong. During the first year, $100,000 will be spent on marketing research to buy store audits and consumer panel information to monitor the market's reaction and buying rates.

The third part of the marketing-strategy statement describes the intended long-run sales and profit goals and marketing-mix strategy over time. For the breakfast drink the statement might read:

The company intends to ultimately capture 25 percent market share and realize an aftertax return on investment of 12 percent. To achieve this, product quality will start high and be further improved over time through technical research. Price will initially be set at a skimming level and lowered gradually to expand the market and meet competition. The total promotion budget will be boosted each year about 20 percent, with the initial advertising/sales promotion split of 63:37 evolving eventually to 50:50. Marketing research will be reduced to $60,000 per year after the first year.

BUSINESS ANALYSIS

Once management has developed a satisfactory product concept and a tentative marketing strategy, it is in a position to do a hardheaded analysis of the business attractiveness of the proposal. Management must review the future sales, costs, and profit estimates as to whether they satisfy the company's objectives. If they do, the product concept can be moved to the product-development stage. As new information comes in, some revision will probably have to take place in the product concept and marketing strategy, calling for revised estimates of sales, costs, and profits. Thus business analysis, which starts in this stage, will be revised at critical review periods during the product's development.

Estimating Sales   The key to whether a product should be developed is whether its sales will be high enough to return a satisfactory profit to the firm. One can obtain some helpful benchmarks by carefully examining the history of previous (analogous) products and surveying market opinion. At the very least, management finds it

helpful to have estimates of minimum and maximum sales to provide some indication of the risk involved.

Estimation methods differ depending upon whether they are designed to
estimate the sales of a one-time purchased product, an infrequently purchased
product, or a frequently purchased product. Figure 13–3A illustrates the product life-cycle sales that can be expected for one-time purchased products. Sales
rise at the beginning, peak, and later approach zero as the number of potential
buyers is exhausted. If new buyers keep entering the market, the curve will not
go down quite to zero.

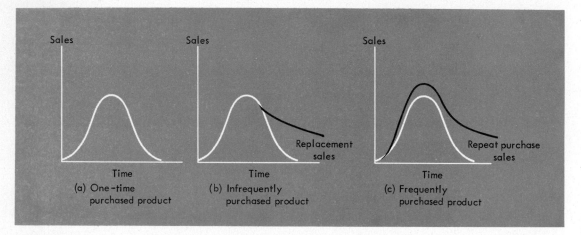

FIGURE 13–3

Product Life-Cycle Sales for Three Types of Products

Infrequently purchased products are exemplified by many durable goods,
such as automobiles, toasters, and industrial equipment. These goods exhibit replacement cycles, dictated either by their physical wearing out or their obsolescence associated with changing styles, features, and tastes. Sales forecasting for
this category of products consists of separately estimating sales and replacement
sales (see Figure 13–3B).

Frequently purchased products, such as consumer and industrial nondurables, have product life-cycle sales resembling Figure 13–3C. The number of
first-time buyers first increases and then decreases as there are fewer left (assuming a fixed population). Repeat-purchase sales occur soon, provided that the
product satisfies some fraction of people who become steady customers. The
sales curve eventually falls to a plateau level representing a level of steady repeat purchase volume; by this time the product is no longer in the class of new
products.

Estimating first-time sales The first task, regardless of the type of product, is to
estimate first-time purchases of the new product in each period. Three examples
will be described.

MEDICAL EQUIPMENT A medical-equipment manufacturer developed a
new instrument for rapidly analyzing blood specimens for various potential-

illness indicators. To estimate market potential, the company first defined the various market segments—they included hospitals, clinics, and unaffiliated laboratories. For each segment, management defined the minimum-size facility that would be a potential customer for the instrument. Then it turned to data indicating the number of such units in each segment. It reduced the number by the estimated purchase probability, which varied from segment to segment. It then cumulated the number of remaining potential customers over the segments and called this the *market potential*. *Market penetration* was then estimated, based on the amount of advertising and personal selling effort per period, the rate of favorable word of mouth, the price set on the machine, and the activity of competitors. These two estimates were then multiplied to form an estimate of sales.

ROOM AIR CONDITIONERS   A number of investigators have proposed that models of epidemics (sometimes called contagion models) provide a useful analogy to the new-product diffusion process. Bass has used an equation based on an epidemic model to forecast future sales of major appliances, including room air conditioners, electric refrigerators, home freezers, black-and-white television, and power lawn mowers.[17] He used sales data for only the first few years of product introduction to estimate sales for the subsequent years, until replacement demand became a big factor. For example, his sales projection for room air conditioners fit the pattern of actual sales with a coefficient of determination, R^2 = .92. The predicted time of peak was 8.6 years as against an actual time of peak of 7.0 years, and the predicted magnitude of peak was 1.9 million as against an actual peak of 1.8 million.

CONSUMER NONDURABLES   Fourt and Woodlock developed a useful first-time sales model that they tested against several new consumer nondurable products.[18] Their observation of new-product market penetration rates showed that (1) cumulative sales approached a limiting penetration level of less than 100 percent of all households, frequently far less, and (2) the successive increments of gain declined. Their equation is

$$q_t = r\bar{q}(1 - r)^{t-1} \tag{13–1}$$

where:

q_t = percentage of total U.S. households expected to try the product in period t

r = rate of penetration of untapped potential

$\bar{q}$ = percentage of total U.S. households expected to eventually try the new product

t = time period

Assume that a new product is about to be introduced where it is estimated that 40 percent of all households will eventually try the new product ($\bar{q}$ = .4). Furthermore, it is estimated that in each period 30 percent of the remaining new-buyer potential is penetrated (r = .3). Therefore the percentage of U.S. households trying the product in each of the first four periods will be

[17] Frank M. Bass, "A New Product Growth Model for Consumer Durables," *Management Science*, January 1969, pp. 215–17.

[18] Louis A. Fourt and Joseph N. Woodlock, "Early Prediction of Market Success for New Grocery Products," *Journal of Marketing*, October 1960, pp. 31–38.

$$q_1 = r\bar{q}(1 - r)^{1-1} = (.3)(.4)(.7^0) = .120$$
$$q_2 = r\bar{q}(1 - r)^{2-1} = (.3)(.4)(.7^1) = .084$$
$$q_3 = r\bar{q}(1 - r)^{3-1} = (.3)(.4)(.7^2) = .059$$
$$q_4 = r\bar{q}(1 - r)^{4-1} = (.3)(.4)(.7^3) = .041$$

As time goes to infinity, the incremental trial percentage goes to zero. To estimate dollar sales from new triers in any period, the estimated trial rate for the period given by equation (13–1) is multiplied by the total number of U.S. households times the expected first-purchase expenditure per household on the product.

Estimating replacement sales   To estimate replacement sales, management has to research the *survival-age distribution* of its product. The lower end of the distribution will indicate when the first replacement sales are expected to take place. The actual timing of replacement will be influenced by such factors as the customer's economic outlook, cash flow, and product alternatives as well as the company's prices, financing terms, and sales effort. Since replacement sales are difficult to estimate before the product is in actual use, some manufacturers prefer to rest the case for launching the new product solely on the basis of first-time sales.

Estimating repeat sales   For a frequently purchased new product, the seller has to estimate repeat as well as first-time sales. This is because the unit value of frequently purchased products is low, and repeat purchases take place soon after the introduction. A high rate of repeat purchasing means buyer satisfaction with the product; sales are likely to remain high even after all first-time purchases take place. The seller should note the percentage of repeat purchases that take place in each *repeat purchase class:* those who buy once, twice, three times, and so on. Some products and brands are bought a few times and then dropped. It is important to estimate whether the repeat-purchase ratio is likely to rise or fall, and at what rate, with deeper repeat-purchase classes.[19]

Estimating Costs and Profits

After preparing the sales forecast, management can proceed to estimate the expected costs and profits of this venture. The costs are gathered through discussions with the R&D and manufacturing departments and include the planned marketing costs described in the marketing strategy statement. Table 13–3 illustrates a five-year projection of sales, costs, and profits for the instant breakfast drink product.

Row 1 shows the projected sales revenue over the five-year period. The company expects to sell $11,889,000 (approximately 500,000 cases at $24 per case) in the first year. Sales are expected to rise around 28 percent in each of the next two years, increase by 47 percent in the fourth year, and then slow down to 15 percent growth in the fifth year. Behind this increasing series is a specific set of assumptions about the rate of market growth, the company's market share, and the factory-realized price.

[19] See Robert Blattberg and John Golanty, "Tracker: An Early Test Market Forecasting and Diagnostic Model for New Product Planning," *Journal of Marketing Research*, May 1978, pp. 192–202.

	YEAR 0	YEAR 1	YEAR 2	YEAR 3	YEAR 4	YEAR 5
1. Sales revenue	0	11,889	15,381	19,654	28,253	32,491
2. Cost of goods sold	0	3,981	5,150	6,581	9,461	10,880
3. Gross margin	0	7,908	10,231	13,073	18,792	21,611
4. Development costs	− 3,500	0	0	0	0	0
5. Marketing costs	0	8,000	6,460	8,255	11,866	13,646
6. Allocated overhead	0	1,189	1,538	1,965	2,825	3,249
7. Gross contribution	− 3,500	− 1,281	2,233	2,853	4,101	4,716
8. Supplementary contribution	0	0	0	0	0	0
9. Net contribution	− 3,500	− 1,281	2,233	2,853	4,101	4,716
10. Discounted contribution (15%)	− 3,500	− 1,113	1,691	1,877	2,343	2,346
11. Cumulative discounted cash flow	− 3,500	− 4,614	− 2,922	− 1,045	1,298	3,644

Row 2 shows the *cost of goods sold,* which hovers around 33 percent of sales revenue. This cost is found by estimating the average cost of labor, ingredients, and packaging per case.

Row 3 shows the expected *gross margin,* which is the difference between sales revenue and cost of goods sold.

Row 4 shows anticipated *development costs* of $3.5 million for researching and preparing to produce the new product. The development costs are made up of three components. The first is the *product-development costs* of researching, developing and testing the physical product. The second is the *marketing research costs* of fine-tuning the marketing program and assessing the market's likely response. It covers the estimated costs of package testing, in-home placement testing, name testing, and testmarketing. The third is *the manufacturing-development costs* of new equipment, new or renovated plant, and inventory investment.

Row 5 shows the estimated *marketing costs* over the five-year period to cover advertising, sales promotion, marketing research, and an amount allocated for sales-force coverage and marketing administration. In the first year, marketing costs stand at a high 67 percent of sales and by the fifth year are estimated to run at 42 percent of sales.

Row 6 shows the *allocated overhead* to this new product to cover its share of the cost of executive salaries, heat, light, and so on.

Row 7, the *gross contribution,* is found by subtracting the previous three costs from the gross margin. Years 0 and 1 involve losses and thereafter the gross contribution becomes positive and is expected to run as high as 15 percent of sales by the fifth year.

Row 8, *supplementary contribution,* is used to list any change in income from other products of the company that is due to the introduction of the new product. *Dragalong income* is the name given to any increase in the income on other company products resulting from adding a product to the line. *Cannibalized income* is the name given to any decrease in the income on other company products (such as replaced products) resulting from adding a product to the line.[20]

Row 9 shows the *net contribution,* which in this case is the same as the gross contribution since there was no supplementary contribution.

Row 10 shows the *discounted contribution,* that is, the present value of each of the future contributions discounted at 15 percent compounded per annum. For example, the company will not receive the contribution of $4,716,000 until the fifth year, which means that it is worth only $2,346,000 today if the company can normally earn 15 percent on its money.[21]

Finally, row 11 shows the *cumulative discounted cash flow,* which is the cumulation of the annual contributions in row 10. This cash flow is the key series on which management bases its decision on whether to go forward into product development or drop the project. Two things are of central interest. The first is the *maximum investment exposure,* which is the highest loss that the project can create. We see that the company will be in the hole for a maximum of $4,614,000 in year 1; this will be the company's loss if it terminates the project. The second is the *payback period,* which is the time when the company recovers all of its investment including the built-in return of 15 percent. The payback period here is approximately three and a half years. Management therefore will have to decide whether it can expose itself to a maximum investment loss of $4.6 million and wait three and a half years for payback.[22]

PRODUCT DEVELOPMENT

A product concept that scores high in a business analysis is now ready to be turned over to the R&D and/or engineering departments to be developed into a physical product. Up to now, it existed only as a word description, a drawing, or a very crude mock-up. This next step calls for a large jump in investment, which dwarfs the idea-evaluation costs incurred in the earlier stages. Much time and many dollars go into trying to develop a technically feasible product. This stage will provide an answer as to whether the product idea can be translated into a

[20] See Roger A. Kerin, Michael G. Harvey, and James T. Rothe, "Cannibalism and New Product Development," *Business Horizons,* October 1978, pp. 25–31.

[21] The *present value (V)* of a future sum *(I)* to be received *t* years from today and discounted at the interest rate *(r)* is given by $V = I_t/(1 + r)^t$. Thus $\$4,716/(1.15)^5 = \$2,346$.

[22] Companies use other financial measures to evaluate the merit of a new-product proposal. The simplest is *breakeven analysis,* where management figures out how many cases of the product the company would have to sell to break even with the given price and cost structure. If management is confident that the company can sell at least the breakeven number of cases, then it would probably move the project into product development. The most complex method is *risk analysis.* The basic approach is to obtain three estimates (optimistic, pessimistic, and most likely) for each uncertain variable affecting profitability under an assumed marketing environment and marketing strategy for the planning period. The computer simulates possible outcomes from which a rate-of-return probability distribution is drawn, showing the range of possible rates of returns and their probabilities. See David B. Hertz, "Risk Analysis in Capital Investment," *Harvard Business Review,* January–February 1964, pp. 96–106.

technically and commercially feasible product. If not, the company's accumulated investment will be lost except for any by-product information gained in the process.

Three steps involved in the product-development stage: prototype development and testing, branding, and packaging.

Prototype
Development and
Testing

The R&D department will undertake developing one or more physical versions of the defined product concept. It succeeds if it finds a prototype that satisfies the following criteria:

1. The prototype is seen by consumers as successfully embodying the key attributes of the product concept.
2. The prototype performs safely under normal use and conditions.
3. The prototype can be produced for the budgeted manufacturing costs.

The work of developing a successful product prototype can take days, weeks, months, or even years. Designing a new commercial aircraft, for example, will take several years of development work. Even developing a new taste formula can take time. For example, the Maxwell House Division of General Foods discovered, through consumer research, a strong preference for a brand of coffee that would strike the consumer as "bold, vigorous, deep tasting."[23] Its laboratory technicians spent over four months working with various coffee blends and flavors to formulate a corresponding taste. Even then it turned out to be very expensive to produce, and the company took steps to "cost reduce" the blend to meet the target manufacturing cost. This compromised the taste, however, and the new coffee brand failed to do well in the marketplace.

The lab scientists must know not only how to design the required functional characteristics but also how to convey the psychological aspects of the product concept through *physical cues*. This requires knowing how consumers react to different colors, sizes, weights, and other physical cues. In the case of a mouthwash, for example, a yellow color supports an "antiseptic" claim (Listerine), a red color "supports" a refreshing claim (Lavoris), and a green color supports a "cool" claim (Micrin). Or, to support the claim that a lawnmower is powerful, the lab people have to design a heavy frame and a noisy engine. Marketers often work with the lab people, who fill them in on how consumers make their judgments about product qualities they are seeking.

When the prototypes are ready, they must be put through a series of rigorous functional and consumer tests. The *functional tests* are conducted under laboratory and field conditions to make sure that the product performs safely and effectively. The new aircraft must be able to fly; the new snack food must be shelf-stable; the new drug must not create dangerous side effects. Functional product testing of new drugs now takes years of laboratory work with animal subjects and then human subjects before they obtain Federal Drug Administration approval. In the case of equipment testing, consider the experience of the Bissell Company with a combination electric vacuum and floor scrubber:

... four were left with the research and development department for continued tests on such things as water lift, motor lift, effectiveness in cleaning, and dust

[23] See "Maxwell House Division (A)" (Boston: Intercollegiate Case Clearing House, ICH 13M83, 1970).

bag design. The other eight were sent to the company's advertising agency for test by a panel of fifty housewives. The research and development department found some serious problems in their further tests of the product. The life of the motor was not sufficiently long, the filter bag did not fit properly, and the scrubber foot was not correct. Similarly, the consumer tests brought in many consumer dissatisfactions that had not been anticipated: the unit was too heavy, the vacuum did not glide easily enough, and the scrubber left some residue on the floor after use.[24]

Consumer testing can take a variety of forms from bringing consumers into a lab to test and rate the product versions to giving them samples to use in their normal settings. *In-home product-placement tests* are common with products ranging from ice cream flavors to new appliances. When Du Pont developed its new synthetic carpeting, it installed free carpeting in several homes in exchange for the homeowners' willingness to report from time to time their likes and dislikes about the new carpeting in relation to conventional carpeting. Consumer-preference testing draws on a variety of techniques, such as paired comparisons, multiple choices, and ranking procedures, each with its own advantages and biases.[25]

Branding

The brand name should not be a casual afterthought but an integral reinforcer of the product concept. Among the desirable qualities for a brand name are:

1. *It should suggest something about the product's benefits.* Examples: Coldspot, Beautyrest, Craftsman, Accutron.
2. *It should suggest product qualities, such as action, color, or whatever.* Examples: Duz, Sunkist, Spic and Span, Firebird.
3. *It should be easy to pronounce, recognize, and remember.* Short names help. Examples: Tide, Crest.
4. *It should be distinctive.* Examples: Mustang, Kodak.

Some marketing research firms have developed elaborate name-research procedures including *association tests* (what images come to mind), *learning tests* (how easily is the name pronounced), *memory tests* (how well is the name remembered), and *preference tests* (which names are preferred).

The goal of many firms is to build a unique brand name that will eventually become identified with the generic product. Such brand names as Frigidaire, Kleenex, Levis, Jello, Scotch tape, and Fiberglas have succeeded in this way. However, their very success has threatened some of the companies with the loss of exclusive rights to the name. Cellophane and shredded wheat are now names in the common domain. Because of legal action, Du Pont has to describe its product as Du Pont Cellophane and Nabisco has to describe its product as Nabisco Shredded Wheat.

Packaging

Some years ago, packaging was a minor element in the marketing mix for a product. The traditional packaging concerns of manufacturers are product *protection* and *economy*. A third packaging objective, which comes closer to consid-

[24] Ralph Westfall and Harper W. Boyd, Jr., *Cases in Marketing Management* (Homewood, Ill.: Richard D. Irwin, 1961), p. 365.

[25] See Paul E. Green and Donald S. Tull, *Research for Marketing Decisions*, 4th ed. (Englewood Cliffs, N.J.: Prentice-Hall, 1978), chap. 6.

ering the consumer, is *convenience*. This means such things as size options and packages that are easy to open. A fourth packaging objective, *promotion*, has received increasing recognition from manufacturers. And a fifth objective, *ecology*, is becoming increasingly important as people become concerned with the disposal of packaging material and its effects on the environment.

Various factors account for the growing recognition of packaging as an independent and potent selling tool:

Self-service   An increasing number of products are sold on a self-service basis as a result of the growth of supermarkets and discount houses. The package must now perform many of the sales tasks. It must attract attention, describe the product's features, give the consumer confidence, and make a favorable overall impression.

Consumer affluence   The rise in consumer affluence has meant that consumers are willing to pay a little more for the convenience, appearance, dependability, and prestige of better packaging.

Company and brand image   Companies are recognizing the power of well-developed packaging to contribute to instant consumer recognition of the company or brand. There is hardly a film buyer who does not immediately recognize from a distance the familiar yellow packaging of Kodak film. Packaging is a tool not only in creating category identification but also in carrying out the brand's positioning concept in terms of quality, costs, and other factors.

Innovational opportunity   Innovative packaging can bring about large sales gains. The first companies to move into pop top cans and aerosol cans attracted many brand switchers. Hanes Corporation's L'eggs hosiery is one of the best recent examples of an innovative packaging approach—in this case, mass-marketed hosiery packaged in a unique egg-shaped container merchandised in free-standing display units. Hanes quickly gained a 10 percent share of the hosiery market with this product.

Developing the package for a new product requires a large number of decisions. The first task is to establish the *packaging concept*. The packaging concept is a definition of what the package should basically *be* or *do* for the particular product. Should the main function(s) of the package be to offer superior product protection, introduce a novel dispensing method, suggest certain qualities about the product or the company, or something else?

> General Foods developed a new dog-food product in the form of meatlike patties. Management decided that the unique and palatable appearance of these patties demanded the maximum visibility. Visibility was defined as the basic packaging concept, and management considered alternatives in this light. It finally narrowed down the choice to a tray with a film covering.[26]

A host of further decisions must be made on the component elements of package design—*size, shape, materials, color, text,* and *brand mark*. Decisions must be made on much text or little text, cellophane or other transparent film, a plastic or a laminate tray, and so on. Each packaging element must be harmo-

---

[26] See "General Foods—Post Division (B)," Case M-102, Harvard Business School, 1964.

nized with the other packaging elements; size suggests certain things about materials, materials suggest certain things about colors, and so forth. The packaging elements also must be guided by decisions on pricing, advertising, and other marketing elements.

After the packaging is designed, it must be put through a number of tests. *Engineering tests* are conducted to insure that the packaging stands up under normal conditions; *visual tests*, to insure that the script is legible and the colors harmonious; *dealer tests*, to insure that dealers find the packages attractive and easy to handle; and *consumer tests*, to insure favorable consumer response.

In spite of these precautions, a packaging design occasionally gets through with some basic flaw that is discovered belatedly:

> Sizzl-Spray, a pressurized can of barbecue sauce developed by Heublein, . . . had a potential packaging disaster that was discovered in the market tests. . . . "We thought we had a good can, but fortunately we first test marketed the product in stores in Texas and California. It appears as soon as the cans got warm they began to explode. Because we hadn't gotten into national distribution, our loss was only $150,000 instead of a couple of million."[27]

It should be clear why developing packaging for a new product may cost a few hundred thousand dollars and take from several months to a year. This may sound like excessive attention to pay to packaging, but for those who recognize the several functions it performs in consumer attraction and satisfaction, the attention is well warranted.

MARKET TESTING

After management is satisfied with the product's functional performance, the product moves into further market testing. Market testing is the stage where the product and marketing program are introduced into more authentic consumer settings to learn how well the product will do before making a final decision to launch it in the marketplace.

Not all companies choose the route of market testing. A company officer of Revlon, Inc., stated:

> In our field—primarily higher-priced cosmetics not geared for mass distribution— it would be unnecessary for us to market test. When we develop a new product, say an improved liquid makeup, we know it's going to sell because we're familiar with the field. And we've got 1,500 demonstrators in department stores to promote it.[28]

Most companies, however, know they can pick up valuable information about the users, trade, marketing program effectiveness, market potential, and other matters from market testing. The main issues are, how much market testing and what kind?

The amount of market testing is influenced by the amount of *investment*

---

[27] "Product Tryouts: Sales Tests in Selected Cities Help Trim Risks of National Marketings," *Wall Street Journal*, August 10, 1962, p. 1.

[28] Ibid.

cost and *risk* on the one hand, and the *time pressure* and *research cost* on the other. Products involving a substantial investment deserve to be market tested so as not to make a mistake; the cost of the market tests will be an insignificant percentage of the cost of the project itself. Products involving high risk—those that create new-product categories (first instant breakfast) or have novel features (first fluoride toothpaste)—warrant more market testing than those that represent simple modifications (another toothpaste brand). On the other hand, the amount of market testing may have to be severely limited if the company is under great pressure to introduce its brand, as might happen if the season is just starting or if competitors are about to rush their products into the market. The company may prefer the risk of a product failure to the risk of losing distribution or market penetration on a highly successful product. The cost of market testing will also make a difference in how much is done and what kind.

Market-testing methods differ somewhat in the testing of consumer versus industrial products, and they shall be discussed separately.

Consumer-Goods Market Testing

The purpose of consumer-goods market testing is to find out how consumers and the trade react to handling, using, and repurchasing the product, and how large the market is.

In testing consumers, the company is interested in forming estimates of the main components of sales, specifically *trial, first repeat, adoption,* and *frequency of purchase.* The company hopes to find all of these at high levels. In some cases, it will find many consumers trying the product but not rebuying it, showing a lack of product satisfaction. Or it might find high first-time repurchase but then a rapid wear-out effect. Or it might find high permanent adoption but low frequency of purchase (such as in the case of gourmet frozen food) because the buyers have decided to use the product only on special occasions.

In testing the trade, the company wants to learn how many and what types of dealers will handle the product, under what terms, and with what shelf-position commitments.

The major methods of consumer-goods market testing, going from the less to the more costly, are described in the following paragraphs.[29]

Sales-wave research Sales-wave research is an extension of the ordinary home-use testing in which consumers who initially try the product at no cost are offered the opportunity to obtain more of the product, or any competitor's products, at slightly reduced prices. They may be reoffered the product as many as three to five times (sales waves), the company noting each time how many consumers selected that company's product again and what comments they reported about usage. Sales-wave research can also include exposing consumers to one or more advertising concepts in rough form to see what impact the advertising has on subsequent repeat-purchase behavior.

The main advantage of sales-wave research is that the company can estimate the repeat-purchase rate under conditions where consumers are spending their own money and have a choice among competitors' brands. Another advantage is that the company can gauge the impact of alternative advertising concepts on consumer repurchase behavior. Finally, sales-wave research can be

---

[29] See Edward M. Tauber, "Forecasting Sales Prior to Test Market," *Journal of Marketing,* January 1977, pp. 80–84.

conducted under relative competitive security, implemented in a short time, and carried out without needing to develop final packaging or advertising.

On the other hand, sales-wave research does not indicate the trial rates that would be achieved by a given-size promotion budget, since the consumers are preselected to try the product. Nor does it indicate anything about the brand's power to gain distribution and favorable shelf position from the trade.

A variation of sales waves is the *printed-shopping-list method*. This method uses a special consumer panel whose members continually buy products from a printed shopping list, which are then delivered to their homes. New products are inconspicuously added to the long shopping list from time to time and promoted earlier by a direct-mail piece to the home. The company can learn the trial and repeat-purchase rates without exposing the product to competitors in the open market. However, the company is not allowed to interview panel members for more information, and it has to worry about possible panel biases. The advertising exposure is limited to printed material, and therefore there is no test of the impact of a full advertising program.

Simulated store technique The simulated store technique (also called "laboratory test markets," "purchase laboratories," or "accelerated test marketing") calls for finding thirty to forty shoppers (at a shopping center or elsewhere) and inviting them to a brief screening of some television commercials. Included are a number of well-known commercials and some new ones, and they cover a range of products. One of the commercials advertises the new product, but it is not singled out for attention. The consumers are given a small amount of money and invited into a store where they may use the money to buy any items or they may keep the money. The company notes how many consumers buy the new product and competing brands. This provides a measure of product trial and of the commercial's effectiveness against competing commercials. The consumers reconvene and are asked the reasons for their purchases or nonpurchases. Some weeks later they are reinterviewed by phone to determine product attitudes, usage, satisfaction, and repurchase intention and are also offered an opportunity to repurchase any products.

This method has several advantages, including the measuring of trial rates (and repeat rates if extended), advertising effectiveness, speedy results, and competitive security. The results are usually incorporated into mathematical models that are used to project ultimate sales levels. Marketing research firms that offer this service report surprisingly accurate prediction of sales levels of products that are subsequently launched in the market.[30]

Controlled test marketing Several research firms have arranged controlled panels of stores that have agreed to carry new products for a certain fee. The company with the new product specifies the number, store types, and geographical locations it wants. The research firm takes responsibility for delivering the product to the participating stores, and for controlling shelf location, num-

---

[30] The best-known systems are Yankelovich's "Laboratory Test Market," Elrick and Lavidge's "Comp," and Management Decision Systems' "Assessor." For a description of "Assessor," see Alvin J. Silk and Glen L. Urban, "Pre-Test Marketing Evaluation of New Packaged Goods: A Model and Measurement Methodology," *Journal of Marketing Research*, May 1978, pp. 171–91.

ber of facings, displays and point-of-purchase promotions, and pricing, according to prespecified plans. Sales results can be audited both from shelf movement and from consumer diaries kept by a sample of consumers who stop at these stores. The company may also test small-scale advertising in local newspapers in conjunction with the test.

Controlled testing (also called "minimarket testing") allows the company to gauge the effectiveness of in-store factors and limited advertising on consumers' buying behavior toward a new product without the consumers' being contacted in advance or during the process. A sample of consumers could be interviewed later to gather their impressions of the product. The company does not have to use its sales force, give trade allowances, or take the time to buy into distribution. There are also disadvantages, in that this technique does not provide the company with experience in the problems of selling the new product to the trade. This technique also involves a greater exposure of the product to competition.

Test markets Test markets are the ultimate form of testing a new consumer product in a situation resembling the one that would be faced in a full-scale launching of the product. The company usually works with an outside research firm to locate a small number of representative test cities in which the company's sales force will try to sell the trade on carrying the product and giving it good shelf exposure. The company will put on a full advertising and promotion program in these markets similar to the one that would be used in national marketing. It is a chance to do a dress rehearsal of the total plan. Test marketing can cost the company several hundred thousand dollars, depending upon the number of cities tested, the duration of the test, and the amount of data the company plans to collect.

Test marketing is expected to yield several benefits. The primary motive is to *achieve a more reliable forecast of future sales.* If product sales fall below target levels, the company may have to drop or modify the product.

A second motive is to *pretest alternative marketing plans.* Some years ago Colgate-Palmolive used a different marketing mix in each of four cities to test market a new soap product.[31] The four approaches were: (1) an average amount of advertising coupled with free samples distributed door to door, (2) heavy advertising plus samples, (3) an average amount of advertising linked with mailed redeemable coupons, and (4) an average amount of advertising with no special introductory offer. Colgate found that the third alternative generated the best sales and profit level.

Through test marketing, the company may discover a product fault that escaped its attention in the product-development stage. It may pick up valuable clues to distribution-level problems. And the company may gain better insight into the behavior of different market segments.

Test marketing calls for several decisions.[32]

---

[31] *Wall Street Journal,* "Product Tryouts."

[32] For some good discussions, see N. D. Cadbury, "When, Where and How to Test Market," *Harvard Business Review,* May–June 1975, pp. 96–105; and Jay E. Klompmaker, G. David Hughes, and Russell I. Haley, "Test Marketing in New Product Development," *Harvard Business Review,* May–June 1976, pp. 128–38.

1. **How many test cities?** Most tests use between two and six cities, with an average of four. In general, a larger number of cities should be used, (1) the greater the maximum possible loss and/or the probability of loss from going national, (2) the greater the number of alternative marketing plans and/or the greater the uncertainty surrounding which is best, (3) the greater the number of regional differences, and (4) the greater the chance of calculated test-market interference by competitors.

2. **Which cities?** No single city is a perfect microcosm of the nation as a whole. Some cities, however, typify aggregate national or regional characteristics better than others and have become popular for test-marketing purposes, among them Syracuse, Dayton, Peoria, and Des Moines. Each company develops its own test-city selection criteria. One company looks for test cities that have diversified industry, good media coverage, cooperative chain stores, average competitive activity, and no evidence of being overtested. Additional test-city selection criteria may be introduced because of the special characteristics of the product. Patio Foods, in testing a new line of frozen Mexican dinners, selected cities according to the incidence of travel to Mexico, the existence of a Spanish-language press, and good retail sales of prepared chili and frozen Chinese food.

3. **Length of test?** Test markets have lasted anywhere from a few months to several years. The longer the product's *average repurchase period*, the longer the desired test period, to observe repeat-purchase rates. On the other hand, the period should be cut down if competitors are rushing to the market.

4. **What information?** Management must decide on the type of information to collect in relation to its value and cost. *Warehouse shipment data* will show gross inventory buying but not indicate weekly sales at retail. *Store audits* will show actual retail sales and competitors' market shares but will not indicate anything about the characteristics of the buyers buying the different brands. *Consumer panels* will indicate what people are buying what brands, and their loyalty and switching rates. *Buyer surveys* can be conducted to obtain information in depth about consumer attitudes, usage, and satisfaction. Among other things that can be studied during the test-market period are trade attitudes, retail distribution, and the effectiveness of advertising, promotion, and point-of-sale material.

5. **What action to take?** Table 13–4 shows four possible test-market findings bearing on trial and repeat-purchase rates. If the test markets show a high trial and high repurchase rate, this suggests the desirability of a GO-decision. If the test markets show a high trial and a low repurchase rate, then the customers are not satisfied with the product and it should be either redesigned or abandoned. If the test markets show a low trial and a high repurchase rate, then the product is essentially appealing but more people have to be influenced to try it earlier: this means increasing advertising and sales promotion. Finally, if the trial and repurchase rates are both low, then the product should be dropped.

TABLE 13–4
Alternative Actions Following Test-Market Results

TRIAL RATE	REPURCHASE RATE	ACTION
High	High	Commercialize the product
High	Low	Redesign product or drop it
Low	High	Increase advertising and sales promotion
Low	Low	Drop the product

In spite of the benefits of test marketing, some experts question its value. Achenbaum lists five concerns:

1. There is the problem of obtaining a set of markets that is reasonably representative of the country as a whole.
2. There is the problem of translating national media plans into local equivalents.
3. There is the problem of estimating what is going to happen next year based on what has happened in this year's competitive environment.
4. There is the problem of competitive knowledge of your test and of deciding whether any local counteractivities are representative of what competition will do nationally at a later date.
5. There is the problem of extraneous and uncontrollable factors such as economic conditions and weather.[33]

Achenbaum contends that test marketing's main value lies not in sales forecasting but in learning about unsuspected problems and opportunities connected with the new product. He points to the large number of products that failed after successful test-market results. Some large companies are beginning to skip the test-marketing stage altogether and are relying on the earlier market-testing methods.

Industrial-Goods Market Testing

New industrial goods typically undergo extensive *product testing* in the labs to measure performance, reliability, design, and operating costs. Following satisfactory results, many companies will proceed to commercialize the product by listing it in the catalog and turning it over to the sales force. Today, however, an increasing number of companies are turning to *market testing* as an intermediate step. Market testing can indicate: (1) how the product performs under actual operating conditions in the customer's hands; (2) who are the key buying influences; (3) how different buying influences react to alternative prices and sales approaches; (4) what is the market potential; and (5) what are the best market segments.

Test marketing is not typically used in the market testing of industrial products. It is too expensive to produce a small sample of Concordes or new computers, let alone actually put them up for sale in a select set of markets to see how they sell. Industrial buyers won't buy durable goods that are being test marketed only, since they want assurances of service and parts. Furthermore, marketing research firms have not generally built the test market systems in industrial markets that are found in consumer markets. Therefore, industrial-goods manufacturers generally have to use other methods to research the market's reactions to a new industrial product.

The most common method is a *product-use test*, similar to the in-home use test for consumer products.[34] The manufacturer selects a small group of potential customers who agree to use the new product for a limited period. The product may be used at the manufacturer's site but is more typically used at the customer's site. The manufacturer's technical people observe how the customer's

[33] Alvin A. Achenbaum, "The Purpose of Test Marketing," in *The Marketing Concept in Action*, ed. Robert M. Kaplan (Chicago: American Marketing Association, 1964), p. 582.

[34] The discussion of this and other methods draws heavily on Morgan B. MacDonald, Jr., *Appraising the Market for New Industrial Products* (New York: Conference Board, 1967), chap. 2.

workers use the product, which often exposes unanticipated problems of safety and servicing. This clues the manufacturer about customer training and servicing requirements. After the test, the customer is given an opportunity to express purchase intent and other reactions.

A second common market-test method is to introduce the new industrial product at *trade shows*. Trade shows draw a large number of buyers to view new exhibits in a few concentrated days. The manufacturer can see how much interest buyers show in the new product, how they react to various features and terms, and how many orders or purchase intentions they express. The disadvantage is that the trade show reveals the product to all competitors, and the manufacturer should be fairly ready to launch it at that point.

The new industrial product can also be tested in *distributor and dealer display rooms*, where it may stand next to the manufacturer's other products and possibly competitors' products. This method yields preference and pricing information in the normal selling atmosphere for the product. The disadvantages are that the customers may want to place orders that cannot be filled, and those customers who come in might not be representative of the total market.

Controlled or test marketing has been used by some manufacturers. They will produce a limited supply of the product, often through subcontractors, and give it to the sales force to sell in a limited set of geographical areas that will be given promotional support, printed catalogue sheets, and so on. In this way, management can gain experience about what might happen under full-scale marketing and be in a better position to make the final decision about launching.

COMMERCIALIZATION

At this point, management presumably has enough information to make a final decision about whether to launch the new product. If the company goes ahead with commercialization, it will face its largest costs to date. The company will have to build or rent a full-scale manufacturing facility. The size of the plant will be a critical decision variable. The company can build a smaller plant than called for by the sales forecast, to be on the safe side. This is what Quaker Oats did when it launched its 100% Natural brand of breakfast cereal. The demand so far exceeded their sales forecast that for about a year they could not supply enough product to the stores. Although they were gratified with the response, the low forecast cost them a considerable amount of lost profits.

Another major cost is marketing. To introduce a major new household detergent into the national market may require $10 to $20 million for advertising and promotion alone in the first year. In the introduction of new food products, marketing expenditures typically represent 57 percent of sales during the first year.

The decision to commercialize involves four component decisions.

When (Timing)   The first decision concerns *timing* questions. If the new product replaces another product, the new product's introduction might be delayed until the old product's stock is drawn down through normal sales. If the demand is highly seasonal, the new product should not be introduced until the seasonal timing is right. If the new product could be improved further, the company may prefer to miss the selling season in order to come out with a better product.

Where (Geographical Strategy)

The next decision is whether the company should launch the new product in a *single locality*, a *region*, a *set of regions*, the *national market*, or the *international market*. Few companies have the confidence, capital, and capacity to put new products into full national distribution from the start. Instead, they will develop a *planned market rollout* over time. Small companies, in particular, will select an attractive city and put on a blitz campaign to win share. They will spread out to further cities as they gain footholds. Large companies will generally introduce their product into a whole region and then move on to the next region. A few companies with large national distribution networks, like the auto companies, will launch their new models in the national market unless there are production shortages.

In rollout marketing, the company has to rate the alternative markets for their attractiveness. The various candidate markets can be listed as rows, and rollout attractiveness criteria can be listed as columns. The major rating criteria are: *market potential, company's local reputation, cost of filling the pipeline, quality of research data in that area, influence of area on other areas,* and *competitive penetration.* In this way the company determines the prime markets and develops a geographical rollout plan.

The factor of competitive presence is very important. Suppose McDonald's wants to launch a new chain of fast-food pizza parlors. Suppose Shakey's, a formidable competitor, is strongly entrenched on the East Coast. Another pizza chain is entrenched on the West Coast but is considered weak. The Midwest is the battleground between two other chains. The South is open, but Shakey's is planning to move in. We can see that McDonald's faces quite a complex decision in choosing a rollout strategy.

To Whom (Target Market Prospects)

Within the rollout markets, the company must target its distribution and promotion to the best prospect groups. Presumably the company has already profiled the prime prospects on the basis of data gathered in the market testing or earlier stages. Prime prospects for a new consumer product would ideally have four characteristics:

1. They would be early adopters of the product.
2. They would be heavy users of the product.
3. They would give the product good word of mouth and influence others to buy it.
4. They could be reached at a low cost.[35]

Few profiled groups have all of these characteristics. The company can rate the various prospect groups by these characteristics and then target its initial efforts to them. The aim is to generate high sales as soon as possible to motivate the sales force and attract other new prospects.

How (Introductory Marketing Strategy)

The final step is to develop the marketing strategy for introducing the new product in the rollout markets. It calls for allocating the marketing budget among the marketing-mix elements and sequencing the various activities. Thus a new car might be launched by developing publicity several months before the product is available, then switching to advertising when the car is in the showrooms, and

[35] Philip Kotler and Gerald Zaltman, "Targeting Prospects for a New Product," *Journal of Advertising Research*, February 1976, pp. 7–20.

later developing promotional incentives to draw more people to the showrooms. To sequence and coordinate the multitude of activities involved in launching a new product, management increasingly is using network planning techniques, such as critical-path scheduling.[36]

THE CONSUMER-ADOPTION PROCESS

The *consumer-adoption process* begins where the *firm's innovation process* leaves off. It deals with the process by which potential customers come to learn about the new product, try it, and eventually adopt or reject it. It underlies the introduction and rapid growth stages of the product life cycle. The company must understand this process so that it can bring about early market awareness and trial usage. The *consumer-adoption process* should be distinguished from the *consumer-loyalty process*, which is the concern of the established producer.

The earliest approach used by new-product marketers for launching a new product was to distribute it widely and inform everyone who might be a potential purchaser. This *mass-market approach*, however, has two drawbacks: (1) it requires heavy marketing expenditures, and (2) it involves a substantial number of wasted exposures to nonpotential and low-potential buyers. These drawbacks have led to a second approach called *heavy-user target marketing*, that of directing the product to the group that tends to account for a substantial share of all purchasing. This makes sense, provided heavy users are identifiable and among the first to try the new product. But it was noticed that even within the heavy-user group, persons differed in how much interest they showed in new products and in how fast they could be drawn into trying them. Certain persons tended to be earlier adopters than others. The import of this finding is that the new-product marketer ought to direct marketing effort to those persons who are most likely to adopt the product early. *Early-adopter theory* grew around this view and held that:

1. Persons within a target market will differ in the amount of time that passes between their exposure to a new product and their trial of the new product.
2. Early adopters are likely to share some traits in common that differentiate them from late adopters.
3. There exist efficient media for reaching early-adopter types.
4. Early-adopter types are likely to be high on opinion leadership and therefore helpful in "advertising" the new product to other potential buyers.

We now turn to the theory of innovation diffusion and adoption, which provides clues to identifying the best early prospects.

Concepts in Innovation Diffusion and Adoption

The central concept is that of an *innovation*, which refers to any good, service, or idea that is *perceived* by someone as new. The idea may have had a long history, but it is still an innovation to the person who sees it as being new.

Innovations are assimilated into the social system over time. *Diffusion process* is the name given to "the spread of a new idea from its source of inven-

---

[36] See Yung Wong, "Critical Path Analysis for New Product Planning," *Journal of Marketing*, October 1964, pp. 53–59.

tion or creation to its ultimate users or adopters."[37] The *adoption process*, on the other hand, focuses on "the mental process through which an individual passes from first hearing about an innovation to final adoption." *Adoption* itself is a decision by an individual to use an innovation regularly.

The differences among individuals in their response to new ideas is called their *innovativeness*. Specifically, innovativeness is "the degree to which an individual is relatively earlier in adopting new ideas than the other members of his social system." On the basis of their innovativeness, individuals can be classified into different *adopter categories* (see p. 344).

Individuals also can be classified in terms of their influence on others with respect to innovations. *Opinion leaders* are "those individuals from whom others seek information or advice." Individuals or firms who actively seek to change other people's minds are called *change agents*.

Propositions about the Consumer-Adoption Process

We are now ready to examine the main generalizations drawn from hundreds of studies of how people accept new ideas.

Stages in the adoption process   The first proposition is that *the individual consumer goes through a series of stages of acceptance in the process of adopting a new product*. The stages are classified by Rogers as follows:

1. *Awareness:* the individual becomes cognizant of the innovation but lacks information about it.
2. *Interest:* the individual is stimulated to seek information about the innovation.
3. *Evaluation:* the individual considers whether it would make sense to try the innovation.
4. *Trial:* the individual tries the innovation on a small scale to improve his or her estimate of its utility.
5. *Adoption:* the individual decides to make full and regular use of the innovation.

The value of this model of the adoption process is that it requires the innovator to think carefully about new-product acceptance. The manufacturer of electric dishwashers may discover that many consumers are frozen in the interest stage; they cannot move to the trial stage, because of their uncertainty and the large investment. But these same consumers would be willing to use an electric dishwasher on a trial basis for a small fee. Recognizing this, the manufacturer may institute a trial-use plan with option to buy.

Individual differences in innovativeness   The second proposition is that *people differ markedly in their penchant for trying new products*. In each product area, there are apt to be "consumption pioneers" and early adopters. Some women are the first to adopt new clothing fashions or new appliances, such as the microwave oven, some doctors are the first to prescribe new medicines,[38] and some farmers are the first to adopt new farming methods.[39]

---

[37] The following discussion leans heavily on Everett M. Rogers, *Diffusion of Innovations* (New York: Free Press, 1962).

[38] See James Coleman, Elihu Katz, and Herbert Menzel, "The Diffusion of an Innovation among Physicians," *Sociometry*, December 1957, pp. 253–70.

[39] See J. Bohlen and G. Beal, *How Farm People Accept New Ideas*, Special Report No. 15 (Ames: Iowa State College Agricultural Extension Service, November 1955).

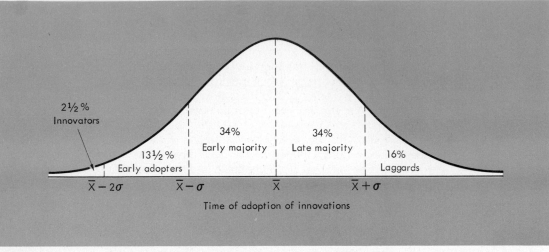

FIGURE 13–4
Adopter Categorization on the Basis of Relative Time of Adoption of Innovations

Other individuals, however, tend to adopt innovations much later. This has led to a classification of people into the adopter categories shown in Figure 13–4. The adoption process is represented as following a normal (or near normal) distribution when plotted over time. After a slow start, an increasing number of people adopt the innovation, the number reaches a peak, and then it diminishes as fewer persons remain in the nonadopter category.

Convenient breaks in the distribution are used to establish adopter categories. Thus innovators are defined as the first 2½ percent of the individuals to adopt a new idea; the early adopters are the next 13½ percent who adopt the new idea, and so forth. Although this partitioning in terms of unit standard deviations is somewhat arbitrary, the model provides the needed standardization for comparing different studies of product adoption.

Rogers has characterized the five adopter groups in terms of ideational values. The dominant value of innovators is *venturesomeness;* they like to try new ideas, even at some risk, and are cosmopolite in orientation. The dominant value of early adopters is *respect;* they enjoy a position in the community as opinion leaders and adopt new ideas early but with discretion. The dominant value of the early majority is *deliberateness;* these people like to adopt new ideas before the average member of the social system, although they rarely are leaders. The dominant value of the late majority is *skepticism;* they do not adopt an innovation until the weight of majority opinion seems to legitimize its utility. Finally, the dominant value of the laggards is *tradition;* they are suspicious of any changes, mix with other tradition-bound people, and adopt the innovation only because it has now taken on a measure of tradition itself.

The marketing implication of the adopter classification is that an innovating firm should direct its communications to those people who are likely to be early in adopting the innovation; messages reaching late adopters and laggards are wasted.

The identification of early adopters is not easy. So far no one has demonstrated the existence of a general personality factor called innovativeness. Individuals tend to be innovative in certain areas and laggard in others. We can think of a businessman who dresses conservatively but who delights in trying unfamiliar cuisines. The firm's problem is to identify the characteristics of those who are likely to be early adopters in its product area. The probability of being an early adopter may turn out to be related to easily identified economic, educational, social, or personality characteristics. For example, studies show that innovative farmers are likely to be better educated and more efficient than noninnovative farmers. Innovative housewives are more gregarious and usually of a higher social status than noninnovative housewives. Certain communities, especially those with higher than average mobility, tend to be more ready to accept new ideas. Drawing on several studies, Rogers offered the following hypotheses about early adopters:

> The relatively earlier adopters in a social system tend to be younger in age, have higher social status, a more favorable financial position, more specialized operations, and a different type of mental ability from later adopters. Earlier adopters utilize information sources that are more impersonal and cosmopolite than later adopters and that are in closer contact with the origin of new ideas. Earlier adopters utilize a greater number of different information sources than do later adopters. The social relationships of earlier adopters are more cosmopolite than for later adopters, and earlier adopters have more opinion leadership.[40]

Once the characteristics of early adopters are identified, a marketing communications program can be developed for the new product calculated to reach and interest these people. The known media habits of these people can be used to increase the effectiveness of the company's advertising. The company can also supply samples to community leaders and utilize store demonstrations to attract the early adopters.

Role of personal influence The third proposition is that *personal influence plays a very large role in the adoption of new products.* By *personal influence* is meant the effect of product statements made by one person on another's attitude or probability of purchase. Katz and Lazarsfeld reported:

> About half of the women in our sample reported that they had recently made some change from a product or brand to which they were accustomed to something new. The fact that one third of these changes involved personal influences indicates that there is also considerable traffic in marketing advice. Women consult each other for opinions about new products, about the quality of different brands, about shopping economies and the like.[41]

Although personal influence is an important factor throughout the diffusion process, its significance is greater in some situations and for some individuals

---

[40] Rogers, *Diffusion of Innovations,* p. 192.

[41] Elihu Katz and Paul F. Lazarsfeld, *Personal Influence* (New York: Free Press, 1955), p. 234.

than for others. Personal influence seems to be more important in the evaluation stage of the adoption process than in the other stages. It seems to have more influence on the later adopters than the earlier adopters. And it appears to be more important in risky situations than in safe situations.

Influence of product characteristics on the rate of adoption   The fourth proposition is that *the character of the innovation itself affects the rate of adoption.* Five characteristics seem to have an especially important influence on the adoption rate. The first is the innovation's *relative advantage,* or the degree to which it appears superior to previous ideas. The greater the perceived relative advantage, whether in terms of higher profitability, reliability, or ease of operation, the more quickly the innovation will be adopted.

The second characteristic is the innovation's *compatibility,* or the degree to which it is consistent with the values and experiences of the individuals in the social system.

Third is the innovation's *complexity,* or the degree to which it is relatively difficult to understand or use. The more complex innovations are likely to take a longer time to diffuse, other things being equal.

Fourth is the innovation's *divisibility,* or the degree to which it may be tried on a limited basis. The evidence of many studies indicates that divisibility helps to increase the rate of adoption.

The fifth characteristic is the innovation's *communicability,* or the degree to which the results are observable or describable to others. Innovations that lend themselves to better demonstration or description of advantage will diffuse faster in the social system.

Other characteristics have also been found to influence the rate of adoption, such as initial cost, continuing cost, risk and uncertainty, scientific credibility, and social approval. The new-product marketer has to research the role of all these factors and give the key ones maximum attention in developing the new-product and marketing program.

Influence of organizational buyers' characteristics on the rate of adoption   The fifth proposition is that *organizations, like individuals, can be classified as to their likely rate of trying and adopting a new product.* Thus, the producer of a new teaching method would want to identify the schools that rank high in adoption probability. The producer of a new piece of medical equipment would want to identify hospitals that rank high in adoption probability. Some of the characteristics might be associated with the organization's environment (community progressiveness, community income), the organization itself (size, profits, pressure to change), and the administrators (education level, age, cosmopolitanism). Once a set of useful indicators are found, they can be used to identify the best target organizations.

SUMMARY   More and more organizations are recognizing the advantages, indeed the necessity, of developing new products and services. If anything, their current offerings are facing shortening life spans and must be replaced by newer products.

New-product development, however, is not a primrose path. The risks of innovation are as great as the rewards. A large percentage of new products fail in the marketplace, and a still larger number have to be dropped before commercialization. The key to successful innovation lies in developing better organizational arrangements for handling new-product ideas and developing sound research and decision procedures.

The new-product-development process consists of eight stages: idea generation, idea screening, concept development and testing, marketing strategy and development, business analysis, product development, test marketing, and commercialization. The purpose of each successive stage is to decide whether the idea should be further developed or dropped. The company seeks decision criteria for each stage that minimize the chances of poor ideas moving forward and good ideas being rejected. The last stage, commercialization, involves the introduction of the products that have passed the previous tests; it is benefited by marketing planning and strategy based on an understanding of the consumer-adoption process.

QUESTIONS AND PROBLEMS

1. The new-product development process starts with a search for good ideas. Suggest some concepts that can guide a company's search effort.

2. A candy store chain is seeking ideas for a new sales promotion campaign. Show how morphological analysis might be used to generate a large number of ideas for a campaign.

3. Complained a research executive: "Would fluorocarbon resins, nylon, or polyethylene have come out of a screening formula—or a check list, for that matter? The important things are intuition and judgment. Research is a creative art." Is this a valid argument against formal screening devices? Can you name any advantages of using formal screening devices?

4. (a) Expected profit and risk are two major dimensions for determining whether to introduce a new product nationally. Can you develop a diagram using these two dimensions to show how critical limits might be set up by a firm before a market test to guide its decision after the test? (b) Suppose a firm finds that the test-market results are borderline and concludes that the product would probably yield a below-average return. It has sunk a lot of money into the development of the product. Should it introduce the product nationally or drop it? (c) State the two opposing risks that a firm faces when it bases its new-product decision on test-market results. How can it reduce these risks? (d) In the test marketing of Colgate's new soap (described in the text), the third marketing mix yielded the highest sales. Does this mean that it should be preferred to the other mixes if the product is launched nationally?

5. In 1950, Charles Saunders introduced a store called the Keedozall. The customer would pass a series of closed displays and insert a key into slots for wanted merchandise. He would take a resulting punched tape to a check-out cashier who fed the tape to a register. The amount would be totaled and the assembled merchandise delivered at the check-out point. Do you think this innovation in retailing was successful? Why or why not?

6. General Foods developed a new dog food product, PC-33. Not a canned or dry dog food, this product had a meat formulation and the appearance of hamburgers and could be sold on the regular grocery shelves. It offered a new combination of convenience and nutritional values. Develop four alternative product concepts for this new dog food.

7. A school furniture company is eager to develop a new line of lightweight chairs for elementary school classrooms. Recommend a set of steps for researching, developing, and testing these chairs.

8. A company president asked his new product manager what a proposed new product

would earn if launched. "Profits of three million dollars in five years." Then he asked whether the product might fail. "Yes." "What would we lose if the product fails?" "One million dollars." "Forget it," said the president. Do you agree with the president's judgment?

9. The International Harvester Company is planning to introduce a new line of trucks with luxury cabin features. Propose a plan for encouraging the dealers to sell these trucks and to promote these trucks to their target customers.

Assembling the Marketing Mix

4

PRODUCT DECISIONS

We are now ready to examine, in the chapters of Part 4, each of the major elements of the marketing mix. It is appropriate that we begin with product, the most important element of the marketing mix. In the first part of this chapter we will explore the concept of "product," and then we will examine the various decisions that management must make at the level of its overall product mix, product lines, brands, and services.

THE CONCEPT OF A PRODUCT

The word "product" has several meanings. We shall define it in the following way:

> A *product* is anything that can be offered to a market for attention, acquisition, use, or consumption; it includes physical objects, services, personalities, places, organizations, and ideas.

Other names for a product would be the offering, offer, value package, or benefit bundle.

"Product" has three senses that are worth distinguishing.

At the most fundamental level we can talk about the *core product*. The core product answers the question, "What is the buyer really buying?" The product is simply the packaging of a problem-solving service. The woman purchasing lipstick is not buying a set of chemical and physical attributes for their own sake; she is buying hope. The woman buying a camera is not buying a mechanical box for its own sake; she is buying pleasure, nostalgia, a form of immortality. The marketer's job is to sell *core benefits*, not *product features*. Notice that the core benefit is the center of Figure 14–1.

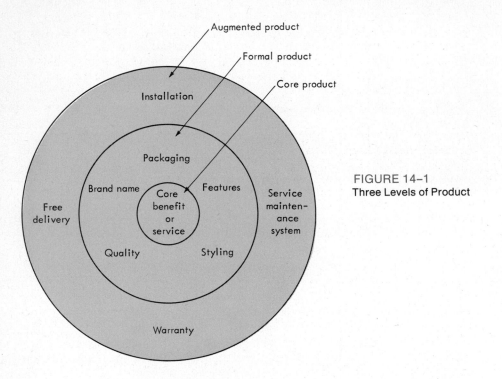

FIGURE 14–1
Three Levels of Product

The *formal product* is the larger "packaging" of the core product. It is what the target market recognizes as the tangible offer. Lipsticks, computers, educational seminars, political candidates, are all formal products. If the formal product is a physical object, it may be recognized by the market as having up to five characteristics: a *quality level, features, styling,* a *brand name,* and *packaging.* If it is a service, it may have some or all of these facets in an analogous manner. We can say that the U.S. Income Tax Advisory Service exhibits a certain quality level in that government tax advisers have a certain degree of competence. The service has certain features, such as being offered at no charge and usually requiring some waiting time. The service has a certain styling, such as being brief, cursory, and impersonal. The service has a certain formal name, that of "Federal Income Tax Advisory Service." Finally, the service is packaged within branch offices located in various cities.

Finally, the *augmented product* is the totality of benefits that the person receives or experiences in obtaining the formal product. The augmented product of IBM is not only the computer but a whole set of accompanying services, including instruction, canned software programs, programming services, maintenance and repairs, guarantees, and so on. IBM's outstanding position in the computer field is due in part to its early recognition that the customer wants all of these things when buying a computer. This recognition leads to the notion of *systems selling;* the company is selling a system, not just a computer.[1] It leads the sellers to look at the buyer's total *consumption system*—"the way a purchaser of a product performs the total task of whatever it is that he or she is trying to accomplish when using the product."[2] As a result, sellers are able to recognize many opportunities for augmenting their product offering as a competitive maneuver. According to Levitt, the *new competition* is not between what companies produce in their factories, but between *what they add to their factory output in the form of packaging, services, advertising, customer advice, financing, delivery arrangements, warehousing, and other things that people value.*[3] The firm that develops the right augmented product will thrive in this competition.

Product Hierarchy

Each product is related in a hierarchical fashion to a whole set of other products. We can postulate the existence of product hierarchies stretching from basic needs down to very particular items that might satisfy those needs. We can identify seven levels of the product hierarchy. Here they are defined and illustrated for life insurance.

1. *Need family.* The core need that actualizes the product family. Example: security.
2. *Product family.* All the product classes that can satisfy a core need with more or less effectiveness. Example: savings and income.
3. *Product class.* A group of products within the product family that are recognized as having a certain functional coherence. Example: financial instruments.
4. *Product line.* A group of products within a product class that are closely related, either because they function in a similar manner, are sold to the same customer groups, are marketed through the same types of outlets, or fall within given price ranges. Example: life insurance.
5. *Product type.* Those items within a product line that share one of several possible forms of the product. Example: term life.
6. *Brand.* The name associated with one or more items in the product line that is used to identify the source or character of the item(s). Example: Prudential.
7. *Item.* A distinct unit within a brand or product line that is distinguishable by size, price, appearance, or some other attribute. The item is sometimes called a *stockkeeping unit,* a product variant, or subvariant. Example: renewable.

---

[1] Systems selling really originated as systems buying, to describe government procurement practices in buying a major weapons or communication system. Instead of purchasing and putting all the components together, the government would solicit bids from prime contractors who would be willing to assemble the package or system. The winning prime contractor would then buy or bid for the subcomponents. Sellers have increasingly recognized that buyers like to purchase in this way and have responded with augmented-product offerings.

[2] See Harper W. Boyd, Jr., and Sidney J. Levy, "New Dimensions in Consumer Analysis," *Harvard Business Review,* November–December 1963, pp. 129–40.

[3] Theodore Levitt, *The Marketing Mode* (New York: McGraw-Hill Book Company, 1969), p. 2.

Another example: the need "hope" gives rise to a product family called toiletries and a product class within that family called cosmetics, of which one line is lipstick, which has different product forms, such as tube lipstick, which is offered as a brand called Revlon in a particular size, such as economy size.

Two other terms frequently arise. A *product system* is a group of diverse but related items that function in a compatible manner. For example, the Nikon Company offers a basic 35mm camera along with an extensive set of lenses, filters, and other options that collectively constitute a product system. A *product mix* (or *product assortment*) is the set of all products and items that a particular seller makes available to the buyers.

PRODUCT-MIX DECISIONS

Most companies, whether in manufacturing, wholesaling, or retailing, handle more than one product. The average supermarket handles 6,800 items, the American Optical Company manufactures over 30,000 items, and General Electric manufactures over 250,000 items.

The General Electric Company manages its incredible number of items by dividing its enterprise into several *sectors* headed by sector vice-presidents; each sector is divided into several *groups;* each group consists of several *divisions;* each division consists of several *product lines;* and each product line consists of several *products, brands, and items.* All of these products constitute the company's *product mix.*

Width, Depth, and Consistency of the Product Mix

The product mix of a company can be described as having a certain width, depth, and consistency. The *width* of the product mix refers to *how many different product lines are found within the company.* The Bissell Company at one time produced only one product line, carpet sweepers. General Electric, on the other hand, produces transformers, light bulbs, toasters, radios, jet engines, and scores of other product lines. The width of the product mix depends on the definitions established for product-line boundaries.

The *depth* of the product mix refers to the *average number of items* (or *length) offered by the company within each product line.* The Toni Company produces its Home Permanent Waves in nine versions to accommodate different hair types and styles and produces its Deep Magic Skin Creme in two versions to accommodate regular and dry skin. These and other product-line depths can be averaged to indicate the typical depth of the company's product mix.

The *consistency* of the product mix refers to *how closely related the various product lines are in end use, production requirements, distribution channels, or in some other way.* Contrast the product mixes of General Electric and Hunt Foods & Industries, Inc. In spite of the large number of General Electric's lines, there is an overall consistency in that most products involve electricity in one way or another. Hunt, on the other hand, produces tomato products, paint, matches, magazines, metal and glass containers, and steel.

All three dimensions of the product mix have a market rationale. Through increasing the width of the product mix, the company hopes to capitalize on its good reputation and skills in present markets. Through increasing the depth of its product mix, the company hopes to entice the patronage of buyers of widely differing tastes and needs. Through increasing the consistency of its product mix, the company hopes to acquire an unparalleled reputation in a particular area of endeavor.

The concepts of width, depth, and consistency are related to those of product item, lines, and mix. Figure 14–2 illustrates these relationships for a hypothetical company's product mix. The mix consists of twelve products, made up of four product lines with an average depth of three items to a line.

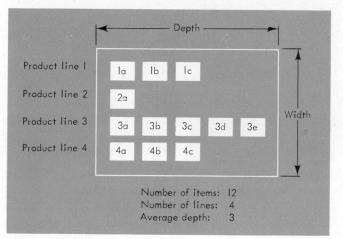

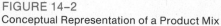
FIGURE 14–2
Conceptual Representation of a Product Mix

The illustration helps clarify the major issues in product policy. Product policy at the level of the product mix involves the issues of what lines to add, strengthen, or delete. Product policy at the level of the product line involves the issues of product-line stretching, filling, and pruning. Product policy at the level of the product item involves the issues of adding, modifying, or dropping individual items.

Evaluation of the Current Product Mix

The product mix of a company is the direct responsibility of top management. Top management must periodically review whether the current mix of product lines represent a good balance in terms of future sales growth, sales stability, and profitability. Markets are continuously changing in their needs and preferences; competitors keep entering and altering their marketing strategies; and the environment keeps changing. All of these changes favor certain of the company's product lines and hurt others. Some of the lines will just begin to show a profit, others will continue to produce good profits, and still others will be slipping badly.

This is illustrated in Figure 14–3. The company produces three product lines—A, B, and C. Projected earnings for the next six years are shown. A produces about 60 percent of the company's total profits, B about 30 percent, and C the remaining 10 percent. Typically, a small percentage of a firm's products account for a large percentage of its earnings. Looking ahead, the company expects A's earnings to decline, B's earnings to grow and then decline, and C's earnings to grow. By the sixth year, C will be contributing most of the profit, followed by B and A. The disturbing development is that the three product lines will not in total earn enough to sustain the company's desired profit-growth rate.

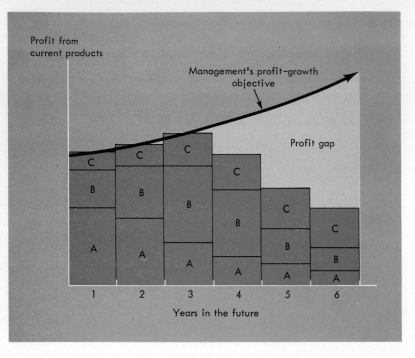

FIGURE 14-3
Projected Profit Growth
from Current Products

The shaded area in the figure shows a profit gap that must be filled in one of two ways: (1) improving the performance of the current product lines; (2) adding new product lines.

Improving the Performance of the Current Product Lines

Top management must take a hard look at its current product lines to see whether resources can be reallocated among the lines to improve the mix's overall performance. In the past, companies tended to give all their product lines support that was proportionate to their sales or profit levels. Those lines that contributed the bulk of the sales and profits received more resources. However, companies lacked a definitive product-classification scheme to guide their resource allocation.

The answer came in the form of business portfolio analysis as developed by the Boston Consulting Group and General Electric and described earlier.[4] The various portfolio grids can be applied to strategic business units, product lines, as individual products in the line. Their application enables the company to decide which products to build, hold, harvest, and divest.

Adding New Product Lines

The other way to close a profit gap is to seek additional product lines to add to the current product mix. Here the company is guided by its corporate mission, natural growth opportunities, and kinds of strengths that give it a differential advantage in particular product markets. The company might also seek new lines whose sales behavior over time will balance the sales of its current lines. The company wants to avoid high sales variability because this means periodic excess capacity, employee layoffs, and so on.

[4] See chap. 4, pp. 75–80.

We are now ready to define *product-mix optimization*. The static product-mix optimization problem is defined as follows: Given n possible products, choose m of them (when $m < n$) such that profit is maximized subject to a given level of risk and other constraints.

This problem is found in a number of situations. Retailers and wholesalers typically have to ration scarce shelf space among a large competing set of products; candy manufacturers have to decide on the best mix of candies to produce and package; and companies facing equipment, labor, or material shortages have to decide which products to produce. The problem may be solvable through mathematical programming, the most important condition being the absence of strong demand and cost interactions among the various products being considered.

The dynamic product-mix optimization problem is the problem of timing deletions and additions to the product mix in response to changing opportunities and resources so that the product mix remains optimal through time. A logical approach would be to simulate possible sequences and timings of planned product deletions and additions over some future time period. The computer's contribution would be to present management with the profit, stability, and growth characteristics of the different possible transformations of the product mix through time.

PRODUCT-LINE DECISIONS

Each product line within a company or division is usually the responsibility of some particular executive. In General Electric's Consumer Appliance Division, for example, there are product-line managers for refrigerators, stoves, washing machines, dryers, and other appliances. In Northwestern University, there are separate academic deans for the medical school, law school, business school, music school, speech school, journalism school, and the college of liberal arts. Often there is arbitrariness in what a company or industry designates as product lines. Consider an office supply manufacturer whose products consist of staplers, staples, staple removers, electric pencil sharpeners, and sharpening blades. Are there five product lines? Or is there a line of staples and accessories and another line of electric pencil sharpeners and accessories? Or are there three lines: staples, electric pencil sharpeners, and accessories? If staplers are divided into home and office staplers, should they be treated as one or two product lines?

The real issue is, What is the best way to organize and manage these various products? If the accessories to the main products yield a high profit, the company will want to manage accessories as a separate product line. Ultimately, the question is, What is the best way to serve the customers and compete effectively in the marketplace?

Product-Line
Analysis Product-line managers must master their lines in two important ways. First, they must know the sales and profits of the various items in the line. Second, they must know how the product line stacks up against the competitors' product lines in the same markets.

Product-line sales and profits The various items in a product line contribute differentially to total sales and profits. The product-line manager should prepare an exhibit showing the percentage of total sales and profits contributed by each item in the line. An example of a product line with five products is shown in Figure 14–4.

According to the figure, the first item in the product line accounts for 50 percent of the product line's sales and 30 percent of its profits. The first two items account for 80 percent of the product line's sales and 60 percent of the product line's profits. If these two items were hit hard by a competitor, the product line's sales and profitability would decline drastically. A high concentration of sales in a few items means some vulnerability. These items must be carefully monitored and protected. At the other end, the last item only constitutes 5 percent of the product line's sales and profits. The product-line manager will want to consider whether this slow seller should be dropped from the line.

FIGURE 14–4
Product Item Contributions to a
Product Line's Total Sales and Profits

Product-line market profile   The product-line manager must also review how the product line is positioned against competitors' product lines. Consider a paper company with a product line consisting of paper board.[5] Two of the major attributes of paper board are the paper weight and the finish quality. Paper weights are usually offered at standard levels of 90, 120, 150, and 180 weight. Finish quality is offered at three standard levels. Figure 14–5 is a product map showing the location of the various items in the product lines of company X and four competitors, A, B, C, and D. Competitor A offers two product items in the extra-high weight class with variable finish quality. Competitor B offers four items that vary in weight and finish quality. Competitor C offers three items such that the greater their weight, the greater their finish quality. Competitor D offers three items, all of which are lightweight but varying in finish quality. Fi-

    [5] This illustration is found in Benson P. Shapiro, *Industrial Product Policy: Managing the Existing Product Line* (Cambridge, Mass.: Marketing Science Institute, September 1977), pp. 3–5, 98–101.

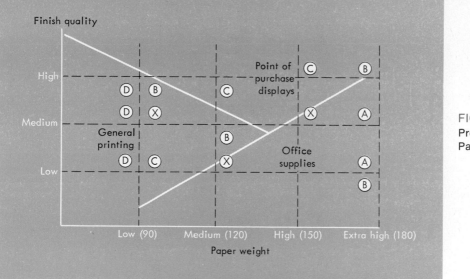

FIGURE 14–5
Product Map for a
Paper-Product Line

SOURCE: Benson P. Shapiro, *Industrial Product Policy: Managing the Existing Product Line* (Cambridge, Mass.: Marketing Science Institute, September 1977), p. 101.

nally, company X offers three items that range in weight and vary between low and medium finish quality.

This product mapping of the product line is highly useful for designing marketing strategy. It shows which competitors' items are competing against each of company X's items. For example, company X's low-weight/medium-quality paper competes against competitor D's paper. On the other hand, its high-weight/medium-quality paper has no direct competitor. The map reveals locations for possible new-product items. For example, no manufacturer offers a high-weight/low-quality paper. This product gap can be explained in one of four ways:

1. It is not technologically possible to produce this kind of paper.
2. It is not economically feasible to produce this kind of paper.
3. There is low or inadequate demand for paper of this kind.
4. This is a good opportunity, and the company is the first to discover it.

Another benefit of the product map is that it is possible to identify market segments and even particular customers according to their paper buying preferences. Figure 14–5 shows the types of paper, by weight and quality, preferred by the general printing industry, the point-of-purchase display industry, and the office-supply industry, respectively. The map shows that company X is well positioned to serve the needs of the general printing industry, but is on the borderline of serving the other two industries and will stay there unless it brings out more paper types that meet their needs.

Another chart that is helpful for marketing strategy is shown in Figure 14–6. The chart shows: (1) the number of items offered by the industry in each

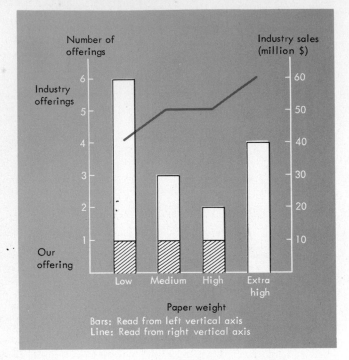

FIGURE 14–6

Number of Offerings and Sales in Each Paper-Weight Category

paper-weight class; (2) the number of items offered by the company in each paper-weight class; and (3) the industry sales of each paper-weight class. Thus, the industry offers six items in the low-paper-weight class (company X offers one of these), and the total sales are only $40 million. On the other hand, sales are $60 million in the extra-high-paper-weight class, and the company does not offer any items in this class. It looks like the company's market coverage is not broad enough and may in fact be mismatched to the real opportunities.

Product-Line Length   One of the major issues facing product-line managers is what the length (the number of items) of the product line should be. The line is too short if the manager could increase profits by adding items; the line is too long if the manager could increase profits by dropping items.

The question of the optimal length of the product line goes back to the company's objectives. Companies that want to be positioned as full-line companies and/or are seeking high market share and market growth will tend to have longer lines. They are less concerned that some items don't contribute an adequate amount of profit. Companies that are keen on high profitability, on the other hand, will carry shorter lines consisting of "cherry-picked" items.

Product lines show a strong tendency to lengthen over time, in an almost unplanned fashion. Several forces are at work:[6]

1. Excess manufacturing capacity puts pressure on the product-line manager to dream up new items.
2. New items are easy to design because they are variations on the existing items.

[6] See the discussion in Shapiro, *Industrial Product Policy*, pp. 9–10.

3. Sales personnel and distributors put pressure on the product-line manager for a more complete product line to satisfy their customers.

4. The product-line manager sees opportunities for additional product items in specific products and markets.

As a result, the product-line manager gradually adds items to the product line in the search for more volume and profits. But as items are added, the following costs go up: (1) designing and engineering costs, (2) inventory carrying costs, (3) manufacturing changeover costs, (4) order processing costs, (5) transportation costs, and (6) promotional costs to introduce the new items.

Eventually something happens to call a halt to the mushrooming growth of the product line. Manufacturing capacity may be in short supply and top management refuses to let the line grow any further. Or the controller raises questions about the line's profitability, and a study is instituted to improve margins. In the latter case, the study will show a large number of money-losing items, and they will be pruned from the line in one major effort to increase profitability. This pattern of gradual line growth followed by sudden line retrenchment will repeat itself many times, resulting in an undulating life-cycle pattern.

We are now ready to look at the major decisions product-line managers face in managing the product line. The decisions include stretching, filling, modernizing, featuring, pricing, and pruning the product line.

Line-Stretching Decision

Every company product line stretches over a certain range of the total range offered by the industry as a whole. For example, Lincoln automobiles are located in the high range of the automobile market, Granadas in the middle range, and Pintos in the low range. "Line stretching" is the act of lengthening the company's product line beyond its current range. It may be motivated by a desire to reach new customer groups, to adapt to changing customer desires, or to become a full-line company. Line stretching should be distinguished from line filling, the latter being concerned with adding items within the current range. Line-filling decisions are largely tactical, whereas line-stretching decisions are largely strategic. We shall examine three types of line-stretching decisions: a downward stretch, an upward stretch, and a two-way stretch.

Downward stretch Many companies establish themselves initially at the high end of a market and subsequently add products for the lower end. Here are two examples:

Caterpillar. For years, Caterpillar has been the dominant supplier of tractors above 100 horsepower (with five models), while John Deere has dominated the lower-horsepower end of the market (with three models). In the early 1970s, each company decided to invade the other's market segment. Caterpillar teamed up with a Japanese supplier to build a lighter tractor. Deere went for a high-end stretch by designing its first large tractor. Caterpillar's move toward the low end of the market was motivated by the wish to participate in a growing market segment that it was neglecting by not having lighter tractors.

IBM. IBM has historically operated in the large main-frame end of the computer market, leaving minicomputer manufacture to other firms, such as Digital Equipment or Data General. However, the slowdown in growth of the large-batch-oriented data processing units had led IBM to enter minicomputer manufacture as an avenue to further growth. IBM's interest in minicomputers is further stimulated by its growing interest in computer networks and distributed data processing systems.

Thus a company may decide to stretch toward the lower end of the market for any of the following reasons:

1. The company finds that slower growth is taking place at the high end and is forced to stretch its product line downward.
2. The company is attacked at the high end and decides to counterattack by invading the low end.
3. The company originally entered the high end in order to establish an image of quality and intended all the time to roll downward.
4. The company adds a low-end unit to fill a hole that otherwise would attract and give a start to a competitor.

In making a downward stretch, the company faces certain risks. The first is that it might provoke low-end companies to counterattack by moving into the higher end. The second is that the company's dealers may not be willing to handle or emphasize the lower-end products. For example, International Harvester truck dealers do not like to sell the lighter trucks because there is much less profit in them. The company may have to establish a second dealership system for its low-end trucks. Still another risk is that low-end items may dilute the company's quality image. If Cadillac added an inexpensive car bearing its name, this would detract from the prestigious Cadillac name. It would be better for Cadillac to design a second, less expensive line not bearing the Cadillac name.

Upward stretch   Companies that are positioned at the low end of the market may want to enter the higher end of the market for any of the following reasons:

1. The company may be attracted by the potential for faster growth rate or higher margins at the upper end of the market.
2. The company may evaluate the competitor(s) at the higher end as weak and easy to displace.
3. The company may want to reposition itself as a full-line manufacturer.

An upward-stretch decision is accompanied by several risks. Not only may the upper-end competitors be well entrenched but the move might tempt them to enter the lower end of the market. Prospective customers may not believe that the company has the wherewithal to produce quality products for the higher end of the market. Finally, the company's sales representatives and distributors may not have the talent or training to serve the higher end of the market, thus requiring intensive training or new sales reps and distributors.

Two-way stretch   Companies that are positioned strongly in the mid-range of a market may decide to go after market dominance by stretching their line in both directions. Texas Instruments' (TI) strategy in the electronic hand-calculator market provides an excellent illustration of a two-way stretch. Before TI entered this market, the market was dominated primarily by Bowmar at the low-price/low-quality end and Hewlett-Packard at the high-price/high-quality end (see Figure 14–7). TI introduced its first calculators in the medium-price, medium-quality end of the market. Gradually it added more machines at each end. It offered better calculators than Bowmar at the same price or lower, ultimately destroying it; and it designed high-quality calculators selling at a much lower price than Hewlett Packard calculators, taking away a good share of HP's sales at the higher end. This two-way stretch won TI the indisputable leadership position in the hand calculator market.

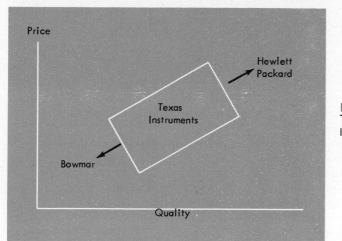

FIGURE 14–7
Two-Way Product-Line Stretch
Illustrated in the Hand-Calculator Market

Line-Filling Decision

A product line can also be lengthened by adding more items within the present range of the line. Looking back at Figure 14–5, we can spot several items that paper company X could add to its line. It can add items at standard levels that are not offered by anyone, such as a high-paper-weight/low-finish-quality paper. It can introduce items between the standard paper weights and/or finish quality levels. It can add items that competitors offer, pricing them the same as, a little higher, or a little lower than competitors' items.

The main motives for line filling are: (1) reaching for incremental profits; (2) trying to satisfy dealers who complain about lost sales because of missing items in the line; (3) trying to utilize excess capacity during slow times; (4) trying to be the leading full-line house; and (5) trying to keep the competitors from finding holes and getting in.

Line filling can be overdone, resulting in cannibalization and customer confusion. The company should strive to make each item differentiable in the consumer's mind. Each item should possess a *just noticeable difference*. According to Weber's Law, customers are more attuned to relative than to absolute differences.[7] They will perceive the difference between boards 2 and 3 feet long and between boards 20 and 30 feet long, but not between boards 29 and 30 feet long. The company should make sure that product item differences within its line are at least as large as just noticeable differences.

The company should check that the proposed item enjoys some market demand and is not being filled in simply to satisfy an internal gap. The famous Edsel automobile, on which Ford lost $350 million, was a case of line filling that met Ford's internal positioning needs but not the market's needs. Ford had no-

[7] See Steuart Henderson Britt, "How Weber's Law Can Be Applied to Marketing," *Business Horizons*, February 1975, pp. 21–29.

ticed that Ford car owners would trade up to General Motors' products like Oldsmobile or Buick rather than step up to a Mercury or Lincoln. Ford decided to create a stepping-stone car to fill its line. The Edsel was created, but it failed to meet a market need since a sufficient number of similar cars were available to the same buyers, and many buyers were beginning to switch to smaller cars.

Once the product-line manager decides to add another item to sell at a certain price, the task of designing it is turned over to the company engineers. The planned price will dictate how the item is designed, rather than the design dictating the price that will be charged.

Line-Modernization Decision

In some cases, the product line is adequate in length but has become old-fashioned looking over time. The line needs to be modernized. For example, a company's line of machine tools may have a 1920s look and lose out to better-styled competitors' lines.

When a company recognizes that its line needs modernization, the issue is whether to overhaul the line piecemeal or in one fell swoop. A piecemeal approach allows the company to test how customers and dealers feel about the new style before committing the whole line to that style. Furthermore, piecemeal modernization poses less of a drain on the company's cash flow. A major disadvantage of piecemeal modernization is that it allows competitors to see what the company is doing and gives them breathing time to redesign their own line.

Line-Featuring Decision

The product-line manager typically selects one or a few items for special featuring to draw attention to the line. Sometimes managers promote items at the low end of the line to serve as "traffic builders." Thus Sears will announce a special low-priced sewing machine to bring people into the sewing machine department. Recently Rolls Royce announced an economy model selling for only $49,000—in contrast to its high-end model selling for $108,000—to bring people into its showrooms. Once the customers arrive, some sales people will try to influence them to buy at the higher end of the line by disparaging the low-end model. (This is called bait-and-switch selling and could be held illegal.)

At other times, managers will feature a high-end item to give the product line "class." Stetson promotes a man's hat selling for $150, which few people buy but which acts as a flagship to enhance the whole line.

Sometimes a company finds one end of its line selling well and the other end poorly. The company may try to boost the demand for the slower sellers, especially if the slower sellers are produced in a separate factory that is idled by the lack of demand. This situation faced Honeywell when its medium-size computers were not selling as well as its large computers. But things are not this simple. It could be argued that the company should be promoting the product items that are selling well in a drive to achieve dominance in that segment of the market, rather than trying to stimulate demand where it is weak. Recently, the author of a successful textbook complained to his publisher that not enough money was being spent promoting his successful textbook, only to hear the editor say that promotion money should be used for the books that were not selling!

Line-Pricing Decision

A major task facing product-line managers is pricing the various items in their lines. Here we want to discuss two special situations. (Also see chap. 15, pp. 407–9 for additional discussion.)

The first has to do with a product line that consists of main products and satellite products. The satellite products take two forms. The first consists of *optional products* or *product features*. Here the buyer of the main product is free to buy none, one, or more optional products or features. The automobile customer can order such options as electric window controls, defoggers, and light dimmers. The restaurant customer can order or skip liquor in addition to the main course. The seller's task is to decide on prices for the optional items. If the prices are too high, customers will either forego purchase of the options or eventually switch to other sellers who price these options lower. Management can choose between pricing these options high in order to make them serve as an independent profit source or to price them low in order to act as a traffic builder. Many restaurants choose to price their liquor high and their food low. The food revenue covers the cost of the food and operating the restaurant, and the liquor produces the profit. This explains why customers may be looked at askance when they don't order something to drink from the bar. Other restaurants will price their liquor low and food high to draw in a crowd that likes to drink.

The other type of satellite product is a *captive product* (or *after-market product*). Examples are razor blades, camera film, and copier supplies. Manufacturers of the main products (razors, cameras, and copiers) often price them low in order to stimulate purchase and then make their profit through a high markup on the supplies. Thus Kodak prices its cameras low because it makes its money on the film. Those camera makers who do not sell film have to price their cameras higher than Kodak in order to make the same overall profit. As for the copier market, the early copier companies (such as Apeco and 3M) made their money selling specially coated paper that had to be used with their copiers. Part of Xerox's success lay in introducing a copying machine that did not require special paper, thus offering customers a way to save money on their copying costs.

The other interesting line-pricing situation arises in connection with *by-products*. In the production of processed meats, petroleum products, and other chemicals, there will often be by-products. If the by-products have no value, and in some cases a cost of disposal, this will have to be considered in pricing the main product. The manufacturer will normally have a strong incentive to develop value either through finding a market for the product in its raw state or processing it into a valued product, where the processing cost is less than its value. The manufacturer should be willing to accept any price for the by-product that covers more than its cost of processing and delivery, since this will conribute to profit or enable the seller to reduce the price of the main product to make it more competitive in the market.

Line-Pruning Decision

Product-line managers must periodically give consideration to pruning their product lines. There are two occasions for pruning. One occasion is when management notices that the product line includes deadwood that is acting as a drag on profits. The weak products can be identified through sales and cost analysis following the method outlined in Chapter 12, pages 299–301. Recently RCA cut down the number of its color television sets from 69 to 44 models, and a chemical company cut down its products from 217 to the 93 with the largest volume, contribution to profits, and long-term potential. Many companies that have implemented major prunings have often achieved stronger long-term profits.

The other occasion for product pruning is when the company is facing high demand and does not have the production capacity to produce all of the items in their desired quantities. Here the company should examine its profit margins and concentrate on the production of the higher-margin items, dropping temporarily or permanently some of the low-margin or losing items. Typically companies shorten their lines in periods of tight demand and lengthen their lines in periods of slow demand.

BRAND DECISIONS

Brand strategy is an intimate aspect of product strategy. A marketer has to decide which products to brand, how to brand them, and how to manage the brands.

First, some definitions are in order. A *brand* is "a name, term, sign, symbol, or design, or a combination of them which is intended to identify the goods or services of one seller or group of sellers and to differentiate them from those of competitors."[8] A *brand name* is "that part of a brand which can be vocalized—the utterable." Well-known brand names include Chevrolet, Coke, and Comet.

A *brand mark* is that part of a brand that can be recognized but is not utterable, such as a symbol, design, or distinctive coloring or lettering. Well-known brand marks include the Playboy bunny and the Metro-Goldwyn-Mayer lion. Finally, a *trademark* is "a brand or part of a brand that is given legal protection because it is capable of exclusive appropriation. . . ." Thus a trademark is essentially a legal term protecting the seller's exclusive rights to use the brand name and/or brand mark. *Branding* will be used as a general term describing the establishing of brand names, marks, or trade names for a product.

The Branding Decision	The first of several decisions in brand strategy is whether the company should even put a brand name on one or more of its products. The alternative to branding is simply to sell the product in bulk to middlemen or the final customers. Until recent times, most staple products—sugar, salt, bacon, cloth—went unbranded. Producers shipped their goods to middlemen who would sell them out of barrels, bins, or cases without any identification of the supplier. Finer goods were branded in some cases—Rubens paintings—and in other cases were unbranded—fine Chinese jade carvings.

A change began in the 1890s with the growth of national firms and national advertising media. The growth of brand names has been so dramatic that today, in the United States, hardly anything is sold unbranded. Salt is packaged in distinctive manufacturers' containers, oranges are stamped, common nuts and bolts are packaged in cellophane with a distributors' label, and various parts of an automobile—spark plugs, tires, filters—bear visible brand names different from that of the automobile itself.

In some industries today, there are occasional reappearances of unbranded, or "generic," goods, primarily as an effort by someone in the marketing system to offer consumers a low-cost alternative to branded goods. Thus, the Jewel Food Company has introduced a product line of plain-wrapped staples—soup, soap, toilet paper—with no brand name and carrying a low price. In many health food stores, several products are spooned from bins without supplier identification. In the pharmaceutical industry, many drugs are supplied in generic form.

[8] This and the following definitions are taken from *Marketing Definitions: A Glossary of Marketing Terms.*

366

Indeed, why should a producer rush into branding when it clearly involves a cost—packaging, stamping, legal protection—and a risk, if the product should prove unsatisfying to the user? It turns out that branding can perform a number of useful functions:

1. The producer may want a brand mark for identification purposes to simplify handling or tracing.
2. The producer may want a legal trademark and patent to protect unique product features from being imitated.
3. The producer may want to emphasize a certain quality level in the offer and make it easy for satisfied customers to find the product again.
4. The producer may see the brand name as an opportunity for endowing the product with an inherent drama that may create the basis for price differentiation.

Sometimes the pressure for branding comes not from the purchaser but from the distributor or ultimate buyer. Distributors may want brand names as a means of making the product easier to handle, identifying suppliers, holding production to certain quality standards, and increasing buyer preference. Ultimate buyers may want brand names to help them identify the products they want.[9] The brand name has informational value to buyers; without it, how could they shop in the modern supermarket with its 6,800 items?

Brand-Sponsor Decision

In branding, producers may use their own name(s) (*manufacturers' brands*), middlemen's names (*middleman brands*), or follow a mixed-brand policy, producing some output under their own name(s) and some output under middlemen's names.[10] For example, Kellogg's, International Harvester, and IBM produce virtually all of their output under their own brand names. A manufacturer such as Warwick Electronics produces virtually all of its output under various distributors' names. Whirlpool produces output both under its own name and under distributors' names.

Manufacturers' brands tend to dominate the American scene. Consider such well-known brands as Campbell's Soup and Heinz Ketchup. In recent times, however, large retailers and wholesalers have turned to developing their own brands. Middlemen are often able to make more profit because they do not bear the manufacturers' heavy promotional expenses. Their own brands give them more control over pricing and some measure of control over suppliers because they can threaten to change suppliers. Middlemen's brands have become an important factor in brand competition. Consider that over 90 percent of Sears products are under its own label, and that 25 percent of A&P's products are under its own label. More and more department stores, service stations, clothiers, drugstores, and appliance dealers are responding to these advantages by launching their own brands.

---

[9] Until recently, Soviet factories did not brand their products but used identification marks indicating the factory. Because of the variable quality, consumers began to buy the products produced at the better-known factories. Before long, state-sponsored advertising agencies emerged to tell consumers about the quality of the various factories.

[10] *Manufacturers' brands* also go under such names as national brands, regional brands, and advertising brands. *Middlemen's brands* also go under a variety of names: distributors' brands, private brands, store brands, dealer brands, house brands, and ghost brands. See Thomas F. Schutte, "The Semantics of Branding," *Journal of Marketing*, April 1969, pp. 5–11.

The competition between manufacturers' and middlemen's brands is called the "battle of the brands." In this confrontation, middlemen have many advantages. Retail shelf space is scarce, and many manufacturers, especially newer and smaller ones, cannot introduce products into distribution under their own name. Middlemen take special care to maintain the quality of their brands, building consumers' confidence. Many buyers know that the private label brand is often manufactured by one of the larger manufacturers anyway. Middlemen's brands are often priced lower than comparable manufacturers' brands, thus appealing to budget-conscious shoppers, especially in times of inflation. Middlemen give more prominent display to their own brands and make sure they are better stocked. For these and other reasons, the former dominance of the manufacturers' brands is weakening. Indeed, some marketing commentators predict that middlemen's brands will eventually knock out all but the strongest manufacturers' brands.

Manufacturers of national brands are in a very trying situation. Their instinct is to spend a lot of money on consumer-directed advertising and promotion to maintain strong brand preference. Their price has to be somewhat higher to cover this promotion. At the same time, the mass distributors put strong pressures on them to put more of their promotional money toward trade allowances and deals if they want adequate shelf space. Once manufacturers start giving in, they have less to spend on consumer promotion, and their brand leadership starts slipping. This is the national brand manufacturers' dilemma.[11]

Brand-Quality Decision

In developing a brand, the manufacturer has to establish the brand's quality level and other attributes that will support the brand's targeted position in the marketplace. Quality is one of the major positioning tools of the marketer. But what is quality and how is it measured? Quality stands for *the rated ability of the brand to perform its functions*. It is an overall measure reflecting the product's standings on durability, reliability, precision, ease of operation and repair, and other valued attributes. Some of these attributes can be measured objectively and combined, using a set of importance weights, into an index of quality. From a marketing point of view, however, quality is better measured in terms of the buyers' perceptions of quality. Buyers can be asked to rate a given set of brands on a quality scale.

Manufacturers do not all attempt to build the highest-quality products. Higher-quality products will cost consumers more. There will be markets for each quality level. Each manufacturer faces two decisions: (1) where to locate the brand's initial quality and (2) how to manage the brand's quality level through time.

Most brands can be established initially at one of four quality levels: low, average, above average, and superior.[12] The PIMS study attempted to determine the relationship between a brand's profitability (ROI) and its quality.[13] The in-

[11] See E. B. Weiss, "Private Label?" *Advertising Age*, September 30, 1974, pp. 27 ff. For an excellent example of decision theory, applied to a national bakery facing this dilemma, see Robert D. Buzzell and Charles C. Slater, "Decision Theory and Marketing Management," *Journal of Marketing*, July 1962, pp. 7–16.

[12] Or six levels could be used: shoddy quality, below-average quality, average quality, plus quality, double-plus quality, finest quality.

[13] See chap. 11, footnote, pp. for references.

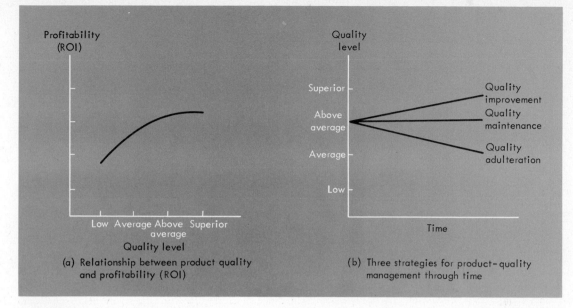

FIGURE 14–8
Brand-Quality Strategies and Profitability

vestigators found that profitability rose with brand quality but not in a linear fashion. The estimated relationship between quality level and profitability is shown in Figure 14–8A. This suggests that companies should aim to deliver above-average quality. Superior quality increases profitability only slightly, while inferior quality hurts profitability substantially. Furthermore, high marketing expenditures tend not to compensate for inferior product quality. "It doesn't pay to promote a poor product."

The other issue is how the company should manage brand quality through time. The three options are illustrated in Figure 14–8B: improve quality, maintain quality, or reduce quality. The first option, where the manufacturer invests in continuous research and development to make the product better, usually produces the highest return and market share. Procter & Gamble is a major practitioner of product-improvement strategy, which, combined with the high initial product quality, helps explain their leading position in many markets. The second option is to maintain product quality. Many companies leave their quality unaltered after its initial formulation unless glaring faults or opportunities occur. The third option is to reduce product quality through time. The company may experience a cost-price squeeze and decide to substitute cheaper materials. If they do this a number of times, the brand's deterioration will eventually be noticed.[14] A few companies will adulterate their products quite deliberately as a

[14] An interesting example is the Simmons Corporation, which substituted cheaper materials in its Beautyrest mattresses to fight rising costs. Consumers and retailers soon noticed the difference. Sales stagnated, market share fell, and profits plummeted. Now Simmons is engaged in a valiant effort to improve its product and image. See "Simmons: A Turnaround Proves Hard to Bring Off," *Business Week*, June 5, 1978, pp. 146–50.

way to increase profits, at least in the short run. The products that get the most adulteration are those in a late stage of their life cycle where they are being harvested or readied for withdrawal.

As a side note, many Japanese and German companies regard product quality as the major selling tool and pay great attention to statistical quality control. They want their products to come as close to zero defects as possible. In these cases, quality control is part of the marketing mix rather than regarded as only part of the production mix.

Family-Brand Decision

Manufacturers who choose to produce most of their output under their own name still face several choices. At least four brand-name strategies can be distinguished:

1. *Individual brand names.* This policy is followed by such companies as Procter & Gamble (Tide, Bold, Dash, Cheer, Gain, Oxydol, Duz) and Genesco, Inc. (Jarman, Mademoiselle, Johnson & Murphy, and Cover Girl).
2. *A blanket family name for all products.* This policy is followed by such companies as Heinz and General Electric.
3. *Separate family names for all products.* This policy is followed by Sears (Kenmore for appliances, Kerrybrook for women's clothing, and Homart for major home installations).
4. *Company trade name combined with individual product names.* This policy is followed by Kellogg's (Kellogg's Rice Krispies and Kellogg's Raisin Bran).

Competitors within the same industry may adopt quite different brand-name strategies. In the soap industry, for example, Procter & Gamble favors individual brand names. The name P&G will be used with new products during the first six weeks of television promotion and then be deemphasized. P&G wants each product to make it on its own. Colgate, on the other hand, makes much use of the phrase "the Colgate family" to help its individual products along.

What are the advantages of an individual-brand-names strategy? A major advantage is that the company does not tie its reputation to the product's acceptance. If the product fails, it is not a bad mark for the manufacturer. Or if the new product is of lower quality, the company does not dilute its reputation. The manufacturer of a line of expensive watches or of high-quality food products can introduce lower-quality lines without using its own name. On the positive side the individual-brand-names strategy permits the firm to search for the best name for each new product. Another advantage is that a new name permits the building of new excitement and conviction.

The opposite policy, that of using a blanket family name for all products, also has some advantages if the manufacturer is willing to maintain quality for all items in the line. The cost of introducing the product will be less because there is no need for "name" research, or for expensive advertising to create brand-name recognition and preference. Furthermore, sales will be strong if the manufacturer's name is good. Thus Campbell's is able to introduce new soups under its brand name with extreme simplicity and instant response. On the other hand, Phillips in Europe uses its name on all of its products, but since its products differ greatly in quality, most people expect only average quality in a Phillips product. That hurts the sales of its superior products; here is a case where individual branding might be better, or the company might decline to put its own name on its weaker products.

Where a company produces or sells quite different types of products, it may not be appropriate to use one blanket family name. Thus Swift and Company, in producing both hams and fertilizers, developed separate family names (Premium and Vigoro). When Mead Johnson developed a diet supplement for *gaining* weight, it created a new family name, Nutriment, to avoid confusion with its family brand for weight-*reducing* products, Metrecal. Companies will often invent different family brand names for different quality lines within the same product class. Thus A&P sells a primary, secondary, and tertiary set of brands—Ann Page, Sultana, Iona, respectively.

Finally, some manufacturers will want to associate their company name along with an individual brand for each product. In these cases, the company name legitimizes, and the individual name individualizes, the new product. Thus the Quaker Oats in *Quaker Oats Cap'n Crunch* allows the new product to benefit from the company's reputation in the breakfast cereal field, and Cap'n Crunch allows room to individualize and dramatize the product.

Brand-Extension Decision

A brand-extension strategy is any effort to use a successful brand name to launch product modifications or additional products. In the case of product modifications, it is commonplace in the detergent industry to talk about brand X, then the new, improved brand X, then the new brand X with additives. Brand extension also covers the introduction of new package sizes, flavors, and models. More interesting is the use of a successful brand name to launch new products. After Quaker Oats's success with Cap'n Crunch dry breakfast cereal, it used the brand name and cartoon character to launch a line of ice cream bars, T-shirts, and other products. Brand extension has also been used by Armour Dial soap to cover a variety of new products that could not easily find distribution without the strength of the Dial name.[15]

Another kind of brand extension occurs when durable-goods manufacturers add stripped-down models to the lower end of their line in order to advertise their brand as starting at a low price. Thus Sears may advertise room air conditioners as "starting at $120," and General Motors may advertise a new Chevrolet at $3,400. In both cases, these "fighter" or "promotional" models are used to draw in customers on a price basis who, upon seeing the better models, usually decide to trade up. This is a common strategy but must be used carefully. The "promotional" brand, although stripped, must be up to the brand's quality image. The seller must be sure to have the promotional product in stock when it is advertised. Consumers must not get the feeling they were taken, or else they may switch suppliers.

Multibrand Decision

A multibrand strategy is the development by a particular seller of two or more brands that compete with each other. Procter & Gamble pioneered this strategy. Following the phenomenal success of its Tide detergent brand introduced after World War II, it introduced another brand, Cheer, in 1950. Cheer took some sales away from Tide, but the combined sales volume was larger than if P&G had sold only Tide. P&G subsequently introduced other brands of detergents,

[15] See Theodore R. Gamble, "Brand Extension," in *Plotting Marketing Strategy*, ed. Lee Adler (New York: Simon and Schuster, 1967), pp. 170–71.

each launched with a claim of somewhat different performance. Other manufacturers in the soap field began to follow a multibrand strategy.

There are several reasons why manufacturers turn to multibrand strategy. First, there is the severe battle for shelf space in the nation's supermarkets. Each brand that the distributors accept gets some allocation of shelf space. By introducing several brands, a manufacturer ties up more of the available shelf space, leaving less for competitors.

Second, few consumers are so loyal to a brand that they won't occasionally try another. They respond to cents-off deals, gifts, and new-product entries that claim superior performance. The manufacturer who never introduces another brand entry will almost inevitably face a declining market share. The only way to capture the "brand switchers" is to be on the offering end of a new brand.

Third, creating new brands develops excitement and encourages efficiency within the manufacturer's organization. Companies such as General Motors and P&G see their individual managers competing to outperform each other.

Fourth, a multibrand strategy enables the company to take advantage of different market segments. Consumers respond to various benefits and appeals, and even marginal differences between brands can win a large following.

In deciding whether to introduce another brand, the manufacturer should consider such questions as

Can a unique story be built for the new brand?

Will the unique story be believable?

How much will the new brand cannibalize the sales of the manufacturer's other brands versus the sales of competitors' brands?

Will the cost of product development and promotion be covered by the sales of the new brand?

A major pitfall is introducing a number of multibrand entries, each of which obtains only a small share of the market and none of which is particularly profitable. In this case, the company has dissipated its resources over several partially successful brands instead of concentrating on a few brands and building each one up to highly profitable levels. Such companies should weed out the weaker brands and establish tighter screening procedures for choosing new brands to introduce. Ideally, a company's brands should cannibalize the competitors' brands and not each other.[16]

Brand-Repositioning Decision

However well a brand is initially positioned in a market, a number of circumstances may call for repositioning thinking:

A competitor may have placed its brand next to the company's brand, thus cutting into its market share in that segment.

Customer preferences may have shifted, leaving the company's brand less in the center of a preference cluster.

New customer preference clusters may have formed that represent attractive opportunities.

A classic repositioning success story is the campaign developed by Seven-Up. Seven-Up was one of many soft drinks on the market and was bought pri-

---

[16] For an excellent discussion of multibrand strategies, see Robert W. Young, "Multibrand Entries," in Adler, *Plotting Market Strategy*, pp. 143–64.

marily by older people who wanted a fairly bland, lemon-flavored drink. Some research indicated that while a majority of soft-drink consumers preferred a cola, they did not prefer it all the time, and furthermore, many consumers were noncola drinkers. Seven-Up decided to establish leadership in the noncola market and executed a brilliant campaign, calling itself the Uncola. The Uncola was featured as a youthful and refreshing drink in its own right, the one to reach for instead of a cola. Seven-Up thus created a new way for consumers to view the market, as consisting of primarily colas and uncolas, with Seven-Up leading the uncolas.

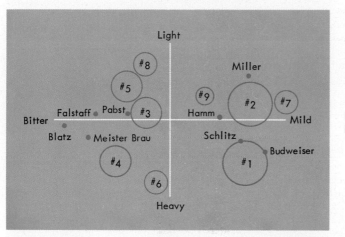

FIGURE 14–9

Distribution of Perceptions and Preferences in the Beer Market

SOURCE: Richard M. Johnson, "Market Segmentation: A Strategic Management Tool," *Journal of Marketing Research*, February 1971, p. 16.

The problem and method of analysis for considering repositioning alternatives for a brand can be illustrated in connection with Hamm's position in the beer market. Figure 14–9 shows the distribution of beer brand perceptions and taste preferences on two attributes: lightness and mildness. The dots represent the perceived positions of the various brands, and the circles represent preference clusters. The larger circles represent more-intense densities of preference. This information would reveal that Hamm no longer meets the preferences of any distinct segment.

To remedy this, Hamm's task is to identify the best preference cluster in which to reposition Hamm. Preference cluster #1 would not be a good choice because Schlitz and Budweiser are well entrenched. Preference cluster #2 seems like a good choice because of its size and the presence of only one competitor, Miller. Preference cluster #9 would be another possibility, although it is relatively small. Hamm can also think about a long-shot repositioning toward the supercluster #3, #5, and #8 or the supercluster #4 and #6.

Management must weigh two factors in making its choice. The first is the *cost* of shifting the brand to that segment. The cost includes changing the product's qualities, packaging, advertising, and so on. In general, the repositioning cost *rises* with the repositioning distance. The more radical the brand-image change that is contemplated, the greater the investment required to alter people's images. Hamm would need more money to reposition its brand in segment #8 than segment #2. It might be better for Hamm to create a new brand for segment #8 than to reposition its present brand.

The other factor is the *revenue* that would be earned by the brand in the new position. The revenue depends upon (1) the number of consumers in the preference segment, (2) their average purchase rate, (3) the number and strength of competitors already in that segment or intending to enter it, and (4) the price normally charged for brands selling to that segment.

CUSTOMER-SERVICE DECISIONS

A company's offer to the marketplace usually includes some service component. The service component can be a minor or major part of the total offer. In fact, the offer can range from a pure good on the one hand to a pure service on the other. Four categories of offer can be distinguished:

1. *A pure good.* Here the offer consists primarily of a tangible good such as soap, toothpaste, or salt. No explicit services accompany the product.
2. *A core good with associated services.* Here the offer consists of a core good along with one or more adjunct services that enhance its utility. For example, an automobile manufacturer sells an automobile that is accompanied by a warranty, service and maintenance instructions, and so on. Levitt observes: "The more technologically sophisticated the generic product (e.g., cars and computers), the more dependent are its sales on the quality and availability of its accompanying customer services (e.g., display rooms, delivery, repairs and maintenance, application aids, operator training, installation advice, warranty fulfillment). In this sense, General Motors is probably more service intensive than manufacturing intensive. Without its services, its sales would shrivel."[17]
3. *A core service with adjunct goods or services.* Here the offer consists of a core service along with some additional services and/or supporting goods. Examples include airline travel and car rental. Airline passengers essentially are buying transportation service. They arrive at their destinations without anything tangible to show for their expenditure. However, the trip included some tangibles such as food and drinks, a plane ticket stub, and an airline magazine. The service required a capital-intensive good called an airplane for its realization, but the primary item was a service.
4. *A pure service.* Here the offer consists of a core service and possibly some adjunct services. Examples include psychotherapy and massages. The client of a psychoanalyst receives a pure service with the only tangible elements in the service situation consisting of an office and a couch.

Thus the company's core product can be a good, or service and additional services might be included. We define a *service* as *activity that has value to a buyer.* A service is not a physical thing but rather an energy expenditure. It cannot be stored. A service that is not purchased at the moment it is available perishes. Thus while a car will stay in inventory until it is sold, an unoccupied seat on a particular flight is lost forever when the flight departs. Furthermore, a

---

[17] Theodore Levitt, "Production-Line Approach to Service," *Harvard Business Review*, September–October 1972, pp. 41–42.

service tends to be more variable in quality than a physical product, since it is often inseparable from the person offering it.

The services that accompany a core product or service can be extremely influential in the company's market share. As noted by Levitt:

> Whether the product is cold-rolled steel or hot-cross buns, whether accountancy or delicacies, competitive effectiveness increasingly demands that the successful seller offer his prospect and his customer more than the generic product itself. He must surround his generic product with a cluster of value satisfactions that differentiates his total offerings from his competitors! He must provide a total proposition, the content of which exceeds what comes out at the end of the assembly line.[18]

The marketer faces three decisions with respect to customer service: (1) what elements of customer service should be included in the customer-services mix? (2) what level of service should be offered? and (3) in what forms should the services be provided?

The Service-Elements Decision

The first task is to identify the main service elements in the industry and their relative importance to customers. Customers can be asked to name service elements that they consider important. Once a list is settled upon, customers can be asked to rank or rate the importance of these elements. For example, Canadian buyers of industrial equipment ranked thirteen service elements in the following order of importance: (1) delivery reliability, (2) prompt quotation, (3) technical advice, (4) discounts, (5) after-sales service, (6) sales representation, (7) ease of contact, (8) replacement guarantee, (9) wide range of manufacturer, (10) pattern design, (11) credit, (12) test facilities, and (13) machining facilities.[19] These importance rankings suggest that the company should at least match competition on delivery reliability, prompt quotation, and technical advice and other elements deemed most important by the customers.

But the issue of which service elements to emphasize is more subtle than this. It goes back to the discussion of the difference between the importance and determinance of an attribute (see chap. 6, pp. 162–63). A customer-service element can be highly important and yet not a determinant of customer preference if all of the suppliers are perceived to be equal on this attribute. Consider the following example.

> The Monsanto Company was seeking a way to improve its customer-services mix. Purchasing agents were asked to rate Monsanto, Du Pont, and Union Carbide on several attributes. All three companies, it turned out, were seen by customers as offering high delivery reliability and having good sales representatives. These were not determinant attributes. All three companies, however, were viewed as rendering insufficient technical service. Monsanto then carried out a study to find out how important technical service is to chemical buyers. Their study showed that buyers attached a high importance to technical service. Monsanto then proceeded to hire and train additional technical people. Shortly thereafter, it launched a campaign describing itself as the leader in technical service. The discovery gave Monsanto an opportunity to develop a valued difference in the minds of buyers.

[18] Levitt, *The Marketing Mode*, p. 2.

[19] Peter G. Banting, "Customer Service in Industrial Marketing: A Comparative Study," *European Journal of Marketing* 10, no. 3 (1976): 140.

Customers not only expect important service elements to be included in the product offer but also want the services to be offered in the right amount and quality. If bank customers face lengthy waits in line or confront frowning bank tellers, they will be inclined to switch their business to other banks.

Normally, higher levels of customer service produce higher customer satisfaction and therefore higher repeat purchases. We can use the right-hand diagram of Figure 10–1 on page 256 to illustrate various relationships that might exist between sales and service level. A shows the benchmark case where a particular customer service, no matter how well it is provided, does not make a difference to the sales level. For example, a supermarket chain may offer additional labeling to help consumers understand nutrition, and this may not draw more sales. B shows a case where sales respond in a linear fashion to the level of service offered. For example, sales might rise linearly with the degree of ease of contact with the sales rep. C shows sales responding very rapidly to a service and increasing with higher levels of this service at a diminishing rate. Adding one sales person to a department in a store makes a big difference; adding a second person makes a smaller difference; adding a third person makes an even smaller difference. D shows a case where offering a small amount of a service has little impact on sales; the impact increases as more is offered; and later it falls off. An example would be a new automobile warranty. If the warranty covers thirty days, it is not very impressive; a year—it is more impressive; three years—it is still more impressive but may not produce that much more in sales.

Companies must maintain a constant check on their own and competitors' service levels in relation to customers' expectations. The company can monitor service deficiencies through a number of devices: comparison shopping, periodic customer surveys, suggestion boxes, and complaint-handling systems. The task is not to minimize complaining behavior but in fact to maximize it so that the company can really know how it is doing, and the disappointed customers can get satisfaction.

A useful device is to periodically survey a sample of customers to find out how they feel about each service element in terms of its importance and performance. An example is shown in Figure 14–10A. Fourteen different service attributes of an automobile dealer's service department were rated by customers on importance and performance. The importance of the service attribute was rated on a four-point scale of "extremely important," "important," "slightly important," and "not important." The dealer's performance was rated on a four-point scale of "excellent," "good," "fair," and "poor." For example, the first service attribute, "Job done right the first time," received a mean importance rating of 3.83 and a mean performance rating of 2.63, indicating that customers felt it was highly important, although not being performed that well by this service department. The ratings of the fourteen attributes are displayed in Figure 14–10B. The figure is divided into four quadrants. Quadrant A shows the important service attributes that are not being offered at the desired performance levels; they include attributes 1, 2, and 9. Dealers should concentrate their attention on improving their performance on these attributes. Quadrant B shows important service elements where the company is performing well; its job is to maintain the high performance. Quadrant C shows minor service elements that are delivered in a mediocre way but do not need any attention since they are not very important. Quadrant D shows a minor service element, "Send out maintenance notices," which is being performed in an excellent manner, a case of

ATTRIBUTE NUMBER	ATTRIBUTE DESCRIPTION	MEAN IMPORTANCE RATING[a]	MEAN PERFORMANCE RATING[b]
1	Job done right the first time	3.83	2.63
2	Fast action on complaints	3.63	2.73
3	Prompt warranty work	3.60	3.15
4	Able to do any job needed	3.56	3.00
5	Service available when needed	3.41	3.05
6	Courteous and friendly service	3.41	3.29
7	Car ready when promised	3.38	3.03
8	Perform only necessary work	3.37	3.11
9	Low prices on service	3.29	2.00
10	Clean up after service work	3.27	3.02
11	Convenient to home	2.52	2.25
12	Convenient to work	2.43	2.49
13	Courtesy buses and rental cars	2.37	2.35
14	Send out maintenance notices	2.05	3.33

[a] Ratings obtained from a four-point scale of "extremely important," "important," "slightly important," and "not important."

[b] Ratings obtained from a four-point scale of "excellent," "good," "fair," and "poor."

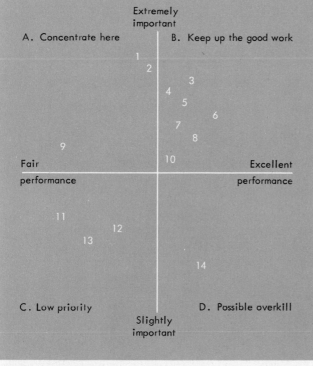

FIGURE 14–10
Importance and Performance Ratings
for Automobile Dealer's Service Department

SOURCE: John A. Martilla and John C. James, "Importance-Performance Analysis," *Journal of Marketing*, January 1977, pp. 77–79.

possible "overkill." This classification of service elements according to their importance and performance provides marketers with guidelines as to where they should concentrate their effort.

The Service-Form Decision

Marketers must also decide on the forms in which to offer various service elements. First, there is the question of how to price the service element. Consider, for example, what Zenith should do in connection with offering repair services on its television sets. Zenith has three pricing options:

1. Zenith could offer free television-repair service for a year with the sale of its set.
2. Zenith could offer the customer an option to buy a service contract.
3. Zenith could decide not to offer any repair service, leaving it to independent television-repair specialists.

Second, there is the question of how the repair service should be provided. Zenith has three choices:

1. Zenith can hire and train its own service repair people and locate them throughout the country.
2. Zenith can make arrangements with distributors and dealers to provide the repair services.
3. Zenith can leave it to independent companies to provide the necessary repair services.

For each such service element, various options exist on how it could be provided to customers. The company's decision depends very much on customers' preferences as well as competitors' strategies.

The Customer-Service Department

Given the importance of customer service as a competitive weapon, companies would do well to consider developing a strong customer-service department reporting to the vice president of marketing. Customer-service departments are found in many companies, although their scope and authority vary widely. Ideally, these departments should integrate and be responsible for a number of customer services, the most important of which are:[20]

1. *Complaints and adjustments.* The company should set up procedures for facilitating and handling complaints. By keeping statistics on the types of complaints, the customer-service department can recognize problems and press for changes in product design, quality control, high-pressure selling, and so on. It is much less expensive to preserve the goodwill of existing customers than to attract new customers or woo back lost customers.
2. *Credit service.* The company should offer customers a number of options in financing their purchase, including installment credit contracts, open book credit, loans, and leasing options. The costs of extending credit are usually more than made up by the gross profit on the additional sales and the reduced cost of marketing expenditures to overcome the customers' objection of not having enough money.
3. *Maintenance service.* The company should make provisions for supplying customers with a parts and service system that is effective, speedy, and reasonable in

[20] See Ralph S. Alexander and Thomas L. Berg, *Dynamic Management in Marketing* (Homewood, Ill.: Richard D. Irwin, 1965), pp. 419–28.

378

cost. While maintenance service is often run by the production department, marketing should monitor customers' satisfaction with this service.

4. **Technical service.** The company should provide customers who buy complex materials and equipment with technical services such as custom design work, installation, customer training, applications research, and process-improvement research.

5. **Information service.** The company should consider setting up an information unit that is responsible for answering customer inquiries and disseminating information on new products, features, processes, expected price changes, order backlog status, and new company policies. The information can be disseminated through company newsletters and selectively to specific customers.

All of the preceding services should be coordinated and used as tools in creating customer satisfaction and loyalty.

SUMMARY

Product is the most important element in the marketing mix. By a product, we mean anything that can be offered to a market for attention, acquisition, use, or consumption. Each product has three aspects. The core product is the essential service that the buyer is really buying. The formal product is made up of the features, styling, quality, brand name, and packaging that constitute the tangible product. The augmented product is the formal product plus the various services accompanying it, such as installation, service maintenance, and free delivery. Each product, furthermore, can be interpreted as fitting somewhere in a product hierarchy consisting of a need family, product family, product class, product line, product type, brand, and item.

Most companies handle more than one product, and their product mix can be described as having a certain width, depth, and consistency. The various lines making up the product mix have to be periodically evaluated for profitability and growth potential. The company's better lines should receive disproportionate support; weaker lines should be phased down or out; and new lines should be added in the effort to fill the profit gap.

Each product line should have a separate manager. The manager should study the sales and profit contributions of each item in the product line as well as how the items are positioned in the market against competitors' items. This provides information needed for making several product-line decisions. Line stretching involves the question of whether a particular line should be stretched downward, upward, or two ways. Line filling raises the question of whether additional items should be added within the present range of the line. Line modernization raises the question of whether the line needs a new look, and whether the new look should be installed piecemeal or all at once. Line featuring raises the question of which end of the line should be featured in promotions of the line. Line pricing raises the question of how optional features, by-products, and various satellite services should be priced. Line pruning raises the question of how to detect and remove weaker product items from the line.

Companies also develop a set of brand policies concerning whether to sell their products under their own name, distributors' names, or both, and whether to develop family or individual brands. Many manufacturers of consumer goods employ brand-extension and multibrand strategies.

Finally, companies have to develop a set of customer services that are wanted by customers and are effective against competitors. The company has to decide on the most important service elements to offer, the level at which each element should be offered, and the form in which each element should be provided. The service offer can be coordinated by a customer-service department that is responsible for complaints and adjustments, credit, maintenance, technical service, and information service.

QUESTIONS AND PROBLEMS

1. Define the primary want-satisfying purpose(s) of the following goods: (a) cars; (b) bread; (c) oil; (d) pillows; (e) pens; (f) novels; (g) textbooks; (h) uniforms; (i) watches; (j) detergents.

2. Offer a definition of the basic business of each of the following large companies: (a) General Motors; (b) Bayer's (maker of aspirins); (c) Massachusetts Investors Trust (a mutual fund); (d) Sears; and (e) *Time* magazine.

3. Most firms prefer to develop a diversified product line to avoid overdependence on a single product. Yet there are certain advantages that accrue to the firm that produces and sells one product. Name them.

4. "As a firm increases the number of its products arithmetically, management's problems tend to increase geometrically." Do you agree?

5. Does the ranking of a company's products according to their relative profit contribution indicate the best way to allocate the marketing budget to these products? If yes, how should the budget be allocated to the products? If no, why?

6. Draw a graph showing how the length of a product line behaves over time.

7. Some supermarket chains have recently introduced a line of generic (unbranded) products, including soups, paper goods, dog food, and so on. Why are generics emerging now and how far are they likely to go?

8. Determine the category of the service component of each of the following items and list some of the elements in their service mixes: (a) museum tour; (b) food processor; (c) photocopies obtained from a coin-operated photocopy machine; (d) facial tissue.

PRICE DECISIONS

15

All profit organizations and many nonprofit organizations face the task of setting a price on their products or services. Price goes by many names: fares, fees, charges, tuitions, rents, assessments, and plain old price. Originally, price was considered one of the top two or three influences on buyer choice behavior. In the 1950s and 1960s, nonprice factors grew relatively more important and reached a point where over half of a sample of company managers "did not *select* pricing as *one of the five most important* policy areas in their firm's marketing success."[1] More recently, because of worldwide inflation, price has again attracted considerable attention and is now viewed by many marketers as the most important element in the marketing mix, following the product.[2]

Price is the only element in the marketing mix that creates sales revenue; the other elements are costs. In spite of the importance of setting the right price, most companies do not handle pricing well. The most common mistakes are the following: pricing is too cost oriented in that companies fail to take sufficient account of demand intensity and customer psychology, price is not revised often

---

[1] See Jon G. Udell, "How Important Is Pricing in Competitive Strategy?" *Journal of Marketing*, January 1964, pp. 44–48; also see Robert A. Robicheaux, "How Important Is Pricing in Competitive Strategy?" in *Proceedings: Southern Marketing Association*, ed. Henry W. Nash and Donald P. Robin, January 1976, pp. 55–57.

[2] See "Pricing Strategy in an Inflation Economy," *Business Week*, April 6, 1974, pp. 43–49.

enough to capitalize on changed conditions in the marketplace; price is too often set independently of the rest of the marketing mix rather than as an intrinsic element of market-positioning strategy; and price is not varied enough for different product items and market segments.

The pricing function is handled in a variety of ways in different companies. In small companies, pricing is often a decision of top management and may be out of the hands of the marketing or sales department. In large companies, price determination is typically in the hands of divisional and product-line managers. Even here, top management sets the general pricing objectives and policies and often has to approve the prices proposed by lower levels of management. In industries where pricing is a key factor (aerospace, railroads, oil companies), companies will often establish a separate pricing department to set prices or assist others in the determination of appropriate prices. This department reports in some cases to the marketing department and in other cases to top management. Others who exert an influence on pricing include sales managers, production planners and managers, finance specialists, and accountants.

Pricing is a problem in four general types of situations. It is a problem *when a firm must set a price for the first time.* This happens when the firm develops or acquires a new product, when it introduces its regular product into a new distribution channel or geographical area, or when it regularly enters bids on new contract work. Pricing is a problem *when circumstances lead a firm to consider initiating a price change.* The firm may wish to review whether its price is right in relation to its demand, costs, and competitors' prices. Repricing can be triggered by inflation, shortages, or excess inventories. Pricing is a problem *when competition initiates a price change.* The firm has to decide whether to change its own price, and if so, by how much. Finally, pricing is a problem *when the company produces several products that have interrelated demands and/or costs.* The problem is one of determining optimal price relationships for the products in the line.

SETTING PRICES

Pricing is a problem when a company develops a new product and must set its price for the first time. We can distinguish between pricing strategy and pricing tactics. *Pricing strategy* is the task of defining the price range and price movement through time that would support the sales and profit objectives and marketing positioning of the product in the target market. Thus if a television producer designs a new super-screen TV set that it wishes to position as the Cadillac of the industry, price and quality will have to be set high to support this positioning. *Pricing tactics* is the task of setting specific price levels and terms and altering them within the general parameters of the price strategy as conditions change.

The setting of price is rarely a simple matter. It is only simple in a *price-taking* market, that is, a market where each seller must charge the going price. As conditions approach perfect competition (i.e., homogeneous product, high information, and high mobility of resources), such as is found in several raw material markets, suppliers pretty much have to charge the same as their competitors. If they charge more (without offering any extra services), no one will buy; and there is no reason to charge less as long as buyers are paying the going price.

Most markets, however, do not meet the conditions of perfect competition and call for *price making.* Here the pricing decision can be very complex. The following example is presented to sensitize the reader to the complicated issues involved in price setting.[3]

Pricing a new mobile home   Modern Mobile Homes manufactures a single mobile home called the Knight, which is sold through its own franchised dealers at a retail price of $7,000. The dealers have been pressuring the company to add a second mobile home to the line at the higher end. In response, the company has designed the Queen and is about to set its dealer and retail price. Here are the major facts:

1. The company has enough extra plant capacity to produce up to 500 units a year. Any more than this would require investing in new plant capacity.
2. The fixed costs of producing the Queen are estimated at $120,000. The direct costs are estimated at $6,000 a unit.
3. There is one major competitor producing a high-quality mobile home, which is retailing for $7,800. The competitor charges its dealers $6,400, which is approximately an 18 percent dealer discount off the list price. The company estimates that the competitor's direct cost is $5,800, which means that the competitor makes $600 a unit. The competitor sells about 600 units a year.
4. The company would like to price the Queen to sell for at least $800 more than the Knight to establish its superior quality in the product line.
5. The company displayed the Queen at the latest retail trade show and over 60 percent of the visitors reported that the Queen seemed better designed than the competitor's model.

With this information, what dealer and retail price should Modern Mobile Homes establish for the Queen? If the company is cost-oriented, it could simply start with the fact that each unit costs $6,000 to manufacture and add a markup for the profit it wants per unit. If the company wants $600 profit, the dealers would pay $6,600 and in turn mark it up for the profit they want per unit. The fault with this approach is that it ignores the competitor's price and the relative perceived value of the Queen.

A market-oriented approach would attempt to start with what value potential buyers put on the Queen. For example, if market testing indicates that potential buyers think that the Queen is worth at least $200 more than the competitor's mobile home, then the company might consider a retail price of $8,000. It might decide to offer its dealers a 20 percent dealer discount to motivate them more highly than the competitor's dealers. Under that plan, dealers would pay $6,400, and the company would make $400 per unit. This pricing strategy, which is one of many possible ones, is displayed in Figure 15–1, along with the other information in this case.

What are the implications of pricing the Queen at $8,000? The first thing

[3] This example is adapted with several changes from David J. Schwartz, *Marketing Today: A Basic Approach,* 2nd ed. (New York: Harcourt Brace Jovanovich, 1977), pp. 542–44.

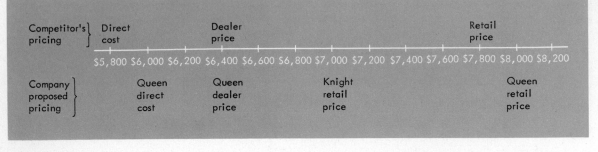

FIGURE 15–1
Illustration of a Pricing Problem

the company has to consider is how many units it would have to sell at $6,400 to break even. The *breakeven volume* is given by:

$$Q_B = \frac{F}{(P\text{-}c)} = \frac{\$120,000}{(\$6,400\text{-}\$6,000)} = 300 \text{ units} \qquad (15\text{-}1)$$

where:

F = fixed cost
P = price
c = direct cost

The competitor is currently selling 600 units. If this is the total market potential, then Modern Mobile Homes will have to achieve a 50 percent market share to break even. And it would have to achieve this market share in spite of charging $200 more per unit. On the other hand, if the market potential might grow in response to strong market effort, then the company might feel more confident about being able to sell at least 300 units a year.

The company will also want to consider other pricing alternatives. The Queen might be priced slightly below $8,000 (say at $7,950) because buyers have a tendency to think of it as selling in the $7,000 rather than $8,000 price range. This is called *odd pricing* and assumes a certain buyer psychology. Or the Queen might be priced at the competitor's price of $7,800 so that the companies are left to fight for market share on the basis of nonprice competition. Or the company might price the Queen below the competitor's price to grab for a higher market share. However, this violates the wish to price the Queen at $800 more than the Knight; also, it could lead to a higher volume of orders than the company can fill, and this would require increased investment. On the other hand, the company might want to consider pricing the Queen higher than $8,000, to suggest a real Cadillac (called *prestige pricing*). For each possible price level, management would have to figure out the breakeven volume and its probability of attainment, the competitor's likely price and marketing-mix response, and the dealers' discount that makes sense.

Modern Mobile Homes's pricing problem is even more complicated. The company can produce the Queen with optional features (better plumbing, lighting, and so on) and will have to figure out a price structure for the different options. Price will also depend on the size of the planned marketing budget because that will make a difference in the company's ability to convince the market to pay a high price. The Queen could cannibalize some of the sales of the Knight, depending on how closely the Queen is priced to the Knight. Or conversely, the Queen could increase the sales of the Knight, since the dealers will be able to attract more traffic with the longer product line. The company will face opportunities to sell the Queen to large mobile-park developers and will have to decide whether these sales will be handled through their franchised dealers or through a national accounts sales department in the home office, and if so, at what price. The company may not have the freedom to charge less than dealer cost to mobile-park developers in order not to be charged with price discrimination under the Robinson-Patman Act. Finally, the example assumed only one competitor where normally several competitors would operate and complicate the pricing problem.

Thus actual pricing strategies require taking many factors into account. A company has to proceed by clarifying its *pricing objectives,* then considering the *policy constraints,* and then choosing a *pricing procedure.*

Pricing Objectives

A company must be clear on what it is trying to achieve in the way of overall business and marketing objectives before it can set the price on a product. Each possible price has a different implication for profits, sales revenue, and market share. This is shown in Figure 15–2 for a hypothetical product. If the company wants to maximize pretax profits, it should set a price of $97. If it wants to maximize sales revenue, it should set a price of $86. If it wants to maximize its market share, it should set an even lower price.

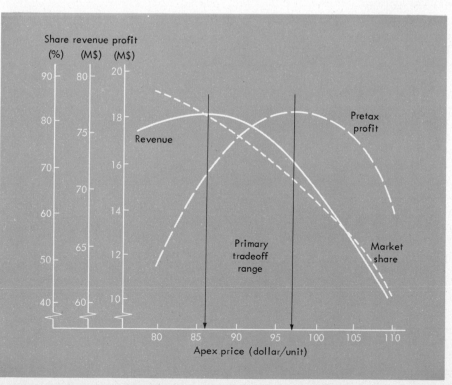

FIGURE 15–2
Relation Between Price,
Revenue, Market Share,
and Profits

SOURCE: Franz Edelman, *Decision Making in Marketing* (New York: Conference Board, 1971).

Here we will examine six frequently found pricing objectives.

Profit-maximization pricing One of the most common pricing objectives is to maximize current profits. Economists have worked out a simple yet elegant model for pricing to maximize current profits. The model assumes that the firm has, or can acquire, knowledge of its demand and cost functions for the product in question. The demand function describes the estimated quantity (Q) that would be purchased per period at various prices (P) that might be charged. Suppose the firm is able to determine through statistical demand analysis that its *demand equation* is

$$Q = 1,000 - 4P \qquad (15\text{-}2)$$

This equation expresses the law of demand—less will be bought at higher prices.

The cost function describes the estimated total cost (C) for alternative quantities per period (Q) that might be produced. In the simplest case, the total cost function can be described by the linear equation $C = F + cQ$ where F is total fixed cost and c is unit variable cost. Suppose the company estimated the following *cost equation* for its product:

$$C = 6,000 + 50Q \qquad (15\text{-}3)$$

The company is almost in a position to determine the current profit maximizing price. It needs only two more equations, both definitional in nature. First, *total revenue* (R) is defined as equal to price times quantity sold—that is,

$$R = PQ \qquad (15\text{-}4)$$

Second, *total profits* (Z) are defined as the difference between total revenue and total cost—that is,

$$Z = R - C \qquad (15\text{-}5)$$

The company can now determine the relationship between profits (Z) and price (P) by starting with the profit equation (15–5) and going through the following derivation:

$$Z = R - C$$
$$Z = PQ - C$$
$$Z = PQ - (6,000 + 50Q)$$
$$Z = P(1,000 - 4P) - 6,000 - 50(1,000 - 4P)$$
$$Z = 1,000P - 4P^2 - 6,000 - 50,000 + 200P$$
$$Z = -56,000 + 1,200P - 4P^2$$

Total profits turn out to be a quadratic (that is, second-degree) function of price. It is a hatlike figure (a parabola), and profits reach their highest point ($34,000) at a price of $150.[4]

---

[4] The optimal price of $150 can be found by drawing the parabola with some sample prices and locating the high point; or by using calculus.

The economist's model has value in showing the role played by the demand and cost function in setting price. But it also has several limitations in practice. (1) It assumes that the other marketing-mix variables are held constant, when in fact they would have to be adjusted for different price settings. (2) It assumes that competitors don't change their prices, when in fact they will react with different prices to different price settings of the company. (3) It ignores the reaction of other parties in the marketing system—government, suppliers, dealers, and so on—to various prices that might be charged. (4) It assumes that the demand and cost functions can be reliably estimated, when in fact great difficulties exist.[5]

Market-share pricing   A company could choose to set a price that maximizes its market-share penetration even though it foregoes current profits. An increasing number of companies believe that long-run profitability rises with market share.[6] Texas Instruments and other companies have set out to dominate their markets through *market-penetration pricing*. They will build excess plant capacity to produce a huge volume, set the price at or below competitors to win share, and keep bringing down their price as their costs fall. They will lose money for the first few years but make it up later when they dominate the market and have the lowest costs.

Any of several conditions might favor setting a low price:[7] (1) The market appears to be highly price sensitive, and therefore a low price will stimulate more rapid market growth. (2) The unit costs of production and distribution fall with accumulated production experience. (3) A low price would discourage actual and potential competition.

Market skimming   Firms may want to take advantage of the fact that some buyers stand ready to pay a much higher price than others because the product has high present value to them. They will initially price to yield a high profit margin per unit sold. This makes sense under the following conditions: (1) There are enough buyers whose demand is relatively inelastic. (2) The unit production and distribution costs of producing a smaller volume are not so much higher that they cancel the advantage of charging what some of the traffic will bear. (3) There is little danger that the high price will stimulate the emergence of rival firms. (4) The high price creates an impression of a superior product.

As time passes, the firm will lower its price to draw in the more price-elastic segments of the market. Du Pont is a prime practitioner of market-skimming pricing, particularly on patent-protected discoveries. They used it with cellophane and nylon, for instance. They will charge a high initial price and only lower it gradually over the years to bring in new price-sensitive segments. Polaroid is another practitioner. It will introduce an expensive version of a new camera and only gradually introduce lower-priced models in a bid for the mass market.

[5] Cost function estimation is described in Jack Johnston, *Statistical Cost Analysis* (New York: McGraw-Hill Book Company, 1960). Demand function estimation is described in Leonard J. Parsons and Randall L. Schultz, *Marketing Models and Econometric Research* (New York: North-Holland, 1976).

[6] See Chapter 11, pp. 279–80.

[7] See Joel Dean, *Managerial Economics* (Englewood Cliffs, N.J.: Prentice-Hall, 1951), pp. 420 ff.

Current-revenue pricing   A company may wish to set the price to maximize current sales revenue. This is a matter of finding the price/quantity combination that yields the largest sales revenue. The firm's interest in early cash recovery could arise because it is strapped for funds or regards the future as too uncertain to justify patient market development.

Target-profit pricing   Some companies describe their pricing objective as the achievement of a satisfactory rate of return. The implication is that although another price might produce an even larger return over the long run, the firm is satisfied with a return that is conventional for the given level of investment and risk. Target pricing (see pp. 390–91) is an example of this.

Promotional pricing   Firms will occasionally set a price designed to enhance the sales of the entire line rather than to yield a profit on the product by itself. An example is *loss-leader pricing*, in which a popular product is priced low to attract a large number of buyers who can be expected to buy the firm's other products. Another example is *prestige pricing*, in which a high price is set on a product item to enhance the quality image of the product line.

Pricing Policies and Constraints

A company's pricing policies answer such questions as the pricing image the company wants, its attitude toward price discounts, and its philosophy of meeting competitors' prices. Thus if Modern Mobile Homes wants an image as a high-quality manufacturer, its pricing policies would rule against introducing models at the low-price, low-quality end.

In setting prices, the decision maker has to consider the reaction of various parties affected by the pricing decision. The following parties are important.

Distributors   The firm must think through its pricing strategy for its distributors and dealers. Some companies set a price for distributors and allow them to set whatever final price they wish. This is done where it is thought that each distributor is in the best position to determine the price suited to local conditions and to set it high enough to provide sufficient selling incentive. The disadvantage is that the manufacturer relinquishes control over the final price. The other approach is for the manufacturer to determine the final price and how much of a distributor's margin is necessary to provide sufficient distributor incentive. The distributors must recognize that the important incentive variable is not the difference between the distributor's and final price (the margin) but rather the margin times the sales volume stimulated by the particular final price.

Competitors   The firm must consider how current competitors will react to its price. Competitors can do nothing, adjust their prices, and/or adjust other elements of their marketing mix. In addition, the price chosen is likely to influence the entry rate of new competitors.

Suppliers   The company's suppliers of materials, funds, and labor also must be considered. Many suppliers interpret the product's price as indicating the level of the firm's profits from the product. The reaction of labor unions will be that a high price, or price increase, constitutes grounds for higher wages. Farmers believe they deserve higher cattle prices if retail meat prices are high. The firm's bank often feels uneasy if product prices are on the low side.

Government   Another price-interested party is the government. Under the Robinson-Patman Act, the seller cannot charge different prices to comparable customers unless the price differences are based strictly on cost differences. Under the Miller-Tydings Act, the seller may or may not be able to require retailers to sell their branded products at a uniform list price, depending upon the state laws. Public utilities must justify their rates before regulatory commissions. At various times, pricing in the steel, auto, meat, drug, and heavy-equipment industries has been subject to government pressure. The prices of agricultural goods and of imported goods are affected by agricultural and tariff legislation, respectively. And various state and local governmental units pass legislation and rulings affecting the prices that can be set by sellers.

Company executives   Price is a concern of different parties within the company. The sales manager wants a low price so that the sales representatives can "talk price" to customers. The controller likes to see a price that will lead to an early payout. The price makes an important difference to the advertising manager as to copy and media tactics. The production planner is interested because the price will affect the rate of sales. These and other executives in the organization can be expected to have strong views on where to set the price.

Pricing Procedures

There is widespread agreement that actual price setting should be based on the three factors of *cost*, *demand*, and *competition*. Yet various pricing procedures used in practice will often pay undue attention to one of these factors. We shall examine cost-oriented, demand-oriented, and competition-oriented pricing procedures in this section.

Cost-oriented pricing   A great number of firms set their prices largely or even wholly on the basis of their costs. Typically, all costs are included, including a usually arbitrary allocation of overhead made on the basis of expected operating levels.

MARKUP PRICING   The most elementary examples of cost-oriented pricing are markup pricing and cost-plus pricing. In both cases price is determined by adding some fixed percentage to the unit cost. Markup pricing is most commonly found in the retail trades where the retailer adds predetermined but different markups to various goods. Cost-plus pricing is most often used to describe the pricing of jobs that are nonroutine and difficult to "cost" in advance, such as construction and military-weapon development.

Markups vary considerably among different goods. Some common markups on the retail price in department stores are 20 percent for tobacco goods, 28 percent for cameras, 34 percent for books, 41 percent for dresses, 46 percent for costume jewelry, and 50 percent for millinery.[8] In the retail grocery industry, items like coffee, canned milk, and sugar tend to have low average markups, while items like frozen foods, jellies, and some canned products have high average markups. In addition, quite a lot of dispersion is found around the averages. Within the category of frozen foods, for example, one study showed the markups on retail price to range from a low of 13 percent to a high of 53 percent.[9]

[8] *Departmental Merchandising and Operating Results of 1965* (New York: National Retail Merchants Association, 1965).

[9] See Lee E. Preston, *Profits, Competition, and Rules of Thumb in Retail Food Pricing* (Berkeley: University of California Institute of Business and Economic Research, 1963), p. 31.

Many hypotheses have been advanced to explain the variations in markups within selected product groups. Preston conducted a study to examine how much of the markup variance within common grocery-product groups could be explained by differences in unit costs, turnover, and manufacturers' versus private brands.[10] The principal finding was that over 40 percent of the variation remained unexplained in most product categories and was probably due to erratic decisions, random factors, and frequently better adaptations to the current market than could be provided by these factors.

Does the use of a rigid customary markup over cost make logical sense in the pricing of products? Generally, no. Any model that ignores current demand elasticity in setting prices is not likely to lead, except by chance, to the achievement of maximum profits, in either the short or long run. As demand elasticity changes, as it is likely to do seasonally, cyclically, or over the product life cycle, the optimal markup would also change.

Still, markup pricing remains popular for a number of reasons. First, there is generally less uncertainty about costs than about demand. By pinning the price to unit costs, sellers simplify their own pricing task considerably; they do not have to make frequent adjustments as demand conditions change. Second, where all firms in the industry use this pricing approach, their prices are likely to be similar if their costs and markups are similar. Price competition is therefore minimized, which would not be the case if firms paid attention to demand variations when they priced. Third, there is the feeling that cost-markup pricing is fairer to both buyers and sellers. Sellers do not take advantage of buyers when the latter's demand becomes acute; yet the sellers earn a fair return on their investment.

TARGET PRICING   A common cost-oriented pricing procedure is that of *target pricing*, in which the firm tries to determine the price that would give it a specified target rate of return on its total costs at an estimated standard volume. This pricing approach has been most closely associated with General Motors, which prices its automobiles so as to achieve a long-run average rate of return of 15 to 20 percent on its investment. It is also closely associated with the pricing policies of public utilities, which have a large investment and are constrained by regulatory commissions, in view of their monopoly position, to seek a fair rate of return on their costs.

The pricing procedures can be illustrated in terms of the breakeven chart in Figure 15–3. Management's first task is to estimate its total costs at various levels of output. The total-cost curve is shown rising at a constant rate until capacity is approached. Management's next task is to estimate the percentage of capacity at which it is likely to operate in the coming period. Suppose the company expects to operate at 80 percent of capacity. This means that it expects to sell 800,000 units if its capacity is 1 million units. The total cost of producing this volume, according to Figure 15–3, is $10 million. Management's third task is to specify a target rate of return. If the company aspires for a 20 percent profit over costs, then it would like absolute profits of $2 million. Therefore one point on its total-revenue curve will have to be $12 million at a volume of 80 percent of capacity. Another point on the total-revenue curve will be $0 at a volume of zero percent of capacity. The rest of the total-revenue curve can be drawn between these two points.

[10] Ibid., pp. 29–40.

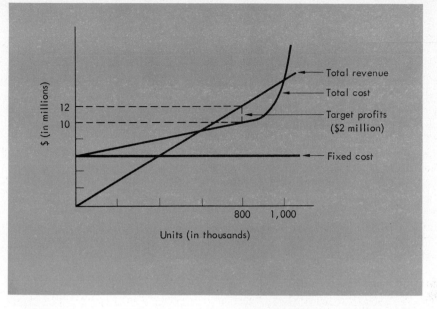

FIGURE 15–3
Breakeven Chart for
Determining Target Price

Where does price come in? The slope of the total-revenue curve is price. In this example, the slope is $15 a unit. Thus if the company charges $15 a unit and manages to sell 800,000 units, it will attain the target rate of return of 20 percent, or $2 million.

Target pricing, however, has a major conceptual flaw. The company used an estimate of sales volume to derive the price, but price is a factor that influences sales volume! A price of $15 may be too high or too low to move 800,000 units. What is missing is a demand function, showing how many units the firm could expect to sell at different prices. With an estimate of the demand curve and with the requirement to earn 20 percent on costs, the firm could solve for those prices and volumes that would be compatible with each other. In this way, the firm would avoid setting a price that failed to generate the estimated level of output.

Demand-oriented pricing   Demand-oriented pricing calls for setting a price based on consumer perceptions and demand intensity rather than on cost.

PERCEIVED-VALUE PRICING   An increasing number of companies are basing their price on the product's "perceived value." They see the buyers' perception of value, not the seller's level of cost, as the key to pricing. They attempt to measure the relative perceived value of their offer and utilize this in setting the price.[11]

Perceived-value pricing is in line with modern market-positioning thinking. A company develops a product for a particular target market with a particular market positioning in mind with respect to price, quality, and service. Thus, it makes an initial decision on offer value and price. Then the company

[11] See Daniel A. Nimer, "Pricing The Profitable Sale Has a Lot to Do With Perception," *Sales Management*, May 19, 1975, pp. 13–14.

estimates the volume it can sell at this price. This suggests the needed plant capacity, investment, and unit costs. Management then figures out whether the product would yield a satisfactory profit at the chosen price and cost. If the answer is yes, the company goes ahead with product development. Otherwise, the company drops the idea.

Among the major practitioners of perceived value pricing are Du Pont and Caterpillar. When Du Pont developed its new synthetic fiber for carpets, it demonstrated to carpet manufacturers that they could afford to pay Du Pont as much as $1.40 a pound for the new fiber and still make their current profit. Du Pont calls this the *value-in-use price*. Du Pont recognized, of course, that pricing the new material at $1.40 a pound would leave the market indifferent. So they set the price somewhat lower than $1.40, depending on the rate of market penetration they were seeking. Du Pont did not take into consideration its own unit-manufacturing cost in setting the price but only in judging whether there was enough profit to go ahead in the first place.

Caterpillar uses perceived value to set prices on its construction equipment. It might price a tractor at $24,000 although a competitor's similar tractor is priced at $20,000. And Caterpillar will get more sales than the competitor! When prospective customers ask a Caterpillar dealer why they should pay $4,000 more for the Caterpillar tractor, the dealer answers:

$20,000 is what the tractor's price would be if it were equivalent to the competitor's tractor
$ 3,000 is the price premium for superior durability
$ 2,000 is the price premium for superior reliability
$ 2,000 is the price premium for superior service
$ 1,000 is the price premium for the longer warranty on parts
_____
$28,000 is the price to cover the value package
−$ 4,000 discount
_____
$24,000 final price

The stunned customers learn that although they are asked to pay a $4,000 premium for the Caterpillar tractor, they are in fact getting a $4,000 discount! They end up choosing the Caterpillar tractor because they are convinced that the lifetime operating costs of the Caterpillar tractor will be smaller.

The key to perceived-value pricing is to make an accurate determination of the market's perception of the value of the total offer. Sellers with an inflated view of the value of their offer may be overpricing their product. In some cases, they underestimate the perceived value and are charging less than they could. Market research has to be carried out to establish the market's perceptions.

Suppose three companies, A, B, and C, produce rapid-relay switches, and a sample of industrial buyers are asked to examine and rate the respective companies' offers. Three alternative methods can be used.

Direct price-rating method. Here the buyers are asked to estimate a price for each switch that they think reflects the total value of buying the switch from each company. For example, they may assign $2.55, $2.00, and $1.52 respectively.

Direct perceived-value-rating method. Here the buyers are asked to allocate 100 points to the three companies to reflect the total value of buying the switch from each company. Suppose they assign 42, 33, 25 respectively. If the average market price of a relay switch is $2.00, we would conclude that the three firms could charge, respectively, $2.55, $2.00, and $1.52 and reflect the perceived value.

Diagnostic method. Here the buyers are asked to rate the three offers on a set of, say, four attributes. They are to allocate 100 points to the three companies with respect to each attribute. They are also asked to distribute 100 points to reflect the relative importance of the attributes. Suppose the results are those shown below:

| IMPORTANCE | | PRODUCTS | | |
WEIGHT	ATTRIBUTE	A	B	C
25	Product durability	40	40	20
30	Product reliability	33	33	33
30	Delivery reliability	50	25	25
15	Service quality	45	35	20
100	(Perceived value)	(41.65)	(32.65)	(24.9)

By multiplying the importance weights against each company's ratings, we find that company A's offer is perceived to be above average (at 42), company B's offer is perceived to be average (at 33), and company C's offer is perceived to be below average (at 25).

Company A, according to these findings, can set a high price for its switches because it offers more, and the buyers perceive this. If it wants to price proportionally to its perceived value, it can charge around $2.55 (= $2.00 for an average quality switch $\times \frac{42}{33}$). If all three companies set their price proportional to perceived value, they all would enjoy some market share since they all offer the same value-to-price.

If a company prices at less than the perceived value of its offer, it would gain a higher-than-average market share because buyers will be getting more value for their money by dealing with this company. This is illustrated in Figure 15–4. The three offers, A, B, and C, initially lie on the same value/price line. Respective market shares will depend upon the relative density of ideal points (not shown) surrounding the three locations. Now suppose company A decides to lower its price to A'. This means its value/price is on a higher line (the dashed line), and it will pull market share away from both B and C, particularly B because it offers more value at the same price as B. B will be pressed to either lower its price or raise its perceived value. In the latter case, B would have to design better qualities and services and effectively inform the market. If the cost of doing this is less than the loss in revenue that would result from a lower price, B would probably invest in strengthening its perceived value.

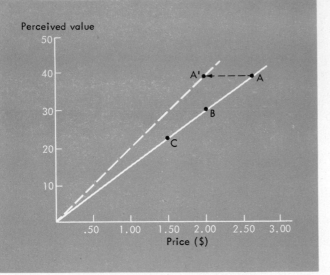

FIGURE 15–4
Perceived-Value Analysis

DEMAND-DIFFERENTIAL PRICING   Another form of demand-oriented pricing is demand-differential pricing (also called *price discrimination*), in which a product or service is sold at two or more prices that do not reflect a proportional difference in marginal costs. Price discrimination takes various forms:

1. *Customer basis.* Here different customers pay different amounts for the same product or service. One car buyer pays the full list price and another car buyer bargains and pays a lower price.

2. *Product-form basis.* Here different versions of the product are priced differently but not proportionately to their respective marginal costs. An electric dishwasher with a $5 Formica top might be priced at $260 and the same dishwasher with a $10 wooden top might be priced at $280.

3. *Place basis.* Here different locations are priced differently, even though there is no difference in the marginal cost of offering the locations. A theatre varies its seat prices because of the different intensities of demand for the various locations.

4. *Time basis.* Here different prices are charged seasonally, by the day, and even by the hour. Public utilities typically vary their prices to commercial users by time of day and weekend versus weekday.

For price discrimination to work, certain conditions must exist.[12] First, the market must be segmentable, and the segments must show different intensities of demand. Second, there should be no chance that the members of the segment paying the lower price could turn around and resell the product to the segment paying the higher price. Third, there should be little chance that competitors will undersell the firm in the segment being charged the higher price. Fourth, the cost of segmenting and policing the market should not exceed the extra revenue derived from price discrimination. Fifth, the practice should not breed customer resentment and turning away.

[12] See George Stigler, *The Theory of Price*, rev. ed. (New York: Macmillan Company, 1952), pp. 215 ff.

Competition-oriented pricing   When a company sets its prices chiefly on the basis of what its competitors are charging, its pricing policy can be described as competition oriented. It is not necessary to charge the same price as competition, although this is a major example of this policy. The competition-oriented-pricing firm may seek to keep its prices lower or higher than competition by a certain percentage. The distinguishing characteristic is that it does *not* seek to maintain a rigid relation between its price and its own costs or demand. Its own costs or demand may change, but the firm maintains its price because competitors maintain their prices. Conversely, the same firm will change its prices when competitors change theirs, even if its own costs or demand have not altered.

GOING-RATE PRICING   The most popular type of competition-oriented pricing is that in which a firm tries to keep its price at the average level charged by the industry. Called *going-rate pricing*, it is popular for several reasons. Where costs are difficult to measure, it is felt that the going price represents the collective wisdom of the industry concerning the price that would yield a fair return. It is also felt that conforming to a going price would be least disruptive of industry harmony. The difficulty of knowing how buyers and competitors would react to price differentials is still another reason for this pricing.

Going-rate pricing primarily characterizes pricing practice in homogeneous product markets, although the market structure itself may vary from pure competition to pure oligopoly. The firm selling a homogeneous product in a *highly competitive market* has actually very little choice but to set the going price. In *pure oligopoly*, where a few large firms dominate the industry, the firm also tends to charge the same price as competition, although for different reasons. Since there are only a few firms, each firm is quite aware of the others' prices, and so are the buyers. The slightest price difference would attract business to the lower-price firm. The individual oligopolist's demand curve has a kink in it at the level of the present prices. The demand curve tends to be elastic above the kink because other firms are not likely to follow a raise in prices; the demand curve tends to be inelastic below the kink because other firms are likely to follow a price cut. An oligopolist can gain little by raising its price when demand is elastic or by lowering its price when demand is inelastic.

In markets characterized by *product differentiation*, the individual firm has more latitude in its price decision. Product and service differences desensitize the buyer to existing price differentials. Firms try to establish themselves in a pricing zone with respect to their competitors, assuming the role of a high-price, medium-price, or low-price firm. Their product and marketing programs are made compatible with this chosen pricing zone or vice versa. They respond to competitive changes in price to maintain their pricing zone.

SEALED-BID PRICING   Competitive-oriented pricing also dominates in those situations where firms compete for jobs on the basis of bids, such as original equipment manufacture and defense contract work. The bid is the firm's offer price, and it is a prime example of pricing based on expectations of how competitors will price rather than on a rigid relation based on the firm's own costs or demand. The objective of the firm in the bidding situation is to get the contract, and this means that it hopes to set its price lower than that set by any of the other bidding firms.

Yet the firm does not ordinarily set its price below a certain level. Even when it is anxious to get a contract in order to keep the plant busy, it cannot quote a price below marginal cost without worsening its position. On the other hand, as it raises its price above marginal cost, it increases its potential profit but reduces its chance of getting the contract.

The net effect of the two opposite pulls can be described in terms of the *expected profit* of the particular bid. Suppose a bid of $9,500 would yield a high chance of getting the contract, say .81, but only a low profit, say $100. The expected profit with this bid is therefore $81. If the firm bid $11,000, its profit would be $1,600, but its chance of getting the contract might be reduced, say to .01. The expected profit would be only $16. Table 15–1 shows these and some other bids and the corresponding expected profits.

TABLE 15–1
Effect of Different Bids on Expected Profit

COMPANY'S BID	COMPANY'S PROFIT	PROBABILITY OF GETTING AWARD WITH THIS BID (ASSUMED)	EXPECTED PROFIT
$ 9,500	$ 100	.81	$ 81
10,000	600	.36	216
10,500	1,100	.09	99
11,000	1,600	.01	16

One logical bidding criterion would be to state the bid that would maximize the expected profit. According to Table 15–1, the best bid would be $10,000, for which the expected profit is $216.

The use of the expected-profit criterion makes sense for the large firm that makes many bids and is not dependent on winning any particular contract. In playing the odds, it should achieve maximum profits in the long run. The firm that bids only occasionally and/or may need a particular contract badly will probably not find it advantageous to use the expected-profit criterion. The criterion, for example, does not distinguish between a $1,000 profit with a .10 probability and a $125 profit with an .80 probability. Yet the firm that wants to keep production going is likely to prefer the second contract to the first. In other words, the dollar value of expected profits may not reflect the utility value.[13]

INITIATING PRICE CHANGES

Pricing is a challenge not only when the firm sets a price for the first time but also when it is about to initiate a price cut or increase. We will examine these two moves and then consider how to estimate the likely reactions of various parties, particularly buyers and competitors, to these moves.

Initiating Price Cuts

Several circumstances may lead a firm to consider cutting its price even though such a move may threaten industrial harmony and provoke a price war. One circumstance is *excess capacity*. Here the firm needs additional business and pre-

---

[13] For further discussion, see C. West Churchman, Russell L. Ackoff, and E. Leonard Arnoff, *Introduction to Operations Research* (New York: John Wiley & Sons, 1957), pp. 559–73.

sumably has failed to generate it through increased sales effort, product improvement, and other normal means of sales expansion. In the mid-1970s, prices remained remarkably sticky in spite of widespread overcapacity, showing that firms preferred high margins on low sales to low margins on higher sales.[14] But in the late 1970s various companies, particularly small ones, began to break ranks with "follow the leader pricing" and turned to "flexible pricing" to gain as much business as they could.[15]

Another circumstance is *falling market share* in the face of vigorous price competition. Several American industries—such as automobiles, consumer electronics, cameras, watches, and steel—have been losing market share, particularly to Japanese competitors whose high-quality goods carry lower prices than American products. This has led Zenith, General Motors, and others to take more aggressive pricing action. GM, for example, has begun to price by geography and cut its subcompact car prices by 10 percent on the West Coast, where Japanese competition is stiffest.

Still another circumstance provoking price cutting is a *drive for dominance through lower costs*. Either the aggressive pricer starts with lower costs than its competitors or it initiates price cuts in the hope of gaining market share, which would lead to falling costs through larger volume.

Initiating Price Increases

Many companies have had to raise prices in recent years. They do this in spite of the fact that the price increases will be resented by customers, dealers, and even the company's own sales force. A successful price increase can increase profits considerably. For example, if the company's profit margin is 3 percent of sales, a 1 percent price increase will increase profits by 33 percent if sales volume is unaffected.

A major circumstance calling for upward price revision is the persistent worldwide *cost inflation* in recent years. Rising costs unmatched by productivity gains squeeze profit margins and lead companies to regular rounds of price hikes. Prices are often raised by more than the cost increases in anticipation of further inflation or government price controls. Companies hesitate to make price commitments in long-term contracts for fear that cost inflation will erode their profit margins. Companies have become adept at inflation pricing through such measures as:[16]

1. Adopting delayed quotation pricing
2. Writing escalator clauses into contracts
3. Unbundling goods and services and pricing them separately[17]
4. Reducing cash and quantity discounts and off-list pricing by sales force
5. Increasing minimum-acceptance order sizes
6. Putting more sales power behind higher marginal products and markets
7. Reducing product quality, features, or service

[14] See "Prices Rise in Spite of Spare Capacity," *Business Week*, March 21, 1977, pp. 120–26.

[15] See "Flexible Pricing," *Business Week*, December 12, 1977, pp. 78–88.

[16] See "Pricing Strategy in an Inflationary Economy," *Business Week*, December 12, 1977; and Norman H. Fuss, Jr., "How to Raise Prices—Judiciously—to Meet Today's Conditions," *Harvard Business Review*, May–June 1975, pp. 10 ff.

[17] The classic unbundling story is told of a customer buying an automobile in Mexico when inflation was at its worst. After the customer agreed to buy the car at the stated price, the salesperson asked if he also wanted to order tires and a steering wheel!

The other major circumstance leading to price increases is *overdemand.* When a company cannot supply all of its customers, it can raise its price, use allocation quotas, or both. Prices may be raised relatively invisibly through dropping discounts and adding higher-priced units to the line. Or prices may be pushed up boldly. U.S. Gypsum faced this problem when it fell into an oversold position on wallboard, fully recognizing that it would probably catch up with demand in six months and move to an undersold position. The issue was whether it should put through a sharp price increase then, followed by a sharp price decrease six months later, or a small price increase then and a small price decrease six months later. It decided on the former because it felt dealers were more concerned with availability than price and would make good money even at the higher price.

In passing price increases on to customers, the company should show a concern for their situation and not act as a ruthless price gouger. The price increases should be accompanied by a well-thought-out communication program in which the customers are told why the prices are being increased and how they might economize. The company's sales force should make regular calls on the customers and attempt to help them solve their problems.

Buyers' Reactions to Price Changes

Whether the price is to be moved up or down, the action is sure to affect buyers, competitors, distributors, and suppliers, and may interest government as well. The success of the move depends critically on how major parties, particularly buyers and competitors, respond.

The traditional analysis of buyers' reactions to price change utilizes the concept of *price elasticity of demand.*

Price elasticity of demand This term refers to the ratio of the percentage change in demand (quantity sold per period) caused by a percentage change in price. In symbols:

$$Eqp = \frac{(Q_1 - Q_0)/\tfrac{1}{2}(Q_0 + Q_1)}{(P_1 - P_0)/\tfrac{1}{2}(P_0 + P_1)} \qquad (15\text{--}7)$$

where:

Eqp = elasticity of quantity sold with respect to a change in price
Q_0,Q_1 = quantity sold per period before and after price change
P_0,P_1 = old and new price

A price elasticity of -1 means that sales rise (fall) by the same percentage as price falls (rises). In this case, total revenue is unaffected. A price elasticity greater than -1 means that sales rise (fall) by more than price falls (rises) in percentage terms; in this case, total revenue rises. A price elasticity less than -1 means that sales rise (fall) by less than price falls (rises) in percentage terms; in this case, total revenue falls.

As an example, suppose a company lowers its price from \$10 to \$5 and, as a result, its sales rise from 100 units to 150 units. According to (15–7):

$$\frac{(150 - 100) / \tfrac{1}{2}(100 + 150)}{(\$5 - \$10) / \tfrac{1}{2}(\$10 + \$5)} = \frac{.40}{-.67} = -.60$$

Thus the demand elasticity is less than −1, or inelastic, and we know that total revenue will fall. Checking this, we note that the total revenue fell from $1,000 to $750.

Price elasticity of demand gives precision to the question of whether the firm's price is too high or too low. From the point of view of maximizing *revenue,* price is too high if demand is elastic and too low if demand is inelastic. Whether this is also true for maximizing *profits* depends on the behavior of costs.

In practice, price elasticity is extremely difficult to measure. There are definitional as well as statistical hurdles. Definitionally, price elasticity is not an absolute characteristic of the demand facing a seller but rather a conditional one. Price elasticity depends on the magnitude of the contemplated price change. It may be negligible with a small price change (one below the threshold level) and substantial with a large price change. Price elasticity also varies with the original price level. A 5 percent increase over current prices of $1 and $1.20, respectively, may exhibit a quite different elasticity. Finally, long-run price elasticity is apt to differ from short-run elasticity. Buyers may have to continue with their current supplier immediately after a price increase because choosing a new supplier takes time, but they may eventually switch suppliers. In this case, demand is more elastic in the long run than in the short run.[18] Or the reverse may happen: buyers drop a supplier in anger after being notified of a price increase but return later. The significance of this distinction between short-run and long-run elasticity is that sellers will not know for a while the total effect of their price change.

Major statistical estimation problems face the firm wishing to evaluate price elasticity. Different techniques have evolved, none completely appropriate or satisfactory in all circumstances. The problem can be brought into focus by considering the following case:

> One of the telephone companies in the Bell chain was considering a rate reduction on the extension (or second) phone, which it installed in a home for an extra monthly charge of 75 cents. The company had been using heavy promotion to sell families on second phones, but the advertising stimulation appeared to be showing diminishing returns. The company was wondering how many additional extension phones would be ordered if the charge was reduced to fifty cents.

A telephone company would not have any competitive reactions to worry about in contemplating a price change. The company could proceed to estimate the likely reactions of the ultimate customers, using one of four methods.

DIRECT ATTITUDE SURVEY   The company could interview a sample of potential users as to whether they would add another phone if the monthly service charge was lowered to fifty cents. The percentage who said yes could then be applied against the known total number of potential users to find the number of extra extensions this would mean.

STATISTICAL ANALYSIS   This could take the form of either a historical or a cross-sectional analysis of the relationship between price and quantity. A historical analysis consists in observing how extension usage was affected in the past by

---

[18] Stigler suggests that demand is generally more elastic in the long run because the short run is marked by the difficulty of rapid adjustment, the existence of market imperfections, and the presence of habit. Stigler, *Theory of Price,* pp. 45–47.

rate reductions. A cross-sectional analysis consists in observing how extension usage varies with the rates charged by different companies in the Bell System.

MARKET TEST   The company could offer a representative sample of potential users the chance to have an extension phone for fifty cents a month if they acted on the offer within a specified time period. The percentage who took advantage could then be applied against the estimated number of potential users.

ANALYTIC INFERENCE   The company could conjecture how many additional families would be likely to find a second phone worthwhile at the lower price. The issue of a second phone would be one of convenience versus cost. The company could segment the market into dwelling units of different sizes and different income levels. A family in a large home with a good income would tend to be more receptive to a second phone. The company could estimate how many families in this segment were without second phones and apply the probability that they would acquire the phone at the reduced rate. This could be done for all the segments, to build up an estimate.

Perceptual factors in buyers' response   Perceptual factors constitute an important intervening variable in explaining market response to price changes. In the Bell case, this turned out to be particularly true. In a direct attitude survey, potential extension users were asked what they thought the extension service cost. Over 80 percent of the respondents named a price above seventy-five cents a month, in some cases as high as two dollars. The amount of price misinformation was profound, and this could be an important deterrent of purchase. The policy implication is quite interesting. It means that *bringing people closer to an understanding of the correct price would be tantamount to a price reduction*. If a housewife thought the monthly charge was one dollar and then learned that it was only seventy-five cents, this is tantamount to a price reduction *in her mind* of 25 percent. Rather than reducing the monthly rate to fifty cents, the company might gain more through an advertising campaign that clarified the current price.

Customers will not always put the most straightforward interpretation on a price change when it occurs.[19] A price reduction, which would normally attract more buyers, could mean other things to the buyers:[20]

The item is about to be superseded by a later model.
The item has some fault and is not selling well.
The firm is in financial trouble and may not stay in business to supply future parts.
The price will come down even further and it pays to wait.[21]
The quality has been reduced.

[19] For an excellent review, see Kent B. Monroe, "Buyers' Subjective Perceptions of Price," *Journal of Marketing Research*, February 1973, pp. 70–80.

[20] See Alfred R. Oxenfeldt, *Pricing for Marketing Executives* (San Francisco: Wadsworth Publishing Company, 1961), p. 28.

[21] Economists use the concept of *elasticity of expectations* to convey this possibility. The elasticity of expectations is the ratio of the future expected percentage change in price to the recent percentage change in price. A positive elasticity means that buyers expect a price reduction (increase) to be followed by another reduction (increase).

A price increase, which would normally deter sales, may carry a variety of different meanings to the buyers:

The item is very "hot" and may be unobtainable unless it is bought soon.
The item represents an unusually good value.[22]
The seller is greedy and is charging what the traffic will bear.

Buyers' reactions to price changes will also vary with the buyers' perceptions of the product's cost in their total scheme of purchases. Buyers are most price sensitive to products that cost a lot and are bought frequently, whereas they hardly notice higher prices on small items that they buy infrequently. In addition, buyers are normally less concerned with the product's *price* than its *total costs*, where the costs include obtaining, operating, and servicing the product. A seller can charge a higher price than competition and still get the business if he or she is able to convince the customer that the total costs are low.

Competitors' Reactions to Price Changes

A firm contemplating a price change has to worry about competitors' as well as customers' reactions. Competitors' reactions are particularly important where the number of firms is small, the product offering is homogeneous, and the buyers are discriminating and informed.

How can the firm estimate the likely reaction of its competitors? Let us assume that the firm faces only one large competitor. The likely behavior of this competitor can be approached from two quite different starting points. One is to assume that the competitor has a set policy for reacting to price changes. The other is to assume that the competitor treats each price change as posing a fresh challenge. Each assumption has different research implications.

If the competitor has a set price-reaction policy, there are at least two ways to fathom it—through inside information and through statistical analysis. Inside information can be obtained in many ways, some quite acceptable and others verging on cloak-and-dagger methods. One of the more respectable methods is hiring an executive away from a competitor. In this way the firm acquires a rich source of information on the competitor's thought processes and patterns of reaction. It may even pay to set up a unit of former employees whose job is to think like the competitor. Information on the thinking of a competitor can also come through the financial community, suppliers, dealers, and the business community at large.

A set policy toward meeting price changes may be discerned through a statistical analysis of the firm's past price reactions. We can employ the concept "conjectural price variation" (V), defined as the ratio of the competitor's reactive price change to the company's previous price change. In symbols:[23]

$$V_{A,t} = \frac{P_{B,t} - P_{B,t-1}}{P_{A,t} - P_{A,t-1}} \qquad (15\text{-}8)$$

---

[22] A cosmetics company introduced a new low-priced lipstick line, and it did not sell. The company raised its price substantially, and it began to sell extremely well. Price is taken by many buyers as an indicator of quality. See André Gabor and C. W. J. Granger, "Price as an Indicator of Quality," *Economica*, February 1966, pp. 43–70.

[23] See William Fellner, *Competition among the Few* (New York: Alfred A. Knopf, 1949); and Richard M. Cyert and James G. March, *A Behavioral Theory of the Firm* (Englewood Cliffs, N.J.: Prentice-Hall, 1963), chap. 5, esp. pp. 88–90.

where:

$$V_{A,t} = \text{the change in competitor B's price during period } t \text{ as a}$$
$$\text{proportion of company A's price change during period } t$$
$$P_{B,t} - P_{B,t-1} = \text{the change in competitor B's price during period } t$$
$$P_{A,t} - P_{A,t-1} = \text{the change in company A's price during period } t$$

The last-observed $V_{A,t}$ can be used by the company as an estimate of the probable reaction of the competitor. If $V_{A,t} = 0$, then the competitor did not react last time. If $V_{A,t} = 1$, then the competitor fully matched the company's price change. If $V_{A,t} = \frac{1}{2}$, then the competitor only matched half of the company's price change. However, it could be misleading to base the analysis only on the last price reaction. It would be better to average several of the past V terms, giving more weight to the more recent ones because they are reflections of more current policy. A possible estimate of future competitive price reaction $(V_{A,t+1})$ might be

$$V_{A,t+1} = .5V_{A,t} + .3V_{A,t-1} + .2V_{A,t-2} \tag{15-9}$$

where three past conjectural price-variation terms are combined in a weighted average.

The statistical method makes sense if the competitor shows a fairly consistent price reaction. Otherwise it would be better to assume that the competitor decides afresh on each occasion of a price increase what response to make. An analysis must be made of the competitor's self-interest. His current financial situation should be researched, along with recent sales and capacity, customer loyalty, and corporate objectives. If evidence points to a market-share objective, then the competitor is likely to match the price change. If evidence points to a profit-maximization objective, the competitor may react on some other policy front, such as increasing the advertising budget or improving the product quality. The task is to get into the mind of the competitor through inside and outside sources of information.

The problem is complicated because each price change by the company occurs under unique circumstances, and the competitor is capable of putting different interpretations on it. The competitor's reaction to a price reduction will depend on whether it is interpreted to mean:

The company is trying to steal the market.

The company is not doing well and is trying to improve its sales.

The company is hoping that the whole industry will reduce its prices in the interests of stimulating total demand.

When there is more than one competitor, the company must estimate each competitor's likely reaction. If all competitors behave alike, this amounts to analyzing only a typical competitor. If the competitors cannot be expected to react uniformly because of critical differences in size, market shares, or policies, then separate analyses are necessary. If it appears that a few competitors will match the price change, then there is good reason to expect the rest will also match it.

The following case illustrates how a major chemical company analyzed the probable reactions of various parties to a contemplated price reduction.[24]

> A large chemical company had been selling a plastic substance to industrial users for several years and enjoyed a 40 percent market share. The management became worried about whether its current price of one dollar per pound could be maintained for much longer. The main source of concern was the rapid buildup of capacity by its three competitors and the possible attraction of further competitors by the current price. Management saw the key to the problem of possible oversupply to lie in further market expansion. The key area for market expansion lay in an important segment of the market that was closely held by a substitute plastic product produced by six firms. This substitute product was not as good, but it was priced lower. Management saw a possible solution in displacing the substitute product in the recalcitrant segment through a price reduction. If it could penetrate this segment, there was a good chance it could also penetrate three other segments, which had resisted the displacement.

The first task was to develop a decision structure for the problem in which all components would be related. This meant defining the objectives, price alternatives, and key uncertainties. It was decided that the objective would be to maximize the present value of future profits over the next five years. Management decided to consider the four alternatives of maintaining the price at one dollar or reducing the price to ninety-three, eighty-five, and eighty cents, respectively. The following were considered among the key uncertainties that had to be evaluated:

How much penetration in the key segment would take place without a price reduction?

How would the six firms producing the substitute plastic react to each possible price reduction?

How much penetration in the key segment would take place for every possible price reaction of the suppliers of the substitute plastic?

How much would penetration into the key segment speed up penetration into the other segments?

If the key segment were not penetrated, what would be the probability that the company's competitors would initiate price reductions soon?

What would be the impact of a price reduction on the decision of existing competitors to expand their capacity and/or potential competitors to enter the industry?

The data-gathering phase consisted mainly in asking key sales personnel to place subjective probabilities on the various possible states of the key uncertainties. Meetings were held with the sales personnel to explain the concept of expressing judgments in the form of probabilities. The probabilities were filled out on a long questionnaire. For example, one question asked for the probability that the producers of the substitute product would retaliate if the company

[24] See Paul E. Green, "Bayesian Decision Theory in Pricing Strategy," *Journal of Marketing*, January 1963, pp. 5–14.

reduced its price to ninety-three cents per pound. On the average, the sales personnel felt that there was only a 5 percent probability of a full match, a 60 percent probability of a half match, and a 35 percent probability of no retaliation. They were also asked for probabilities if price were reduced to eighty-five and to eighty cents. The sales personnel indicated, as expected, that the probability of retaliation increased with an increase in price reduction.

The next step was to estimate the likely payoffs of different courses of action. A decision-tree analysis revealed that there were over four hundred possible outcomes. For this reason, the estimation of expected payoffs was programmed on a computer. The computer results indicated that in all cases a price reduction had a higher expected payoff than status quo pricing, and, in fact, a price reduction to eighty cents had the highest expected payoff. To check the sensitivity of these results to the original assumptions, the results were recomputed for alternative assumptions about the rate of market growth and the appropriate cost of capital. It was found that the ranking of the strategies was not affected by the change in the assumptions. The analysis clearly pointed to the desirability of a price reduction.

RESPONDING TO PRICE CHANGES

Let us reverse the previous question and ask how a firm should respond to a price change initiated by a competitor.

In some market situations the firm has no choice but to meet a competitor's price change. This is particularly true when the price is cut in a homogeneous product market. Unless the firm meets the price reduction, most buyers will shift their business to the lowest-price competitor.

When the price is raised by a firm in a homogeneous product market, the other firms may or may not meet it. They will comply if the price increase appears designed to benefit the industry as a whole. But if one firm does not see it that way and thinks that it or the industry would gain more by standing pat on prices, its noncompliance can make the leader and the others rescind any price increases.

In nonhomogeneous product markets, a firm has more latitude in reacting to a competitor's price change. The essential fact is that buyers choose the seller on the basis of a multiplicity of considerations: service, quality, reliability, and other factors. These factors desensitize many buyers to minor price differences. The reacting firm has a number of options: doing nothing and losing few or many customers, depending upon the level of customer loyalty; meeting the price change partly or fully; countering with modifications of other elements in its marketing mix.

The firm's analysis should take the form of estimating the expected payoffs of alternative possible reactions. It should consider the following questions:

Why did the competitor change the price? Is it to steal the market, to utilize excess capacity, to meet changing cost conditions, or to evoke a calculated industry-wide price change to take advantage of total demand?

Is the competitor intending to make the price change temporary or permanent?

What will happen to the company's market share and profits if it ignores the price change? Are the other companies going to ignore the price change?

What is the competitor's (and other firms') response likely to be to each possible reaction?

Market leaders, in particular, are frequent targets of aggressive price cutting by smaller firms trying to build market share. One only has to think of Fuji Film's attack on Kodak, Bic's attack on Gillette, and Datril's attack on Tylenol.[25] When the attacking firm brings a comparable quality to the market, its lower price will cut increasingly into the market leader's share. The leader at this point has several options.

1. *Price maintenance.* The leader might choose to maintain its price and profit margin. It may believe that (a) it would lose too much profit if it reduced its price on all the units it sells; (b) it would not lose much market share; and (c) it would be easy to regain market share when necessary. It may also feel that it could hold on to the good customers, giving up only the poorer ones to the competitor. The argument against price maintenance, however, is that the attacker gets more confident, the leader's sales force gets demoralized, and the leader ends up losing more share than expected. The leader then panics, lowers price in order to regain share, and finds it more difficult and costly to regain share than expected.

2. *Price maintenance with nonprice counterattack.* If the leader chooses to maintain price, it should take some steps to strengthen the value of its offer. It should improve its product, services, and communications so that customers see themselves as getting more value per dollar from the company than from its competitor. The firm will often find it cheaper to maintain its price and spend money to improve the value of its offer than to cut its price and operate at a lower margin.

3. *Price reduction.* The leader might prefer to lower its price to the competitor's price to hold its market share. It may choose this course of action because (a) its costs fall with volume; (b) it believes that the market is very price sensitive and it will lose a substantial market share; and (c) it believes that it would be hard to rebuild its market share once it is lost. This action will cut its profits in the short run. Some firms will be tempted to reduce their product quality, services, and marketing communications to maintain profits but this is shortsighted and can ultimately hurt their long-run market share. The company should try to maintain the value of its offer as it cuts prices.

4. *Price increase with product counterattack.* The leader, instead of maintaining or lowering its price, might raise it along with introducing some new brands to bracket the attacking brand. Heublein, Inc., used this strategy when its Smirnoff's vodka, which had 23 percent of the American vodka market, was attacked by another brand, Wolfschmidt, priced at one dollar less a bottle. Instead of Heublein's lowering the price of Smirnoff by one dollar, it raised the price by one dollar and put the increased revenue into its advertising. At the same time, Heublein introduced a new brand, Relska, to compete with Wolfschmidt and also introduced Popov, a low-priced vodka. This strategy effectively bracketed Wolfschmidt and gave Smirnoff an even more elite image.

The best response requires an analysis of the particular situation. The company under attack has to consider the product's stage in the life cycle, its importance in the company's portfolio, the intentions and resources of the competitor, the price sensitivity versus value sensitivity of the market, the behavior of costs with volume, and the company's alternative opportunities.

An extended analysis of company alternatives is not always feasible at the time of a price change. The competitor who initiated the price change may have spent considerable time in preparing for this decision, but the company may

[25] See "The Market Manhandles a Blue Chip," *Business Week*, June 20, 1977, p. 70 ff; "Razor Fighting," *Newsweek*, November 22, 1976, p. 103; and "A Painful Headache for Bristol-Myers?" *Business Week*, October 6, 1975, pp. 78–80.

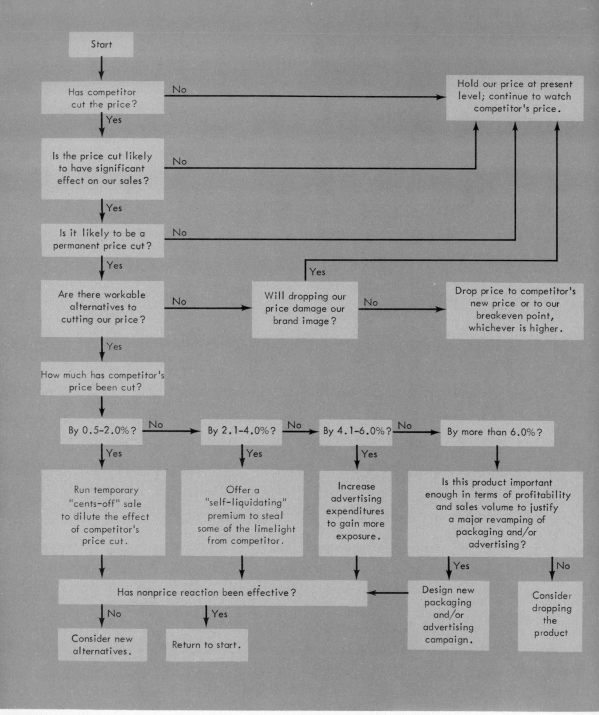

SOURCE: Redrawn, with permission, from an unpublished paper by Raymond J. Trapp, Northwestern University, 1964.

FIGURE 15–5
Decision Program for Meeting a Competitor's Price Cut

have to react decisively within hours or days. About the only way to place such decisions on a sure footing is to anticipate their possible occurrence and to prepare an advanced program to guide managers' responses. An example of such a program to meet a possible price cut is shown in Figure 15–5. Reaction programs for meeting price changes are likely to find their greatest application in industries where price changes occur with some frequency and where it is important to react quickly. Examples could be found in the meat-packing, lumber, and oil industries.[26]

PRICING THE PRODUCT LINE

The logic of setting or changing a price on an individual product has to be modified when the product is a member of a product line. In the latter case, the quest is for a set of mutual prices that maximizes the profits of the line. This quest is made difficult because various company products are interrelated in demand and/or cost and are subject to different degrees of competition.

Interrelated Demand Two products are interrelated in demand when the price (or some other element of the marketing mix) of one affects the demand for the other. Economists use the concept of "cross-elasticity of demand" to express the interaction.[27] A positive cross-elasticity means that two goods are *substitutes*, a negative cross-elasticity means that two goods are *complements*, and a zero cross-elasticity means that two goods are *unrelated* in demand. If a television manufacturer lowered the price of its color television sets, this would decrease the demand for its black-and-white sets (substitutes), increase the demand for the components of its color sets (complements), and probably not affect the demand for its pocket radios. Before changing the price of any single item in its line, the seller should consider the various cross-elasticities to determine the overall impact of this move.

Interrelated Cost Two products are interrelated in cost when a change in the production of one affects the cost of the other. By-products and joint products are related in this sense. If the production of ham is cut down, the production of pork will be also. As a result, the unit cost of the pork will rise because the overhead is spread over fewer units. More generally, any two products using the same production facilities are interrelated on the cost side even if they are not joint products. This is largely because accounting practice requires a full allocation of costs. The significance of all this is that if the company increases the price of A, for example, and causes its sales to fall, the cost of the other products, assuming they are not complementary goods, will be higher. Thus management must examine the cost interactions before it changes the price of a single product in the line.

[26] See, for example, William M. Morgenroth, "A Method for Understanding Price Determinants," *Journal of Marketing Research*, August 1964, pp. 17–26.

[27] Technically, the cross-elasticity of demand (E_c) is the percentage change in quantity sold of product B associated with a percentage change in price of product A.

Various products in a company line are exposed to different degrees of competition. The seller may have little latitude in pricing products in the line where existing or potential competition is keen and will have varying degrees of price discretion in the other cases. Therefore the prices of the products in the line should not simply be proportional to costs, for this would overlook profit opportunities that are associated with taking advantage of different degrees of competition.

In practice, costs have provided the usual starting point for determining the prices of interrelated products in the line. Even here there seems to be considerable disagreement over which costs should be used. The three most popular cost bases are full costs, incremental costs, and conversion costs. The price structures resulting from using these respective cost bases are illustrated for a hypothetical soap manufacturer in Table 15–2.

The soap manufacturer makes two types of specialty soap. The second soap requires more labor cost but less material cost per bar than the first soap. The second soap also requires more manufacturing overhead than the first. The specific costs per bar are shown in Table 15–2A.

The first pricing principle calls for pricing the soaps proportionately to their full costs. Since both soaps have the same full costs, they will bear the same price (here forty-two cents because of a 20 percent markup). The chief criticism against using the full cost is that the allocation of overhead unavoidably involves some arbitrariness. Therefore the resulting prices take on a partly arbitrary character. As a result, the company may be blind to profit opportunities that would exist if the prices of the two soaps were not geared so tightly to the recovery of a somewhat arbitrary overhead burden.

The second pricing principle calls for setting prices that are proportional

---

TABLE 15–2
Illustration of Alternative Product-line Pricing Principles

A. PRODUCT-LINE COST STRUCTURE

	SOAP 1	SOAP 2
1. Labor cost	.10	.15
2. Material cost	.20	.10
3. Overhead cost	.05	.10
Full cost (1 + 2 + 3)	.35	.35
Incremental cost (1 + 2)	.30	.25
Conversion cost (1 + 3)	.15	.25

B. ALTERNATIVE PRODUCT-LINE PRICES

	MARKUP	SOAP 1	SOAP 2
1. Full cost pricing	20%	.42	.42
2. Incremental cost pricing	40%	.42	.35
3. Conversion cost pricing	180%	.42	.70

to incremental costs. The underlying theory is that the company should charge customers proportionately to the extra costs it has to bear in supplying additional units of the two soaps. In the example, supplying an additional unit of soap 2 imposes less additional cost than supplying another unit of soap 1. The net effect of pricing on an incremental cost basis is to shift sales toward the soap that absorbs more company overhead.[28]

The third pricing principle calls for setting prices that are proportional to conversion costs. Conversion costs are defined as the labor and company overhead required to convert purchased materials into finished products. Conversion costs thus amount to the "value added" by the firm in the production process; it can be found by subtracting purchased material costs from the allocated full costs. The argument that has been advanced for using conversion costs is that the firm's profits should be based on the value its own operations add to each soap. The net effect of pricing on a conversion cost basis is to shift sales toward the soap that has more material cost. This pricing principle economizes on the use of scarce company resources, such as labor and machines.

Although costs can represent a starting point for developing the pricing structure, they hardly represent sufficient criteria. Incremental costs provide the lower limit to individual product pricing (except in special circumstances, such as loss leading). But a *uniform* markup over incremental or any other costs is fallacious in that it ignores the different demand intensities, cross-elasticities, competitive conditions, and life-cycle characteristics of each product.

SUMMARY

In spite of the increased role of nonprice factors in the modern marketing process, price remains an important element and especially challenging in certain situations.

In setting a price, the firm must pay attention to pricing objectives, policies, and procedures. The firm can draw guidance from the theoretical pricing model of the economists. The model suggests how the firm can find the short-run profit-maximizing price when estimates of demand and cost are available. The model, however, leaves out several factors that have to be considered in actual pricing situations, such as the presence of other objectives, multiple parties, marketing-mix interactions, and uncertainties surrounding the estimates of demand and cost. In practice, companies tend to orient their pricing toward cost (as in markup pricing and target pricing), or demand (as in perceived-value pricing and differential-demand pricing), or competition (as in going rate pricing and bidding).

When a firm considers changing its established price, it must carefully consider customers' and competitors' reactions. The probable reaction of customers is summarized in the concept of price elasticity of demand. There are several ways to estimate price elasticity and some problems in interpreting it, but it is a key factor in the determination of how much would be gained by the price change. Competitors' reactions also must be taken into account, and they depend very much on the nature of the market structure and the degree of product

---

[28] The principle of marking up incremental costs is analyzed and defended for retail pricing in Malcolm P. McNair and Eleanor G. May, "Pricing for Profit, A Revolutionary Approach to Retail Accounting," *Harvard Business Review*, May–June 1957, pp. 105–22.

homogeneity. Competitors' reactions may be studied on the assumption either that they flow from a set reaction policy or that they flow from a fresh appraisal of the challenge each time. The firm initiating the price change must also consider the probable reactions of suppliers, middlemen, and government.

The firm that faces a competitor's price change must try to understand the competitor's intent and the likely duration of the change. If swiftness of reaction is desirable, the firm should preplan its reactions to different possible pricing developments.

Pricing is complicated when it is realized that various products in a line typically have important demand and/or cost interrelationships. Then the objective is to develop a set of mutual prices that maximize the profits on the whole line. Most companies develop tentative prices for the products in the line by marking up full costs or incremental costs or conversion costs and then modifying these prices by individual demand and competitive factors.

QUESTIONS AND PROBLEMS

1. Does an "early cash recovery" pricing objective mean that the firm should set a high rather than a low price on its new product?

2. The statement was made that a firm might set a low price on a product to discourage competitors from coming in. Are there any situations (aside from anti-trust reasons) when a firm might deliberately want to attract competitors into a new market and set a high price for this reason?

3. Four different methods of estimating the price elasticity of demand for extension telephones were described in the text. What are the limitations of each method?

4. Xerox developed an office copying machine called the 914. The machine was more expensive than competitive machines but offered the user superior copy and lower variable costs: 1 cent per copy as opposed to between 4 and 9 cents for competing processes. The machine cost around $2,500 to produce, and management was considering pricing it at either $3,500 or $4,500. How could it estimate unit sales at the two alternative price levels?

5. Bell and Howell was the first company to develop an electric-eye camera by combining a regular $70 camera with a $10 electric-eye mechanism. What price do you think might be charged for the new camera?

6. A group of people were asked to choose between two raincoats, one bearing a brand label and a higher price and another bearing a store label and a lower price. The two coats happened to be identical, but the customers were not told this. If customers were completely knowledgeable, (a) what percentage would choose the higher-priced coat, and (b) what percentage do you think actually chose the higher-priced coat?

7. In principle, a reduction in price is tantamount to an increase in marketing effort. How can the price reduction be monetized into its equivalent in increased marketing effort?

8. The leading manufacturer of a food flavor intensifier has recently watched its market share fall from 100 percent to 85 percent. Its declining share is due to its insistence on maintaining a high price in the face of new competitors who have introduced the same product for substantially less. The company has fought the new competition by increasing its advertising expenditures and dealer promotions. Does this make as much sense as cutting its price?

9. Restate the following prose description of a pricing procedure in either (a) mathematical or (b) logical flow diagram form.

Given that my competitor is operating at or above his breakeven point with a price equal to mine, then: If I cut my price, my competitor will cut his to match mine providing the price cut is likely to be permanent and the competitor can break even at my new price. If I do not cut my price, my competitor will not cut his either. If I cut my price, and the price cut is not likely to be permanent, my competitor will watch price and volume but will do nothing now. If I cut my price, and if the price cut is likely to be permanent and my competitor cannot break even at my new price, he will cut his price down to his breakeven point.

10. How can a company increase its profits without raising a single price and managing to lower any of its costs?

11. Four companies, W, X, Y, and Z, produce electric can openers. Research asking consumers to allocate 100 points among the companies' products for each of four attributes produced the following results.

IMPORTANCE WEIGHT	ATTRIBUTE	COMPANY PRODUCTS			
		W	X	Y	Z
.35	Durability	30	15	40	15
.15	Attractiveness	20	20	30	30
.25	Noiselessness	30	15	35	20
.25	Safety	25	25	25	25

An average electric can opener sells for $20. What should company W do about the pricing of its product if company Y charges $22?

Marketing-Channels Decisions

> The middleman is not a hired link in a chain forged by a manufacturer, but rather an independent market, the focus of a large group of customers for whom he buys. . . . As he grows and builds a following, he may find his prestige in his market is greater than that of the supplier whose goods he sells.
>
> PHILLIP McVEY

In today's economy, most producers do not sell their goods directly to the final users. Between them and the final users stands a host of marketing intermediaries performing a variety of functions and bearing a variety of names. Some intermediaries—such as wholesalers and retailers—buy, take title to, and resell the merchandise; they are called *merchant middlemen*. Others—such as brokers, manufacturers' representatives, and sales agents—search for customers and may negotiate on behalf of the producer but do not take title to the goods; they are called *agent middlemen*. Still others—such as transportation companies, independent warehouses, banks, and advertising agencies—assist in the performance of distribution but neither take title to goods nor negotiate purchases or sales; they are called *facilitators*.

Two aspects of channel decisions place them among the most critical marketing decisions of management. The first is that *the channels chosen for the company's products intimately affect every other marketing decision*. The firm's pricing decisions depend upon whether it seeks a few franchised high-markup dealers or mass distribution; the firm's advertising decisions are influenced by the degree of cooperation from channel members; the firm's sales-force decisions depend upon whether it sells directly to retailers or uses manufacturers' representatives. This does not mean that channel decisions are always made prior to other decisions, but rather that they exercise a powerful influence on the rest of the mix.

The second reason for the significance of channel decisions is that *they involve the firm in relatively long-term commitments to other firms.* When an automobile manufacturer signs up independent franchised dealers to merchandise its automobiles, it cannot easily replace them with company-owned outlets if conditions change. When a drug manufacturer relies on independent retail druggists for the distribution of most of its products, it must heed them when they object to its entering its products into mass-distribution chain stores. Corey has observed:

> A distribution system . . . is a key *external* resource. Normally it takes years to build, and it is not easily changed. It ranks in importance with key *internal* resources such as manufacturing, research, engineering, and field sales personnel and facilities. It represents a significant corporate commitment to large numbers of independent companies whose business is distribution—*and* to the particular markets they serve. It represents, as well, a commitment to a set of policies and practices that constitute the basic fabric on which is woven an extensive set of long-term relationships.[1]

Thus there is a powerful tendency toward status quo in channel arrangements. Therefore, management must choose its channels carefully, with an eye on tomorrow's likely selling environment as well as today's.

THE NATURE OF MARKETING CHANNELS

Every producer seeks to link together the set of marketing intermediaries that best fulfill the firm's objectives. This set of marketing intermediaries is called the *marketing channel* (also trade channel, channel of distribution). We shall use Bucklin's definition of a marketing channel: "A *channel of distribution* shall be considered to comprise a set of institutions which performs all of the activities (functions) utilized to move a product and its title from production to consumption."[2]

Number of Channel Levels

Marketing channels can be characterized according to the number of channel levels. Each institution that performs some work to bring the product and its title to the point of consumption constitutes a *channel level.* Since both the producer and the ultimate consumer perform some work in bringing the product and its title to the point of consumption, they are included in every channel. We will use the number of *intermediary levels* to designate the *length* of a channel. Figure 16–1 illustrates several marketing channels of different lengths.

A zero-level channel, often called a *direct marketing channel,* consists of a manufacturer selling directly to a consumer. Many examples can be found. Avon's sales representatives sell cosmetics directly to homemakers on a door-to-door basis; IBM's sales representatives sell computer equipment directly to user firms; and Bell Apple Orchard invites the public to pick their own apples at a flat price per bushel.

A one-level channel contains one selling intermediary. In consumer mar-

---

[1] E. Raymond Corey, *Industrial Marketing: Cases and Concepts* (Englewood Cliffs, N.J.: Prentice-Hall, 1976), p. 263.

[2] Louis P. Bucklin, *A Theory of Distribution Channel Structure* (Berkeley: Institute of Business and Economic Research, University of California, 1966), p. 5.

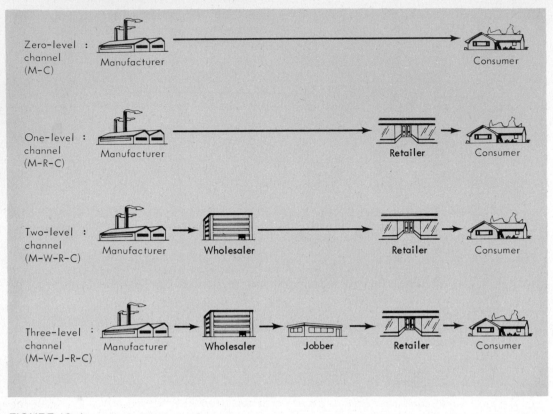

Zero-level
channel
(M–C)

Manufacturer   Consumer

One-level
channel
(M–R–C)

Manufacturer   Retailer   Consumer

Two-level
channel
(M–W–R–C)

Manufacturer   Wholesaler   Retailer   Consumer

Three-level
channel
(M–W–J–R–C)

Manufacturer   Wholesaler   Jobber   Retailer   Consumer

FIGURE 16–1
Examples of Different-Level Channels

kets this intermediary is typically a retailer (R); in industrial markets, it is often a sales agent or a broker.

A two-level channel contains two intermediaries. In consumer markets they are typically a wholesaler and a retailer; in industrial markets they may be a sales agent and a wholesaler.

A three-level channel contains three intermediaries. An example is found in the meat-packing industry, where a jobber usually intervenes between the wholesalers and the retailers. The jobber buys from wholesalers and sells to the smaller retailers, who generally are not serviced by the large wholesalers.

Higher-level marketing channels are also found, but with less frequency. From the producer's point of view the problem of control increases with the number of levels, even though the manufacturer typically deals only with the adjacent level.

Types of Channel Flows   The various institutions that make up a marketing channel are connected by several distinguishable types of flows. The most important are the physical flow, title flow, payment flow, information flow, and promotion flow. These are illustrated in Figure 16–2 for the marketing of forklift trucks.

The *physical flow* describes the actual movement of physical products from raw materials to final customers. In the case of a forklift-truck manufacturer, such as Allis-Chalmers or Clark Equipment, raw materials, subassemblies, parts, and engines flow from suppliers via transportation companies (transporters) to the manufacturer's warehouses and plants. The finished trucks are warehoused and later shipped to dealers in response to their orders. The dealers in turn sell and ship them to customers. Large orders may be supplied directly from the company warehouses or even from the plant itself. At each stage of movement, one or more modes of shipment may be used, including railroads, trucks, and air freight.

The *title flow* describes the actual passage of title (of ownership) from one marketing institution to another. In the case of forklift trucks, title to the raw materials and components passes from the suppliers to the manufacturer. The title to the finished trucks passes from the manufacturer to the dealers and then to the customers. If the dealers only hold the trucks on *consignment*, they would not be included in the diagram.

The *payment flow* shows customers paying their bills through banks and other financial institutions to the dealers, the dealers remitting payment to the manufacturer (less the commission), and the manufacturer making payments to the various suppliers. There will also be payments made to transporters and independent warehouses (not shown).

The *information flow* describes how information is exchanged among the

FIGURE 16–2
Five Different Marketing Flows in the Marketing Channel for Forklift Trucks

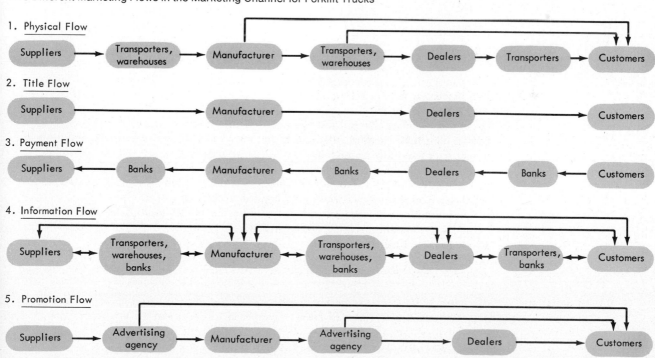

institutions in the marketing channel. A two-way information exchange takes place between each successive stage in the channel, and there are several information flows between nonadjacent institutions.

Finally, the *promotion flow* describes directed flows of influence (advertising, personal selling, sales promotion and publicity) from one party to other parties in the system. Suppliers promote their name and products to the manufacturer. They may also promote their name and products to final customers in the hope of influencing the manufacturer to prefer products embodying their parts or materials. A promotion flow is also directed by the manufacturer to dealers (trade promotion) and final customers (end-user promotion).

Were all of these flows superimposed on one diagram, they would emphasize the tremendous complexity of even simple marketing channels. This complexity goes even further, once we start distinguishing among different types of intermediaries, and customers.

Channels in the Service Sector

The concept of marketing channels is not limited to the distribution of physical goods. Producers of services and ideas also face the problem of making their output *available* and *accessible* to target populations.[3] "Educational-dissemination systems" and "health-delivery systems" are simply names for marketing channels to distribute services in the nonprofit sector. The problem is one of developing and locating a set of agencies and facilities to provide services to a spatially distributed population.

> Hospitals must be located in geographic space to serve the people with complete medical care, and we must build schools close to the children who have to learn. Fire stations must be located to give rapid access to potential conflagrations, and voting booths must be placed so that people can cast their ballots without expending unreasonable amounts of time, effort or money to reach the polling stations. Many of our states face the problem of locating branch campuses to serve a burgeoning and increasingly well educated population. In the cities we must create and locate playgrounds for the children. Many overpopulated countries must assign birth control clinics to reach the people with contraceptive and family planning information.[4]

Channels of distribution are also used in "person" marketing. A professional comedian seeking an audience before 1940 had available seven different channels: vaudeville houses, special events, nightclubs, radio, movies, carnivals, and theaters. In the 1950s television emerged as a strong channel and vaudeville disappeared. Politicians also must find cost-effective channels—mass media, rallies, coffee hours—for distributing their ideas to the voters.

Channels normally are thought to describe routes for the forward movement of products. Increasingly there is talk about the development of *backward channels:*

[3] *Availability* means that the goods and services could be obtained by consumers with a reasonable (not excessive) amount of effort. *Accessibility* means that the consumers feel comfortable in dealing with the channel outlets. For example, poor people might know that medical services are *available* from a particular hospital, but various social and psychological barriers might exist to make the hospital seem of low *accessibility*.

[4] Ronald Abler, John S. Adams, and Peter Gould, *Spatial Organization* (Englewood Cliffs, N.J.: Prentice-Hall, 1971), pp. 531–32.

The recycling of solid wastes is a major ecological goal. Although recycling is technologically feasible, reversing the flow of materials in the channel of distribution—marketing trash through a "backward" channel—presents a challenge. Existing backward channels are primitive, and financial incentives are inadequate. The consumer must be motivated to undergo a role change and become a producer—the initiating force in the reverse distribution process.[5]

The authors of this statement go on to identify several types of middlemen that can play a role in the backward channel, including (1) manufacturers' redemption centers; (2) "Clean-Up Days" community groups; (3) traditional middlemen such as soft-drink middlemen; (4) trash-collection specialists; (5) recycling centers; (6) modernized "rag and junk men"; (7) trash-recycling brokers; and (8) central-processing warehousing.

Why Are Middlemen Used?

Why is the producer generally willing to delegate some of the selling job to intermediaries? The delegation usually means the relinquishment of some control over how and to whom the products are sold. The producer appears to be placing the firm's destiny in the hands of intermediaries.

Since producers are free in principle to sell directly to final customers, there must be certain advantages or necessities for using middlemen. Some of the major factors are described below.

Many producers lack the financial resources to embark on a program of direct marketing. For example, General Motors's new automobiles are marketed by over 18,000 independent dealers; even as the world's largest manufacturing corporation, General Motors would be hard pressed to raise the cash to buy out its dealers.

Direct marketing would require many producers to become middlemen for the complementary products of other producers in order to achieve mass-distributional efficiency. For example, the Wm. Wrigley Jr. Company would not find it practical to establish small retail gum shops throughout the country or to sell gum door to door or by mail order. It would have to tie gum in with the sale of many other small products and would end up in the drugstore and foodstore business. It is much easier for Wrigley to work through the existing and extensive network of privately owned distribution institutions.

Those producers who have the required capital to develop their own channels often can earn a greater return by increasing their investment in other parts of their business. If a company is earning a 20 percent rate of return on its manufacturing operation and foresees only a 5 percent rate of return on investing in direct marketing, it would not make sense to put money toward vertically integrating its channels.

The use of middlemen boils down largely to their superior efficiency in making goods widely available and accessible to target markets. Marketing intermediaries, through their experience, their specialization, their contacts, and their scale, offer the firm more than it can usually achieve on its own.

Figure 16–3 shows just one source of the economies effected by the use of middlemen. Part A shows three producers using direct marketing to reach each of three customers. This system requires nine different contacts. Part B shows

[5] William G. Zikmund and William J. Stanton, "Recycling Solid Wastes: A Channels-of-Distribution Problem," *Journal of Marketing*, July 1971, p. 34.

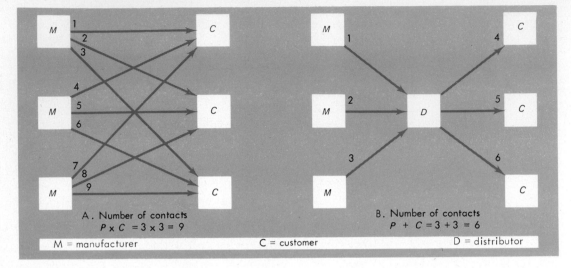

FIGURE 16–3
How a Distributor Effects an Economy of Effort

the three producers working through one distributor, who in turn contacts the three customers. This system requires only six contacts. Thus the use of middlemen reduces the amount of work that must be done.

From the point of view of the economic system, the basic role of marketing channels is to transform the heterogeneous supplies found in nature into meaningful goods assortments desired by humans:

> The materials which are useful to man occur in nature in heterogeneous mixtures which might be called conglomerations since these mixtures have only random relationship to human needs and activities. The collection of goods in the possession of a household or an individual also constitutes a heterogeneous supply, but it might be called an assortment since it is related to anticipated patterns of future behavior. The whole economic process may be described as a series of transformations from meaningless to meaningful heterogeneity.[6]

Alderson has summarized this in the statement that "the goal of marketing is the matching of segments of supply and demand."[7]

Marketing-Channel Functions A marketing channel is essentially a method of organizing the work that has to be done to move goods from producers to consumers. The purpose of the work is to overcome various gaps that separate the goods and services from those who

[6] Wroe Alderson, "The Analytical Framework for Marketing," *Proceedings—Conference of Marketing Teachers from Far Western States* (Berkeley: University of California Press, 1958).

[7] Wroe Alderson, *Marketing Behavior and Executive Action: A Functionalist Approach to Marketing Theory* (Homewood, Ill.: Richard D. Irwin, 1957), p. 199.

would use them. The work of middlemen is designed to create *form, time, place,* and *possession utilities.* Several *functions* or tasks are involved in this work. The major marketing-channel functions are:[8]

1. **Research.** The gathering of information necessary for planning and facilitating exchange.
2. **Promotion.** The development and dissemination of persuasive communications about the offer.
3. **Contact.** The searching out and communicating with prospective buyers.
4. **Matching.** The shaping and fitting of the offer to the buyer's requirements. Includes such activities as manufacturing, grading, assembling, and packaging.[9]
5. **Negotiation.** The attempt to reach final agreement on price and other terms of the offer so that transfer of ownership or possession could be effected.
6. **Physical distribution.** The transporting and storing of the goods.
7. **Financing.** The acquisition and dispersal of funds to cover the costs of the channel work.
8. **Risk taking.** The assumption of risks in connection with carrying out the channel work.

The first five functions deal primarily with consummating transactions, while the last three act as facilitating functions.

It is not a question of whether these functions must be performed in order to bridge the gaps between producer and customer—they must be—but rather who is to perform them. All of the functions have three things in common: they use up scarce resources, often they can be performed better through specialization, and they are shiftable. To the extent that the manufacturer performs them, its costs go up and its prices have to be higher. When some of these tasks are delegated to middlemen, the producer's costs and prices are lower, but the middlemen must add a charge to cover the use of scarce resources. The issue of who should perform various channel tasks is largely one of relative efficiency and effectiveness. To the extent that specialist intermediaries achieve economies through their scale of operation and their knowhow, the producer can gain by transferring some of the channel functions to their charge.

A major point to keep in mind is that marketing functions are more basic than the institutions that at any given time appear to perform them. Changes in the number of channel levels and/or channel institutions largely reflect the discovery of more efficient ways to combine or separate the economic work that must be carried out if useful assortments of goods are to be provided to target customers.

[8] For other lists, see Edmund D. McGarry, "Some Functions of Marketing Reconsidered," in *Theory in Marketing,* eds. Reavis Cox and Wroe Alderson (Homewood, Ill.: Richard D. Irwin, 1950), pp. 269–73; and Bucklin, *Theory of Distribution Channel Structure,* pp. 10–15.

[9] Alderson adds the concept of *sorting* as part of the matching process. Sorting consists of four basic processes. *Sorting out* is separating a heterogeneous collection into homogeneous groupings. *Accumulation* is the building up of larger homogeneous collections out of smaller ones. *Allocation* is breaking down large homogeneous collections into smaller ones to meet the requirements of various markets. *Assorting* is the building up of a heterogeneous collection from various sources to meet the requirements of some market. See Alderson, *Marketing Behavior and Executive Action,* chap. 7.

TABLE 16–1
Definitions of Various Marketing Intermediaries

Agent. A business unit which negotiates purchases or sales or both but does not take title to the goods in which it deals. The agent usually performs fewer marketing functions than does the merchant. He commonly receives his remuneration in the form of a commission or fee. Examples are: broker, commission merchant, manufacturers agent, selling agent, and resident buyer.

Broker. An agent who does not have direct physical control of the goods in which he deals but represents either buyer or seller in negotiating purchases or sales for his principal. The broker's powers as to prices and terms of sale are usually limited by his principal.

Commission house (sometimes called *Commission merchant*). An agent who usually exercises physical control over and negotiates the sale of the goods he handles. The commission house usually enjoys broader powers as to prices, methods, and terms of sale than does the broker, although it must obey instructions issued by the principal. It generally arranges delivery, extends necessary credit, collects, deducts its fees, and remits the balance to the principal.

Dealer. A firm that buys and resells merchandise at either retail or wholesale.

Distributor. In its general usage this term is synonymous with "wholesaler."

Facilitating agencies in marketing. Those agencies which perform or assist in the performance of one or a number of the marketing functions, but which neither take title to goods nor negotiate purchases or sales. Common types are banks, railroads, storage warehouses, commodity exchanges, stock yards, insurance companies, graders and inspectors, advertising agencies, firms engaged in marketing research, cattle loan companies, furniture marts, and packers and shippers.

Jobber. This term is widely used as a synonym of "wholesaler" or "distributor." The term is sometimes used in certain trades and localities to designate special types of wholesalers.

Manufacturer's agent. An agent who generally operates on an extended contractual basis; often sells within an exclusive territory; handles noncompeting but related lines of goods; and possesses limited authority with regard to prices and terms of sale. He may be authorized to sell a definite portion of his principal's output.

Merchant. A business unit that buys, takes title to, and resells merchandise. The distinctive feature of this middleman lies in the fact that he takes title to the goods he handles. Wholesalers and retailers are the chief types of merchants.

Middleman. A business concern that specializes in performing operations or rendering services directly involved in the purchase and/or sale of goods in the process of their flow from producer to consumer. Middlemen are of two types, *merchants* and *agents.*

Retailer. A merchant, or occasionally an agent, whose main business is selling directly to the ultimate consumer.

Selling agent. An agent who operates on an extended contractual basis, sells all of a specified line of merchandise or the entire output of his principal, and usually has full authority with regard to prices, terms, and other conditions of sale. This functionary is often called a "sales agent."

Wholesaler. A business unit which buys and resells merchandise to retailers and other merchants and/or to industrial, institutional, and commercial users, but which does not sell in significant amounts to ultimate consumers. Those who render all the services normally expected in the wholesale trade are known as *service wholesalers;* those who render only a few of the wholesale services are known as *limited-function wholesalers.* The latter group is composed mainly of *cash-and-carry wholesalers,* who do not render the credit or delivery service; *drop-shipment wholesalers,* who sell for delivery by the producer direct to the buyer; *truck wholesalers,* who combine selling, delivery, and collection in one operation; and *mail-order wholesalers,* who perform the selling service entirely by mail.

SOURCE: *Marketing Definitions: A Glossary of Marketing Terms,* compiled by the Committee on Definitions of the American Marketing Association, Ralph S. Alexander, Chairman (Chicago: American Marketing Association, 1960).

Channel Institutions   We have been talking about various channel institutions, such as wholesalers, jobbers, and retailers, without defining them. The fact is that a large number of different channel institutions exist, each performing one or more functions in the channel. Table 16–1 provides a set of definitions of the more common channel institutions.

CHANNEL DYNAMICS

Channel institutions, like products, are subject to life cycles. A particular channel institution may emerge suddenly, enjoy rapid growth, reach a point of relative maturity, and eventually move into a period of slow decline. A major force behind the channel life cycle is changing economics, which makes new combinations of marketing functions suddenly more efficient than previous ones.

Evolution of Retailing Institutions   In retailing, totally new institutions have appeared in an industry that a hundred years ago consisted only of small general and specialty stores. *Department stores* first came on the American scene in the 1860s, about a decade after they started in Europe. Shortly thereafter *mail-order houses,* such as Montgomery Ward (1872) and Sears Roebuck (1886), were established. During the 1910s and 1920s, *chain-store organizations* emerged and entered a period of rapid growth. The principal retailing innovation in the 1930s was the *supermarket.* The late 1940s were marked by the appearance of *planned suburban shopping centers.* The major retailing development in the early 1950s was the *discount house.* The 1950s also produced a rapid expansion of *automatic merchandising,* that is, vending machines. The 1960s witnessed the rapid growth of *fast-food service outlets, superstores* and *hypermarkets,* and *convenience stores.* The 1970s marked the rapid development of *boutiques, discount grocery stores, home improvement centers, furniture warehouse showrooms,* and *catalog showrooms.* None of these retailing forms have passed out of existence, but they show changing capacities over time to deliver what the consumer wants.

The newer retailing forms appear to be reaching maturity much faster than earlier retailing forms, that is, institutional life cycles seem to be growing shorter. The time required to reach maturity was eighty years for department stores (1860–1940), forty-five years for variety stores (1910–1955), and thirty-five years for supermarkets (1930–1965), twenty years for discount department stores (1950–1970), and fifteen years for home improvement centers (1965–1980).[10]

Retailing innovations are emerging all the time in a dynamic economy. A soft-drink manufacturer opened a chain of soft-drink stores for the take-home market that sell private-brand colas, ginger ale, and so on, at substantial savings. American Bakeries started Hippopotamus Food Stores, featuring large institutional-sized packages at a 10 to 30 percent savings. One of the large New York banks recently instituted "house-call loans," for which they will qualify an applicant over the phone and then deliver the money in person. Adelphi University in New York developed a "commuter train classroom" in which executives who commute daily between Long Island and Manhattan can earn M.B.A.'s by sitting in on fifty-minute classes held in specially reserved cars on the commuter train. Marketers are continually seeking new ways to distribute their products and services.

[10] William R. Davidson, Albert D. Bates, and Stephen J. Bass, "The Retail Life Cycle," *Harvard Business Review,* November–December 1976, p. 94.

What explains the emergence of new retailing forms and decline of old retailing forms?[11] One major hypothesis is called the *wheel of retailing*.[12] According to this hypothesis, many new types of retailing institutions begin as low-status, low-margin, low-price operations. They become effective competitors of more conventional outlets, which have grown "fat" over the years. Their success gradually leads them to upgrade their facilities and proffer additional services. This increases their costs and forces price increases until they finally resemble the conventional outlets that they displaced. They, in turn, become vulnerable to still newer types of low-cost, low-margin operations. This hypothesis appears to explain the original success and later troubles of department stores, supermarkets, and, more recently, discount houses. On the other hand, it does not explain the growth of suburban shopping centers and automatic retailing, both of which started out as high-margin and high-cost operations.

When new institutions first appear, the typical pattern is one of institutional *conflict* followed later by *accommodation*. The established institutions band together and use all their power to thwart the new institution. They may threaten to break off business relations with those who supply the new institution. This happened when national-brand appliance manufacturers started dealing with discount houses, when milk producers allowed their brands to appear in vending machines, and when drug manufacturers started to sell their products through food outlets. The established retailers will also lobby for restrictive legislation against the new retailing outlets. They try to pass laws placing special taxes on these organizations, or restricting their hours of operation, or preventing them from selling certain goods.

But the newer firms, where they bring real advantages, generally survive this onslaught, and in the next phase the more progressive established firms begin to accommodate to the new ones. They reduce their margins, cut down some of their frills, form chains, expand their parking space, and in general reduce the competitive advantage of the newer firms. In time, the differences diminish.

Evolution of Wholesaling Institutions

Wholesalers are essentially middlemen who market products to retailers, other wholesalers, or industrial users. There are many types of wholesalers as indicated in the definition in Table 16-1. *Merchant wholesalers* buy title to the merchandise and resell it to others. *Agent wholesalers* buy and sell goods for others without taking title and receive fees or commissions. *Miscellaneous-type wholesalers* are usually found in specialized sectors of the economy such as the agricultural market (farm product assemblers) and the petroleum market (petroleum bulk plants and terminals).

Not all wholesalers are independent businesses, and in fact an increasing volume of products is going through producer-owned and retail-owned wholesalers. *Producer-owned wholesalers* include sales offices (which sell and promote

---

[11] Four theories of retail institutional change are described in Ronald E. Gist, *Retailing: Concepts and Decisions* (New York: John Wiley and Sons, 1968), chap. 4.

[12] Malcolm P. McNair, "Significant Trends and Developments in the Postwar Period," in *Competitive Distribution in a Free, High-Level Economy and Its Implications for the University*, ed. A. B. Smith (Pittsburgh: University of Pittsburgh Press, 1958), pp. 1–25. Also see the critical discussion by Stanley C. Hollander, "The Wheel of Retailing," *Journal of Marketing*, July 1960, pp. 37–42.

but do not stock product) and sales branches (which carry a limited inventory in addition to selling and promoting and customer services). *Retailer-owned whole-salers* have been set up by many large retailers to bypass independent whole-salers and include purchasing offices, warehouses, and wholesale cooperatives.

Changes in wholesaling have been less dramatic than changes in retailing, but no less important. At one time wholesalers dominated the marketing chan-nels. Small manufacturers and small retailers could not operate without their services. But as manufacturers and retailers grew in size, the larger ones were able to find ways to avoid or reduce the charges of wholesaling middlemen. Dur-ing the 1920s, many thought that the majority of wholesalers were doomed by the growth of chain operations. Wholesalers declined in relative importance from 1929 on, and did not regain their former relative position until as late as 1954. Absolute wholesale sales volume has continued to grow, but in relative terms wholesalers have just been holding their own. During the period 1950–1972, they suffered a major decline in their profitability, productivity, and liquidity.

The wholesalers who fell into deep trouble were those who failed to adapt to the dramatic changes taking place in retailing, materials-handling technology, and manufacturers' new marketing policies. Many wholesalers had enjoyed a protected position and had grown "fat and lazy." Their main activities were to break bulk-and-fill customer orders, rather than to carry on aggressive selling programs. They tended to render similar services and charges to all customers, even though some customers wanted more services and others wanted less. It is understandable why both manufacturers and retailers continually sought ways to circumvent the wholesaler.

The progressive wholesalers were those who were willing to change their ways to meet the challenges of chain organizations, discount houses, and rising labor costs. This meant (1) seeking to adapt their services to a clearer target group of customers and (2) seeking cost-reducing methods of transacting busi-ness. Wholesalers became much more selective in choosing their customers, pre-ferring to drop those who appeared to be unprofitable according to an analysis of sales and service costs. They placed more emphasis on increasing order size and promoting the higher-profit merchandise. They offered assistance to custom-ers in locating, leasing, designing, opening, and modernizing stores and in doing a better job of selling, advertising, promoting, and displaying their wares. Pro-gressive wholesalers selected and trained their salesmen better. Many whole-salers met the threat of chain organizations by organizing smaller retailers into voluntary chains. Many wholesalers went into private branding, supplying their customers with less expensive products. Others went into cash-and-carry or cost-plus wholesaling. Still others met the challenge by becoming specialty whole-salers and taking on functions that neither manufacturers nor customers were performing.

To meet the challenge of rising costs, alert wholesalers turned to advanced systems of material handling, billing, and shipping. Material-handling costs were brought down by time-and-motion studies of work procedures and ultimately by automating the warehouse so that orders could be processed through computers and items picked up by mechanical devices and conveyed on a belt to the ship-ping platform, where they were assembled. Billing, inventory control, and forecasting were improved through computerization and office automation. Finally, alert wholesalers were able to bring down their shipping costs by finding the right combinations of rail, truck, barge, and air freight.

Although the overwhelming majority of goods and services are still sold through marketing intermediaries, a growing number of producers have turned to direct marketing to either bypass or supplement their use of middlemen. Direct marketing (sometimes called in-home buying or nonstore retailing) in 1977 accounted for $75 billion or 12 percent of all consumer purchases. It takes four major forms:

1. *Mail-order selling.* Direct-mail expenditures reached $5 billion in 1975, or 15 percent of all advertising expenditures. Over sixty-five hundred companies sent out more than 2.26 billion catalogs targeted to appropriate households. Large general merchandise mail-order houses like Sears sent out general and specialized catalogs, and smaller operators sent out specialized ones. Catalog buying, while it normally does not save the buyer money, especially in the light of rising freight and postal charges, does offer a convenient way to shop and makes available certain goods that are absent or difficult to obtain in the buyer's home area. Direct mail also takes the form of mailed letters and foldouts promoting a particular item (books, insurance, magazine subscriptions) or making an appeal for funds for worthy causes (in 1975, nonprofit organizations raised $21.4 billion through the mail, or 80 percent of their total contributions).

2. *Mass-media selling.* Many direct marketers place direct-response ads in newspapers, magazines, radio, and television to sell phonograph records and tapes, small appliances, and myriad other items.

3. *Telephone selling.* The telephone is increasingly being used as a selling tool for selling everything from home repair services to newspaper subscriptions to zoo memberships. Some telephone marketers have developed computerized phoning systems where households are dialed automatically and computerized messages presented. Telephone selling has incurred the opposition of several groups who consider it an invasion of privacy and are proposing laws to ban or limit it.

4. *On-premise selling.* This old form of selling, which started centuries ago with itinerant peddlers, has burgeoned into a $6 billion industry, with over six hundred companies either selling *door to door* or arranging *home demonstration parties.* The industry still contains Fuller Brush and many encyclopedia- and bible-selling companies and their paid staffs of mainly male workers. But new personnel and selling concepts have emerged—for example, World Book enlists school teachers to sell encyclopedias to their neighbors; Avon trains attractive young women to sell cosmetics and act as beauty consultants to their neighbors; Tupperware has been a pioneer in home-demonstration cookware parties for small neighborhood groups.[13]

Why the boom in direct marketing? Direct marketing meets the needs of people who cannot easily find certain goods, are too busy to shop, or do not like to shop because of the crowds, parking difficulties, and poorly trained sales clerks. As the nation's educational level and affluence rise, people find their time growing scarcer, and also they feel more competent to select goods in private.

[13] See "How the 'New Sell' is Raking in Billions," *U.S. News and World Report,* May 8, 1978, pp. 74–75.

Add to this the improvements in communication technology and promotional techniques, and it becomes clear why direct marketing is soaring.[14]

Growth of Vertical
Marketing
Systems While the retailing, wholesaling, and direct marketing sectors undergo their individual evolutions, a very significant development is occurring that cuts across all of these levels. This development is the emergence of *vertical marketing systems* (VMS).[15] To understand them, we should first define *conventional marketing channels*. Conventional channels are "highly fragmented networks in which loosely aligned manufacturers, wholesalers, and retailers have bargained with each other at arm's length, negotiated aggressively over terms of sale, and otherwise behaved autonomously."[16] By contrast, *vertical marketing systems* are "professionally managed and centrally programmed networks, pre-engineered to achieve operating economies and maximum market impact."[17] These systems offer effective competition to conventional marketing channels because they achieve impressive scale economies through their size, bargaining power, and elimination of duplicated services. In fact, they have emerged in the consumer-goods sector of American economy as the preferred mode of distribution, accounting for as much as 64 percent of the available market.

Corporate VMS Three types of vertical marketing systems can be distinguished. A *corporate vertical marketing system* has as its distinguishing characteristic the combining of successive stages of production and distribution under a single ownership. As examples:

> . . . Sherwin-Williams currently owns and operates over 2,000 retail outlets . . . Sears reportedly obtains 50 percent of its throughput from manufacturing facilities in which it has an equity interest. . . . Holiday Inns is evolving into a self-supply network that includes a carpet mill, a furniture manufacturing plant, and numerous captive redistribution facilities. In short, these and other organizations are massive, vertically integrated systems. To describe them as "retailers," "manufacturers," or "motel operators" oversimplifies their operating complexities and ignores the realities of the marketplace.[18]

Administered VMS An *administered vertical marketing system*, by contrast, achieves coordination of successive stages of production and distribution not through common ownership but through the size and power of one of the parties within the system. Thus, manufacturers of a dominant brand are able to secure strong trade cooperation and support from resellers. Such companies as General Electric, Procter & Gamble, Kraftco, and Campbell Soup are able to command

---

[14] Direct marketers must be skilled at prospect identification, communication planning, and promotion testing. For an excellent text, see Bob Stone, *Successful Direct Marketing Methods* (Chicago: Crain Books, 1975).

[15] The following discussion is indebted to Bert C. McCammon, Jr., "Perspectives for Distribution Programming," in *Vertical Marketing Systems*, ed. Louis P. Bucklin (Glenview, Ill.: Scott, Foresman & Company, 1970), pp. 32–51.

[16] Ibid., p. 43.

[17] Ibid.

[18] Ibid., p. 45.

unusual cooperation from their resellers and retailers in connection with displays, shelf space, promotions, and price policies.

Contractual VMS A *contractual vertical marketing system* consists of independent firms at different levels of production and distribution integrating their programs on a contractual basis to obtain more economies and/or sales impact than they could achieve alone. Contractual VMSs have expanded the most in recent years and constitute one of the most significant developments in the economy. There are three major types of contractual VMSs:

1. *Wholesaler-sponsored voluntary chains.* These originated in the effort of wholesalers to save the independent retailers they served against the competition of large chain organizations. The wholesaler develops a program in which independent retailers join together to standardize their practices and/or to achieve buying economies that enable them to stand as a group against the inroads of the chains.

2. *Retailer cooperatives.* These arose through the efforts of groups of retailers to defend themselves against the corporate chains. The retailers organize a new business entity to carry on wholesaling and possibly production. Members are expected to concentrate their purchases through the retailer co-op and plan their advertising jointly. Profits are passed back to members in the form of patronage refunds. Nonmember retailers may also be allowed to buy through the co-op but do not receive patronage refunds.

3. *Franchise organizations.* Here several successive stages in the production-distribution process are linked under an agreement with one entity of the system, which is considered the franchiser. Franchising has been the fastest growing and most interesting retailing development in recent years. Although the basic idea is an old one, some forms of franchising are quite recent. In fact, three forms of franchises can be distinguished.

The first is the *manufacturer-sponsored retailer franchise system,* exemplified in the automobile industry. A car manufacturer such as Ford licenses dealers to sell its cars, the dealers being independent business who agree to meet various conditions of sales and service.

The second is the *manufacturer-sponsored wholesaler franchise system,* which is found in the soft-drink industry. The soft-drink manufacturer licenses bottlers (wholesalers) in various markets who buy its concentrate and then carbonate, bottle, and sell it to retailers in local markets.

The third is the *service-firm-sponsored retailer franchise system.* Here a service firm organizes a whole system for bringing its service efficiently to consumers. Examples are found in the auto rental business (Hertz and Avis), fast-food service business (McDonald's, Burger King), and motel business (Howard Johnson, Ramada Inn). The motel franchiser, for example, uses its mass-purchasing power to obtain favorable terms from suppliers; in some cases it buys an equity interest or owns them entirely. The motels are standardized in their appearances, procedures, and services, allowing travelers to know what to expect in advance. The franchiser provides the franchisees with a large number of services, such as *national advertising and sales promotion, site selection, motel design, employee and management training, centralized reservation system, market surveys and management consulting.* In return, the franchisees buy certain equipment and supplies through the franchiser and pay franchising fees and a percentage of their revenue. No wonder individually owned motels and hotels are at a disadvantage in competing with these franchised systems. Franchising systems are rapidly replacing the "opportunistic and ad hoc linkages" that have historically prevailed in many lines of trade.[19]

Many independents, if they have not joined VMSs, have become specialty-store operators, serving special segments of the market that are not available or attractive to the mass merchandisers. Thus there is a polarization in retailing, with large vertical marketing organizations on the one hand and specialty independent stores on the other. This development creates a problem for independent manufacturers. They are strongly aligned with the traditional outlets, which they cannot easily give up. At the same time, they must eventually realign themselves with the high-growth vertical marketing systems. The manufacturers will probably have to accept less attractive terms from these large buying organizations. Vertical marketing systems can always decide to bypass large manufacturers and set up their own manufacturing. *The new competition in retailing is no longer between independent business units but rather between whole systems of centrally programmed networks (corporate, administrative, and contractual) competing against each other to achieve the best economies and customer response.*

Growth of Horizontal Marketing Systems

Another significant development is the readiness of two or more companies to form alliances to jointly exploit an emerging marketing opportunity. Neither firm is able to amass the capital, know-how, production or marketing facilities to venture alone; or it prefers not to because of the high risk; or it envisions a substantial synergy in the proposed relationship. The companies may set up temporary or permanent arrangements to work with each other, or to create a third entity owned by the two parents. Such developments in horizontal marketing systems have been described by Adler as *symbiotic marketing*.[20] Here are two examples:

> In spite of Pillsbury Company's acceptance in grocery outlets, it lacked the resources to market its new line of refrigerated doughs for biscuits, cookies, and rolls because merchandising these products required special refrigerated display cases. But Kraft Foods Company was expert at selling its cheeses in this manner. Accordingly, the two firms set up an arrangement whereby Pillsbury makes and advertises its dough line while Kraft sells and distributes it.
>
> In the advertising field, *Million Market Newspapers, Inc.*, is the sales company held in common by five newspapers—*St. Louis Post-Dispatch, Washington Star, Boston Globe, Philadelphia Bulletin*, and *Milwaukee Journal-Sentinel*. By selling these five markets in one convenient package, a beneficial synergistic effect is created.

Growth of Multichannel Marketing Systems

Another important channel development is the movement of companies toward developing multichannel systems that reach the same or different markets, where some of these channel systems are in competition with each other. Here

[19] For background on franchising systems, see Dov Izraeli, *Franchising and the Total Distribution System* (London: Longman Group, 1972); and Charles L. Vaughn, *Franchising: Its Nature, Scope, Advantages, and Development* (Lexington, Mass.: Lexington Books, 1974).

[20] Lee Adler, "Symbiotic Marketing," *Harvard Business Review*, November-December 1966, pp. 59–71.

are examples of companies that have designed two or more channel systems for reaching the same customer level.

> The John Smythe Company, a Chicago-based furniture retailer, sells a full line of furniture through its company-owned conventional furniture stores as well as through its Homemakers Division, which runs furniture warehouse show-rooms. Furniture shoppers can spot many similar items in both types of outlets, usually finding lower prices at the latter.
>
> A large liquor distiller in Kentucky bottles bourbon under 4,000 different labels for various distributors, chains, and supermarkets. Shoppers in a particular town buying different brands and paying different prices might unknowingly be getting the bourbon that came out of the same barrels of this Kentucky dis-tiller.
>
> J.C. Penney operates department stores, mass-merchandising stores (called The Treasury), and specialty stores.

Tillman has labelled large retailing stores with diversified retailing chan-nels "merchandising conglomerates" or "conglomerchants" and defined them as "a multiline merchandising empire under central ownership, usually combining several styles of retailing with behind-the-scenes integration of some distribution and management functions."[21]

A growing number of companies can also be found that operate multi-channels that serve two different customer levels. This is called *dual distribution* and can be a source of many conflicts for the sponsoring company.[22] Some exam-ples are:

> Shell Oil sells its gasoline through company dealerships and also to inde-pendent gasoline-marketing companies. Conflicts arise during gasoline short-ages when the independent gasoline companies accuse Shell of favoring its own dealers with sure supplies and also of engaging in price squeezing.
>
> General Electric sells large home appliances through independent dealers (department stores, discount houses, catalog retailers) and also directly to large tract builders. The independent dealers would like General Electric to get out of the business of selling to tract developers because it competes with the retailers. General Electric defends its position by pointing out that builders and retailers are different classes of customers.

**Alternative Roles
of Individual
Firms in a
Channel**

Our discussion of direct, vertical, horizontal, and multichannel marketing sys-tems underscores the dynamic and changing nature of channels. Each firm in an industry has to define its relation to the dominant channel type and its pricing policies, advertising, and sales promotion practices. McCammon has distin-guished five types of relationship of an individual firm to the dominant channel.[23]

[21] Rollie Tillman, "Rise of the Conglomerchant," *Harvard Business Review*, Novem-ber–December 1971, pp. 44–51.

[22] See Robert E. Weigand, "Fit Products and Channels to Your Markets," *Harvard Business Review*, January–February 1977, pp. 95–105.

[23] Bert C. McCammon, Jr., "Alternative Explanations of Institutional Change and Channel Ev-olution," in *Toward Scientific Marketing*, ed. Stephen A. Greyser (Chicago: American Marketing As-sociation, 1963), pp. 477–90.

The *insiders* are the members of the dominant channel who enjoy continuous access to preferred sources of supply and high respect in the industry. They have a vested interest in perpetuating the existing channel arrangements and are the main enforcers of the industry code. The *strivers* are those firms who are seeking to become insiders but have not yet arrived. They have discontinuous access to preferred sources of supply, which can disadvantage them in periods of short supply. They adhere to the industry code because of their desire to become insiders. The *complementors* neither are nor seek to be part of the dominant channel. They perform functions not normally performed by others in the channel, or serve smaller segments of the market, or handle smaller quantities of merchandise. They usually benefit from the present system and tend to respect the industry code. The *transients,* like the complementors, are outside of the dominant channel and do not seek membership. They go in and out of the market or move around as opportunities arise, but are really members of another channel. They have short-run expectations and little incentive to adhere to the industry code. Finally, the *outside innovators* are the real challengers and disrupters of the dominant channels. They come with an entirely new system for carrying out the marketing work of the channel; if successful, they cause major structural realignments. They are companies like McDonald's, Avon, and Holiday Inn, who doggedly develop a new system to challenge the old.

Another important role is that of *channel captain.* The channel captain is the dominant member of a particular channel, the one who organized it and leads it. For example, General Motors is the channel captain of a system consisting of a huge number of suppliers, dealers, and facilitators. The channel captain is not always a manufacturer, as the examples of McDonald's and Sears show. Some channels do not have an acknowledged captain in that the various firms do not even recognize that they are acting as part of a system.

Channel Cooperation, Conflict, and Competition

It should be clear that within and between marketing channels there are different degrees of cooperation, conflict, and competition.

Channel cooperation is usually the dominant theme among members of the same channel. The channel represents a coalition of dissimilar firms that have banded together for mutual advantage. Manufacturers, wholesalers, and retailers complement each other's needs and their partnership normally produces greater profits for each participant than could have been secured by trying to carry out individually all of the channel's work. The need for channel cooperation is a natural extension of the *marketing concept* in that firms are trying to effectively sense, serve, and satisfy the needs of the target market.

Channel conflict, nevertheless, also tends to occur within each channel system. *Horizontal channel conflict* refers to conflict between firms at the same level of the channel. Some Ford car dealers in Chicago may complain about other Ford dealers in the city being too aggressive in their pricing and advertising and stealing sales from them. Some Pizza Inn franchisees may complain about other Pizza Inn franchisees cheating on the ingredients, maintaining poor service, and hurting the overall Pizza Inn image. In cases of horizontal channel conflict, the responsibility lies with the *channel captain* to set clear and enforceable policies, to encourage information about intralevel channel conflict to flow upward to management, and to take quick and definitive action to reduce or control this type of conflict, which, if left unchecked, could hurt the channel's image and cohesiveness.

Vertical channel conflict is even more common and refers to conflicts of interest between different levels of the same channel. Consider the following examples:

> Auto manufacturers threaten to drop dealers who refuse to comply with the manufacturers' policies on service, pricing, or advertising.
>
> Toy wholesalers boycott those toy manufacturers who sell direct to large retail discounters.
>
> Drug retailers threaten to drop drug manufacturers who put their lines in supermarket outlets.

Some amount of vertical channel conflict is healthy, and the problem is not one of eliminating it but of managing it better. The solution lies in two possible directions. The first is the effort on the part of the channel captain to develop *superordinate goals* for the system, from which everyone would gain. Superordinate goals would include trying to minimize the total cost of moving the product through the system, improving information flows within the system, and cooperating to increase consumer acceptance of the product. The second is to develop *administrative mechanisms* that increase participation and trust and help to resolve conflicts, such as dealer and distributor councils and various conciliation, mediation, and arbitration mechanisms.[24]

Channel competition is another phenomenon of channel relations and describes the normal competition between firms and systems trying to serve the same target markets. *Horizontal channel competition* occurs between firms at the same channel level competing for sales in the same target market. Thus various appliance retailers, such as department stores, discount stores, and catalog houses, all compete for the consumer's appliance dollar. This competition is healthy and should result in consumers' enjoying a wider range of choice in the way of products, prices, and services. *Channel system competition* describes the competition between different whole systems serving a given target market. For example, are food consumers better served by conventional marketing channels, corporate chains, wholesale-sponsored voluntary chains, retailer cooperatives, or food-franchise systems? While each system will have some loyal followers, the share of the different systems in the total food business will shift over time in favor of those systems that are best able to meet consumer needs at the time.

CHANNEL-DESIGN DECISIONS

We shall now look at channel decision problems from the point of view of the producer. In the last section of this chapter, we will examine the channel-management decisions facing resellers.

In developing channels of distribution, producers have to struggle with what is ideal and what is available. In the typical case, a new firm starts as a local or regional operation selling to a limited market. Since it has limited capital, it usually utilizes existing middlemen. The number of middlemen in any local market is apt to be limited: a few manufacturers' sales agents, a small number of

---

[24] For an excellent summary of interorganizational conflict and power in marketing channels, see Louis W. Stern and Adel I. El-Ansary, *Marketing Channels* (Englewood Cliffs, N.J.: Prentice-Hall, 1977), chap. 7.

wholesalers, an established set of retailers, a few trucking companies, and a few warehouses. The best channels may be a foregone conclusion. The problem may be to convince one or a few of the available middlemen to handle the line.

If the new firm is successful, it may branch out to new markets. Again, the producer will tend to work through the existing intermediaries, although this may mean using different types of marketing channels in different areas. In the smaller markets, the firm may sell directly to the retailers; in the larger markets, it may work only through distributors. In rural areas, it may work with general-goods merchants; in urban areas, with limited-line merchants. In one part of the country it may grant exclusive franchises because the merchants are accustomed to work this way; in another, it may sell through any and all outlets willing to handle the merchandise. In this way, the producer's channel system evolves as an expedient adaptation to local opportunities and conditions.

Determining Channel Objectives and Constraints

The starting point for the effective planning of channels is a determination of which markets are to be reached by the company. In practice, the choice of markets and choice of channels may be interdependent. The company may discover that markets it would like to serve cannot be served profitably with the available channels.

> A producer of gypsum wallboard defined its target market as all contractors and dry-wall applicators. But this firm could not get lumber yards to handle its product, since existing lumber yards were tied to existing competitors. This led the firm to change its target market to large tract builders who wanted to deal directly with the producer rather than through lumber yard intermediaries. Thus the choice of market target was redetermined after the consideration of channels.

Each producer develops its channel objectives in the context of constraints stemming from the customers, products, intermediaries, competitors, company policies, and the environment.

Customer characteristics In designing their channels, producers are greatly influenced by customer characteristics. When the *number* of customers is large, producers tend to use long channels with many middlemen on each level. The importance of the number of buyers is modified somewhat by their degree of *geographical dispersion*. It is less expensive for a producer to sell directly to five hundred customers who are concentrated in a few geographical centers than to sell them if they are scattered over five hundred locations. Even number and geographical dispersion are further qualified by the *purchasing pattern* of these buyers. Where the ultimate customers purchase small quantities on a frequent basis, lengthier marketing channels are desirable. The high cost of filling small and frequent orders leads manufacturers of such products as hardware, tobacco, and drug sundries to rely chiefly on wholesalers. At the same time, these same manufacturers may also bypass their wholesalers and sell direct to certain larger customers (retail chains and cooperative associations) who can place larger and less frequent orders. The buyers' *susceptibilities to different selling methods* also influence the producer's channel design. For example, a growing number of furniture retailers prefer to make selections at trade shows, and that has increased the popularity of this channel.

Product characteristics   Product characteristics also influence channel design. *Perishable* products require more direct marketing because of the dangers associated with delays and repeated handling. Products that are *bulky* in relation to their value, such as building materials or soft drinks, usually require channel arrangements that minimize the shipping distance and the number of handlings in the movement from producer to ultimate customers. *Unstandardized* products, such as custom-built machinery and specialized business forms, are usually sold directly by company salesmen because of the difficulty of finding middlemen with the requisite technical knowledge. Products requiring installation and/or maintenance *services* usually are sold and maintained directly by the company or by dealers given exclusive franchises. Products of *high unit value* are often sold through a company sales force rather than through middlemen.

Middleman characteristics   Channel design must take into account the strengths and weaknesses of different types of intermediaries in handling various tasks. For example, manufacturers' representatives are able to contact customers at a relatively low cost per customer because the total cost is shared by several clients. But the selling effort per customer during the contact is often less intense than if the company's salesmen were doing the selling. In general, intermediaries differ in their aptitude for performing such functions as promotion, negotiation, storage, and contact, as well as in their requirements for credit, return privileges, training, and frequency of shipment.

Competitive characteristics   Channel design is influenced by the channels that competitors use. The producers in some industries want their products to compete in or near the same outlets carrying the competitors' products. Thus food producers want their brands to be displayed next to competitive brands, and this means using the same middlemen. The marketing channels used by competitors sometimes define what the producer wants to avoid rather than imitate. Avon decided not to compete with other cosmetics manufacturers for scarce and inconspicuous positions in retail stores and established instead a profitable door-to-door selling operation.

Company characteristics   Company characteristics play an important role in channel selection. The company's overall *size* determines the extent of its markets, the size of its larger accounts, and its ability to secure the cooperation of intermediaries it elects to use. Its *financial resources* determine which marketing functions it can handle and which ones to delegate to intermediaries. A financially weak company tends to employ commission methods of distribution and tries to use intermediaries who are able and willing to absorb some of the storage, transit, and customer-financing costs. The company's *product* mix influences its channel pattern. The wider the company's product mix, the greater the ability of the company to deal with its customers directly. The greater the average depth of the company's product mix, the more it is likely to favor exclusive or selective dealers. The more consistent the company's product mix, the greater the homogeneity of its marketing channels. The company's *past channel experience* and *current marketing policies* influence channel design. A policy of speedy delivery to ultimate customers affects the functions the producer wants intermediaries to perform, the number of final-stage outlets and stocking points, and the type of transportation system used. A policy of heavy advertising leads the producer to seek intermediaries willing to handle displays and join in cooperative advertising programs.

Environmental characteristics Channel design is further influenced by environmental factors. When *economic conditions* are depressed, producers want to move their goods to market in the most economical way. This means using shorter channels and dispensing with inessential services that add to the final price of the goods. *Legal regulations and restrictions* also affect channel design. The law has sought to prevent channel arrangements that "may tend to substantially lessen competition or tend to create a monopoly." The most sensitive areas have to do with agreements by manufacturers not to sell to certain types of outlets, attempts by a manufacturer to offer its line to dealers on condition they do not carry competitive lines, attempts by a manufacturer to force its full line on dealers, arbitrary action by a manufacturer in the withdrawal of or refusal to renew dealer franchises, and attempts to set up territorial restrictions that substantially lessen competition.

Identifying the Major Channel Alternatives

After specifying channel objectives and constraints, the firm should proceed to identify its major channel alternatives. A channel alternative specifies four elements:

The basic *types of business intermediaries* that will be involved in selling and facilitating the movement of the goods to the market

The *number of intermediaries* that will be used at each stage of distribution

The particular *marketing tasks* of the participating intermediaries

The *terms and mutual responsibilities* of the producer and intermediaries

Types of intermediaries The firm should first identify the alternative intermediaries available to carry on its channel work. Consider the following industrial example:[25]

A manufacturer of test equipment for public utilities developed an audio device for detecting poor mechanical connections in any machinery with moving parts. The company executives felt that this product would have a market in all industries where electric, combustion, or steam engines were either used or manufactured. This meant such industries as aviation, automobile, railroad, food canning, construction, and oil. The existing sales force was small, and the problem was how to reach these diverse industries in an effective way. The following channel alternatives came out of management discussions:

1. **Company sales force.** Expand the company's direct sales force. Assign sales representatives to territories and give them responsibility for contacting purchasing agents in the relevant industries. Or specialize the company sales force by end-use industries.

2. **Manufacturers' agencies.** Hire manufacturers' agencies operating in different regions or end-use industries to sell the new test equipment.

3. **Industrial distributors.** Find distributors in the different regions and/or end-use industries who will buy and carry the new line. Give them exclusive distribution, adequate margins, product training, and promotional support.

---

[25] Adapted from David E. Faville, *Selected Cases in Marketing Management* (Englewood Cliffs, N.J.: Prentice-Hall, 1961), pp. 98–101. For further reading on industrial distributors, see Frederick E. Webster, Jr., "The Role of the Industrial Distributor," *Journal of Marketing*, July 1976, pp. 10–16.

Here is another example:

A consumer electronics company decided to use its excess capacity to produce FM car radios. In considering channels of distribution, it came up with the following alternatives:

1. **OEM market.** The company could seek a contract with one or more automobile manufacturers to buy its radios for factory installation on original equipment. OEM stands for *original equipment manufacture.*

2. **Auto dealer market.** The company could sell its radios to various auto dealers for replacement sales when they service cars.

3. **Retail automotive parts dealers.** The company could sell its radios to the public through retail automotive parts dealers. They could reach these dealers through a direct sales force or through distributors.

4. **Mail-order market.** The company could arrange to have its radios advertised in mail-order catalogs.

Not only do conventional channel arrangements suggest themselves, but sometimes more innovative possibilities. This happened when the Conn Organ Company decided to merchandise organs through department and discount stores, thus drawing more attention to them than they ever enjoyed in the small music stores where they had always been merchandised. A daring new channel was exploited when a group decided to merchandise books through the mails in the now famous Book-of-the-Month Club. Other sellers, perceiving the success of the Book-of-the-Month Club, developed Record-of-the-Month clubs, Candy-of-the-Month clubs, and dozens of others.

Number of intermediaries   The number of intermediaries to use at each stage is influenced by the degree of *market exposure* sought by the company. Three degrees of market exposure can be distinguished.

INTENSIVE DISTRIBUTION   Producers of convenience goods and common raw materials generally seek *intensive distribution*—that is, the stocking of their product in as many outlets as possible. The dominant factor in the marketing of these goods is their place utility. The producers of cigarettes, for example, try to enlist every possible retail outlet and device to create maximum brand exposure and convenience. This policy has culminated in the use of over 1 million outlets, which is about as intensive as distribution can get.

EXCLUSIVE DISTRIBUTION   Some producers deliberately limit the number of intermediaries handling their products. The extreme form of this is *exclusive distribution,* a policy of granting dealers exclusive rights to distribute the company's products in their respective territories; it often goes along with *exclusive dealing,* where the manufacturer requires the dealers not to carry competing lines. The latter is found at the retail level with respect to the distribution of new automobiles, some major appliances, and some brands of women's apparel. But why would a manufacturer want to limit its products' market exposure? Obviously, it must be gaining other advantages in limiting its distribution. Through granting exclusive distribution privileges, the manufacturer hopes to gain a more aggressive selling effort and be able to exercise more direct controls over intermediaries' policies on prices, promotion, credit, and various services. Exclusive distribution also tends to enhance the prestige or image of the product and allow higher markups.

SELECTIVE DISTRIBUTION   Between the two extreme policies of intensive distribution and exclusive distribution stand a whole range of intermediate arrangements that have been called *selective distribution*. Selective distribution involves the use of more than one but less than all of the intermediaries who are willing to carry a particular product. It is used both by established companies with good reputations and by new companies seeking to get distributors by promising them selective distribution. The company does not have to dissipate its efforts over a lot of outlets, many of which would be marginal. It can develop a good working understanding with the selected intermediaries and expect a better-than-average selling effort. In general, selective distribution enables the producer to gain adequate market coverage with more control and less cost than intensive distribution.

Specific marketing tasks of channel members   Every producer faces several tasks in moving goods to the target markets. Looking at a channel as a sequence of tasks rather than a linkage of business entities makes it immediately apparent that every producer faces a large number of alternatives, even when there is little choice regarding the basic types of intermediaries and the best degree of market exposure.

Assume that the following four tasks have to be performed:

T = *transit,* the work of transporting the goods toward the target markets
A = *advertising,* the work of informing and influencing buyers through advertising media
S = *storage,* the work of carrying an inventory out of which orders are filled
K = *contact,* the work of searching for and communicating with buyers.

Assume that there are three channel members—manufacturer (M), wholesaler (W), and retailer (R)—and each can perform one or more of these tasks. There are many possible patterns of task allocation to the various members of the channel. For example:

$$M(TA\text{--}) \rightarrow W(T\text{-}S\text{-}) \rightarrow R(\text{-}A\text{-}K)$$

In this channel, the manufacturer transports the goods and advertises them. (A dash means the absence of the corresponding task.) The wholesaler takes responsibility for transporting and storing the goods and therefore resembles a warehouse agent rather than a full-service wholesaler. The retailer is responsible for further advertising and contact work.

A different marketing channel is implied by the pattern

$$M(T\text{-}S\text{-}) \rightarrow W(\text{----}) \rightarrow R(\text{-}A\text{-}K)$$

Here the manufacturer is reduced to a private-brand producer who stocks and ships on order, the wholesaler is eliminated, and the retailer assumes the complete selling function. This is the marketing channel developed by mail-order houses for many of their products.

There are a great number of other possible patterns of task allocation in a marketing channel.[26] Many can be ruled out because they would be uneconomic, unstable, or illegal. Management's task is to identify the feasible alternatives and select the one that promises the highest degree of effectiveness in serving customers relative to competition.

Terms and responsibilities of channel members In conceiving the tasks to be performed by different channel members, the producer must also determine the mix of conditions and responsibilities that must be established among the channel members to get the tasks performed effectively and enthusiastically. The "trade-relations" mix is capable of many variations and introduces a still further dimension of alternatives.

The main elements in the trade-relations mix are the *price policies, conditions of sale, territorial rights,* and *the specific services to be performed by each party.*

Price policy is one of the major elements in the trade-relations mix. The producer usually establishes a list price and then allows discounts from it to various types of intermediate customers and possibly for various quantities purchased. In developing the schedule of discounts, the producer must proceed carefully because intermediate customers have strong feelings about the discounts they and others are entitled to.

Conditions of sale refers to the payment terms and to producer guarantees. Most producers grant discounts to their distributors for early payment. For example, "2 percent in 10 days, net 30" means that distributors can deduct 2 percent from the invoice price if they pay within ten days, or otherwise they must pay the full price within thirty days. The producer may also extend certain guarantees to distributors regarding defective merchandise or price declines. The offer of a guarantee against price declines may be necessary to induce distributors to buy in large quantities rather than on a hand-to-mouth basis.

Distributors' territorial rights are another element in the trade-relations mix. Distributors want to know where the producer intends to enfranchise other distributors. They also would like to receive full credit for all sales taking place in their territory, whether or not the sales were stimulated through their personal efforts.

Mutual services and responsibilities are a fourth element of the trade-relations mix. These are likely to be comprehensive and well defined in franchised and exclusive-agency channels where the relation between producer and distributor is close. For example, the Howard Johnson Company provides the restaurant leaseholders with the building, promotional support, a record-keeping system, training, and general administrative and technical assistance. In turn, the leaseholders are supposed to meet company standards regarding physical facilities, cooperate with new promotional programs, furnish requested information, and buy specified food products.

Evaluating the Major Channel Alternatives By this time, the producer will have identified several major channel alternatives for reaching the market. The problem is to decide which of the alternatives would best satisfy the long-run objectives of the firm. Each alternative must be rated against *economic, control,* and *adaptive* criteria.

---

[26] The number of possible patterns of task allocation in a marketing channel is given by $(2^n)^m$, where n represents the number of tasks and m represents the number of channel members. In the example, there are $(2^4)^3 = 4,096$ possible task allocations.

Economic criteria   Of the three, economic criteria are the most important, since the firm is not pursuing channel control or adaptability as such but is pursuing profits. True, channel control and adaptability have implications for long-run profit, but the more outstanding a channel alternative is from an economic point of view, the less important are its potentialities for conflict and rigidity.

DIRECT SALES FORCE VERSUS MANUFACTURERS' SALES AGENCY   Economic analyses can be illustrated with the familiar problem facing many manufacturers: Should they hire their own sales force or use a manufacturers' sales agency?

> A company wishes to reach a large number of retailers in a certain region of the country. One alternative is to hire and train ten company sales representatives who would operate out of a sales office in the region. They would be paid a base salary with the opportunity for further earnings through a commission plan. The other alternative is to use a manufacturers' sales agency in the region that has developed extensive contacts with retailers. The agency has thirty sales representatives, who would receive commissions on the goods sold.

Each alternative will produce a different level of sales and costs. The better system is not the one producing the greater sales or the lesser cost but rather the one producing the higher profit.

The analysis should begin with an estimate of *sales* under each system, because some costs will be dependent upon the level of sales. Will more sales be produced through a company sales force or a manufacturers' agency? Most marketing managers believe that a company sales force will sell more. Company sales representatives concentrate entirely on the company's products; they are better trained to sell the company's products; they are more aggressive because their future depends on the company; they are more successful because customers prefer to deal directly with the company.

But these are abstract arguments. It is conceivable that the manufacturers' agency could produce as many or more sales than a company sales force. In the first place, the producer is considering hiring ten new company sales representatives versus using thirty agency sales representatives. The sheer difference in the size of the sales force could lead to more sales through the agency. Second, the agency's sales force may be just as aggressive as a direct sales force. This depends on how much pay incentive the line offers them in relation to the other lines they represent. Third, it is not unconditionally true that customers prefer to deal with company sales representatives over agents. Where the product and terms are standard, the customers may be quite indifferent. They may prefer dealing with the agent who represents a larger number of manufacturers to dealing with a salesperson representing a single company. Fourth, one of the chief assets of the agency is the extensive contacts built up over the years. A company sales force would have to cultivate contacts from scratch. The agency can often obtain more sales for the manufacturer, at least in the first few years.

Thus, estimates of the sales potential with a company sales force versus a manufacturer's agency require a detailed analysis of the concrete plans for each. Sales estimates can be developed by soliciting the opinions of experienced managers and experts in the field.

The next step calls for estimating the costs associated with selling different

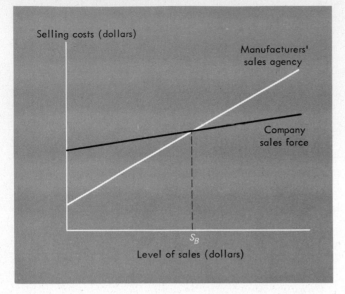

Selling costs (dollars)

Manufacturers'
sales agency

Company
sales force

S_B

Level of sales (dollars)

FIGURE 16–4
Breakeven Cost Chart for the Choice
Between a Company Sales Force
and a Manufacturers' Sales Agency

volumes under each system. They are shown in Figure 16–4. The fixed costs of engaging a manufacturers' agency are lower than those of conducting a sales office operation. On the other hand, costs rise faster with additional sales through a manufacturers' agency than through a company sales force. The reason is that sales agents get a larger fixed percentage of sales than company sales representatives, who are only on part commission.

Looking at the figure, we see one sales level (S_B) at which selling costs would be the same for the two channels. The sales agency would constitute a superior channel at any volume of sales below S_B, and the company sales branch would constitute a superior channel at any volume higher than S_B. This analysis accords with common observations of the circumstances under which the two channels have been used. Sales agents tend to be engaged by smaller firms, or by larger firms in their smaller territories, because in both cases the sales volume is too low to justify a fixed investment in a company sales force.

Control criteria   The evaluation of the economics of sales agents versus a company sales force provides a rough guide to the probable economic superiority of one channel over the other. The evaluation must now be broadened by a consideration of the motivational, control, and conflict aspects of the two channel alternatives.

The use of sales agents can give rise to a number of control problems. The central fact is that the manufacturers' sales agency is an independent business interested in maximizing its own profits. The agent may not cooperate with the client's agent in an adjacent territory. The agent concentrates calls on the customers that are most important to the agency in terms of the total assortment of goods rather than on the customers who are most important to the client. The agent's sales force may not take the time to master the technical details concerning the client's product or to make use of the client's promotion materials carefully.

438

Adaptive criteria One other criterion should be considered—that of the producer's freedom to adapt to changing conditions. Each channel alternative involves some duration of commitment and loss of flexibility. A manufacturer who decides to use a sales agent may have to offer a five-year contract; during this period, other means of selling, such as direct mail, might become more efficient, but the manufacturer is not free to drop the sales agent. A channel alternative involving a long commitment must appear to be greatly superior on economic or control grounds in order to be considered.

CHANNEL-MANAGEMENT DECISIONS

After a company has determined its basic channel design, individual middlemen must be *selected, motivated,* and *evaluated.*

Selecting Channel Members

Producers differ in their ability to recruit qualified middlemen for the proposed channel operation. Some producers have no trouble finding specific business establishments to join the channel. Their proposal attracts more than enough middlemen either because of the high prestige of the firm or because the specific product or line appears to be a good moneymaker. For example, Ford was able to attract twelve hundred new dealers for its ill-fated Edsel. In some cases the promise of exclusive or selective distribution will influence a sufficient number of middlemen to join the channel. The main problem for the producer who can attract enough middlemen is one of selection. The producer must decide on what middlemen characteristics provide the best indication of their competence.

At the other extreme are producers who have to work hard to line up the desired number of qualified middlemen. U.S. Time Company found it very hard to line up jewelry stores to carry its inexpensive Timex watches and was forced to go to mass-merchandising outlets. When Polaroid started, it could not get photographic-equipment stores to carry its new cameras and was forced to go to mass-merchandising outlets. Often small producers of new food products find it very hard to get shelf space in food outlets. The producer should study how middlemen make their buying decisions—specifically, how much weight they give to gross margin, planned advertising and promotion, return guarantees, and so on. The producer must develop an offer that promises to make a lot of money for the middlemen.

Whether producers find it easy or difficult to recruit middlemen, they should determine what characteristics distinguish the better middlemen from the poorer ones. They will want to evaluate the middlemen's number of years in business, growth record, solvency, cooperativeness, and reputation. If the middlemen are sales agents, producers will also want to evaluate the number and character of other lines carried and the size and quality of the sales force. If the middleman is a department store being considered for exclusive distribution, the producer wants to evaluate the store's location, future growth potential, and type of clientele.

Motivating Channel Members

Middlemen must be motivated to do their best job. The factors and terms that led them to join the channel provided some of the motivation, but these must be supplemented by continuous supervision and encouragement from the producer. The producer must sell not only through the middlemen but to them. The question of motivation is a complex one, since there are grounds for both cooperation and conflict between producers and their distributors.

The job of stimulating channel members to top performance must start with the manufacturer's attempting to understand the needs and psychology of the particular middlemen. Middlemen are often criticized by manufacturers, according to McVey:

> for failure to stress a given brand, or for the poor quality of his salesmen's product knowledge, his disuse of suppliers' advertising materials, his neglect of certain customers (who may be good prospects for individual items but not for the assortment), and even for his unrefined systems of record keeping, in which brand designations may be lost.[27]

However, what are shortcomings from the manufacturer's point of view may be quite understandable from the middleman's point of view. McVey listed the following four propositions to help understand the middlemen:

> The middleman is not a hired link in a chain forged by a manufacturer, but rather an independent market. ... After some experimentation, he settles upon a method of operation, performing those functions he deems inescapable in the light of his own objectives, forming policies for himself wherever he has freedom to do so. ...
>
> [The middleman often acts] primarily as a purchasing agent for his customers, and only secondarily as a selling agent for his suppliers. ... He is interested in selling any product which these customers desire to buy from him. ...
>
> The middleman attempts to weld all of his offerings into a family of items which he can sell in combination, as a packaged assortment, to individual customers. His selling efforts are directed primarily at obtaining orders for the assortment, rather than for individual items. ...
>
> Unless given incentive to do so, middlemen will not maintain separate sales records by brands sold. ... Information that could be used in product development, pricing, packaging, or promotion-planning is buried in nonstandard records of middlemen, and sometimes purposely secreted from suppliers.[28]

These propositions serve as a provocative departure from otherwise stereotyped thinking about the performance of middlemen. The first step in motivating others is to see the situation from their viewpoint.

Producers vary in their level of sophistication with respect to handling distributor relations. We can distinguish between three approaches: *cooperation, partnership,* and *distribution programming.*[29]

Most producers see the problem of motivation as one of figuring out ways to gain *cooperation* from independent and sometimes difficult middlemen who "aren't loyal" or "are lazy." They will use the carrot-and-stick approach. They will dream up positive motivators, such as higher margins, special deals, premiums, cooperative advertising allowances, display allowances, and sales con-

---

[27] Phillip McVey, "Are Channels of Distribution What the Textbooks Say?" *Journal of Marketing,* January 1960, pp. 61–64.

[28] Ibid.

[29] See Bert Rosenbloom, *Marketing Channels: A Management View* (Hinsdale, Ill.: Dryden Press, 1978), pp. 192–203.

tests. If these don't work, they will apply negative sanctions, such as threatening to reduce the margins, slow down service, or terminate the relationship. The basic problem with this approach is that the producer has not really studied the needs, problems, strengths, and weaknesses of the distributors. Instead, the producer puts together a miscellaneous set of devices that are based on crude stimulus-response thinking. McCammon notes:

> Many programs (developed by the manufacturer) consist of hastily improvised trade deals, uninspired dealer contests, and unexamined discount structures. . . . This traditional attitude toward distributor programming is a luxury that no longer can be easily afforded.[30]

More-sophisticated companies try to forge a long-term *partnership* with their distributors. This calls for the manufacturer's developing a clear sense of what it wants from its distributors and what its distributors can expect from the manufacturer in terms of market coverage, product availability, market development, account solicitation, technical advice and services, and market information. It seeks agreement from the channel members on these policies and may even set up compensation based on adherence to these policies. In one case, the company, instead of paying a straight 25 percent sales commission, pays the following:

1. Five percent for carrying the proper level of inventory
2. Another 5 percent for meeting the sales quotas
3. Another 5 percent for servicing the customers effectively
4. Another 5 percent for proper reporting of final customer purchase levels
5. Another 5 percent for proper accounts receivables management

Distribution programming is still a further stage in the possible relation between manufacturers and their distributors. McCammon defines this as building a planned, professionally managed, vertical marketing system that incorporates the needs of both manufacturer and distributors.[31] The manufacturer sets up a special department within the marketing department called distributor relations planning, whose job is to identify the distributors' needs and build up the programmed merchandising and other programs to help each distributor operate as optimally as possible. This department and the distributors jointly plan the merchandising goals, inventory levels, space and visual merchandising plans, sales-training requirements, and advertising and promotion plans. The aim is to convert the distributors from the idea that they make their money primarily on the buying side (through an adversarial relation with the supplier) to the realization that they make their money on the selling side through being part of a sophisticated vertical marketing system.

Evaluating Channel Members

The producer must periodically evaluate middleman performance against certain standards. Where a middleman's performance is below standard, it is necessary to determine the underlying causes and to consider the possible remedies. The producer may have to tolerate the unsatisfactory performance if dropping

[30] Bert C. McCammon, Jr., "Perspectives for Distribution Programming," in *Vertical Marketing Systems*, ed. Louis P. Bucklin (Glenview, Ill.: Scott, Foresman & Co., 1970), p. 32.

[31] Ibid., p. 43.

or replacing the middleman would lead to even worse results. But if there are attractive alternatives to the use of this middleman, then the producer should require the middleman to reach a certain level of performance within a stated time or be dropped from the channel.

Much grief can be avoided if standards of performance and sanctions are agreed upon at the very beginning between the producer and the channel members. The areas posing the greatest need for explicit agreement concern sales intensity and coverage, average inventory levels, customer delivery time, treatment of damaged and lost goods, cooperation in company promotional and training programs, and middleman services owed to the customer.

The producer typically issues sales quotas to define current performance expectations. Automobile manufacturers and many appliance dealers set quotas not only for total units to be sold but often for types of units. In some cases these quotas are treated only as guides; in others, they represent serious standards. Some producers list the sales of various middlemen after each sales period and send the rankings out. This device is intended to motivate middlemen at the bottom of the list to do better for the sake of self-respect (and continuing the relationship) and middlemen at the top to maintain their performance out of pride.

A simple ranking of the middlemen by level of sales is not necessarily the best measure. Middlemen face varying environments over which they have different degrees of control; the importance of the producer's line in their assortments also varies. One useful measure is to compare each middleman's sales performance against its performance in the preceding period. The average percentage of improvement (or decline) for the group can be used as a norm. Another useful measure is to compare each middleman's performance against assigned quotas based on an analysis of the sales potential in the respective territories. After each sales period, middlemen are ranked according to the ratio of their actual sales to their sales potential. Diagnostic and motivational effort can then be focused on those middlemen who have underachieved.

CHANNEL-MODIFICATION DECISIONS

A producer must do more than design a good channel system and set it into motion. Every so often the system requires modification to meet new conditions in the marketplace.

This fact struck a large manufacturer of major household appliances who had been marketing exclusively through franchised dealers. A relative loss in market share made the producer take stock of several distributional developments that had taken place since the original channel was designed:

> An increasing share of major-brand appliances were being merchandised through discount houses.
>
> An increasing share of major appliances were being sold on a private-brand basis through large department stores.
>
> A new market was developing in the form of volume purchases by tract home builders who preferred to deal directly with the manufacturers.
>
> Door-to-door and direct-mail solicitation of orders was being undertaken by some dealers and competitors.

The only strong independent dealers were those in small towns, and rural families were increasingly making their purchases in large cities.

These and other developments in the ever-changing distribution scene led this manufacturer to undertake a major review of possible channel modifications.

Three different levels of channel change should be distinguished. The change could involve adding or dropping individual channel members; adding or dropping particular market channels; or developing a totally new way to sell goods in all markets.

The decision to add or drop particular middlemen usually requires a straightforward incremental analysis. The economic question is, What would the firm's profits look like with this middleman and without this middleman? The incremental analysis could be complex if the decision would have many repercussions on the rest of the system. An automobile manufacturer's decision to grant another dealer franchise in a city will require taking into account not only that dealer's probable sales but the possible losses or gains in the sales of the manufacturer's other dealers.[32]

Sometimes a producer contemplates dropping not an isolated middleman but all middlemen who fail to bring their unit sales above a certain level within a certain period. This happened when a large manufacturer of motor trucks selling through a network of franchised dealers noted that at least 5 percent of its dealers were selling fewer than three or four trucks a year. According to the controller's calculation, it cost more for the company to service these small dealers than the sale of three or four trucks was worth. If the issue were a matter of dropping a few of these weak dealers, then an incremental analysis would probably indicate that company profits would rise. But the decision to drop most of these dealers could have such large repercussions on the system as a whole that an incremental analysis would not suffice. Such a decision would raise the unit costs of producing trucks, since the overhead would have to be spread over fewer trucks; some employees and equipment would be idled; some business in the markets where the smaller dealers were cut out would go to competitors; and other company dealers might be made insecure by the decision. Nothing short of a detailed, total systems simulation would be adequate for comprehending all the effects.

A producer sometimes faces the question of whether its channel for reaching a particular geographical area or customer type is still optimal. A breakeven or rate-of-return analysis could be made of the present and alternative systems. The most difficult "channel-change" decision involves the revision of the overall system of distribution. For example, an automobile manufacturer may consider replacing independent dealers with company-owned dealers; a soft-drink manufacturer may consider replacing local franchised bottlers with centralized bottling and direct sales. These are decisions made at the highest level, decisions that not only change the channels but necessitate a revision of most of the marketing-mix elements and policies to which the firm is accustomed. Such decisions have so many ramifications that any quantitative modeling of the problem can only be a first approximation.

[32] See T. E. Hlavac, Jr., and John D. C. Little, "A Geographical Model of an Urban Automobile Market," in *Proceedings of the Fourth International Conference on Operational Research*, ed. David B. Hertz and Jacques Melese (New York: John Wiley & Sons, 1966), pp. 302–11.

In analyzing the desirability of changing a channel, the task is one of determining whether the channel is in equilibrium.[33] A channel is in equilibrium when there is no structural or functional change that would lead to increased profits. A structural change is one involving the addition or elimination of some middleman level in the channel. A functional change is one involving the reallocation of one or more channel tasks among the channel members. A channel is ripe for change when it is in disequilibrium—that is, when it provides an opportunity for gain through a structural or functional modification.

A simple example will convey the concept of channel disequilibrium. Assume there is a channel of the manufacturer-wholesaler-retailer type (M-W-R). (See Figure 16–5.) Each channel member makes a set of decisions on price, advertising, and distribution (P,A,D). For simplicity, assume that these decisions mainly affect the succeeding stage. Thus the producer makes decisions $(P,A,D)_1$, which influence the quantity (Q_1) ordered by the wholesaler. The producer calculates net profits (Z_1) by subtracting its costs from its revenue from the wholesaler. In the same fashion, each channel member makes an independent set of decisions that influence its revenue and cost and bring about a particular net profit.

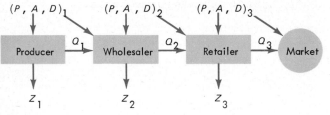

FIGURE 16–5

Conceptual Picture of the Profits in a Marketing Channel

SOURCE: Redrawn, with modifications, from Stanley Stasch, "A Method of Dynamically Analyzing the Stability of the Economic Structure of Channels of Distribution" (Ph.D. dissertation, School of Business, Northwestern University, 1964), p. 63.

Looking at the channel as a whole, a set of independent decisions is made $[(P,A,D)_1, (P,A,D)_2, (P,A,D)_3]$ that results in some total channel profit $(Z_1 + Z_2 + Z_3)$. The concept of channel disequilibrium can now be defined precisely. The channel is in disequilibrium if there exists an alternative set of decisions $[(P,A,D)_1, (P,A,D)_2, (P,A,D)_3]^\circ$ that would result in a different total channel profit $(Z_1 + Z_2 + Z_3)^\circ$ that is greater than $(Z_1 + Z_2 + Z_3)$. If this is the case, the channel presents an opportunity for increased profit. But the alternative decisions are not likely to be made as long as the channel members make their decisions independently. The greater the difference between $(Z_1 + Z_2 + Z_3)^\circ$ and $(Z_1 + Z_2 + Z_3)$, the greater will be the incentive of the channel members to pursue joint planning or for some channel member to absorb one or more of the others to achieve the extra profits from integrated decision making.

[33] This section leans heavily on Stanley Stasch's "A Method of Dynamically Analyzing the Stability of the Economic Structure of Channels of Distribution" (Ph.D. dissertation, School of Business, Northwestern University, 1964).

Let us turn from the channel decisions facing manufacturers to those facing middlemen, particularly wholesalers and retailers. We will look at the marketing decisions made by resellers in the areas of product, price, promotion, and place.[34]

Product Decisions of Resellers

Resellers have to make product decisions with respect to the assortment they will carry, the buying policies they will implement, and the services they will provide to customers.

A reseller's *product assortment* can be described in terms of decisions on width (narrow or wide) and depth (shallow or deep). Consider the restaurant business. A small lunch counter offers a food assortment that is narrow and shallow—a few sandwiches and some egg dishes. A delicatessen's assortment is narrow but deep—essentially smoked meat and smoked fish products with many varieties. A cafeteria usually offers a wide assortment of foods lacking much depth in any category. Finally, a major restaurant offers a wide assortment of foods with many variations of each. In the food store business, mom-and-pop stores, health food stores, convenience food stores, and supermarkets differ primarily in the width and depth dimensions of their respective assortments. In the area of industrial wholesaling, assortment profiles vary. For example, a rack jobber carries a narrow line of sundries that is shallow in depth. On the other hand, a full-line wholesaler carries a wide and deep assortment by definition. Typically, resellers begin as small-business people, with narrow and shallow lines. If successful, they expand by increasing either the width or the depth of their assortment. Those that are ultimately successful are able to carry assortments that are both wide and deep.

Resellers make their profit on the difference between what they pay for their merchandise and what they get for it. Because margins are usually small, they are under great pressure to buy carefully. Often they can make as much or more money through adept buying as adept pricing. So the *buying function* is usually a key resource that must be expertly staffed. The buying group develops product specifications, often invites competitive bidding, and buys from multiple sources.

Resellers also make decisions of the *mix of services* they will provide their customers. The old mom-and-pop grocery stores offered home delivery, credit, and conversation to their customers—services that today's modern supermarkets have completely eliminated. In industrial wholesaling, cash-and-carry operations offer minimal services whereas full-line wholesalers offer delivery, credit, sales aids and training, cooperative advertising, and return privileges to their customers.

Pricing Decisions of Resellers

Resellers typically base their prices on conventional markups over the costs of the original goods. For example, wholesalers average a gross margin of 20 percent. Gross margin is the difference between their selling price and their cost price of the goods sold. This gross margin has to cover their expenses, which may

---

[34] See Ben Enis, *Marketing Principles: The Management Process,* 2nd ed. (Pacific Palisades, Cal.: Goodyear Publishing Co., 1977), pp. 428–36.

run an average of 17 percent, leaving a profit margin of around 3 percent. The gross margins in retailing average 35 to 40 percent, but here too expenses consume most of the gross margin. There are wide variations around these margins for different types of wholesalers and retailers. For example, grocery wholesalers and retailers work with an average profit margin of less than 2 percent.

Resellers are continually looking for ways to improve their gross margin through smarter pricing. They will often put a low markup on a few items to act as *loss leaders* (or *traffic builders*) and put high markups on other items, hoping that buyers will buy them once the buyers are on the premises. They will also place the higher-markup items in prime exposure locations.

Promotion Decisions of Resellers

Resellers make regular use of the normal tools of promotion, such as advertising, personal selling, sales promotion, and publicity. In the case of wholesalers, they use both push and pull methods of promotion. Their sales force acts as a push force in calling on prospective and current customers, offering special prices and premiums, and asking for orders. Wholesalers use pull force by advertising their assortments and certain manufacturers' brands in media reaching retailers and ultimate consumers. The advertising is supplemented with such promotional tools as special discounts for off-season purchase and premiums.

Retailers use a number of promotion tools to reach final consumers. The major tool is advertising, and in many areas it takes the form of newspaper advertising to announce sales prices or special merchandise. The advertising is occasionally supplemented by hand-delivered circulars or direct-mail pieces. Sales promotion takes the form of in-store demonstrations, trading stamps, grand prizes, and visiting celebrities. Much effort goes into the designing of effective atmospheres for the retailing establishment that reinforce impulses to buy or consume the products.

Place Decisions of Resellers

Resellers compete in creating place utility for their customers. Wholesalers must develop well-located stocking points, carry sufficient inventories, and use reliable means of transportation to be able to fill customers' orders fast. In the case of retailers, their choice of locations will be a key competitive factor in their attraction of customers. For example, the major factor in the consumer's choice of a bank is its nearness to the customer. Department store chains, oil companies, and major fast-food franchisers must be particularly adept in making their location decisions, and the use of advanced methods of site selection and evaluation is critical.

SUMMARY

Marketing-channel decisions are among the most complex and challenging facing the firm. Each firm usually confronts a number of alternative ways to reach the market. They vary from direct selling, to using one, two, three, or more intermediaries. The firms making up the marketing channel are connected in different ways by physical, title, payment, information, and promotion flows. Marketing channels do not stay static but are characterized by continuous and sometimes dramatic change. Four of the most significant recent trends are direct, vertical, horizontal, and multichannel marketing systems.

Each channel system has a different potential for creating sales and producing costs. Once a particular marketing channel is chosen, the firm must usually adhere to it for a substantial period. The chosen channel will significantly affect and be affected by the rest of the marketing mix.

Good channel design should proceed with a clarification of channel objectives, alternatives, and likely payoffs. The objectives are conditioned by the particular characteristics of customers, products, middlemen, competitors, and environment. The alternatives are usually numerous because of the variety of types of intermediaries, the different possible intensities of market coverage, the various ways in which channel tasks can be allocated among channel members, and the many possible trade-relations mixes. Each feasible alternative way to reach the market has to be spelled out and evaluated according to economic, control, and adaptive criteria.

After the basic design of the channel is determined, the firm faces the task of effective channel management. It has to select particular firms to work with or find business firms willing to work with it. It has to supplement the motivations provided to channel members through the trade-relations mix by special incentives and supervision. It has to periodically evaluate the performance of individual channel members against their own past sales, other channel members' sales, and, possibly, sales quotas.

Because markets and the marketing environment are continually changing, the firm must be prepared to make channel revisions: individual members may be dropped or added, the channels in specific markets may be modified, and sometimes the whole channel system may have to be redesigned. Evaluating a proposed channel change may be approached through incremental analysis if only the particular unit or channel is affected; it may require a systems-level analysis if the change is likely to affect other units. The greater the disequilibrium in a channel, the more apparent it will be to observers that channel modification would lead to increased profits.

QUESTIONS AND PROBLEMS

1. If there are five producers and five customers in a market, how many contacts would have to be made (a) without a middleman? (b) with a middleman? What are the general formulas?

2. Explain how the characteristics of (a) peaches and (b) cement affect the channels for them.

3. Suggest some alternative channels for (a) a small firm which has developed a radically new harvesting machine; (b) a small plastic manufacturer who has developed a picnic pack for keeping bottles and food cold; and (c) a manufacturer of expensive watches.

4. Is the following channel pattern plausible? What kinds of institutions are implied?

$$M(---K) \rightarrow W(-AS-) \rightarrow R(TA--)$$

5. Produce a checklist of questions for rating prospective applicants for a distributorship.

6. "Discussions of merchandising practices in the oil industry have often proceeded from the premise that the existing distributive channel structure for gasoline is a millstone around the industry's neck." Can you think of innovations for improving the distribution of automobile fuel or for improving the profitability of service stations?

7. Can you think of a radically different way to organize the distribution of (a) automobiles; (b) beer?

8. "Middlemen are parasites." This allegation has been made by many over the centuries. Is this likely to be the case in a competitive economic system? Why or why not?

9. There is often conflict between manufacturers and retailers. What does each party really want from the other and why does this give rise to conflict?

Physical-Distribution Decisions

When is a refrigerator not a refrigerator? . . . when it is in Pittsburgh at the time it is desired in Houston.
J. L. HESKETT, N. A. GLASKOWSKY, R. M. IVIE

17

Throughout the years, the term *marketing* has connoted two different but related processes, the first dealing with the *search for and stimulation of buyers* and the second with the *physical distribution of goods*. With the increased competition for markets, marketing executives have devoted the bulk of their time to the search and stimulation function. Their attention has been given over to developing a mix of products, prices, promotion, and channels that would keep demand high and growing. They have viewed physical distribution, or the logistics of getting goods to the buyers, as a supportive and subsidiary activity.

More recently, several developments have awakened management's interest in the logistics problem and led them to wonder whether they were not overlooking many opportunities to increase customer service, outperform competition, and effect cost savings.

One of the alerting factors is the steady climb in the bill for such physical-distribution services as freight, warehousing, and inventory. Freight and warehousing bills are rising as a result of increased labor, energy, and equipment costs. The inventory bill is rising because buyers are tending to place smaller orders more frequently, and manufacturers are tending to expand the width and depth of their product lines. Many executives have been shocked to learn that the total costs of storing, handling, and moving their products are anywhere between 19 and 22 percent of their net sales![1] One study showed the cost breakdown as follows: inventory (44 percent), traffic service and customer freight (23 percent), warehousing and shipping (16 percent), interplant freight (9 percent), and sales order processing (8 percent).[2]

Authorities in increasing numbers argue that substantial savings can usually be effected in the physical-distribution area, which has been variously described as "the last frontier for cost economies"[3] and "the economy's dark continent."[4] There is much evidence that uncoordinated physical-distribution decisions result in profit suboptimization. Not enough use is being made of modern decision tools for blending economic levels of inventories, efficient modes of shipment, and sound plant, warehouse, and store locations.

Furthermore, physical distribution is a potent tool in the demand-stimulation process. Companies can attract additional customers by offering better service or by cutting prices through successfully reducing physical-distribution costs.

THE SCOPE OF PHYSICAL DISTRIBUTION

Physical distribution comprises the set of tasks involved in planning and implementing the physical flows of materials and final goods from points of origin to points of use or consumption to meet the needs of customers at a profit.

At least fourteen tasks are involved in physical distribution and they are shown in Figure 17–1. The system starts with sales forecasting, which allows the company to formulate plans with respect to production and inventory levels. The production plans suggest the materials that must be ordered by the purchasing department, and these arrive through inbound transportation, enter the receiving area, and are stored in raw material inventory. Raw materials are converted into finished goods. Finished goods inventory is the link between customers' orders and the company's manufacturing activity. Customers' orders draw down the finished goods inventory level, and manufacturing activity builds it up. Finished goods flow off the assembly line, and pass through packing, in-plant warehousing, shipping-room processing, outbound transportation, field warehousing, and customer delivery and servicing.

Under traditional thinking, physical distribution starts with goods at the plant and tries to find efficient ways to get them to customers. Under marketing thinking, physical-distribution planning should start with market considerations and work all the way back to raw material needs and sources. The company should start with its target customers, their locations, and their needs for product delivery and availability. It should know the service levels offered by competitors and plan to match or exceed these levels, or at least compensate for

[1] For further discussion of physical-distribution costs, see Ronald H. Ballou, *Basic Business Logistics* (Englewood Cliffs, N. J.: Prentice-Hall, 1978), pp. 17–19.

[2] Bernard J. LaLonde, "Integrated Distribution Management: The American Perspective," *Journal of Long-Range Planning*, December 1969, p. 64.

[3] Donald D. Parker, "Improved Efficiency and Reduced Cost in Marketing," *Journal of Marketing*, April 1962, pp. 15–21.

[4] Peter Drucker, "The Economy's Dark Continent," *Fortune*, April 1962, pp. 103 ff.

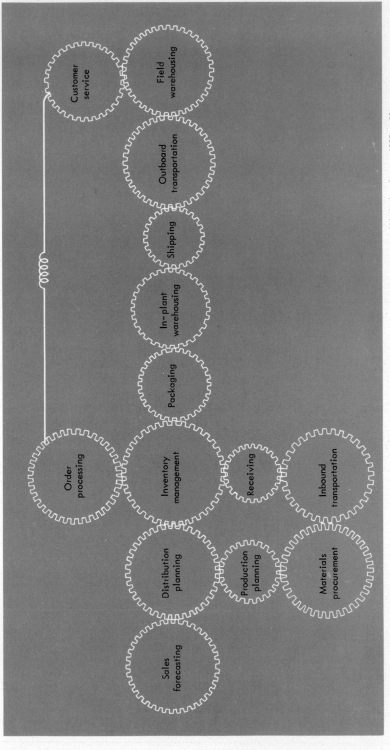

SOURCE: Redrawn, with modifications, from Wendell M. Stewart, "Physical Distribution: Key to Improved Volume and Profits," *Journal of Marketing*, January 1965, p. 66.

FIGURE 17–1
Major Activities Involved in Physical Distribution

them by other features of its offer. The company then makes an integrated set of decisions on warehouse and plant locations, inventory levels, and transportation modalities that are designed to supply the target levels of service to the target customers.

A growing number of practitioners prefer to call this way of thinking "market logistics" rather than "physical distribution." Too often, physical distribution is a planning of physical flows of the existing finished goods from the company out to the marketplace at the least cost. A market-logistics viewpoint reverses this thinking and often leads to an innovative approach to physical distribution. Consider the following case:

> In Germany, soft drinks are typically purchased from retailers in individual bottles. A soft-drink manufacturer, looking for an advantage, decided to design a six-pack. He tested the idea with consumers who responded positively to the convenience aspect of carrying bottles in a six-pack. The retailers also responded positively because the bottles could be loaded faster on the shelves and could lead to the purchase of more bottles per occasion. The company designed the six-packs to fit on the shelf in a way that maximized utilization of the shelf space. Then it designed cases and pallets that would bring these six-packs to the store's receiving rooms efficiently. The plant operations were redesigned to produce the new bottles and six-packs. The purchasing department let out bids for the new needed materials. When implemented, this new way of packaging soft drinks was an instant hit with consumers, and the manufacturer's market share increased substantially. A market-logistics viewpoint led to a creative physical-distribution breakthrough.

THE PHYSICAL-DISTRIBUTION OBJECTIVE

Many companies state their physical-distribution objective as *getting the right goods to the right places at the right time for the least cost.* Unfortunately, this provides little actual guidance. No physical-distribution system can simultaneously maximize customer service and minimize distribution cost. Maximum customer service implies such policies as large inventories, premium transportation, and many warehouses, all of which raise distribution cost. Minimum distribution cost implies such policies as slow and cheap transportation, low stocks, and few warehouses.

The physical-distribution objective can be defined more carefully by introducing the notion of an *efficient system.* System efficiency is a matter of the ratio of a system's output to its input. By clarifying what the outputs and inputs are in a physical-distribution system, we can come closer to defining a clear objective for such a system.

Level of Service (Output)

A basic output of a physical-distribution system is the *level of customer service.* Customer service represents one of the key competitive benefits that a company can offer potential customers in order to attract their business. From the customer's view, customer service means several things:

1. The speed of filling and delivering normal orders
2. The supplier's willingness to meet emergency merchandise needs of the customer
3. The care with which merchandise is delivered, so that it arrives in good condition

4. The supplier's readiness to take back defective goods and resupply quickly
5. The availability of installation and repair services and parts from the supplier
6. The number of options on shipment loads and carriers
7. The supplier's willingness to carry inventory for the customer
8. The service charges, that is, whether the services are "free" or separately priced

The company's task is to research the relative importance and determinance of these various customer services to the target customers and what competitors are offering. The company then decides on a competitively viable mix of customer services.

Of all the services listed above, the first one, *delivery time,* is typically the most important to customers. Customers want the ordered merchandise or service delivered at the promised time. Late delivery of needed parts or service can idle expensive equipment, labor, and even whole factories. Actual delivery time is made up of two components, order cycle time and delivery reliability. *Order cycle time* is the normal time the company takes to fill an order after receiving it. It is what the company's sales representatives state as the expected time for delivery, such as "one-week delivery." *Delivery reliability* is the percentage of times the company actually fills the order within the stated order cycle time. Thus "60 percent reliability" means that the company meets the promised delivery date only 60 percent of the time.

The company can improve actual delivery time by cutting down the order cycle time, increasing delivery reliability, or both. Suppose a company has been operating on an order cycle time of seven days with a 60 percent reliability. In a bid for more customers, it is considering cutting delivery time down to five days with a 95 percent reliability. This will substantially increase its physical distribution costs. The trick is to measure whether this move will produce enough increased sales and profits to cover the added costs. To the extent that the management is able to estimate the relationship between levels of service and sales, it will have a means of determining the optimal level of customer service.

Several factors influence the optimal level of customer service. The *competitors' normal delivery time* is a major factor in that the company risks losing or failing to attract customers if it offers a lower standard; and to offer a higher standard would be costly and might even lead competitors to increase their service levels, thus raising everyone's costs. Another factor is the *degree of criticality of the needed parts or service;* delivery times have to be faster when expensive operations are dependent upon delivery. Still another factor is the *differential advantage or loyalty* enjoyed by the company; the higher this is, the less it has to offer in the way of a delivery-time advantage. Finally, the *cost of supplying higher levels of service* will influence the normal delivery time; a company is not going to improve the delivery time at a high cost unless this will substantially improve sales.

Once it decides on a delivery-time standard, the company can design the physical distribution system to meet that standard with a high degree of reliability. Pillsbury defines its delivery-time standard as "third-morning rail delivery anywhere in the U.S." Xerox defines its service-delivery standard as being able "to put a disabled machine anywhere in the continental United States back into operation within three hours after receiving the service request." To accomplish this, Xerox has a separate division consisting of 12,000 service personnel and parts managers.

A company bears certain costs, of which freight, inventory, and warehousing are the main ones, in providing its present level of customer service. Often the total bill is not known because companies typically lack centralized management and accounting of their physical-distribution activities. These costs, however, must be measured as a prerequisite for distribution planning and control.

The present system can be said to be efficient if no reorganization of logistical inputs could reduce the costs *while maintaining the present service level.* Many companies think their physical-distribution system is efficient because each decision center—inventory, warehousing, and traffic—appears to do a good job of keeping down its own costs. However, this is an area where the sum of distribution costs is not necessarily minimized by a set of uncoordinated efforts to minimize the separate costs. As Parker points out:

> Pressures are applied by top management which encourage the separate functional units to control and reduce their costs of operation. Cost reduction becomes the primary way for these functional units to call attention to themselves. . . . As a result, when decisions are made about transportation, warehousing, packaging, inventory levels . . . they are based on an analysis of alternatives within that specific function, without regard for the possible effects upon other closely related functions. Functional costs are considered, but the all-important total cost of the related functions is ignored.[5]

Various physical-distribution costs interact, often in an inverse way:

> The traffic manager favors rail shipment over air shipment whenever possible. This reduces the company's freight bill. However, because the railroads are slower, this ties up company capital longer, delays customer payment, and may cause customers to buy from competitors offering more rapid service.
>
> The shipping department uses cheap containers to minimize shipping costs. This leads to a high damage rate of goods in transit and the loss of customer goodwill.
>
> The inventory manager favors holding low inventories to reduce total inventory cost. However, this results in many stockouts, backorders, accompanying paperwork, special production runs, and high-cost fast-freight shipments.

The import is that since physical-distribution activities are highly interrelated, decisions must be made on a total system basis.

We are now ready to define the objective of physical-distribution design. A physical-distribution system consists of a set of decisions on the number, location, and size of warehouses; freight policies; and inventory policies. Each possible physical-distribution system implies a total distribution cost, as given by the expression:

$$D = T + FW + VW + S \qquad (17\text{--}1)$$

[5] Parker, "Improved Efficiency in Marketing," p. 17.

where:

D = total distribution cost of proposed system

T = total freight cost of proposed system

FW = total fixed warehouse cost of proposed system

VW = total variable warehouse costs (including inventory) of proposed system

S = total cost of lost sales due to average delivery delay under proposed system[6]

The choice of a physical-distribution system calls for examining the total distribution cost associated with different proposed systems and selecting the system that minimizes total distribution cost. Alternatively, if it is hard to measure S in (17–1), the company should aim to minimize the distribution cost $T + FW + VW$ of reaching a *given level of customer service*.

MAJOR ALTERNATIVES IN PHYSICAL-DISTRIBUTION STRATEGY

A firm faces a large number of alternatives in designing its physical-distribution system. The variety increases in number and complexity as we go from a firm with a single plant serving a single market to a firm with multiple plants and multiple markets. Many firms, in fact, follow a "logistic life cycle" going from a single plant in a single market to one of multiple plants in multiple markets, calling for various changes in physical-distribution arrangements along the way.

Single Plant, Single Market

The vast majority of the three hundred thousand manufacturers in the United States are single-plant firms doing business in single markets. The single markets served may be a small city, as in the case of small bakeries and printing firms, or a region, as in the case of local breweries and boat manufacturers.

Does the single-plant firm generally locate in the midst of its market? It often does, for the cost of serving a market increases with the distance. The distant firm has to absorb higher outbound freight costs and is normally at a competitive disadvantage.

Yet in some cases there are offsetting economies in locating a plant at some distance from the market. The higher market transportation cost may be offset by lower costs of land, labor, energy, or raw materials.

> A pickling plant serving the Chicago market was deliberately located in the midst of a cucumber-growing region two hundred miles from Chicago. This gave the company better control over crop selection. Labor costs were lower because pickling and packing were done only in certain months, when farmers had surplus time on their hands. Finally, the acreage for the plant cost only a fraction of what it would have cost near the city.

The merits of locating a plant near the market or near its sources depend

[6] Adapted from Alfred A. Kuehn and Michael J. Hamburger, "A Heuristic Program for Locating Warehouses," *Management Science*, July 1963, pp. 657–58.

mainly on relative transfer and processing costs. A substantial change in certain costs could upset the balance of advantages. The firm choosing between two alternative plant sites must carefully weigh not only present alternative costs but expected future alternative costs.

Single Plant, Multiple Markets

The firm having a single plant and selling in a dispersed set of markets has a choice of several physical-distribution strategies. Consider a midwestern manufacturer who wishes to expand its operation into the East. The manufacturer can serve the eastern market in four ways: (1) *direct shipments* to customers on the East Coast, (2) *carload shipments to a warehouse* on the East Coast, (3) *fabricated-parts shipments to an assembly plant* on the East Coast, or (4) *establishment of a manufacturing plant* on the East Coast.

Direct shipments to customers   Any proposed system of physical distribution must be evaluated in terms of customer service and cost. The direct-shipment proposal would normally score poorly on both of these counts. Direct shipment implies slower delivery than shipments to the customer from an eastern-based warehouse. Direct shipment also implies higher cost, because the typical customer order is normally smaller than carload size. Carload rates (CL) are often 50 percent lower than less-than-carload rates (LCL).

But whether direct shipment does involve these disadvantages depends upon a number of things. It is conceivable that direct shipment from a distant plant could effect *faster* delivery than shipment from a nearby warehouse. A Kansas City manufacturer of colored, flavored ice cream cones learned that its customers in the East could receive shipments sooner by air freight direct from Kansas City than by truck shipments out of New York City. Furthermore, direct shipment of less-than-carload orders must be measured against the cost of maintaining warehoused inventories in the East. The decision on whether to use direct shipment depends on such factors as the nature of the product (its unit value, perishability, and seasonality), the required speed and cost of delivery, the size and/or weight of the typical customer order, and the geographical distance and direction.

The cost of direct shipment varies with selection of waterways, railroad, motor carriers, air freight, or some combination. Figure 17–2A shows how the cost of different modes of transportation may be compared. If the company receives eastern orders for shipments averaging less than ten pounds, it could minimize transportation cost by using air freight; between ten and thirty-five pounds, motor freight; over thirty-five pounds, rail freight.

This analysis is incomplete because each transportation alternative implies a different average delivery time. We can assume a higher cost of lost sales for longer delivery delays. Thus the slower modes of transportation cost less for freight but more in sales. These two diverging cost functions of delivery time are shown in Figure 17–2B. By adding the two cost curves vertically, we can find a total-cost curve. The total-cost curve tends to be U-shaped, and by projecting its minimum point down to the days-of-delivery axis, we can estimate the optimum delivery delay, D. This delay has the property that the marginal savings in freight from a slightly longer delay would just equal the marginal cost of lost patronage.

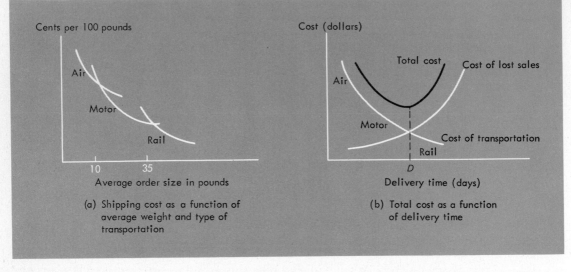

Cents per 100 pounds

Air

Motor

Rail

10   35

Average order size in pounds

(a) Shipping cost as a function of
average weight and type of
transportation

Cost (dollars)

Total cost   Cost of lost sales

Air

Motor

Cost of transportation

Rail

D

Delivery time (days)

(b) Total cost as a function
of delivery time

FIGURE 17–2
Costs as a Function of Shipping Mode and Average Weight

Bulk shipments to a warehouse near the market   The firm may find it less expensive to make bulk shipments to a regional warehouse in the East and to fill customer orders from that regional warehouse. The savings would arise mainly because of the substantial difference between carload and less-than-carload shipping rates. Suppose the midwestern manufacturer expects to sell 5,000 units annually in the East, and virtually all of the individual orders call for less-than-carload shipments. Assume that the shipping cost is $8 per unit on a carload basis, and $12 per unit on a less-than-carload basis. The cost of shipping the 5,000 units directly to customers at less-than-carload rates would be $60,000 (5,000 × $12). The cost of shipping carloads to a warehouse would be $40,000 (5,000 × $8). This represents a gross cost saving of $20,000.

From this, we have to subtract the cost of local delivery from the warehouse to the customer and the cost of warehousing. Suppose the typical local delivery charge is $1 a unit; then local delivery charges of $5,000 (5,000 × $1) must be subtracted from the gross savings, leaving savings of $15,000. Suppose the average unit stays in the warehouse one week before shipment and the warehouse charge per unit per week is $2, including handling, insurance, and all other charges. Then the annual warehousing bill would be $10,000 (5,000 × $2), leaving net savings of $5,000. Given these figures, the midwestern manufacturer could save $5,000 a year by making bulk shipments to a warehouse in the East as an alternative to direct shipments to customers.

To this possible freight savings should be added another advantage accruing from the use of a market-located stocking point. A regional warehouse typically makes it possible to make faster deliveries to customers and thereby increase customer patronage. In general, the optimizing rule for adding regional warehouses is simple enough. A regional warehouse should be added *if the freight savings and increased patronage resulting from faster delivery exceed the incremental costs of operating the warehouse.*

456

Large manufacturers must consider a whole system of regional warehouses, or stocking points, to serve a national market. Maytag, a large manufacturer of home laundry equipment, has over one hundred regional stocking points. Instead of sending small-volume orders of washing machines to over fifteen thousand different dealers, the company sends carload shipments to its various stocking points. In this way it can promise speedier delivery and also save considerably on freight costs.

But an extensive regional warehouse system raises a number of new problems: (1) What is the best number of stocking points?; (2) Where should they be located?; (3) What is the best inventory level to hold at each? Paper-and-pencil analysis is exceedingly inadequate to answer these questions. Companies are turning increasingly to computer models. Gerson and Maffei have described a computer simulation program for evaluating a system of up to forty warehouses, four thousand customers, and ten factories.[7] This program can be used to estimate quickly the cost of alternative arrangements in the existing number and locations of factories and warehouses. Other models are available, which use mathematical programming or heuristic techniques to determine the optimal distribution system.[8]

Fabricated-parts shipments to an assembly plant near the market A third alternative for the midwestern manufacturer is to establish an assembly plant near the market. Parts are shipped in carload quantities to the regional assembly plant at lower freight charges. The presence of a regional plant also stimulates the increased interest of local salesmen, dealers, and the community at large. Against this the company must consider the sunk investment cost in additional facilities.

Establishment of a regional manufacturing plant The midwestern manufacturer's fourth alternative is to establish a regional plant in the East. The decision to build a regional manufacturing plant requires the most detailed factual information and analysis of the local scene. Many factors are involved, including the availability and costs of manpower, energy, land, transportation, and, not the least important, the legal and political environment.

One of the most important factors is the nature of mass-production economies in the industry. In industries requiring a relatively heavy fixed investment, a plant has to be quite large in order to achieve cost economies. If unit costs of manufacture decrease continuously with the scale of plant, then one plant could logically supply the entire company volume at minimum *production* costs. However, it would be fallacious to ignore distribution costs, because they tend to be higher at higher volumes. The two considerations are combined in Figure 17–3. Unit production costs decline steadily as increased volume is produced by a single plant, while unit distribution costs tend to rise as the volume requires direct shipment to more distant markets. When the two curves are summed vertically, total costs may in fact rise as a result of using only one plant location. The company should consider a second plant as an alternative to expanding the size of a single plant much past V. It is conceivable in this case that two plants, each involving higher unit production costs, may effect a large enough saving in distribution costs to constitute the better arrangement.

[7] Martin L. Gerson and Richard B. Maffei, "Technical Characteristics of Distribution Simulators," *Management Science*, October 1963, pp. 62–69.

[8] See Kuehn and Hamburger, "Locating Warehouses."

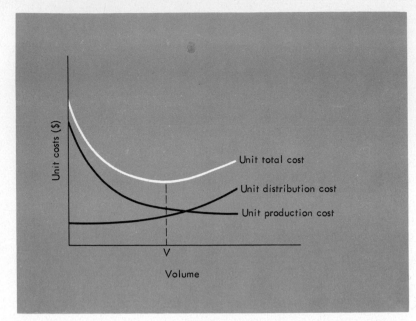

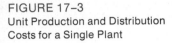

FIGURE 17–3
Unit Production and Distribution
Costs for a Single Plant

**Multiple Plants,
Multiple Markets**
Many of the large companies that do not require extremely large plants to
achieve production economies utilize a physical-distribution system consisting of
many plants and many warehouses. These companies face two optimization
tasks. The first is to set a factory-to-warehouse shipping pattern that minimizes
total freight costs, given the present plant and warehouse locations. The second
is to determine the number and location of facilities that will minimize total
distribution costs. Here system simulation is a potent technique. A physical-
distribution simulation at General Electric showed how a subsidiary with $50
million sales could save $2.9 million a year through system redesign.[9]

The physical-distribution system must be designed not so much for maximum economy for the present as for maximum flexibility for the future, even if
present costs must be a little higher in order to gain this flexibility. The company's plans for entering new-product markets, for introducing new-product
styles and models, and for changing the number of distributors all should count
in designing the system. The system should be planned with an awareness of
technological developments, particularly in the areas of communications, transportation, and automation. Such innovations as automated warehouses, piggyback freight, electronic hookups between computers in different locations,
containerization, and air freight are all factors to consider.

INVENTORY DECISIONS

While marketing management generally does not have control over inventory
policy, it is inclined to seek a strong voice in the making of inventory policy.
The marketer's chief concern lies in providing a high level of customer service.
Inventory policy is thus a tool in the demand-creation and demand-satisfaction
process. The marketer would like to promise customers that all their orders would

[9] "The Case for 90% Satisfaction," *Business Week*, January 14, 1961.

be filled immediately and would be shipped by the most rapid transportation. However, it is not realistic from a cost point of view for a company to carry the amount of stock that would virtually guarantee no stockouts. A major reason is that *inventory cost increases at an increasing rate as the customer-service level approaches 100 percent.* A typical cost relationship is illustrated in Figure 17–4A. To be able to fill 85 percent of the total received orders from existing stock, the company has to carry an inventory valued at $400,000. To raise the customer-service standard by five percentage points, to 90 percent, inventory investment must be increased by $100,000. To raise the customer-service standard another five percentage points, to 95 percent, inventory investment must now be increased by $200,000.

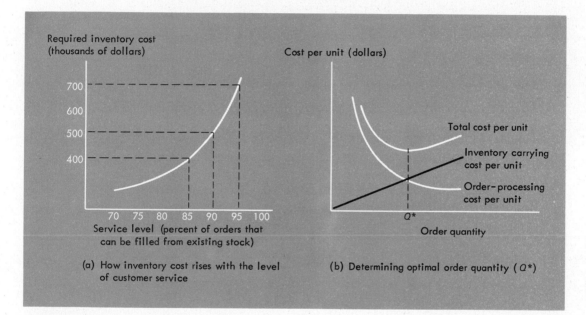

(a) How inventory cost rises with the level of customer service

(b) Determining optimal order quantity (Q^*)

FIGURE 17–4
Important Inventory Relationships

This acceleration of inventory cost does not mean that increases in customer service are never warranted. Increases in service spell increases in patronage and sales. But how much do sales increase with service? The graph only tells us that an increase from 90 to 95 percent service requires another $200,000 of inventory investment. We need to know whether sales and profits would increase enough to justify the higher investment.

Types of Inventory Decisions

Inventories are carried because *producing* and *using* activities typically take place at different times, in different locations, and at different rates. In the case of agricultural food crops, rate of usage is usually even throughout the year, but harvesting occurs at discrete times. In the case of manufacturing output, factories achieve production economies by producing large runs of items infrequently. The savings in producing large runs generally exceed the cost of storing the goods over the period required for their complete sale.

Inventory decision making can be thought of as a two-step decision process: (1) when to order (order point), and (2) how much to order (order quantity).

When to order   The basic characteristic of an inventory is that it is drawn down during the period. This calls for a determination of the level at which the remaining stock justifies the placement of a new order. This level is called the *order (or reorder) point*. An order point of 20 would mean that when the seller's supply of an item falls to 20 units, an order for more stock should be placed.

The determination of the order point depends upon the order lead time, the usage rate, and the service standard. The higher these are, the higher the order point. Furthermore, if the order lead time and customer usage rate are variable, the order point would have to be higher by an amount of *safety stock*. The final order point is set on the basis of balancing the risks of stockouts against the costs of overstock.

How much to order   The decision the firm makes on how much to order directly influences how often it has to order. The larger the quantity ordered, the less often an order has to be placed.

Order-processing costs are somewhat different for the distributor and the manufacturer. The distributor's processing costs consist of whatever materials, machine accounting time, and labor are used up every time an order is placed, received, and inspected. Distributors have variously estimated their order-processing costs anywhere from a few dollars to one hundred dollars an order. The figure used makes quite a difference in the final determination of optimal order quantity.

Order-processing costs for a manufacturer consist of *setup costs* and *running costs* for the item. If setup costs are very low, the manufacturer can produce the item often and the cost per item is pretty constant and equal to the running costs. However, if setup costs are high, the manufacturer can reduce the average cost per unit by producing a long run and carrying more inventory.

Order-processing costs must be compared with *inventory carrying costs*. The larger the average stock carried, the higher the inventory carrying costs. These carrying costs include (1) storage charges, (2) cost of capital, (3) taxes and insurance, and (4) depreciation and obsolescence. Inventory carrying costs may run as high as 30 percent of the inventory value. That is a higher figure than the estimate used by many businessmen, but there is growing recognition that the cost is this high. This means that marketing managers who want their companies to carry larger inventories must be able to convince top management that the higher inventories will yield new sales with an incremental gross profit that would more than cover the incremental inventory carrying costs.

Many companies have higher inventory carrying costs than necessary because they try to offer their customers the same service standard on all their goods. It would be better for these companies to distinguish between their fast-moving, moderately moving, and slow-moving items and handle them differently. The fast-moving items would be highly stocked and carried in several locations, whereas the slow-moving items would be kept low in stock, carried in only one location, and possibly shipped by air freight when badly needed. Customers would expect to wait longer for nonstandard items, and the company will save a lot of money.[10]

[10] See James L. Heskett, "Logistics—Essential to Strategy," *Harvard Business Review*, November–December 1977, pp. 85–96.

The optimal order quantity can be determined by observing how order-processing costs and inventory carrying costs sum up at different possible order levels. In Figure 17–4B, the order-processing cost per unit is shown to fall with the number of units ordered, because the order costs are spread over more units. Inventory carrying charges per unit are shown to rise with the number of units ordered because each unit remains longer in inventory. The two cost curves are summed vertically into a total-cost curve. The lowest point on the total-cost curve is projected down on the horizontal axis to find the optimal order quantity Q^*.[11]

LOCATION DECISIONS

Marketing managers have a keen interest in the location decisions made by the firm. Retail outlets must be carefully located near the greatest number of potential customers, because of the importance of shopper convenience in store patronage. Even warehouse locations should be located near the customer concentration points to ensure fast and cheap delivery to customers.

Types of Location Decisions

Location decision making can be thought of as a two-step decision process: (1) selecting a general area, and (2) selecting a specific site.

We can illustrate the major issues in retail location by citing the experience of the Rayco Manufacturing Company.[12] Rayco was formed after World War II as a manufacturer of automobile seat covers. Its distribution network consisted of independently financed, franchised dealers who merchandised Rayco products exclusively. By 1955, it had over one hundred fifty dealers operating in sixty different cities. Its national retail structure continued to grow, and new lines were added: convertible tops, automobile replacement parts, and a line of home-furnishing fabrics. But auto seat covers remained its main product.

Selecting the area Rayco's Research Division has the responsibility of evaluating the profit potential of various areas of the country. The areas might be cities, standard metropolitan areas, or some other geographical unit. Suppose a set of n areas $(1, 2, 3, \ldots, i, \ldots, n)$ is to be evaluated. Let Z_i represent the expected profit potential of the ith area. Let X_i be a proposed company dollar investment in developing area i. The expected profit potential will vary with development expenses. That is, $Z_i = f(X_i)$. A larger outlet, a better dealer, or a larger promotion budget invested in a particular area would create higher profits, although the rate of profit increase can be expected to diminish beyond some level of investment.

[11] The optimal order quantity is given mathematically by the formula

$$Q^* = \sqrt{\frac{2DS}{IC}}$$

where D = annual demand, S = cost to place one order, and IC = annual carrying cost per unit. Known as the economic-order quantity formula, it assumes a constant ordering cost, a constant cost of carrying an additional unit in inventory, a known demand, and no quantity discounts. For the derivation of this and more complex formulas, see Martin K. Starr and David W. Miller, *Inventory Control: Theory and Practice* (Englewood Cliffs, N.J.: Prentice-Hall, 1962).

[12] The discussion that follows is adapted from "Rayco Manufacturing Company, Inc.: Pinpointing Store Locations by Electronic Computer," Case 3M38, Intercollegiate Case Clearing House. Harvard Graduate School of Business Administration, Boston, by permission of the author, Charles H. Dufton, Northeastern University, Boston.

461

Rayco's task is to estimate, for each candidate area, how profits would behave at different levels of investment. Once it derives a set of area profit functions, it can allocate its total "new locations" budget to these areas in such a way that the marginal profit is the same in all areas.

Although the area investment problem turns out to be simple to solve in principle, everything hinges on being able to estimate expected profits as a function of investment: $Z_i = f(X_i)$. Area profits are a complex function of area cost and area demand characteristics. The relevant cost characteristics of an area, such as land costs and advertising rates, are fairly easy to determine. It is the area's demand potential that is usually hard to determine.

Rayco initially identified about three hundred variables that could influence area sales. The Research Division examined the logical rationale for each variable and was able to reduce the set to seventy-four. Included were such variables as "average January temperature," "percent of the dwellings that were one-unit detached structures," and an "index for the physical appearance of a store." An equation was fitted to these seventy-four variables based on data from 150 existing outlets. Several of the variables failed to pass tests of statistical significance, and in the final equation, thirty-seven variables were retained, yielding an R^2 of .92. Rayco felt it could now estimate the "market potential" of any new area by inserting thirty-seven characteristics into the formula.

Selecting the site   After determining the areas of high potential, the firm must decide how many outlets to establish and where they should be specifically situated. If San Francisco appeared to be a high-potential market, Rayco could establish, for about the same investment, one large outlet in a central location or a few smaller outlets in separate parts of the city. If consumers behaved as though auto seat covers were specialty goods, they would be willing to travel longer distances, and this would favor one large, centrally located store. If consumers regarded Rayco's products as convenience goods, this would favor Rayco's establishing a few smaller outlets.

A store's trading area or reach is affected by a number of other factors besides the type of merchandise. One is the number of different items carried by the store. Baumol and Ide have developed an analysis in which they visualize each consumer as calculating his or her net gain from patronizing a store with N items at a distance D.[13] They assume that increases in N more than compensate for increases in D up to a point. Beyond this point, the cost of traveling to the store, and within the store, become dominant. The cost of traveling within a store, which is a function of N, would never reach discouraging proportions in the case of a Rayco outlet but could be a real factor in very large supermarkets and department stores, especially for the shopper who plans to purchase only a few items.

The *utility* expected by a consumer in location i of shopping at an outlet in location j is affected by many variables in addition to N and D. Included are such factors as store image, delivery, credit, service policies, promotion, parking facilities, and air conditioning. If consumer utility as a function of these variables could be measured, the choice of the best site and store size from a list of alternatives is solvable in principle.[14] Suppose there are three alternative proposed

[13] See William J. Baumol and Edward A. Ide, "Variety in Retailing," *Management Science*, October 1956, pp. 93–101.

[14] See David L. Huff, "Defining and Estimating a Trading Area," *Journal of Marketing*, July 1964, pp. 34–38.

sites—1, 2, and 3—offering utilities 40, 30, and 10, respectively, to a consumer in location i. The probability that this consumer would shop at site 1 is the ratio of the utility of site 1 to the total utility, in this case .50 ($= 40/80$). If there are 1,000 similar consumers clustered at location i, then half of them, or 500, can be expected to patronize proposed site 1. In a more advanced analysis, it would be desirable to distinguish major socioeconomic types of consumers at location i, because there are strong interactions of consumer type and store type.

In practice, firms vary considerably in how analytically they investigate the trade potential of proposed sites. Small firms rely on population census data and on simple traffic counts. Large firms carry out expensive surveys of consumer shopping habits and make extensive calculations of expected sales volume.

In undertaking a detailed *trade analysis* for a proposed site, the large firm first prepares area maps indicating density and the location of competitive intercepting facilities. An overlay on this map indicates major arteries to pinpoint traffic flows. Additional information is obtained by surveying the license plates in the parking lots of competitive facilities and through inquiries at noncompeting stores as to customer sources.

The real estate department then determines the availability and cost of potential sites within the general area. The trade potential of each site is then evaluated. A series of circles is drawn around each site at varying distances to indicate the primary trading area, the secondary trading area, and the fringe trading area. The secondary and fringe areas are further away from the new site and closer to competitive sites; they can be expected to contribute a progressively smaller amount of per capita sales.

The major chains utilize elaborate site-location checklists in their evaluation of sites. Nelson has published a very elaborate checklist containing over thirty factors, each of which has to be rated excellent, good, fair, or poor in evaluating a proposed site.[15] These factors relate to the site's trading area potential, accessibility, growth potential, competitive interception, and site economics. Some of the large chain organizations have gone beyond checklists into elaborate computer models for site location. One very large merchandising organization dropped its location consultant firm when it realized that the methods being used were at the checklist stage and undertook to build its own internal consultancy group for sophisticated location research.

ORGANIZATIONAL RESPONSIBILITY FOR PHYSICAL DISTRIBUTION

Divided Authority

By now it should be abundantly clear that decisions on warehousing, transportation, inventory levels, and location require the highest degree of coordination. Yet in the typical company, physical-distribution responsibilities tend to be divided in an ill-coordinated and often arbitrary way among several company departments. Furthermore, each department tends to adopt a narrow view of the company's physical-distribution objective. *Traffic managers* seek to minimize the freight bill. They prefer less-expensive modes of transportation and infrequent and large shipments. *Sales managers* seek to maximize the level of customer service. They prefer large inventories and premium transportation. *Inventory-control managers* seek to minimize inventory costs. They prefer small inventories because inventory carrying costs tend to be more tangible than

[15] Richard L. Nelson, *The Selection of Retail Locations* (New York: F. W. Dodge Corporation, 1958), pp. 349–50.

stockout costs. Various managers jealously guard their prerogatives. The result is system suboptimization.

Organizational Alternatives

Companies are increasingly recognizing the potential benefits of developing some coordinating mechanism and have generally chosen one of two forms. Many companies have set up a permanent committee, composed of personnel responsible for different physical-distribution activities, that meets periodically to work out policies for increasing the efficiency of the overall distribution system. A small number of companies have centralized their physical-distribution activities in the hands of a single authority.[16]

The example of the Burroughs Corporation is particularly illuminating.[17] Burroughs organized the Distribution Services Department to centralize control over its physical-distribution activities. Within two and one-half years following the reorganization, the company claimed savings of over $2 million annually (on $200 million of sales), plus a higher level of service to field branches and customers.

When a company establishes a separate department with responsibility for physical distribution, the major issue is whether the new department should have separate status or be placed within one of the major existing departments. For example, Heinz created a new department of coordinate stature with Marketing and Production which was headed by a vice-president of Distribution. Heinz hoped that this arrangement would guarantee respect for the department, develop a greater degree of professionalism and objectivity, and avoid partisan domination by Marketing or Production.

On the other hand, Burroughs placed its new Distribution Services Department within the Marketing Department. By this move, Burroughs was expressing the great importance it attached to good customer service relative to the costs of providing it. Wherever marketing is the crucial factor in competitive success, physical distribution is usually placed under the marketing department. This is especially true in such competitive industries as soap, food, and cosmetics, where marketing and physical distribution must be coordinated not only to minimize costs but also to harmonize distribution with frequent advertising campaigns and customer and dealer promotions.

But the location of the department, or even its creation, is a secondary concern. The important thing is the recognition by the company that if it does not coordinate the planning and operation of its physical-distribution activities, it is missing the opportunity for often sizable cost savings and service improvements. When this fundamental awareness takes place, each company can then make a determination of what would constitute the most appropriate coordinative mechanism.

SUMMARY

Just as the marketing concept is receiving increasing recognition by business firms, a growing number of firms are beginning to heed the physical-distribution concept. Physical distribution is an area of high potential cost savings, improved

---

[16] But in half the cases, the heads of distribution manage only transportation and warehousing and not the other physical distribution functions. See Robert S. Jeffries, Jr., "Distribution Management: Failures and Solutions," *Business Horizons*, April 1974, pp. 55–66. Also see Stephen B. Oresman and Charles D. Scudder, "A Remedy for Maldistribution," *Business Horizons*, June 1974, pp. 61–72.

[17] See L. O. Browne, "Total Distribution in an Age of Computers," *Distribution Age*, July 1964, pp. 33–40.

customer satisfaction, and competitive effectiveness. When traffic managers, inventory managers, and warehouse planners make decisions only with reference to their own framework, they affect each other's costs and demand-creation influences but do not take them into consideration. The physical-distribution concept calls for treating all these decisions within a unified total systems framework. Then the important task becomes that of designing physical-distribution arrangements that minimize the cost of providing a given level of customer service.

The firm can choose from a number of alternative physical-distribution strategies, ranging from direct shipment to field warehousing to local assembly plants to local manufacturing plants. It must develop inventory policies that reconcile the value of a high level of customer service with the need to economize on inventory carrying costs. It must find more accurate ways to evaluate alternative general areas and specific sites for marketing expansion. It must review the whole question of organizational responsibility for physical distribution, particularly how to coordinate the various decisions and where leadership should be located in the organization.

We have deliberately emphasized the planning rather than the operations aspects of physical distribution. Physical distribution is an area where good systems design counts for as much as or more than good operations management. Nevertheless, many of the potential economies come from improved management of the existing system.

**QUESTIONS
AND
PROBLEMS**

1. Does it follow that the company offering a high customer service level tends to bear high physical distribution costs in relation to sales?

2. A small midwestern boat company with good sales wants to expand into the eastern part of the country. What physical distribution strategy might it use to bring its boats to the East?

3. A national can manufacturer operates many local plants because cans are a low-cost, low-price product that has a relatively high transportation cost when shipped assembled, being mostly "air." Some of its plants appear uneconomic, and it is considering closing them. Much depends upon whether customers in the affected areas would accept a longer delivery time, switch business to a competitor's local plant, or manufacture their own cans. Develop a flow diagram showing how the company might analyze probable customer reactions to the elimination of a local plant.

4. What are the two inventory-production policy alternatives facing a seasonal producer?

5. Suppose a company's inventory carrying cost is 30 percent. A marketing manager wants the company to increase its inventory investment from $400,000 to $500,000, believing this would lead to increased sales of $120,000 because of greater customer loyalty and service. The gross profit on sales is 20 percent. Does it pay the company to increase its inventory investment?

6. The text mentioned that Rayco approached the problem of finding the characteristics of good locations through multiple regression. (a) Suggest some of the various ways in which the dependent variable, sales, might be defined. (b) How could the research department further reduce the number of independent variables in the market evaluation formula?

7. Suppose you are the marketing manager of a medium-sized manufacturing company. The president has just made the following statement: "The distribution activity is not a concern of the marketing department. The function of the marketing department is to sell the product . . . let the rest of the company handle production and distribution." How would you reply to this statement?

Marketing Communications Decisions

> People no longer buy shoes to keep their feet warm and dry. They buy them because of the way the shoes make them feel— masculine, feminine, rugged, different, sophisticated, young, glamorous, "in." Buying shoes has become an emotional experience. Our business now is selling excitement rather than shoes.
>
> FRANCIS C. ROONEY

Modern marketing calls for more than developing a good product, pricing it attractively, and making it readily accessible to target customers. The company must design and disseminate information about the product's existence, features, and terms and how these will benefit the target market. Every company is inevitably cast into the role of a communicator and promoter.

Companies have responded by hiring sales forces to carry persuasive messages, advertising agencies to develop attention-getting ads, sales promotion specialists to develop sales campaigns; and public relations firms to enhance the company's image. They all continue to spend large and growing sums for promotion. For most companies the question is not whether to promote, but how much to spend and in what ways.

The company's communications responsibilities go beyond disseminating information to target customers. The company must communicate effectively with other parties in its *task environment*, particularly its dealers and suppliers. It must communicate with major *external publics*, such as its stockholders, the financial community, the media, and various government units. It must communicate effectively with its *internal publics*, particularly its directors, middle management, sales force, and wage workers.

This means that the company must know how to market itself to various groups in order to gain their confidence and goodwill. It must develop a clear corporate identity. This involves answering an extremely difficult question, What does it want to be? Whether or not the company answers this question, it *will be* something to its customers and other publics. Its products, employees, and actions will communicate something. And what is communicated should not be left to chance.

The company that can establish a reputation for trustworthiness, progressiveness, and social responsibility starts with an advantage over other firms in the minds of actual and potential customers and other publics. The corporate aura lends a halo effect to the individual corporate divisions, product lines, and brands. Many buyers, when it comes to explaining why they chose one company over another, in the end say they have more confidence in that company. Customer confidence is built through a combination of satisfying offers and effective communications. Neither alone will do the job. Companies are increasingly recognizing the value of creating an integrated communications program that reflects the company's identity in all of the things that it does.

This chapter will look at the major tools in the marketing communications mix and then at a model of the marketing communications process. Finally we will discuss planning the marketing communications program. The following three chapters will take up advertising, sales promotion and publicity, and sales force, and examine the major decisions involved in each.

THE MARKETING COMMUNICATIONS MIX

One can take a broad or a narrow view of the tools in the marketing communications mix. The broad view says that each of the four *P*s belongs in the marketing communications mix. The product's styling, the color and shape of the packaging, and the price all communicate something. Once the company decides on a target market position, all the marketing-mix tools should reinforce this position.

The narrow view says the marketing communications mix consists of the subset of marketing tools that are primarily "communicational" in nature. They are the tools normally classified under promotion, one of the four *P*s. They are called *promotools,* and include various forms of advertising, packaging, sales presentations and demonstrations, point-of-purchase displays, sales aids (catalogs, literature, films), incentive tools (contests, trading stamps, premiums, free samples, coupons), and publicity programs.

Each of these promotools has specific potentialities and complexities that could justify managerial specialization. Yet a company, even a very large one, typically does not have a specialist in each area but only in those areas where the importance and usage frequency of the tool warrant specialization. Historically, companies first made a separate function out of *personal selling,* later out of *advertising,* still later out of *sales promotion,* and ultimately out of *publicity.* These four major tools are defined as follows:

Advertising. Any paid form of nonpersonal presentation and promotion of ideas, goods, or services by an identified sponsor.

Personal selling. Oral presentation in a conversation with one or more prospective purchasers for the purpose of making sales.

Sales promotion. Short-term incentives to encourage purchase or sale of a product or service.

Publicity. Nonpersonal stimulation of demand for a product, service, or business unit by planting commercially significant news about it in a published medium or obtaining favorable presentation of it upon radio, television, or stage that is not paid for by the sponsor.[1]

Here we will discuss the special qualities of each promotional component.

Advertising

Advertising comes in many forms and has many uses. It involves such varied media as magazines and newspapers, radio and television, outdoor displays (such as posters, signs, skywriting), direct mail, novelties (matchboxes, blotters, calendars), cards (car, bus), catalogs, directories, and circulars. It can be carried out for such diverse purposes as long-term buildup of the company name (*institutional advertising*), long-term buildup of a particular brand (*brand advertising*), information dissemination about a sale, service, or event (*classified advertising*), announcement of a special sale (*sales advertising*), and so on.

Because of the many forms and uses of advertising, it is hard to advance all-embracing generalizations about its distinctive qualities as a component of the marketing communications mix. Yet the following qualities can be noted:

1. *Public presentation.* Advertising, unlike personal selling, is a highly public mode of communication. Its public nature confers a kind of legitimacy to the product and also suggests a standardized offering. Because many persons receive the same message, buyers know that their motives for purchasing the product will be publicly understood.
2. *Pervasiveness.* Advertising is a pervasive medium that permits the seller to repeat a message many times. It also allows the buyer to receive and compare the messages of various competitors. Large-scale advertising by a seller says something positive about the seller's size, popularity, and success.
3. *Amplified expressiveness.* Advertising provides opportunities for dramatizing the company and its products through the artful use of print, sound, and color. Sometimes the tool's very success at expressiveness may, however, dilute or distract from the message.
4. *Impersonality.* Advertising, in spite of being public, pervasive, and expressive, cannot be as compelling as a company sales representative. The audience does not feel obligated to pay attention or respond. Advertising is only able to carry on a monologue, not a dialogue, with the audience.[2]

Personal Selling

Personal selling also takes several forms, such as sales calls by a field representative (field selling), assistance by a salesclerk (retail selling), and a golf invitation from one company president to another (executive selling). It can be used for many purposes, such as creating product awareness, arousing interest, developing product preference, negotiating prices and other terms, closing a sale, and

[1] These definitions, with the exception of the one for sales promotion, came from *Marketing Definitions: A Glossary of Marketing Terms* (Chicago: American Marketing Association, 1960). The AMA definition of sales promotion covers, in addition to incentives, such marketing media as displays, shows and exhibitions, and demonstrations that can better be classified as forms of advertising, personal selling, or publicity. Some marketing scholars have also suggested adding packaging as a fifth element of the promotion mix, although others classify it as a product element.

[2] The distinctive qualities of advertising and personal selling, are adapted from Sidney J. Levy, *Promotional Behavior* (Glenview, Ill.: Scott, Foresman & Company, 1971), chap. 4.

providing posttransactional reinforcement. Personal selling has certain distinctive qualities:

1. *Personal confrontation.* Personal selling involves an alive, immediate, and interactive relationship between two or more persons. Each party is able to observe at close hand the characteristics and needs of the other and make immediate adjustments. Each party has the potentiality to help or hurt the other by showing interest or lack of it, and this can make the encounter stressful.

2. *Cultivation.* Personal selling permits all kinds of relationships to spring up, ranging from a matter-of-fact selling relationship to a deep personal friendship. In most cases, the sales representative must use art to woo the buyer. The sales representative at times will be tempted to put on pressure or to dissemble to get an order, but normally will keep the customer's long-run interests at heart.

3. *Response.* Personal selling, in contrast with advertising, makes the buyer feel under some obligation for having listened to the sales talk or using up the sales representative's time. The buyer has a greater need to attend and respond, even if the response is a polite "thank you."

Sales Promotion

Sales promotion is the catchall for various promotools that are not formally classifiable as advertising, personal selling, or publicity. These tools may be subclassified into items for *consumer promotion* (e.g., samples, coupons, money-refund offers, prices-off, premiums, contests, trading stamps, demonstrations), *trade promotion* (e.g., buying allowances, free goods, merchandise allowances, cooperative advertising, push money, dealer sales contests), and *sales-force promotion* (e.g., bonuses, contests, sales rallies).

Although sales promotion tools are a motley collection, they have two distinctive qualities:

1. *Insistent presence.* Many sales promotion tools have an attention-getting, sometimes urgent, quality that can break through habits of buyer inertia toward a particular product. They tell the buyers of a chance that they won't have again to get something special. This appeals to a broad spectrum of buyers, although particularly to the economy minded, with the disadvantage that this type of buyer tends to be less loyal to any particular brand in the long run.

2. *Product demeaning.* Some of these tools suggest that the seller is anxious for the sale. If they are used too frequently or carelessly, they may lead buyers to wonder whether the brand is desirable or reasonably priced.

Publicity

A company and its products can come to the attention of the public through being newsworthy. The seller pays nothing for the news coverage. The results of free publicity can sometimes be spectacular. Consider the case of the diet drink Metrecal:

> Almost overnight, Metrecal became part of the American tribal customs, fashions and language. The signs were everywhere. Drugstores served Metrecal across soda fountains. Newspapers printed Metrecal-inspired cartoons. Fashionable luncheon clubs served Metrecal cocktails. Steve Allen and a probate judge in Charleston, South Carolina, wrote songs about Metrecal. Don Wilson, the announcer, danced "The Metrecal Bounce" on television. Overweight football players in Chicago ate at "the Metrecal table."[3]

[3] Peter Wyden, *The Overweight Society* (New York: William Morrow & Co., 1965), p. 50.

Publicity has three distinctive qualities:

1. *High credibility.* News stories and features seem to most readers to be authentic, media-originated reports. They have a higher degree of credibility than if they came across as sponsored by a seller.
2. *Off guard.* Publicity can reach many potential buyers who otherwise avoid salesmen and advertisements. This is because the message is packaged in a way that gets to the buyers as news rather than as a sales-directed communication.
3. *Dramatization.* Publicity has, like advertising, a potential for dramatizing a company or product.

A MODEL OF THE COMMUNICATIONS PROCESS

We are now ready to examine how the process of communications works. Years ago, Lasswell suggested that communications involve five major questions: *who . . . says what . . . in what channel . . . to whom . . . with what effect.*[4] These can be rephrased into saying that communications consist of a *sender* transmitting a *message* through *media* to a *receiver* who *responds.* Communications specialists spend their time doing source analysis, message analysis, media analysis, audience analysis, and response analysis.

We will use a slightly expanded version of this model, the one shown in Figure 18–1. The model consists of eight major communications elements. Two of them (in rectangles) represent the major parties in a communication—sender and receiver. Two others (in diamonds) represent the major communications tools—message and media. The remaining four (in ovals) represent major communication functions—encoding, decoding, response, and feedback. Each of these is defined below.

> *Sender.* The party sending the message to another party (also called the *source* or *communicator*).
>
> *Encoding.* The process of putting thought into symbolic form.
>
> *Message.* The set of symbols that the sender transmits.
>
> *Media.* The paths through which the message moves from sender to receiver.
>
> *Decoding.* The process by which the receiver assigns meaning to the symbols transmitted by the sender.
>
> *Receiver.* The party receiving the message sent by another party (also called the *audience* or *destination*).
>
> *Response.* The set of reactions that the receiver has after being exposed to the message.
>
> *Feedback.* The part of the receiver's response that the receiver communicates back to the sender.

The model indicates the factors in effective communications. Senders must know what audiences they want to reach and what responses they want. They must be skillful in encoding messages that take into account how the target audience tends to decode messages. They must transmit the message over efficient media that reach the target audience. They must develop feedback channels so that they can monitor whether the audience got the intended message.

[4] Harold D. Lasswell, *Power and Personality* (New York: W. W. Norton & Company, 1948), pp. 37–51.

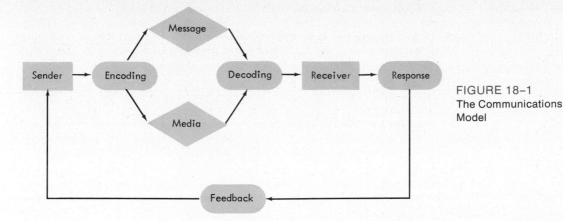

FIGURE 18–1
The Communications
Model

This might suggest that skillful communicators can exercise great powers of persuasion over their audiences, a view propounded in *The Hidden Persuaders*[5] and other books criticizing marketing communicators. However, the same model shows this is not the case. The audience is far from manipulable. The model shows an active rather than passive audience.[6] The audience, because of decoding, does not necessarily receive all of the message or receive it in the intended way.[7] Furthermore, the audience can show a wide variety of responses after decoding or interpreting the message. Finally, the audience may initiate or control the feedback to the sender, thus also playing the role of communicator. The audience, far from being passive, is an active party in the marketing dialogue.

The model permits the drawing together of many interesting findings about the communications process that have a bearing on effective marketing communications planning. We will discuss the elements not in the order of the *message flow* (from communicator to audience) but mainly in terms of the *planning flow* (from target audience backward to the communicator). The marketing communicator must make decisions on the following elements:

1. Who is the target audience? (Receiver)
2. What response should be sought? (Response and decoding)
3. What message should be developed? (Message and encoding)
4. What media should be used? (Media)
5. What source attributes should accompany the message? (Sender)
6. What feedback should be collected? (Feedback)

[5] Vance Packard, *The Hidden Persuaders* (New York: Pocket Books, 1957).

[6] See Joseph T. Klapper, *The Effects of Mass Communication* (New York: Free Press, 1960); Raymond A. Bauer, "The Limits of Persuasion," *Harvard Business Review*, September–October 1958, pp. 105–10; and Bauer, "The Initiative of the Audience," *Journal of Advertising Research*, June 1963, pp. 2–7.

[7] For example, an audience survey showed that many viewers of the popular "All in the Family" CBS program viewed Archie Bunker as a hero rather than as a narrow-minded and prejudiced American. See Neil Bidmar and Milton Rokeach, "Archie Bunker's Bigotry: A Study in Selective Perception and Exposure," *Journal of Communication*, winter 1974, pp. 36–47.

| Who Is the Target Audience? | A marketing communicator must start with a clear target audience in mind. The audience may be potential buyers of the company's products or current users, deciders, or influencers. The audience may be individuals, groups, particular publics, or the general public. The target audience will critically determine *what* is to be said, *how* it is to be said, *when* it is to be said, *where* it is to be said, and *who* is to say it. |

Given the target audience, the communicator has to research several audience characteristics, such as the audience's image of the company and its products, cognitive processing approach, needs and wants, product and brand preferences, and media habits. We will examine the first two characteristics here, the others being treated elsewhere in the book.

Audience image   A major part of audience analysis is to assess the audience's current image of the company, its products, and its competitors. People's attitudes and actions toward an object are highly conditioned by their beliefs about the object. *Image* is the term used to describe the *set of beliefs that a person or group holds of an object.*

At any point in time, the current image of an object is likely to lag behind the reality of the object. For example, a particular company may continue to be seen as the market leader long after its quality has started to slip. Another company might have a second-class image long after it has transformed itself into a first-class institution. Images can be five to ten years obsolete in the same way that we are not seeing a real star in the sky but an image of that star as it was earlier, since light takes time to travel. *Image persistence* is the result of people continuing to see what they expect to see, rather than what is. This means that it is very hard for a company to improve its image in a short time, even given a willingness to spend a great deal of money.

Furthermore, a company cannot change its image simply through communications effort. The image is a function of "good deeds plus good words." The company must live out what it wants to be and must use communications to tell the story. Some companies attempt to create phony images through slick communications campaigns, but this rarely succeeds because there is too much discrepancy between the message and the reality.

The communicator's task is to research the current image as a basis for deciding on communications objectives. This requires contacting a sample of people in the target audience and using some instrument to measure their image of the object in question. There are many instruments for image measurement,[8] but we shall describe here the popular one known as the *semantic differential*.[9]

The semantic differential involves creating a set of attribute scales with each attribute defined by bipolar adjectives. Figure 18–2 shows a set of nine scales used to measure the image of three brewing companies. The scales each have seven intervals, although there could have been five, nine, or some other number. More scales could have been added, but many would be redundant, since only a certain number of basic image dimensions exist. In fact, the creators

---

[8] For a discussion of various image-measurement techniques, see the author's *Marketing for Nonprofit Organizations* (Englewood Cliffs, N.J.: Prentice-Hall, 1975), pp. 131–37.

[9] The semantic differential technique was originally developed in C. E. Osgood, C. J. Suci, and P. H. Tannenbaum, *The Measurement of Meaning* (Urbana: University of Illinois Press, 1957).

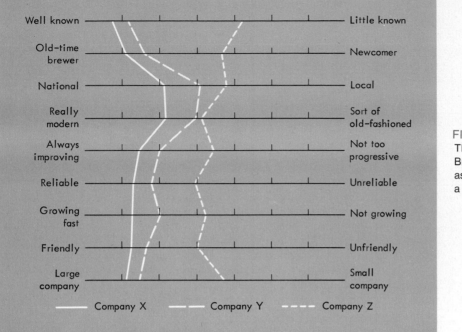

FIGURE 18–2
The Images of Three
Brewing Companies
as Measured by
a Semantic Differential

SOURCE: William A. Mindak, "Fitting the Semantic Differential to the Marketing Problem," *Journal of Marketing*, April 1961, pp. 28–33.

of the semantic differential suggest that images are measurable along three basic factors:

1. Evaluation (the good-bad qualities of the image)
2. Potency (strong-weak qualities)
3. Activity (active-passive qualities)

The various image attributes in Figure 18–2 all reflect either evaluation ("reliable, unreliable"), potency ("large company, small company"), or activity ("growing fast, not growing"). The image researcher simply has to make sure that enough scales have been developed to reflect these basic factors. Normally, the new instrument is tested on a small sample of people so that it can be refined before using it on a larger group.

Respondents are asked to place a mark on each scale according to their impression of the degree to which the object possesses that attribute. The image researcher then averages the responses on each scale and represents this average by a point. The points of the various scales are connected vertically, forming an image profile of the object. In Figure 18–2, company X has the best standing on each image attribute.[10] That is not always the case. More often, each company

[10] When administering the instrument, all of the favorable adjectives should not be on the same side, lest the respondents answer carelessly on the basis of a halo effect.

excels on certain attributes and lags on others. Even here, company X has some communication work to do in not being sufficiently "national" or "really modern." But even before concluding this, company X should ascertain where consumers see the ideal company (not shown) by asking them how "national" and how "modern" they would expect the ideal company to be.

To gain additional value from the data, the image profile should be recalculated for major groups in the market. For example, people in various parts of the country may hold different images of the same company. This would make a difference in establishing communications objectives for each group. Even within a given group, the image researcher should calculate the variance as well as the mean on each image attribute. We can imagine two extremes. The first is where there is high *image consistency,* in that most of the respondents see the object in approximately the same way. The way may or may not please the company, but nevertheless it is consistent. The other is where there is high *image diffusedness,* in that the respondents vary considerably in how they see the object. The company should not necessarily be disturbed by image diffusedness, and in fact, it may have deliberately cultivated some image ambiguity. This is essentially what politicians do who are running for office. They try to attain different images among diverse groups. Our main point is that the communicator will have to start with the existing images in the marketplace in determining the communication objectives.

Audience cognitive processing The communicator should also probe how the particular target audience processes incoming information. For example, people differ in cognitive complexity as a result of their native intelligence and education. A highly educated audience will be able to handle a larger and more complex set of symbols than will a group with a poor educational background. The communicator will want to know the tendencies of the target audience toward selective perception, distortion, and recall because this will affect the persuasive effectiveness of the message.

Of particular interest is the degree to which various audience groups are persuasible. Communicators have been looking for audience traits that correlate with persuasibility. For example, intelligence is widely thought to be negatively correlated with persuasibility, but the evidence is inconclusive. Women have been found to be more persuasible than men, but men who feel socially inadequate also show this trait.[11] Persons who accept external standards to guide their behavior and who have a weak self-concept appear to be more persuasible. Persons who are low in self-confidence are also thought to be more persuasible. However, research by Cox and Bauer and later by Bell showed a curvilinear relation between self-confidence and persuasibility, with those moderate in self-confidence being the most persuasible.[12] In general, the communicator should consider this research, look for audience traits that correlate with differential persuasibility, and use them to guide the message and media development.

[11] I. L. Janis and P. B. Field, "Sex Differences and Personality Factors Related to Personality," in *Personality and Persuasibility,* ed. C. Hovland and I. Janis (New Haven: Yale University Press, 1958), pp. 55–68.

[12] Donald F. Cox and Raymond A. Bauer, "Self-confidence and Persuasibility in Women," *Public Opinion Quarterly,* fall 1964, pp. 453–66; and Gerald D. Bell, February 1967, pp. 46–53: However, see the attempted refutation by Abe Shuchman and Michael Perry, "Self-confidence and Persuasibility in Marketing: A Reappraisal." *Journal of Marketing Research,* May 1969, pp. 146–54.

What Response Should Be Sought?

The next task of the marketing communicator is to define the target response it seeks. The ultimate response, of course, is purchase behavior. But purchase behavior does not occur *in vacuo*. In most cases, the consumer goes through a series of stages before deciding to purchase a product. It is critical that the marketing communicator know these buyer-readiness stages and assess where the target audience is at a particular time.

The marketer may be seeking a *cognitive, affective,* or *behavioral* response from the target audience. In other words, the purpose may be to put something into the consumer's mind, to change the consumer's attitude, or to get the consumer to undertake a specific action. Even here, there are different models of what each response consists of. Figure 18–3 shows four of the better-known *response hierarchy models.*

The AIDA model shows the buyer as passing through successive stages of awareness, interest, desire, and action. The "hierarchy-of-effects" model shows the buyer as passing through stages of awareness, knowledge, liking, preference, conviction, and purchase. The "innovation-adoption" model shows the buyer as passing through stages of awareness, interest, evaluation, trial, and adoption. The "communications" model shows the buyer as passing through stages of ex-

FIGURE 18–3
Response Hierarchy Models

Stages	"AIDA" Model[a]	"Hierarchy-of-Effects" Model[b]	"Innovation-Adoption" Model[c]	"Communications" Model[d]
			Models	
Cognitive stage	Attention	Awareness ↓ Knowledge	Awareness	Exposure ↓ Reception ↓ Cognitive response
Affective stage	Interest ↓ Desire	Liking ↓ Preference ↓ Conviction	Interest ↓ Evaluation	Attitude ↓ Intention
Behavior stage	Action	Purchase	Trial ↓ Adoption	Behavior

SOURCES: (a) E. K. Strong, *The Psychology of Selling* (New York: McGraw-Hill Book Company, 1925), p. 9; (b) Robert J. Lavidge and Gary A. Steiner, "A Model for Predictive Measurements of Advertising Effectiveness," *Journal of Marketing,* October 1961, p. 61; (c) Everett M. Rogers, *Diffusion of Innovations* (New York: Free Press, 1962), pp. 79–86; (d) Various sources.

475

posure, reception, cognitive response, attitude, intention, and behavior. Most of these differences are semantic.

The communicator normally assumes that buyers pass through these stages in succession on the way to purchase. However, there is some evidence that the stages can occur in different orders. Ray has distinguished three plausible response models.[13]

Learning response model The learning response model is the hierarchy showing a person passing from *cognition to affect to behavior.* It is particularly applicable where the buyer feels *involved* and there are *clear differences among alternatives.* It applies to high-involvement goods such as automobiles, washing machines, and computers. It suggests that the marketer should plan a communication campaign to first build product awareness and knowledge, then interest and conviction, and finally motivation to purchase.

Dissonance-attribution response model This model describes situations where buyers go through a *behavioral-affective-cognitive* sequence. They buy the product through the recommendation of a personal source, then their attitude changes through experience with the object, and then they learn about the product's attributes by paying attention to messages supporting that product. An example would be the purchase of insurance where a general agent recommends a particular policy and company, the customers buy it, then their attitude starts changing, and they watch for messages about this company. Their attitude changes after purchase to reduce dissonance, and their learning takes place as they attribute the purchase to their own volition. *Attribution (or self-perception) theory* says that when people are uncertain they develop their attitudes largely from making choices in actual situations rather than coming to these situations with strongly set attitudes.[14] This model applies primarily to situations where the audience is *involved,* but the alternatives are almost *indistinguishable.* For the marketer, it suggests that the main task is to induce trial or purchase through effective sales promotion incentives rather than relying on advertising to build up a favorable attitude. Attribution researchers have particularly investigated the effectiveness of the communication strategies of "foot-in-the-door" (making a small request as a prelude to a larger request) and "door-in-the-face" (making a large request that will probably be refused as a prelude to making a smaller request).[15] As for the role of mass media, according to this response model, its task is primarily to reduce dissonance *after* purchase and promote learning.

Low-involvement response model Here the consumer is thought to pass from *cognition to behavior to attitude change.* Krugman proposed this sequence for products where there is *low involvement* or *minimal differences* between alter-

[13] Michael L. Ray, *Marketing Communication and the Hierarchy-of-Effects* (Cambridge, Mass.: Marketing Science Institute, November 1973).

[14] D. Bem, "Self-Perception Theory," in *Advances in Experimental Social Psychology,* ed. L. Berkowitz (New York: Academic Press, 1972).

[15] A. Cann, S. Sherman, and R. E. Elkes, "Effects of Initial Request Size and Timing of a Second Request on Compliance: The Foot in the Door and the Door in the Face," *Journal of Personality and Social Psychology,* 32, 1975, pp. 774–82.

natives (e.g., detergents, flour).[16] Low involvement means that there is a low "number of conscious 'bridging experiences,' connections, or personal references per minute that the viewer made between his own life and the stimulus." Television advertising for these products is a low-involvement learning experience where many messages penetrate the person's normal perceptual defenses (because of low involvement) and create gradual perceptual shifts, such as awareness, but not attitude change. In the purchase situation, the consumer recognizes the product and buys it, and a change in attitude occurs after use. According to this model, the function of marketing communications is to build product awareness and to support favorable attitudes after purchase.

We will now look more closely at the response variables that the communicator wants to influence. We will use the response variables listed in the "communications model" in Figure 18–3.

Exposure   The first thing the communicator must do is to expose the message to the target audience. Exposure means that *the message physically appears in the target audience's immediate environment.* Thus a member of the target audience reads the newspaper or magazine, listens to the radio or television station or comes into contact with the person carrying the message.

To achieve exposure, the communicator must study the media habits of the target audience. Most media vehicles publish data, with varying degrees of accuracy, on the size and composition of their audiences. The communicator is guided by the media cost in relation to the size of the target audience delivered by a given vehicle. The most common measure of exposure efficiency is *cost-per-thousand exposures.* The communicator seeks to select media that minimize the cost-per-thousand exposures.

Reception   Given an exposure, the next question is whether there is reception of the message. Did the message actually enter the receiver's consciousness? This breaks down into two issues: whether there is message *attention* and whether there is message *comprehension* by the receiver.

Any receiver who is exposed to a particular media vehicle has an *attention probability* somewhere between zero and one. Attention is a function of (1) the amount and strength of competing stimuli in the immediate environment, (2) the receiver's traits, (3) the receiver's media-using habits, and (4) the situational context. The receiver is bombarded by approximately fifteen hundred commercial messages every day. This gives rise to a condition known as *sensory overload.* The receiver copes with sensory overload by ignoring most of the messages in the environment. Receivers vary, of course, in the messages that they pay attention to, a phenomenon known as *selective attention.* A person in the market for a car will notice automobile advertising, whereas this advertising will be lost on other people. People also vary in their media-using habits. Thus some readers of *Newsweek* will read every ad of every issue (probability of attention = 1), other readers will read about half of the ads of every issue (probability of attention = ½), and still others will read about half of the ads in half of the issues (probability of attention = ¼). Finally, the situational context will influence attention, as when a person has an hour to read *Newsweek* versus only five minutes because of having to be somewhere.

[16] Herbert E. Krugman, "The Impact of Television Advertising: Learning without Involvement," *Public Opinion Quarterly*, fall 1965, pp. 349–56.

The challenge to the communicator is to design a message that wins attention in spite of the surrounding distractions. Schramm has suggested that the likelihood that a potential receiver will attend to a message is given by:[17]

$$\frac{\text{Likelihood}}{\text{of attention}} = \frac{\text{(Perceived reward strength)} - \text{(Perceived punishment strength)}}{\text{Perceived expenditure of effort}}$$

This explains why ads with bold headlines promising something, such as "How to Make a Million," along with an arresting illustration and little copy have a high likelihood of grabbing attention. For very little effort, the reader has an opportunity to gain a great reward.

Communicators have developed several devices for attracting attention, including *novelty and contrast, arresting pictures or headlines, distinctive formats, message size and position,* and *color, shape, and movement.*[18]

Achieving attention is not enough. The communicator also wants the receiver to correctly *comprehend* the message. Comprehension is measured by asking people who have been exposed to a message to play it back or describe its intent. The more complex the message, the poorer the comprehension is likely to be. Some people will get the intended message, others will forget some important parts, and still others will completely misconstrue the major points. Loss of comprehension efficiency is due to audience tendencies toward *selective attention, recall,* and *distortion.* Receivers often add things to the message that are not there (*amplification*) and do not notice other things that *are* there (*leveling*). The communicator's task is to do the best job possible in achieving message simplicity, clarity, interest, and repetition to get the main points across.

Cognitive response   The communicator is really aiming to get the message accepted and assimilated into the receiver's long-term memory. Long-term memory is the repository for all information one has ever processed. In entering the receiver's long-term memory, the message has a chance of modifying the receiver's beliefs and attitudes. But first the message has to enter the receiver's short-term memory, which is conceived as a limited-capacity store that represents and processes incoming information. Whether the message actually passes from the receiver's short-term to long-term memory depends upon the amount and type of *message rehearsal* by the receiver. Rehearsal does not mean simple message repetition but rather the receiver's elaborating on the meaning of the information in a way that retrieves into short-term memory related thoughts in the receiver's long-term memory. If the receiver's initial attitude toward the object is positive and he or she rehearses support arguments, the message is likely to be accepted and have high recall. If the receiver's initial attitude is negative and the person rehearses counterarguments, the message is likely to be rejected but to stay in long-term memory. If there is no rehearsal of arguments but simply, "I've heard this before" or "I don't believe it," there is not likely to be high

[17] Wilbur Schramm and Donald F. Roberts, eds., *The Process and Effects of Mass Communication* (Urbana: University of Illinois Press, 1971), p. 32.

[18] For a summary of some findings on these attention-attracting devices, see James F. Engel, Roger D. Blackwell, and David T. Kollat, *Consumer Behavior,* 3rd ed. (Hinsdale, Ill.: Dryden Press, 1978), pp. 346–48.

recall or any attitude change. Generally speaking, much of what is called persuasion is self-persuasion.[19]

Attitude To the extent that the acceptance of a message alters the beliefs about the object or their relative weights, the receiver's attitude toward the object will be altered. This supposition is based on Fishbein's model showing attitudes as a function of beliefs (see expectancy value model, p. 160). An effective message will predispose the consumer to view the object more favorably. Since we have discussed attitude elsewhere, we will not elaborate on it here.

Intention People who have a positive attitude toward an object will not necessarily buy it. A person must form an intention to buy. The person has to feel like the kind of person who buys this object and must see others whom he respects as approving of the purchase. Fishbein calls these *personal normative beliefs* and *social normative beliefs* and says that they must support the person's attitude toward the object for a buying intention to be formed.

What can the communicator do to increase the person's intention to buy the object? The communicator can develop messages that weaken objections, such as that the product costs too much, or that it does not fit the buyer's personality, or that friends will look askance. Furthermore, the communicator can try to create a sense of urgency to buy the product now, such as implying that prices will go up or that the goods will go out of stock. Sales representatives use a number of devices to get a buyer to act, such as asking when the buyer will make a decision, or offering a discount or premium if the order is placed now.

Behavior We know that buyers do not always carry out their intentions. Their stated intentions are not the same as commitments; they are simply their own predictions as to what they might do. The main factors causing intentions not to be carried out are inertia or the occurrence of unpredictable events. The buyer might never quite make it to the auto showroom, dislike the salesperson, or lose a job. The communicator cannot do much to counteract extraneous events that undermine the buyer's purchase intention.

The communicator is interested not only in whether the consumer buys, but also in whether and how the consumer talks about the product to others. Part of the message strategy of the marketer is to provide information that will reduce postpurchase dissonance, refute inaccurate impressions, and provide a language for speaking favorably about the product.

What Message Should Be Developed?

Knowing the target audience and the desired response, the communicator can proceed to formulate an appropriate message. The communicator has to solve three problems: what to say (*message content*), how to say it logically (*message structure*), and how to say it symbolically (*message format*).

Message content The communicator has to figure out what to say to the target audience that will produce the desired response. This has been variously called the *appeal, theme, idea,* or *unique selling proposition*. It amounts to formulating

[19] A. Greenwald, "Cognitive Learning, Cognitive Response to Persuasion, and Attitude Change," in *Psychological Foundations of Attitudes*, ed. A. Greenwald, T. Brock, and T. Ostrom (New York: Academic Press, 1968).

some kind of benefit, motivator, identification, or reason why the audience should think or do something.

Ever since Aristotle, it has been traditional to distinguish between rational, emotional, and moral appeals. *Rational appeals* are appeals directed to the rational self-interest of the audience. They attempt to show that the product will yield the expected functional benefits. Examples would be messages demonstrating a product's quality, economy, value, or performance. It is widely believed that industrial buyers are most responsive to rational appeals. They are knowledgeable about the product class, trained to recognize value, and accountable to others for their choice. They have the time and incentive to compare different suppliers' offers and choose the best. Consumers, when they buy big-ticket items, are also thought to gather information and make careful comparisons of alternative offers. They will respond to quality, economy, performance, and other appeals.

Emotional appeals are appeals designed to stir up some negative or positive emotion that will motivate product interest or purchase. Communicators have worked with such negative emotional appeals as fear, guilt, and shame, especially in connection with getting people to start doing things they should (e.g., brushing their teeth, having an annual health checkup) or stop doing things they shouldn't (e.g., smoking, overdrinking of alcohol, drug abuse, overeating).

The use of fear appeals has been studied more than any other negative emotional appeal, not only in marketing communications but also in politics and child rearing. It used to be held that the message's effectiveness increased with the level of fear presented. The more fear building, the more tension, and the greater the drive to reduce the tension. Then the famous study of Janis and Feshbach, in which they tested the effectiveness of different fear levels in a dental-hygiene message directed to high school students, indicated that the strong fear appeal was less effective than a moderate one in producing adherence to a recommended dental hygiene program.[20] For a while, this finding became the standard, that neither extremely strong nor weak fear appeals were as effective as moderate ones. Ray and Wilke supported this position by hypothesizing two types of effects as fear increases:

> First, there are the facilitating effects that are most often overlooked in marketing. If fear can heighten drive, there is the possibility of greater attention and interest in the product and message than if no drive were aroused. . . . But fear also brings the important characteristic of inhibition into the picture. . . . If fear levels are too high, there is the possibility of defensive avoidance of the ad, denial of the threat, selective exposure or distortion of the ad's meaning, or a view of the recommendations as being inadequate to deal with so important a fear.[21]

Other researchers have found cases where high fear appeals appear maximally effective. This may mean that the buyers have different tolerances for fear, and the level of the fear message should be set separately for different segments. Further, if the fear message is to be maximally effective, the communication should

---

[20] Irving L. Janis and Seymour Feshbach, "Effects of Fear-Arousing Communications," *Journal of Abnormal and Social Psychology*, January 1953, pp. 78–92.

[21] Michael L. Ray and William L. Wilkie, "Fear: The Potential of an Appeal Neglected by Marketing," *Journal of Marketing*, January 1970, pp. 55–56.

promise to relieve in a believable and efficient way the fear it arouses; otherwise the buyers will ignore or minimize the threat.[22]

What about the effectiveness of positive emotional appeals, such as love, humor, pride, and joy? For example, a recent campaign to encourage young people to attach their auto seat belts showed a young man asking his woman friend to put on her belt as a way of saying, "I love you." Motivation researchers have found that persons may more often undertake to do something out of love for others than out of fear of harm to themselves. Marketers have also successfully used messages communicating joy (e.g., some soft-drink ads) associated with using the product. As for humor, the evidence has not established that a humorous message is necessarily more effective than a straight version of the same message.[23] On the positive side, humorous messages probably attract more attention and create more liking and belief in the source; but humor may also detract from comprehension. David Ogilvy, head of a major advertising agency, believes that humor is overused: "People are amused by clowns—they don't buy from them. . . . So many people in advertising are compulsive entertainers who seek applause rather than sales."

Moral appeals are appeals to the receiver's sense of what is right and proper to do. They are often used in messages exhorting people to support high-consensus social causes such as a cleaner environment, better race relations, equal rights for women, and aiding the disadvantaged. An example is the March of Dimes appeal: "God made you whole. Give to help those He didn't." They are less often used in connection with mundane products. This society is not highly responsive to moral appeals as such, although in many societies moral appeals are highly effective.

Message structure The persuasive effect of a communication is affected not only by its content but also by the manner in which it is structured. Research carried on many years ago by Hovland and his associates at Yale shed much light on the major issues in message structure, namely, conclusion drawing, one- versus two-sided arguments, and order of presentation.

Conclusion drawing raises the question of whether the communicator should draw a definite conclusion for the audience or leave it to them. In a laboratory-type experiment, Hovland and Mandell found that more than twice as many persons changed in the direction advocated when the conclusion was stated than when they were left to form their own conclusions.[24] However, other studies produced conflicting results, and it appears that some situations are unfavorable to conclusion drawing:

1. If the communicator is seen as untrustworthy, the audience may resent the attempt to influence them.

---

[22] See Carl I. Hovland, Irving L. Janis, and Harold H. Kelley, *Communication and Persuasion* (New Haven: Yale University Press, 1953), pp. 87–88.

[23] See Brian Sternthal and C. Samuel Craig, "Humor in Advertising," *Journal of Marketing*, October 1973, pp. 12–18.

[24] Carl I. Hovland and Wallace Mandell, "An Experimental Comparison of Conclusion-Drawing by the Communication and by the Audience," *Journal of Abnormal and Social Psychology*, July 1952, pp. 581–88.

2. If the issue is simple, or the audience is intelligent, the audience may be annoyed at the attempt to explain the obvious.

3. If the issue is highly personal, the audience may resent the communicator's interference.

Sometimes drawing too explicit a conclusion, especially in the area of new products, can overly limit the product's acceptance. If the Mustang people had hammered away at the point that the car was for young people, this strong definition might have ruled out the many other age groups who were attracted to it. Some *stimulus ambiguity* can play a definite role in leading to a broader market definition and more spontaneous uses of new products. It permits more people to read their own meaning into the product. Conclusion drawing seems better suited for complex or specialized products where a single and clear use is intended.

One- or two-sided arguments raise the question of whether the communicator should only praise the product or also mention or anticipate some of its shortcomings. Intuitively, it would appear that the best effect is gained by a one-sided presentation: this is the predominant approach in sales presentations, political contests, and child rearing. Yet the answer is not so clear-cut. It depends on such things as the initial position of the audience, the audience's level of education, and the audience's exposure to subsequent communication.[25] (1) *One-sided messages tend to work best with audiences that are initially favorably predisposed to the communicator's position, whereas two-sided arguments tend to work best with audiences who are opposed.* A seller of a new brand whose other products are well accepted might think of favorably mentioning the existing products and then going on to praise his new product. (2) *Two-sided messages tend to be more effective with better-educated audiences.* A salesperson dealing with engineers might not pretend his or her product has it all over competing products but mention more factually where it excels and where it lags. (3) *Two-sided messages tend to be more effective with audiences who are likely to be exposed to counterpropaganda.* By mentioning a minor shortcoming in the product, a salesperson takes the edge off this mention when it comes from a competitor, much as a small discomforting inoculation now prevents a greater sickness later. But he or she must be careful to inoculate only enough negative vaccine to make the buyer resistant to counterpropaganda, not to his or her own product. The success of some products that emphasize minor limitations, such as Benson & Hedges, Volkswagen, and Avis, derives from a two-sided message strategy.

Order of presentation raises the question of whether a communicator should present his or her strongest arguments first or last. In the case of a one-sided message, presenting the strongest argument first has the advantage of establishing attention and interest. This may be especially important in newspapers and other media where the audience does not attend to all of the message. However, it means an anticlimactic presentation. If the audience is captive, as in a sales presentation or conference, then a climactic presentation may be more effective. Studies have yielded both findings, and we can say only that the strongest arguments do *not* belong in the middle of the message. In the case of a two-sided message, the issue is whether to present the positive argument

[25] See C. I. Hovland, A. A. Lumsdaine, and F. D. Sheffield, *Experiments on Mass Communication*, vol. III (Princeton, N.J.: Princeton University Press, 1948), chap. 8.

first (primacy effect) or last (recency effect). If the audience is initially opposed, it would appear that the communicator would be smarter to start with the other side's argument. This will tend to disarm the audience and allow him to conclude with his strongest argument. It does not appear that either the primacy or the recency effect dominates in all or most situations, and more research is needed into the underlying processes.

Message format   The remaining task in message development is to choose the most effective symbols to implement the message content and structure strategy. If the message is to be carried in a print ad, the communicator has to develop the format elements of headline, copy, illustration, and color. A good message strategy can be ruined by a poor message format. If the message is to be carried over radio, the communicator has to choose words, voice qualities (speech rate, rhythm, pitch, articulation) and vocalizations (pauses, sighs, yawns). The sound of an announcer promoting used automobiles has to be different from the sound of an announcer advertising a soft, comfortable bed mattress. If the message is to be carried over television or in person, then all of these elements plus body language (nonverbal clues) have to be planned. Thus politicians have to pay as much attention to their facial expressions, gestures, dress, posture, and hair style as to what they are saying. Finally, if the message is to be carried by a product and its packaging, the message designer will have to pay attention to texture, scent, noise, color, size, and shape. For example, it is well known that color plays an important communication role in food preference. When housewives sampled four cups of coffee next to brown, blue, red, and yellow containers (all the coffee was identical, although this was unknown to the housewives), 75 percent felt the coffee next to the brown container tasted too strong; nearly 85 percent judged the coffee next to the red can to be the richest; nearly everyone felt the coffee next to the blue can was mild and next to the yellow can was weak.

What Media Should Be Used?

Knowing the target audience, desired response, and message, the communicator can now turn to the selection of efficient media, that is, channels of communication or influence. Channels of communication are of two broad types, *personal* and *nonpersonal*.

Personal influence channels are means of direct contact with target individuals or groups. Three types can be distinguished. *Advocate channels* consist of company representatives in personal contact with the buyers, trying to influence them. *Expert channels* consist of independent persons (consultants, authorities) exercising an influence on the buyers through their expertise. *Social channels* consist of the buyers' associates, neighbors, friends, or family who may exercise an influence on the buyers. This last channel is also known as *word-of-mouth influence,* and it may be the strongest of the three personal channels, especially in the consumer-products area.

Nonpersonal influence channels are media that carry influence without involving direct contact. Three types of nonpersonal media can be distinguished. *Mass and selective media* consist of newspapers, magazines, radio, television, and billboards that people might buy or perceive. Mass media are aimed at large, often undifferentiated audiences; selective media are aimed at specialized audiences. *Atmospheres* are environments that are designed to create or reinforce the buyer's leanings toward purchase or consumption of the product. Thus dentists, lawyers, and boutique stores each design atmospheres that communicate confidence and other things that might be valued by the clients.[26] *Events* are occurrences that are designed to communicate particular messages to target audiences. Modern organizations, through their public relations department, arrange events that they hope will be newsworthy enough to be picked up and amplified by the news media.

We shall now look more closely at the major channels of influence.

Person-to-person communication   There has been much discussion of the relative effectiveness of personal versus nonpersonal influence in changing attitudes and behavior. Most observers believe that personal influence is generally the more potent of the two, especially in two cases:

1. *Where the product is expensive, risky, or purchased infrequently.* In such cases, buyers are likely to be high information seekers. They will probably go beyond mass-media information and seek out the product experiences and opinions of knowledgeable and trusted sources.
2. *Where the product has a significantly social, as opposed to private, character.* Such products as automobiles, clothing, and even beer and cigarettes have significant brand differentiation that implies something about the status or taste of the users. Here users are likely to choose brands acceptable to their groups.

This should normally incline marketers to favor personal influence channels over mass media. Unfortunately, marketers have limited control over personal influence channels. They cannot hire neighbors and friends to speak favorably about their products. Ironically what little control they have comes through the mass media! According to Klapper: "Personal influence may be more effective than persuasive mass communication, but at present mass communications seems the most effective means of stimulating personal influence."[27]

Thus the relationship and relative influence of personal influence and mass communication is more complicated than it at first appears. Many observers hold that mass communications affect personal attitudes and behavior through a *two-step flow-of-communication process.* "Ideas often flow from radio and print to opinion leaders and from these to the less active sections of the population."[28]

If true, this hypothesis has several significant implications. First it says that mass media's influence on mass opinion is not as direct, powerful, and automatic as supposed. It is mediated by *opinion leaders,* persons who are members of primary groups and whose opinions tend to be sought out in one or more areas. Opinion leaders are more exposed to mass media than the people they influence. They are the carriers of the messages to people who are less exposed to media, thus extending the influence of the mass media; or they may carry altered or no messages, thus acting as *gatekeepers.*

[26] See Philip Kotler, "Atmospherics as a Marketing Tool," *Journal of Retailing,* winter 1973–74, pp. 48–64.

[27] Joseph T. Klapper, *The Effects of Mass Communication* (New York: Free Press, 1960), p. 72.

[28] P. F. Lazarsfeld, B. Berelson, and H. Gaudet, *The People's Choice,* 2nd ed. (New York: Columbia University Press, 1948), p. 151.

Second, the hypothesis challenges the notion that persons are influenced in their consumption styles primarily from a "trickle-down" effect from the higher-status classes. Since people primarily interact with others in their own social class, they pick up their fashion and other ideas in this way—from people like themselves who are opinion leaders.

A third implication is that the mass communicator may accomplish message dissemination more efficiently by using a lower advertising budget and directing it specifically at opinion leaders, letting them carry the message to others. Thus a pharmaceutical firm may direct new-drug promotion to influential doctors. In many markets, however, opinion leaders and the people whom they influence are very much alike. It is hard to identify opinion leaders, aim communications specifically at them, and trust that they will say positive things about the product.

Although the two-step flow-of-communication hypothesis opened up some important new understandings about the flow of influence, it also has certain difficulties as a theory, and it could be misleading if used literally. The following qualifications must be made:

1. Opinion leadership is not a dichotomous trait. It is a matter of degree. All group members may have some opinion leadership in certain areas of consumption.

2. Opinion followers do not get their information only from opinion leaders. They too are in touch with mass media, although a little less so.

3. An effective mass-media strategy might be to aim messages at everyone and stimulate *opinion seeking;* this is a useful way to use opinion leaders.[29]

More recently, communications researchers have been moving toward a social structure view of interpersonal communication.[30] They see society as made up of *cliques,* that is, social subsystems whose members interact with each other relatively more frequently than with other members of the social system. The members of the cliques are highly similar, thus constituting an "interlocking network." Their similarity and close attraction facilitate effective communication but also act as barriers to new ideas entering the network. The challenge is to create more system openness whereby cliques exchange more information with each other and the larger environment. This is accomplished by persons who play roles as liaisons and bridges. A *liaison* is a person who interpersonally connects two or more cliques without belonging to either clique. A *bridge* is a person who is a member of one clique and who has a link to a person who is a member of another clique. Word-of-mouth communications flow most readily within cliques, and the problem is one of facilitating a communication flow between cliques.

Companies can take some steps to stimulate personal influence channels to work on their behalf, even if their actual control is somewhat limited. Among the things they can do are:

[29] For further discussion, see Elihu Katz, "The Two-Step Flow of Communication," *Public Opinion Quarterly,* spring 1957, pp. 61–78; and Everett M. Rogers, *Modernization among Peasants: The Impact of Communication* (New York: Holt, Rinehart and Winston, 1969), p. 222.

[30] See Everett M. Rogers, "New Product Adoption and Diffusion," *The Journal of Consumer Research,* March 1976, pp. 290–301.

1. Observe whether certain individuals or companies seem to stand out as influentials in their groups and devote extra effort to them, either through personal attention, direct mail, or advertising.

2. Create opinion leaders out of certain persons, by supplying them with the product on attractive terms, or selecting them as company representatives.

3. Work through community influentials such as disc jockeys, class presidents, and presidents of women's organizations.

4. Let the advertising feature interpersonal discussion of products or testimonials by influentials as part of the content.

5. Develop advertising that is high in conversational value.

6. Choose salesmen who are of the same general social status as their prospects.[31]

Mass communication   Mass-communication channels tend to have a less insistent presence than personal communication channels, which means that audience members can more easily avoid or tune them out. Even during high-saturation campaigns, many members of the audience will not be reached. Three psychological processes, commonly referred to as factors of *perceptual defense,* operate to cut down the reach and impact of mass media. *Selective attention* means that a person notes only a small fraction of all the media vehicles and only a small fraction of their content. *Selective distortion* means that the person perceives the content differently than intended—because it is filtered through personal needs and beliefs. *Selective retention* means that the person remembers certain things better than others—again because of the personal needs and beliefs.

Thus the communicator's ability to reach and persuade a target audience is highly constrained. The communicator's best course of action is to identify the major channels of influence that reach the target audience: groups they are in touch with, newspapers and magazines they read, people they respect. These are then rated according to the influence they have on members of the target audience and the costs of trying to activate them to carry the message. For each communication channel, a benefit-cost analysis is made. The communicator then develops a media mix that optimizes message distribution and impact for a given budget or minimizes the message cost of achieving a given level of message distribution and impact. We shall say more about media selection in chapter 19, pages 508–16.

What Source Attributes Should Accompany the Message?

Communicators influence their audience through their choice of message and media and through how they are perceived by the audience. The latter is called the *source effect.*

Source credibility   Marketers have known for years that messages delivered by highly credible sources will add to the persuasiveness of a message. Pharmaceutical companies will quote doctors' opinions to testify to their products' benefits because doctors have high credibility. Antidrug crusaders will use former drug addicts to warn high school students against drugs because exaddicts have higher credibility than teachers. Other marketers will hire well-known personalities, such as newscasters or athletes, to carry their messages.

But what factors underlie source credibility? The three factors most often

[31] These and other points are discussed in Thomas S. Robertson, *Innovative Behavior and Communication* (New York: Holt, Rinehart and Winston, 1971), chap. 9.

identified are expertise, trustworthiness, and likability.[32] *Expertise* is the degree to which the communicator is perceived to possess the necessary authority for what is being claimed. Doctors, scientists, and professors rank high on expertise where their advocacy pertains to their field of specialization. *Trustworthiness* is related to how objective and honest the source is perceived to be. Friends are perceived to be more trustworthy than strangers or salespeople. *Likability* is related to how attractive the source is to the audience. Qualities such as candor, humor, and naturalness tend to make a source more likable.

The most highly credible source, then, would be a person who scored high on all three dimensions. If such a message carrier could not be found, it would be helpful to know the relative influence of expertness, trustworthiness, and likability on message acceptance. This will of course vary for different products and situations.

Source incongruity   If a person has a positive attitude toward a source and a message—or a negative attitude toward both—a state of congruity is said to exist. But what happens if the person holds one attitude toward the source and the opposite toward the message? Suppose, for example, a homemaker hears a celebrity whom she likes praise a brand that she dislikes. Osgood and Tannenbaum posit that *attitude change will take place in the direction of increasing the amount of congruity between the two evaluations.*[33] In this example, the homemaker will end up respecting the celebrity somewhat less and respecting the brand somewhat more. If on further occasions she encounters the same celebrity praising other negatively valued brands, she will eventually develop a negative evaluation of the celebrity and maintain her negative attitudes toward the brands. The principle of congruity says that communicators can use their own good image to reduce some negative feelings toward a brand, but in the process may lose some of their trusted standing, especially if they do that often.

What Feedback Should Be Collected?

After the messages have been developed and distributed, the communicator must research the effects that these messages have on the target audience. This generally involves contacting a sample of members of the target audience and asking them whether they recognize or recall seeing or hearing the message, how many times, what points they recall, how they felt about the message, and their previous and current attitudes toward the product and company. Ultimately, the communicator would like to collect behavioral measures of audience response, such as how many people were moved to buy the product or to talk about it to others. Many companies settle for low-level measures of communications effectiveness, such as recall scores, when in fact the correlation of these measures with actual behavior may be very weak or even negative. If people counterargue with specific message content, they will recall counterarguments, associate them with message arguments, and exhibit good recall—but reject the message. Companies tend to spend comparatively little money researching what they are accomplishing with their communications, and yet careful monitoring of the results is at the heart of improving the impact of their communications.

[32] Herbert C. Kelman and Carl I. Hovland, " 'Reinstatement' of the Communicator in Delayed Measurement of Opinion Change," *Journal of Abnormal and Social Psychology*, 48 (1953), 327–35.

[33] C. E. Osgood and P. H. Tannenbaum, "The Principle of Congruity in the Prediction of Attitude Change," *Psychological Review*, 62 (1955), 42–55.

THE MARKETING COMMUNICATIONS PLANNING PROCESS

Having examined how the process of communications works and the various factors that influence communications effectiveness, we can appreciate the challenging task facing management. Management must make three major decisions in the communications arena:

1. What are the company's major communications objectives?
2. What total communications budget is necessary to accomplish these objectives?
3. How should the total communications budget be divided among the major communications tools?

Communications Objectives

Communications planning requires that the company has already developed its strategic management and marketing thrust, as discussed in chapter 4. It knows the business that it is in, the product/markets and market segments that it wants to reach, the product positions that it is aiming for, the resources and strengths that it has, and the basic marketing mix that it will use. It has analyzed the target markets with respect to awareness, knowledge, attitude, and buying behavior toward the company's and the competitors' products.

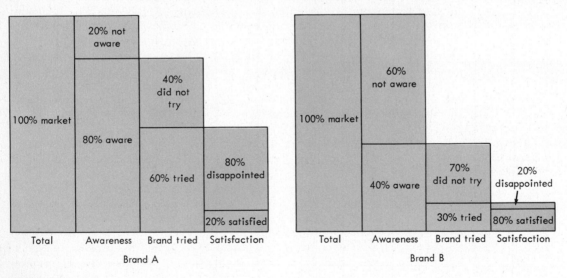

FIGURE 18–4
Current Consumer States for Two Brands

Communications objectives can be derived from analyzing how the target market is currently distributed over various states of readiness to buy the product. Consider a company that is preparing to set marketing communication objectives for two of its brands, A and B. For each brand the company has conducted marketing research to ascertain how many persons are in the market and the percentage distribution of these persons in three classes: awareness, brand trial, and satisfaction. The results are shown in Figure 18–4. As for brand A, 80 percent of the total market is aware of the brand, 60 percent have tried it and 20 percent of those who tried it are satisfied.[34] On the other hand, only 40 percent of the total market are aware of brand B, only 30 percent have tried it, and 80 percent of those who have tried it are satisfied. Clearly, these two profiles have very different implications for advertising objectives and strategy. The market is highly aware of brand A, but a substantial portion of those who have tried it are disappointed. This indicates that the advertising exposure schedule and creative message are effective in creating awareness but the product fails to live up to the claims. Brand B has the opposite problem. The advertising has produced only 40 percent awareness, and only 12 percent of the market have tried the product. But of those who have tried brand B, satisfaction runs in the order of 80 percent. In this case the entire advertising program, including the media, the message, and the level of expenditure may be much too weak to take advantage of the satisfaction-generating power of the brand.

Ottesen has suggested an alternative device called a *market map* for determining communication objectives (see Figure 18–5).[35] The horizontal dimension shows the current percentage of the market that has knowledge of the brand. This percentage increases through the life cycle of the brand, and in the illustration stands at 90 percent, indicating a mature brand. The vertical dimension shows the percentage of the market that has tried the brand. In this case, 80 percent of those who know the brand have tried it, another indication that the brand has been around for a while. There is a further breakdown of the knowers-triers into those who prefer (25 percent), are indifferent (50 percent), and have

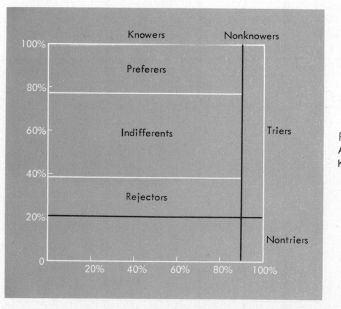

FIGURE 18–5
A Market Map Showing Percentage of Brand Knowers and Triers

[34] For a system for measuring these relationships, see John C. Maloney, "Attitude Measurement and Formation," a paper presented at the American Marketing Association Test Market Design and Measurement Workshop, Chicago, April 21, 1966.

[35] Otto Ottesen, "The Response Function," in *Current Theories in Scandinavian Mass Communications Research,* ed. Mie Berg (Grenaa, Denmark: G.M.T., 1977).

rejected (25 percent) the brand. We can imagine (not shown) a similar break-down of knower-nontriers into those who have a positive, indifferent, and negative attitude toward the brand.

The task is to set communications objectives for this brand. Since 90 percent of the target market already know the brand, it would not make sense to devote a large effort to building awareness in the remaining 10 percent. Ninety percent is a fairly high awareness level in the population. The 10 percent who do not know this brand consist of many persons who are not in the mainstream, who are unaware of most things, and who don't have much income. It gets increasingly expensive to reach these people and usually is not worth it.

What about using communications to get more knower-nontriers to try the product? This is a worthy objective and can be best accomplished through sales promotion (free samples, cents-off coupons, and so on) rather than through additional advertising or personal selling. Since 25 percent of the current triers prefer the brand, we cannot expect that more than 25 percent of the new triers will go for the brand. If so, the communicator should calculate whether achieving this number of new-trier preferers would be worth the cost of the contemplated sales promotion campaign.

Another possible communications objective is to try to increase the proportion of triers who prefer this brand to other brands. This is a difficult task since consumer attitude is largely a function of how the consumer experiences the value of the offer—e.g., performance and price rather than the communications appeal. If the company wants to increase preference, that is better accomplished through product improvement and lower prices.

Looking at the three trier attitude groups, the following conclusions can be drawn. Communication to those who already prefer the brand is usually not very productive unless there is high consumer forgetfulness or a high level of competitors' expenditure aimed at preferers. Communication directed to the rejectors is probably wasted because the rejectors are not likely to pay attention to the advertising and probably would not re-try the brand. Communication directed to the indifferents will probably be effective in attracting a proportion of their purchases, especially if the advertising has some point to make to this audience.

The main conclusion is that the communications objectives depend very much on the state of the market. When a brand is new, there are few knowers and triers, and communication can be very effective in increasing their number. When the brand is in the mature stage of its life cycle, it makes sense to try to convert nontriers into triers through sales promotion and to fight for a normal share of the indifferent triers; it makes less sense to try to increase the percentage of knowers, or reinforce preferers, or try to get rejectors to re-try the brand.

The Total Communications Budget

The total communications budget should be set at the level necessary to accomplish the communications objectives. The budget can be established by using "objectives-and-tasks" thinking; that is, deciding on the tasks that have to be performed to accomplish the communication objectives and then estimating their costs. Here is an example:

1. We want to convince 100,000 people to try our brand.
2. This means getting our message into the attention set of 1,000,000 people since only 1 in 10 will try the product after hearing about it.

3. We will need 8,000,000 exposures because only 1 in 8 exposures gains attention.

4. The average cost-per-thousand exposures to the type of audience we want is $6. Therefore we can buy 8,000,000 exposures for a total budget of around $48,000 (= $6 × 8,000,000/1,000).

In this way, management is able to estimate a total budget to accomplish a specific communication task.

The Communications Mix

Most companies set their total communications budget first and then divide it among the alternative communications tools. The most striking fact about the various communications tools is that they can be interchanged with each other and with other marketing mix elements. It is possible to achieve a given sales level by increasing advertising expenditures, personal selling, or sales promotion. It is also possible to achieve the same sales level by product improvement, lower prices, or additional customer services. This substitutability explains why marketing departments are increasingly trying to achieve administrative coordination over all of the tools of communications and marketing.

In allocating the communications budget to the various tools, companies should pay attention to the following four factors: (1) the type of product—consumer versus industrial, (2) the communications task to be accomplished, (3) the stage of the product life cycle, and (4) the economic outlook.

Type of product—consumer versus industrial Historically, there has been a considerable difference in the communication mixes used by consumer and industrial marketers. The mix differences are illustrated in Figure 18–6A. Advertising is widely felt to be the most important promotool in consumer marketing, and personal selling the most important promotool in industrial marketing. Sales promotion is considered of equal, though smaller, importance in both markets. And publicity is considered to have even smaller, but equal, importance in both markets.

FIGURE 18–6
Communications Mix as a Function of Type of Market and Buyer Readiness Stage

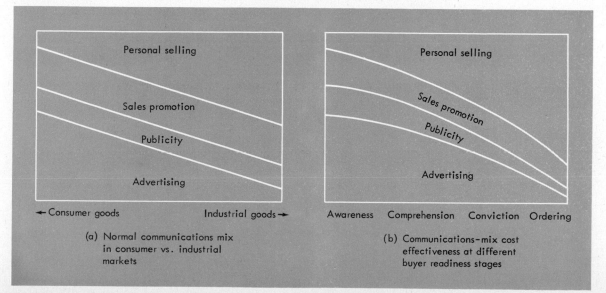

(a) Normal communications mix in consumer vs. industrial markets

(b) Communications-mix cost effectiveness at different buyer readiness stages

This view leads some marketers to act as if advertising is unimportant in industrial marketing and as if personal selling is unimportant in consumer marketing. Such conclusions are erroneous and can be refuted both in terms of common sense and by some recent studies.

While sales calls will normally have more impact than advertising in industrial marketing situations, especially where the product is complex, advertising can perform several useful functions:

1. *Awareness building.* Prospects who are not aware of the company or product may refuse to see the sales representative. Furthermore, the sales representative may have to use up a lot of time describing the company and its products.

2. *Comprehension building.* If the product embodies new features, some of the burden of explaining them can be effectively carried on by advertising.

3. *Efficient reminding.* If prospects know about the product but are not ready to buy, advertisements reminding them of the product would be much more economical than sales calls.

4. *Lead generation.* Advertisements carrying return coupons are an effective way to generate leads for sales representatives.

5. *Legitimation.* Sales representatives can use tear sheets of the company's advertisements to legitimatize their company and products.

6. *Reassurance.* Advertising can remind customers how to use the product and reassure them about their purchase.

A study by Theodore Levitt sought to determine the relative roles of the company's reputation (built mainly by advertising) and the company's sales presentation (personal selling) in producing industrial sales.[36] The experiment consisted of showing various groups of purchasing agents different filmed sales presentations of a new, but fictitious, technical product for use as an ingredient in making paint. The variables were the quality of the presentation and whether the sales person represented a well-known company, a less known but creditable company, or an unknown company. The reactions and ratings of the purchasing-agent groups were collected after the films and then again five weeks later. The findings were:

1. A company's generalized reputation (the source effect) has a positive influence on sales prospects in improving the chances of (a) getting a favorable first hearing and (b) getting an early adoption of the product. Therefore, to the extent that corporate advertising can build up the company's reputation (other factors also shape its reputation), the company's sales representatives will be helped.

2. Sales representatives from well-known companies have an edge in getting the sale, provided that their sales presentation is up to the expected standard. If, however, a sales representative from a less known company makes a highly effective sales presentation, that can overcome the disadvantage. To this extent, smaller companies may find it better to use their limited funds in selecting and training better sales representatives than in advertising.

3. Company reputations tend to have the most effect where the product is complex, the risk is high, and the purchasing agent is less professionally trained.

---

[36] Theodore Levitt, *Industrial Purchasing Behavior: A Study in Communications Effects* (Boston: Division of Research, Harvard Business School, 1965).

In general, the findings confirm the constructive role of both advertising and the source effect in the industrial marketing process.[37] Findings such as these have been developed by Cyril Freeman into a formal model for apportioning promotional funds between advertising and personal selling on the basis of the selling tasks that each performs more economically.[38]

In the same way that industrial marketers tend to play down the role of advertising, many consumer marketers tend to play down the role of the sales force. Many consumer companies use their inside sales force or an outside sales force mainly to collect weekly orders from dealers and to see that sufficient stock is on the shelf. The common feeling is that "salesmen put products on shelves and advertising takes them off." Yet even here, an effectively trained sales force can make three important contributions:

1. *Increased stock position.* Persuasive sales representatives can influence dealers to take more stock or devote more shelf space to the company's brand.
2. *Enthusiasm building.* Persuasive sales representatives can build dealer enthusiasm for a new product by dramatizing the planned advertising and sales promotion back-up.
3. *Missionary selling.* Sales representatives are crucial in any effort to sign up more dealers to carry the company's brands.

Within the same consumer industry, companies can be found that put quite different relative emphasis on the advertising, personal-selling mix. Nabisco and Kraftco rely very heavily on sales-force "push," while many of their competitors rely more heavily on advertising "pull." Revlon puts most of its promotional money into advertising, while Avon puts most of it into personal selling.

The communications task The optimal communication mix also depends on the nature of the communications task or objective. Communications tools differ in their cost effectiveness in accomplishing different objectives. For example, although industrial marketers will generally spend far more on personal selling than on advertising, it would be inefficient to use the sales force for all communications purposes. Figure 18–6B shows the general findings that have come out of a number of studies.[39] Advertising, sales promotion, and publicity are the most cost-effective tools in building buyer awareness, more than "cold calls" from sales representatives. Advertising is highly cost effective in producing comprehension, with personal selling coming in second. Buyer conviction is influenced most by personal selling, followed by advertising. Finally, placing an order is predominantly a function of the sales call, with an assist from sales promotion.

[37] Also see John E. Morrill, "Industrial Advertising Pays Off," *Harvard Business Review*, March–April 1970, pp. 4ff.

[38] Cyril Freeman, "How to Evaluate Advertising's Contribution," *Harvard Business Review*, July–August 1962, pp. 137–48.

[39] "What IBM Found About Ways to Influence Selling," *Business Week*, December 5, 1959, pp. 69–70; and Harold C. Cash and William J. Crissy, "Comparison of Advertising and Selling," in vol. 12 of *The Psychology of Selling* (Flushing, N.Y.: Personnel Development Associates, 1965).

These findings have important practical implications. First, the company could effect promotional economies by cutting back on the involvement of salespeople in the early stages of the selling job so that they can concentrate on the vital phase: closing the sale. Second, when advertising is relied on to do more of the job, it should take different forms, some addressed to building product awareness and some to producing comprehension.

The stage of the product life cycle The effectiveness of communications expenditures varies at different stages of the product life cycle.

Promotion is particularly important in the introduction stage because the market is not aware of the product. This task is carried out best by advertising and sales promotion, both of which can be conducted on a low-cost-per-thousand-people-reached basis. Sales promotion, particularly trade and consumer deals, facilitates interest and trial of the new product.

In the growth stage, word-of-mouth processes begin to work hard for the new product and partially replace or supplement company promotion efforts. If the company wants to build its market share, it should continue to promote vigorously during the growth stage.

The maturity stage is marked by intensified promotional expenditures to meet competition and to advertise new-product uses and features. There is generally an increase in *dealing* effort relative to *advertising* effort.

In the decline stage, many companies reduce their promotion expenditures to improve their profit margins. Publicity is cut down to zero; salesmen give the product only minimal attention; and advertising is cut down to a reminder level. Dealing is probably the most exercised promotion tool at this stage.

The economic outlook Companies would do well to revise their communications mixes with shifts in the economic outlook. During inflation, for example, buyers become highly price conscious. They will be on the lookout for value. The enterprising company can do at least three things to respond: (1) it can increase its sales promotion relative to advertising, since people are looking for deals; (2) it can emphasize value and price in its communications; and (3) it can develop messages that help customers know how and where to buy intelligently.

Responsibility for Marketing Communications Planning

Members of the marketing organization have strong and varied feelings about the proper proportions of the company's communications budget to spend on the different promotools. The sales manager finds it hard to understand how the company could get more value by spending $80,000 to buy a single exposure of a thirty-second television commercial than by hiring three or four additional sales representatives for a whole year. The public relations manager feels that the company can gain by transferring some of the advertising budget to publicity.

Historically, companies left these decisions to different people. No one was given the responsibility for thinking through the roles of the various promotional tools and coordinating the company's communication mix. Today companies are moving toward the concept of *integrated communications*. This concept calls for:

1. Developing a corporate position, such as marketing communications director, who has overall responsibility for the company's persuasive communications efforts

2. Working out a philosophy of the role and the extent to which the different promotools are to be used

3. Keeping track of all promotional investments by product, promotool, stage of product life cycle, and observed effect, as a basis for improving subsequent effective use of each tool

4. Coordinating the promotional activities and their timing when major campaigns take place

Integrated management of promotional activities promises more consistency in the company's *meaning* to its buyers and publics. It places a responsibility in someone's hand—where none existed before—to constructively unify and manage the company's image as it comes through the thousand activities the company carries on. It leads to the determination of a total marketing communications strategy aimed at showing how the company can help customers solve their problems.

SUMMARY

Marketing communications is one of the four major elements of the company's marketing mix. The instruments of marketing communications—advertising, personal selling, sales promotion, and publicity—have separate and overlapping capabilities, and their effective coordination requires careful definition of communications goals.

In preparing specific activities in marketing communications, the communicator has to understand the eight elements of any communication process: sender, receiver, encoding, decoding, message, media, response, and feedback. The communicator's first task is to identify the target audience, particularly to understand how they view the company and its product and how they process information. Next, the communicator has to establish the sought response, whether it is awareness, interest, desire, or action. Then a message must be constructed containing an effective content, structure, and format. Then media must be selected, for both person-to-person communication and mass communication. The message must be delivered by someone with good source credibility, particularly expertise, trustworthiness, and likability. Finally, the communicator must monitor how much of the market becomes aware and tries the product and is satisfied in the process.

The overall company planning of marketing communications requires establishing clear communications objectives, setting a communications budget that will achieve these objectives, and developing the most effective communications mix. In allocating the communications budget to different communications tools, the planner is guided by the type of product, the communications task, the stage of the product life cycle, and the economic outlook. Companies are increasingly coordinating the various departments that carry on communications work, in order to achieve a consistent and synergistic impact on their target markets.

1. Draw up a list of sales situations which can be aided by (a) atmospherics; (b) event management.

2. The dairy industry would like to interest teenagers in drinking more milk. Outline a nationwide promotion campaign using all the promotools and making use of the planning paradigm: audience, channels, message, and communicator.

3. An advertising agency is preparing a cake mix commercial. It is trying to choose between two copy versions. Version A allows the audience to share the entire product experience from the moment of purchase through the act of baking the cake and the family enthusiastically receiving it. Version B stops short of completing the process, hoping to involve the audience in imagining the rest. Which version do you think will be more effective and why?

4. A marketing research agency was asked to find out what consumers thought of the soft drink, Seven-Up. The agency found that most consumers regarded it as a wholesome drink. The company was pleased with this finding. Should they be?

5. The various mass media—newspapers, magazines, radio, television, and outdoor media—show striking differences in their capacity for dramatization, credibility, attention getting, and other valued aspects of communication. Describe the special characteristics of each media type.

6. Develop a set of thematic guidelines that laundry soap companies might follow in preparing soap ads aimed at upper-lower and lower-middle-class housewives in the 24–45 age bracket.

7. What types of consumer responses over time should be aimed for in communication strategies for the following products: legal services, frozen pizzas, veterinarian services, sewing machines, pianos, telephone answering services, hammers?

Advertising Decisions

If you think advertising doesn't pay—we understand there are twenty-five mountains in Colorado higher than Pike's Peak. Can you name one?

THE AMERICAN SALESMAN

19

Advertising is one of the four major tools companies use to direct persuasive communications to target buyers and publics. It consists of *nonpersonal forms of communication conducted through paid media under clear sponsorship.* This form of communication runs up a bill of over $33 billion a year in the United States. It is a tool by no means restricted to commercial firms. Advertising is used by the U.S. Army, museums, fund raisers, and various social-action organizations to bring messages about their causes and organizations to various target publics.

Within the commercial sector, the top 125 national advertisers account for as much as one-fifth of all national advertising. The five top spenders are Procter & Gamble ($460 million), General Motors ($312 million), General Foods ($300 million), Sears ($290 million), and K-Mart ($210 million). The highest absolute spenders are found in soaps and cleaners, drugs and cosmetics, autos, food, and tobacco. The highest relative advertising spenders (as a percentage of sales) are found in drugs and cosmetics (between 10 percent and 20 percent), gum and candy (12 percent), and soaps (6 to 12 percent).[1]

[1] For this information, see the special issue of *Advertising Age* on the one hundred leading national advertisers, August 28, 1978, esp. p. 29.

497

Purpose of Advertising

People have sought for years to define the purpose of advertising. In his *Madison Avenue, U.S.A.*, Martin Mayer sounded a skeptical note by saying: "Only the very brave or the very ignorant . . . can say exactly what advertising does in the marketplace." It is fairly clear, however, what advertising is *supposed* to do. In ultimate terms, advertising is undertaken to increase company sales and/or profits over what they otherwise would be. Advertising, however, is rarely able to create sales by itself. Whether the customer buys also depends upon the product, price, packaging, personal selling, services, financing, and other aspects of the marketing process.

More specifically, the purpose of advertising is to enhance potential buyers' responses to the organization and its offerings. It seeks to do this by providing information, by channelizing desires, and by supplying reasons for preferring a particular organization's offer.

What Are the Major Advertising Decisions?

This chapter will examine the following major decisions called for in the realm of advertising:

1. How much should be spent for overall company advertising? *(Money)*
2. What message should be used? *(Message)*
3. What media should be used? *(Media)*
4. How should the advertising be phased during the year? *(Motion)*
5. What are the best methods for knowing what the advertising is accomplishing? *(Measurement)*

SIZE OF THE ADVERTISING BUDGET

Common Methods for Setting the Advertising Budget

Each year the firm must decide how much to spend on advertising. Four of the more common methods are described below.[2]

"Affordable" method   Many companies set the advertising budget on the basis of what they think the company can afford. As explained by one advertising executive:

> Why it's simple. First I go upstairs to the controller and ask how much they can afford to give us this year. He says a million and a half. Later, the boss comes to me and asks how much we should spend, and I say "Oh, about a million and a half." Then we have an advertising appropriation.[3]

Setting budgets in this manner is tantamount to saying that the relationship between advertising expenditure and sales results is at best tenuous. If the company has enough funds, it should spend them on advertising as a form of insurance.

The basic weakness of the affordable approach is that it leads to a fluctuating advertising budget that makes it difficult to plan for long-range market development.

[2] See Joel Dean, *Managerial Economics* (Englewood Cliffs, N.J.: Prentice-Hall, 1951), pp. 363–75; and David L. Hurwood and James K. Brown, *Some Guidelines for Advertising Budgeting* (New York: Conference Board, 1972).

[3] Quoted in Daniel Seligman, "How Much for Advertising?" *Fortune*, December 1956, p. 123.

Percentage-of-sales method   Many companies set their advertising expenditures at a specified percentage of sales (either current or anticipated) or of the sales price. A railroad company executive said:

> We set our appropriation for each year on December 1 of the preceding year. On that date we add our passenger revenue for the next month, and then take 2 percent of the total for our advertising appropriation for the new year.[4]

Automobile companies typically budget a fixed percentage for advertising based on the planned price for each car, and oil companies tend to set the appropriation as some fraction of a cent for each gallon of gasoline sold under their own label.

A number of advantages are claimed for this method. First, the percentage-of-sales method means that advertising expenditures are likely to vary with what the company can "afford." This pleases the more financially minded members of top management, who feel that expenses of all types should bear a close relation to the movement of corporate sales over the business cycle. Second, this method encourages management to think in terms of the relationship between advertising cost, selling price, and profit per unit. Third, the method encourages competitive stability to the extent that competing firms spend approximately the same percentage of their sales on advertising.

In spite of these advantages, the percentage-of-sales method has little to justify it. It uses circular reasoning in viewing sales as the cause of advertising rather than as the result. It leads to an appropriation set by the availability of funds rather than by the opportunities. It discourages experimentation with countercyclical advertising or aggressive spending. The dependence of the advertising budget on year-to-year fluctuations in sales militates against the planning of long-range advertising programs. The method does not provide a logical basis for the choice of a specific percentage, except what has been done in the past, or what competitors are doing, or what the costs will be. Finally, it does not encourage the constructive development of advertising appropriations on a product-by-product and territory-by-territory basis but instead suggests that all allocations be made at the same percentage of sales.

Competitive-parity method   Some companies set their advertising budgets specifically to match competitors' outlays—that is, to maintain competitive parity. This thinking is illustrated by the executive who asked a trade source, "Do you have any figures that other companies in the builders' specialties field have used that would indicate what proportion of gross sales should be given over to advertising?"[5]

Two arguments are advanced for this method. One is that competitors' expenditures represent the collective wisdom of the industry. The other is that maintaining a competitive parity helps to prevent advertising wars.

Neither of these arguments is valid. There are no a priori grounds for believing that the competition is using more logical methods for determining outlays. Advertising reputations, resources, opportunities, and objectives are likely to differ so much among companies that their budgets are hardly a guide for an-

[4] Albert Wesley Frey, *How Many Dollars for Advertising?* (New York: Ronald Press Company, 1955), p. 65.

[5] *Ibid.*, p. 49.

other firm to follow. Furthermore, there is no evidence that appropriations based on the pursuit of competitive parity do in fact stabilize industry advertising expenditures.

Knowing what the competition is spending on advertising is undoubtedly useful information. But it is one thing to know this and another to follow it blindly.

Objective-and-task method The objective-and-task method calls upon advertisers to develop their budget by (1) defining their advertising objectives as specifically as possible, (2) determining the tasks that must be performed to achieve these objectives, and (3) estimating the costs of performing these tasks. The sum of these costs is the proposed advertising budget.

Advertising goals should be formulated as specifically as possible in order to guide the copy development, media selection, and results measurement. The stated goal, "to create brand preference," is much weaker than "to establish 30 percent preference for brand X among Y million housewives by next year." Colley listed as many as fifty-two specific communication goals, including:

> Announce a special reason for "buying now" (price, premium, and so on).
> Build familiarity and easy recognition of package or trademark.
> Place advertiser in position to select preferred distributors and dealers.
> Persuade prospect to visit a showroom, ask for a demonstration.
> Build morale of company sales force.
> Correct false impressions, misinformation and other obstacles to sales.[6]

The method has strong appeal and popularity among advertisers. Its major limitation is that it does not indicate how the objectives themselves should be chosen and whether they are worth the cost of attaining them.

Decision Models for Setting Advertising Budgets In recent years various researchers have proposed several decision models for setting the advertising budget. These models differ in the advertising situation to which they are addressed and the type and number of variables they include. We shall review four of the models here.

Sales response and decay models The earliest advertising-budgeting models attempted to measure the shape of the advertising sales response function. Given this function, the profit-maximizing advertising outlay can be determined. As for the shape itself, the evidence is mixed. Many analysts hold that the sales/advertising curve is S-shaped. This curve implies initial advertising economies of scale. According to Joel Dean:

> Larger appropriations may make feasible the use of expert services and more economical media. More important than specialization usually are economies of repetition. Each advertising attack starts from ground that was taken in previous forays, and where no single onslaught can overcome the inertia of existing spending patterns, the hammering of repetition often overcomes skepticism by attrition.[7]

---

[6] See Russell H. Colley, ed., *Defining Advertising Goals* (New York: Association of National Advertisers, 1961); and H. D. Wolfe, J. K. Brown, and G. C. Thompson, *Measuring Advertising Results,* Studies in Business Policy, no. 102 (New York: Conference Board, 1962), pp. 62–68.

[7] Dean, *Managerial Economics,* p. 357.

Dean has also spelled out the reasons why diminishing returns to advertising can eventually be expected to set in:

> Presumably the most susceptible prospects are picked off first, and progressively stiffer resistance is encountered from layers of prospects who are more skeptical, more stodgy about their present spending patterns, or more attached to rival sellers. The rise may also be caused by progressive exhaustion of the most vulnerable geographical areas or the most efficient advertising media. Promotional channels that are ideally adapted to the scale and market of the firm are used first.[8]

Other studies of the advertising sales response function indicate that it is concave rather than S-shaped, which suggests that incremental advertising expenditures are increasingly less efficient. Simon, in a review of several studies, concluded that "there was no single piece of strong empirical support for the belief in *any* economies of scale in advertising, and . . . there was large evidence to the contrary."[9] From this he concluded:

> If diminishing returns rather than economies of scale are the case, then advertising expenditures should be dispersed rather than concentrated. That is, it would pay for a firm to: divide its advertising among several equally likely media buys rather than concentrate it in one; spread the advertising evenly over weeks and months, rather than concentrating in a few time periods; use two copy approaches if both are equally strong; disperse the advertising geographically (making allowance for variations in market potentials); use smaller-size ads; increase the number of brands marketed.[10]

One of the earliest and best models of the response of sales to advertising was developed by Vidale and Wolfe.[11] In their model, the change in the *rate of sales* at time t is a function of four factors: the *advertising budget,* the *sales response constant,* the *saturation level of sales,* and the *sales decay constant.* Their basic equation is

$$\frac{dS}{dt} = rA\frac{M-S}{M} - \lambda S \qquad (19\text{--}1)$$

where:

S = rate of sales at time t

$\dfrac{dS}{dt}$ = change in the rate of sales at time t ⎫ *variables*

A = rate of advertising expenditure at time t ⎭

r = sales response constant (defined as the sales generated per advertising dollar when $S = 0$)

M = saturation level of sales ⎬ *parameters*

λ = sales decay constant (defined as the fraction of sales lost per time unit when $A = 0$)

[8] *Ibid.,* p. 358.

[9] Julian L. Simon, "New Evidence for No Effect of Scale in Advertising" *Journal of Advertising Research,* March 1969, pp. 38–41.

[10] Julian L. Simon, "Are There Economies of Scale in Advertising?" *Journal of Advertising Research,* June 1965, pp. 15–20.

[11] M. L. Vidale and H. B. Wolfe, "An Operations-Research Study of Sales Response to Advertising," *Operations Research,* June 1957, pp. 370–81.

The equation says that the change (increase) in the rate of sales will be higher, the higher the sales response constant, the higher the advertising expenditure, the higher the untapped sales potential, and the lower the decay constant. Suppose, for example, the sales response to advertising dollars is estimated at 4, current sales are $40,000, saturation-level sales are $100,000 and the company loses .1 of its sales per period if no advertising expenditure is made. In this case, by spending $10,000 in advertising, the company can hope to achieve an additional $20,000 of sales:

$$\frac{dS}{dt} = 4(10,000)\ \frac{100,000 - 40,000}{100,000} - .1(40,000) = \$20,000$$

If the profit margin on $20,000 is better than 50 percent, it pays to spend the $10,000 on advertising.

The Vidale-Wolfe model can be embedded in a long-run profit equation and used to estimate the profit consequences of alternative advertising-budgeting strategies. Its main significance is that it brings together and relates three useful concepts for determining the proper size of the advertising budget.

Some models of sales response to advertising go beyond the Vidale-Wolfe model in the number of factors they postulate. A notable example is Kuehn's model.[12] Here company sales are a function of the percentage of customers with brand loyalty and the rate of decay in this brand loyalty; the percentage of customers not committed to this firm or its main competitor; the size and rate of growth of the total market; the relative influence of product characteristics, price, advertising, and distribution as selling influences; the relative influence of the *interaction* of product characteristics and advertising as a selling influence; and the relative share and effectiveness of this company's advertising expenditure. Using this model to describe company sales for the case of two-firm competition, Kuehn derived an optimal formula for setting advertising expenditures.

Communication-stage models   Communication-stage advertising models arrive at an advertising budget by noting its effects on several intermediate variables that link advertising expenditures to ultimate sales. Ule developed an example to show how a manufacturer of a brand new filter-tip cigarette, Sputniks (name fictitious), could establish the necessary advertising budget.[13] The steps are as follows:

1. *Establish the market-share goal.* The advertiser wants 8 percent of the market. There are 50 million cigarette smokers, which means the company wants to attract 4 million regular Sputnik smokers.
2. *Determine the percent of the market that should be reached by Sputnik advertising.* The advertiser hopes to reach 80 percent (40 million smokers) with the advertising campaign.
3. *Determine the percent of aware smokers that should be persuaded to try the*

[12] Alfred A. Kuehn, "A Model for Budgeting Advertising," in *Mathematical Models and Methods in Marketing*, ed. Frank M. Bass *et al.* (Homewood, Ill.: Richard D. Irwin, 1961), pp. 302–53.

[13] G. Maxwell Ule, "A Media Plan for 'Sputnik' Cigarettes," *How to Plan Media Strategy*, American Association of Advertising Agencies, 1957 Regional Conventions, pp. 41–52.

brand. The advertiser would be pleased if 25 percent of aware smokers, or 10 million smokers, tried Sputnik because it is estimated that 40 percent of all triers, or 4 million persons, would become loyal users. That is the market goal.

4. ***Determine the number of advertising impressions per one percent trial rate.*** The advertiser estimates that forty advertising impressions (exposures) for every one percent of the population would bring about a 25 percent trial rate.

5. ***Determine the number of gross rating points that would have to be purchased.*** A gross rating point is one exposure to one percent of the target population. Since the company wants to achieve forty exposures to 80 percent of the population, it will want to buy 3,200 gross rating points.

6. ***Determine the necessary advertising budget on the basis of the average cost of buying a gross rating point.*** To expose one percent of the target population to one impression costs an average of $3,277. Therefore 3,200 gross rating points would cost $10,486,400 (= $3,277 × 3,200) in the introductory year.

Ule's method is essentially an implementation of the objective-and-task method. It has the advantage of requiring management to spell out its assumptions about the relations between dollars spent, exposure levels, trial rates, and regular usage. Its major conceptual weakness is that the market-share goal is set arbitrarily without being derived from a profit-maximizing approach to sales.

Adaptive-control models   Adaptive advertising-budgeting models make the assumption that the parameters of the advertising sales response function are not stable but change through time. If they were stable, it would pay the company to make a big effort to measure the functions as soon and as accurately as possible because the benefits in achieving optimization would extend far into the future. However, there is good reason to believe that the parameters are not stable because of continuously changing competitive activity, advertising copy, product design, and national economic activity. In this case it would not pay to invest heavily in learning the exact parameters of the sales response function in the current period. Suppose the parameters change slowly through time. Then the best research strategy would be to collect some new information each time about the current parameters and combine it with the old information to produce new estimated parameters for the sales response function on which the current outlay for advertising can be based.

The manner in which the periodic data can be collected and used to determine an optimal advertising expenditure has been described by Little.[14] Advertising expenditures should be set each period in such a way as to yield information about the current levels of the sales response parameters. Suppose the company has picked an advertising expenditure rate for the coming period on the basis of applying profit-maximization criteria to its most current information on the sales function. It then decides to spend this rate in all markets except a subset of $2n$ of them randomly drawn. In n of the test markets the company will spend a deliberately low amount of dollars, and in the other n it will spend a deliberately high amount of dollars. This experiment will yield information on the average sales created by the low, medium, and high rates of advertising, and this will provide the best estimate of the current sales response function. In turn,

[14] John D. C. Little, "A Model of Adaptive Control of Promotional Spending," *Operations Research*, November 1966, pp. 1075–97.

this estimate is used to determine the best promotional rate for the next period. If this procedure is carried out each period, actual advertising expenditures will track closely to the optimal advertising expenditures.

Competitive-share models The preceding models do not explicitly take competitors' expenditures into account. This omission is valid where there are many competitors, none of whom is large; or where it is difficult for companies to know what others are spending for advertising. In many situations, however, firms know what others are spending and try to maintain a competitive parity. In these situations a firm must take competitive reactions into account in determining its own advertising appropriation.

Under certain assumptions, the problem can be treated with some of the techniques of game theory. Friedman has developed some models to show how fixed advertising budgets should be allocated by two duopolists to different territories under the assumption that each is interested in taking maximum advantage of the other's mistakes.[15] He distinguishes between the case where resulting company sales are proportional to the company's share of advertising expenditures and the case where the company with 50-plus percent of the total advertising takes the whole market (as when a single customer is at stake).

MESSAGE DEVELOPMENT

Many studies of the effect of advertising expenditures on sales neglect the message factor. Some analysts rationalize this by arguing that all large advertising agencies are equally creative, and therefore differences in individual campaigns tend to "wash out." But it is precisely the differences in individual campaigns that advertisers want to note and exploit. The consequence of leaving out the creative factors is that a substantial part of the movement of market shares remains "unexplained."

One study claims to have overcome the neglect of the message factor.[16] A five-year study of sixty-seven different television campaigns led to the development of a multiple-regression formula that "explained" 73 percent of the fluctuations in market shares. What is most interesting is that one of the three independent variables was a measure of the effectiveness of the message. The study's major conclusion is that a campaign's quality is far more important than the number of dollars spent. Whether this is actually so, there is no doubt that differences in creative strategy are very important in advertising success.

Advertisers go through three stages to develop their message: message generation, evaluation and selection, and execution.

Message Generation Message generation is the activity of developing a number of alternative possible messages about the product. Many things can be said about any product. No ad should say more than a few things, and in fact, a case could be made that an ad, to gain distinctiveness, should emphasize one theme. This theme should

[15] Lawrence Friedman, "Game-Theory Models in the Allocation of Advertising Expenditures," *Operations Research*, September–October 1958), pp. 699–709.

[16] See "New Study Tells TV Advertisers How Advertising Builds Sales and Share of Market," *Printer's Ink*, May 8, 1964, pp. 27–38.

reinforce the product's positioning in the marketplace. The challenge is to develop a few major alternative messages that could be pretested to find the best one.

Creative people use different methods to generate possible advertising appeals. Many creative people proceed *inductively*. They talk to consumers, dealers, experts, and competitors to spot ideas. Consumers are by far the most important source of good ideas. Their feelings about the strengths and shortcomings of existing brands provide the most important clues to creative strategy. A leading hair-spray company, for example, carries out consumer research annually to determine consumer dissatisfaction with existing brands. If it turns out that consumers would like stronger holding power, the company would use this appeal, assuming that the company's brand promises good holding power or can be reformulated to meet this claim.

Today there is increasing interest in *deductive* frameworks for generating advertising appeals. Maloney proposed one possible framework.[17] He suggested that buyers may be expecting any of four types of reward from an offering: *rational, sensory, social,* or *ego satisfaction*. And they may visualize these rewards from *results-of-use experience, product-in-use experience,* or *incidental-to-use experience*. Crossing the four types of rewards with the three types of experience gives twelve different modes of buyer evaluation to be found concurrently in the marketplace. The advertiser can generate a theme for each of the twelve cells as possible messages for his product. For example, the appeal "gets clothes cleaner" is a rational reward promise following results-of-use experience; and the phrase "real gusto in a great light beer" is a sensory-reward promise connected with product-in-use experience.

Message Evaluation and Selection

The task of selecting the best message out of a large number of possibilities calls for the introduction of criteria for judging the communication potency of different messages. Twedt has suggested that the contending appeals be rated on three scales: *desirability, exclusiveness,* and *believability*.[18] He believes that the communication potency of an appeal is a function of a multiplicative relationship among the three named factors—multiplicative because if any of the three has a low rating, the appeal's communication potency will be greatly reduced. The appeal must first say something desirable or interesting about the product. That is not enough, however: many brands will be making the same claim. Therefore the statement must also say something exclusive or distinctive that does not apply to every brand in the product category. Finally, the statement must be believable or provable. By getting a sample of consumers to rate different product statements on the three scales of desirability, exclusiveness, and believability, these statements can be numerically rated for communication potency.

For example, the March of Dimes was searching for an advertising theme to raise money for its fight against birth defects.[19] A brainstorming session came

[17] John C. Maloney, "Marketing Decisions and Attitude Research," in *Effective Marketing Coordination,* ed. George L. Baker, Jr., (Chicago: American Marketing Association, 1961), pp. 595–618.

[18] Dik Warren Twedt, "How to Plan New Products, Improve Old Ones, and Create Better Advertising," *Journal of Marketing,* January 1969, pp. 53–57.

[19] See William A. Mindak and H. Malcolm Bybee, "Marketing's Application to Fund Raising," *Journal of Marketing,* July 1971, pp. 13–18.

up with more than twenty possible themes. A group of young married parents were asked to rate each theme for interest, distinctiveness, and believability, assigning up to 100 points for each. For example, the theme "500,000 unborn babies die each year from birth defects" scored 70, 60, and 80 on interest, distinctiveness, and believability, while the theme "your next baby could be born with a birth defect" scored 58, 50, and 70. The first theme dominates the second. If one theme does not dominate, then weights would be assigned to the three criteria to reflect their assumed importance.

Consumer ratings of ad appeals are not that reliable, however; they reflect opinion and not necessarily behavior. The advertiser should employ some pretest procedure to determine which final appeals are the strongest. For example, the Washington State Apple Commission was trying to decide which of two advertising themes for apples appealed more to housewives.[20] One theme stressed the various *uses* of apples; the other, the *healthful* qualities of apples. An experiment was carried out in seventy-two self-service food stores in six midwestern cities for sixteen weeks. An analysis of the final sales results revealed that the apple-use theme was significantly more effective in promoting sales than the health theme.

Message Execution

The impact of an advertisement depends not only upon what is said but also upon how it is said. In fact, message execution can be decisive for those products that are essentially the same as the competition, such as detergents, cigarettes, coffee, and beer. The advertiser has to put the message across in a way that will win attention and interest on the part of the target audience.

To guide the development of message execution, the advertiser usually prepares a *copy strategy statement* describing the objective, content, support, and tone of the desired ad. Here is a copy strategy statement for a Pillsbury product called 1869 Brand Biscuits:

The *objective* of the advertising is to convince biscuit users that now, for the first time, they can buy a canned biscuit that's as good as homemade—Pillsbury's 1869 Brand Biscuits.

The *content* consists of emphasizing the following product characteristics of the 1869 Brand Biscuits:
1. They look like homemade biscuits.
2. They have the same texture as homemade biscuits.
3. They taste like homemade biscuits.

Support for the "good as homemade" promise will be twofold:
1. 1869 Brand Biscuits are made from a special kind of flour (soft wheat flour) traditionally used to make homemade biscuits but never before used in making canned biscuits.
2. The use of traditional American biscuit recipes.

The *tone* of the advertising will be news announcement, yet tempered by a warm, reflective mood emanating from a look back at traditional American baking quality.

It is the task of the creative people in the advertising agency to find the *style, tone, words,* and *format factors* that make for effective message execution.

[20] See Peter L. Henderson, James F. Hind, and Sidney E. Brown, "Sales Effects of Two Campaign Themes," *Journal of Advertising Research*, December 1961, pp. 2–11.

Any message can be put across in different *execution styles*, such as:

1. *Slice-of-life.* This shows one or more persons using the product in a normal setting. A family might be shown at the dinner table expressing satisfaction with a new brand of biscuits.
2. *Life style.* This emphasizes how a product fits in with a life style. The Revlon ads of the Charlie fragrances show an adventuresome, rule-breaking young woman going after the things she wants in life and getting them.
3. *Fantasy.* This creates a fantasy about what might happen in connection with the use of the product. A woman sprays on a certain brand of perfume and suddenly becomes irresistible to every man she meets.
4. *Mood or image.* This builds an evocative mood or image around the product—beauty, love, or serenity. No claim is made about the product except through suggestion. Many cigarette ads, such as Salems and Newport, create moods.
5. *Musical.* This shows one or more persons or characters singing a song or jingle involving the product. Many cola ads have used this format.
6. *Personality symbol.* This creates a character that represents or personifies the product. The character might be *animated* (Green Giant, Cap'n Crunch, or Mr. Clean) or *real* (Marlboro man, Morris the Cat). The Chicago advertising agency of Leo Burnett has been very successful in creating memorable characters around mundane products.
7. *Technical expertise.* This features the care that the company exercises and the experience it has in selecting the ingredients for this product or in manufacturing the product. Thus Hills Brothers shows one of its buyers carefully selecting the coffee beans and Italian Swiss Colony emphasizes the many years of experience the company has in winemaking.
8. *Scientific evidence.* This presents survey or scientific evidence that the brand is preferred to or outperforms one or more other brands. For years, Crest toothpaste has featured scientfic evidence to convince toothpaste buyers of the superior cavity-fighting properties of Crest.
9. *Testimonial evidence.* This features a highly credible or likable source endorsing the product. It could be a celebrity like O. J. Simpson (Hertz Rent-a-Car) or ordinary people saying how much they like the product.

The communicator must also choose an effective *tone* for the ad. Procter & Gamble advertising, for example, is consistently positive in its tone: their ads say something superlatively positive about the product in the clearest possible way. Humor is avoided so as not to take attention away from the message. On the other hand, Volkswagen's ads for its famous "beetle" automobile typically took on a humorous and self-deprecating tone ("the Ugly Bug").

Words must be found that are memorable and attention getting. This is nowhere more apparent than in the development of headlines and slogans to lead the reader into an ad. There are six basic types of headlines: *news* ("New Boom and More Inflation Ahead . . . and What You Can Do About It"); *question* ("Have You Had It Lately?"); *narrative* ("They Laughed When I Sat Down at the Piano, but When I Started to Play!"); *command* ("Don't Buy Until You Try All Three"); *1-2-3 ways* ("12 Ways to Save on Your Income Tax"); and *how-what-why* ("Why They Can't Stop Buying").[21] Look at the care that airlines

---

[21] See "Powerful Headlines Uncover Basic Wants," *Marketing Insights*, May 19, 1969, pp. 16–17.

have lavished on finding the right way to describe their airline as safe without explicitly mentioning safety as an issue:

"The Friendly Skies of United" (United)

"The Wings of Man" (Eastern)

"The World's Most Experienced Airline" (Pan American)

Format elements such as ad size, color, and illustration can make a large difference in an ad's impact, as well as its cost. A minor rearrangement or alteration of mechanical elements within the advertisement can improve its attention-gaining power by several points. Larger-size ads gain more attention, though not necessarily by as much as their difference in cost. The use of four-color illustrations instead of black and white increases ad effectiveness and also ad cost.[22]

How Many Advertisements Should Be Created?

The client typically wants the advertising agency to create and test several alternative ideas before making a selection. The more ads created, the higher the probability that the agency will find a first-rate one. Yet the more time it spends creating alternative ads, the higher the costs. Therefore it would seem that there must be some optimal number of alternative ads that an agency should try to create and test for the client.

If the agency were reimbursed by the client for the cost of creating ads, the agency would create the optimal number. Under the present commission system, however, the agency does not like to go to the expense of creating and pretesting many ads. In an ingenious study, Gross concluded that agencies generally create too few advertisement alternatives for their clients.[23] The advertiser does not get a very good ad but only the best (one hopes) of the few that have been created.

Gross estimates that advertising agencies spend from 3 to 5 percent of their media income on creating and testing advertising, whereas he estimates they should be spending closer to 15 percent. He thinks agencies should devote a larger part of their budget to finding the best ad and somewhat less to buying media. He proposed splitting advertising agencies into two types, purely creative agencies and marketing agencies. The company hires a marketing agency, and this agency in turn hires several creative agencies to create advertisements, from which the best one is selected.

MEDIA SELECTION

Media selection is the *problem of finding the best way to deliver the desired number of exposures to the target audience.* But what do we mean by the desired number of exposures? Presumably the advertiser is seeking a certain response

---

[22] Twedt regressed the readership scores of 137 advertisements in *The American Builder* against a large number of variables and found that size of the advertisement, size of illustration, and number of colors accounted for over 50 percent of the variance in advertising readership. See Dik Warren Twedt; "A Multiple Factor Analysis of Advertising Readership," *Journal of Applied Psychology,* June 1952, pp. 207–15. Also see Daniel S. Diamond, "A Quantitative Approach to Magazine Advertisement Format Selection," *Journal of Marketing Research,* November 1968, pp. 376–87.

[23] Irwin Gross, "An Analytical Approach to the Creative Aspects of Advertising Operations" (Ph.D. dissertation, Case Institute of Technology, November 1967).

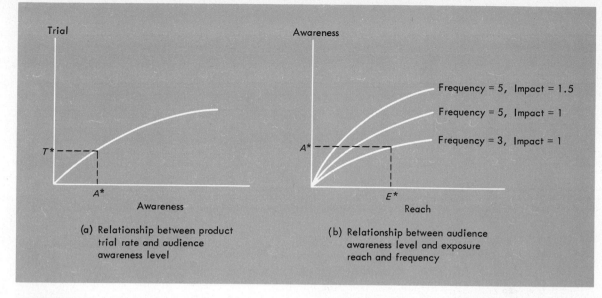

FIGURE 19–1

Relationship Between Trial, Awareness, and the Exposure Function

from the target audience, for example, a certain level of *product trial*. Now the rate of product trial will depend, among other things, on the level of audience brand awareness. Suppose the rate of product trial increases at a diminishing rate with the level of audience awareness, as shown in Figure 19–1A. If the advertiser wants to achieve a product trial rate of (say) T^*, it will be necessary to achieve a brand awareness rate of A^*.

Exposure Reach, Frequency, and Impact

The next task is to find out how many exposures, E^*, will be needed to produce a level of audience awareness of A^*. The effect of exposures on audience awareness depends on the exposures' reach, frequency, and impact. These terms are defined below:

> *Reach (R):* the number of different persons or households exposed to a particular media schedule at least once during a specified time period

> *Frequency (F):* the number of times within the specified time period that an average person or household is exposed to the message

> *Impact (I):* the qualitative value of an exposure through a given medium (thus a food ad in *Good Housekeeping* would have a higher impact than in the *Police Gazette*)

Figure 19–1B shows the relationship between audience awareness and reach. Audience awareness will be greater, the higher the exposures' reach, frequency, and impact. The media planner recognizes important trade-offs between reach, frequency, and impact. Suppose the media planner has an advertising budget of $1,000,000 and the cost per thousand exposures of average quality is $5. This means that the advertiser can buy 200,000,000 exposures

($= \$1,000,000 \div 1000/\$5$). If the advertiser seeks an average exposure frequency of 10, then the advertiser can reach 20,000,000 people ($= 200,000,000 \div 10$) with the given budget. Now if the advertiser wants higher-quality media costing $10 per thousand exposures, the advertiser will be able to reach only 10,000,000 people unless he or she is willing to lower the desired exposure frequency.

The relationship between reach, frequency, and impact is captured in the following concepts:

Total number of exposures (E). This is the reach times the average frequency, that is, $E = R \times F$. It is also called the *gross rating points* (GRP). If a given media schedule reaches 80 percent of the homes with an average exposure frequency of 3, the media schedule is said to have a GRP of 240 ($= 80 \times 3$). If another media schedule has a GRP of 300, it can be said to have more weight but we cannot tell how this weight breaks up into reach and frequency.

Weighted number of exposures (WE). This is the reach times the average frequency times the average impact, that is, $WE = R \times F \times I$.

The media planning challenge is as follows. With a given budget, what is the most cost-effective combination of reach, frequency and impact to buy? Suppose the media planner is willing to use average impact media. This leaves the task of deciding how many people to reach with what frequency. It would make sense to settle the issue of frequency first. How many exposures does an average member of the target audience need for the advertising to work? Once this target frequency is decided, then reach will fall into place.

Many advertisers have operated on the theory that members of the target audience need a large number of exposures for the advertising to work. Too few repetitions may be a waste, according to Lucas and Britt: "It can be reasoned that introductory advertisements make too weak an impression to initiate much interest in buying. Succeeding advertisements may sometimes be more effective by building up already established weak impressions to the action level."[24] Other advertising researchers doubt the value of many exposures. They feel that after people see the same ad a few times, they either act on it, get irritated by it, or stop noticing it. Krugman has made the case that three exposures may be enough:

The first exposure is by definition unique. As with the initial exposure to anything, a "What is it?" type of cognitive response dominates the reaction.
The second exposure to a stimulus . . . produces several effects. One may be the cognitive reaction that characterized the first exposure, if the audience missed much of the message the first time around. . . . More often, an evaluative "What of it?" response replaces the "What is it?" response. . . .
The third exposure constitutes a reminder, if a decision to buy based on the evaluations has not been acted on. The third exposure is also the beginning of disengagement and withdrawal of attention from a completed episode.[25]

[24] Darrell B. Lucas and Steuart Henderson Britt, *Measuring Advertising Effectiveness* (New York: McGraw-Hill Book Company, 1963), p. 218.

[25] See Herbert E. Krugman, "What Makes Advertising Effective?" *Harvard Business Review,* March–April 1975, pp. 96–103, here p. 98.

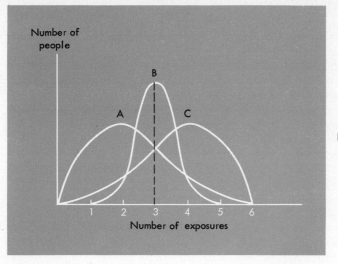

FIGURE 19–2
Exposure-Frequency Distributions

Let us assume for the moment that Krugman is right. Then advertisers should be concerned with the exposure-frequency distribution that a particular advertising campaign is achieving. An *exposure-frequency distribution* shows how many persons are receiving 0, 1, 2, . . . n exposures to the same ad in a given time period. Figure 19–2 shows three different exposure-frequency distributions. The media plan delivering the B distribution is the most efficient because most people are receiving three exposures. Distribution C overdoes repetition while distribution A underdoes the desired frequency of exposure.

Krugman's thesis favoring three exposures has to be qualified. He is using exposures to mean actual attention episodes on the part of the target audience. The advertiser would have to buy more exposures than three to insure that the audience actually sees three ads. Also, there is a forgetting factor that operates. The job of advertising repetition is partly to put the message back into memory. The higher the forgetting rate associated with that brand, product category, or message, the higher the warranted level of repetition.[26]

Choosing among Major Media Types

Given the reach, frequency, and impact objectives, the media planner has to review each major media type for its capacity to deliver the particular objectives. The major media types and the 1976 level of expenditures on each are as follows (in millions): newspapers, $9,910; television, $6,622; direct mail, $4,754; radio, $2,277; magazines, $1,789; outdoor, $383; and miscellaneous, $7,725. The total is $33,460.[27]

These major media types vary in their reach, frequency, and impact values.[28] For example, television typically delivers much more reach than maga-

---

[26] One of the best summaries of research in this area is *The Repetition of Advertising* (New York, N.Y.: Batten, Barton, Durstine, & Osborn, February 1967).

[27] *Statistical Abstract of the U.S., 1977,* p. 845.

[28] For a discussion of how the effectiveness of different media types might be compared, see Allan Greenberg, "Intermedia Comparisons," *Journal of Advertising Research,* October 1972, pp. 47–49.

zines. Outdoor delivers much more frequency than magazines. Magazines deliver more impact than newspapers.

The experienced media planner knows the special characteristics of each media type. *Newspapers* have the advantages of flexibility, timeliness, good local market coverage, broad acceptance, and high believability. Their disadvantages are a short life, poor reproduction quality, and a small "pass-along" audience. *Magazines* have the advantages of high geographic and demographic selectivity, credibility and prestige, high-quality reproduction, long life, and good pass-along readership. They have the disadvantages of long ad-purchase lead time, some waste circulation, and no guarantee of position. *Radio* has the advantages of mass use, high geographic and demographic selectivity, and low cost. It has the disadvantages of audio presentation only, lower audience attention than television, nonstandardized rate structures, and fleeting exposure. *Television* has the advantages of combining sight, sound, and motion, appealing to the senses, high attention, and high reach. It has the disadvantages of high absolute cost, high clutter, fleeting exposure, and less audience selectivity. *Direct mail* has the advantages of audience selectivity, flexibility, no ad competition within the same medium, and personalization. It has the disadvantages of relatively high cost and a "junk mail" image. Finally, *outdoor* has the advantages of flexibility, high repeat exposure, low cost, and low competition. It has the disadvantages of no audience selectivity and creative limitations.

In choosing a combination of media types, the media planner will consider:

1. ***Target audience media habits.*** For example, the most effective medium for reaching stamp collectors is stamp collector magazines.
2. ***Product.*** A product like women's dresses might be shown to best advantage in color magazines, and Polaroid cameras might be best demonstrated on television. Media types have different potentialities for demonstration, visualization, explanation, believability, and color.
3. ***Message.*** A message announcing a major sale tomorrow will require radio or newspaper. A message containing a great deal of technical data might require specialized magazines or mailings.
4. ***Cost.*** Television is very expensive, and newspaper advertising is inexpensive. What counts, of course, is the cost per thousand exposures rather than the total cost.

Assumptions about media impact and cost must be reexamined from time to time. For a long time, television enjoyed the supreme position in the media mix, and magazines and other media were neglected. Then media researchers began to notice television's reduced effectiveness owing to increased clutter. Advertisers are beaming shorter and more numerous commercials at the television audience, resulting in poorer attention and registration. Furthermore, television advertising costs have been rising faster than other media costs. Several companies have found that a combination of print ads and television commercials often do a better job than television commercials alone. This illustrates how advertisers must reevaluate periodically what they are getting for their money from different media.

On the basis of these characteristics, the media planner has to decide on how to allocate the given budget to the major media types. For example, a firm launching a new biscuit mix may decide to allocate $6,000,000 in the following way:

MEDIA TYPES	AMOUNT	PERCENTAGE
Daytime network television	$3,000,000	50
Women's magazines	2,000,000	33
Daily newspapers in 20 major markets	1,000,000	17
	$6,000,000	100

Selecting Specific Media Vehicles

The next step is to choose the specific media vehicles within each media type that would deliver the desired response in the most cost-effective way. Consider for example, the category of women's magazines, which includes *Cosmopolitan, Family Circle, Good Housekeeping, Ladies' Home Journal, McCall's, Ms, Redbook, Seventeen,* and *Woman's Day*. The media planner turns to several volumes put out by Standard Rate and Data that provide circulation and costs for different ad sizes, color options, ad positions, and quantities of insertions. Beyond this, the media planner evaluates the different magazines on qualitative characteristics such as credibility, prestige, geographical editioning, reproduction quality, editorial climate, lead time, and psychological impact. The media planner makes a final judgment as to which specific vehicles will deliver the best reach, frequency, and impact for the money.

The cost-per-thousand criterion Media planners calculate the *cost per thousand persons* reached by a particular vehicle. If a full-page, four-color advertisement in *Time* costs $50,000 and *Time's* estimated readership is 10 million persons, then the cost of reaching each one thousand persons is $5. The same advertisement in *Business Week* may cost $15,000 but reach only 2 million persons, at a cost per thousand of $7.50. The media planner would rank the various magazines according to cost per thousand and place advertisements in those magazines with the lowest cost per thousand.

The cost-per-thousand criterion, at least in its simple form, has come under increasing attack. Its major fault is that it uses the figure for the total readership of the magazine instead of weighing the different readership groups by their *exposure value*. For a baby lotion advertisement, the exposure value might be 1 million if all the readers are young mothers and zero if all the readers are old men.

The second weakness has to do with the varying probability of attention for different media. The media planner is interested in the number of persons who will see the ad, not the number who are exposed. Readers of certain magazines, such as *Vogue*, look at a higher percentage of the ads than readers of other magazines, say *Time*.

A third weakness of cost per thousand is that it neglects qualitative differences that might exist in the impact of different magazines. Even if two magazines reach the same number of target buyers, an advertisement may take on more believability, prestige, or other qualities in one magazine than the other.

A fourth weakness of cost per thousand is that it tends to be used in an average sense rather than in a marginal sense. If a magazine retains its lowest-cost-per-thousand standing independently of how much it is used, then logically the entire magazine budget should be spent on it. In reality, the magazine may quickly lose its cost-per-thousand advantage as more advertisements are placed in it. This is because successive-issue ads are seen largely by the same people, with diminishing impact in relation to what could be achieved by exposing new readers to the advertisement through new magazines.

Computerized Media Selection

An increasing number of agencies are using a computer program to develop their initial advertising media plan. At least three different basic types of models are in use.

Linear programming Linear programming seems like a natural format for analyzing the media-selection problem. The method can be used to discover the media mix that will maximize the number of effective exposures subject to a set of constraints—in this case the advertising budget, minimum and maximum media availabilities, and minimum desired exposure rates.

Figure 19–3 shows a linear programming statement of the media-selection problem. In the sample problem, the total advertising budget is $500,000, and at least $250,000 must be spent on medium 1. Medium 1 gives 3,100 (in thousands) effective exposures with each use and costs $15,000. It is possible to buy any-

FIGURE 19–3
Linear Programming Model for a Media Selection

Sample statement

$$\text{Maximize } E = e_1 X_1 + e_2 X_2 + \ldots + e_n X_n \quad \left.\right\} \begin{array}{l}\text{effectiveness}\\\text{function}\end{array}$$

$$E = 3,100X_1 + 2,000X_2 + \ldots + 2,400X_n$$

$$\text{subject to } c_1 X_1 + c_2 X_2 + \ldots + c_n X_n \leq B \quad \left.\right\} \begin{array}{l}\text{budget}\\\text{constraint}\end{array}$$

$$15,000X_1 + 4,000X_2 + \ldots + 5,000X_n \leq 500,000$$

$$c_1 X_1 + c_2 X_2 \leq B_1 \quad \left.\right\} \begin{array}{l}\text{media category}\\\text{usage constraint}\end{array}$$

$$15,000X_1 \geq 250,000$$

$$X_1 \geq k_{1L}$$

$$X_1 \geq 0$$

$$X_1 \leq k_{1U}$$

$$X_1 \leq 52$$

$$X_2 \geq k_{2L} \quad \left.\right\} \begin{array}{l}\text{individual}\\\text{medium}\end{array}$$

$$X_2 \geq 1$$

$$X_2 \leq k_{2U} \quad \left.\right\} \begin{array}{l}\text{usage}\\\text{constraints}\end{array}$$

$$X_2 \leq 8$$

$$X_n \geq k_{nL}$$

$$X_n \geq 6$$

$$X_n \leq k_{nU}$$

$$X_n \leq 12$$

where:

E = total exposure value (number of rated exposures)

e_i = exposure value of one ad in medium i

X_i = number of ads placed in medium i

c_i = cost of one ad in medium i

B = total advertising budget

B_1 = part of advertising budget

k_{1L} = minimum number of units to purchase of medium i

k_{1U} = maximum number of units to purchase of medium i

where between zero and fifty-two advertisements in medium 1 over a year's time. The other values are similarly interpreted. Given these concrete values, a mathematical solution technique is used to find the precise optimum solution to the problems as stated.[29]

The problem, as stated, unfortunately contains a number of artificialities. The four most important limitations are: (1) linear programming assumes that repeat exposures have a constant marginal effect; (2) it assumes constant media costs (no discounts); (3) it cannot handle the problem of audience duplication; and (4) it fails to say anything about when the advertisement should be scheduled.

Heuristic programming An alternative technique proceeds with a sequential rather than a simultaneous selection of media. The basic idea is to start with the media available in the first week of the year and select the single best buy. After this selection is made, the remaining media choices are reevaluated to take into account audience duplication and potential media discounts. A second selection is made for the same week if the *achieved* exposure rate for the week is below the *optimal* rate. The latter is a complex function of several marketing and media variables. This process continues until the optimal exposure rate for the week is reached, at which point new media choices are considered for the following week. This cycling process continues until the year's schedule is completed.[30]

The sequential procedure has four advantages: (1) it develops a schedule simultaneously with the selection of media; (2) it handles the audience-duplication problem; (3) it handles the media-discount problem; and (4) it incorporates theoretically important variables such as brand-switching rates and multiple-exposure coefficients.

Simulation model A simulation model does not profess to find the "best" media plan but rather to estimate the exposure value of any given media plan. For example, the Simulmatics media model consists of a sample universe of 2,944 make-believe media users representing a cross section of the American population by sex, age, type of community, employment status, and education. Each individual's media choices are determined probabilistically as a function of the person's socioeconomic characteristics and location in one of ninety-eight American communities. A particular media schedule is exposed to all the persons in this hypothetical population. The computer tabulates the number and types of people being exposed. Summary graphs and tables are prepared at the end of the hypothetical year's run, and they supply a multidimensional picture of the schedule's probable impact. The advertiser examines these tabulations and decides whether the audience profile and the reach and frequency characteristics of the proposed media schedule are satisfactory.

Simulation complements rather than competes with the preceding models. Its major limitations are: (1) simulation normally does not include an overall effectiveness function; (2) it lacks a procedure for finding better schedules; and (3) the representativeness of the hypothetical population is always suspect.

[29] See James F. Engel and Martin R. Warshaw, "Allocating Advertising Dollars by Linear Programming," *Journal of Advertising Research*, September 1964, pp. 41–48.

[30] For an example, see William T. Moran, "Practical Media Decisions and the Computer," *Journal of Marketing*, July 1963, pp. 26–30.

Other models   Current media models have gone beyond these simple ones to incorporate additional variables and complexities. Little and Lodish created one of the best models, which they call MEDIAC.[31] MEDIAC handles in an analytical fashion a large number of marketing and advertising facets of the real media problem, such as market segments, sales potentials, exposure probabilities, diminishing marginal response rates, forgetting, seasonality, and cost discounts. It is programmed for on-line access in a conversational mode so that the user can follow the model's logic, supply the requested data, and receive in a matter of minutes an optimal media schedule. The user can easily change the data inputs and note the effect on the media schedule.

Computerized media-selection models should be thought of as an aid to, rather than a substitute for, executive judgment. The computer can produce or "test" in a matter of hours a media plan that formerly might have taken days or weeks. The plan itself must be regarded only as a starting point. This sounds paradoxical, because it may represent the optimum solution to a mathematical programming statement of the media problem. But it must be remembered that the programming statement is somewhat artificial in the weights used and the constraints set up. The media planner will want to bring judgment to bear on the quality of the plan as a whole as well as on its parts. The planner may want to revise some of the specifications in the programming statement of the problem. A great advantage of the computer is that new plans can be quickly generated to show the significance of changes made in problem specifications. The final media plan should be the joint product of the machine's ultralogical mind and man's imagination and judgment.

TIMING OF ADVERTISING EXPENDITURES

Another major advertising decision is the optimal timing of advertising expenditures throughout the year. We shall distinguish between the macroscheduling problem and the microscheduling problem.

Macroscheduling Problem   The macroscheduling problem involves deciding how to allocate advertising expenditures over the year in response to the seasonal pattern of industry sales. Suppose industry sales of a particular product peak in December and wane in March. Any individual seller in this market has three broad options. The firm can vary its advertising expenditures to follow the seasonal pattern; it can vary its advertising expenditures to oppose the seasonal pattern; or it can hold its expenditures constant throughout the year. The vast majority of firms tend to pursue a policy of seasonal rather than constant or counterseasonal advertising. Even here, the firm faces options. It has to decide whether its advertising expenditures should lead or coincide with seasonal sales. It also has to decide whether its advertising expenditures should be more intense, proportional, or less intense than the seasonal amplitude of sales.

Forrester has proposed using his "industrial dynamics" methodology to test alternative seasonal advertising policies.[32] He visualizes advertising as hav-

---

[31] John D. C. Little and Leonard M. Lodish, "A Media Planning Calculus," *Operations Research.* January–February 1969, pp. 1–35.

[32] See Jay W. Forrester, "Advertising: A Problem in Industrial Dynamics," *Harvard Business Review,* March–April 1959, pp. 100–110.

ing a lagged impact on consumer awareness; awareness in turn has a lagged impact on factory sales; and factory sales have a lagged impact on advertising expenditures. He suggests that these time relationships be studied for the individual company and formulated mathematically into a digital computer simulation model. The parameters for this model would be estimated from company data supplemented by executive judgment. Alternative timing strategies would be stimulated in an effort to assess their differential impacts on company sales, costs, and profits.

Kuehn developed a model to explore how advertising should be "timed" for frequently purchased, highly seasonal, low-cost grocery products. He adopted the following product and market assumptions for illustrative purposes:

> The long-run demand for the particular product is stable. The product, however, is subject to a seasonal demand. The timing and magnitude of industry advertising expenditures does not affect the seasonal demand. A company's advertising only influences the company's share of industry demand. Advertising has no effect on retailers. There are two dominant competitors, who develop their timing patterns independently of each other, but optimally. The gross margin from sales is constant throughout the year (no price or cost changes). Other brand merchandising variables, such as product characteristics, retail availability, and competing brand prices, maintain a constant relative appeal to consumers throughout the sales cycle.[33]

Kuehn showed that the appropriate timing pattern depends upon the *degree of advertising carry-over* and the *amount of habitual behavior in customer brand choice*. Carry-over refers to the rate at which the effect of an advertising expenditure decays with the passage of time. A carry-over of .75 per month means that the current effect of a past advertising expenditure is 75 percent of its level last month, whereas a carry-over of only .10 per month means that only 10 percent of last month's effect is carried over. Habitual behavior, the other variable, indicates how much brand holdover occurs by reason of habit, inertia, or brand loyalty, independently of the level of advertising. High habitual purchasing, say .90, means that 90 percent of the buyers repeat their purchase of the brand regardless of the marketing stimuli.

Kuehn found that in the case of no advertising carry-over and no habitual purchasing, the decision maker is justified in using a percentage-of-sales rule in budgeting advertising. The optimal timing pattern for advertising expenditures coincides with the expected seasonal pattern of industry sales. But, if there exists any advertising carry-over and/or habitual purchasing, the percentage-of-sales budgeting method is not optimal. In all these cases it would be better to time advertising to lead the sales curve. The peak in advertising expenditures should come before the expected peak in sales, and the trough in advertising expenditures should come before the trough in sales. Lead time should be greater, the higher the carry-over. Furthermore, advertising expenditures should be steadier, the greater the extent of habitual purchasing.

Microscheduling Problem

The microscheduling problem involves how to allocate a set of advertising exposures over a short period of time to obtain the maximum impact. Suppose the

---

[33] See Alfred A. Kuehn, "How Advertising Performance Depends on Other Marketing Factors," *Journal of Advertising Research*, March 1962, pp. 2–10.

firm has decided to buy thirty radio spot announcements in the month of September.

One way to classify the multitude of possible patterns is shown in Figure 19-4. The left side shows that advertising messages for the month can be concentrated in a small part of the month ("burst" advertising), dispersed continuously throughout the month, or dispersed intermittently throughout the month. The top side shows that the advertising messages can be beamed with a level frequency, a rising frequency, a falling frequency, or an alternating frequency. The advertiser's problem is to decide which of these twelve general patterns would represent the most effective distribution plan for the messages.

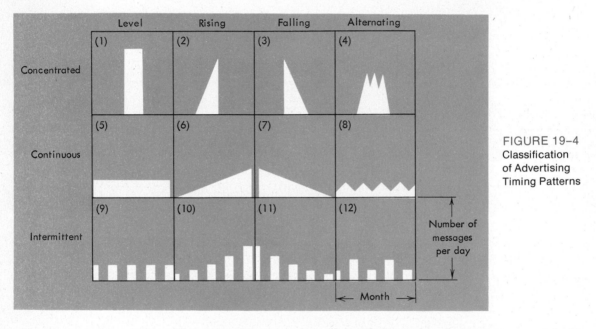

FIGURE 19-4
Classification
of Advertising
Timing Patterns

The most effective pattern depends upon the advertising communication objectives in relation to the nature of the product, target customers, distribution channels, and other marketing factors. Consider the following cases:

A *retailer* wants to announce a preseason sale of skiing equipment. She recognizes that only certain people will be interested in the message. Furthermore she recognizes that the target buyers need to hear the message only once or twice to know whether they are interested. Her objective is to maximize the *reach* of the message, not the *repetition*. She decides to concentrate the messages on the days of the sale at a level rate, but to vary the time of day to avoid the same audiences. She uses pattern (1).

A *muffler manufacturer-distributor* wants to keep his name before the public. Yet he does not want his advertising to be too continuous because only 3 to 5 percent of the cars on the road need a new muffler at any given time. He has therefore chosen to use intermittent advertising. Furthermore, he recognizes that Fridays are paydays for many potential buyers, and this would influence their interest in replacing a worn-out muffler. So he sponsors a few messages on a midweek day and more messages on Friday. He uses pattern (12).

The timing pattern should take into account three general factors. *Buyer turnover* expresses the rate at which new buyers appear in the market; the higher this rate, the more continuous the advertising ought to be to reach these new buyers. *Purchase frequency* is the number of times during the period that the buyer buys the product; the higher the purchase frequency, the more continuous the advertising ought to be to keep the brand on the buyer's mind. The *forgetting rate* is the rate at which the buyer forgets the brand in the absence of stimuli; the higher the forgetting rate, the more continuous the advertising ought to be to keep the brand in the buyer's mind.

In launching a new product, advertisers must make a choice between a campaign based on continuity versus flighting. *Continuity* is achieved by scheduling exposures evenly within a given time period. *Flighting* (or *pulsing*) refers to scheduling exposures unevenly over the same time period. Thus fifty-two exposures could be scheduled continuously at one a week throughout the year or flighted in bursts of thirteen exposures in each of four months, say January, April, July, October. Those who favor flighting feel that the resulting reduction in continuity is more than compensated for by the increased learning that takes place. They cite Ebbinghaus's finding that information learned more quickly is retained better than information learned more slowly.[34] However, the issue requires more research, and the decision model must take into account product, consumer, and competitive factors at the time of product introduction.[35]

When the decisions are made on the media vehicles and their timing, they should be displayed in a chart to give a bird's-eye view of the total media schedule. The media vehicles can be listed as rows and the months as columns, with the cells indicating when each media vehicle will be used.

MEASURING ADVERTISING EFFECTIVENESS

Good planning and control of advertising depend critically on measures of advertising effectiveness. Yet the amount of fundamental research on advertising effectiveness is appallingly small. According to Forrester:

> I doubt that there is any other function in industry where management bases so much expenditure on such scanty knowledge. The advertising industry spends 2 or 3 percent of its gross dollar volume on what it calls "research," and even if this were really true research, the small amount would be surprising. However, I estimate that less than a tenth of this amount would be considered research plus development as these terms are defined in the engineering and product research departments of companies . . . probably no more than 1/5 of 1 percent of total advertising expenditure is used to achieve an enduring understanding of how to spend the other 99.8 percent.[36]

Most of the measurement of advertising effectiveness is of an applied nature, dealing with specific advertisements and campaigns. Of the applied part, most of the money is spent by agencies on *pretesting* the given advertisement or

[34] Hermann Ebbinghaus, *Memory* (New York: Columbia University Press, 1913).

[35] See Ambar G. Rao, *Quantitative Theories in Advertising* (New York: John Wiley & Sons, 1970), pp. 60–79.

[36] Forrester, "Advertising," p. 102.

campaign before launching it into national circulation. Relatively less tends to be spent on *posttesting* the effect of given advertisements and campaigns.

The research techniques used to measure advertising effectiveness vary with what the advertiser is trying to accomplish. The behavioral change of ultimate interest to the advertiser is the act of purchase. One would expect to find that research on the "sales effect" of advertising predominates. Actually, sales-effect research tends to be meager in comparison with "communication-effect" research—research to determine the effect of given advertising on buyers' knowledge, feelings, and convictions. Many advertisers feel that the links between sales and advertising are too tenuous, complicated, and long-term to permit measuring the direct impact. They feel instead that the more short-term communication effects of given advertisements should be measured.

Communication-Effect Research

Communication-effect research seeks to discover whether the advertising is achieving the intended communication effects. There are various ways to evaluate the communication effectiveness of, say, an individual ad.[37] Called *copy testing,* it can be used both before and after an ad has been printed or broadcast. The purpose of *ad pretesting* is to make improvements in the advertising copy to the fullest extent possible prior to its release. There are three major methods of ad pretesting:

1. *Direct ratings.* Here a panel of target consumers or advertising experts examine alternative ads and fill out rating questionnaires. Sometimes a single question is raised, such as "Which of these ads do you think would influence you most to buy the product?" Or a more elaborate form consisting of several rating scales may be used, such as the one shown in Figure 19–5. Here the person evaluates the ad's at-

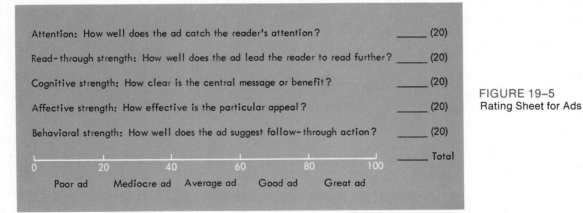

FIGURE 19–5
Rating Sheet for Ads

tention strength, read-through strength, cognitive strength, affective strength, and behavioral strength, assigning a number of points up to a maximum in each case. The underlying theory is that an effective ad must score high on all of these properties if it is ultimately to stimulate buying action. Too often ads are evaluated only on their attention- or comprehension-creating abilities. At the same

[37] For an excellent survey of research methods, see Lucas and Britt, "Measuring Advertising Effectiveness."

time, it must be appreciated that direct rating methods are less reliable than harder evidence of an ad's actual impact on target consumers. Direct rating scales help primarily to screen out poor ads rather than identify great ads.

2. *Portfolio tests.* Here respondents are given a dummy portfolio of ads and asked to take as much time as they want to read them. After putting them down, the respondents are asked to recall the ads they saw—unaided or aided by the interviewer—and to play back as much as they can about each ad. The results are taken to indicate the ability of an ad to stand out and of its intended message to be understood.

3. *Laboratory tests.* Some researchers assess the potential effect of an ad by measuring physiological reactions—heart beat, blood pressure, pupil dilation, perspiration—with such equipment as galvanometers, tachistoscopes, size-distance tunnels, and pupil-dilation-measuring equipment. These physiological tests at best measure the attention-getting power of an ad rather than any impact it has on beliefs, attitudes, or intentions.

There are two popular *ad posttesting* methods, the purpose of which is to assess the actual communication impact of the ad after it has appeared in media:

1. *Recall tests.* Recall tests involve finding persons who are regular users of the media vehicle and asking them to recall advertisers and products contained in the issue under study. They are asked to recall or play back everything they can remember. The administrator may or may not aid them in their recall. Recall scores are prepared on the basis of their responses and are used to indicate the power of the ad to be noticed and retained.

2. *Recognition tests.* Recognition tests call for sampling the readers of a given issue of, say, a magazine, asking them to point out what they recognize as having seen and/or read. For each ad, three different Starch readership scores (named after Daniel Starch, who provides the leading service) are prepared from the recognition data:

    Noted. The percentage of readers of the magazine who say they have previously seen the advertisement in the particular magazine.

    Seen/associated. The percentage of readers who say they have seen or read any part of the ad that clearly indicates the names of the product or service of the advertiser.

    Read most. The percentage of readers who not only looked at the advertisement but say that they read more than half of the total written material in the ad.

    The Starch organization also furnishes Adnorms, that is, average scores for each product class for the year, and separately for men and women for each magazine, to enable advertisers to evaluate their ads in relation to competitors' ads.

It should be noted that most of these efforts rate the attention and comprehension effectiveness of the ad and not necessarily its impact on attitude or behavior. Too many advertisers and agencies unfortunately stop short of investing the necessary money to really measure what the ad is accomplishing.

Sales-Effect Research Communication-effect advertising research undoubtedly helps advertisers improve the quality of message content and presentation, but it reveals little about how much sales may be affected, if at all. What *sales* conclusion can the advertiser draw in learning that its recent campaign has increased brand awareness by

20 percent and brand comprehension by 10 percent? What has the advertiser learned about the sales productivity of its advertising dollars and therefore how much to spend?

The sales effect of advertising will generally be more difficult to measure than the communication effect. Advertising sales effectiveness is easiest to measure in mail-order situations and hardest to measure in brand or corporate-image-building advertising. Efforts to measure the sales impact of advertising usually follow one of two approaches.

The *historical approach* involves the researcher in fitting past company sales to past company advertising expenditures on a current or lagged basis using least-squares regression. One of the best studies of this type was conducted by Palda to estimate the effect of advertising expenditures on the sales of Lydia Pinkham's Vegetable Compound between 1908 and 1960. Fortunately, the marketing factors in this market were minimal:

> The firm spent a very high proportion (40–60 percent) of its sales on advertising. Furthermore, it did not employ many of the customary "parameters" of marketing action: sales force, credit, discounts, frequent changes in package, point of purchase efforts, special offerings, etc. The assumption thus could safely be made that advertising had a measurable effect on Pinkham's sales. The product itself, Lydia Pinkham's Vegetable Compound, had no close substitutes. Competitors' marketing action was not, therefore, a complicating factor to be coped with. By the same token certain allied issues, such as the geographic distribution of Pinkham's marketing effort, could be ignored.[38]

Palda's equation was shown in chapter 9, page 235. He was able to calculate both the short-term and long-term marginal sales effects of advertising. The marginal advertising dollar seemed to increase sales by only $.50 in the short term, seeming to suggest that Pinkham appropriated too much for advertising. But the long-term marginal sales effect was three times as large; the marginal advertising dollar increased sales by $1.63 in the long term. Palda went on to calculate the posttax marginal rate of return on the company's invested advertising dollar. He found it to be in the neighborhood of 37 percent over the whole period, not an implausible figure for a well-established monopolist.

A marketing communications study by Montgomery and Silk estimated the sales response to three different communication tools used in the pharmaceutical industry.[39] A particular drug company spent 38 percent of its communication budget on direct mail, 32 percent on samples and literature, and 29 percent on journal advertising. Yet the sales-effects research indicated that journal advertising, the least used communication element, had the highest long-run advertising elasticity, here .365; samples and literature had an elasticity of .108; and direct mail had an elasticity of only .018. It thus appeared that the company was overdoing direct mail and underdoing journal advertising.

Other investigators applying multiple-regression methods to historical data have also produced useful advertising impact-on-sales measures for such

[38] Kristian S. Palda, *The Measurement of Cumulative Advertising Effect* (Englewood Cliffs, N.J.: Prentice-Hall, 1964), p. 87.

[39] David B. Montgomery and Alvin J. Silk, "Estimating Dynamic Effects of Market Communications Expenditures," *Management Science*, June 1972, pp. 485–501.

items as cigarettes, branded gasoline, coffee, and other products.[40] In all cases, these investigators have had to cope with the following problems: (1) autocorrelation of annual advertising and sales series, respectively; (2) high intercorrelation among the explanatory variables; (3) confounding of the sales/advertising response coefficient by the fact that many companies set advertising as a percentage of sales; and (4) insufficient number of years of data to fit the required number of variables.

These problems have led a growing number of companies to rely on a second method of measuring the sales impact of advertising, that of *experimental design*. Du Pont, for example, was one of the earliest firms to use experimental design principles to measure the effects of varying levels of advertising expenditure on sales. In the case of one Du Pont brand, management thought that the advertising budget was too low.[41] There were fifty-six sales territories, and they were divided into three groups: high, average, and low market share. (See Figure 19–6.) In a third of the territories, Du Pont spent the normal amount for advertising in the next period; in another third, two and a half times the normal amount; and in the remaining third, four times the normal amount. At the end of the experimental period, Du Pont was able to estimate how much extra sales were created by higher levels of advertising expenditure. Du Pont found that higher levels of advertising expenditure led to increased sales at a diminishing rate; and that the sales response was less pronounced in the areas where Du Pont had a higher market share.

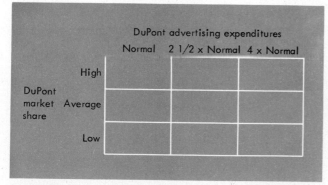

FIGURE 19–6
Experimental Design for Testing the Effect of Three Levels of Advertising Expenditure on Market Share

SOURCE: From p. 166, *Mathematical Models and Marketing Management*, by Robert Buzzell. Boston: Division of Research, Graduate School of Business Administration, Harvard University, 1968.

Anheuser-Busch uses advertising experiments in its beer markets to estimate sales response functions for different brands, market segments, and sales territories. This knowledge has enabled them to bring down their advertising ex-

---

[40] For a good review, see Nariman K. Dhalla, "Assessing the Long-term Value of Advertising," *Harvard Business Review*, January–February 1978, pp. 87–95.

[41] See Robert D. Buzzell, "E. I. Du Pont de Nemours & Co.: Measurement of Effects of Advertising," in his *Mathematical Models and Marketing Management* (Boston: Division of Research, Graduate School of Business Administration, Harvard University, 1968), pp. 157–79.

penditures per case while at the same time increasing their market share.[42] In general, a growing number of companies are striving to measure the sales effect of advertising expenditures rather than settling for lower-order measures such as ad recall or noting scores.

SUMMARY

Advertising—the use of paid media by a seller to communicate persuasive information about its products, services, or organization—is a potent promotional tool. American marketers spend over $33 billion annually on advertising. This includes many types of advertising (national, regional, local; consumer, industrial, retail; product, brand, institutional; and so on) designed to achieve a variety of objectives (immediate sales, brand recognition, preference, and so on).

The size of the advertising budget is commonly determined in a number of ways—according to what can be afforded, or as a regular percentage of the company's sales dollar, or to match competitors' expenditures, or by defining the cost of accomplishing specific communication goals. Four types of new decision models for setting the advertising budget are (1) sales response and decay models, (2) communication-stage models, (3) adaptive-control models, and (4) competitive-share models. The effectiveness of the advertising dollar will also depend upon the development of good message development and execution. The advertising copy must be placed in the most effective media, a problem that is increasingly being assisted by computerized media-selection models. The budget must be set over the business cycle, the seasons, the months, and even the days, with a careful consideration for delays in impact and the psychology of repetition. A continuous effort must be made to research the communication and sales effects of advertising programs before they are run, while they are running, and after they are terminated.

QUESTIONS AND PROBLEMS

1. Consider the following two statements: "The purpose of advertising is to create sales." "The purpose of advertising is to improve the buyers' disposition toward the company's products." Which comes closer to the truth?

2. The advertising manager of a large firm asks the executive committee to approve a $100,000 increase in the advertising budget. He submits that this extra money will probably increase company sales by $500,000 over what they would otherwise be. What other information would you want in order to judge the budget request?

3. A company's advertising expenditures average $5,000 a month. Current sales are $29,000, and the saturation sales level is estimated at $42,000. The sales response constant is $2, and the sales decay constant is 6 percent per month. Use the Vidale-Wolfe formula to estimate the probable sales increase next month.

4. A canned dog food manufacturer is trying to decide between media A and B. Medium A has 10,000,000 readers and charges $20,000 for a full page ad ($2.00 per 1,000). Medium B has 15,000,000 readers and charges $25,000 for a full page ad ($1.67 per 1,000). Is there any other calculation which might be made before assuming that B is the better medium?

5. A large oil company allocates its advertising budget to its territories according to current territorial sales. The advertising manager justifies using a constant advertising-to-sales ratio by saying that the company loses a certain percentage of its customers in

---

[42] See Russell L. Ackoff and James R. Emshoff, "Advertising Research at Anheuser-Busch, Inc. (1963–68)," *Sloan Management Review,* winter 1975, pp. 1–15.

each market each year and that advertising's most important job is to get new customers to replace them. What assumptions underlie this reasoning?

6. At one time, executives at Alberto-Culver expressed the following view about the relationship between increased advertising and sales: "We have found an astounding fact: the more we invest in advertising, the less our advertising-to-sales ratio becomes . . . once we get a brand off the ground, its ability to grow and return profits to the company accelerates at a much greater rate than the increased advertising expenditure." Is this plausible?

7. Hershey Foods for many years had the distinction of no consumer advertising. In spite of this, its candy bar sales continued to grow. Does this suggest that companies with excellent products may need little or no advertising?

8. Suggest some rules for developing effective advertising headlines and copy.

9. "The art department in an advertising agency is properly called the creative department. Media is not a creative function." Do you agree?

10. Is industrial advertising harder to measure for its communication effectiveness than consumer advertising?

11. Maloney's deductive scheme for generating advertising messages provides twelve ways to advertise a product. Develop an appeal illustrating each of the twelve types of messages.

Sales Promotion and Publicity Decisions

> *Gifts are like hooks.*
> MARTIAL (86 A.D.)
>
> *We despise no source that can pay us a pleasing attention.*
> MARK TWAIN

In this chapter, we turn to sales promotion and publicity. They are often viewed as playing a secondary role to the major tools of advertising and personal selling. Yet these tools can make a major contribution to marketing performance. They tend to be less well understood by marketing practitioners. Although some companies have created sales promotion departments, most companies do not have a sales promotion manager and leave it up to the individual product and brand managers to choose their own promotions. Many companies do not have a publicity director and borrow resources from the public relations department to help in product publicity. The recent high rate of inflation, however, has led companies to use these promotional tools more aggressively in showing customers ways to save money and gain more value in the marketplace.

SALES PROMOTION

Sales promotion comprises a wide variety of tactical promotion tools of a short-term incentive nature, designed to stimulate earlier and/or stronger target market response. Among the more popular ones are *coupons, premiums,* and *contests* for consumer markets; *buying allowances, cooperative advertising al-*

lowances, and *free goods* for distributors and dealers; *discounts, gifts,* and *extras* for industrial users; and sales contests and special bonuses for members of the sales force.

Sales promotion tools are used by a large variety of organizations, including manufacturers, distributors, retailers, trade associations, and various non-profit groups. As examples of the latter—churches sponsor bingo games, theatre parties, testimonial dinners, and raffles.

Rapid Growth of Sales Promotion

Sales promotion activities have grown rapidly in recent years. Between 1969 and 1976, sales promotion expenditures grew at an average rate of 9.4 percent per year, compared to 5.4 percent for advertising, and were estimated at over $30 billion in 1976.[1] Furthermore, sales promotion expenditures are expected to continue to grow faster than advertising. Consider the following:

> A technique of particularly high growth has been consumer couponing. The A. C. Nielsen Company reports that the number of consumer coupons distributed jumped from 23.4 billion in 1972 to 45.8 billion in 1976. The proportion of households using coupons rose from 58 percent to 77 percent between 1971 and 1977. However, redemption rates for coupons was relatively low in the 2.8 percent to 5.4 percent range for newspapers and magazines, 10.2 percent for direct mail, and up to 22.2 percent for "in" or "on" rack couponing.[2]

A number of factors contributed to the rapid growth of sales promotion in recent years, particularly in consumer markets.[3] Internal factors include: (1) promotion has become more acceptable to top management as an effective means to stimulate sales; (2) more product managers are qualified to use sales promotion tools; and (3) product managers are under greater pressure to obtain quick sales response. External factors include: (1) brands have increased in numbers; (2) competitors have become more promotion minded; (3) inflation and recession have made consumers more deal oriented; (4) trade pressure for more manufacturers' deals has grown; and (5) there is a belief that advertising efficiency has declined because of costs, media clutter, and government control.

Purpose of Sales Promotion

No single purpose can be advanced for sales promotion tools since they are so varied in form. A free sample stimulates consumer trial, while a free management-advisory service cements a long-term relationship with a retailer. Sales promotion techniques make three contributions to exchange relationships:

1. **Communication.** They gain attention and usually provide information that may lead the consumer to the product.
2. **Incentive.** They incorporate some concession, inducement, or contribution designed to represent value to the receiver.
3. **Invitation.** They include a distinct invitation to engage in the transaction now.

Incentive promotions are adopted by sellers to attract nonbrand users to

---

[1] Reprinted by permission of the *Harvard Business Review.* "Sales Promotion—Fast Growth, Faulty Management," by Roger A. Strang (July–August 1976). Copyright © 1976 by the President and Fellows of Harvard College; all rights reserved.

[2] "A Look At Sales Promotion," *The Nielsen Researcher,* no. 4, 1977, p. 8.

[3] Strang, "Sales Promotion," pp. 116–19.

try the brand and/or to reward brand-loyal users for their loyalty. Since both types of buyers will buy during the promotion period, both purposes are served, although the primary purpose is usually to attract nonbrand users to the brand. The nonbrand users are of two types, those who are loyal to other brands and those who are normal brand switchers. Incentive promotions primarily attract the brand switchers because the brand-loyal users of other brands do not always notice or act on the promotion. Since brand switchers are what they are, sales promotions are unlikely to turn them into loyal brand users. Incentive promotions used in markets of high brand similarity produce a high sales response in the short run but little permanent gain. In markets of high brand dissimilarity, incentive promotions are more likely to permanently alter market shares.

Incentive promotions essentially offer something extra to the customer and therefore attract the more price-conscious or premium-conscious customers. The extent to which the offer will be taken advantage of varies with the type of promotion, size of the incentive, ease of acting on the offer, and amount of advertising announcing the offer.

Sellers usually think of sales promotion as an activity designed to break down brand loyalty, and advertising as an activity designed to build up brand loyalty. Therefore an important issue for marketing managers is how to divide the budget between promotion and advertising. Companies can be found dividing their funds in ratios of anywhere from 20:80 to 80:20 on sales promotion and advertising respectively. This ratio has been rising over the past several years in response to the consumers' heightened sensitivity to price. Management should resist letting this ratio get too high. When a brand is on deal too much of the time, the dealing dilutes the brand image. The consumer begins to think of it as a cheap brand. No one knows when this happens but probably there is risk in putting a well-known brand on deal more than 30 percent of the time. In fact, dominant brands should use dealing infrequently, since most of it only gives a subsidy to current users.

Most observers feel that dealing activities do not build any long-term consumer franchise in contrast to advertising. Brown's study of 2,500 instant coffee buyers indicated that:

1. Sales promotions yield faster responses in sales than advertising.
2. Sales promotions do not tend to yield new, long-term buyers in mature markets because they attract mainly deal-prone consumers who switch among brands as deals become available.
3. Loyal brand buyers tend not to change their buying patterns as a result of competitive promotion.
4. Advertising appears to be capable of increasing the "prime franchise" of a brand.[4]

Prentice, however, has suggested that sales promotion tools can be divided into two groups, those that are "consumer franchise building" and those that are not.[5] The former imparts a selling message along with the deal, as in the case of

[4] Robert George Brown, "Sales Response to Promotions and Advertising," *Journal of Advertising Research*, August 1974, pp. 33–39, here pp. 36–37.

[5] See Roger A. Strang, Robert M. Prentice, and Alden G. Clayton, *The Relationship Between Advertising and Promotion in Brand Strategy* (Cambridge, Mass.: Marketing Science Institute, 1975), chap. 5.

free samples, coupons when they include a selling message, and premiums when they are related to the product. Sales promotion tools that are not consumer franchise building include price-off packs, consumer premiums not related to a product, contests and sweepstakes, consumer refund offers, and trade allowances. Sellers are urged to use consumer franchise-building promotions when possible because they enhance the brand's value in the mind of the consumers.

Ultimately, sales promotion seems most effective when used in conjunction with advertising.

> In one study, point-of-purchase displays related to current TV commercials were found to produce 15 percent more sales than similar displays not related to such advertising. In another, a heavy sampling approach along with TV advertising proved more successful than either TV alone or TV with coupons in introducing a product.[6]

Despite these research findings, there is a general lack of research studies to guide the sales promotion planner.[7] A systematic approach to sales promotion planning involves the following steps:

1. Establishing the sales promotion objectives
2. Selecting the sales promotion tools
3. Constructing the sales promotion program
4. Pretesting the sales promotion program
5. Implementing and controlling the sales promotion program
6. Evaluating the sales promotion results

Establishing the Sales Promotion Objectives

Sales promotion objectives are derived from basic *marketing communication objectives,* which in turn are derived from more basic *marketing objectives* developed for the product. Within this context, the specific objectives set for sales promotion will vary with the type of target market:

For *consumers,* objectives include encouraging more usage and purchase of larger-sized units by users, building trial among nonusers, attracting trial by other brand users.

For *retailers,* objectives include inducing retailer stocking of new items or larger volume, encouraging off-season buying, encouraging stocking of related items, offsetting competitive promotions, building brand loyalty of retailer, gaining entry into new retail outlets.

For *sales force,* objectives include encouraging support of a new product or model, encouraging more prospecting, stimulating sales in off-season.

Selecting the Sales Promotion Tools

A wide range of sales promotion tools are available to accomplish the various objectives. What is more, variations are continually being developed. The selection decision must take into account the type of market, sales promotion objec-

---

[6] Strang, "Sales Promotion," (1976), p. 124.

[7] For some interesting efforts, see *Promotional Decisions Using Mathematical Models* (Boston, Mass.: Allyn & Bacon, 1967); and Carl-Magnus Seipel, "Premiums—Forgotten by Theory," *Journal of Marketing,* April 1971, pp. 26–34.

tives, competitive conditions, and cost and effectiveness of each tool. The main tools for the markets and objectives are discussed below.

Use by manufacturers in consumer markets   If the objective is to offset a competitor's promotion, then *price-off packs* provide a quick, defensive response. On the other hand, if the objective is to generate initial trial of a product that is considered to have distinct competitive advantages, a *product sampling* program is an effective technique. For example, Lever Brothers had so much confidence in the superiority of its new mouthwash called Signal that it decided to distribute a free sample to two out of three American households at a cost of $15 million in 1978.

In launching a new consumer brand, the seller will typically use heavy sales promotion and advertising to achieve the objective of early and heavy trial. For example, P&G's plan for breaking into the Pittsburgh market in 1977 with its Folger brand included: (1) a 28 percent *discount* off wholesale price to retailers, (2) a thirty-five-cent *coupon* discount on a one-pound can mailed to area homes, (3) *coupon in can* for ten cents off, and (4) extensive area television advertising so the retailer couldn't refuse to carry the new brand.

In the case of mature brands, sales promotions are primarily designed to defend the current market share. Retailers often are unhappy about the form and amount of consumer deals they have to handle. They would much prefer to receive trade deals rather than handle consumer deals. According to Chevalier and Curhan:

> Retailers view promotional efforts initiated by manufacturers as encouraging profitless brand switching rather than increasing sales or profits. Manufacturers, on the other hand, complain that retailer-initiated promotions sometimes damage brand franchises which have been carefully and expensively nurtured over many years. Worse yet, manufacturers complain that retailers frequently take advantage of them by "absorbing" deals without passing their benefits along to consumers.[8]

Use by retailers in consumer markets   The retailer is concerned with building patronage and store traffic, and most sales promotion tools are selected with this objective in mind. The use of *specials* or *loss leaders* is prevalent in retailing, especially among food chains. *Trading stamps* emerged after World War II and boomed into the 1960s, only to fade in use when mass adoption of trading stamps removed competitive distinctiveness. *Sweepstakes,* and to a lesser extent *contests,* have emerged as popular techniques, with success being a function of factors such as the form and number of prizes.

Use by manufacturers for retailers and wholesalers   Manufacturers have a number of objectives for which sales promotions are usually effective. Basically, they are trying to secure the cooperation of wholesalers and retailers in carrying out their marketing strategy. These middlemen require some benefit, usually one that will be directly reflected in profit contribution. Manufacturers may offer a deal such as a *buying allowance* in order to stimulate middlemen to carry mer-

---

[8] Michel Chevalier and Ronald C. Curhan, *Temporary Promotions as a Function of Trade Deals: A Descriptive Analysis* (Cambridge, Mass.: Marketing Science Institute, 1975), p. 2.

chandise or to increase sales efforts. *Advertising allowances* and *display allowances* provide an indirect benefit to middlemen, since they contribute to promotional objectives. The manufacturer will normally want to run trade and consumer promotion in tandem. The use of promotions by manufacturers for the sole purpose of loading up the trade with merchandise is a short-sighted perspective. Trade deals must be coordinated with consumer promotional programs for long-run effectiveness.

Use by manufacturers for distributor salespersons   Direct stimulation of the distributor's salespersons is often undertaken by manufacturers where these salespersons handle a large number of different brands and are in a position to recommend them to customers. *Sales bonuses* and *gift incentive programs* are two devices that can be used effectively to enlist brand support from salespersons working for distributors.

Use by manufacturers in industrial markets   Industrial marketers use a whole range of sales promotion tools to stimulate sales and build stronger relationships with industrial customers. According to Shapiro:

> Technically oriented companies often offer design guides, or user brochures which provide a great deal of information. Some offer special calculation aids (e.g., specialized slide rules) or small pieces of equipment particularly suited to the industry (e.g., tape measure, magnifying glasses, magnets to detect iron and steel, and so on). Business gifts are perhaps more prevalent in the industrial area where buyer-seller relationships seem more permanent and are closer because of intimate design and production scheduling activities.[9]

Developing the Sales Promotion Program

A sales promotion program involves more than selecting the type of promotion. The marketer must make some additional decisions to define the full promotion program. The main decisions are size of incentive, conditions for participation, distributor vehicle for promotion, duration of promotion, timing of promotion, and overall budget for promotion.

Size of incentive   The marketer has to determine the most cost-effective size of the incentive. We start with the assumption that sales response will increase with the size of the incentive. Thus a fifteen-cents-off coupon will bring about more consumer trial than a five-cents-off coupon. But we cannot say that there will be three times as much response. In fact, the sales response function is normally S-shaped. That is, if the incentive size is small, there may be very little response. A certain minimum incentive size must be reached for the promotion to start drawing sufficient attention. Beyond some point, higher incentives produce more sales response at a diminishing rate. By examining the relative rates of sales and cost increase, the marketer can determine the optimal size incentive to offer.

Some of the large consumer-packaged-goods firms have a sales promotion manager who keeps records on the effectiveness of different promotions used throughout the company and correlates their incentive value with the sales re-

---

[9] Benson P. Shapiro, "Improve Distribution with Your Promotional Mix," *Harvard Business Review*, March–April 1977, p. 123.

sponse in order to gain insight into the sales response function. As a result, the sales promotion manager can recommend incentive levels with a degree of expertise that would not normally be possessed by individual brand managers who carry out only one or two promotions a year.

Conditions for participation Another decision in using a promotion is the conditions for participation. For example, a premium offer may be made available to anyone or only to those who turn in boxtops or other evidence of consumption. Sweepstakes may be limited to certain states and not made available to families of company personnel or to persons under a certain age. By carefully choosing conditions for participation, the seller can selectively discourage those who are unlikely to become regular users of the product. On the other hand, if the conditions are too restrictive, only the most loyal or deal-prone consumers will participate.

Distribution vehicle for promotion The marketer must decide how to promote and distribute the promotion program to the target audience. Suppose the promotion is a coupon that will entitle the buyer to fifteen cents off the list price. The coupon could be made available to prospective customers in at least four ways: (1) in or on the package or related packages. (2) in the store, (3) in the mail, and (4) in advertising media. Each vehicle involves a different level of reach and cost. For example, in-pack coupons primarily reach current users, whereas mailed coupons can be directed at nonbrand users, although at a greater cost.

Duration of promotion Another issue is the length of the period sales promotions should be run. If they are offered for too short a period, many prospects would not have a chance to take advantage, since they may not be repurchasing at the time or be too busy with other things. If the promotion runs for a long period, then the customers may begin to view this as a long-term price concession and the deal will lose some of its "act now" force and also raise questions about the brand's quality. Stern reports, on the basis of a number of studies, that an optimal frequency appears to be about three weeks per quarter and optimal duration is the length of the average purchase cycle.[10] This varies, of course, with the promotion objectives, customer buying habits, competitors' strategies, and other factors.

Timing of promotion A schedule of sales promotion will usually be constructed by brand managers, subject to sales department requirements. This schedule will be studied and evaluated by divisional marketing management in terms of total divisional marketing strategy. The schedule is a planning instrument and requires careful timing to allow for production, salespersons, and distribution coordination. At the same time, some unplanned promotions will be needed under tactical pressure and will have to be prepared on short notice.

Overall sales promotion budget The overall budget for sales promotion can be arrived at in two ways. It can be built from the ground up, where the marketer

---

[10] Arthur Stern, "Measuring the Effectiveness of Package Goods Promotion Strategies," a paper presented at a meeting of the Association of National Advertisers, Glen Cove, N.Y., February 1978.

decides on the various promotions to sponsor during the year and estimates the cost of each. The cost of a particular promotion consists of the total *administrative cost* (printing, mailing, and promoting the deal) and the *incentive cost* (cost of premium or cents-off, including rate of redemption), multiplied by the *expected number of units* that will be sold on deal.

> Suppose a brand of after-shave lotion will be marked down 9¢ for a limited period. The item regularly sells for $1.09, of which 40¢ represents a contribution to the manufacturer's profit before marketing expense. The brand manager expects a million bottles to be sold under this deal. Thus the incentive cost of the deal will be $90,000 (= .09 × 1,000,000). Suppose the administrative cost is estimated at $10,000. Then the total cost is $100,000. In order to break even on this deal, the company will have to sell 250,000 (= $100,000 ÷ .40) more units than would have occurred over the same period without the deal.

In the case of a coupon deal, the cost would take into account the fact that only a fraction of the consumers will redeem the coupons. In the case of an in-pack premium, the deal cost must include the costs of procurement and packaging of the premium offset by any price increase on the package.

The other, more common way to arrive at an overall budget for sales promotion is to resort to a conventional proportion of the total budget for advertising and sales promotion. For example, toiletries may get a sales promotion budget of 20 to 40 percent of the total promotion budget, whereas packaged goods may get as much as 30 to 60 percent. These proportions vary substantially for different brands in different markets and are influenced by the product stage of the life cycle and competitive expenditures on promotion.

Organizations with multiple brands should insure that brand budgets are coordinated in order to gain economies from sales promotion activities. Although not all sales promotion activities can be preplanned, coordination gives cost-saving advantages such as single mailings of multiple coupons to consumers.

Strang, in his study of sales promotion in seventeen leading U.S. consumer goods manufacturers and advertising agencies, found a number of inadequacies in budgeting proceedings.[11] These included:

1. Lack of consideration of cost effectiveness.
2. Use of simplistic decision rules, such as extensions of last year's spending, percentage of expected sales, maintenance of a fixed ratio to advertising, and the "leftover approach" where promotion gets what is left from a fixed percentage of sales after the advertising budget has been removed.
3. Advertising and promotional budgets being prepared independently.

Pretesting the Sales Promotion Program

Although sales promotion programs are designed on the basis of experience, pretests should be conducted whenever possible to determine if (1) the tools are appropriate, (2) the size of the incentive is optimal, and (3) the method for presentation is likely to be efficient. A survey by the Premium Advertisers Association indicated that fewer than 42 percent of premium offerers ever tested their effectiveness.[12] Strang maintains that promotions can usually be tested quickly and in-

[11] Strang, "Sales Promotion," p. 119.

[12] Russell D. Bowman, "Merchandising and Promotion Grow Big in Marketing World," *Advertising Age*, December 1974, p. 21.

expensively, and that some large companies test alternative strategies in selected market areas with each of their national promotions.[13]

Sales promotions directed at consumer markets can be readily pretested. Groups of consumers can be asked to rate or rank different possible deals according to their preference. Or trial tests can be run in limited geographical areas.

Implementing and Controlling the Sales Promotion Program

Effective control of sales promotions requires that specific goals and implementation plans for individual promotions be established. Program implementation must cover two critical time factors, lead time and sell-off time. Lead time is the time necessary to bring the program up to the point of announcing the deal.

> It covers initial planning, design, and approval of package modifications or material to be mailed or distributed to the home, preparation of conjunctive advertising and point-of-sale materials, notification of field sales personnel, establishment of allocations for individual distributors, purchasing and printing of special premiums or packaging materials, production of advance inventories and staging at distribution centers in preparation for release at a specific date, and, finally, the distribution to the retailer.[14]

Sell-off time begins at the date of release and ends when approximately 90 to 95 percent of the deal merchandise is in the hands of consumers, which may take one to several months, depending on the deal duration.

Evaluating the Sales Promotion Results

Evaluation is a crucial requirement for improving any program. Yet according to Strang:

> Evaluation of promotion programs receives . . . little attention. Even where an attempt is made to evaluate a promotion, it is likely to be superficial. . . . Evaluation in terms of profitability is even less common.[15]

Evaluation procedures vary with the type of market. For example, manufacturers usually measure the effectiveness of retail trade promotions by checking on store delivery volume, store shelf-space allocation, and cooperative advertising placed by retailers. Manufacturers measure the effectiveness of consumer promotions using any of four methods: sales performance movement, analysis of consumer-panel data, consumer surveys, and experimental studies.

The most common consumer promotion evaluation technique is to compare sales or market share before, during, and after a promotion. Increased sales are attributed to the impact of the sales promotion program, all other things being equal. Figure 20–1 shows the type of deal results that manufacturers would like to see. In the prepromotion period, the company's brand enjoyed a 6 percent share of the market. During the promotion period, the company's brand share rose to 10 percent. This share gain of 4 percent is made up of (1) deal-prone consumers who switched to this brand to take advantage of the deal and (2) brand-loyal customers who increased their purchases in response to the price

[13] Strang, "Sales Promotion," p. 122.

[14] Kurt H. Schaffir and H. George Trentin, *Marketing Information Systems* (New York: Amacom, 1973), p. 81.

[15] Strang, "Sales Promotion," p. 120.

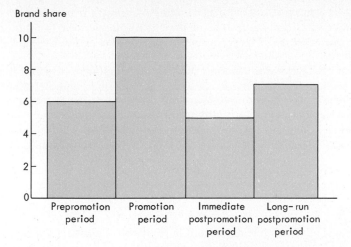

Brand share

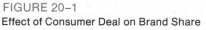

FIGURE 20–1
Effect of Consumer Deal on Brand Share

incentive. Immediately after the promotion ended, the brand share fell to 5 percent because consumers were overstocked and they were working down their inventory. After this stock adjustment period, brand share went up to 7 percent, showing a one percentage point increase in the number of loyal customers. This is likely to be the case when the brand has good qualities that many nonbrand users had not known about.

In many cases, the results are less satisfactory. We can imagine two different situations. In the first one, brand share jumps up to 10 percent in the promotion period, falls to 2 percent in the immediate postpromotion period, and then returns to 6 percent. This pattern suggests that the existing customers were the main buyers during the promotion period and they stocked up on this brand; then they consumed out of stock immediately after the promotion period; and they ultimately returned to their normal rate of purchase. Thus the effect of the deal was largely to alter the time pattern of purchase rather than the permanent level of purchase. This is not necessarily wasteful, especially if pipeline inventories are excessive and the company wants to clear them earlier and, in the meantime, cut production.

We can imagine another case where brand share rises little or not at all during the promotion period and falls and remains below the normal level after the promotion period. This situation suggests a brand that is basically on a downward sales trend, which the promotion simply slowed down but did not halt or reverse. Peckham reports some brands where the promotion slowed down the rate of decline, but did not stop it.[16]

Another way to measure the effect of a sales promotion program is to interview a sample of consumers in the target market, attempting to learn how many consumers recall the promotion, what they thought of it, how many took advantage of it, and how it affected their subsequent brand-choice behavior. This method would not be used for each promotion but only selectively to research the effect of that type of sales promotion on consumers.

Deals can also be studied through carefully arranged experiments that vary such deal attributes as incentive value, deal duration, and deal-distribution

[16] See James O. Peckham, Sr., *The Wheel of Marketing* (Chicago: A. C. Nielsen, 1973).

media. By varying the deal attributes offered to matched groups or matched geographical areas, inferences can be drawn on their sales impact. At the same
time, experiments need some follow-up consumer study to understand the reasons why the deal attributes produced different levels of response.

Consumer-panel data can also be used to evaluate consumer response to
sales promotion. A consumer-panel data study by Dodson, Tybout, and Sternthal
found that deals generally enhance brand switching, the rate depending on the
type of deal. Media-distributed coupons induce substantial switching, cents-off
deals induce somewhat less switching, and package coupons hardly affect brand
switching. Furthermore consumers generally return to their preferred brands after the deal.[17]

PUBLICITY

Another major marketing communications tool is *publicity*. Publicity has been
defined as the activity of "securing editorial space, as divorced from paid space,
in all media read, viewed, or heard by a company's customers or prospects, for
the specific purpose of assisting in the meeting of sales goals."[18] To the extent
that an organization can create events and news around a marketable entity, it is
using publicity.

What kinds of entities can be publicized? Almost anything. Publicity is
used to promote various brands, products, persons, places, ideas, activities, organizations, and even nations. For example, trade associations representing
products whose primary demand has fallen—such as eggs, milk, potatoes—have
developed publicity campaigns to renew interest in and increase use of these
products. Publicity is commonly used in the launching of new products and
brands as well as in efforts to rekindle interest in mature brands. Organizations
suffering from low visibility have resorted to publicity to create more awareness,
while organizations with poor public images have attempted to improve their
image by engaging in and publicizing positive actions. Nations that are seeking
more tourists, foreign investment, or international support often use publicity
toward these purposes.

Publicity is part of a larger concept, that of public relations. Today's public relations practitioners perform the following functions:

1. *Press relations.* The aim of press relations is to place newsworthy information
   into the news media to attract attention to a person, product, or service.
2. *Product publicity.* Product publicity involves various efforts to publicize through
   news media and other means specific products and happenings related to
   products.
3. *Corporate communications.* This activity covers internal and external communications to give attention and understanding to the institution.
4. *Lobbying.* Lobbying refers to the effort to deal with legislators and government
   officials to defeat unwanted legislation and regulation and/or to promote wanted
   legislation and regulation.

[17] Joe A. Dodson, Alice M. Tybout, and Brian Sternthal, "Impact of Deals and Deal Retraction
on Brand Switching," *Journal of Marketing Research*, February 1978, pp. 72–81, here p. 79.

[18] George Black, *Planned Industrial Publicity* (Chicago: Putnam Publishing, 1952), p. 3.

5. *Counseling.* Counseling is the provision of general advice to the company about what is happening in the society and what the company might do in the way of changing its ways or improving its communications.[19]

Since publicity is part of public relations, those skilled in publicity are usually found not in the company's marketing department but in its public relations department. The public relations department is typically located at corporate headquarters rather than in the various divisions; and its staff is so busy dealing with various publics—stockholders, employees, legislators, city officials—that publicity to support product marketing objectives may be neglected. One frequent solution is to establish a publicity unit within the marketing department.

Publicity is often described as a marketing stepchild because it is relatively underutilized in relation to the real contribution it can make. Publicity has created in many cases memorable impacts on public awareness that advertising alone could not have accomplished, at least not at the same low cost. The company does not pay for the space or time in the media. It does pay for the staff time used to develop the stories and induce the media to use them, but this cost is relatively small. If the company has a real story to tell, it could be picked up by all the news media and be worth millions of dollars in equivalent advertising. Furthermore, it would possess more credibility as news than if it had been delivered as advertising.

In considering when and how to use product publicity, management should approach the publicity function as it does any function. Management should define the publicity objectives; develop and carry out an effective publicity plan; and evaluate the results. We now turn to these decisions.

Establishing the Publicity Objectives

We will assume that an organization is engaged in developing a marketing plan for a brand, product, or other marketable entity. The organization has identified the target market and the target response that it wants in the coming period. It considers the role of different marketing communication tools in contributing to the target response. It decides to use advertising as the primary means of building or expanding market awareness and sales promotion as the primary means of stimulating trial. What can publicity contribute?

The first thing to recognize is that the usefulness of publicity varies from product to product. Publicity's potential contribution is stronger, the stronger the following variables:

1. *Newsworthiness.* Products that can support interesting stories that news editors will accept are the best candidates for publicity.

2. *Stimulus for sales force and dealers.* Publicity can be useful in boosting the enthusiasm of the sales force and dealers when it might be lacking. For example, news stories appearing about a new product before it is launched will help the sales force gain a hearing from retailers.

3. *Need for credibility.* Publicity introduces an element of credibility by virtue of communicating the message in an editorial context. Credibility is needed by new products as well as by mature products that the market has questioned.

4. *Small budget.* Publicity, while it is not without cost, tends to be low in cost for producing exposures in comparison with direct mail and media advertising. The

---

[19] Adapted from Scott M. Cutlip and Allen H. Center, *Effective Public Relations*, 3rd ed. (Englewood Cliffs, N.J.: Prentice-Hall, 1964), pp. 10–14.

smaller the company's marketing communications budget, the stronger the case for using imaginative publicity to neutralize the advantage of a competitor who has more money to spend on advertising.

If the product has one or more of these characteristics, publicity should be considered as a potentially useful tool in the marketing communications mix.

Now the task is to set specific objectives for the publicity. As an example, the Wine Growers of California hired the public relations firm of Daniel J. Edelman, Inc., in 1966 to create a publicity program to support two major marketing objectives: (1) to convince Americans that wine drinking is a pleasurable part of good living; and (2) to improve the image and market share of California wines among all wines. To contribute to these marketing objectives, the following publicity objectives were established: (1) to develop magazine stories about wine and get them placed in top magazines (*Time, House Beautiful*) and in newspapers (food columns, feature sections); (2) to develop stories directed to the medical profession on wine's many health values; and (3) to develop special programs for the young adult market, college market, governmental bodies, and various ethnic communities.

Where possible, objectives such as these should be translated into specific goals for audience response variables so that results can be evaluated at the end of the publicity campaign.

Choosing the Publicity Messages and Vehicles

After establishing the objectives, the publicist sets about determining whether there are any interesting stories to tell about the product. As an example, suppose a college with low visibility adopts the objective of achieving more public recognition. The publicist will review the college's various components to see whether any natural stories exist. Do any faculty members have unusual backgrounds or are any of them working on unusual projects? Are any novel courses being taught? Are any unusual students enrolled? Are any interesting events taking place on campus? Is there a story about the architecture, history, or aspirations of the college? Usually a search along these lines will uncover hundreds of stories that can be fed to the press with the effect of creating much more public recognition of the college. Ideally, stories should be chosen that symbolize the kind of college this college wants to be. The stories should support its desired market positioning.

If the number of good stories is insufficient, the publicist then dreams up newsworthy events that the college could sponsor. Here the publicist gets into *creating news* rather than *finding news.* Among the ideas are hosting major academic conventions, featuring well-known speakers, and developing news conferences. Each event is an opportunity to develop a host of stories directed to relevant media vehicles and audiences.

Event creation is a particularly important skill in publicizing fund-raising drives for nonprofit organizations. Fund raisers have developed a large repertoire of special events, including *anniversary celebrations, art exhibits, auctions, benefit evenings, bingo games, book sales, cake sales, contests, dances, dinners, fairs, fashion shows, parties in unusual places, telethons, rummage sales, tours,* and *walkathons.* No sooner does one type of event get created, such as a walkathon, than competitors spawn new versions such as read-a-thons, bike-a-thons, and jog-a-thons.

A publicist is able to find or create stories on behalf of even mundane products. Some years ago, the Potato Board, an association of more than fifteen thousand U.S. potato growers, decided to finance a publicity campaign to encourage more potato consumption.[20] A national attitude and usage study indicated that many consumers perceived potatoes as too fattening, not nutritious enough, and not a good source of vitamins and minerals. These attitudes were being disseminated by various opinion leaders, such as food editors, diet advocates, and doctors. In truth, potatoes have far fewer calories than people imagine and contain several important vitamins and minerals. The Potato Board decided to develop separate publicity programs for each major audience: consumers, doctors, dieticians, nutritionists, home economists, and food editors. The consumer program called for generating many stories about the potato for network television and national women's magazines, developing and distributing *The Potato Lover's Diet Cookbook*, and placing articles and recipes in food editors' columns. The food editors' program consisted of organizing seminars conducted by nutrition experts and a tour of major markets by a leading diet authority, who talked with food editors.

Publicity can also be highly effective in brand promotion. One of the top brands of cat food is Star-Kist Foods's 9-Lives. Its brand image revolves around one of the most famous felines in the world, the now-deceased Morris the Cat. The advertising agency of Leo Burnett, which created Morris for its ads, wanted to make him more of a living, breathing, real-life feline to whom cat owners and cat lovers could relate. They hired a public relations firm, which then proposed and carried out the following ideas: (1) launch a Morris "look-alike" contest in nine major markets, with Morris being booked for personal appearances, and extensive stories appearing about the search for a look-alike; (2) write a book called *Morris, An Intimate Biography*, describing the adventures of this famous feline; (3) establish a coveted award called The Morris, a bronze statuette given to the owners of award-winning cats selected at local cat shows; (4) sponsor Adopt-A-Cat Month with Morris as the official "spokescat" for the month, urging people to adopt stray cats as Morris once was; and (5) distribute a booklet called *The Morris Method*, on cat care. All of these publicity steps strengthened the brand's market share in the cat food market.

Implementing the Publicity Plan

Implementing publicity requires a great deal of care. Take the matter of placing stories in the media. A great story is easy to place, no matter who does the placing. But most stories are less than great and may not get through busy editors. One of the chief assets of publicists is the personal relationships they have established with media editors. Publicists are typically exjournalists who know a number of the media editors and know what they want. Media editors want interesting, well-written stories, and easy access to sources of further information. Publicists look at media editors as a market to satisfy so that in turn these editors will be inclined to "buy" their stories.

Publicity also requires extra care when it involves staging special events such as testimonial dinners, news conferences, and national contests. Publicists need a good head for detail and also for coming up with quick solutions when things go wrong.

---

[20] For details, see Joseph M. Coogle, Jr., "Media, Advertising, and Public Relations," in *Review of Marketing 1978*, eds. Gerald Zaltman and Thomas V. Bonoma (Chicago: American Marketing Association, 1978), pp. 481–84.

Evaluating the Publicity Results

The most difficult thing about measuring publicity's contribution is that it is typically used with other marketing communication tools, and its contribution is hard to separate out. If it is used before the other tools come into action, as often happens in launching a new product, its contribution is easier to evaluate.

Publicity is designed with certain audience-response objectives in mind, and these objectives form the basis of what is measured. The major response measures are exposures, awareness/comprehension/attitude change, and sales.

Exposures The easiest and most common measure of publicity effectiveness is the number of exposures created in the media. Most publicists supply the client with a clippings book, showing all the media that carried news about the product and a summary statement such as:

> Media coverage included 3,500 column inches of news and photographs in 350 publications with a combined circulation of 79.4 million; 2,500 minutes of air time on 290 radio stations and an estimated audience of 65 million; and 660 minutes of air time on 160 television stations with an estimated audience of 91 million. If this time and space had been purchased at advertising rates, it would have amounted to $1,047,000.[21]

The purpose of citing the equivalent advertising cost is to make a case for publicity's cost effectiveness, since the total publicity effort must have cost less than $1,047,000. Furthermore, publicity is usually more read and believed than ads.

Still, this exposure measure is not very satisfying. There is no indication of how many people actually read, saw, or heard the message, and what they thought afterwards. Furthermore, there is no information on the net audience reached since publications have overlapping readership.

Awareness/comprehension/attitude change A better measure calls for finding out what change in product awareness/comprehension/attitude occurred as a result of the publicity campaign (after allowing for the impact of other marketing communications). This requires the use of survey methodology to measure the before-after levels of these variables. The Potato Board carried out this type of evaluation and learned, for example, that the number of people who agreed with the statement "potatoes are rich in vitamins and minerals" went from 36 percent before the campaign to 67 percent after the campaign, a significant improvement in product comprehension.

Sales and profit contribution Sales and profit impact is the most satisfactory measure if obtainable. For example, 9-Lives sales had increased 43 percent at the end of the Morris the Cat publicity campaign. However, advertising and other marketing communications had been stepped up, and it was not possible to attribute all the increased sales to publicity alone. It is necessary to make some assumption as to the role that publicity played in the total impact. Sup-

[21] Arthur M. Merims, "Marketing's Stepchild: Product Publicity," *Harvard Business Review,* November–December 1972, pp. 111–12. The value of "equivalent advertising" was arrived at by summing the total number of publicity exposures, which is 235.4 million; then figuring that it costs (at that time) approximately $4.45 per thousand exposures with advertising media, or a total advertising cost of $1,047,000 (= $4.45 × 235,400).

pose total sales have increased $1,500,000, and management conservatively estimates that publicity contributed 15 percent of the total sales increase. Then the return on publicity investment is calculated as follows:

Total sales increase	$1,500,000
Estimated sales increase due to publicity (15%)	225,000
Contribution margin on product sales (10%)	22,500
Total direct cost of publicity program	−10,000
Contribution margin added by publicity investment	$ 12,500
Return on publicity investment ($12,500/$10,000) =	125%

SUMMARY   Sales promotion and publicity are two important tools of marketing communication that are often not as well understood by many marketing practitioners as advertising and personal selling. Yet their potential impact on sales and profit is substantial.

Sales promotion covers a wide variety of short-term incentive tools—such as coupons, premiums, contests, and buying allowances—designed to stimulate earlier and/or stronger market response. They can be used to stimulate consumer markets, the trade, and the organization's own sales force. Sales promotion expenditures now exceed advertising expenditures and have been growing at a faster rate than advertising in recent times. The effective use of sales promotion requires careful planning, consisting of six steps. The first step is to develop clear objectives for sales promotion that derive from the larger marketing communication objectives and still broader marketing objectives set for the product. The second step calls for choosing the sales promotion tools that can accomplish these objectives in the most cost-effective way. The third step calls for rounding out the sales promotion program by making decisions on the specific size of the promotion incentive, conditions for participation, distribution vehicles, duration and timing of promotion, and the overall budget for promotion. The fourth step calls for pretesting the proposed promotion in a limited geographical area or market group to assess its effectiveness. The fifth step calls for the careful implementation and control of the sales promotion program. Finally, the sixth step calls for evaluating the sales promotion results to improve the future use of this tool.

Publicity tends to be the least utilized of the major marketing communication tools, although it has great potential for building awareness and preference in the marketplace. Publicity resources in organizations tend to be located in public relations departments rather than in marketing departments, and this accounts for some of its relative neglect. Publicity is especially useful for organizations that have a good story to tell but have too limited a budget to support large-scale advertising. There are four steps in the effective use of publicity. The first step is to establish the objectives for publicity in support of the broader marketing objectives. The second step is to select the publicity messages and vehicles that would be most cost effective. The third step calls for implementing the publicity plan through seeking the cooperation of media people and arranging planned events. The final step is to evaluate the publicity results in terms of the number of exposures achieved, changes in awareness/comprehension/attitude in the target audience and, ultimately, increases in sales and profits.

1. A major basketball team has recently experienced a decline in home game attendance. The team's owner decided to hire a marketing person to stimulate attendance. What are some of the steps that can be taken?

2. A nationwide trucking company uses a combination of advertising and personal selling to stimulate demand for its services. Can you envision roles for publicity and sales promotion in the promotion of trucking services? What percentages of the total promotion budget should go into advertising, personal selling, publicity, and sales promotion?

3. Joe Pringle, a product manager at the XYZ Snacks Company, is concerned about falling sales in recent months. His inventory is high. He is contemplating a sales promotion to reverse the sales trend and reduce inventories. He is thinking of offering a case allowance to the trade. He expects sales to be 40,000 cases in the absence of promotion. The case price is $10 and the gross profit contribution is .40. He is currently thinking of offering a $1 case allowance. He expects increased sales of 20,000 cases during the promotion period. The estimated cost of developing this promotion is $12,000. (a) Will he make a profit on this promotion? (b) What is the breakeven sales increase that will justify this case allowance? (c) If he offered only a $.50 case allowance, he expects additional net sales of 12,000. Should he offer a $1 or $.50 case allowance?

4. Indicate how the movie industry is currently using publicity to promote its major new pictures. Give some examples.

5. Much of the public relations work done by business firms consists of miscellaneous and unrelated activities. Can you suggest an underlying public relations orientation a company could adopt that would provide a focus for many publicity activities?

6. Select a product or service of your choice and recommend which sales promotion tools should be used to build its consumer franchise.

Sales-Force Decisions

Every organization contains one or more persons who have direct responsibility for contacting and dealing with prospects and customers. We call this group the sales force. Sales forces are found not only in commercial companies but in non-profit organizations as well. College recruiters represent a sales-force arm of the college seeking to sell prospective students on coming to that college. Churches form membership committees, which are responsible for attracting new members. The U.S. Agricultural Extension Service consists of agricultural specialists who try to educate and sell farmers on using the latest technology. Hospitals, museums, and other organizations use a staff of fund raisers to contact prospective donors and sell them on supporting the organization.

The traditional term used to describe the persons in the sales force is *salesmen*. However, this term is becoming obsolete because of the increasing number of women who are taking on sales responsibilities. We will use *sales representatives* and *salespersons*, although *salesmen* will be used occasionally where appropriate. Many other terms have come into use to describe people who work in sales, including account executive, sales consultant, field representative, manufacturers' representative, agent, service representative, and marketing representative.

Organizations have a choice between engaging a direct and a contractual sales force. A *direct (or company) sales force* consists of full or part-time paid employees who work exclusively for the company. This sales force may in turn consist of two groups: *inside sales personnel,* who conduct their business from their offices, using the telephone and receiving visits from prospective buyers, and *field sales personnel,* who travel and visit customers. A company can also use a *contractual sales force* such as manufacturers' reps, sales agents, or brokers, who are paid a commission on the sales they generate.

The sales force, to get its job done, requires the support of other personnel, such as:

1. *Top management.* Top management is increasingly getting involved in the sales process,[1] especially when *national accounts*[2] or *major sales*[3] are at stake.
2. *Technical sales personnel.* They are technical people who work with the sales representatives to supply technical information needed by the customer before, during, or after the purchase of the product.
3. *Customer service representatives.* They provide installation, maintenance, and other services to the customer.
4. *Office staff.* This group consists of sales analysts, order expediters, and secretarial personnel.

In 1976, American firms spent approximately $100 billion on personal selling compared with $33 billion on advertising. Over 5.4 million Americans work in sales and related occupations. Sales personnel serve as the company's unique link to the customers. The sales representative *is* the company to many of its customers. The sales representative tailors the company's offer to the individual customer and in turn brings back to the company much needed intelligence about the customer.

In this chapter, we will examine the major decisions involved in developing and managing personal selling resources. These decisions consist of defining tasks and objectives for the sales force, determining the size of the sales force, designing the sales organization and territories, and recruiting, selecting, training, compensating, supervising, and evaluating sales representatives.

SALES-FORCE TASKS AND OBJECTIVES

Sales-force objectives must be based on the character of the company's target markets and the company's sought position in these markets. The company must consider the unique role that personal selling can play in the marketing mix to serve customer needs in a competitively effective way. Personal selling happens to be the most expensive contact and communications tool of the company, costing companies an average of $59 a sales call in 1978.[4] Therefore it must be used

---

[1] "Executive Suite Salesmanship," *Business Week,* October 20, 1975, pp. 70, 74.

[2] Roger M. Pegram, *Selling and Servicing the National Account* (New York: Conference Board, Report No. 557, 1972).

[3] William H. Kaven, *Managing the Major Sale* (New York: American Management Association, 1971); and Benson P. Shapiro and Ronald S. Posner, "Making the Major Sale," *Harvard Business Review,* March–April 1976, pp. 68–78.

[4] John Steinbrink, *Compensation of Salesmen: Dartnell's 19th Biennial Survey* (Chicago: Dartnell Corp., 1978).

sparingly. Personal selling is also the most effective tool at certain stages of the buying process, such as the buyer-education, negotiation, and sales-closing stages. It is important that the company think out carefully when and how to use sales representatives to facilitate the marketing task.

Types of Sales Positions

There are probably more stereotypes about sales representatives than about any other group. The salesman is likely to conjure up an image of Arthur Miller's pitiable Willy Loman or Meredith Willson's ebullient Harold Hill from "The Music Man"—the latter a glib, boisterous character always ready with a glad hand and a racy story. Sales representatives are typically pictured as loving sociability—in spite of some recent evidence that many sales representatives actually dislike it. They are criticized for aggressively foisting goods on people—in spite of the fact that buyers often search out sales representatives.

Actually, the term *sales representative* covers a broad range of positions in our economy, within which the differences are often greater than the similarities. McMurry offered the following classification of sales positions:

1. Positions where the "salesperson's" job is predominantly to deliver the product, e.g., milk, bread, fuel, oil.
2. Positions where the salesperson is predominantly an inside order-taker, e.g., the haberdashery salesperson standing behind the counter.
3. Positions where the salesperson is also predominantly an order-taker but works in the field, as the packing-house, soap, or spice salesperson does.
4. Positions where the salesperson is not expected or permitted to take an order but is called on only to build goodwill or to educate the actual or potential user . . . the distiller's "missionary person" or the medical "detailer" representing an ethical pharmaceutical house.
5. Positions where the major emphasis is placed on technical knowledge, e.g., the engineering salesperson who is primarily a consultant to the "client" companies.
6. Positions which demand the creative sale of tangible products like vacuum cleaners, refrigerators, siding, and encyclopedias.
7. Positions requiring the creative sale of intangibles, such as insurance, advertising services, or education.[5]

The positions move along a spectrum ranging from the least to the most creative types of selling. The earlier jobs call primarily for maintaining accounts and taking orders, while the latter require hunting down prospects and creating new sales. Most of the discussion here will deal with the more creative types of selling.

Types of Selling Situations

Most people visualize selling as consisting of a single seller talking to a single buyer. This is really one of five types of selling situations. The five are:

1. *Sales representative to buyer.* Here a single sales representative talks to a single prospect or customer in person or over the phone.
2. *Sales representative to buyer-group.* Here a sales representative appears before a buying committee to make a sales presentation about a specific product.

[5] Robert N. McMurry, "The Mystique of Super-Salesmanship," *Harvard Business Review,* March–April 1961, p. 114.

3. *Sales team to buyer-group.* Here a sales team (such as a company officer, sales representative, and sales engineer) makes a sales presentation to a buying group.

4. *Conference selling.* Here the sales representative brings resource people from the company to meet with one or more buyers to discuss problems and mutual opportunities.

5. *Seminar selling.* Here a company team of technical people presents an educational seminar to a technical group in a customer company about recent state-of-the-arts developments. The aim is to enhance customer knowledge and loyalty rather than to make a specific sale.

Thus we see that the sales representative does not always do the whole selling job and may serve as a "matchmaker" bringing together company and customer personnel. The sales representative acts as "account manager" whose job it is to initiate and facilitate transactions between two companies.

The Buyer-Seller Relationship

Effective selling is in large part a matter of having the correct attitude toward the customer. *The customer wants help in solving problems. An effective sales representative recognizes the customer's problems and knows how to be of help.* A vice president of a major food company spent one week watching fifty sales presentations to a busy buyer for a major supermarket chain. Here are some of his experiences:

> I watched a soap company representative come in to the buyer. He had three separate new promotional deals to talk about with six different dates. He had *nothing* in writing. . . . After the salesman left, the buyer looked at me and said, "It will take me fifteen minutes to get this straightened out." I watched another salesman walk in to the buyer and say, "Well, I was in the area, and I want you to know that we have a great new promotion coming up next week." The buyer said, "That's fine. What is it?" He said, "I don't know . . . I'm coming in next week to tell you about it." The buyer asked him what he was doing there today. He said, "Well, I was in the area." Another salesman came [and] said, "Well, it's time for us to write that order now . . . getting ready for the summer business." The buyer said, "Well, fine, George, how much did I buy last year in total?" The salesman looked a little dumfounded and said, "Well, I'll be damned if I know. . . ." The majority of salesmen were ill-prepared, unable to answer basic questions, uncertain as to what they wanted to accomplish during the call. They did not think of the call as a studied, professional presentation. They didn't have a real idea of the busy retailer's *needs and wants.*[6]

Companies are striving to overcome these problems through better selection and training of their sales force. They are wary of "the old drummer type of salesman." Much of the old sales job has been taken over by mass media and nonpersonal retailing. The new breed of sales representative is better schooled and able to absorb a vast amount of information about many products and customers. He or she is likely to have technical training and be backed by a top-flight team of engineers and market researchers. The sales representative knows how to read the needs of customers and recognizes their growing interest in buying systems and service packages rather than single products. He or she goes after the *long-run relationship* rather than the *quick sale.* As technology grows

---

[6] From an address by Donald R. Keough at the 27th Annual Conference of the Super-Market Institute in Chicago, April 26–29, 1964.

more complex and competition more keen, one can expect to see more of this new type of sales representative.[7]

A Sales Representative's Tasks Selling is only one of several tasks of the sales representative. He or she may perform as many as six different activities:

1. *Prospecting.* The company does its best to generate leads for the sales representative, but he or she is expected to search for additional prospects.
2. *Communicating.* Much of a sales representative's work consists of communicating information to existing and potential buyers about the company's products and services.
3. *Selling.* The sales representative engages in the "art of salesmanship"—approaching, presenting, answering objections, and closing sales.
4. *Servicing.* The sales representative provides various services to the customers—consulting on their problems, rendering technical assistance, arranging financing, and expediting delivery.
5. *Information gathering.* The sales representative conducts market research and intelligence work and is responsible for supplying regular reports on call activity.
6. *Allocating.* The sales representative helps evaluate customer profitability and advises on allocating scarce products to customers in times of product shortages.

The sales representative's actual mix of tasks varies with the character of the purchase decision process, company marketing strategy, and the economy. The nature of the purchase decision process establishes the kinds of activities that the sales representative must perform in order to develop and maintain satisfied customers. The sales activities required to handle straight rebuy situations are different from those required to "crack open" new accounts.

Sales-force strategy is also influenced by company marketing strategy. In the food industry, many manufacturers use a *pull strategy*, relying on massive consumer advertising to draw customers into the retailers' establishments to ask for their brands. The company sales representatives play a servicing role of seeing to it that the retailers carry a sufficient stock, give good shelf space, and cooperate in sales promotion programs. Other food manufacturers use a *push strategy*, primarily relying on their sales representatives to sell the trade on carrying their brands. Companies also will vary in how much time they want their sales representatives to spend on selling their established brands versus new ones and on calling on current customers versus prospects.

The sales representative's mix of tasks also varies with the state of the economy. When widespread product shortages appeared in 1973, sales representatives in many industries found themselves with nothing to sell. Some observers jumped to the conclusion that sales representatives were redundant and could be retrenched. But this thinking overlooked the other roles of the salesperson—allocating the product, counseling unhappy customers, communicating company plans on remedying the shortage, and selling the company's other products that were not in short supply.

Sales-Force Objectives There are two schools of thought about what the sales force should be good at doing. The traditional view is that the job of sales representatives is to produce

[7] See Carl Rieser, "The Salesman Isn't Dead–He's Different," *Fortune*, November 1962, pp. 124ff; and "The New Supersalesmen: Wired for Success," *Business Week*, January 6, 1973, pp. 58–62.

sales volume. They must know the art of promoting the company's products and getting orders. The newer view says that the job of sales representative is to produce profit. They must know the cost and profit potential of various products and customers and manage their territories as profit centers.

These two views lead to different conceptions of the proper training of sales representatives. The traditional view emphasizes training sales personnel in the art of salesmanship. The new school emphasizes training sales personnel to use planning and marketing concepts. One marketing vice president complained recently: "It takes me about five years to train sales people to think like marketers. I want them to know how to find and solve customers' problems, bring intelligence back to the company, and make decisions that will maximize profit rather than sales volume."

At times, it seems that marketing management and sales management represent completely opposite cultures. Sales executives focus on sales volume planning, short-run sales goals, individual customers, customer contact work, and price as a marketing tool. Marketing executives focus on profit planning, long-run sales goals, market segments, analytical work, and perceived value as a marketing tool. Marketers believe that a marketing-oriented rather than a sales-oriented sales force will be most effective in the long run.

SALES-FORCE SIZE

Once the company clarifies the tasks and objectives of the sales force in the marketing mix, it is ready to consider the question of sales-force size. Sales representatives are among the most productive and expensive assets in a company. Increasing their number will increase both sales and costs. We shall describe two analytical approaches to determining the optimal sales-force size.

Productivity Approach

Semlow proposed a solution to the problem of sales-force size that requires measuring the sales productivity of sales representatives in different-size territories.[8] He noted that sales representatives in territories rated as having higher sales potential produced more sales but that their sales were less than proportionate to the increase in sales potential. Citing a particular company's case, Semlow found that the sales in a territory with 1 percent of total national potential were $160,000 and sales in a territory with 5 percent of total potential were $200,000. In the latter case, there was only $40,000 in sales for every 1 percent of potential.

Now if the company employed one hundred sales representatives and wanted them all to work territories of equal potentials, it would create one hundred territories, each with 1 percent of total potential. This means that sales would average $160,000 in each territory, according to the previous analysis. Since there are one hundred sales representatives, total company sales would be $16 million.

If the company employed a sales force of only twenty, it would create twenty territories, each with 5 percent of the total potential. In this case, sales would average $200,000 in each territory, according to the previous analysis.

[8] Walter J. Semlow, "How Many Salesmen Do You Need?" *Harvard Business Review*, May–June 1959, pp. 126–32.

Since there were twenty sales representatives, total company sales would be only $4,000,000. Semlow applied the same reasoning to other possible sizes of the sales force. For each size, he projected to total sales volume, based on the estimated productivity of sales representatives in different-size territories.

His final step was to convert each sales volume into operating profit on investment. He first estimated the operating profit before variable selling cost on each sales volume. Then he deducted the variable selling cost, specifically the size of the sales force times the cost per sales representative. This left an estimate of operating profit on that sales volume. Then he estimated the working capital and plant investment required at alternative sales volumes. Finally, he expressed the estimated operating profit as a ratio to the required investment. In his example, the operating profit on investment was 11.6 percent with a sales force of one hundred and only 8.7 percent with a sales force of twenty. The optimal-size sales force called for sixty-five sales representatives, with the estimated rate of return of 22.0 percent.

Semlow's method depends on having a sufficient number of existing territories to allow making a statistical estimate of creating territories of equal sales potential. It also assumes that sales productivity is a function only of territory sales potential, neglecting the variations that might be produced by the mix of accounts in the territory, their geographical dispersion, and other factors.[9]

Workload Approach

Talley proposed an approach based on equalizing the workload of sales representatives rather than territory sales potential.[10] His method assumes that management has determined the economic number of calls to make on accounts of different sizes. The method consists of the following steps:

1. Customers are grouped into size classes according to their annual sales volume.
2. The desirable call frequencies (number of sales calls on an account per year) are established for each class.
3. The number of accounts in each size class are multiplied by the corresponding call frequency to arrive at the total workload for the country, in sales calls per year.
4. The average number of calls a sales representative can make per year is determined.
5. The number of sales representatives needed is determined by dividing the total annual calls required by the average annual calls made by a sales representative.

Suppose, for example, the company estimates that there are one thousand A-accounts and two thousand B-accounts in the nation; and A-accounts require thirty-six calls a year and B-accounts twelve calls a year. This means the company needs a sales force that can make sixty thousand sales calls a year. Suppose the average sales representative can make one thousand calls a year. The company would need sixty full-time sales representatives.

---

[9] For a criticism of Semlow's findings and an alternative method, see Henry C. Lucas, Jr., Charles B. Weinberg, and Kenneth W. Clowes, "Sales Response as a Function of Territorial Potential and Sales Representative Workload," *Journal of Marketing Research*, August 1975, pp. 298–305.

[10] Walter J. Talley, "How to Design Sales Territories," *Journal of Marketing*, January 1961, pp. 7–13.

SALES-FORCE DESIGN

Sales-Force Structure

The effectiveness of a sales force depends a great deal on how it is organized. A sales force can be organized around company territories, products, customers, or some mixture of the three.

Territory-structured sales force In the simplest sales organization each sales representative has an exclusive territory in which he or she represents the company's full line. This sales structure has a number of advantages. First, it results in a very clear definition of the salesperson's responsibilities. As the only salesperson working the territory, he or she bears the credit or blame for area sales to the extent that personal selling effort makes a difference. This tends to encourage a high level of effort, especially when management is able to gauge fairly accurately the area's sales potential. Second, responsibility for a definite territory increases the sales representative's incentive to cultivate local business and personal ties. These ties tend to improve the quality of the sales representative's selling effectiveness and personal life. Third, travel expenses are likely to be relatively small, since each sales representative's travel takes place within the bounds of a small geographical territory.

The territorial form of sales organization works quite well in companies with a relatively homogeneous set of products and customers. But these same companies, as their products and markets become diversified, find this form increasingly less effective. At the heart of the problem is the fact that the sales representative, to be effective, must know the company's products and markets. But there is a clear limit to how much knowledge a sales representative can acquire about different types of products and customers.

Product-structured sales force The importance of sales representatives' knowing their products, together with the development of product divisions and management, has led many companies to structure their sales force along product lines. Specialization of the sales force by product is particularly warranted where the products are (1) technically complex, (2) highly unrelated, and/or (3) very numerous.

The mere existence of different company products, however, is not a sufficient argument for such specialization. A major drawback may exist if the company's separate product lines are bought by many of the same customers. For example:

> The *American Hospital Supply Corporation* has several divisions and subsidiaries, each with its own sales force. All of these sales forces call on the same hospitals. It is conceivable that as many as seven different sales representatives of the American Hospital Supply Corporation could call on the same hospital on the same day.[11]

This means that company sales personnel travel over the same routes, and each one uses up valuable time waiting in the outer office to see the customer's purchasing agents. These extra costs must be weighed against the benefits that may result from the higher level of customer service and more knowledgeable product representation.

[11] See Ralph Westfall and Harper C. Boyd, Jr., *Cases in Marketing Management* (Homewood, Ill.: Richard D. Irwin, 1961), pp. 376–83.

Customer-structured sales force   Companies often specialize their sales forces along customer lines. Separate sales forces may be set up for different industries, customer sizes, national accounts, and new business. The most obvious advantage of customer specialization is that each sales force can become more knowledgeable about specific customer needs. At one time General Electric's sales representatives specialized in specific products (fan motors, switches, and so forth), but later they changed to specialization in markets, such as the air conditioning market, because this is how the customer saw the problem of fan motors, switches, and so on. A customer-specialized sales force can also sometimes reduce total sales-force costs. A large pump manufacturer at one time used a single sales force of highly trained sales engineers to sell to both original equipment manufacturers (who needed to deal with technical representatives) and to jobbers (who did not need to deal with technical representatives). Later the company split its sales force and staffed the one selling to jobbers with less highly trained sales representatives.

The major disadvantage of customer-structured sales forces arises if the various types of customers are scattered evenly throughout the country. This means an overlapping coverage of territories, which is always more expensive.

Complex sales-force structures   When a company sells a wide variety of products to many types of customers over a broad geographical area, it often combines several principles of sales-force structure. Sales representatives may be specialized by territory-product, territory-customer, product-customer, or ultimately by territory-product-customer. A salesman may then be responsible to one or more line managers and/or one or more staff managers.

Territorial Design

The great majority of companies assign their sales representatives to specific territories whether or not they are further specialized by product or type of customers. The territories are aggregated into larger groupings called *districts*, and in turn these districts may be aggregated into major sales *regions*. Many of the larger companies, for example, utilize an eastern, southern, central, and western regional plan for field operations.

In designing a system of territories, the company generally tries to achieve the following territorial characteristics: the territories are easy to administer; their sales potential is easy to estimate; they keep down total travel time; and they provide a sufficient and equitable workload and sales potential for each sales representative. These characteristics are achieved through decisions about the size and shape of territorial units.

Territory size   One approach calls for forming territories of *equal sales potential,* and the other calls for forming territories of *equal workload.* Each principle offers advantages at the cost of some real dilemmas.

The logic of creating territories of *equal potential* is to provide each sales representative with the same income opportunities and to provide the company with a means of evaluating performance. Persistent differences in sales yield by territory are assumed to reflect differences in the ability or effort of individual sales representatives. Awareness of that will encourage salespersons to work at their top capacity.

But because customer geographical density almost always varies, territories with equal potential typically cover vastly different areas. For example, the potential for the sale of large drill presses is as large in Detroit as it is in a number of the western states. A sales representative assigned to Detroit can cover the same potential with far less effort than the sales representative who sells in the territory spanning the several western states.

The problem is that sales representatives assigned to the larger and sparser territories are either going to end up with fewer sales and less income for equal effort or with equal sales only through extraordinary effort. Is there any way around the problem? One possibility is to pay the western sales representatives more to compensate for the extra effort. But this reduces the profits on sales in the western territories. An alternative is to acknowledge that territories differ in attractiveness and assign the better or more senior sales representatives to the better territories.

The alternative principle for creating territories is to try to *equalize the sales workloads*. The objective is to permit each sales representative to cover his or her territory adequately. However, this principle generally results in some variation in territory sales potentials. That is not a concern when the sales force is on straight salary. But where sales representatives are compensated partly on the basis of their sales, territories definitely vary in their attractiveness even though the workloads are approximately equalized. The same solutions appear. A lower compensation rate can be paid to sales representatives in the territories with the higher sales potential, or the territories with the better potential can go to the higher performers.

Territory shape   Territories are formed by combining smaller units, such as counties or states, until they add up to a territory of a given potential or workload. They are put together with reference to the location of natural barriers, the compatibility of adjacent areas, the adequacy of transportation, and so forth. Many companies also try to achieve a certain territory shape because this can influence the cost and ease of coverage and the sales representatives' satisfaction. The most common shapes are circular, cloverleaf, and wedge-shaped territories.

Computer models are being increasingly used to design sales territories that achieve some balance of workload, sales potential, compactness, and routing efficiency.[12] The efficient routing of sales calls through a territory to reduce travel time or cost is being assisted by computer programs based on the "traveling salesman problem."[13]

RECRUITING AND SELECTING SALES REPRESENTATIVES

Up to now, we have considered sales-force tasks and objectives, sales-force size, and sales-force structure. We now want to turn to the day-to-day concerns of sales management in operating an effective sales force. Sales management has to

[12] A computer-based method that creates territories that are compact and equal in workload is described in Sidney W. Hess and Stuart A. Samuels, "Experiences with a Sales Districting Model: Criteria and Implementation," *Management Science*, December 1971, pp. 41–54. Also see Leonard M. Lodish, "Sales Territory Alignment to Maximize Profit," *Journal of Marketing Research*, February 1975, pp. 30–36; and Andris A. Zoltners, "Integer Programming Models for Sales Territory Alignment to Maximize Profit," *Journal of Marketing Research*, November 1976, pp. 426–30.

[13] See John D. C. Little et al., "An Algorithm for the Traveling Salesman Problem," *Operations Research*, November–December 1963, pp. 972–89.

recruit, select, train, compensate, supervise, and evaluate sales representatives. Various strategies and policies guide these decisions.

Importance of Careful Selection

At the heart of a successful sales-force operation is the selection of good sales representatives. The performance levels of an average and a top sales representative are quite different. A survey of more than five hundred companies revealed that 27 percent of the sales force brought in over 52 percent of the sales.[14] Beyond the differences in sales productivity are the great wastes in hiring the wrong persons. Of the sixteen thousand sales representatives who were hired by the surveyed companies, only 68.5 percent still worked for their company at the end of the year, and only 50 percent were expected to remain through the following year. The cost of recruiting, training, and supervising an individual sales person for one year was estimated at the time at $8,730. As a result, the surveyed companies were expected to lose around $70 million, or half their investment. This loss would be much larger in today's dollars.

The financial loss due to turnover is only part of the total cost. The new sales representative who remains with the company receives a direct income averaging around half of the direct selling outlay. If he or she receives $14,000 a year, another $14,000 may go into fringe benefits, expenses for travel and entertainment, supervision, office space, supplies, and secretarial assistance. Consequently, the new sales representative should be capable of creating sales on which the gross margin at least covers the selling expenses of $28,000. If this margin was 10 percent, for example, he or she would have to sell at least $240,000 of product to constitute a breakeven resource for the company.

What Makes a Good Sales Representative?

Selecting sales representatives would not be such a problem if one knew the characteristics of an ideal salesperson. If ideal salespersons are outgoing, aggressive, and energetic, it would not be too difficult to check for these characteristics in applicants. But a review of the most successful sales representatives in any company is likely to reveal a good number who are introverted, mild-mannered, and far from energetic. The successful group will also include men and women who are tall and short, articulate and inarticulate, well groomed and slovenly.

Nevertheless, the search for the magic combination of traits that spells sure-fire sales ability continues unabated. The number of lists that have been drawn up is countless. Most of them recite the same qualities. McMurry wrote:

> It is my conviction that the possessor of *effective* sales personality is *a habitual "wooer," an individual who has a compulsive need to win and hold the affection of others.* . . . His wooing, however, is not based on a sincere desire for love because, in my opinion, he is convinced at heart that no one will ever love him. Therefore, his wooing is primarily exploitative . . . his relationships tend to be transient, superficial and evanescent.[15]

McMurry went on to list five additional traits of the supersalesperson: a high level of energy, abounding self-confidence, a chronic hunger for money, a well-

---

[14] The survey was conducted by the Sales Executives Club of New York and was reported in *Business Week*, February 1, 1964, p. 52.

[15] McMurry, "Mystique of Super-Salesmanship," p. 117.

553

established habit of industry, and a state of mind that regards each objection, resistance, or obstacle as a challenge.[16]

Mayer and Greenberg offered one of the shortest lists of traits exhibited by effective sales representatives.[17] Their seven years of field work led them to conclude that the effective salesperson has at least two basic qualities: (1) *empathy,* the ability to feel as the customer does; and (2) *ego drive,* a strong personal need to make the sale. Using these two traits, they were able to make fairly good predictions of the subsequent performance of applicants for sales positions in three different industries.

It may be true that certain basic traits may make a person effective in any line of selling. From the viewpoint of a particular company, however, these basic traits are rarely enough. Each selling job is characterized by a unique set of duties and challenges. One only has to think about insurance selling, computer selling, and automobile selling to realize the different educational, intellectual, and personality requirements that would be sought in the respective sales representatives.

How can a company determine the characteristics that its prospective sales representatives should "ideally" possess? The particular duties of the job suggest some of the characteristics to look for in applicants. Is there a lot of paperwork? Does the job call for much travel? Will the salesperson confront a high proportion of refusals? In addition, the traits of the company's most successful sales representatives suggest additional qualities to look for. Some companies compare the standing of their best versus their poorest sales representatives to see which characteristics differentiate the two groups.

Recruitment Procedures

After management develops general criteria for new sales personnel, it has the job of attracting a sufficient number of applicants. The recruiting is turned over to the personnel department, which seeks applicants through various means, including soliciting names from current sales representatives, using employment agencies, placing job ads, and contacting college students. As for college students, companies have not found it easy to sell them on selling. A survey of one thousand male students in 123 colleges indicated that only one in seventeen college students showed an interest in selling.[18] The reluctant ones gave as reasons the fear of insecurity and a dislike of travel and being away from their families. To counter these objections company recruiters emphasized starting salaries, income opportunities, and the fact that one-quarter of the presidents of large U.S. corporations started out in marketing and sales.

Applicant Rating Procedures

Recruitment procedures, if successful, will lead to the development of more applicants than jobs, and the company's task is to select the better applicants. The selection procedures vary in elaborateness from a single informal interview to prolonged testing and interviewing, not only of the applicant but also of her or his family.

An increasing number of companies are giving formal tests to applicants for sales positions. Although test scores are only one information element in a set

---

[16] *Ibid.,* p. 118.

[17] David Mayer and Herbert M. Greenberg, "What Makes a Good Salesman?" *Harvard Business Review,* July–August 1964, pp. 119–25.

[18] "Youth Continues to Snub Selling," *Sales Management,* January 15, 1965, p. 69.

that includes personal characteristics, references, past employment history, and interviewer reactions, they are weighed quite heavily by some companies, including IBM, Prudential, Procter & Gamble, and Gillette. Gillette claims that the use of tests has resulted in a 42 percent reduction in turnover and that test scores have correlated well with the subsequent progress of new sales representatives in the sales organization.

The choice of an appropriate battery of tests is not simple. Standard tests are available to measure intelligence, interests, personality, interpersonal skills and sales aptitude. There are also tailor-made tests for special selling situations. These tests vary considerably in reliability and validity. Furthermore, many of them are vulnerable to manipulation by the applicant. A person, for example, can spot a red-herring question such as "Do you prefer golf or reading?" Whyte laid down the following rules for the job applicant who takes company psychological tests: (1) Give the most conventional answer; (2) show that you like things as they are; (3) indicate that you never worry; and (4) deny any taste for books or music.[19]

TRAINING SALES REPRESENTATIVES

Not too long ago many companies sent their new salespeople out into the field almost immediately after hiring them. The sales representative would be supplied with a pack of samples, order books, and instructions to sell west of the Mississippi. Training programs were considered luxuries. A training program meant large outlays for instructors, materials, and space; the payment of a base salary to a person who was not selling; and lost opportunities because he or she was not in the field.

Nowadays new sales representatives can expect to spend from a few weeks to many months in the limbo state known as training. In industries such as steel or data processing new sales representatives are not on their own for two years!

IBM expects its sales representatives to spend 15 percent of their time each year in additional training. The sales-training bill for a major U.S. corporation can run into millions of dollars each year. Several factors have convinced sales management that extended training may add more value than cost. The sales representative of today is selling to more cost-conscious and value-conscious buyers. Furthermore, he or she is selling a host of products, often loosely related, and sometimes technically complex. More reports are expected of this person. The company wants to be represented by a mature and knowledgeable sales representative.

The purpose of the training is to instill certain information and attitudes in the sales force and teach certain skills:

The sales representative should know the company and identify with it. Most companies devote the first part of the training program to describing the history and objectives of the company, the organizational setup and lines of authority, the names of the chief officers, the company's financial structure and facilities, and the company's chief products and sales volume.

The sales representative should know the company's products. The sales trainee is shown how the products are produced and how they function in various uses.

[19] William H. Whyte, Jr., *The Organization Man* (New York: Simon and Schuster, 1956), pp. 405–10.

The sales representative should know customers' and competitors' characteristics. The sales representative is introduced to the different types of customers and their needs, buying motives, and buying habits. He or she learns about the company's and competitors' strategies and policies.

The sales representative should learn how to make effective sales presentations. The sales representative is trained in the basic principles of salesmanship. Part of the training time is used to develop the sales representative's personality and interpersonal skills. In addition, the company outlines the major sales arguments for each product, and some go so far as to provide a sales script.

The sales representative should be introduced to field procedures and responsibilities. The sales representative should know how to divide time between active accounts and potential accounts; how to use the expense account, prepare reports, and route effectively.

New methods of training are continually being sought to speed up and deepen skill development and understanding. Among the instructional approaches are role playing, sensitivity training, cassette tapes, videotapes, programmed learning, and films on salesmanship and company products.[20]

Does all this sales training pay off? Unless the sales training department of the company can show bottom-line results, they will be one of the first to have their budget cut in hard times. There is no one way to evaluate the training results, but training departments should make an effort to collect as much concrete evidence of improved sales performance as possible.[21] Besides a demonstrable change in the sales personnel's knowledge, skills, and attitudes, there should be a measurable impact on such variables as: (1) sales-force turnover, (2) sales volume, (3) absenteeism, (4) average sale size, (5) calls-to-close ratio, (6) customer complaints and compliments, (7) new accounts per time unit, and (8) volume of returned merchandise.

The substantial costs of company training programs raise the question of whether a company would be better off to hire experienced sales representatives away from other companies. The gain is often illusory, however, because the experienced salesperson is brought in at a higher salary, which sometimes may simply represent a capitalization of the equivalent training costs. From a national point of view, there is probably a net loss when an industry practices pirating on a large scale. Some of the representatives' specific training and company experience is wasted when he or she transfers to another company. Within some industries, companies tacitly agree not to hire sales personnel away from each other.

Principles of Salesmanship

One of the major objectives of sales-training programs is to train company sales personnel in the art of selling. The sales-training industry today involves expenditures of hundreds of millions of dollars in training programs, books, cassettes and other materials. Almost a million copies of books on selling are purchased every year, bearing such provocative titles as *How to Outsell the Born Salesman, How to Sell Anything to Anybody, The Power of Enthusiastic Selling, How Power Selling Brought Me Success in 6 Hours, Where Do You Go From No?*

[20] For a good overview, see Morgan B. MacDonald, Jr., and Earl L. Bailey, *Training Company Salesmen* (New York: Conference Board, 1967).

[21] See Ron Zemke, "Sales Training and the Bottom Line: Is There a Measurable Relationship?" *Training HRD*, October 1976, pp. 36–41.

and *1,000 Ways a Salesman Can Increase His Sales.* One of the most enduring books is Dale Carnegie's *How to Win Friends and Influence People.*

All of the sales-training approaches are designed to convert a salesperson from being a passive *order taker* to a more active *order getter.* Order taking is based on the notion that: (1) the customers are aware of their own needs; (2) they cannot be influenced or would resent any attempt at influence; and (3) they prefer salespersons who are courteous and self-effacing. An example of an order-taking mentality would be a Fuller Brush salesman who knocks on dozens of doors each day, simply asking if the consumer needs any brushes.

In training salespersons to be order getters, there are two basic approaches, a sales-oriented approach and a customer-oriented approach. The first one trains the salesperson to be adept in the use of *high-pressure selling techniques,* such as those used in selling encyclopedias or automobiles. The techniques include overstating the product's merits, critizing competitive products, using a slick, canned presentation, selling yourself, and offering some concession to get the order on the spot. The assumptions behind this form of selling are that: (1) the customers are not likely to buy except under pressure; (2) they are influenced by a slick presentation and ingratiating manners; and (3) they won't regret the transaction after signing the order, or if they do, it doesn't matter.

The other approach attempts to train sales personnel in *customer problem solving.* Here the salesperson studies the customers' needs and wants and proposes profitable solutions. An example would be a sales representative who examines a customer's situation and proposes a plan that would make or save the customer money. Here the salesperson does what is good for the customer, not what is immediately good for the salesperson. The assumptions behind this approach are that: (1) the customers have latent needs that constitute opportunities for the sales representative; (2) they appreciate good suggestions; and (3) they will be loyal to sales representatives who have their long-term interests at heart. Certainly the problem solver is a more compatible image for the salesperson, under the marketing concept, than is the hard seller or order taker.[22]

Blake and Mouton see the problem of selling in terms of two dimensions, the salesperson's *concern for the sale* and *concern for the customer.*[23] These two dimensions give rise to the *sales grid* shown in Figure 21–1A, which describes five types of salespersons. Type 1,1 is very much the order-taker mentality, and 9,1 is the hard-seller mentality. Type 5,5 is a soft-sell mentality, while type 1,9 is a sell-myself mentality. Type 9,9 epitomizes the problem-solving mentality, which is most consistent with the marketing concept.

Blake and Mouton go on to say that no one type of sales style is going to work with all buyers because buying styles are just as varied as salespersons. Figure 21–1B exhibits a *customer grid* and defines five types of customers based on their degree of *concern for the purchase* and *concern for the salesperson.*[24] One can begin to appreciate the difficulty—or low probability—of achieving com-

---

[22] The problem-solving salesperson is good at "consultative selling." See Mark Hanan, James Cribbin, and Herman Heiser, *Consultative Selling* (New York: American Management Association, 1970).

[23] Robert R. Blake and Jane S. Mouton, *The Grid for Sales Excellence: Benchmarks for Effective Salesmanship* (New York: McGraw-Hill Book Company, 1970), p. 4.

[24] *Ibid.,* p. 10.

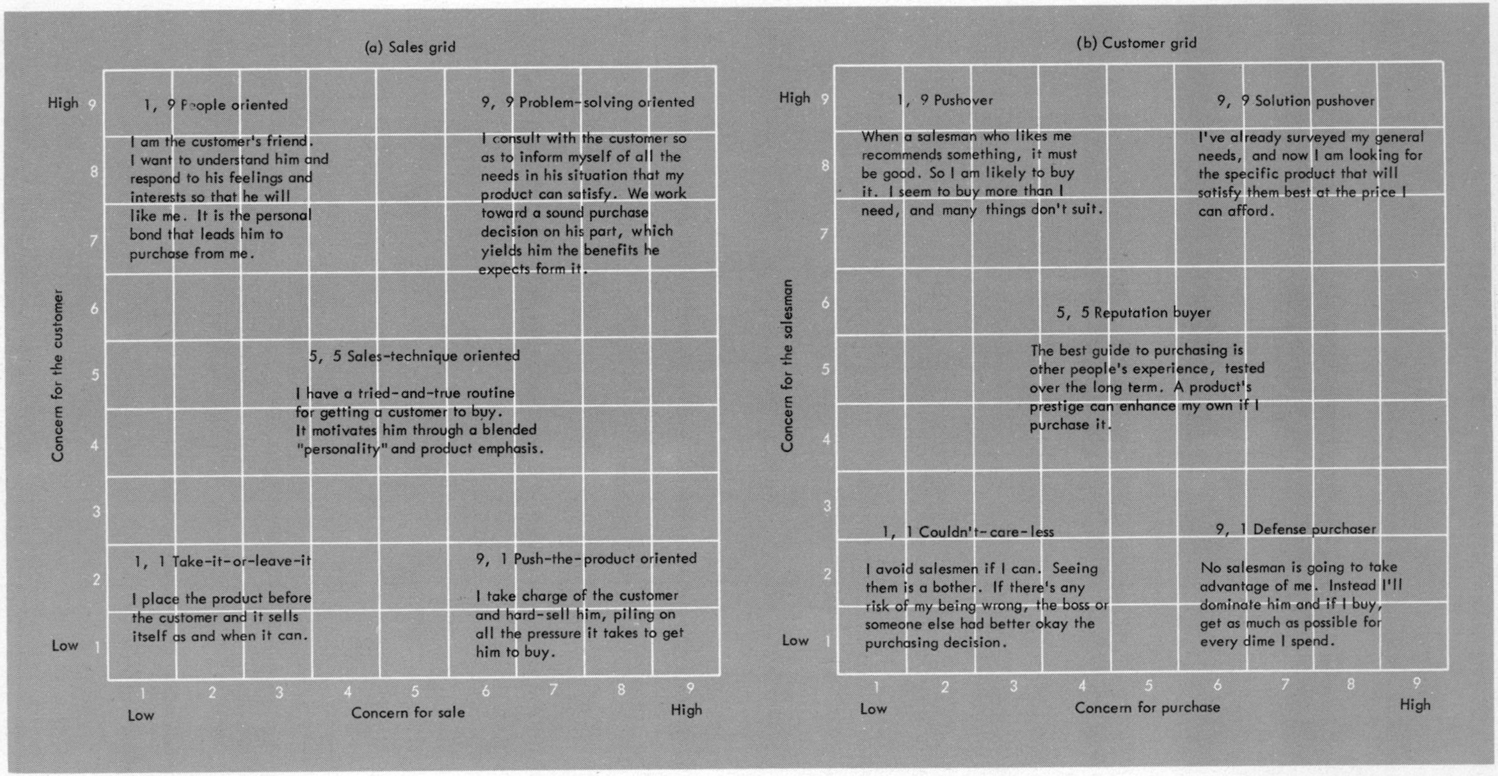

(a) Sales grid

Concern for the customer (vertical axis: High 9 → Low 1)
Concern for sale (horizontal axis: Low 1 → High 9)

1, 9 People oriented
I am the customer's friend. I want to understand him and respond to his feelings and interests so that he will like me. It is the personal bond that leads him to purchase from me.

9, 9 Problem-solving oriented
I consult with the customer so as to inform myself of all the needs in his situation that my product can satisfy. We work toward a sound purchase decision on his part, which yields him the benefits he expects form it.

5, 5 Sales-technique oriented
I have a tried-and-true routine for getting a customer to buy. It motivates him through a blended "personality" and product emphasis.

1, 1 Take-it-or-leave-it
I place the product before the customer and it sells itself as and when it can.

9, 1 Push-the-product oriented
I take charge of the customer and hard-sell him, piling on all the pressure it takes to get him to buy.

(b) Customer grid

Concern for the salesman (vertical axis: High 9 → Low 1)
Concern for purchase (horizontal axis: Low 1 → High 9)

1, 9 Pushover
When a salesman who likes me recommends something, it must be good. So I am likely to buy it. I seem to buy more than I need, and many things don't suit.

9, 9 Solution pushover
I've already surveyed my general needs, and now I am looking for the specific product that will satisfy them best at the price I can afford.

5, 5 Reputation buyer
The best guide to purchasing is other people's experience, tested over the long term. A product's prestige can enhance my own if I purchase it.

1, 1 Couldn't-care-less
I avoid salesmen if I can. Seeing them is a bother. If there's any risk of my being wrong, the boss or someone else had better okay the purchasing decision.

9, 1 Defense purchaser
No salesman is going to take advantage of me. Instead I'll dominate him and if I buy, get as much as possible for every dime I spend.

SOURCE: Robert R. Blake and Jane S. Mouton, *The Grid For Sales Excellence: Benchmarks for Effective Salesmanship* (New York: McGraw-Hill Book Company, 1970), p. 4.

FIGURE 21-1
Sales Types and Customer Types

patibility between a buyer and a seller. Consider, for example, the incompatibility of a 9,1 customer (defensive purchaser) and a 9,1 sales representative (product pusher). The purpose of these two grids is to provide diagnostics to the salesperson for analyzing a particular buyer and determining the best selling style to use.

The view that effective selling depends on matching *buyer and seller styles* is an alternative to the traditional view seeking to train salespersons in one particular selling style. It suggests that the buyer plays an active role in determining the outcome. Evans sees selling as a *dyadic process* where the outcome depends primarily on the match of *buyer and seller characteristics* even more than *buying and selling styles.*[25] He found, for example, that people tended to buy insurance from people very much like themselves. This was true for such factors as age, height, income, political opinions, religious beliefs, and smoking. What mattered was the perceived similarity more than the actual similarity. Evans proposed that insurance companies should hire all types of salespersons if they want to achieve broad market penetration. The only requirement is that they exhibit the intelligence and kinds of abilities effective in selling insurance.

Company sales-training programs differ depending on management's view of what constitutes an effective selling approach for the type of selling situation the company faces. Programs can be found that are based on stimulus-response thinking, formulated-steps thinking, or need-satisfaction thinking.[26] Regardless of the underlying model, most sales-training programs view the selling process as consisting of a set of steps that the salesperson has to carry out, each involving certain skills. The major steps are: *prospecting, preapproach, approach, demonstration, handling objections, closing,* and *follow-up.*[27]

Prospecting   The first step in the sales process is to identify prospects. Although the company can supply leads, the sales representatives also need skills in developing their own leads. Leads can be developed in the following ways:

1. Asking current satisfied customers for the names of other potential buyers
2. Cultivating other referral sources, such as suppliers, dealers, noncompeting sales representatives, bankers, and trade association executives
3. Joining organizations where there is a high probability of meeting or learning about new prospects
4. Engaging in speaking and writing activities that are likely to increase the salesperson's visibility
5. Examining various data sources (newspapers, directories) in search of names
6. Using the telephone and mail to track down leads
7. Dropping in cold on various offices (cold canvassing)

Sales representatives also need to know how to screen the leads to avoid wasting valuable time on poor leads. Prospects can be qualified by examining their finan-

[25] Franklin B. Evans, "Selling as a Dyadic Relationship—a New Approach," *The American Behavioral Scientist,* May 1963, pp. 76–79, at p. 76, 78. Also see Harry L. Davis and Alvin J. Silk, "Interaction and Influence Processes in Personal Selling," *Sloan Management Review,* winter 1972, pp. 59–76.

[26] See W. J. E. Crissy, William H. Cunningham, and Isabella C. M. Cunningham, *Selling: The Personal Force in Marketing* (New York: John Wiley & Sons, 1977), pp. 119–29.

[27] The following discussion draws in part from Crissy et al., *Selling.*

cial ability, volume of business, special requirements, location, and likelihood of continuous business. The salesperson should phone or write to prospects to see if they are worth pursuing further.

Preapproach This step involves the salesperson's learning as much as possible about the company (what it needs, who is involved in the purchase decision) and the buyers (their personal characteristics and buying styles). The salesperson can consult standard sources (such as *Moody's, Standard and Poor, Dun and Bradstreet*), acquaintances, and others to learn about the company. The salesperson should determine *call objectives,* which may be to qualify the prospect, or to gather information, or to make an immediate sale. Another task is to decide on the best *approach,* which might be a personal visit (possibly with a respected intermediary), a phone call, or a letter. The best *timing* should be thought out because many prospects are especially busy at certain times of the year. Finally, the salesperson should give thought to an overall strategy to use in the approach stage.

Approach This stage involves the salesperson's knowing how to meet and greet the buyer to get the relationship off to a good start. The salesperson's looks, opening lines, and follow-up remarks are all important factors. The salesperson's looks include his or her appearance, manner, and mannerisms. The salesperson is encouraged to wear clothes similar to the clothes buyers usually wear and is reminded to have a neat appearance, to show courtesy and attention to the buyer, and to avoid distracting mannerisms, such as pacing the floor or staring at the customer. The opening line should be positive and pleasant—"Mr. Smith, I am Bill Jones from the ABC Company. My company and I appreciate your willingness to see me. I will do my best to make this visit profitable and worthwhile for you and your company." This opener might be followed by some light talk to further the acquaintance, some key questions, or the showing of a display or sample to attract the buyer's attention and curiosity.

Demonstration After getting acquainted and sizing up the buyer, the salesperson attempts to relate the company's products to the buyer's situation. The aim is to demonstrate the want-satisfying characteristics of the company and its products. The salesperson may follow the AIDA approach in presenting the product in a way that gains attention, holds interest, builds desire, and leads to purchase action. The salesperson covers the *features* of the product but concentrates on selling the *benefits.*[28] Emphasis is placed on how the product will save or make money for the buyer. The salesperson may use aids, such as attractive literature, an audiovisual presentation, or an actual physical demonstration. During the demonstration, the salesperson will apply a mix of five influence strategies.[29]

---

[28] A feature is a characteristic of a product, such as its portability. A benefit is any advantages the buyer obtains from this feature, such as less exertion or lower cost. A common mistake in selling is to dwell on product features (a product orientation) instead of user benefits (a marketing orientation). See the feature-benefit matrices in Crissy et al., *Selling,* pp. 247–50.

[29] See Rosann L. Spiro and William D. Perreault, Jr., "Influence Use by Industrial Salesmen: Influence Strategy Mixes and Situational Determinants," unpublished paper, Graduate School of Business Administration, University of North Carolina, 1976.

1. *Legitimacy.* The salesperson will attempt to convince the buyer of the relevant reputation and experience of the salesperson's company.

2. *Expertise.* The salesperson will attempt to demonstrate strong knowledge of the buyer's situation and of his or her own company's products, doing this without being overly "smart."

3. *Referent power.* The salesperson will attempt to build on any shared characteristics, interests, and acquaintances to deepen their personal relationship.

4. *Ingratiation.* The salesperson may attempt to provide personal favors (a free lunch, promotional gratuities) to the customer to strengthen affiliation and reciprocity feelings.

5. *Impression management.* The salesperson may manipulate impressions of self in order to achieve a more favorable response.

Handling objections Customers will almost always pose objections during the demonstration or when asked to place an order. Their sales resistance could take a psychological or logical form. Psychological sales resistance includes: (1) resistance to interference, (2) preference for established habits, (3) apathy, (4) reluctance to give up something, (5) unpleasant associations with other person, (6) tendency to resist domination, (7) predetermined ideas, (8) dislike of making decisions, and (9) neurotic attitude toward money.[30] Logical resistance might consist of objections to the price, delivery schedule, or certain products or company characteristics. To handle these objections, the salesperson uses such techniques as maintaining a positive approach, trying to have the buyer clarify and define the objections, questioning the buyer in a way that the buyer has to answer his or her own objections, denying the validity of the objections, and turning the objection into a reason for buying. The salesperson needs training in the broader skills of negotiation, of which handling objections is a part.[31]

Closing In this stage, the salesperson attempts to close the sale. Some salespeople do not handle this stage effectively. They lack confidence in themselves or their company or product; or feel guilty about asking for the order; or don't recognize the right psychological moment to close the sale. Salespersons have to be trained in recognizing specific closing signals from the buyer including physical actions, statements or comments, and questions signaling a possible readiness to close. Salespersons can then use one of several closing techniques. They can ask the prospect for the order (direct method), recapitulate the points of agreement (summative method), offer to help the secretary write up the order (assumptive method), ask whether the buyer wants A or B (positive-choice method), get the buyer to make minor choices such as the color or size (minor-decision method), or indicate what the buyer will lose if the order is not placed now (scare method). The salesperson may offer the buyer specific inducements to close, such as a special price, an extra quantity at no charge, or a gift.

Follow-up This last stage is necessary if the salesperson wants to assure customer satisfaction and repeat business. Immediately after closing, the sales-

---

[30] Crissy et al., *Selling*, pp. 289–94.

[31] See Gerald I. Nierenberg, *The Art of Negotiation* (New York: Hawthorn Books, 1968); and Chester L. Karrass, *The Negotiating Game* (Cleveland, Ohio: World Publishing Co., 1970).

person should attempt to complete any necessary details on delivery time, purchase terms, and other matters. The salesperson should also consider scheduling a follow-up call when the initial order is received to make sure there is proper installation, instruction, and servicing. This visit is designed to detect any problems, to assure the buyer of the salesperson's interest and service, and to reduce any cognitive dissonance that might have arisen.

COMPENSATING SALESMEN

The major requirements for building a topflight sales force are (1) attracting good people, (2) motivating them, and (3) keeping them. In all three areas company compensation policies can make the crucial difference.

It is not easy to formulate a compensation plan that can be trusted to attract, motivate, and keep good sales personnel. Sales representatives and management tend to seek different, and often conflicting, objectives. Sales representatives would like a plan that offers the following features:

Income regularity. Since sales are influenced by many factors beyond the sales representative's control, he or she wants to be assured of some regular base income regardless of sales. This minimum income will help pay bills in periods of poor sales.

Reward for above-average performance. Most sales representatives think they can sell more than the average salesperson and want a compensation plan that provides superior income for superior performance.

Fairness. Sales representatives want to feel that their pay is about right in relation to their experience and ability, the earnings of coworkers and competitors' sales representatives, and the cost of living.

On the other hand, an ideal compensation plan from management's point of view would emphasize:

Control. Management likes a plan that facilitates its control over how sales representatives spend their time.

Economy. Management wants to establish a level of pay that is reasonable in relation to the value of the sales representatives' efforts and the cost and value of company products.

Simplicity. Management prefers a plan that is simple to administer from a payroll point of view, simple to explain to sales personnel, and simple to change as product situations and business conditions change.

Management is obviously hard pressed to reconcile all these objectives in one plan. Plans with good control features are generally not simple. Management objectives, such as economy, will conflict with sales representatives' objectives, such as financial security. In the light of these conflicting objectives, it is understandable why compensation plans exhibit a tremendous variety, not only among industries but among companies within the same industry.

The Level of Compensation Management must determine the level, components, and structure of an effective compensation plan. The level must bear some relation to the "going market price" for the type of sales job and abilities required. For example, the average earnings of the experienced salesperson in 1977 were $24,500.[32] If the market price for salespersons is well defined, the individual firm has little choice but to pay the going rate. To pay less would not bring forth the desired quantity or quality of applicants, and to pay more would be unnecessary. More often, however, the market price for salespersons is not well defined. For one thing, company plans vary in the importance of fixed and variable salary elements, fringe benefits, and expense allowances. And data on the average take-home pay of sales representatives working for competitive firms can be misleading because of significant variations in the average seniority and ability levels of the competitors' sales force. Published comparisons of industry-by-industry sales-force compensation levels are infrequent and generally lack sufficient detail.

The theoretical solution to the problem of the optimal compensation level is the same as shown in Figure 10–2, p. 259. Assume a company that is preparing to establish a specialized sales force of ten sales representatives to handle a new product. They will be paid on a straight salary. Higher salary levels would allow the company to recruit better applicants and lead to higher sales volumes. The sales curve can be assumed to be S-shaped with respect to the sales impact of greater total expenditures on the sales force. From the estimated sales curve would be deducted all costs before the total sales-force expenditures, to find gross profits. Then total sales-force expenditures would be deducted from gross profits, to find net profits. At the point where net profits are highest, the optimal total sales-force expenditure is found. This figure can be divided by the planned size of the sales force, here ten, to find the optimal salary level.

The Elements of Compensation

After a firm decides on the average pay level, it must determine the appropriate mix of the four basic elements of sales-force compensation—a fixed amount, a variable amount, expenses, and fringe benefits. The fixed amount, which might be salary or a drawing account, is intended to satisfy the sales representatives' need for some stability of income. The variable amount, which might be commissions, bonus, or profit sharing, is intended to stimulate and reward greater effort. Expense allowances are intended to enable the sales representatives to undertake selling efforts that are considered necessary or desirable. And fringe benefits, such as paid vacations, sickness or accident benefits, pensions, and life insurance, are intended to provide security and job satisfaction.

Top sales management must decide which elements should be in the compensation plan and their relative importance. A popular rule seems to favor making about 70 percent of the salesperson's total income fixed and allocating the remaining 30 percent among the other elements. But the variations around this average are so pronounced that it can hardly serve as a sufficient guide in planning. For example, fixed compensation should have more emphasis in jobs with a high ratio of nonselling duties to selling duties and in jobs where the selling task is technically complex. Variable compensation should have more emphasis in jobs where sales are cyclical and/or depend on the personal initiative of the sales representative.

Fixed and variable compensation taken alone give rise to three basic types of sales-force compensation plans—straight salary, straight commission, and

[32] John P. Steinbrink, "How to Pay Your Sales Force," *Harvard Business Review*, July–August 1978, pp. 111–22.

combination salary and commission. In one study, 28 percent of the companies paid straight salary, 21 percent paid straight commission, and 51 percent paid salary plus commission.[33] Figure 21–2 illustrates how the monthly compensation level of the sales representative is affected by his or her sales performance under four different plans. Clearly these different plans will have different effects on sales-force motivation and performance. More confident sales representatives will favor plans B and D because of the opportunity to earn more if they are high producers. More conservative sales representatives will favor plans A or C. The plans will also have different impacts on company costs and profits. Here we will examine the major strengths and drawbacks of each plan.

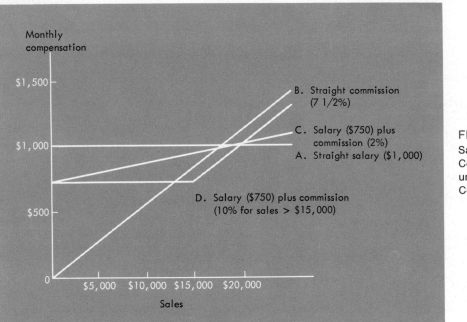

FIGURE 21–2
Sales-Force
Compensation
under Different
Compensation Plans

Straight salary   With this plan, the sales representative receives a fixed salary in total payment for services. Generally he or she also receives an amount to cover expenses incurred in performing various duties. Occasionally, this will be additional compensation in the way of discretionary bonuses or sales-contest prizes.

From management's point of view, a number of advantages are secured under a straight salary plan. The primary one is that management has more freedom to direct and alter sales duties without incurring strong opposition from the sales personnel affected. In addition, straight salary plans are generally less costly to administer and easier to explain. They also simplify the task of projecting the sales payroll for the coming year. Finally, by providing the sales

[33] *Ibid.*

force with security through stability of income, the straight salary plan may lead to a greater evenness in the morale of the sales force.

The chief weakness of the straight salary plan is that it does not present the sales force with any direct incentive to do a better-than-average selling job. This puts a greater supervision burden on management to control, evaluate, and reward the performances of individual sales representatives. Other problems posed by straight salary plans are an inflexible selling-expense burden during downswings in business; the danger that during upswings sales representatives on fixed salaries do not have sufficient incentive to exploit the increased business potential; thorny questions in salary adjustment for ability, rising living costs, length of service; and the probability that the more hard-driving type of salesperson will not be easy to attract.

Straight commission   This plan pays the sales representative some fixed or sliding rate related to his or her sales or profit volume. The sales representative may or may not also receive reimbursement for expenses incurred in performing the selling function. Straight commission plans are particularly prominent in the selling of insurance and investment securities, furniture, office equipment, small office machines, clothing, the textile and shoe industries, and drug and hardware wholesaling.

The straight commission plan offers at least three advantages. The most obvious one is that it provides a maximum financial incentive for the sales representative to work to capacity. A second advantage is that a straight commission plan leads to selling expenses more closely related to funds either currently available or becoming available through sales revenues. A third advantage is that commission plans enable management to employ financial incentives to direct sales representatives in their use of selling time.

These advantages come at a substantial price, however. The major difficulty is that management encounters great resistance when it tries to get the sales force to do things that do not generate immediate sales, such as following up leads, filling out reports, or providing sufficient customer service. Their personal financial involvement in getting the sale may lead them to use high-pressure tactics or price discounting, which in the long run may damage customer goodwill and company profits. Second, straight commission plans are generally more costly to administer. Third, straight commission plans provide little security and could have a deteriorative effect on the morale of sales representatives when sales fall through no fault of their own.

Management has several options regarding the commission base, the nature of commission rates, and the starting point for commissions. The *commission base* may be gross sales volume, net sales after returns, gross margins, or net profits. The *commission rates* may be identical for all sales or differentiated by customers and/or products; they may be constant with sales volume or vary in a progressive or regressive fashion. The *starting point for commissions* may be the first sale or sales beyond the established minimum quota. Most companies base sales commissions on sales volume because of administrative simplicity and because of sales management's traditional interest in promoting volume. But sales commissions based on sales volumes may not properly relate selling effort to company profitability. The payment of commissions on *gross margin* has been recommended as a better base and one that is practical to administer. Commissions tied to product gross margins should do a superior job of motivating sales representatives to improve their product and customer mix and, therefore, company profits.[34]

Combination salary and commission   The great majority of firms use a combination of salary and commission features in the hope of achieving the advantages of each while avoiding the disadvantages. The combination plan is especially appropriate where sales volume depends upon the sales representative's motivation and yet where management wants some control over the amount of nonselling duties performed by the sales representative. The plan also means that during downswings the company is not stuck with rigid selling costs, but neither does the sales representative lose his or her whole income.

Bonus   Many companies pay *bonuses* as a supplement or a substitute for commission-type incentives. Bonuses are noncontractual payments for extra effort or merit or for results beyond normal expectations. They are used to reward sales representatives for performing tasks that are desirable but not rewardable through commissions, for example, preparing prompt reports, supplying useful selling ideas, protecting the customer's inventory interests, and developing unusual product or market knowledge. The main problem with bonuses is that managerial judgment enters into their determination, and this can raise questions of fairness in the minds of individual sales representatives.

Other costs   Besides salary, commission, and bonus, the company's selling costs include the following additional elements:

1. *Selling expenses* (travel, lodging, telephone, entertainment, samples promotion, and office and/or clerical expenses)
2. *Fringe benefits* (hospitalization insurance, life insurance, pension plan, association memberships, and moving expenses)
3. *Special incentives* (contests, service awards)
4. *Staff back-up costs* (cost of technical and customer-service people, sales analysts, computer time, and sales-training programs)

Thus the cost of running a sales force adds up to much more than the direct compensation elements alone.

SUPERVISING SALES REPRESENTATIVES

The new sales representative is given more than a territory and a compensation package—he or she is given supervision. Supervision is the fate of everyone who works for someone else. It is the expression of employers' natural and continuous interest in the activities of their agents. Through supervision, employers hope to direct and motivate the sales force to do a better job.

[34] See Ralph L. Day and Peter D. Bennett, "Should Salesmen's Compensation Be Geared to Profits?" *Journal of Marketing Research*, May 1964, pp. 39–43; and John U. Farley and Charles B. Weinberg, "Inferential Optimization: An Algorithm for Determining Optimal Sales Commissions in Multiproduct Sales Forces," *Operational Research Quarterly*, June 1975, pp. 413–18.

Directing Sales Representatives

Companies differ in the extent to which they try to prescribe to their sales representatives what they should be doing. Much depends upon the nature of the selling job. Sales representatives who are paid largely on commission and who are expected to hunt down their own prospects are generally left on their own. Those who are largely salaried and who must cover a definite set of accounts are likely to receive substantial supervision.

A major purpose of supervision is to help the sales representatives use their major resource, which is *time*, effectively and efficiently. The effective use of time means that the sales representatives make good decisions as to which customers and prospects to spend the time on in the first place. The efficient use of time means that the sales representatives are able to plan their call time so as to maximize the ratio of selling to nonselling time.

Developing Customer Targets and Call Norms

Most companies classify their customers into a number of types, reflecting the sales volume or profit potential of the different accounts. They establish a certain desired number of calls per period that their sales force should make to each customer type. They might label the customer types A, B, and C. A accounts may receive nine calls a year, B six calls, and C three calls. The exact levels that are set depend upon competitive call norms and expected account profitability.

These call norms are to be taken as rough guidelines only.[35] The real issue is how much sales volume could be expected from a particular account as a function of the annual number of calls made to that account. In one current computer model for sales-call planning, the sales representative is asked to estimate sales for each account for five different possible call levels. The computer then calculates the optimal number of calls to make on each account, given these subjective sales response functions, the accounts' profit margins, and the total available sales call time.[36]

It may be possible to determine the sales-call response function experimentally. Magee described an experiment where sales representatives were asked to vary their call pattern in a particular way to determine what effect this would have on sales.[37] The experiment called first for sorting accounts into major classes. Each account class was then randomly split into three sets. The respective sales representatives were asked, for a specified period of time, to spend less than five hours a month with accounts in the first set, five to nine hours a month with the second set, and more than nine hours a month with the third set. The results demonstrated that additional call time increases sales volume, leaving only the question of whether the magnitude of sales increase was sufficient to justify the additional increase in call time.

---

[35] The story is told about a salesman who thought he literally had to make twelve prospect calls a day. At 4:45 P.M. he was still talking with the eleventh prospect, who was getting increasingly interested in the company's products. "Tell me more, young man," said the prospect. "I'm sorry, sir," replied the salesman. "There are only fifteen minutes left, and I must leave to make my last call."

[36] Leonard M. Lodish, "Callplan: An Interactive Salesman's Call Planning System," *Management Science*, December 1971, pp. 25–40. For company applications, see "Computers Route the Salesmen," *Business Week*, July 1, 1972.

[37] See John F. Magee, "Determining the Optimum Allocation of Expenditures for Promotional Effort with Operations Research Methods," in *The Frontiers of Marketing Thought and Science*, Frank M. Bass, ed. (Chicago: American Marketing Association, 1958), pp. 140–56. See also Arthur A. Brown, Frank T. Hulswit, and John D. Kettelle, "A Study of Sales Operations," *Operations Research*, June 1956, pp. 296–308.

Developing prospect targets and call norms   Companies like to specify to their sales force how much time to spend prospecting for new accounts. For example, Spector Freight wants its sales force to spend 25 percent of their time prospecting and to stop calling on a prospect after three unsuccessful calls.

There are a number of reasons why companies try to set up a minimum requirement for the canvassing of new accounts. If left alone, many sales representatives will spend most of their time in the offices of current customers. Current customers are better-known quantities. The sales representatives can depend upon them for some business, whereas a prospect may never deliver any business or deliver it only after many months of effort. Unless the sales representative receives a bonus for opening new accounts, he or she may underdo new account development. Some companies have decided to rely on a salaried, missionary sales force to open new accounts.

The key issue in developing prospect call norms is to have a way to estimate the *value of any given prospect*. This problem is especially acute in situations where there are more prospects than time available for developing them. They must be ranked so that sales representatives can concentrate on the best prospects. A useful model can be formulated by looking at the value of an account in terms of investment theory. First the sales representative should estimate the value of the prospect's business if the prospect were converted to a customer. The value of the prospect's business may be represented in terms of a discounted income stream lasting so many years. Specifically,

$$Z = \sum_{t=1}^{\bar{t}} \frac{mQ_t - X}{(1 + r)^t} \tag{21-1}$$

where:

Z = present value of the future income from a new customer
m = gross margin on sales
Q_t = expected sales from new customer in year t
X = cost of maintaining customer contact per year
r = company discount rate
t = a subscript for year
$\bar{t}$ = number of years that this new customer is expected to remain a customer

Thus the sales representative estimates that this prospect, if converted to a customer, would annually purchase from the company Q_t units with a profit per unit of m less a customer-contact cost (X) and that this will last for t periods. Future income is discounted at an interest rate r.

The next step is to consider the investment necessary to convert this prospect to a customer. The investment can be described as:

$$I = nc \tag{21-2}$$

where:

I = investment in trying to convert the prospect to a customer
n = number of calls to convert the prospect into a customer
c = cost per call

The number of calls to the prospect will influence the probability of conversion—that is,

$$p = p(n) \qquad (21\text{–}3)$$

The value of the prospect's business should be scaled down by this probability. Putting the previous elements together, the following investment formula emerges for the value (V) of a prospect:

$$V = p(n) \sum_{t=1}^{\bar{t}} \frac{mQ_t - X}{(1 + r)^t} - nc \qquad (21\text{–}4)$$

According to this formula, the value of a prospect depends on the difference between the expected present value of the income stream and the investment made in prospect conversion. Both the expected present value and the investment depend in turn on the intended number of calls, n, upon the prospect. The intended number of calls should be the optimal number of calls, and this can be found mathematically if the probability-of-conversion function is known.

The formula could easily be incorporated into a computer program wherein the sales representative sits down at a terminal, types in a set of estimates for each prospect regarding the expected volume of the prospect's business, the maximum probability of conversion, and so on, and receives back a ranking of all the prospects in order of their investment value along with the suggested number of calls to make on each.

Using sales time efficiently The sales representative should also know how to schedule planned sales calls and use his or her time efficiently. One tool is the preparation of an annual call schedule showing which customers and prospects to call on in which months and which activities to carry out. The activities include such things as participating in trade shows, attending sales meetings, and carrying out marketing research projects. For example, the sales force in the various Bell Telephone Company subsidiaries plan their calls and activities around three concepts. The first is *market development*—various efforts to educate customers, cultivate new business, and gain greater visibility in the buying community. The second is *sales-generating activities*—direct efforts to sell particular products to customers on particular calls. The third is *market protection activities*—various efforts to learn what competition is doing and to protect relations with existing customers. The sales force is supposed to aim for some balance among these activities, so that the company does not achieve high current sales at the expense of long-run market development.

Sales representatives also have to be good at time management. They allocate their time to the following activities:

Travel. Travel time is the time spent in travel between rising in the morning and arriving at lodging in the evening. It can amount in some jobs to as much as 50 percent of total time. Travel time can be cut down by substituting faster for slower means of transportation, recognizing, however, that this will increase costs. More companies are encouraging air travel (commercial or private plane) for their sales force in order to increase their ratio of selling to total time. They are also encouraging the sales force to fill out reports while traveling or to listen to cassettes describing company products, customers, or policies.

Food and breaks. Some portion of the sales force's workday is spent in eating and breaks. If this involves dining with a customer, it will be classified as selling time, otherwise as food and breaks.

Waiting. Waiting consists of time spent in the outer office of the buyer. This is dead time unless the sales representative uses it to plan or fill out reports.

Selling. Selling is the time spent with the buyer in person or on the phone. It breaks down into "social talk," which is the time spent discussing other things, and "selling talk," which is the time spent discussing the company and its products.

Administration. This is a miscellaneous category consisting of the time spent in report writing and billing, attending sales meetings, and talking to others in the company about production, delivery, billing, sales performance, and other matters.

No wonder actual selling time may amount in some companies to as little as 15 percent of total working time! If it could be raised from 15 percent to 20 percent, it would be a 33 percent improvement. Companies are constantly seeking ways to help their sales representatives use their time more efficiently. They do so by training them in the effective use of the telephone ("phone power"), simplifying the record-keeping forms and requirements, using the computer to develop call and routing plans, and supplying marketing research reports on the customer.

Motivating Sales Representatives

A small percentage of sales representatives in any sales force can be expected to do their best without any special prompting from management. To them, selling is the most fascinating job in the world. They are ambitious and are self-starters. But the majority of sales representatives on nearly every sales force require personal encouragement and special incentives to work at their best level. This is especially true for creative field selling, for the following reasons:

The nature of the job. The selling job is one of frequent frustration. Sales representatives usually work alone, the hours are irregular, and they are often away from home. They confront aggressive competing sales representatives; they have an inferior status relative to the buyer; they often do not have the authority to do what is necessary to win an account; they lose large orders that they have worked hard to obtain.

Human nature. Most people operate below capacity in the absence of special incentive. They won't "kill themselves" without some prospect of financial gain or social recognition.

Personal problems. The sales representative, like everyone else, is occasionally preoccupied with personal problems, such as sickness in the family, marital discord, or debt.

Management can affect the morale and performance of the sales force through its organizational climate, sales quotas, and positive incentives.

Organizational climate Organizational climate describes the feeling that the sales force get from their company regarding their opportunities, value, and rewards for a good performance. Some companies treat their sales force as being of minor importance. Other companies treat their sales representatives as the prime movers and allow unlimited opportunity for income and promotion. The company's attitude toward its sales representatives acts as a self-fulfilling prophecy: if they are held in low regard, there is much turnover and poor performance; if they are held in high regard, there is little turnover and high performance.

The quality of personal treatment from the sales representative's immediate supervisor is an important aspect of the organizational climate. An effective supervisor keeps in touch with the members of the sales force through regular correspondence and phone calls, personal visits in the field, and evaluation sessions in the home office. At different times the supervisor is the sales representative's boss, companion, coach, and confessor.

Sales quotas Many companies set sales quotas for their sales representatives specifying what they should sell during the year. Compensation is often, though not always, related to their degree of quota fulfillment.

Sales quotas are set each year in the process of developing the annual marketing plan. The company first decides on a sales forecast that is reasonably achievable. This becomes the basis of planning production, work-force size, and financial requirements. Then management establishes sales quotas for all of its regions and territories, which typically add up to more than the sales forecast. Sales quotas are set higher than the sales forecast in order to move the sales managers and sales representatives to their best effort. If they fail to make their quotas, the company nevertheless may make its sales forecast.

Each field sales manager takes his or her quota and divides it up among the sales representatives. Actually, there are three schools of thought on quota setting. The *high-quota school* sets quotas that are above what most sales representatives will achieve but that are possible for all. Advocates of this system are of the opinion that high quotas spur extra effort. The *modest-quota school* sets quotas that a majority of the sales force can achieve. The feeling is that the sales force will accept the quotas as fair, will be able to attain them, and will gain confidence from attaining them. Finally, the *variable-quota school* thinks that individual differences among sales representatives warrant high quotas for some, modest quotas for others. According to Heckert:

> Actual experience with sales quotas, as with all standards, will reveal that sales representatives react to them somewhat differently, particularly at first. Some are stimulated to their highest efficiency, others are discouraged. Some sales executives place considerable emphasis upon this human element in setting their quotas. In general, however, good men will in the long run respond favorably to intelligently devised quotas, particularly when compensation is fairly adjusted to performance.[38]

More formally, the variable-quota school will base quotas for the individual sales representative on a number of considerations, including the person's sales performance in the previous period, his or her territory's estimated potential, and a judgment of his or her aspiration level and reaction to pressure and incentive. Some propositions in this area are:

1. The sales quota for salesperson j at time t, Q_{jt}, should generally be set above his or her sales in the year just ending, $S_{j,t-1}$; that is,

$$Q_{jt} > S_{j,t-1}$$

[38] J. B. Heckert, *Business Budgeting and Control* (New York: Ronald Press Company, 1946), p. 138.

2. The sales quota for salesperson j at time t should be higher, the greater the positive gap between the estimated sales potential of the salesperson's territory, S_{Pjt}, and his or her sales in the year just ending; that is,

$$Q_{jt} \sim (S_{Pjt} - S_{j,t-1})$$

3. The sales quota for salesperson j at time t should be higher, the more positively he or she responds to pressure, E_j; that is,

$$Q_{jt} \sim E_j$$

These three propositions can be combined in an equation for setting a salesperson's quota:

$$Q_{jt} = S_{j,t-1} + E_j(S_{Pjt} - S_{j,t-1}) \qquad (21\text{--}5)$$

Thus, salesperson j's quota at time t should be at least equal to his or her actual sales in the previous period, plus some fraction, E_j, of the difference between estimated territorial sales potential and his or her sales last year; the more positively he or she reacts to pressure, the higher the fraction.

Positive incentives Companies use a number of positive motivators to stimulate sales-force effort. Periodic *sales meetings* provide a social occasion, a break from routine, a chance to meet and talk with "company brass," a chance to air feelings and to identify with a larger group. Companies also sponsor *sales contests* when they want to spur the sales force to make a special selling effort above what would be normally expected. Other motivators include honors and awards, profit-sharing plans, and vacations with pay.

EVALUATING SALES REPRESENTATIVES

We have been describing the "feed-forward" aspects of supervision—the efforts of management to communicate to the sales representatives what they should be doing and to motivate them to do it. But good feed-forward requires good feedback. And good feedback means getting regular information from and about sales representatives to evaluate their performance.

Sources of Information Management gains information about its sales representatives through a number of channels. Probably the most important source of information is the sales representative's periodic reports. Additional information comes through personal observation, through customers' letters and complaints, and through conversations with other sales representatives.

A distinction can be drawn between sales reports that represent *plans for future activities* and those that represent *write-ups of completed activities*. The best example of the former is the *salesperson's work plan*, which most sales representatives are required to submit for a specified future period, usually a week or a month in advance. The plan describes the calls they will make and the routing they will use. This report serves the purposes of encouraging the sales force to plan and schedule their activities, informing management of their whereabouts, and providing a basis for comparing their plans with their accomplishments. Sales representatives can be evaluated on their ability to "plan their work and work their plan." Occasionally, management contacts individual sales representatives after receiving their plans to suggest improvements.

Companies moving toward annual marketing planning in depth are beginning to require their sales representatives to draft an annual *territory marketing plan* in which they outline their program for developing new accounts and increasing business from existing accounts. The formats vary considerably, some asking for general ideas on territory development and others asking for detailed volume and profit estimates. This type of report reflects the conception of sales representatives as market managers and profit centers. The plans are studied by the immediate supervisors and become the bases for rendering constructive suggestions to sales representatives and developing branch sales objectives and estimates for higher-level management.

Several forms are used by sales representatives to write up their completed activities and accomplishments. Perhaps the best known is the *call report* on which the salesperson records pertinent aspects of his or her dealings with a customer, including competitive brands used, best time for calling, degree and type of resistance, and future account promise. Call reports serve the objectives of keeping sales management informed of the salesperson's activities, indicating the status of the customers' accounts, and providing information that might be useful in subsequent calls.

Sales representatives also report *expenses* incurred in the performance of selling duties, for which they are partly or wholly reimbursed. The objective from management's standpoint is primarily to exercise control over the type and amount of expenses and secondarily to have the requisite expense data for income-tax purposes. It is also hoped that the sales representatives will exercise more care in incurring expenses when they must report them in some detail.

Additional types of reports that some companies require from their sales representatives are:

A report on new business secured or potential new business. This alerts management to new accounts and new prospects for which it can formulate special marketing plans in the form of direct mail, team selling, and so on. It is also used to evaluate the extent and effectiveness of the sales representative's prospecting work.

A report on lost business. This report enables the company to keep abreast of competitive efforts and needed product or service improvements and, not the least important, to evaluate the effectiveness of the individual salesperson.

A periodic report on local business and economic conditions. This report aids the development of territory norms and sales programs, although it must be recognized that sales representatives sometimes distort the local picture to defend their own performance.

The reports that companies require their sales representatives to submit contain a wealth of information. Sales representatives, however, frequently complain that they have to devote too much time to writing when they should be selling and that their reports are not read. Management must guard against these criticisms by thinking through carefully the intended uses of the information. The forms should be brief and easy to fill out. Management should make a point of regularly responding to the information.

Formal Evaluation of Performance

The sales force's reports along with other reports from the field and the manager's personal observations supply the raw materials for formally evaluating members of the sales force. Formal evaluation procedures lead to at least three benefits. First, they lead management to develop specific and uniform standards for judging sales performance. Second, they lead management to draw together all its information and impressions about individual sales representatives and make more systematic, point-by-point evaluations. Third, they tend to have a constructive effect on the performance of sales representatives. The constructive effect comes about because the sales representatives know that they will have to sit down one morning with their supervisor and explain certain facets of their routing or sales-call decisions or their failure to secure or maintain certain accounts.

Salesperson-to-salesperson comparisons   One type of evaluation frequently made is to compare and rank the sales performance of the various sales representatives. Such comparisons, however, can be misleading. Relative sales performances are meaningful only if there are no variations from territory to territory in the market potential, workload, degree of competition, company promotional effort, and so forth. Furthermore, sales are not the best denominator of achievement. Management should be more interested in how much each sales representative contributed to net profits. And this cannot be known until the sales representatives' sales mix and sales expenses are examined. A possible ranking criterion would be the sales representative's *actual contribution to company net profits as a ratio to his or her territory's potential contribution to company net profits*. A ratio of 1.00 would mean that the sales representative delivered the potential sales in his or her territory. The lower a sales representative's ratio, the more supervision and counseling he or she needs.

Current-to-past-sales comparisons   A second common type of evaluation is to compare a sales representative's current performance with his or her past performance. This should provide a more direct indication of progress. An example is shown in Table 21–1.

Many things can be learned by the sales manager about John Smith from the information in this table. One of the first things to note is that Smith's total sales increased every year (line 3). This does not necessarily mean that Smith is doing a better job. The product breakdown shows that he has been able to push further the sales of product B than product A (lines 1 and 2). According to his quotas for the two products (lines 4 and 5), his success in increasing sales of product B may be at the expense of product A. According to gross profits (lines 6 and 7), the company earns about twice as much on A as B. The picture begins to emerge that Smith may be pushing the higher-volume, lower-margin product at the expense of the more profitable product. In fact, although he increased total sales by $1,100 between 1978 and 1979 (line 3), the gross profits on his total sales actually decreased by $580 (line 8).

Sales expense (line 9) shows a steady increase, although total expense as a percentage of total sales seems to be under control (line 10). The upward trend in Smith's total dollar expense does not seem to be explained by any increase in the number of calls (line 11), although it may be related in part to his success in acquiring new customers (line 14). However, there is a possibility that in pros-

TABLE 21–1
Form for Evaluating Sales Representative's Progress

TERRITORY: MIDLAND	SALES REPRESENTATIVE: JOHN SMITH		
	1976	1977	1978	1979
1. Net sales product A	$251,300	$253,200	$270,000	$263,100
2. Net sales product B	423,200	439,200	553,900	561,900
3. Net sales total	674,500	692,400	823,900	825,000
4. Percent of quota product A	95.6	92.0	88.0	84.7
5. Percent of quota product B	120.4	122.3	134.9	130.8
6. Gross profits product A	50,260	50,640	54,000	52,620
7. Gross profits product B	42,320	43,920	55,390	56,190
8. Gross profits total	92,580	94,560	109,390	108,810
9. Sales expense	10,200	11,100	11,600	13,200
10. Sales expense to total sales (%)	1.5	1.6	1.4	1.6
11. Number of calls	1,675	1,700	1,680	1,660
12. Cost per call	6.09	6.53	6.90	7.95
13. Average number of customers	320	324	328	334
14. Number of new customers	13	14	15	20
15. Number of lost customers	8	10	11	14
16. Average sales per customer	2,108	2,137	2,512	2,470
17. Average gross profit per customer	289	292	334	326

pecting for new customers, he is neglecting present customers, as indicated by an upward trend in the annual number of lost customers (line 15).

The last two lines show the level and trend in Smith's sales per customer and the gross profits on his sales per customer. These figures become more meaningful when they are compared with overall company averages. For example, if John Smith's average gross profit per customer is lower than the company's average, he may be concentrating on the wrong customers or may not be spending enough time with each customer. Looking back at his annual number of calls (line 11), it may be that Smith is making fewer annual calls than the average salesman. If distances in his territory are not much different, this may mean he is not putting in a full workday, he is poor at planning his routing or minimizing his waiting, or he spends too much time with certain accounts.

Qualitative appraisal of sales representatives   The appraisal usually includes an evaluation of the salesperson's knowledge, personality, and motivation. The salesperson can be rated on the extent of his or her knowledge of the company, products, customers, competitors, territory, and responsibilities. Personality characteristics can be rated, including general manner, appearance, speech, and temperament. The supervisor can also consider any problems in motivation or compliance. Since an almost endless number of qualitative factors might be included, each company must decide what would be most useful to know. It should also inform the sales representatives of these criteria so that they are aware of how their performance is judged.

SUMMARY

The great majority of companies utilize sales representatives, and many assign them the pivotal role in the creation of sales. Because sales representatives are capable of performing a wide variety of tasks, each company must decide exactly what it expects to accomplish through direct selling. The objectives set for the sales force influence the strategies and tactical decisions arising in the management of an effective sales operation.

At the strategic level, the company must decide on the size of its sales force and how it should be organized. In principle, the sales force should be expanded up to the point where an additional sales representative would impose more cost on the company than he or she generates in the way of a gross margin on sales. In practice, sales-force-size decisions are made on estimates of sales productivity in different territories or feasible territory workloads. Effective sales forces can be organized along territorial, product, or customer lines, and sales territories should be thoughtfully designed in terms of size and shape.

Sales representatives must be continuously recruited and selected on the basis of scientific procedures to hold down the high costs of hiring the wrong persons. Sales-training programs are growing more elaborate and are designed to familiarize the salesperson with the company's history, products, and policies, the characteristics of the market and competitors, and the art of selling. Compensation is probably the most important single element in sales-force motivation and should somehow provide a measure of both incentive and security to be maximally effective. The average salesperson needs supervision and continuous encouragement because he or she must make a large number of decisions and is subject to many frustrations. Periodically the person's performance must be formally evaluated to help him or her do a better job.

QUESTIONS AND PROBLEMS

1. A district sales manager voiced the following complaint at a sales meeting: "The average salesman costs our company $40,000 in compensation and expenses. Why can't we buy a few less $40,000 full-page advertisements in *Time* magazine and use the money to hire more men? Surely one man working a full year can sell more products than a one-page ad in one issue of *Time*." Evaluate this argument.

2. The text described some of the characteristics that might be looked for in sales representatives. What characteristics should be looked for in selecting district sales managers? What about the top sales manager?

3. (a) Show diagrammatically, in terms of distances traveled, why a product-structured sales force involves more total travel distance than an unspecialized sales force. (b) Show diagrammatically why a customer-structured sales force involves more total travel distance than an unspecialized sales force.

4. The sales manager of a large company would like to determine how many sales calls per month the sales force should make to average-size accounts. Describe how an experiment might be set up to answer the question.

5. A sales manager is trying to figure out the most that should be spent to win a particular account. This account would produce sales of $10,000 a year, and the company is likely to retain it for at least four years. The company's profit margin on sales is 15 percent. The company wants its various investments to earn 8 percent. What is the most that the company should spend to win this account?

6. Suppose a sales representative in a particular industry can make an average of 1,600 calls a year. If he or she has been writing $420,000 worth of business a year, how many calls can the sales representative afford to make to a $10,000-a-year account without diluting the total business written during the year?

7. Describe several types of selling situations where a straight salary plan seems appropriate.

8. A company regularly asks for its sales representatives' views on such questions as whether to introduce a new product or to raise the price on one of its products. How unbiased are the sales representatives' reactions likely to be?

9. Should individual sales representatives participate in the establishment of sales quotas for their territories? What would be the advantages and disadvantages of such participation?

10. Develop a formula showing Talley's method of determining the optimal size sales force.

Administering the Marketing Program

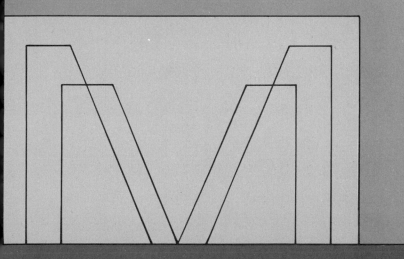

5

MARKETING ORGANIZATION

*Do your work with your whole heart and you will succeed—there
is so little competition!*
ELBERT HUBBARD

We now turn to the administrative side of marketing management to examine how firms organize and control their marketing activities. In this chapter we shall deal with marketing organization, and in the following two chapters, with the firm's marketing information and control systems.

We shall illustrate our discussion of marketing organization mainly in connection with manufacturing companies, where the marketing management function first emerged. The same organizational principles will also apply in such service industries as retailing, banking, and insurance. The marketing management function is even emerging in large nonprofit organizations, such as the U.S. Postal Service, U.S. Army, health maintenance organizations, and mass-transit companies.

THE EVOLUTION OF THE MARKETING DEPARTMENT

The modern marketing department is the product of a long evolution from very humble beginnings. It has evolved through the five stages, and companies can be found today in each of these stages.

Simple Sales Department (Stage One)	All companies start out with three simple functions. Someone must raise and manage capital (finance), produce the product or service (operations), and sell it (sales). The selling function is headed by a sales manager or sales vice president who basically manages a sales force and may do some selling. When the company needs some occasional marketing research or advertising, the sales vice president also handles these because they fall in the selling area. Nevertheless, the sales vice president's heart is in the sales force, and these other assignments are often handled halfheartedly.
Sales Department with Ancillary Functions (Stage Two)	As the company expands, it finds that it needs marketing research, advertising, and customer service on a more continuous and expert basis. The sales vice president hires a few specialists who can perform these functions. A marketing director might be appointed to manage these functions and report to the sales vice president.
Separate Marketing Department (Stage Three)	The continued growth of the company inevitably increases the importance of other marketing functions—marketing research, new-product development, advertising and promotion, customer service—relative to sales-force activity. Nevertheless, the sales vice president continues to give disproportionate time and attention to the sales force. The marketing director will argue that sales could be facilitated by more budget allocation for these other marketing activities. The company president or executive vice president will eventually see the advantage of establishing a marketing department with some independence from the sales vice president. The marketing department will be headed by a marketing director or marketing vice president and will report, along with the sales vice president, to the president or executive vice president. At this stage, sales and marketing are seen as separate and equal functions in the organization that are supposed to work together.
Modern Marketing Department (Stage Four)	Although the sales vice president and the marketing vice president are supposed to work together harmoniously, their relation is often characterized by rivalry and distrust. The sales vice president sees a conspiracy to make the sales force less important in the marketing mix; and the marketing vice president seeks to gain power over all the customer-impinging functions. The sales vice president tends to be short-run oriented and preoccupied with achieving current sales. The marketing vice president tends to be long-run oriented and preoccupied with planning the right products and marketing strategy to meet the customers' long-run needs.

At times it seems that the sales and marketing people represent two different cultures in the organization. The sales people usually have less education, are more practical and "street-wise," whereas the marketing people are younger, more educated, and less experienced in selling. Often the sales people don't trust or believe the marketing people's findings. Some companies arrange for the marketing people to get more selling experience and even hand them a few house accounts to keep them close to the selling situation.

If there is too much conflict between sales and marketing, the company president may (1) eliminate the marketing vice president's office and place marketing activities back under the sales vice president, (2) instruct the executive vice president to handle conflicts that arise, or (3) place the marketing vice president in charge of everything, including the sales force. The last solution is eventually chosen in many companies and forms the basis of the modern marketing department, a department headed by a marketing vice president with subordinates reporting from every marketing function, including sales management.[1]

Modern Marketing Company (Stage Five)

A company can have a modern marketing department and yet not operate as a modern marketing company. Whether it is the latter depends upon how the officers of the company view the marketing function. If they view marketing as primarily a selling function, they are missing the point. The vice president of marketing, no matter how well he or she runs the marketing department, meets frequent resistance from other vice presidents in the matter of carrying out a company-wide customer orientation. The manufacturing vice president holds to the logic of cost minimization and resents interrupting production schedules to please customers. The financial vice president is not sure about the returns from investments in marketing research, communication, and promotion and normally reacts to sales declines by recommending cuts in market-development expenditures. Other departments also resist cooperating to produce satisfied customers. Ultimately the job may call for increasing the power and authority of the marketing vice president over the other business functions. Only a few companies have attained the status of true marketing companies.

WAYS OF ORGANIZING THE MODERN MARKETING DEPARTMENT

An examination of modern marketing departments reveals innumerable arrangements. All marketing organizations must somehow accommodate to four basic dimensions of marketing activity: *functions, geographical units, products,* and *end-use markets.*

Functional Organization

The earliest and still most common form of marketing organization has various functional marketing specialists reporting to a marketing vice president, who is in charge of coordinating all of their activities. Figure 22–1 shows three such specialists, who bear the titles of advertising manager, sales manager, and marketing research manager, respectively. Additional functional specialties might also be present in the marketing department, such as *merchandising, sales promotion, new products, customer service, sales analysis, market planning,* and *marketing administration.*

FIGURE 22–1
Functional Organization

---

[1] For job descriptions of the position of marketing vice president, see David S. Hopkins and Earl L. Bailey, *The Chief Marketing Executive* (New York: Conference Board, 1971), pp. 36–62.

If the number of functions reporting to the marketing vice president becomes large, they may be subgrouped into *operations* functions and *planning* functions. Reporting to the marketing vice president would be a manager of marketing operations responsible for sales, customer services, and advertising, and a manager of marketing planning responsible for marketing research, sales forecasting, and new-product planning. The marketing vice president then has two major functions to think about, planning and doing, instead of several specialties.

The main advantage of a functional marketing organization is its administrative simplicity. On the other hand, this organizational form suffers from certain disadvantages as the company's product line or number of markets increases. First, there is inadequate detailed planning for specific products and markets, since no one is assigned full responsibility for any product or market. Products that are not favorites with various functional specialists tend to get neglected. Second, each functional group develops its own subgoals, which include trying to gain more budget and status vis-a-vis the other functions. The marketing vice president has to constantly sift the claims of competing functional specialists and faces a difficult problem in coordination.

Geographical Organization

A company selling in a national market is likely to set up a vertically structured organization consisting of a sales vice president, regional sales managers, zone sales managers, district sales managers, and finally salespersons. The span of control increases as we move from the sales vice president, who supervises about four regional sales managers (East, West, North, South), to a district sales manager, who might supervise between six and fourteen salespeople. The shorter span allows the manager to give more time to subordinates and is warranted when the sales task is complex, the salespersons are highly paid, and the salespersons' impact on profits is high.

Some companies are now adding *local marketing specialists* to support the sales efforts in high-volume markets. The local marketing specialist for Cleveland, for example, would know everything there is to know about the Cleveland marketing environment. The specialist would prepare and implement a long-range and short-range marketing plan for developing the Cleveland market for the company's products.

Product Management Organization

Companies producing a variety of products and/or brands often establish a product management system (also called a brand management system). The product management system does not replace the functional management system but serves as another layer of management (see Figure 22–2). The functional managers are essentially *resource managers,* and the product managers are essentially *program managers.* This type of organization is called a *matrix organization* because each resource manager gets involved with each program manager. The organization can be visualized as a set of rows representing marketing functions and columns representing products.

The decision to establish a product management system is influenced by the extent of product heterogeneity and the sheer number of products. If the company product lines can benefit from specialized marketing programs, or if the sheer number of products is beyond the capacity of a functional marketing organization to handle, a product management organization is a natural recourse.

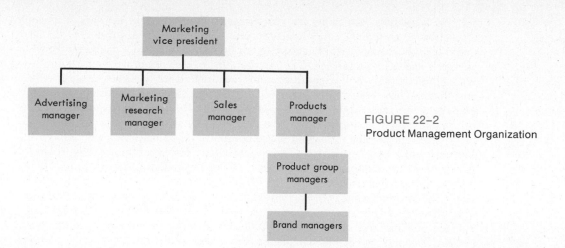

FIGURE 22–2
Product Management Organization

Product management first made its appearance in the Procter & Gamble Company in 1927. A new company soap, Camay, was not doing well, and one of the young men, Neil H. McElroy (later president of P&G), was assigned to give his exclusive attention to developing and promoting this product. This he did successfully, and the company soon afterward added other product managers. Since then a large number of firms, especially in the food, soap, toiletries, and chemical industries, have established product management systems. General Foods, for example, uses a product management system in its Post Division. There are separate product group managers in charge of cereals, pet food, and beverages. Within the cereal product group, there are separate product managers for nutritional cereals, children's presweetened cereals, family cereals, and miscellaneous cereals. In turn, the nutritional-cereal product manager supervises several brand managers.[2]

The product management system creates a focal point of planning and responsibility for individual products. The product manager's role is to create product strategies and plans, see that they are implemented, monitor the results, and take corrective action. This responsibility breaks down into the following six tasks:

1. Developing a long-range growth and competitive strategy for the product
2. Preparing an annual marketing plan and sales forecast
3. Working with advertising and merchandising agencies to develop copy, programs, and campaigns
4. Stimulating interest in and support of the product among the sales force and distributors
5. Gathering continuous intelligence on the product's performance, customer and dealer attitudes, and new problems and opportunities
6. Initiating product improvements to meet changing market needs

These basic functions are common to both consumer and industrial

[2] For details, see "General Foods Corporation: Post Division," in E. Raymond Corey and Steven H. Star, *Organization Strategy: A Marketing Approach* (Boston: Division of Research, Graduate School of Business Administration, Harvard University, 1971), pp. 201–30.

product managers. Yet there are some important differences in their jobs and emphases.[3] Consumer-product managers tend to manage fewer products than industrial-product managers. They spend considerably more time dealing with advertising and sales promotion. They spend most of their time working with others in the company and various agencies and little time in direct contact with customers. They tend to be younger and better educated. Industrial-product managers, by contrast, think more carefully about the technical aspects of their product and possible improvements in design. They spend more time with laboratory and engineering personnel in the company. They work more closely with the sales force and key buyers. They tend to pay less attention to advertising, sales promotion, and promotional pricing. They emphasize rational product factors over emotional ones.

The product management system introduces several advantages in the management of the firm's marketing activity. First, the product manager can balance and harmonize the various functional marketing inputs needed by a product. Second, the product manager is in a position to react quickly to problems in the marketplace without involving several different people in lengthy meetings. Third, smaller brands, because they have a product champion, are not as neglected in this system as they tend to be in functional marketing organizations. Fourth, product management is an excellent training ground for promising young executives, for it involves them in every area of company operations—marketing, production, and finance.

But a price is paid for these advantages. First, the product management system introduces many sources of conflict and frustration that might not otherwise be present.[4] Product managers are not given authority commensurate with their responsibility. They have to rely on persuasive methods to gain cooperation from various resource managers. They spend so much time importuning advertising, sales, and manufacturing for special support that they have little time for planning. They have been told by their superiors that they are minipresidents, but they are often treated like low-level coordinators. They solicit the help of specialists but often do not follow their advice. Sometimes they are forced to go over the heads of others. They are bogged down by a great amount of "housekeeping" paperwork. If this results in a rapid turnover of product managers, it can damage the sound long-range planning of products.

Second, product managers become experts in their product but rarely have a chance to become experts in any of the functions for which they are responsible. They vacillate between posing as an expert and being cowed by real experts. This is particularly unfortunate where the product basically depends on a particular type of expertise, such as advertising; here it would almost make more sense to put the product in the hands of an advertising specialist.

Third, the product management system often turns out to be costlier than anticipated. Originally, one person is appointed to manage each important product. Soon, product managers are appointed to manage even minor products. Each product manager, usually overworked, pleads for and gets an *assistant brand manager*. Later, both of them, still overworked, persuade management to

[3] See Elmer E. Waters, "Industrial Product Manager . . . Consumer Brand Manager: A Study in Contrast," *Industrial Marketing,* January 1969, pp. 45–49.

[4] See David J. Luck, "Interfaces of a Product Manager," *Journal of Marketing,* October 1969, pp. 32–36.

give them a *brand assistant*. Product managers who supervise the more important company products, in their frustration in having to coax time from advertising, packaging, and other specialists, next pressure to hire their own specialists. In one large brewery, the main brand manager has his own advertising department. With all this personnel, payroll costs climb. In the meantime the company continues to increase its number of functional specialists in copy, packaging, media, promotion, market surveys, statistical analysis, and so on. The company soon finds itself stuck with a costly superstructure of product-management people and a superstructure of specialists.

When a company has a product management system that breeds too much conflict or cost, it has four recourses. The first is to try to improve its functioning through better training and procedures. Although P&G managed to achieve over the years a smooth-working product management system, many of its imitators have installed the form without the substance. Pearson and Wilson have suggested five things that will make it work better:

1. *Clearly delineate the limits of the product manager's role and responsibility for the management of a product.* [They are essentially proposers, not deciders.]
2. *Build a strategy development and review process to provide an agreed-to framework for the product manager's operations.* [Too many companies allow product managers to get away with shallow marketing plans featuring a lot of statistics but little strategic rationale.]
3. *Take into account areas of potential conflict between product managers and functional specialists when defining their respective roles.* [Clarify which decisions are to be made by the product manager, which by the expert, and which will be shared.]
4. *Set up a formal process that forces to the top all conflict-of-interest situations between product management and functional line management.* [Both parties might be expected to put all issues in writing and forward them to general management for settlement.]
5. *Establish a system for measuring results that is consistent with the product manager's responsibilities.* [If product managers are to be held accountable for profit, they should be given more control over the factors that affect their profitability.][5]

A second alternative is to switch from a product manager to a product team approach. In fact, there are three types of product team structures in product management. The standard one is called the *vertical product team* and consists of a product manager, assistant product manager, and product assistant (see Figure 22–3A). The product manager is the leader and primarily interacts with other executives trying to gain their cooperation. The assistant product manager helps in these tasks and also does some of the paper work. The product assistant largely does the paperwork and runs various errands. Some companies have moved to a *triangular product team* consisting of a product manager and two specialized product assistants, one who takes care of (say) marketing research and the other, marketing communications (see Figure 22–3B). For example, this design is used at the Illinois Central Railroad where various three-person teams manage different commodities. As another example, the Hallmark Company uses a "marketing team" consisting of a market manager (the leader) and a mar-

[5] Andrall E. Pearson and Thomas W. Wilson, Jr., *Making Your Organization Work* (New York: Association of National Advertisers, 1967), pp. 8–13.

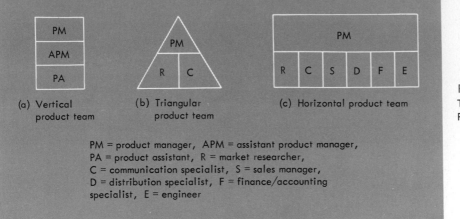

FIGURE 22–3
Three Types of
Product Teams

PM = product manager, APM = assistant product manager,
PA = product assistant, R = market researcher,
C = communication specialist, S = sales manager,
D = distribution specialist, F = finance/accounting
specialist, E = engineer

keting manager and distribution manager. Still other companies have moved to a *horizontal product team* consisting of a product manager and several specialists from within and outside of marketing (see Figure 22–3C). Thus the 3M Company divided its commercial tape division into nine business planning teams, with each team further broken down into team leader and sales, marketing, laboratory, engineering, accounting, and marketing research members. Instead of a product manager's having to bear the entire responsibility for a product plan, the responsibility is shared by representatives from the various key parts of the company, and the opportunity for conflict is lessened. The ultimate step after a horizontal product team is organized is to form a product division around the product.

A third alternative is to eliminate product managers of minor brands and load two or more brands on the existing product managers. This is feasible especially where the company products appeal to a similar set of needs. Thus a cosmetics company does not need separate product managers as much because cosmetics serve one major need—beauty—whereas a toiletries company needs a different manager for headache remedies, toothpaste, soap, and hair shampoo because these products are very different in their use and appeal.

A fourth alternative is to establish divisions around the major company products or product groups and use functional arrangements within divisions. Pearson and Wilson feel that a functional marketing organization "is the oldest, simplest and, in many respects, the soundest form of organization for marketing."[6]

The position of product manager is undergoing important changes.[7] Three particular trends have been accelerated by recent company experiences with shortages, rapid inflation, recession, and consumerism. The first is the greater as-

[6] *Ibid.*, p. 5.

[7] See Richard M. Clewett and Stanley F. Stasch, "Shifting Role of the Product Manager," *Harvard Business Review*, January–February 1975, pp. 65–73; Victor P. Buell, "The Changing Role of the Product Manager in Consumer Goods Companies," *Journal of Marketing*, July 1975, pp. 3–11; and "The Brand Manager: No Longer King," *Business Week*, June 9, 1973.

sumption of profit responsibility by product managers. Cost inflation has led companies to be less satisfied with the sheer volume they sell and more concerned with the profits they make. The product manager is becoming more of a profit center and must put a profit test to the various items in his or her line and to the various marketing expenditures. Some companies are even holding their product managers responsible for excessive costs of inventory and receivables. The second trend is the closer working together of product managers with other managers in the company to find ways of securing scarce supplies, developing substitute ingredients, engineering product economies, smoothing production, and keeping total costs down. The third trend is for people in higher levels of marketing management to have more authority over brand managers. That is in response to the need for more coordinated planning of whole product lines rather than simply of brands and the need for greater responsiveness to consumerists' concerns with advertising truthfulness and product safety.[8]

Market Management Organization

Many companies will sell a product line to a highly diverse set of markets. For example, a paint firm will sell to the consumer, industrial, and government markets. A steel fabricator will sell to the railroad industry, construction industry, and public utilities. A soft-drink company will sell to retail and institutional markets. Where the company sells to customers who fall into distinct user groups having different buying practices or product preferences, some market specialization is desirable in the marketing organization.

The general structure of a market management organization is similar to the product management organization shown earlier in Figure 22–2, except with the substitution of market management for product management. Along with functional managers, there is a *markets manager* who supervises several *market managers* (also called *market development managers* or *market specialists*). The market managers draw upon functional services from the rest of the organization as needed. Market managers of important markets may even have some functional specialists reporting to them.

Market managers are essentially staff, not line, people with similar duties to product managers. Market managers develop long-range and annual plans for the sales and profits in their markets. They have to coax resource help from the other specialists in the organization. This system produces some of the same advantages and disadvantages as the product management system. Its strongest advantage is that the marketing activity is organized to meet the needs of distinct customer groups rather than focusing on marketing functions, regions, or products per se.

An increasing number of companies are reorganizing their management systems along market lines. Hanan calls these *market-centered organizations* and argues that "the only way to insure being market oriented is to put a company's organizational structure together so that its major markets become the centers around which its divisions are built."[9] Xerox has converted from geographical selling to selling by industry. The Mead Company is clustering its marketing activities around home building and furnishings, education, and leisure markets.

[8] See Joseph A. Morein, "Shift From Brand to Product Line Marketing," *Harvard Business Review,* September–October 1975, pp. 56–64.

[9] Mack Hanan, "Reorganize Your Company around Its Markets," *Harvard Business Review,* November–December 1974, pp. 63–74.

One of the most dramatic changes to market centeredness has occurred at the Heinz Company. Before 1964, Heinz was primarily organized around a brand management system, with separate brand managers for soups, condiments, puddings, and so on. Each brand manager, such as the ketchup brand manager, was responsible for both grocery sales and institutional sales. Then in 1964, Heinz created a separate marketing organization for institutional sales. Thus ketchup sales to institutions would be the responsibility of institutional product managers rather than the brand managers. More recently, Heinz split the marketing organization into three broad groups: groceries, commercial restaurants, and institutions. Each group contains further market specialists. For example, the institutional division contains separate market specialists for schools, colleges, hospitals, and prisons.

Product Management/ Market Management Organization

Companies that produce multiple products that flow into multiple markets face a real dilemma. They could utilize a product management system, which requires product managers to be familiar with highly divergent markets. Or they could utilize a market management system, which means that market managers would have to be familiar with highly divergent products bought by their markets. Or they could install both product and market managers, that is, a product/market organization.

Du Pont is an example of a company that has done the latter.[10] Its textile fibers department consists of separate product managers for rayon, acetate, nylon, orlon, and dacron; and also separate market managers for men's wear, women's wear, home furnishings, and industrial markets. The product managers have responsibility for planning the sales and profits of their respective fibers. They are primarily focused on short-run performance and uses of their fiber. Their job is to contact each market manager and ask for an estimate of how much material can be sold in each market. The market managers, on the other hand, have responsibility for developing profitable markets for existing and future Du Pont fibers. They take a long-view of market needs and care more about evolving the right products for their market than pushing specific fibers. In preparing their market plan, they contact each product manager to learn about planned prices and availabilities of different materials. The final sales forecasts of the market managers and the product managers should add to the same grand total.

It would seem that a product management/market management organization would be desirable in a multiple-product, multiple-market company. The rub, however, is that this system is both costly and conflictual. There is the cost of supporting a three-dimensional *matrix organization* (i.e., two layers of program management in addition to one layer of resource management). There are also serious questions as to where authority and responsibility should reside. Here are two of the many dilemmas:

1. How should the sales force be organized? In the Du Pont example, should there be separate sales forces for rayon, nylon, and each of the other fibers? Or should the sales forces be organized according to men's wear, women's wear, and other markets? Or should the sales force not be specialized?

2. Who should set the prices for a particular product/market? In the Du Pont

---

[10] For details, see Corey and Star, *Organization Strategy*, pp. 187–96.

example, should the nylon product manager have final authority for setting nylon prices in all markets? What happens if the men's wear market manager feels that nylon will lose out in this market unless special price concessions are made on nylon?

Some companies are adapting a product/market organization, and others using this organization are having second thoughts. Most agree that only the more important products and markets would justify separate managers. Some observers are not upset about the conflicts in this system on the argument that it provides the company with the benefit of both the short-run and the long-run view and the conflict is healthy.[11]

Corporate-Divisional Organization

As multiproduct companies grow in size, they have a tendency to turn their larger product groups into separate divisions. The larger divisions often set up their own marketing departments on the ground that this will give them more knowledgeable and controllable marketing resources. This poses the question as to what marketing services and activities should be retained at the corporate headquarters level.

Divisionalized companies have reached different answers to this question. Corporate marketing staffs seem to follow any of four models:[12]

1. *No corporate marketing.* Some companies do not have a corporate marketing staff. They don't see any useful function for marketing at the corporate level. Each division has its own marketing department.

2. *Minimal corporate marketing.* Some companies have a small corporate marketing staff that performs a few functions, primarily (a) assisting top management with overall opportunity evaluation, (b) providing divisions with consulting assistance on request, (c) helping divisions that are without marketing or that have weak marketing, and (d) attempting to promote the marketing concept to other departments in the company.

3. *Moderate corporate marketing.* Some companies have a corporate marketing staff that, in addition to the preceding activities, also provides various marketing services to the divisions. The corporate marketing staff might provide certain specialized *advertising services* (e.g., coordination of media buying, institutional advertising, review of division advertising from a taste and image standpoint, auditing of advertising expenditures), *sales promotion services* (e.g., company-wide promotions, central buying of promotional materials), *marketing research services* (e.g., advanced mathematical analysis, research on marketing developments cutting across divisional lines), *sales administration services* (e.g., counsel on sales organization and sales policies, development of common sales reporting systems, management of sales forces selling to common customers), and some miscellaneous services (e.g., counseling of marketing planning, hiring and training of marketing personnel).

4. *Strong corporate marketing.* Some companies have a corporate marketing staff that, in addition to the preceding activities, has the authority to participate strongly in the planning and control of divisional marketing activities.

[11] See B. Charles Ames, "Dilemma of Product/Market Management," *Harvard Business Review,* March–April 1971, pp. 66–74.

[12] See Watson Snyder, Jr., and Frank B. Gray, *The Corporate Marketing Staff: Its Role and Effectiveness in Multi-Division Companies* (Cambridge, Mass.: Marketing Science Institute, April 1971).

The question arises as to whether companies are tending to move toward a particular model of the corporate marketing department. There is no evidence of this. Some companies have recently installed a corporate marketing staff for the first time; others have expanded their department; others have reduced its size and scope; and still others have eliminated it altogether. The potential contribution of a corporate marketing staff varies in different stages of the company's evolution. Most companies begin with weak marketing in their divisions, and these companies often establish a corporate marketing staff whose primary purpose is to bring marketing into the various divisions through education and supplying various services. This begins to work, and some members of the corporate marketing staff join the divisions to head marketing departments. As the divisions grow strong in their marketing, corporate marketing has less to offer them. Some companies decide that corporate marketing no longer has a useful role to play, and it is eliminated.

All said, a corporate staff generally has three justifications. The first is to serve as a corporate focus for review and leadership of overall company marketing activities and opportunities. The second is to offer certain marketing services that could be provided more economically on a centralized basis than by being duplicated in the different divisions. The third is to take responsibility for educating divisional managers, sales managers, and others in the company on the meaning and implementation of the marketing concept.

MARKETING'S INTERFACE WITH OTHER DEPARTMENTS

In principle, business functions should mesh harmoniously to achieve the overall objectives of the firm. In practice, departmental interfaces are often characterized by deep rivalries and misunderstandings that profoundly impede the realization of the company's objectives. Some interdepartmental conflict stems from differences of opinion as to what lies in the best interests of the firm; some from real trade-offs between departmental well-being and company well-being; and some from unfortunate departmental stereotypes and prejudices.

Types of Interdepartmental Conflict

In the typical organization, made up of specialized departments charged with carrying out different company tasks, each department directly or indirectly has an impact on customer satisfaction through its own activities and decisions. Typically these impacts are uncoordinated. Under the marketing concept, it is desirable to coordinate them, because the satisfaction gained by the customer is a function of the *totality* of stimuli, not simply of the stimuli managed by the marketing department.

The marketing department is glad to accept this responsibility and use its influence. The reason for appointing a marketing vice president is twofold: (1) to bring about an integration and coordination of the formal marketing activities of the company, such as sales forecasting, marketing research, advertising, sales force, promotion, and customer service; and (2) to deal with the vice presidents of finance, operations, and so on, on a regular basis to try to develop a deeper appreciation by them of the value and benefits of a customer orientation. But there is little unanimity on how much influence and authority marketing should have over other departments to bring about coordinated marketing.

Other departments naturally resent having to bend their efforts to the will of the marketing department. Just as marketing stresses the customer's point of view, other departments wish to stress the importance of their tasks. Inevitably, departments and individuals define company problems and goals in terms slanted by self-interest. The reason is that each deals continuously with problems in a local portion of the overall system. The major departmental differences in point of view—or organizational conflicts—between marketing and other departments are summarized in Table 22–1. We will briefly examine the typical concerns of each department.

TABLE 22–1
Summary of Organizational Conflicts Between Marketing and Other Departments

DEPARTMENT	THEIR EMPHASIS	MARKETING'S EMPHASIS
R&D	Basic research	Applied research
	Intrinsic quality	Perceived quality
	Functional features	Sales features
Engineering	Long design lead time	Short design lead time
	Few models	Many models
	Standard components	Custom components
Purchasing	Narrow product line	Broad product line
	Standard parts	Nonstandard parts
	Price of material	Quality of material
	Economical lot sizes	Large lot sizes to avoid stockouts
	Purchasing at infrequent intervals	Immediate purchasing for customer needs
Manufacturing	Long production lead time	Short production lead time
	Long runs with few models	Short runs with many models
	No model changes	Frequent model changes
	Standard orders	Custom orders
	Ease of fabrication	Aesthetic appearance
	Average quality control	Tight quality control
Finance	Strict rationales for spending	Intuitive arguments for spending
	Hard and fast budgets	Flexible budgets to meet changing needs
	Pricing to cover costs	Pricing to further market development
Accounting	Standard transactions	Special terms and discounts
	Few reports	Many reports
Credit	Full financial disclosures by customers	Minimum credit examination of customers
	Low credit risks	Medium credit risks
	Tough credit terms	Easy credit terms
	Tough collection procedures	Easy collection procedures

R&D   The company's desire for successful new products is often thwarted by poor working relations between R&D and marketing. In many ways, these groups represent two different cultures in the organization. The R&D department is staffed with scientists and technicians who (1) pride themselves on scientific curiosity and detachment, (2) like to work on challenging technical problems without much concern for immediate sales payoffs, and (3) like to work without much supervision or accountability for research costs. The marketing/sales department is staffed with business-oriented persons who (1) pride themselves on a practical understanding of the world, (2) like to see many new products with sales points that can be talked about to customers, and (3) feel compelled to pay daily attention to the bottom line. Furthermore, each group often carries negative stereotypes of the other group. Marketers see the R&D people as impractical, long-haired, mad-scientist types who don't understand business at all, while R&D people see marketers as gimmick-oriented hucksters who are more interested in sales than in the technical quality of the product. These stereotypes interfere with achieving a good record of successful innovation.

Companies turn out to be either R&D dominated, marketing dominated, or balanced. In *R&D-dominated companies,* the R&D staff goes about researching fundamental problems, looking for major solutions, and striving for technical perfection in product development. In these companies, R&D expenditures tend to be high, and the new product success rate tends to be low, although R&D occasionally comes up with an important new product discovery. In *marketing-dominated companies,* the R&D staff is directed to design products for specific market needs, often involving product modification and the application of existing technologies. In these companies, a higher ratio of new products succeed, but they represent primarily product modifications with relatively short product lives.

A *balanced R&D/marketing company* is one in which effective organizational relations have been worked out between R&D and marketing to share responsibility for successful market-oriented innovation. The R&D staff takes responsibility not for invention alone but for successful innovation. The marketing staff takes responsibility not for new sales features alone but for supporting the discovery of new ways to satisfy needs. R&D/marketing understanding and communication is facilitated in several ways: (1) joint seminars are sponsored to build mutual understanding and respect for each other's goals, working styles, and problems; (2) each new project is assigned to both an R&D person and a marketing person who are in constant communication throughout the life of the project; (3) R&D and marketing personnel are interchanged so that they have a chance to experience each other's work situations. Some R&D people may travel with the sales force, while some marketing people might hang around the lab for a short time; (4) a liaison individual or committee is set up to work out problems that arise between the two groups.[13]

Engineering   Engineering has responsibility for finding practical ways to design new products and new production processes. Engineers are interested in achieving technical quality, cost economy, and manufacturing simplicity. They

---

[13] For further discussion, see William E. Souder, "Effectiveness of Nominal and Interacting Group Decision Processes for Integrating R&D and Marketing," *Management Science,* February 1977, pp. 595–605.

come into conflict with marketing personnel when the latter want several models to be produced, often with product features that require custom components rather than standard components. Engineers see marketers as wanting "bells-and-whistles" on the products rather than more substantial qualities. These problems are less pronounced in companies where the marketing executives have engineering backgrounds and can understand and communicate with the engineers more effectively.

Purchasing   Purchasing executives are responsible for obtaining satisfactory materials and components at the lowest possible cost and in the right quantities from an inventory cost-control point of view. They see marketing executives as pushing for several models in a product line, which requires purchasing small quantities of many inventory items rather than large quantities of a few items. They may think that marketing insists on too high a quality of ordered materials and components. They dislike the inability of marketing to forecast sales accurately—it causes them to have to place rush orders at unfavorable prices and at other times to carry excessive inventories.

Manufacturing   There are many occasions of conflict between manufacturing and marketing managers. Manufacturing people are responsible for the smooth running of the factory to produce the right products in the right quantities at the right time for the right cost. They have spent their lives in the factory, with its attendant problems of machine breakdowns, inventory stockouts, and labor disputes and slowdowns. They see marketers as having little understanding of factory economics or politics. Marketers will complain about insufficient plant capacity, delays in production, poor quality control, and poor customer service. Yet marketers often turn in inaccurate sales forecasts, design products that are difficult to manufacture and come in too many versions, and promise more factory service than is reasonable.

Marketers, being out in the marketplace, do not see the factory's problems but rather the problems of their customers who need the goods quickly, who receive defective merchandise, and who can't get factory service. Marketers show little concern with the extra factory costs of getting something done to make or save a customer. The problem is one not only of poor communication but of actual conflict of interest.

The conflict is settled by companies in different ways. Some companies are *manufacturing dominant,* in that everything is done to insure smooth production and low costs. The company chooses to produce narrow product lines in large quantities. Products are designed simply. Sales promotions calling for quick production are kept to a minimum. Customers on back order have to be patient and wait their turn. Other companies are *marketing dominant,* in that everything is done to serve and satisfy customers. In one large toiletries company, the marketing personnel call the shots, and the manufacturing people have to fall in line, including going overtime, producing short runs, and so on. This results in high and fluctuating manufacturing costs, as well as poor quality control.

Ideally, companies need to move toward a *balanced manufacturing/marketing orientation* in which policies and authority are defined, both sides feel important, and both participate in determining what is best for the company. Solutions take the form of joint seminars to understand each other's viewpoint, joint committees and liaison personnel, personnel exchange programs, and analytical methods to determine the most profitable course for the company to take when there is disagreement.[14]

Finance Financial executives pride themselves on being able to evaluate the profit implications of different business actions. When it comes to marketing expenditures, they frequently feel frustrated. Marketing executives will ask for substantial budgets for advertising, sales promotion, and sales force, without providing dependable forecasts of how much sales will be produced by these different expenditures. Financial executives suspect that the marketers' forecasts are self-serving rather than arrived at by any solid scientific methodology. They think that marketing people don't spend enough time relating their expenditures to sales outcomes and shifting their budgets to more profitable areas. They think that marketers are too willing to slash prices in order to make sales, instead of pricing to make a profit.

In turn, marketing executives often see financial people as controlling the purse strings too tightly and refusing to invest in long-term market development. Financial people seem overly conservative and risk averse, causing many opportunities to be passed over. The solution lies in giving marketing people more training in financial concepts and giving financial people a better understanding of how the market works and responds to different types of marketing effort.

Accounting Accountants see marketing people as lax in providing good sales reports and providing them on time. They also dislike the special deals sales people make with customers who require special accounting procedures. Marketers, on the other hand, are upset by the procedures used by accountants to allocate fixed-cost burdens to different products in the line. Thus brand managers may feel that their brand is more profitable than it looks if it were not for the high overhead assigned to it. They would also like the accounting department to prepare special reports on sales and profitability by different channels, territories, order sizes, and so on, only to hear that the accounting department is too busy to do it.

Credit Credit officers are eager to check out the credit standing of potential customers and to deny or limit credit to the more doubtful ones. They think that marketers are too ready to sell to anyone, even to those from whom payment would be slow or doubtful. Marketers, on the other hand, often feel that credit standards are too high. They think that "zero bad debts" may look good on the credit officers' records but really means that a lot of sales and profits have been lost. They feel that they work too hard to find customers to hear that they are not good enough to sell to.

Strategies for Building a Company-wide Marketing Orientation

Only a handful of American companies—such as P&G, IBM, Caterpillar—are truly marketing oriented. A much larger number of companies are sales oriented, which they confuse with being marketing oriented. At some time in their history, something happens to create a disturbing awareness of their lack of a true marketing orientation. They may lose a major market, experience slow

---

[14] See Benson P. Shapiro, "Can Marketing and Manufacturing Coexist?" *Harvard Business Review*, September–October 1977, pp. 104–14.

growth or low profitability, or find themselves facing more sophisticated competitors. This has happened many times.

For years, General Motors prided itself on a marketing orientation and was able to point to its huge sales volume and market share as evidence. However, as management witnessed the growing share of small cars and foreign cars, they realized that they had not fully monitored the market and responded to consumer desires. They still have not yet learned to design small economy cars that Americans prefer as strongly as some foreign imports.

In the early 1970s, American Telephone and Telegraph (AT&T) suddenly found itself facing keen competition in the sale of switchboards and ancillary telephone equipment. AT&T was totally unprepared to make an effective marketing case to buyers to keep them from buying competitors' equipment selling at lower prices. They realized that they had been pushing sales when they should have been paying attention to changing market forces. They are now involved in a crash effort to acquire marketing know-how.[15]

American Hospital Supply Company enjoys market leadership in the hospital supplies business, based largely on their extensive distribution and sales coverage. They are now facing new sophisticated competitors, such as P&G, who are attacking their established markets. AHS is concerned and is rapidly transforming itself from a sales company to a marketing company.

The Chase Manhattan Bank of New York has watched Citibank, its main competitor, make one smart move after another, each time leaving Chase behind. Citibank has been systematically developing a marketing culture at the bank, while Chase has been running along traditional financial lines. Recently Chase has started to build new marketing resources at the bank.

All of these companies realized that they were weak in marketing and therefore at a great disadvantage when competing against topflight marketing companies. Old-fashioned sales responses are not enough. Sales managers, when faced with sales declines or stagnation, plea to top management for more resources and lower prices. They feel the answer lies in working harder. But top management is becoming less confident in pure sales power. They want those responsible for sales to get smarter, not work harder. They want more-advanced warnings and better analyses of the changing forces in the marketplace; they want better marketing strategies and plans; they want products that meet new and emerging customer needs.

Top management's problem is how to convert the company from a traditional sales company to a modern marketing company. Actually, there are several steps companies have to take to acquire a modern marketing orientation.

Presidential leadership Presidential leadership is a key prerequisite to establishing a modern marketing company. The vice president of marketing cannot unilaterally direct other company officers to bend their efforts to serve customers. The company president must understand marketing and its difference from sales, believe that it is the key to company growth and prosperity, and build it into his speeches and decisions.

---

[15] Bro Uttal, "Selling Is No Longer Mickey Mouse at A.T.&T.," *Fortune*, July 17, 1978, pp. 98–104.

Marketing task force   The president should appoint a marketing task force to develop a strategy for bringing modern marketing into the company. The task force should include the president, executive vice president, the vice presidents of sales, marketing, manufacturing, and finance, and a few other key individuals. They should examine the need for marketing, set objectives, anticipate problems in introducing it, and develop an overall strategy. For the next few years, this committee should meet from time to time to measure progress and take new initiatives.

Outside marketing consultant   The marketing task force would probably benefit from outside guidance and assistance in developing a plan for introducing marketing into the organization.

A corporate marketing department   A key step is to establish a corporate marketing department. The corporate marketing department should review each division's marketing resources and needs with the division's general manager. Often the division's general manager does not understand marketing and confuses it with sales. The division's sales operation is usually headed by a sales vice president who is not marketing oriented. To appoint a marketing vice president over this person would be asking for trouble. Alternative steps might be to add the outside marketer to the division as the executive vice president; or to add this person as a marketing vice president on a parallel level to the sales vice president; or to put this person in charge of divisional planning. Ultimately, each division will need a strong marketing vice president to make marketing headway.

In-house marketing seminars   The new corporate marketing department should develop an extensive program of in-house marketing seminars for top corporate management, divisional general managers, marketing and sales personnel, manufacturing personnel, R&D personnel, and so on. The seminars should start with the higher levels of management and move to lower levels. The aim of the marketing seminars is to bring about changes in the marketing beliefs, attitudes, and behavior of various executive groups.

Hiring marketing talent   The company should also hire marketing talent away from leading marketing companies and also hire new M.B.A.'s receiving their degrees in marketing. For example, when Citibank got serious about marketing some years ago, they hired away several brand managers from General Foods and other companies.

Promoting executives who are market oriented   The company should favor market-oriented individuals in selecting new division managers. A large public-accounting firm that is currently trying to become market-oriented has now sent out signals that it will give preference to marketing- rather than financially-oriented partners in promotions to branch manager.

Installing a modern marketing-planning system   An excellent way to train an organization to think marketing is to install a modern market-oriented planning system. This means that corporate planners will begin their thinking with market opportunity considerations and will formulate marketing strategies to capitalize on these opportunities. Other departments will do their planning around these marketing strategies and forecasts.

The job of implementing a marketing orientation throughout the company is an uphill and never-ending battle. The purpose is not to resolve every issue in favor of the customer, no matter what the cost, but rather to remind others that customers are the foundation of the company's business.[16]

SUMMARY
The modern marketing department evolved through several stages to reach its contemporary form. It started as a simple sales department consisting of only a sales force. Later the sales department took on some ancillary functions, such as advertising and marketing research. As the ancillary functions grew in importance, many companies created a marketing department separate from the sales department to manage these other marketing activities. But the heads of sales and marketing often disagreed on company marketing policy, and eventually the two departments were merged into a modern marketing department headed by the marketing vice-president. A modern marketing department, however, does not automatically create a modern marketing company unless the other officers accept a customer orientation as the hub of the enterprise.

Modern marketing departments are organized in a number of ways. The most common form is the functional marketing organization in which the various marketing functions are headed by separate managers who report to the marketing vice president. Another common form is the product management organization in which major products are the responsibility of product managers who work with the various functional specialists in the company to develop and achieve their plans for the product. Another, less common, form is the market management organization in which major markets are the responsibility of market managers who work with the various functional specialists to develop and achieve their plans for the market. Some large companies use a product management/market management organization, which combines both systems of management. Finally, multidivision companies normally develop a corporate marketing staff and separate marketing departments at the divisions, with some variations as to the division and authority for different services.

Marketing must work smoothly with the other functions in a company. In its pursuit of the customers' interests, marketing frequently comes into conflict with R&D, engineering, purchasing, manufacturing, finance, accounting, credit, and other functions that stress a cost minimization logic. These conflicts can be reduced when the company president commits himself and the company to a customer orientation and when the marketing vice president learns to work effectively with the other officers. Acquiring a modern marketing orientation requires presidential support, a marketing task force, outside marketing consulting help, the establishment of a corporate marketing department, in-house marketing seminars, marketing talent hired from the outside, and a market-oriented marketing-planning system.

[16] For further discussion, see Edward S. McKay, *The Marketing Mystique* (New York: American Management Association, 1972), pp. 22–30.

1. In order to carry out a proposed national sales promotion, describe some of the departments whose efforts must be coordinated with those of the marketing department. Through what kind of planning device might these efforts be integrated?

2. Does it make organizational sense to combine the company's marketing department and public relations department under one vice-president?

3. A major airline's marketing department is presently organized on a functional basis: advertising, field sales, customer services, and so on. The airline is considering setting up a route manager organization, with a manager assigned to each major route who would be to a route what a brand manager is to a brand. Do you think this is a good idea?

4. "In 1945 he had been brought back to Millburgh and made vice-president of sales. At fifty-three, J. Walter Dudley was probably the best-known man in the entire furniture industry. His memory for names and faces was phenomenal. At one Chicago Market . . . two bystanding salesmen had actually kept a count and heard him greet two hundred and eighteen furniture store owners and buyers by name before he was confronted by an individual whose name he did not know. There were hundreds of furniture merchants who would not have thought a market visit complete without having had the opportunity to shake hands with good old Walt Dudley."—Cameron Hawley, *Executive Suite* (Boston: Houghton Mifflin Company, 1952), pp. 133–34. Does J. Walter Dudley sound like the ideal vice-president of marketing?

5. You are being interviewed for the position of brand manager at the Blogg's Blotting Paper Company. Sales of blotters have been declining for several years. Develop a list of questions and suggestions that would reflect well on your qualifications for this position.

6. The General Electric Company does not have a corporate vice-president of marketing. Its vice-presidents of marketing are found in various sections, groups, and divisions. General Electric does have a corporate vice-president of strategic planning. Do you think a corporate vice-president of marketing should be added?

7. In large railroads, the operations department usually holds dominant power. The needs of freight customers were accorded less importance than sticking to schedules. Suggest a strategy for establishing a company-wide marketing orientation.

8. Describe some product and market situations where local marketing specialists would be of particular assistance to a company.

Marketing Research and the Marketing Information System

> To manage a business well is to manage its future; and to manage its future is to manage information.
>
> MARION HARPER, JR.

In the long history of business enterprise, management's overwhelming attention has been devoted to the problems of effectively managing *money, materials, machines,* and *men.* Through time, business has attained increased mastery over these resources. Less attention has been paid historically to the fifth critical resource of the firm: *information.* It is hard to find company executives anywhere who are substantially satisfied with their marketing information. Their complaints include:

There is too much marketing information of the wrong kind.

There is not enough marketing information of the right kind.

Marketing information is so dispersed throughout the company that usually a great effort must be made to locate simple facts.

Important marketing information is sometimes suppressed by subordinates if they believe it will reflect unfavorably on their performance.

Important information often arrives too late to be useful.

Information often arrives in a form that leaves no idea of its accuracy, and there is no one to turn to for confirmation.

The basic fact is that most companies have not yet adapted to the intensified information requirements for effective marketing in a modern economy. Three trends, in particular, render the needs for marketing information stronger than at any time in the past.

The first trend is the shift from local to national and international marketing. The concept of the national and international firm means that company decision makers must make their key decisions on the basis of secondhand information, since they are far removed from the scenes where their products are sold. *The second is the transition from buyer needs to buyer wants.* As the society becomes more affluent, its members' survival needs are increasingly satisfied. Buying becomes a highly expressive personal act, and sellers must depend on systematic research to understand the overt and latent wants of buyers. *The third is the transition from price to nonprice competition.* As sellers increase their reliance on competitive weapons such as branding, product differentiation, advertising, and sales promotion, they require great quantities of information on the effectiveness of these marketing tools. Not only markets but also the tools of marketing must be researched.

The explosive information requirements have been met on the supply side by impressive new information technologies. The last thirty years have witnessed the emergence of the computer, microfilming, closed-circuit television, copy machines, tape recorders, and many other devices that have created a veritable revolution in information-handling capacity.

Most business firms, however, do not operate at a high level of information sophistication. Many firms do not have a marketing research department. Many other firms have small marketing research departments whose work is limited to routine forecasting, sales analysis, and occasional surveys. Only a few firms have developed advanced marketing information systems that provide company management with up-to-date marketing information and analysis.

CONCEPT AND COMPONENTS OF A MARKETING INFORMATION SYSTEM

Every firm is the scene of many information flows affecting marketing management. Each firm has made some arrangements to systematize these flows. These arrangements constitute the firm's *marketing information system:*

> A structured, interacting complex of persons, machines, and procedures designed to generate an orderly flow of pertinent information, collected from both intra- and extra-firm sources, for use as the basis for decision making in specified responsibility areas of marketing management.[1]

Figure 23–1 presents a picture of the main components of a total marketing information system. The *marketing information system* is shown to stand between the *environment* and the *marketing executive-user.* There is a *marketing data flow* from the environment to the marketing information system of the company. The marketing information system turns this data flow into a *marketing information flow* that goes to its executives. On the basis of this information,

---

[1] Samuel V. Smith, Richard H. Brien, and James E. Stafford, eds., *Readings in Marketing Information Systems* (Boston: Houghton Mifflin Company, 1968), p. 7. Also see Kurt H. Schaffir and H. George Trentin, *Marketing Information Systems* (New York: American Management Association, 1973).

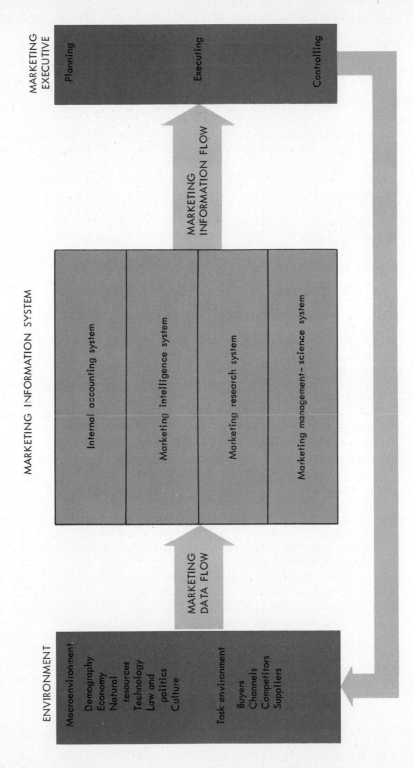

FIGURE 23–1
Components of the Marketing Information System

the executives develop plans and programs, which enter a *marketing decision flow* that goes back to the environment.

We now turn to the main components of the marketing information system.

INTERNAL ACCOUNTING SYSTEM

The earliest and most basic information system used by the marketing executive is the internal accounting system. It is the system that reports orders, sales, inventory levels, receivables, payables, and so on. Through this information the executives can spot opportunities and problems and can compare actual and expected levels of performance.

The Order-Shipping-Billing Cycle

The heart of the accounting system is the order-shipping-billing cycle. Sales representatives, dealers, and customers dispatch orders to the firm. The order department prepares multicopy invoices and dispatches them to various departments. Items that are out of stock are back-ordered. Items that are shipped are accompanied by shipping and billing documents that are also multicopied and go to various departments.

The company has a strong interest in carrying out these steps as quickly and accurately as possible. Sales representatives are supposed to send in their orders every evening, in some cases to phone them in when they are obtained. The order department should process them quickly. The warehouse should send the goods out as soon as possible. And bills should go out as soon as possible. The computer should be harnessed to expedite the order-shipping-billing cycle. Ringer and Howell reported a study of one company's order routine, which resulted in cutting down the elapsed time between the receipt and issuance of an order from sixty-two hours to thirty hours without any change in costs.[2]

Improving the Timeliness of Sales Reports

Marketing executives in many companies receive sales reports some time after the sales have taken place. In consumer food companies, warehouse withdrawal reports are issued with fair regularity, but actual retail purchase reports take about two months, based on special store or consumer panel audits. In the auto industry, executives wait with bated breath for a sales report that comes out every ten days; if sales are down, they can expect ten sleepless nights. Most marketing executives complain that they don't get the sales report fast enough, no matter how often they get it.

Here are three companies that have designed sophisticated sales-reporting systems to increase the value of sales information:

> *General Mills.* The executives at General Mills receive their information daily. The zone, regional, and district sales managers in the Grocery Products Division start their day with a teletype report on orders and shipments in their area the day before. The report also contains progress percentages to compare with target percentages and last year's progress percentages.

[2] Jurgen F. Ringer and Charles D. Howell, "The Industrial Engineer and Marketing," in *Industrial Engineering Handbook,* 2nd ed., ed. Harold Bright Maynard (New York: McGraw-Hill Book Company, 1963), pp. 10, 102–3.

Schenley. Schenley's system allows its key executives to retrieve within seconds, via video-display desk consoles and printers, current and past sales and inventory figures for any brand and package size for each of four hundred distributors; an executive can determine within seconds all areas where sales are lagging behind expectations.

Mead Paper. Mead Paper's system permits its sales representatives in buyers' offices to obtain on-the-spot answers to customers' queries about paper availability. The sales representative dials Mead Paper's computer center. The computer determines whether paper is available at the nearest warehouse and when it can be shipped; if it is not in stock, the computer checks the inventory at other nearby warehouses until one is located. If the paper is nowhere in stock, the computer program goes through a production-scheduling routine to determine where and when the paper can be produced and shipped. The sales representative gets an answer in seconds, and this places him or her in an advantageous position in relation to competitors.

Designing a User-Oriented Reports System

In designing an advanced sales information system, the company should avoid certain pitfalls. First, it is possible to create a system that delivers too much information to the executives. They arrive at their office each morning to face voluminous sales statistics. Second, it is possible to create a system that delivers information that is too current! Executives may end up reacting to sales movements that are essentially random; and their actions may in fact destabilize the market. Third, it is possible that the cost of supplying all of this information at some point will exceed its value.

Cox and Good noted that many companies had not taken advantage of all the existing modern information technology because they recognized the need for a system-manager balance.

> In a "steady state" . . . there usually seems to be a correspondence between management sophistication and information quality. . . . What happens when only the level of information quality is raised significantly? Our prediction is that this would not lead to better decisions. In fact, the reverse may be true, as the result of the confusion and resentment generated by the manager's inability to deal with the more sophisticated information.
>
> Information quality can be upgraded much more rapidly than management quality. It is easy to throw the management system out of balance by installing a sophisticated MIS. . . . A more positive approach is to develop a master plan for improving the system, but make the improvements gradually—say, over several years.[3]

The company's marketing information system should represent a cross between (a) what executives think they need, (b) what executives really need, and (c) what is economically feasible. A useful step is the appointment of a *marketing information-planning committee,* which interviews a cross section of marketing executives—product managers, sales executives, sales representatives, and so on—to find out their information needs. A useful set of questions is shown in Table 23–1. The information-planning committee will want to pay special attention to strong desires and complaints. At the same time, the committee will wisely discount some of the alleged information needs. Executives who have an appetite for information will list a great deal, failing to distinguish between *what is nice*

---

[3] Donald F. Cox and Robert E. Good, "How to Build a Marketing Information System," *Harvard Business Review,* May–June 1967, pp. 145–54.

TABLE 23–1
Questionnaire for Determining Marketing Information Needs

1. What types of decisions are you regularly called upon to make?
2. What types of information do you need to make these decisions?
3. What types of information do you regularly get?
4. What types of special studies do you periodically request?
5. What types of information would you like to get that you are not now getting?
6. What information would you want daily? weekly? monthly? yearly?
7. What magazines and trade reports would you like to see routed to you on a regular basis?
8. What specific topics would you like to be kept informed of?
9. What types of data-analysis programs would you like to see made available?
10. What do you think would be the four most helpful improvements that could be made in the present marketing information system?

to know and *what they need to know.* Other executives will be too busy to give the questionnaire serious thought and will omit many things they ought to know. This is why the information-planning committee must take another step, that of determining what executives *should know* to be able to make responsible decisions. For example, what should brand managers know in order to make truly informed decisions on the size of the advertising budget? They should know something about the degree of market saturation, the rate of sales decay in the absence of advertising, and the spending plans of competitors. The information system should be designed around models for making the key marketing decisions.

MARKETING INTELLIGENCE SYSTEM

Whereas the internal accounting system supplies executives with *results data,* the marketing intelligence system supplies executives with *happenings data.* We shall define the *marketing intelligence system* as *the way in which company executives are kept current and informed about changing conditions in the macroenvironment and task environment.*

All executives engage at different times in four modes of scanning the environment:

1. *Undirected viewing:* general exposure to information where the viewer has no specific purpose in mind.
2. *Conditioned viewing:* directed exposure, not involving active search, to a more or less clearly identified area or type of information.
3. *Informal search:* a relatively limited and unstructured effort to obtain specific information or information for a specific purpose.
4. *Formal search:* a deliberate effort—usually following a preestablished plan, procedure, or methodology—to secure specific information or information relating to a specific issue.[4]

[4] Francis Joseph Aguilar, *Scanning the Business Environment* (New York: Macmillan Company, 1967).

Marketing executives carry on marketing intelligence mostly on their own, being most interested in market news, keeping informed by reading newspapers and trade publications, relying on subordinates for search information, and getting some unsolicited information from outside sources. To the extent that their intelligence work is casual, valuable information will often come in too little or too late. Executives may learn of a competitive move, a new customer need, or a dealer problem too late to make the best response.

Improving Intelligence-Gathering Activity

A company can take three steps to improve the executives' intelligence system: (1) train the sales force to be better at intelligence gathering, (2) utilize additional intelligence resources, and (3) buy information from specialized marketing research services.

Sales representatives as intelligence agents Sales representatives have correctly been called the company's "eyes and ears to the marketplace." They meet the buyers, dealers, and occasionally the competitors. They are in a good position to pick up significant bits of information that would never appear in the usual summary statistics of company sales activity. When these bits and pieces of information are correlated at headquarters, they often yield a revealing picture.

The critical question is whether the sales force feels motivated to look for information and to pass it on to their superiors. In a telling experiment, Albaum arranged with a sample of company customers to pass on six fabricated pieces of market information to the company's sales representatives.[5] Of the six pieces of market information, only two were ever passed on by the sales representatives to their superiors. One arrived in three days but was seriously distorted; the other arrived in about ten days in fairly accurate form. Albaum concluded that there was not a free flow of market intelligence within this company and that, in general, most unmanaged intelligence systems are characterized by information disappearance, delay, and distortion.

The solution requires training sales representatives to be intelligence gatherers for the firm. Their job should be facilitated by designing call reports that are easy to fill out. Sales representatives should know who in the company can use various types of information, so that information does not always have to travel through several relay points before reaching the person who needs it. An intelligence office might be established to receive and disseminate intelligence. Sales managers should make a point of reviewing the intelligence performance of their sales representatives and make it a factor in pay raises.

Other means of gathering competitive intelligence Similar steps should be taken to motivate sales managers, dealers, the advertising agency, and others to pay more attention to gathering and passing along intelligence. It is sometimes desirable to hire one or more full-time specialists in marketing intelligence gathering. This does not necessarily mean industrial espionage agents. Many companies send out comparison shoppers to learn how various brands are selling and how helpful retail sales personnel are. Interviewing customers and dealers to learn about new opportunities and problems is a legitimate intelligence activity. Much can be learned about competitors' activities through such overt means as

[5] Gerald S. Albaum, "Horizontal Information Flow: An Exploratory Study," *Journal of the Academy of Management,* March 1964, pp. 21–33.

(1) pricing or purchasing competitors' products; (2) attending "open houses" and trade shows; (3) reading competitors' published reports and attending stockholders' meetings; (4) talking to competitors' former employees and present employees, dealers, distributors, suppliers, and freight agents; (5) hiring a clipping service; and (6) reading the *Wall Street Journal*, the *New York Times*, and trade-association papers.

Purchase of special marketing intelligence services   Many companies purchase information from outside suppliers. The A. C. Nielsen Company sells bimonthly data (based on a sample of sixteen hundred stores) on brand shares, retail prices, percentage of stores stocking item, and percentage of stock-out stores. The Market Research Corporation of America sells reports (based on the purchase diaries of a representative panel of seventy-five hundred households scattered throughout the country) on weekly movements of brand shares, sizes, prices, and deals. Clipping services may be hired to report on competitive advertising expenditures, media mixes, and advertising appeals.

Improving Intelligence-Processing Activity

The usefulness of gathered intelligence depends on its accuracy, retrievability, and speed in moving to higher management levels where it can be used. A centralized marketing intelligence center can offer several services to improve the processing and dissemination of intelligence.

The first service is intelligence *evaluation*. An analyst trained in data evaluation would be available to examine any information and render a technical opinion as to how much confidence can be placed in it. A second important service is intelligence *abstraction*. Trained abstracters can condense and edit incoming information to make it more useful for executives. *Dissemination* is a third important intelligence-processing service. Dissemination involves getting information to the right people in the right form in the shortest feasible time. Among the devices used are newsletters, telephone calls, cassettes, teletype services, and interconnected company computers. The fourth service is *storage and retrieval*. Each company should develop a master indexing system and organize all the existing information into easily accessible files. The fifth service is *purging*, where old information that is no longer useful is removed, to keep the amount of stored information within limits.

MARKETING RESEARCH SYSTEM

Besides internal accounting information and marketing intelligence, marketing executives need specific studies of problem and opportunity areas. They may need a market survey, a product-preference test, a sales forecast by region, or an advertising-effectiveness study. These studies require the talents of skilled researchers, who can apply principles of sample size, sample design, and questionnaire construction to the task. These researchers usually make up the marketing research department of the company.

Organizational Characteristics of Marketing Research

About 73 percent of all large companies have formal marketing research departments headed by a marketing research manager who reports normally to the marketing vice president and in some cases to top management or other officers. The marketing research manager is considered a major member of the marketing team and performs such roles as study director, administrator, internal company consultant, and advocate. In smaller companies, the department consists of a few professional researchers and in larger companies may comprise one to two dozen full-time employees. The department personnel may be specialized by skill (survey expert, statistician, behavioral scientist), by industry, or by type of project.

The department usually gets a budget anywhere from .01 to 3.50 percent of company sales. The department spends between one-quarter and one-half of this budget on outside services.[6] Bradford lists over three hundred fifty marketing research firms, falling into three major categories:

1. *Full-line marketing research firms.* These firms offer general marketing research services. Their clients range from companies that are too small to support their own marketing research department to large firms who subcontract a portion of their work to relieve backlog or to obtain an independent point of view.
2. *Specialty-line marketing research firms.* These firms specialize in particular marketing research services, such as market analysis and forecasting, survey research work, packaging research, product research, or brand-name testing. They may also specialize in either consumer or industrial goods.
3. *Syndicated information-selling firms.* These firms specialize in gathering continuous trade or consumer data, which they sell to clients on a fee-subscription basis. Well-known examples include A. C. Nielsen Company, Market Research Corporation of America, Daniel Starch, and Gallup-Robinson.[7]

The scope of marketing research   Marketing research departments have been steadily expanding their activities and techniques. Table 23–2 lists thirty-three different marketing research activities and the percentage of companies carrying on each. The ten most common activities are determination of market characteristics, measurement of market potentials, market-share analysis, sales analysis, studies of business trends, competitive-product studies, short-range forecasting, new-product acceptance and potential, long-range forecasting, and pricing studies.[8]

These studies have benefited over the years from increasingly sophisticated techniques. Many of them—such as questionnaire construction and area sampling—came along early and were quickly and widely accepted in the corpus of marketing research practice. Others—such as motivation research and mathematical methods—came in uneasily, with prolonged and heated debates among practitioners over their practical usefulness. But they, too, settled in the corpus of marketing research methodology.

Management's use of marketing research   In spite of the rapid growth of marketing research, there are many companies that are still without it or that use it poorly. Several factors stand in the way of its greater utilization.

A NARROW CONCEPTION OF MARKETING RESEARCH   Many executives see marketing research as only a fact-finding operation. The marketing researcher is

---

[6] For specific statistics, see Dik Warren Twedt, ed., *1978 Survey of Marketing Research: Organization, Functions, Budget, Compensation* (Chicago: American Marketing Association, 1978).

[7] Ernest S. Bradford, *Bradford's Directory of Marketing Research Agencies and Management Consultants in the United States and the World*, 15th ed., 1973–1974 (Middlebury, Vt.: Bradford Co.).

[8] Twedt, *Survey of Marketing Research*, p. 41.

TABLE 23–2
Research Activities of 798 Companies

TYPE OF RESEARCH	PERCENT DOING
Advertising research:	
Motivation research	48
Copy research	49
Media research	61
Studies of ad effectiveness	67
Business economics and corporate research:	
Short-range forecasting (up to 1 year)	85
Long-range forecasting (over 1 year)	82
Studies of business trends	86
Pricing studies	81
Plant and warehouse location studies	71
Product mix studies	51
Acquisition studies	69
Export and international studies	51
MIS (management information system)	72
Operations research	60
Internal company employees	65
Corporate responsibility research:	
Consumers "right to know" studies	26
Ecological impact studies	33
Studies of legal constraints on advertising and promotion	51
Social values and policies studies	40
Product research:	
New-product acceptance and potential	84
Competitive-product studies	85
Testing of existing products	75
Packaging research—design or physical characteristics	60
Sales and market research:	
Measurement of market potentials	93
Market-share analysis	92
Determination of market characteristics	93
Sales analysis	89
Establishment of sales quotas, territories	75
Distribution channels studies	69
Test markets, store audits	54
Consumer-panel operations	50
Sales compensation studies	60
Promotional studies of premiums, coupons, sampling, deals, etc.	52

SOURCE: Dik Warren Twedt, ed., *1978 Survey of Marketing Research* (Chicago: American Marketing Association 1978), p. 41.

supposed to design a questionnaire, choose a sample, carry out interviews, and report results, often without being given a careful definition of the problem or of the decision alternatives before management. As a result, some of the fact finding fails to be useful. This reinforces management's idea of the limited good that can come from marketing research.

UNEVEN CALIBER OF MARKETING RESEARCHERS   Some executives view marketing research as little better than a clerical activity and reward it as such. In these cases, less able individuals are attracted into its ranks, and their weak training and deficient creativity are reflected in their output. The disappointing output reinforces management prejudice against expecting too much from marketing research. Management continues to pay low salaries, perpetuating the basic difficulty.

LATE RESULTS   Marketing research that is carefully designed may take a long time to carry out. Often the report is ready after the decision has had to be made, or when the issue has become less salient to the executives.

OCCASIONAL ERRONEOUS FINDINGS BY MARKETING RESEARCH   Many executives want conclusive information from marketing research, although usually marketing processes are too complex to yield more than tentative findings. The problem is complicated by the low budgets often given to marketing researchers to get the information. Executives become disappointed, and their opinion of the worth of marketing research is lowered.

INTELLECTUAL DIFFERENCES   Intellectual divergences between the mental styles of line managers and researchers often get in the way of productive relationships. All too often the marketing researcher's report is abstruse, complicated, and tentative, whereas the manager wants concreteness, simplicity, and certainty.

Marketing Research Procedure

Marketing research is undertaken in the effort to understand a marketing problem better. The value of the results depends upon the skill with which the marketing research project is designed and implemented. Effective marketing research involves the following five steps: *problem definition, research design, field work, data analysis,* and *report presentation and implementation.*

Problem definition   The first step in the conduct of research calls for a careful definition of the problem. If the problem is stated vaguely, if the wrong problem is defined, or if the uses of the research are not made clear, then the research results may prove useless to the manager.

The poor definition of the problem is often the fault of the manager requesting the study. Thus a top administrator in the U.S. Postal System might ask the marketing research manager to research public attitudes toward the postal system. The marketing research manager has a right to feel uneasy about the assignment. It is too general. It is not clear how much interviewing should be done of home users and business users or what aspects of the postal system they should comment on. This kind of research is called *exploratory research* and is mostly warranted in situations where the organization's ignorance of the marketplace is substantial. Yet research is generally more efficient when the problem and the alternatives are well defined—the cost of research is generally related to the total amount of information gathered, while the value of research is associated only with the proportion of information that is useful.

Research design   The problem definition stage should lead to the development of a clear set of research objectives, stated in writing if possible. The marketing research manager faces a choice among many alternative ways to collect the information that will satisfy the research objectives. The manager must decide on the *data collection method, research instrument,* and *sampling plan.*

DATA COLLECTION METHODS   In simple cases the data needed already exist in an accessible form and merely have to be found. This type of data is called *secondary data.* They might be present in the organization's internal records; in advertising agencies or trade associations; in government, commercial, or trade publications;[9] or purchasable from syndicated services. If the data are found in existing sources, the researcher has saved time and expense. However, the researcher must be careful to evaluate secondary data, since they were collected for a variety of purposes and under a variety of conditions that may limit their usefulness. Marketing researchers should check these data for relevance, impartiality, validity, and reliability.

When satisfactory secondary data are not available, the researcher must collect *primary data.* The data can be gathered from customers, middlemen, salesmen, competitors, or other information sources. There are three basic primary data collection methods.

The first is *observation,* in which case the researcher attempts to learn about the problem by observing the relevant actors. The observational method has been used to study such marketing behaviors: (1) the movement of shoppers through a department store; (2) the number of shoppers who stopped in front of a particular display; (3) the eye movements of the shoppers looking at the display; (4) the selling appeals used by the sales personnel with customers. Its main advantage is that it generally leads to a more objective picture of overt behavior than can be expected from relying on people's accounts of how they behave. On the other hand, this method yields no information about the state of mind, buying motives, or brand images of those being observed.

At the other extreme is *experimentation* as a method of gathering primary data. The experimental method consists of introducing selected stimuli into a controlled environment and systematically varying them. To the extent that extraneous factors are eliminated or controlled, the observed effects can be related to the variations in the stimuli. The purpose of control is to eliminate competing hypotheses that might also explain the observed phenomena. Marketers have applied this data-generation method to such marketing problems as finding the best sales-training method, the best sales promotion, the best price level, and the best ad campaign. Properly used, experimentation is the most reliable and fruitful way to find the answers. But it has rigorous requirements and can be costly. The cooperation of stores, sales forces, and other parties is necessary. There must be enough participating subjects to make a reliable inference. The treatments must be administered uniformly, and the subjects must react as they would under normal circumstances. When these and other conditions are lacking, the usefulness of the experimental results can be questioned.[10]

A third method of generating primary data, and the most common, is *survey research.* Compared with either direct observation or experimentation, surveys yield a broader range of information and are effective for a greater number of research problems. Surveys can produce information on socioeconomic characteristics, attitudes, opinions, motives, and overt behavior. Surveys are an effective way of gathering information for planning product features, advertis-

---

[9] For an excellent guide to major secondary sources in marketing, see Harper W. Boyd, Jr., Ralph Westfall, and Stanley F. Stasch, *Marketing Research: Text and Cases,* 4th ed. (Homewood, Ill.: Richard D. Irwin, 1977), pp. 150–62.

[10] See Seymour Banks, *Experimentation in Marketing* (New York: McGraw-Hill Book Company, 1965).

ing copy, advertising media, sales promotions, channels of distribution, and other marketing variables.

One of the most useful forms of surveys is called the *focus group interview.* From six to fifteen members of the target market are invited to gather for a few hours and discuss a product, service, organization, or other marketing entity. A trained leader probes the group's feelings and behavior toward the object, encouraging as much free discussion as possible. The comments are recorded and subsequently examined by marketing executives for clues about the market's thinking. Several focus group interviews might be held to sample the thinking of different market segments. The findings do not have sampling validity but provide a basis for effective questionnaire construction for a subsequent survey of the market.[11]

RESEARCH INSTRUMENT   The researcher has to use or design a reliable research instrument for gathering information. The observational method makes use of such instruments as tape recorders, cameras, and tally sheets. The experimental method might involve similar instruments if the subjects are put through a task. The survey method and, to some extent, the experimental method commonly rely on questionnaires.

The construction of good questionnaires calls for considerable skill. Every questionnaire should be pretested on a pilot sample of persons before being used on a large scale. A professional marketing researcher can usually spot several errors in a casually prepared questionnaire.

A common type of error occurs in the *types of questions asked:* the inclusion of questions that cannot be answered, or would not be answered, or need not be answered, and the omission of other questions that should be answered. Each question should be checked to determine whether it is necessary in terms of the research objectives. Questions should be dropped that are just interesting (except for one or two to start the interview on a good basis) because they lengthen the time required and try the respondent's patience.

The *form and wording of questions* can make a substantial difference to the response. An open-ended question is one in which the respondent is free to answer in his own words. A close-ended question is one in which the possible answers are supplied. The respondent may be asked to respond in one or two ways (dichotomous questions), to check one of several answers (multiple-choice questions), to place marks along a scale (scaling questions), and so forth. The choice between open-ended and close-ended questions affects the thoughtfulness of responses, the costs of interviewing, and the quality of the subsequent analysis.

The *choice of words* calls for considerable care. The designer should strive for simple, direct, unambiguous, and unbiased wording. A good rule is always to pretest the questions on a sample of respondents before they are used on a wide scale.

Other dos and don'ts arise in connection with the *sequencing of questions* in the questionnaire. The lead questions should create interest, if possible. Open questions are usually better here. Difficult questions or personal questions should be used toward the end of the interview, in order not to create an emotional reaction that may affect subsequent answers or cause the respondent to break off the interview. The questions should be asked in as logical an order as possible in

[11] See Keith K. Cox et al., "Applications of Focus Group Interviews in Marketing," *Journal of Marketing,* January 1976, pp. 77–80.

order to avoid confusing the respondent. Classificatory data on the respondent are usually asked for last, because they tend to be less interesting and are on the personal side.

SAMPLING PLAN   The third element of research design is a sampling plan. The sampling plan answers four questions: who is to be surveyed? (sampling unit); how many are to be surveyed? (sample size); how are they to be selected? (sampling procedure); and how are they to be reached? (sampling media).

Perhaps the basic issue is, Who is to be surveyed? The proper *sampling unit* is not always obvious from the nature of the information sought. In a survey designed to uncover attitudes toward breakfast cereals, should the primary sampling unit be the wife, the husband, the children, or some combination of the three? Where the roles of instigators, influencers, deciders, users, and/or purchasers are not combined in the same person, the researcher must determine not only what information is needed but also who is most likely to have it.

The next issue is *sample size.* Large samples obviously give more reliable results than small samples. However, it is not necessary to sample the entire universe or even a substantial part of it to achieve satisfactory precision. Samples amounting to less than 1 percent of a population can often provide good reliability, given a creditable sample procedure. In exploratory research, very small samples suffice. Much insight about marketing processes and attitudes can be gained from a sample of fewer than one hundred persons. In motivation-research studies, fewer than thirty depth interviews usually suffice to uncover significant attitudes.

Sampling procedure depends upon the research objective. For exploratory research, nonprobability sampling procedure may be adequate. However, to make an accurate estimate of population characteristics, a random (probability) sample of the population should be drawn. Random sampling allows the calculation of confidence limits for sampling error. One could say "the chances are ninety-five in a hundred that the interval '5 to 7 bottles' contains the true number of bottles purchased annually by the typical user of brand X." But random sampling is almost always more costly than nonrandom sampling. Some marketing researchers feel that the extra expenditure for probability sampling could be put to better use. Specifically, more of the money of a fixed research budget could be spent in designing better questionnaires and hiring better interviewers to reduce response and nonsampling errors, which can be just as fatal as sampling errors. This is a real issue, one that the marketing researcher and marketing executives must weigh carefully.

The final issue is *sampling method,* whether the target population should be reached by telephone, mail, or personal interviews. *Telephone interviewing* stands out as the best method for gathering information quickly. It permits the interviewer to clarify questions if they are not understood. The two main drawbacks of telephone interviewing are that only people with telephones can be interviewed, and only short, not too personal, interviews can be carried out. The *mail questionnaire* may be the best way to reach persons who would not give personal interviews or who might be biased by interviewers. On the other hand, mail questionnaires require simple and clearly worded questions, and the return rate is usually low and/or slow. *Personal interviewing* is the most versatile of the three methods. The personal interviewer can ask more questions and can supplement the interview with personal observations. Personal interviewing is the most expensive method and requires much more technical and administrative planning and supervision.

Field work   After the research design has been completed, the research department must supervise, or subcontract, the task of collecting the data. This phase is generally the most expensive and the most liable to error. Four major problems arise:

1. *Not-at-homes.* When no one is home, the interviewer must either call back later or substitute the household next door.
2. *Refusal to cooperate.* After finding the designated individual at home, the interviewer must interest the person in cooperating.
3. *Respondent bias.* The interviewer must encourage accurate and thoughtful answers.
4. *Interviewer bias.* Interviewers are capable of introducing a variety of biases into the interviewing process, through the mere fact of their age, sex, manner, or intonation. In addition, there is the problem of conscious interviewer bias or dishonesty.

Data analysis   The fourth step in marketing research procedure is to extract meaningful information from the data, and there are four steps in this process. The first is to calculate relevant averages and measures of dispersion. The second is to cross-tabulate the data to produce useful relationships. The third is to measure correlation coefficients and perform goodness-of-fit tests. The fourth is to apply *multivariate statistical techniques* to the data in the hope of discovering important relationships. The most important multivariate techniques are described below.[12]

MULTIPLE REGRESSION ANALYSIS   Every marketing problem involves a set of variables. The marketing researcher is interested in one of these variables, such as sales, and seeks to understand the cause(s) of its variation over time and/or space. This variable is called the dependent variable. The researcher hypothesizes about other variables, called independent variables, whose variations over time or space might contribute to the variations in the dependent variable. Regression analysis is the technique of estimating an equation showing the contribution of independent variables to variations in the dependent variable. When one independent variable is involved, the statistical procedure is called simple regression; when two or more independent variables are involved, the procedure is called multiple regression. An example of multiple regression was presented on page 235.

DISCRIMINANT ANALYSIS   In many marketing situations the dependent variable is classificatory rather than numerical. Consider the following situations:

An automobile company wants to explain brand preferences for Chevrolet versus Ford.

A detergent company wants to determine what consumer traits are associated with heavy, medium, and light usage of its brand.

A retailing chain wants to be able to discriminate between potentially successful and unsuccessful store sites.

In all these cases, two or more groups to which an entity (person or object) might belong are visualized. The challenge is to find discriminating variables

---

[12] See David A. Aaker, ed., *Multivariate Analysis in Marketing: Theory and Applications* (Belmont, Calif.: Wadsworth Publishing Co., 1971).

that could be combined in a predictive equation to produce better-than-chance assignment of the entities to the groups. The technique for solving this problem is known as discriminant analysis.

FACTOR ANALYSIS   One of the problems faced in many regression and discriminant analysis studies is multicollinearity—high intercorrelation of the independent variables. The idea in multiple regression is to use variables that are truly independent, both in the sense that they influence but are not influenced by the dependent variable and in the sense that each independent variable is independent of the others. The simple correlation coefficients for all pairs of variables will reveal which variables are highly intercorrelated, and the analyst has the option of dropping one from each pair. Another approach is to factor analyze the set of intercorrelated variables in order to derive a smaller set of factors that are truly independent of each other. Factor analysis is a statistical procedure for trying to discover a few basic factors that may underlie and explain the intercorrelations among a larger number of variables. In the marketing area, factor analysis has been applied to determining the basic factors underlying attitudes toward air travel, alcoholic beverages, and the clustering of media program types.[13]

Report presentation and implementation   The last step is the preparation, presentation, and implementation of a report presenting the major findings and recommendations coming from the study. The report should begin with a short statement of the problem and the major findings. This should be followed by an elaboration of the findings and technical appendices. The report should be discussed and decisions made on the basis of the findings.

Characteristics of Good Marketing Research

Having examined marketing research procedure, we can now advance five characteristics of good marketing research.

Scientific method   Competent marketing research is characterized by an attempt to follow the scientific method: careful observation, formulation of hypotheses, prediction, and testing. An example follows:

> A small mail-order house was suffering from a high rate (30 percent) of merchandise return. Management asked the marketing research manager to uncover the causes of the high return. The research manager proceeded to analyze various characteristics of the returned orders, such as the geographical locations of the customers, the sizes of the returned orders, and the type of merchandise. One hypothesis was that the longer the customer waited for ordered merchandise, the greater the probability of its return. The regression analysis confirmed this hypothesis. The researcher ventured the prediction that the return rate would fall if the company speeded up its delivery time. The company did this, and the prediction proved correct.[14]

[13] William H. Reynolds and George T. Wofford, "A Factor Analysis of Air Traveler Attitudes," *Proceedings of the American Marketing Association* (Chicago: American Marketing Association, June 1966), pp. 640–50; Jean Stoetzel, "A Factor Analysis of the Liquor Preferences of French Consumers," *Journal of Advertising Research*, December 1960, pp. 7–11; and Arthur D. Kirsch and Seymour Banks, "Program Types Defined by Factor Analysis," *Journal of Advertising Research*, September 1962, 29–32.

[14] Horace C. Levinson, "Experiences in Commercial Operations Research," *Operations Research*, August 1953, pp. 220–39.

Research creativity At its best, marketing research develops innovative ways to solve a problem. A classic example of research creativity is described below:

> When instant coffee was first introduced, housewives complained that it did not taste like real coffee. Yet in blindfold tests, many of these same housewives could not distinguish between a cup of instant coffee and real coffee. This indicated that much of their resistance was psychological. The researcher decided to design two almost identical shopping lists, the only difference being that regular coffee was on one list and instant coffee on the other. The regular coffee list was given to one group of housewives and the instant coffee list was given to a different, but comparable, group. Both groups were asked to guess the social and personal characteristics of the woman whose shopping list they saw. The comments were pretty much the same with one significant difference; a higher proportion of the housewives whose list contained instant coffee described the subject as "lazy, a spendthrift, a poor wife, and failing to plan well for her family." These women obviously were imputing to the fictional housewife their own anxieties and negative images about the use of instant coffee. The instant-coffee company now knew the nature of the resistance and could develop a campaign to change the image of the housewife who serves instant coffee.[15]

Multiple methods Competent marketing researchers shy away from over-reliance on any one method, preferring to adapt the method to the problem rather than the other way around. They also recognize the desirability of the simultaneous gathering of information in different ways to give greater confidence than any one method would provide.

Interdependence of models and data Competent marketing researchers recognize that the facts do not speak for themselves but rather derive their meaning from models of the problem. They attempt to guide their search for information on the basis of a useful decision model to help the executive.

Value and cost of information Competent marketing researchers show concern for measuring the value of information against its cost. Value/cost is a consideration when the marketing research department chooses which research projects to conduct, which research design to use, and whether to gather more information.[16]

MARKETING MANAGEMENT-SCIENCE SYSTEM

An increasing number of organizations have been adding a fourth information service to help their marketing executives—management science (also called operations research). A management scientist applies scientific methodology to organizational problems in the search for improved understanding, prediction, and control. Management scientists are often called model builders, and quite appropriately, because "model" is one of the central defining concepts in their

[15] Mason Haire, "Projective Techniques in Marketing Research," *Journal of Marketing*, April 1950, pp. 649–56.

[16] See James H. Myers and A. Coskun Samli, "Management Control of Marketing Research," *Journal of Marketing Research*, August 1969, pp. 267–77.

field. *A model is the specification of a set of variables and their interrelationships designed to represent some real system or process, in whole or in part.*

Although management science is a relative latecomer in marketing, it has already yielded useful insights and decision models in such areas as new-product development, competitive pricing, advertising budgeting and media selection, sales-call time allocation, and marketing-mix planning. Today some models are fully established and running in some larger companies.[17]

Basic Types of Models in Management Science

Marketing executives are in a much better position to understand and evaluate marketing management-science projects when they are aware of the major types of models. A description of model types is provided in Table 23–3.

**TABLE 23–3
A Classification of Models**

I. According to Purpose
A. Descriptive Models
  1. Markov-process model
  2. Queuing model
  3. Simulation
B. Decision Models
  1. Differential calculus
  2. Mathematical programming
  3. Statistical decision theory
  4. Game theory

II. According to Techniques
A. Verbal Models
B. Graphical Models
  1. Logical-flow model
  2. Network-planning model
  3. Causal model
  4. Decision-tree model
  5. Functional-relationship model
  6. Feedback-systems model
C. Mathematical Models
  1. Linear vs. nonlinear model
  2. Static vs. dynamic model
  3. Deterministic vs. stochastic model

Descriptive models Descriptive models are designed to communicate, explain, or predict. They can be built at three levels of detail. A *macromodel* consists of a few variables and a set of relationships among them. An example would be a sales model consisting of a single equation with total sales as the dependent variable and national income, average price, and company advertising expenditures as the independent variables. They are arrived at by fitting the "best" possible equation to the set of variables.

A *microanalytic model* postulates more detailed links between a dependent variable and its determinants. A good example is the DEMON model, in which the effect of total advertising expenditures on total sales is explained through the successive linking of total advertising expenditure, gross number of exposures, reach and frequency, advertising awareness, consumer trial, usage, and usage rate.[18]

---

[17] The factors affecting the likelihood that a marketing model will be used are examined in Jean-Claude Lerréché and David B. Montgomery, "A Framework for the Comparison of Marketing Models: A Delphi Study," *Journal of Marketing Research*, November 1977, pp. 487–98.

[18] David B. Learner, "Profit Maximization through New-Product Marketing Planning and Control," in *Applications of the Sciences to Marketing Management*, ed. Frank M. Bass et al. (New York: John Wiley & Sons, 1968), pp. 151–67.

A *microbehavioral model* creates hypothetical entities (consumers, dealers, and so on) who interact and produce a record of behavior, which is then analyzed. A good example is a consumer model built by Amstutz, in which a population of potential purchasers are exposed to weekly marketing stimuli, and some fraction of them purchase the product.[19]

Two descriptive models in the operations research literature have turned out to be particularly germane to marketing-type problems. The first is the *Markov-process model,* which is useful in describing systems whose next state is influenced by the current state and a set of transitional probabilities. Suppose there are three coffee brands, A, B, and C. Of those consumers who bought brand A last time, suppose 70 percent buy it again, 20 percent buy B, and 10 percent buy C. This information is represented in row one of Figure 23–2, along with further transitional probabilities associated with brands B and C. The brand-switching matrix provides information about:

> The *repeat-purchase rate* for each brand, indicated by the numbers in the diagonal starting at the upper left. Under certain assumptions, the repeat-purchase rate can be interpreted as a measure of brand loyalty.

> The *switching-in and switching-out rate* for each brand, represented by the off-diagonal numbers.

FIGURE 23–2
A Brand-Switching Matrix

		To	
	A	B	C
From A	.70	.20	.10
B	.17	.33	.50
C	.00	.50	.50

If the switching rates are likely to remain constant, at least for the short run, the matrix becomes a useful tool in forecasting both the magnitude and the speed of change in future market shares on the basis of present market shares.[20]

A second descriptive model of relevance to many marketing situations is a *queuing model.* Queuing models are designed to represent waiting-line situations and answer two specific questions: What amount of waiting time may be expected in a particular system? How will this waiting time change as a result of given alterations in the facilities? These questions can be of particular importance to retailing institutions such as supermarkets, gasoline stations, and airline ticket offices. Wherever customers wait, there is the danger that waiting time will become excessive, leading to the loss of some customers to competitors.

[19] Arnold E. Amstutz, *Computer Simulation of Competitive Market Response* (Cambridge: MIT Press, 1967).

[20] See John U. Farley and Alfred A. Kuehn, "Stochastic Models of Brand Switching," in *Science in Marketing,* ed. George Schwartz (New York: John Wiley & Sons, 1965), pp. 446–64.

If the existing system breeds long queues, the decision maker can simulate the effects of different changes. In the case of a supermarket with a serious queuing problem on Saturdays, four possible attacks are indicated by the dimensions. The supermarket can try to influence its customers to do their shopping on other days. The supermarket can decrease the service time, by employing baggers to aid the cashiers. More service channels can be added. Or some of the channels can be specialized to handle smaller orders.

Decision models Decision models are designed to evaluate alternative outcomes associated with different decisions and find the "best" decision. Decision models are subclassified into *optimization* and *heuristic* models. An *optimization model* is one for which computational routines exist for finding the best solution to the problem as stated. A *heuristic model* is one for which computational routines are not available for finding the best solution, but that offers other advantages. The heuristic model may be a much more flexible and complex statement of the problem. To use this model, the analyst applies heuristics, defined as rules of thumb that tend to shorten the time required to find a reasonably good solution. For example, in a model to determine good warehouse locations, the heuristic might be, "Consider locations only in large cities." This may exclude a perfectly good location in a small city, but the savings in having to check far fewer cities is expected to compensate for the omission.

The field of decision models contains four standard models that are of particular relevance to marketing-type problems. The first is *differential calculus,* a mathematical technique that can be applied to well-defined mathematical functions to determine whether the dependent variable has a maximum and/or minimum value(s), and if it does, to which value(s) of the dependent variable(s) it corresponds? Suppose a marketing analyst has determined the profit equation shown in Figure 23–3A. The task is to find the best price—that is, the value of P that will maximize the value of Z. One approach is to draw a picture of the equation and examine it for the profit-maximizing price, here $150. A quicker, more reliable procedure is to apply differential calculus to this equation without bothering to draw a graph.[21]

The second type of decision model is known as *mathematical programming*. Mathematical programming calls for expressing a decision maker's objective(s) in the form of a mathematical function whose value is to be optimized. Various constraints are also introduced in the form of equations and/or inequalities. Consider, for example, the problem in Figure 23–3B. Suppose the marketing analyst has found a profit function relating profits to the amount of funds spent on advertising and distribution. Note that a dollar of advertising appears to contribute $10 profit and a dollar of distribution appears to contribute $20. A set of policy constraints is also introduced. First the total marketing budget, as divided between advertising and distribution, should not exceed $100 (constraint 1). Of this, advertising should receive at least $40 (constraint 2) and no more than $80 (constraint 3); and distribution should receive at least $10 (constraint 4) and no more than $70 (constraint 5). Because of the simplicity of

---

[21] The calculus reader will know that the slope of a tangent to the curve is given by the first derivative of the equation: $dZ/dP = 1,200 - 8P$ But the maximum (or minimum) takes place where the slope is zero: $1,200 - 8P = 0$. Therefore profits are a maximum when $P = \$150$. (The sign of the second derivative must be checked to be sure that $P = \$150$ establishes a maximum and not a minimum.)

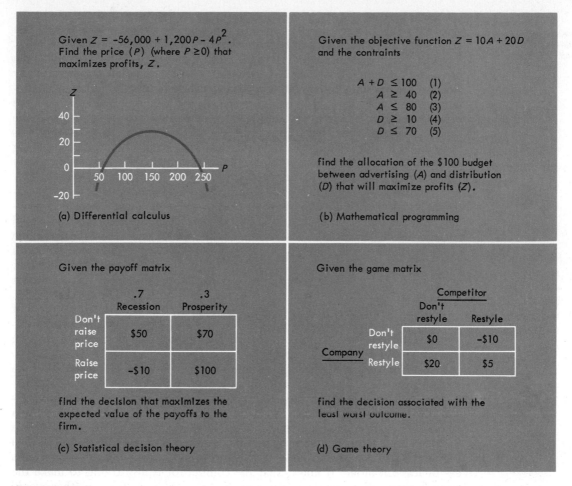

Given $Z = -56,000 + 1,200P - 4P^2$.
Find the price (P) (where $P \geq 0$) that
maximizes profits, Z.

(a) Differential calculus

Given the objective function $Z = 10A + 20D$
and the contraints

$$A + D \leq 100 \quad (1)$$
$$A \geq 40 \quad (2)$$
$$A \leq 80 \quad (3)$$
$$D \geq 10 \quad (4)$$
$$D \leq 70 \quad (5)$$

find the allocation of the $100 budget
between advertising (A) and distribution
(D) that will maximize profits (Z).

(b) Mathematical programming

Given the payoff matrix

	.7 Recession	.3 Prosperity
Don't raise price	$50	$70
Raise price	-$10	$100

find the decision that maximizes the
expected value of the payoffs to the
firm.

(c) Statistical decision theory

Given the game matrix

		Competitor Don't restyle	Restyle
Company	Don't restyle	$0	-$10
	Restyle	$20	$5

find the decision associated with the
least worst outcome.

(d) Game theory

FIGURE 23–3
Four Decision Models

this problem, it is possible to find the best marketing program without invoking
an advanced solution technique. Since distribution dollars are twice as effective
as advertising dollars, it would make sense to spend all that is permitted within
the constraints on distribution. This would appear to be $70, leaving $30 for advertising. However, advertising must receive at least $40 according to constraint
2. Therefore, the optimal marketing-mix allocation would be $40 for advertising
and $60 for distribution; and with this solution, profits will be $10($40) +
$20($60) = $1,600. In larger problems, the analyst would have to resort to spe-
cific solution techniques.

The third type of decision model is called *statistical decision theory* (or
Bayesian decision theory). This model calls for (1) distinguishing major decision
alternatives facing the firm, (2) distinguishing the events (states of nature) that
might, in conjunction with each possible decision, bring about a distinct outcome, (3) estimating the probability of each possible state of nature, (4) estimat-

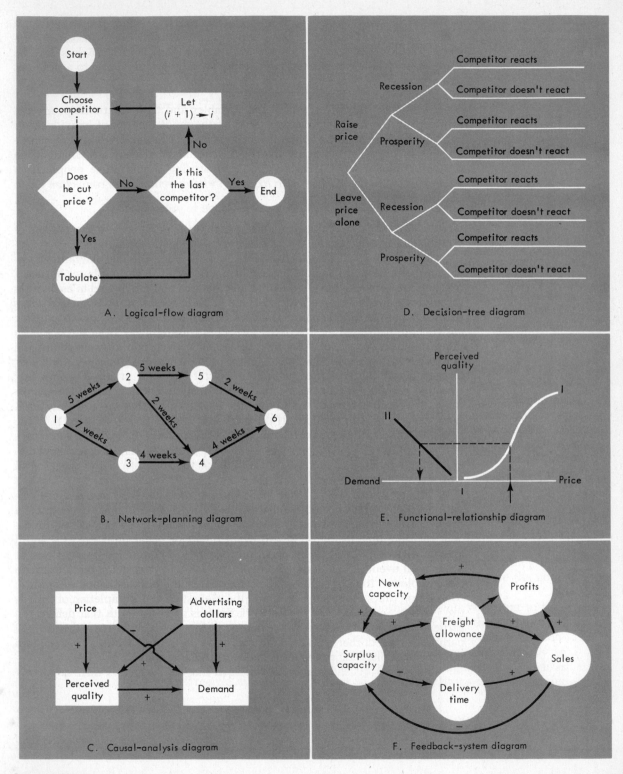

FIGURE 23–4
Six Graphical Models for Marketing Analysis

the directions of influence of various variables on each other. This diagram shows that price has a direct (negative) influence on demand, and an indirect influence also through its positive effects on advertising dollars and perceived quality. A high price leads to high perceived quality and leads the company to spend more on advertising. Both of these in turn have a positive effect on demand. (Not shown is the fact that the level of resulting demand will have a feedback influence on the level of advertising expenditures as well as on the perceived quality.) The value of causal-analysis diagrams is in exposing the complex relationships that the analyst should take into account. They remind us that single-equation relationships between variables may fail to capture the true structure of the phenomena.

Figure 23–4D shows a *decision-tree diagram,* which is used to portray the various decision alternatives and consequences found in a decision situation. The firm is trying to decide between raising its price and leaving it alone. The outcome will be influenced by whether the economy moves toward recession or prosperity, and further by whether or not competitors react. The tree could be extended still further to show other contingencies related to buyer reactions, inventory situations, and so on. By adding payoffs and probabilities to the various branches of the tree, the best decision can be found by using statistical decision theory.

Figure 23–4E is a *functional-relationship diagram,* which is used to portray functional relationship(s) between two or more variables. Quadrant I shows a positive relationship between price and perceived quality. Quadrant II shows a positive relationship between perceived quality and demand. The two quadrants enable the analyst to trace the effect of a *particular* price, through perceived quality, on a *particular* demand level. Thus one can generate a demand function from knowledge of two other functions. Functional graphs can be used to portray sales response functions, probability distributions, and many other relationships.

Figure 23–4F shows a *feedback-system diagram,* which is used to portray any system that yields outputs that return to earlier inputs and act as an influence. This process should not be confused with looping in logical-flow diagrams, which merely returns the procedure to an earlier point without implying any influence on that point. The example given here shows the interactions among sales, profits, capacity, and marketing variables. Surplus capacity leads the company to offer higher freight allowances to customers and reduced delivery time. These lead to higher sales. Increased sales lead to increased profits while drawing down surplus capacity. In the meantime the higher freight allowances reduce profits. If the net effect is a gain in profits, this leads to additional investment in capacity, which increases surplus capacity; and the cycle continues. Thus feedback-system diagrams are useful devices for representing variables that have interactive properties and feedbacks.[25]

Graphical models, in general, have all the virtues that are found in "pictures." A graph strips the phenomenon of inessentials; it allows a viewer to grasp the whole and select which relationships to examine. For marketing analysts, graphs improve exposition, facilitate discussion, and guide analysis.

---

[25] See Jay W. Forrester, "Modeling of Market and Company Interactions," in *Marketing and Economic Development,* ed. Peter D. Bennett (Chicago: American Marketing Association, 1965), pp. 353–64.

Mathematical models   Mathematical models can be subclassified in many ways. A distinction can be drawn between *linear* and *nonlinear models*. In a *linear model* all the relationships between variables are expressed as straight lines. This means that a unit change in one variable has a *constant* marginal impact on a related variable. The advertising-sales relationship would be linear if every $100 increase in advertising created a $1,000 increase in sales, no matter how much had already been spent. This possibility, of course, is unlikely because increasing or diminishing returns to advertising are likely to occur at different points in the relationship. It is also likely that other marketing inputs, such as price and sales-call time, do not relate to sales in a thoroughly linear way. The assumption of linearity is generally useful only as a first approximation for mathematical convenience.

A second distinction can be drawn between *static* and *dynamic models*. A *static model* centers on the ultimate state (or solution) of a system, independent of time. A *dynamic model* brings time explicitly into its framework and allows the observation of the movement of the state (or solution) of the system over time. The elementary demand-supply diagram in beginning economics courses represents a static model of price determination in that it indicates where price and output will be in equilibrium without indicating the path of adjustment through time. Brand-switching models are dynamic in that they predict period-to-period changes in customer states.

A third distinction can be drawn between *deterministic* and *stochastic models*. A *deterministic model* is one in which chance plays no role. The solution is determined by a set of exact relationships. The linear-programming model for determining blends (oils, animal feeds, candies) is deterministic, because the relationships are exact and the cost data are known. A *stochastic model,* on the other hand, is one where chance or random variables are introduced explicitly. Brand-switching models are stochastic in that customer's brand choices are regulated by probabilities.

As marketing management scientists gain acceptance in companies, they will provide a set of statistical procedures and decision models that will greatly enhance the marketing manager's skill at making good decisions. The main need is that the scientists and managers move rapidly toward understanding each other's needs and capacities.

SUMMARY   Marketing information has become the critical element in effective marketing as a result of the trend toward national and international marketing, the transition from buyer needs to buyer wants, and the transition from price to nonprice competition. All firms have a marketing information system connecting the external environment with its executives, but the systems vary greatly in sophistication and the number and quality of services they provide.

Marketing information systems consist of four components. The internal accounting system reports orders, sales, inventory levels, receivables, payables, and so on. Several companies have made large investments in improving the speed, accuracy, and reporting potentials of their order-shipping-billing cycle.

The marketing intelligence system provides executives with current information about developments and changing conditions in the macro and task environments. Executives gather intelligence on their own, but their effectiveness can be augmented by improved training of salesmen in their intelligence responsibilities, the development of a marketing-intelligence center, and the purchase of information when appropriate from specialized intelligence services.

Marketing research provides specific studies of market opportunities, marketing effectiveness, and marketing problems. Marketing research procedure consists of five steps: problem definition, research design, field work, data analysis, and report preparation. Good marketing research is characterized by the scientific method, creativity, multiple methodologies, model building, and cost/benefit measures of the value of information.

The marketing management-science system is responsible for building models to explain, predict, or improve marketing processes. Marketing management scientists may build or use descriptive or decision models and verbal, graphical, or mathematical models to come to grips with marketing problems.

QUESTIONS AND PROBLEMS

1. You are a marketing director. Your boss comes in and wants to know how many stores carry your dry cereal. Since you sell through food brokers, you don't know the answer. He wants the answer in two days. How would you do it?

2. (a) Suggest how a liquor company might estimate the amount of liquor consumed in a legally dry town. (b) Suggest how a research organization might estimate the number of people who read given magazines in a doctor's office. (c) Suggest six different ways in which a sample of men can be gathered to be interviewed on their usage of hair tonics.

3. What is the major issue (impartiality, validity, reliability) that is likely to come up in the following use of secondary data: (a) using a time series of disposable personal income (in current dollars) to indicate the historical trend in consumer purchasing power; (b) using a local chamber of commerce study on the average income of the community; (c) using a man-in-the-street sample to estimate the proportion of men who own dinner jackets.

4. "A manufacturer of automobiles is testing a new direct-mail approach B versus a standard approach A. An experiment is conducted in which each of the two approaches is tried out on random samples of size n (sample size $2n$ in total) from a large national mailing list. Suppose that $n = 100,000$ so that 200,000 is the total sample size of the experiment. During a three-month period, approach B has 761 sales and A has 753." What decision should be made? List the alternatives and the rationale of each.

5. Evaluate the following questions to be asked in a consumer survey: (a) What is your husband's favorite brand of golf balls? (b) What TV programs did you watch a week ago Monday? (c) How many pancakes did you make for your family last year? (d) Tell me your exact income. (e) Can you supply me with a list of your grocery purchases this month?

6. In obtaining estimates from company salesmen, product managers, and other personnel, one must discourage their supplying estimates that are self-serving. Give some examples of self-serving estimates by company personnel and suggest what might be done to discourage this.

7. List and discuss the major criteria for judging the usefulness of a mathematical marketing model.

8. Some marketing men view the emergence of mathematical model building in marketing with hostility. They will make the following statements: (a) we don't use models; (b) models are typically unrealistic; (c) anyone can build a model; (d) a model is of no help unless you can get the data. How would you answer these objections?

9. With the emergence of operations research in marketing, large companies are trying to determine the proper organizational relationship between marketing research activities (MR) and marketing operations research (MOR). Describe five alternative conceptions.

Marketing Control

Having lost sight of our objective, we redoubled our efforts.
OLD ADAGE

In spite of the growing need for better marketing control, many companies use less-than-satisfactory control procedures. This was the conclusion of a major recent private study of seventy-five companies of varying sizes in different industries. The main findings were:

1. Smaller companies have poorer controls than larger companies. They did a poorer job of setting clear objectives and establishing systems to measure performance.
2. Fewer than half of the companies knew the profitability of their individual product lines. About one-third of the companies had no regular review procedure for spotting and deleting weak products.
3. Almost half of the companies failed, on a regular basis, to compare their prices to competition, to analyze their warehousing and distribution costs, to analyze the causes of returned merchandise, to conduct formal evaluations of advertising effectiveness, and to review their sales-force call reports.
4. Management in many companies complained about four-to-eight-week delays in getting many control reports and frequent inaccuracies.

Marketing control, like marketing planning, is far from being a single process. Four different types of marketing control can be distinguished, and they are listed in Table 24–1.

TABLE 24–1
Types of Marketing Control

TYPE OF CONTROL	PRIME RESPONSIBILITY	PURPOSE OF CONTROL	APPROACHES
I. Annual-plan control	Top management Middle management	To examine whether the planned results are being achieved	Sales analysis Market share analysis Sales-to-expense ratios Financial analysis Attitude tracking
II. Profitability control	Marketing controller	To examine where the company is making and losing money	Profitability by: product territory customer group trade channel order size
III. Efficiency control	Line and staff management Marketing controller	To evaluate and improve the spending efficiency and impact of marketing expenditures	Efficiency of sales force advertising sales promotion distribution
IV. Strategic control	Top management Marketing auditor	To examine whether the company is pursuing its best opportunities with respect to markets, products, and channels	Marketing-effectiveness rating instrument Marketing audit

Annual-plan control refers to the steps taken during the year to check on-going performance against plan and to apply corrective actions when necessary. *Profitability control* consists of efforts to measure the actual profitability of different products, territories, end-use markets, and trade channels. *Efficiency control* involves searching for ways to improve the impact of different marketing tools and expenditures. Finally, *strategic control* consists of a systematic examination and appraisal of the overall fit of the company to its marketing environment and opportunities. The following sections will deal with each form of marketing control.

The heart of annual-plan control is the establishment of a system of *management by objectives,* which consists of four elements. First, the annual plan must establish a clear set of *goals* for each responsibility center in the firm. Second, provision must be made for periodic *performance measurement* against the goals to spot any serious performance gaps. Third, performance gaps should be subject to *causal analysis* to determine why they have occurred, that is, whether the environment has changed, the goals were set too high, or the implementers of the plan are not doing their job. Fourth, management must take *corrective action* to close the gap between goals and performance.

This model of control is applied to every level of the organization. Top management is committed to the attainment of certain sales and profit goals for the year. These goals have presumably been elaborated into specific goals for each successively lower level of management. Thus, each product and brand manager is committed to attaining specified levels of sales and costs. Each regional area and district sales manager and sales representative is also committed to specific goals. Each period top management receives summary reports indicating the results attained by the vice presidents, who in turn receive more-detailed reports of the results attained by their subordinates, down to the district sales manager, who observes the results of individual sales representatives in the district.

Managers use five performance tools to check on the progress in reaching the goals in the annual plan.

Sales Analysis

The first performance tool used by managers is sales analysis. *Sales analysis* is the effort to measure and evaluate the actual sales being achieved in relation to the sales goals set for different managers. There are two specific tools in this connection.

Sales variance analysis is an attempt to determine the relative contribution of different factors to a gap in sales performance. Suppose the annual plan called for selling 4,000 widgets in the first quarter at $1 a widget, or $4,000. At quarter's end, only 3,000 widgets were sold at 80¢ a widget, or $2,400. The sales performance variance is −$1,600, or −40 percent of expected sales. The question arises, How much of this underperformance is due to the price decline and how much is due to the volume decline? The following calculation answers this question:

$$\text{Variance due to price decline} = (\$1 - .80)\,(3{,}000) \quad = \$\ \ 600 \qquad 37.5\%$$
$$\text{Variance due to volume decline} = (\$1)\,(4{,}000 - 3{,}000) = \underline{\$1{,}000} \qquad \underline{62.5\%}$$
$$\$1{,}600 \qquad 100.0\%$$

Accordingly, almost two-thirds of the sales variance is due to a failure to realize the volume target. Since sales volume may be under more control than the price, the company should look closely into why its expected sales volume was not achieved.[1]

---

[1] For further discussion, see James M. Hulbert and Norman E. Toy, "A Strategic Framework for Marketing Control," *Journal of Marketing,* April 1977, pp. 12–20.

Microsales analysis may provide the answer. Microsales analysis is an attempt to determine the specific products, territories, and so forth, that failed to produce their expected share of sales. Suppose the company sells in three territories and expected sales were 1,500, 500, and 2,000 units, respectively, adding up to 4,000 widgets. The actual sales volume was 1,400, 525, and 1,075, respectively. Thus territory one showed a 7 percent shortfall in terms of expected sales; territory two, a 5 percent surplus; and territory three, a 46 percent shortfall! It is now clear that territory three is causing most of the trouble. The sales vice president can check into territory three to see which, if any, of the following hypotheses explains the poor performance: (1) territory three's sales representative is loafing or has a personal problem; (2) a major competitor has entered this territory; (3) GNP is depressed in this territory.

Market Share Analysis

A company's sales performance fails to reveal how well the company is performing relative to competitors. Suppose a company's sales increase. That could be due to a general improvement in the economy in which all firms are participating. Or it may be due to improved marketing by this company in relation to its competitors. The normal way to remove the influence of the general environment is to track the company's market share. If the company's market share goes up, it is gaining on competitors; if its market share goes down, it appears to be performing poorer relative to competitors.

Yet these conclusions from market share analysis are subject to certain qualifications.[2]

> *The assumption that outside forces affect all companies in the same way is often not true.* The surgeon general's report on the harmful consequences of cigarette smoking caused total cigarette sales to falter but not equally for all companies. The companies that had established a reputation for a better filter were hit less hard.
>
> *The assumption that a company's performance should be judged against the average performance of all companies also is not always valid.* A company with greater than average opportunities should register a growing market share. If its market share remains constant, this may imply deficient rather than average management.
>
> *If a new firm enters the industry, then every existing firm's market share may fall (again, not necessarily equally).* Here is a case where a fall in the company's market share does not mean that the company is performing below the average of the industry.
>
> *Sometimes the decline in a company's market share is the result of a deliberate policy to improve profits.* Management, for example, may drop unprofitable customers or products, with resulting decline in market share.
>
> *Market share fluctuates for many reasons.* For example, the market share in a particular period can be affected by whether a large sale is made on the last day of the period or at the beginning of the following period. A current shift in market share does not always have a significant marketing implication.

The first step in using market share measurement is to define clearly which measure of market share will be used. Four different measures are available:

[2] See Alfred R. Oxenfeldt, "How to Use Market-Share Measurement," *Harvard Business Review*, January–February 1959, pp. 59–68.

1. ***Overall market share.*** The company's overall market share is its sales expressed as a percentage of total industry sales. Two decisions are necessary to use this measure. The first is whether to use unit sales or dollar sales to express market share. Any changes in unit market share strictly reflect relative volume changes among competitors, whereas changes in dollar market share might reflect volume or price changes.

    The other decision has to do with defining the total industry. Defining the industry or market boundaries is always somewhat arbitrary. For example, suppose Harley Davidson wants to measure its share of the American motorcycle market. Does the motorcycle market include motor scooters and motorized bikes? If so, Harley Davidson's share of this market is lower than if these products are not included. The issue hinges on the degree of consumer perception of the difference between standard motorcycles and these lighter cycles.

2. ***Served-market share.*** The company's served-market share is its sales expressed as a percentage of the total sales to its served market. Its served market is the market (1) that would find the company's offering suitable and (2) that is reached by the company's marketing effort. For example, if Harley Davidson only sells motorcycles costing over $2,000 and sells them only on the East Coast, its served-market share would be its sales as a percentage of the total sales of expensive motorcycles sold on the East Coast. A company's served-market share is always larger than its overall market share. A company could have close to 100 percent of its served market and yet a relatively small percentage of the overall market. A company's first task is to try to get the lion's share of its served market, and as it approaches this, it should add new product lines and territories to enlarge its served market.

3. ***Relative market share (to top three competitors).*** This involves expressing the company's sales as a percentage of the combined sales of the three largest competitors. For example, if this company has 30 percent of the market and its three largest competitors have 20, 10, and 10 percent, then this company's relative market share is 75 percent (= 30/40). If all four companies each had 25 percent of the market, then any company's relative market share would be 33 percent. Relative market shares above 33 percent are considered to be strong.

4. ***Relative market share (to leading competitor).*** Some companies like to track their sales as a percentage of the leading competitor's sales. A relative market share greater than 100 percent suggests that the firm is the market leader. A relative market share of 100 percent means that the firm is tied for the lead. A rise in the company's relative market share means that it is gaining on its leading competitor.

After choosing which market share measure(s) to use, the company faces the task of finding the necessary data. Overall market share is normally the most available measure since it only requires total industry sales, and these are often available in government or trade association publications. Estimating served market share is harder in that the company will have to measure and keep track of its served market, which will be affected by changes in the company's product line and geographical market coverage, among other things. Estimating relative market shares is still harder, because the company will have to estimate the sales of from one to three specific competitors, who do their best to guard these figures. The company has to use indirect means, such as learning about competitors' purchase rate of raw materials, or the number of shifts they are operating. In the consumer-goods area, individual brand shares are measurable and available through syndicated store and consumer panels.

The final requirement is to be able to correctly interpret movements in market share. Market share analysis, like sales analysis, increases in value when the data are disaggregated along various dimensions. The company might watch the progress of its market share by product line, customer type, region, or other breakdowns.

A useful way to analyze market share movements is in terms of the following four components:

$$
\begin{array}{l}
\text{Overall} \\
\text{market} \\
\text{share}
\end{array}
=
\begin{array}{l}
\text{Customer} \\
\text{penetration}
\end{array}
\times
\begin{array}{l}
\text{Customer} \\
\text{loyalty}
\end{array}
\times
\begin{array}{l}
\text{Customer} \\
\text{selectivity}
\end{array}
\times
\begin{array}{l}
\text{Price} \\
\text{selectivity}
\end{array}
\quad (24\text{--}1)
$$

where:

Customer penetration is the percentage of all customers who buy from this company

Customer loyalty is the purchases from this company by its customers expressed as a percentage of their total purchases from all suppliers of the same products

Customer selectivity is the size of the average customer purchase from the company expressed as a percentage of the size of the average customer purchase from an average company

Price selectivity is the average price charged by this company expressed as a percentage of the average price charged by all companies

Now suppose the company's dollar market share falls during the period. Equation (24–1) suggests four possible factors:

1. The company has lost some of its customers (lower customer penetration).
2. The existing customers are buying a smaller share of their supplies from this company (lower customer loyalty).
3. The company's remaining customers are smaller in size (lower customer selectivity).
4. The company's price has slipped relative to competition (lower price selectivity).

By tracking these factors through time, the company can determine the underlying causes of market share changes. Suppose at the beginning of the period, customer penetration was 60 percent, customer loyalty 50 percent, customer selectivity 80 percent, and price selectivity 125 percent. According to (24–1), the company's market share was 30 percent. Suppose that at the end of the period, the company's market share fell to 27 percent. In checking on the market share components, the company finds customer penetration at 55 percent, customer loyalty at 50 percent, customer selectivity at 75 percent, and price selectivity at 130 percent. Clearly, the market share decline was due mainly to a loss of some customers (fall in customer penetration) who normally made larger-than-average purchases (fall in customer selectivity). The manager can now direct attention to finding out why these customers were lost.

Marketing Expense-to-Sales Ratios

Annual-plan control also requires checking on marketing expenses in relation to sales to make sure that the company is not overspending to achieve its sales goals. The key ratio to watch is *marketing expense to sales.* In one company, this ratio is normally 30 percent and is made up of five component expense-to-sales ratios: *sales force to sales* (15 percent); *advertising to sales* (5 percent); *sales promotion to sales* (6 percent); *marketing research to sales* (1 percent); and *sales administration to sales* (3 percent).

Management's job is to monitor the overall and component marketing expense ratios to detect whether any are getting out of control. These ratios will exhibit small random fluctuations that could well be ignored. Only fluctuations in excess of the normal range of variation are a cause for concern. The period-to-period fluctuations in each ratio can be charted on a *control chart* such as the one shown in Figure 24–1. This chart shows that the advertising expense-to-sales ratio normally fluctuates between 8 and 12 percent, say ninety-nine out of one hundred times. In the fifteenth period, however, the ratio exceeded the upper control limit. One of two opposing hypotheses can explain this occurrence:

> **Hypothesis A.** The company still has good control over sales, and this represents one of those rare chance events.
>
> **Hypothesis B.** The company has lost control over this cost as a result of some assignable cause.

If hypothesis A is accepted, no investigation is made to determine whether the environment has changed. The risk in not investigating is that some real change may have occurred, and the company will fall behind. If hypothesis B is accepted, the environment is investigated at the risk that the investigation will uncover nothing and be a waste of time and effort.

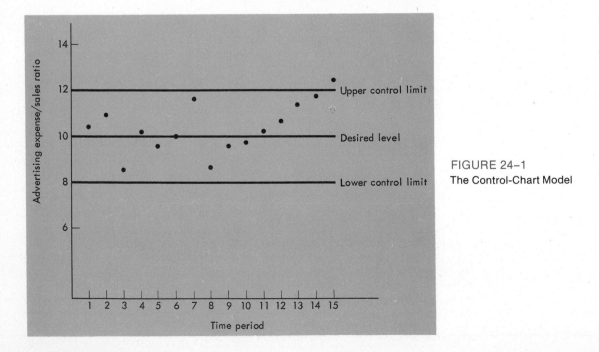

FIGURE 24–1
The Control-Chart Model

The behavior of successive observations even within the control limits should also be watched for patterns that seem difficult to explain by chance. In Figure 24–1 it should be noted that the level of the expense-to-sales ratio rose steadily from the ninth period onward. The probability of encountering a pattern of six successive increases in what should be a random and independent process is only one out of sixty-four.[3] This unusual pattern should have led to an investigation sometime before the fifteenth observation.

When an expense-to-sales ratio gets out of control, disaggregative data may be needed to track down the source of the problem. An *expense-to-sales deviation chart* can be used in this connection. Figure 24–2 shows the perform-

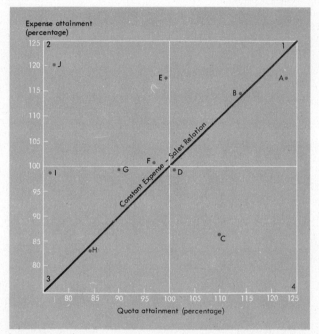
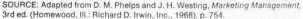

FIGURE 24–2
Comparison of Expense and Revenue
Deviations by District

SOURCE: Adapted from D. M. Phelps and J. H. Westing, *Marketing Management,* 3rd ed. (Homewood, Ill.: Richard D. Irwin, Inc., 1968), p. 754.

ances of different sales districts in terms of their quota attainment and expense attainment (in percentages). For example, district D has accomplished its quota nearly at the expected expense level. District B has exceeded its quota, and its expenses are proportionately higher. The most troubling districts are in the second quadrant. For example, district J has accomplished less than 80 percent of its quota and its expenses are disproportionately high. The next step is to prepare a similar chart for each deviant district that shows sales representatives' standings on percentage of quota attainment and expense attainment. Within

---

[3] There is a chance of ½ that any succeeding observation will be higher and the same chance that it will be lower (excluding the possibility that two successive values are identical). Therefore the probability of finding six successively higher values is given by $(½)^6 = \frac{1}{64}$.

district J, for example, it may turn out that the poor performance is associated with just a few sales representatives.

Financial Analysis

The various expense-to-sales and other ratios should be analyzed by the marketer in an overall framework of financial analysis to determine how and where the company is making its money. Marketers are increasingly being trained to understand and apply financial concepts in the effort to improve their ability to find profitable strategies and not just sales-building strategies.

Financial analysis is directed to identifying the factors that affect the company's *rate of return on net worth*. The main factors are shown in Figure 24–3, along with some illustrative numbers, for a large chain store retailer. The retailer is earning a return on net worth of 12.5 percent. Many professional retailers would argue that this is too low and that retail organizations need at least a 15 percent return if they are to fully satisfy their profit requirements. Some successful retailers routinely earn returns of over 20 percent.

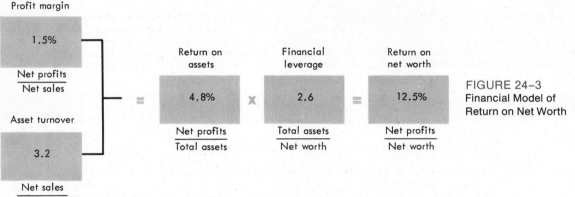

FIGURE 24–3
Financial Model of Return on Net Worth

Next, we notice that the return on net worth is the product of two ratios, the *return on assets* and the *financial leverage* of the company. In order for the company to improve its return on net worth, it must either increase the ratio of its net profits to its assets or increase the ratio of its assets to its net worth. The company should analyze the composition of its assets (i.e., cash, accounts receivable, inventory, and plant and equipment) and see if it can improve its assets management.

The return on assets is itself the product of two ratios, namely the *profit margin* and the *asset turnover*. We note that the profit margin is low, whereas the asset turnover is more normal for retailing. Given the low profit margin, the marketing executive's task is to find ways to increase sales and/or lower costs.

Customer-Attitude Tracking

The preceding annual-plan control measures are largely financial and quantitative in character. They are important but not enough. They fail to give certain qualitative indications of marketplace developments and often come in too late for appropriate action to be taken.

Alert companies set up systems to track the attitudes of customers, dealers, and other marketing system participants as they are occurring. The assumption is that attitude change occurs first, it leads to purchasing behavior change, and then management eventually sees this in sales reports. By monitoring current customer attitudes toward the company and its products, management can take much earlier action.

Companies use the following major systems for tracking customer attitudes:

1. ***Complaint and suggestion systems.*** At a minimum, companies should record, analyze, and respond to any written or oral complaints that come in from customers. The complaints should be tabulated by types of complaint and the more serious and frequent ones should be given early attention. Many retailers, such as hotels, restaurants, and banks, have gone further and provide suggestion cards to encourage customer comments. In fact, the argument can be made that market-oriented companies should strive to maximize the opportunity for consumer complaints so that management can get a more complete picture of consumer reactions to their products and service.[4]

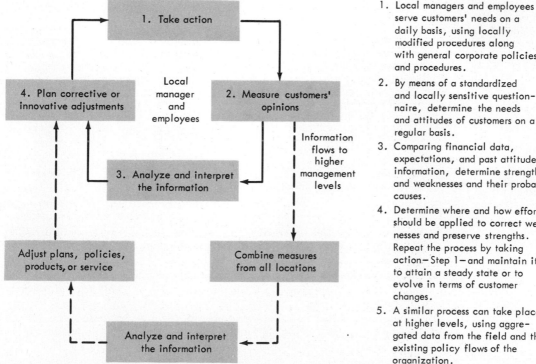

1. Local managers and employees serve customers' needs on a daily basis, using locally modified procedures along with general corporate policies and procedures.

2. By means of a standardized and locally sensitive questionnaire, determine the needs and attitudes of customers on a regular basis.

3. Comparing financial data, expectations, and past attitude information, determine strengths and weaknesses and their probable causes.

4. Determine where and how effort should be applied to correct weaknesses and preserve strengths. Repeat the process by taking action—Step 1—and maintain it to attain a steady state or to evolve in terms of customer changes.

5. A similar process can take place at higher levels, using aggregated data from the field and the existing policy flows of the organization.

SOURCE: Arthur J. Daltas, "Protecting Service Markets with Consumer Feedback," *The Cornell Hotel and Restaurant Administration Quarterly,* May 1977, p. 75.

FIGURE 24–4

A Consumer-Survey Feedback System

[4] See Claes Fornell, "Complaint Management and Marketing Performance," unpublished paper, Graduate School of Management, Northwestern University, Evanston, Ill., October 1978.

2. *Customer panels.* Some companies have created customer panels consisting of a cross-section of customers who have agreed to communicate their attitudes periodically through phone calls or mail questionnaires coming from the company. They are thought to be more representative of the range of customer attitudes than customer complaint and suggestion systems.

3. *Customer-survey systems.* A customer-survey system consists of periodically administering standardized questionnaires to a random sample of customers. Questions may be asked about the friendliness of the staff, the quality of the service, and so on. The customers check off their answers to these questions on a five-point scale (very dissatisfied, dissatisfied, neutral, satisfied, very satisfied). The responses are summarized and go both to local managers and to higher-management levels, as illustrated in Figure 24–4. Local managers receive back reports on how the various components of their service were rated in the current period compared to the last period, to the average of all the local units, and to the goal. Introducing this system has the beneficial effect of improving the staff's motivation to provide good customer service in the knowledge that their ratings will go to higher management.[5]

Corrective Action

We have mentioned corrective action several times. When actual performance deviates too much from the annual-plan goals, companies go through a well-known cycle of defensive maneuvers to correct the situation. Consider the following case:

> A large fertilizer producer found itself falling behind in its sales goals for the year. This was happening to its competitors as well, all of whom had built excess capacity. Some of the competitors were beginning to cut prices in order to achieve their planned sales volume.

In attempting to save and reverse the situation, this company was observed to go through several increasingly drastic steps:

1. *Production cutting.* The company found its inventories rising and proceeded to order cutbacks in production.

2. *Price cutting.* The company began to cut its prices selectively (higher discounts, freight allowances, and so on) to meet competition and retain its share of market.

3. *Increased pressure on sales force.* The company put more pressure on its sales force to meet their quotas. The sales representatives in turn started "beating down" doors, pressuring customers to buy more or buy before the end of the year.

4. *Fringe expenditure cutting.* The company proceeded to cut the budgets for personnel hiring and training, advertising, public relations, charities, and research and development.

5. *Manpower cuts.* The company began to lay off, retire, or fire personnel in various departments, particularly in staff services such as public relations, marketing research, and operations research.

6. *Bookkeeping adjustments.* The company undertook some fancy bookkeeping to bring about a better picture of profits, including changing the depreciation base, recording purchases wherever possible as capital items rather than as expenses, selling some company assets for leaseback in order to increase cash resources, and

---

[5] For an application to a hotel chain, see Arthur J. Daltas, "Protecting Service Markets with Consumer Feedback," *The Cornell Hotel and Restaurant Administration Quarterly*, May 1977, pp. 73–77.

recording sales to phantom buyers, revising them as returned merchandise in the following year.

7. *Investment cutting.* The company began to cut back on its investment in plant and equipment.

8. *Selling property.* The company started to consider selling some of its product lines or divisions to other companies.

9. *Selling the company.* The ultimate step this company considered was selling out or merging with another company that had good finances or some complementarities with this firm.

PROFITABILITY CONTROL

Besides annual-plan control, companies carry on periodic research to determine the actual profitability of their different products, territories, customer groups, trade channels, and order sizes. This task requires an ability to assign marketing and other costs to specific marketing entities and activities.

Methodology of Marketing-Profitability Analysis

Marketing-profitability analysis is a tool for helping the marketing executive determine whether any current marketing activities should be eliminated, added, or altered in scale.[6] The starting point for marketing-profitability analysis is the company's profit-and-loss statement. A simplified profit-and-loss statement is shown in Table 24–2. Profits are arrived at by subtracting cost of goods sold and other expenses from sales. The marketing executive's interest would be in developing analogous profit statements by functional marketing breakdowns, such as products, customers, or territories. To do this, the "natural" expense designations (such as salaries, rent, supplies) would have to be reclassified into "functional" expense designations. Consider the following example:

The marketing vice president of a lawn-mower firm wishes to determine the costs and profits of selling through three different types of retail channels: hardware stores, garden supply shops, and department stores. The company produces only one model of lawn mower. Its profit and loss statement is shown in Table 24–2.

Step 1: Identifying the functional expenses. Assume that the expenses listed in Table 24–2 are incurred to carry out the activities of selling the product, advertising the product, packing and delivering the product, and billing and collecting. The first task is to show how much of each natural expense was incurred in each of these activities.

Suppose that most of the salaries went to sales representatives and the rest went to an advertising manager, packing and delivery help, and an office accountant. Let the breakdown of the $9,300 be $5,100, $1,200, $1,400, and $1,600, respectively. Table 24–3 shows allocation of the salary expense to these four activities.

Table 24–3 also shows the rent account of $3,000 as allocated to the four activities. Since the sales representatives work away from the office, none of the building's rent expense is assigned to the selling activity. Most of the floor space and rental of equipment arises in connection with packing and delivery. A small portion of the floor space is taken up by the activities of the advertising manager and the office accountant.

---

[6] For a basic text, see Donald R. Longman and Michael Schiff, *Practical Distribution Cost Analysis* (Homewood, Ill.: Richard D. Irwin, 1955).

Finally, the supplies account lumps together promotional materials, packing materials, fuel purchases for delivery, and home-office stationery. The $3,500 in this account should be reassigned to the functional uses made of the supplies. The result of this and the previous breakdowns is that the total expenses of $15,800 are reclassified from a natural basis into a functional activity basis.

Step 2: Assigning the functional expenses to the marketing entities. The next task is to determine how much of each activity has gone into serving each type of channel. Consider the selling effort. The selling effort devoted to each channel is approximated by the number of sales calls made in each channel. This is given in the first column of Table 24–4. Altogether 275 sales calls were made during the period. Since the total selling expense amounted to $5,500 (see Table 24–3), then the selling expense per call averaged $20.

As for the advertising expense, Table 24–4 shows this allocated on the basis of the number of advertisements addressed to the different trade channels. Since there were 100 advertisements altogether, the advertising expense of $3,100 means that the average advertisement cost $31.

The basis chosen for allocating the packaging and delivery expense was the number of orders placed by each type of channel; this same basis also was used for allocating the expense of billing and collections.

Step 3: Preparing a profit-and-loss statement for each marketing entity. It is now possible to prepare a profit-and-loss statement for each type of channel. The results are shown in Table 24–5. Since hardware stores accounted for one-half of total sales ($30,000 out of $60,000), this channel is charged with half of the cost of goods sold ($19,500 out of $39,000). This leaves a gross margin from hardware stores of $10,500. From this must be deducted the proportions of the functional expenses that hardware stores consumed. According to Table 24–4 hardware stores received 200 out of 275 total sales calls. At an imputed value of $20 a call, hardware stores have to be charged with $4,000 of the selling expense. Table 24–4 also shows that hardware stores were the target of 50 advertisements. At $31 an advertisement, the hardware stores are charged with $1,550 of the advertising activity. The same reasoning applies in computing the share of the other functional expenses to charge to hardware stores. The result is that hardware stores gave rise to $10,050 of the total expenses. Subtracting this from the gross margin, the profit from the activities of selling to hardware stores is small ($450).

The same analysis is repeated for the other channels. It turns out that the company is losing money in selling through garden supply shops and makes virtually all of its profits from sales to department stores. Clearly, gross sales through each channel is not a reliable indicator of the net profits being made in each channel.

TABLE 24–2
A Simplified Profit-and-Loss Statement

Sales		$60,000
Cost of goods sold		39,000
Gross margin		$21,000
Expenses		
Salaries	$9,300	
Rent	3,000	
Supplies	3,500	
		15,800
Net profit		$ 5,200

TABLE 24–3
Mapping Natural Expenses Into Functional Expenses

NATURAL ACCOUNTS	TOTAL	SELLING	ADVERTISING	PACKING AND DELIVERY	BILLING AND COLLECTING
Salaries	$ 9,300	$5,100	$1,200	$1,400	$1,600
Rent	3,000	—	400	2,000	600
Supplies	3,500	400	1,500	1,400	200
	$15,800	$5,500	$3,100	$4,800	$2,400

TABLE 24–4
Bases for Allocating Functional Expenses to Channels

CHANNEL TYPE	SELLING NO. OF SALES CALLS IN PERIOD	ADVERTISING NO. OF ADVERTISE-MENTS	PACKING AND DELIVERY NO. OF ORDERS PLACED IN PERIOD	BILLING AND COLLECTING NO. OF ORDERS PLACED IN PERIOD
Hardware	200	50	50	50
Garden supply	65	20	21	21
Department stores	10	30	9	9
	275	100	80	80
Functional expense	$5,500	$3,100	$4,800	$2,400
No. of units =	275	100	80	80
Cost per unit =	$20	$31	$60	$30

TABLE 24–5
Profit-and-Loss Statements for Channels

	HARDWARE	GARDEN SUPPLY	DEPT. STORES	WHOLE COMPANY
Sales	$30,000	$10,000	$20,000	$60,000
Cost of goods sold	19,500	6,500	13,000	39,000
Gross margin	$10,500	$ 3,500	$ 7,000	$21,000
Expenses				
Selling ($20 per call)	$ 4,000	$ 1,300	$ 200	$ 5,500
Advertising ($31 per advertisement)	1,550	620	930	3,100
Packing and delivery ($60 per order)	3,000	1,260	540	4,800
Billing ($30 per order)	1,500	630	270	2,400
Total expenses	$10,050	$ 3,810	$ 1,940	$15,800
Net Profit (or loss)	$ 450	$ (310)	$ 5,060	$ 5,200

Determining the Best Corrective Actions

The results of a marketing-profitability analysis do not constitute an adequate informational basis for deciding on corrective action. It would be naive to conclude that garden supply shops (and possibly hardware stores) should be dropped as channels in order to concentrate on department stores. Such information as the following would be needed first on each question:

> To what extent do buyers buy on the basis of the type of retail outlet versus the brand? Would they seek out the brand in those channels that are not eliminated?
>
> What are the future market trends with respect to the importance of these three channels?
>
> Have marketing efforts and policies directed at the three channels been optimal?

On the basis of this and other information, marketing management will want to define the major alternatives open to them:

> *Establish a special charge for handling smaller orders to encourage larger orders.* This move is based on the assumption that small orders are the ultimate cause of the relative unprofitability of dealing with garden supply shops and hardware stores.
>
> *Give more aid to garden supply shops and hardware stores.* This is based on the assumption that the managers of these stores could increase their sales with more training or promotional materials.
>
> *Reduce the number of sales calls and the amount of advertising going to garden supply shops and hardware stores.* This is based on the assumption that some of these costs can be saved without reducing proportionately the level of sales to these channels.
>
> *Do nothing.* This is based on the assumption that current marketing efforts are optimal and that either future marketing trends point to an imminent improvement in the profitability of the weaker channels or dropping any type of channel would reduce rather than improve profits because of repercussions on production costs or on demand.
>
> *Don't abandon any channel as a whole but only the weakest retail units in each channel.* This is based on the assumption that a more detailed cost study would reveal many profitable garden shops and hardware stores whose profits are concealed by the poor performance of other stores in these categories.

To evaluate these alternatives, each would have to be spelled out in greater detail. In general, marketing-profitability analysis provides information on the relative profitability of different channels, products, territories, or other marketing entities.[7] It does not imply that the best course of action is to drop the unprofitable marketing entities, nor does it actually measure the likely profit improvement if these marginal marketing entities are dropped.

Direct versus Full Costing

Like all information tools, marketing-profitability analysis is capable of leading or misleading marketing executives, depending upon the degree to which they understand its procedures and limitations. The example showed some arbitrariness in the choice of bases for allocating the functional expenses to the marketing entities being evaluated. Thus, the "number of sales calls" was used to allocate selling expenses, when in principle "number of sales man-hours" would

---

[7] For another example, see Leland L. Beik and Stephen L. Buzby, "Profitability Analyses by Market Segments," *Journal of Marketing*, June 1973, pp. 48–53.

have been a more accurate indicator of cost. The former base was used because it generally involves less record keeping and computation. Such approximations may not involve the loss of too much accuracy, but marketing executives should be cognizant of this judgmental element in determining distribution costs.[8]

Far more serious may be another judgmental element affecting the computation of marketing costs. This is the matter of whether to allocate *full costs* or only *direct and traceable costs*. The example sidestepped this problem by assuming only simple costs that seemed to fit in with marketing activities. But it cannot be avoided in an actual analysis of marketing costs. Three classes of costs have to be distinguished:

> **Direct costs.** These are costs that can be assigned directly to the marketing entities that give rise to them. For example, sales commissions are a direct cost in a profitability analysis of sales territories, sales representatives, or customers. Advertising expenditures are a direct cost in a profitability analysis of products to the extent that each advertisement promotes only one company product. Other costs that are direct for some purposes are sales-force salaries, supplies, and traveling expenses.
>
> **Traceable common costs.** These are costs that can be assigned only indirectly, but on a plausible basis, to the marketing entities. In the example, rent was analyzed in this way. The company's floor space reflected the need to carry on three different marketing activities, and it was possible to estimate how much floor space supported each activity.
>
> **Nontraceable common costs.** These are costs whose allocation to the marketing entities is necessarily arbitrary. Consider "corporate image" expenditures. It would be arbitrary to allocate them equally among all products, since all products do not benefit equally from corporate image making. It would be arbitrary to allocate them proportionately to the sales of the various products, since relative product sales reflect many factors besides corporate image making. Other typical examples of common costs that are difficult to assign are management salaries, taxes, interest, and other types of overhead.

There is no controversy concerning the inclusion of direct costs in the marketing cost analysis. There is a small amount of controversy concerning the inclusion of traceable common costs. Traceable common costs lump together costs that would change with the scale of the marketing activity and costs that probably would not change in the near future. If the lawn-mower company drops garden supply shops, it is likely to continue to pay the same rent, for contractual reasons or through inertia. In this event its profits would not rise immediately by the amount of the present loss in selling to garden supply shops ($310). The profit figures are more meaningful when fixed traceable costs can be liquidated.

The major controversy concerns whether the nontraceable common costs should be allocated to the marketing entities. This is called the *full-cost approach*, and its advocates defend it on the grounds that all costs ultimately must be imputed in order to determine true profitability. But this argument tends to confuse the use of accounting for financial reporting with the use of accounting to provide a quantitative basis for decision making and profit planning. Full costing has three major weaknesses:

[8] For common bases of allocation, see Charles H. Sevin, *Marketing Productivity Analysis* (New York: McGraw-Hill Book Company, 1965).

The relative profitability of different marketing entities can shift quite radically when one highly arbitrary way to allocate nontraceable common costs is replaced by another. This tends to weaken confidence in the tool.

The arbitrariness leads to argument and demoralization, especially by those who feel that their performance or interest is being judged adversely as a result.

The inclusion of nontraceable common costs may weaken efforts at real cost control. Operating management is most effective in controlling direct costs and traceable common costs. Arbitrary assignments of nontraceable common costs may lead them to spend their time fighting the arbitrary allocations or may altogether discourage them in meeting their cost responsibility.

EFFICIENCY CONTROL

Suppose a profitability analysis reveals that the company is earning poor profits in connection with certain products, territories, or markets. The question is whether there are more efficient ways to manage the sales force, advertising, sales promotion, and distribution.

Sales-Force Efficiency

Sales managers at each level—regional, district, and area—should keep track of several key indicators of sales-force efficiency in their territory. They are:

1. Average number of sales calls per salesperson per day
2. Average sales-call time per contact
3. Average revenue per sales call
4. Average cost per sales call
5. Entertainment cost per sales call
6. Percentage of orders per 100 sales calls
7. Number of new customers per period
8. Number of lost customers per period
9. Sales-force cost as a percentage of total sales

An analysis of these statistics will raise useful questions such as: are sales representatives making too few calls per day? are they spending too much time per call? are they spending too much on entertainment? are they closing enough orders per hundred calls? are they producing enough new customers and holding onto the old customers?

There is much evidence of inefficiency in the way companies manage their personal selling resources. A survey of 257 Fortune-500 companies revealed the following:

- 54 percent have not conducted an organized study of sales representatives' use of time, even though most respondents felt that time utilization represents an area for improvement.
- 25 percent do not have a system for classifying accounts according to potential.
- 30 percent do not use call schedules for their sales force.
- 51 percent do not determine the number of calls it is economical to make on an account.
- 83 percent do not determine an approximate duration for each call.
- 51 percent do not use a planned sales presentation.

- 24 percent do not set sales objectives for accounts.
- 72 percent do not set profit objectives for accounts.
- 19 percent do not use a call report system.
- 63 percent do not use a prescribed routing pattern in covering territories.
- 77 percent do not use the computer to assist in time and territorial management.[9]

When a company becomes serious about improving sales-force efficiency, it often can effect a number of substantial improvements. General Electric was able to reduce the size of the sales force in one of its divisions without losing any sales after discovering that sales representatives were making an excessive number of calls on customers. A large airline found its sales representatives doing both selling and servicing, and took steps to transfer the servicing function to lower-paid clerks. Another company conducted time-and-duty studies and found ways to reduce the ratio of idle to productive time.[10]

Advertising Efficiency

Many managers feel that it is almost impossible to measure what they are getting for their advertising dollars. But an effort should be made to keep track of at least the following statistics:

1. Advertising cost per thousand buyers reached overall, for each media category, and each media vehicle
2. Percentage of audience who noted, saw/associated, and read most for each media vehicle
3. Consumer opinions on the ad content and effectiveness
4. Before-after measures of attitude toward the product
5. Number of inquiries stimulated by the ad
6. Cost per inquiry

Management can undertake a number of steps to improve advertising efficiency, including doing a better job of positioning the product, defining advertising objectives, pretesting messages, using the computer to guide the selection of advertising media, looking for better media buys, and doing advertising post-testing.

Sales Promotion Efficiency

Sales promotion includes dozens of devices for stimulating buyer interest and product trial. In order to improve the efficiency of sales promotion, management should keep records on each sales promotion, its costs, and its impact on sales. Such statistics should be watched as:

1. Percentage of sales sold on deal
2. Display costs per sales dollar
3. Percentage of coupons redeemed
4. Number of inquiries resulting from a demonstration

[9] Robert F. Vizza, "Managing Time and Territories for Maximum Sales Success," *Sales Management,* July 15, 1971, pp. 31–36.

[10] See Charles S. Goodman, *Management of the Personal Selling Function* (New York: Holt, Rinehart and Winston, 1971), pp. 78–80.

By establishing the job position of sales promotion manager, this person can observe the results of different sales promotion instruments and advise product managers on the most cost-effective promotions to use.

Distribution Efficiency

The area of distribution efficiency is one in which management has been active in searching for economies. Considerable work has been done in improving physical-distribution systems, particularly with regard to inventory levels, warehouse locations, and transportation modes. Work has also been done to improve local delivery methods, as the following example shows:

> *Wholesale bakers* face increased competition from chain bakers. They are especially at a disadvantage in the physical distribution of bread. The wholesale bakers must make more stops than the chain bakers and deliver a smaller average volume. Furthermore, the driver typically loads the store's shelf while the chain bakery leaves the bread at the chain's unloading platform to be placed on the shelf by store personnel. This led the American Bakers' Association to investigate whether more efficient bread handling procedures were achievable. A systems engineering study was instituted. The bread delivery operation was studied in minute detail from the time of truck loading to the time of shelving. As a result of riding with the drivers and observing procedures, the engineers recommended a number of changes. Economies could be secured from more scientific routing; from a relocation of the truck's door from the back of the trailer to the driver's side; and from the development of preshelved racks. The interesting thing is that these economies were always available but not recognized until competitive pressure increased the need for improved efficiency.[11]

STRATEGIC CONTROL

From time to time, companies must stand back and undertake a critical review of their overall marketing effectiveness. This goes beyond carrying out annual-plan control, profitability control, and efficiency control. Marketing is one of the major areas where rapid obsolescence of objectives, policies, strategies, and programs is a constant possibility. Because of the rapid changes in the marketing environment, each company should periodically reassess its overall approach to the marketplace. Two tools in this connection are a *marketing-effectiveness rating review* and a *marketing audit*.

Marketing-Effectiveness Rating Review

Consider the following actual situation. The president of a major industrial-equipment company was reviewing the annual business plans of various divisions and found several of the divisional plans lacking in marketing substance. He called in the corporate vice president of marketing and said:

> I am not happy with the quality of marketing in our divisions. It is very uneven. I want you to find out which of our divisions are strong, average, and weak in marketing. I want to know if they understand and are practicing customer-oriented marketing. I want a marketing score for each division. For each deficient division, I want a plan for improving its marketing effectiveness over the next few years. I want evidence next year that each marketing-deficient division is making progress toward a marketing orientation.

[11] See the study by Arthur D. Little, Inc., *Challenge of Distribution in the 60's* (Cambridge, Mass., March 1961).

The corporate marketing vice president agreed to do this, recognizing that it was a formidable task. His first impulse was to base the evaluation of divisional marketing effectiveness on each division's performance in sales growth, market share, and profitability. His thinking was that the high-performing divisions must have good marketing leadership and the poor-performing divisions have deficient marketing leadership.

Actually, marketing effectiveness is not so simple. Good results may be due to a division's being in the right place at the right time, rather than the consequence of effective marketing management. Improvements in that division's marketing might boost results from good to excellent. At the same time, another division might have poor results in spite of the best strategic marketing planning. Replacing the present marketing managers might only make things worse.

The marketing effectiveness of a company or division is reflected in the degree to which it exhibits five major attributes of a marketing orientation: *customer philosophy, integrated marketing organization, adequate marketing information, strategic orientation,* and *operational efficiency.* Each of these attributes can be measured. Table 24–6 presents a *marketing-effectiveness rating instrument* based on these five dimensions. This instrument is filled out by marketing and other managers in the division. The scores are then summarized.

The instrument has been tested in a number of companies, and very few achieve scores within the superior range of 26 to 30 points. The few include well-known master marketers such as Procter & Gamble, Avon, McDonald's, IBM, General Electric, and Caterpillar. Most companies and divisions receive scores in the fair-to-good range, indicating that their own managers feel there is much room for marketing improvement. The breakdown of the total score into the five dimensions indicates which elements of effective marketing action need the most attention. Divisional management can then establish a plan for correcting the major marketing weaknesses over time.[12]

**TABLE 24–6
Marketing Effectiveness Rating Instrument
(Check one answer to each question)**

CUSTOMER PHILOSOPHY

A. Does management recognize the importance of designing the company to serve the needs and wants of chosen markets?

Score

0 ☐ Management primarily thinks in terms of selling current and new products to whoever will buy them.

1 ☐ Management thinks in terms of serving a wide range of markets and needs with equal effectiveness.

2 ☐ Management thinks in terms of serving the needs and wants of well-defined markets chosen for their long-run growth and profit potential for the company.

---

[12] For further discussion of this instrument, see Philip Kotler, "From Sales Obsession to Marketing Effectiveness," *Harvard Business Review,* November–December 1977, pp. 67–75.

TABLE 24–6 continued

648

Marketing Control

    B. Does management develop different offerings and marketing plans for different segments of the market?

0 ☐ No.

1 ☐ Somewhat.

2 ☐ To a good extent.

    C. Does management take a whole marketing system view (suppliers, channels, competitors, customers, environment) in planning its business?

0 ☐ No. Management concentrates on selling and servicing its immediate customers.

1 ☐ Somewhat. Management takes a long view of its channels although the bulk of its effort goes to selling and servicing the immediate customers.

2 ☐ Yes. Management takes a whole marketing systems view recognizing the threats and opportunities created for the company by changes in any part of the system.

INTEGRATED MARKETING ORGANIZATION

    D. Is there high-level marketing integration and control of the major marketing functions?

0 ☐ No. Sales and other marketing functions are not integrated at the top and there is some unproductive conflict.

1 ☐ Somewhat. There is formal integration and control of the major marketing functions but less than satisfactory coordination and cooperation.

2 ☐ Yes. The major marketing functions are effectively integrated.

    E. Does marketing management work well with management in research, manufacturing, purchasing, physical distribution, and finance?

0 ☐ No. There are complaints that marketing is unreasonable in the demands and costs it places on other departments.

1 ☐ Somewhat. The relations are amicable although each department pretty much acts to serve its own power interests.

2 ☐ Yes. The departments cooperate effectively and resolve issues in the best interest of the company as a whole.

    F. How well-organized is the new product development process?

0 ☐ The system is ill-defined and poorly handled.

1 ☐ The system formally exists but lacks sophistication.

2 ☐ The system is well-structured and professionally staffed.

ADEQUATE MARKETING INFORMATION

    G. When were the latest marketing research studies of customers, buying influences, channels, and competitors conducted?

0 ☐ Several years ago.

1 ☐ A few years ago.

2 ☐ Recently.

    H. How well does management know the sales potential and profitability of different market segments, customers, territories, products, channels, and order sizes?

0 ☐ Not at all.

1 ☐ Somewhat.

2 ☐ Very well.

    I. What effort is expended to measure the cost-effectiveness of different marketing expenditures?

0 ☐ Little or no effort.

1 ☐ Some effort.

2 ☐ Substantial effort.

STRATEGIC ORIENTATION

J. What is the extent of formal marketing planning?

0 ☐ Management does little or no formal marketing planning.

1 ☐ Management develops an annual marketing plan.

2 ☐ Management develops a detailed annual marketing plan and a careful long-range plan that is updated annually.

K. What is the quality of the current marketing strategy?

0 ☐ The current strategy is not clear.

1 ☐ The current strategy is clear and represents a continuation of traditional strategy.

2 ☐ The current strategy is clear, innovative, data-based, and well-reasoned.

L. What is the extent of contingency thinking and planning?

0 ☐ Management does little or no contingency thinking.

1 ☐ Management does some contingency thinking although little formal contingency planning.

2 ☐ Management formally identifies the most important contingencies and develops contingency plans.

OPERATIONAL EFFICIENCY

M. How well is the marketing thinking at the top communicated and implemented down the line?

0 ☐ Poorly.

1 ☐ Fairly.

2 ☐ Successfully.

N. Is management doing an effective job with the marketing resources?

0 ☐ No. The marketing resources are inadequate for the job to be done.

1 ☐ Somewhat. The marketing resources are adequate but they are not employed optimally.

2 ☐ Yes. The marketing resources are adequate and are deployed efficiently.

O. Does management show a good capacity to react quickly and effectively to on-the-spot developments?

0 ☐ No. Sales and market information is not very current and management reaction time is slow.

1 ☐ Somewhat. Management receives fairly up-to-date sales and market information; management reaction time varies.

2 ☐ Yes. Management has installed systems yielding highly current information and fast reaction time.

TOTAL SCORE

The instrument is used in the following way. The appropriate answer is checked for each question. The scores are added—the total will be somewhere between 0 and 30. The following scale shows the level of marketing effectiveness:

0–5	= None	16–20	= Good
6–10	= Poor	21–25	= Very good
11–15	= Fair	26–30	= Superior

SOURCE: Philip Kotler, "From Sales Obsession to Marketing Effectiveness," *Harvard Business Review,* November–December 1977, pp 67–75. Copyright © 1977 by the President and Fellows of Harvard College; all rights reserved.

The Marketing Audit

Those companies and divisions that discover through applying the marketing-effectiveness rating instrument that their marketing operations need improvement should consider undertaking a more thorough study known as a *marketing audit.*[13] In its full form, a marketing audit has four basic characteristics.

1. ***Comprehensive.*** The term *marketing audit* should be reserved for a *comprehensive (or horizontal) audit* covering the company's marketing environment, objectives, strategies, organization, and systems. In contrast, a *functional (or vertical) audit* occurs when management decides to take an in-depth look into some key marketing function, such as sales-force management. A functional audit is called by the function that is being audited, such as a sales-force audit, an advertising audit, or a pricing audit. Although functional audits can be useful, they often blind management as to the real source of its problem. Excessive sales-force turnover, for example, may be a symptom not of poor sales-force training or compensation but of poor company products and promotion. A comprehensive marketing audit usually is more effective in locating the real source of the company's marketing problems.

2. ***Systematic.*** The usefulness of a marketing audit will normally increase to the extent that it follows an orderly sequence of diagnostic steps covering the organization's marketing environment, internal marketing system, and specific marketing activities. The diagnosis is followed by a corrective action plan involving both short-run and long-run actions to improve the organization's overall marketing effectiveness.

3. ***Independent.*** A marketing audit can be conducted in six ways:[14] (1) self-audit; (2) audit from across; (3) audit from above; (4) company auditing office; (5) company task-force audit; and (6) outsider audit. Self-audits, where managers use a checklist to rate their own operations, may be useful, but most experts agree that the self-audit lacks objectivity and independence.[15] The 3M Company has made good use of a headquarters-based auditing office, which provides marketing audit services to divisions on request.[16] Generally speaking, however, the best audits are likely to come from experienced outside consultants, who have the necessary objectivity and independence, broad experience in a number of industries, some familiarity with this industry, and the undivided time and attention to give to the audit.

4. ***Periodic.*** Typically, marketing audits are initiated only after sales have turned down sharply, sales-force morale has fallen, and other problems have occurred at the company. The irony is that companies are thrown into a crisis partly because they have failed to review their marketing operations during good times. A periodic marketing audit promises benefits for companies that are in good health as well as companies that are in trouble. "No marketing operation is ever so good that it cannot be improved. Even the best can be made better. In fact, even the best *must* be better, for few if any marketing operations can remain successful over the years by maintaining the status quo."[17]

---

[13] See Philip Kotler, William Gregor, and William Rodgers, "The Marketing Audit Comes of Age," *Sloan Management Review*, Winter 1977, pp. 25–43.

[14] Some of these approaches are briefly discussed by Alfred Oxenfeldt and Richard D. Crisp in their respective articles in *Analyzing and Improving Marketing Performance*, Report No. 32 (New York: American Management Association, 1959).

[15] Many useful checklist questions for marketers are found in C. Eldridge, *The Management of the Marketing Function* (New York: Association of National Advertisers, 1967).

[16] Kotler, Gregor, and Rodgers, "Marketing Audit Comes of Age," p. 31.

[17] Abe Shuchman, "The Marketing Audit: Its Nature, Purposes, and Problems," in Oxenfeldt and Crisp, *Marketing Performance*, pp. 16–17.

650

The preceding ideas on a marketing audit can be brought together into a single definition:

A marketing audit is a comprehensive, systematic, independent, and periodic examination of a company's—or business unit's—marketing environment, objectives, strategies, and activities with a view of determining problem areas and opportunities and recommending a plan of action to improve the company's marketing performance.

Marketing audit procedure   A marketing audit starts with a meeting between the company officer(s) and the marketing auditor(s) to work out an agreement on the objectives, coverage, depth, data sources, report format, and the time period for the audit. The bulk of the auditor's time is then spent in gathering data. A detailed plan as to who is to be interviewed, the questions to be asked, the time and place of contact, and so on, has to be carefully prepared so that auditing time and cost are kept to a minimum. The cardinal rule in data collection is not to rely solely on the company's executives for data and opinion. Customers, dealers, and other outside groups must be interviewed. Many companies do not really know how their customers and dealers see them and their competitors, nor do they fully understand customer needs.

When the data-gathering phase is over, the marketing auditor formally presents the main findings and recommendations. A valuable aspect of the marketing audit is the process that the managers go through to assimilate, debate, and develop new concepts of needed marketing action.

Components of the marketing audit   The marketing audit consists of examining six major components of the company's marketing situation. Each component has a semiautonomous status if a company wants less than a full marketing audit. The six components are described below and the major auditing questions are listed in Table 24–7.

1. *Marketing environment audit.* This audit calls for analyzing the major macro-environment forces that might impact on the company and major trends in the key components of the company's task environment: markets, customers, competitors, distributors and dealers, suppliers, and facilitators.
2. *Marketing strategy audit.* This audit calls for reviewing the company's marketing objectives and marketing strategy to appraise how well these are adapted to the current and forecasted marketing environment.
3. *Marketing organization audit.* This audit calls for evaluating the marketing organization's capability for developing and carrying out the necessary strategy for the forecasted environment.
4. *Marketing systems audit.* This audit involves examining the adequacy of the company's systems for analysis, planning, and control in the marketing area, as well as innovation.
5. *Marketing productivity audit.* This audit calls for examining data on the profitability of different marketing entities and on the cost-effectiveness of different marketing expenditures.
6. *Marketing function audits.* These audits involve carrying out in-depth evaluations of major marketing-mix components, namely products, price, distribution, sales force, advertising, promotion, and publicity.

TABLE 24–7
Components of a Marketing Audit

PART I. THE MARKETING ENVIRONMENT AUDIT

Macroenvironment

A. *Economic-Demographic*

1. What does the company expect in the way of inflation, material shortages, unemployment, and credit availability in the short run, intermediate run, and long run?

2. What effect will forecasted trends in the size, age distribution, and regional distribution of population have on the business?

B. *Technology*

1. What major changes are occurring in product technology? In process technology?

2. What are the major generic substitutes that might replace this product?

C. *Political-Legal*

1. What laws are being proposed that may affect marketing strategy and tactics?

2. What federal, state, and local agency actions should be watched? What is happening in the areas of pollution control, equal employment opportunity, product safety, advertising, price control, etc., that is relevant to marketing planning?

D. *Social-Cultural*

1. What attitudes is the public taking toward business and toward products such as those produced by the company?

2. What changes are occurring in consumer life styles and values that have a bearing on the company's target markets and marketing methods?

Task Environment

A. *Markets*

1. What is happening to market size, growth, geographical distribution, and profits?

2. What are the major market segments? What are their expected rates of growth? Which are high opportunity and low opportunity segments?

B. *Customers*

1. How do current customers and prospects rate the company and its competitors, particularly with respect to reputation, product quality, service, sales force, and price?

2. How do different classes of customers make their buying decisions?

3. What are the evolving needs and satisfactions being sought by the buyers in this market?

C. *Competitors*

1. Who are the major competitors? What are the objectives and strategy of each major competitor? What are their strengths and weaknesses? What are the sizes and trends in market shares?

2. What trends can be foreseen in future competition and substitutes for this product?

D. *Distribution and Dealers*

1. What are the main trade channels bringing products to customers?

2. What are the efficiency levels and growth potentials of the different trade channels?

E. *Suppliers*

1. What is the outlook for the availability of different key resources used in production?
2. What trends are occurring among suppliers in their pattern of selling?

F. *Facilitators*

1. What is the outlook for the cost and availability of transportation services?
2. What is the outlook for the cost and availability of warehousing facilities?
3. What is the outlook for the cost and availability of financial resources?
4. How effectively is the advertising agency performing? What trends are occurring in advertising agency services?

PART II. MARKETING STRATEGY AUDIT

A. *Marketing Objectives*

1. Are the corporate objectives clearly stated, and do they lead logically to the marketing objectives?
2. Are the marketing objectives stated in a clear form to guide marketing planning and subsequent performance measurement?
3. Are the marketing objectives appropriate, given the company's competitive position, resources, and opportunities? Is the appropriate strategic objective to build, hold, harvest, or terminate this business?

B. *Strategy*

1. What is the core marketing strategy for achieving the objectives? Is it a sound marketing strategy?
2. Are enough resources (or too much resources) budgeted to accomplish the marketing objectives?
3. Are the marketing resources allocated optimally to prime market segments, territories, and products of the organization?
4. Are the marketing resources allocated optimally to the major elements of the marketing mix, i.e., product quality, service, sales force, advertising, promotion, and distribution?

PART III. MARKETING ORGANIZATION AUDIT

A. *Formal Structure*

1. Is there a high level marketing officer with adequate authority and responsibility over those company activities that affect the customer's satisfaction?
2. Are the marketing responsibilities optimally structured along functional, product, end user, and territorial lines?

B. *Functional Efficiency*

1. Are there good communication and working relations between marketing and sales?
2. Is the product-management system working effectively? Are the product managers able to plan profits or only sales volume?
3. Are there any groups in marketing that need more training, motivation, supervision, or evaluation?

C. *Interface Efficiency*

1. Are there any problems between marketing and manufacturing that need attention?
2. What about marketing and R&D?

TABLE 24–7 continued

3. What about marketing and financial management?
4. What about marketing and purchasing?

PART IV. MARKETING SYSTEMS AUDIT

A. *Marketing Information System*
1. Is the marketing intelligence system producing accurate, sufficient, and timely information about developments in the marketplace?
2. Is marketing research being adequately used by company decision makers?

B. *Marketing-Planning System*
1. Is the marketing-planning system well conceived and effective?
2. Is sales forecasting and market-potential measurement soundly carried out?
3. Are sales quotas set on a proper basis?

C. *Marketing Control System*
1. Are the control procedures (monthly, quarterly, etc.) adequate to insure that the annual-plan objectives are being achieved?
2. Is provision made to analyze periodically the profitability of different products, markets, territories, and channels of distribution?
3. Is provision made to examine and validate periodically various marketing costs?

D. *New-Product Development System*
1. Is the company well organized to gather, generate, and screen new product ideas?
2. Does the company do adequate concept research and business analysis before investing heavily in a new idea?
3. Does the company carry out adequate product and market testing before launching a new product?

PART V. MARKETING PRODUCTIVITY AUDIT

A. *Profitability Analysis*
1. What is the profitability of the company's different products, served markets, territories, and channels of distribution?
2. Should the company enter, expand, contract, or withdraw from any business segments and what would be the short- and long-run profit consequences?

B. *Cost-Effectiveness Analysis*
1. Do any marketing activities seem to have excessive costs? Are these costs valid? Can cost-reducing steps be taken?

PART VI. MARKETING FUNCTION AUDITS

A. *Products*
1. What are the product line objectives? Are these objectives sound? Is the current product line meeting these objectives?
2. Are there particular products that should be phased out?
3. Are there new products that are worth adding?
4. Are any products able to benefit from quality, feature, or style improvements?

B. *Price*
1. What are the pricing objectives, policies, strategies, and procedures? To what extent are prices set on sound cost, demand, and competitive criteria?

2. Do the customers see the company's prices as being in line or out of line with the perceived value of its offer?

3. Does the company use price promotions effectively?

C. *Distribution*

1. What are the distribution objectives and strategies?

2. Is there adequate market coverage and service?

3. Should the company consider changing its degree of reliance on distributors, sales reps, and direct selling?

D. *Sales Force*

1. What are the organization's sales force objectives?

2. Is the sales force large enough to accomplish the company's objectives?

3. Is the sales force organized along the proper principle(s) of specialization (territory, market, product)?

4. Does the sales force show high morale, ability, and effort? Are they sufficiently trained and are there sufficient incentives?

5. Are the procedures adequate for setting quotas and evaluating performances?

6. How is the company's sales force perceived in relation to competitors' sales forces?

E. *Advertising, Sales Promotion, and Publicity*

1. What are the organization's advertising objectives? Are they sound?

2. Is the right amount being spent on advertising? How is the budget determined?

3. Are the ad themes and copy effective? What do customers and the public think about the advertising?

4. Are the advertising media well chosen?

5. Is sales promotion used effectively?

6. Is there a well-conceived publicity program?

Example of a marketing audit[18] O'Brien Candy Company is a medium-sized candy company located in the Midwest. In the last two years, its sales and profits have barely held their own. Top management feels that the trouble lies with the sales force; somehow they don't "work hard or smart enough." To correct this, management is considering introducing a new incentive-compensation system and hiring a sales-force trainer to train the sales force in modern merchandising and selling techniques. Before doing this, however, they decide to hire a marketing consultant to do a marketing audit. The auditor conducts a number of interviews with management, customers, sales representatives, and dealers and also examines various data. Here is what the auditor finds:

> The company's product line consists primarily of eighteen products, mostly candy bars. Its two leading brands are in the mature stage of their life cycles and account for 76 percent of total sales. The company has looked at the fast-developing markets of chocolate snacks and candies but has not made any moves yet.
>
> The company recently researched its customer profile. Its products appeal especially to lower-income and older people. Respondents who were asked to

[18] This case is adapted with permission from the excellent article by Dr. Ernst A. Tirmann, "Should Your Marketing be Audited?" *European Business*, autumn 1971, pp. 49–56.

assess O'Brien's chocolate products in relation to competitors' products described them as "average quality and a bit old-fashioned."

O'Brien sells its products to candy jobbers and large chains. Its sales force call on many of the small retailers reached by the candy jobbers to fortify displays and provide ideas; its sales force also call on many small retailers not covered by jobbers. O'Brien enjoys good penetration of small retailing, although not in all segments, such as the fast-growing restaurant area. Its major approach to middlemen is a "sell-in" strategy: discounts, exclusivity contracts, and stock financing. At the same time, O'Brien does not do too well in penetrating the various chains. Some of its competitors rely much more heavily on mass consumer advertising and store merchandising and are more successful with the large chains.

O'Brien's marketing budget amounts to about 15 percent of its total sales, compared with competitors' budgets of close to 20 percent. Most of the marketing budget supports the sales force and the remainder supports advertising; consumer promotions are very limited. The advertising budget is spent primarily in reminder advertising for the company's two leading products. New products are not developed often, and when they are, they are introduced to retailers by using a "push" strategy.

The marketing organization is headed by a sales vice president. Reporting to the sales vice president is the sales manager, the marketing research manager, and the advertising manager. Having come up from the ranks, the sales vice president is partial to sales-force activities and pays less attention to the other marketing functions. The sales force is organized by territorial responsibilities headed by area managers.

The marketing auditor came to the firm conclusion that O'Brien's problems would not be solved by actions taken to improve its sales force. The sales-force problem was symptomatic of a deeper company malaise. The auditor prepared and presented a report to management consisting of the findings and recommendations shown in Table 24–8.

TABLE 24–8

SUMMARY OF MARKETING AUDITOR'S FINDINGS AND RECOMMENDATIONS FOR O'BRIEN CANDY COMPANY

FINDINGS

1. The company's product lines are dangerously unbalanced. The two leading products accounted for 76 percent of total sales and have no growth potential. Five of the eighteen products are unprofitable and have no growth potential.

2. The company's marketing objectives are neither clear nor realistic.

3. The company's strategy is not taking changing distribution patterns into account or catering to rapidly changing markets.

4. The company is run by a sales organization rather than a marketing organization.

5. The company's marketing mix is unbalanced, with too much spending on sales force and not enough on advertising.

6. The company lacks procedures for successfully developing and launching new products.

7. The company's selling effort is not geared to profitable accounts.

SHORT-TERM RECOMMENDATIONS

1. Examine the current product line and weed out marginal performers with limited growth potential.
2. Shift some marketing expenditures from supporting mature products to supporting the more recent ones.
3. Shift the marketing-mix emphasis from direct selling to national advertising, especially for new products.
4. Conduct a market-profile study of the fastest growing segments of the candy market and develop a plan to break into these areas.
5. Instruct the sales force to drop some of the smaller outlets and not to take orders for under twenty items. Also, cut out the duplication of effort of sales representatives and jobbers calling on the same accounts.
6. Initiate sales-training programs and an improved compensation plan.

MEDIUM-TO-LONG-TERM RECOMMENDATIONS

1. Hire an experienced marketing vice president from the outside.
2. Set formal and operational marketing objectives.
3. Introduce the product manager concept in the marketing organization.
4. Initiate effective new-product development programs.
5. Develop strong brand names.
6. Find ways to market its brands to the chain stores more effectively.
7. Increase the level of marketing expenditures to 20 percent of sales.
8. Reorganize the selling function by specializing sales representatives by distribution channels.
9. Set sales objectives and base sales compensation on gross profit performance.

THE MARKETING CONTROLLER CONCEPT

We have examined how an outsider called a marketing auditor can contribute to strategic control. Some companies are also establishing inside job positions known as *marketing controllers* to monitor marketing expenses and activities. Marketing controllers are essentially individuals working in the controller office who have a specialization in the marketing side of the business. In the past, the controller's office concentrated on watching manufacturing, inventory, and financial expenses and did not contain individuals who really understood marketing very well. The new marketing controllers are trained in both finance and marketing and can perform a sophisticated financial analysis of past and contemplated marketing expenditures. A survey by Goodman showed that

> large sophisticated companies, such as General Foods, Du Pont, Johnson & Johnson, Trans World Airlines, and American Cyanamid, have all instituted financial control positions which directly oversee advertising and, in some selected cases, merchandising policies. The major functions of these individuals are to verify advertising bills, ensure the optimization of agency rates, negotiate agency contracts, and perform an audit function regarding the client's agency and certain of the suppliers.[19]

[19] Sam R. Goodman, *Techniques of Profitability Analysis* (New York: John Wiley & Sons, 1970), p. 2.

Goodman feels that this is a step in the right direction and advocates even a fuller role for the marketing controller. The marketing controller would:

1. Maintain record of adherence to profit plans;
2. Maintain close control of media expense;
3. Prepare brand manager's budgets;
4. Advise on optimum timing for strategies;
5. Measure the efficiency of promotions;
6. Analyze media production costs;
7. Evaluate customer and geographic profitability;
8. Present sales-oriented financial reports;
9. Assist direct accounts in optimizing purchasing and inventory policies;
10. Educate the marketing area to financial implications of decisions.[20]

The Nestlé Company took a step in this direction in 1965 when a specific segment of the controller operation was made available for marketing planning and control. Marketing-service analysts were assigned to each of Nestlé's six marketing divisions to work for the marketing head. They carried out diverse assignments designed to improve marketing efficiency and performance. Their reports proved helpful, and the position has served as a valuable training ground for future general managers because of their exposure to marketing, production, and finance.

The marketing controller concept is an intriguing one, particularly in organizations where marketing is still practiced with a primary eye toward sales rather than profits. The marketing controller can make a contribution by analyzing how and where the company is making its money. As future marketing managers come on the scene with greater training in financial analysis, they can be expected to do more of this work themselves, with marketing controllers continuing to provide a monitoring function of marketing expenditures.

SUMMARY

Marketing control is the natural sequel to marketing planning. Organizations need to exercise at least four types of marketing control.

Annual-plan control is the task of monitoring the current marketing effort and results to be sure that the annual sales and profit goals will be achieved. The main tools are sales analysis, market share analysis, marketing expense-to-sales ratios, financial analysis, and customer-attitude tracking. If underperformance is detected, the company can implement a variety of corrective measures, including cutting production, changing prices, increasing sales-force pressure, and cutting fringe expenditures.

Profitability control is the task of determining the actual profitability of different marketing entities, such as the firm's products, territories, market segments, and trade channels. Marketing-profitability analysis reveals the weaker marketing entities, although it does not indicate whether the weaker units should be bolstered or phased out.

[20] *Ibid.*, 17–18.

Efficiency control is the task of increasing the efficiency of such marketing activities as personal selling, advertising, sales promotion, and distribution. Managers regularly watch certain key ratios that indicate how efficiently these functions are being performed, and they also implement studies to find ways to improve performance.

Strategic control is the task of making sure that the company's marketing objectives, strategies, and systems are optimally adapted to the current and forecasted marketing environment. One tool, known as the marketing-effectiveness rating instrument, attempts to profile a company or division's overall marketing effectiveness in terms of customer philosophy, marketing organization, marketing information, strategic planning, and operational efficiency. Another tool, known as the marketing audit, is a comprehensive, systematic, independent, and periodic examination of the organization's marketing environment, objectives, strategies, and activities. The purpose of the marketing audit is to determine marketing problem areas and recommend a corrective short-run and long-run action plan to improve the organization's overall marketing effectiveness.

A growing number of companies have established marketing controller positions to monitor marketing expenditures and develop improved financial analyses of the impact of these expenditures.

QUESTIONS AND PROBLEMS

1. Do you foresee a professional marketing auditing association which licenses practitioners, on the model of professional certified public accountants? Why or why not? Do you think it is a good idea?

2. What are the main problems an outside marketing auditor is likely to encounter on a first-time assignment in a company?

3. A sales manager examined his company's sales by region and noted that the East Coast sales were about 2 percent below the quota. To probe this further, the sales manager examined district sales figures. He discovered that the Boston sales district within the East Coast region was responsible for most of the underachievement. He then examined the individual sales of the four salesmen in the Boston district. This examination revealed that the top salesman, Roberts, had filled only 69 percent of his quota for the period. Is it safe to conclude that Roberts is loafing or having personal problems?

4. Suppose a company's market share falls for a couple of periods. The marketing vice-president, however, refuses to take any action, calling it a "random walk." What does he mean? Is he justified?

5. Company XYZ produces five products, and its salesmen represent the full product line on each sales call. In order to determine the profit contribution of each product, salesmen costs (salary, commission, and expenses) have to be allocated among the five products. How should this be done?

6. A large manufacturer of industrial equipment has a salesman assigned to each major industrial city. Regional sales managers supervise the salesmen in several cities. The chief marketing officer wants to evaluate the profit contribution of the different cities. How might each of the following costs be allocated to the cities: (a) billing; (b) district sales manager's expenses; (c) national magazine advertising; (d) marketing research?

7. A company conducts a marketing cost study to determine the minimum size order for breaking even. After finding this size, should the company refuse to accept orders below this size? What issues and alternatives should be considered?

8. The idea of treating the marketing department as a profit center raises several difficult problems. Name them and suggest possible solutions.

9. What is the difference between marketing planning and marketing auditing?

10. What is the difference between the job of a marketing auditor and a marketing controller?

Special Marketing Topics

6

International Marketing

Most American executives think of their market as consumers and business firms located in the United States. American exports, after all, account for only 6 percent of the U.S. gross national product. The American home market has been so large that American thinking has traditionally been directed inward.

When Belgian business executives think of selling their goods, they must include international markets in their thinking. Almost 50 percent of the Belgian national output is sold abroad. In other economies also, such as those of the Netherlands, Denmark, Sweden, and Venezuela, marketing thinking must cover international markets.

Ordinarily, most firms would prefer domestic marketing to foreign marketing. Domestic marketing is generally simpler and safer. The managers do not have to learn another language, deal with a different currency, face political and legal uncertainties, or adapt the product to a different set of needs and expectations. There are mainly two factors that might draw companies into international marketing. First, they might be *pushed* into it by the general lack of opportunity in the home market. The gross national product of the home country may be low or growing very slowly, or their government may be antibusiness or taxing heavily. Second, they might be *pulled* into it by growing opportunities for their product in other countries. Without necessarily abandoning their home market, they may find other markets an attractive place to make a profit, even after allowing for the extra costs and encumbrances they might face in operating abroad.

THE INTERNATIONAL MARKETING ENVIRONMENT

In deciding to sell abroad, a company will have to learn a great many new things. Although international marketing involves no new marketing principles, the company will have to acquire and maintain a good knowledge of the changing international marketing environment. The international marketing environment has undergone significant changes since 1945, creating both new opportunities and new problems. The most significant changes are:

1. The significant internationalization of the world economy reflected in the rapid growth of world trade and investment
2. The gradual erosion of the dominant position of the U.S. and its attendant problems of an unfavorable balance of trade and a falling value of the dollar in world markets
3. The rising economic power of Japan in world markets
4. The establishment of a working international financial system offering improved currency convertibility
5. The shift in world income since 1973 to the oil-producing countries
6. The increasing trade barriers put up to protect domestic markets against foreign competition.[1]

The company also has to know how to research specific foreign markets. American companies that are effective marketers domestically have often forgotten their marketing principles when going abroad, often resulting in costly blunders. They look at foreign markets from an ethnocentric point of view instead of the foreign consumer's point of view. Thus Campbell's bombed when it tried to sell its canned soup in Italy, a country where the way of life clearly rules out canned soup. When Italian housewives were asked, "Would you want your son to marry a canned-soup user?" 99 percent answered no. And the same company failed in some countries to vary the taste of its tomato soup sufficiently to meet varying national and regional taste preferences.

The hundred-odd nations of the world differ greatly in the kinds of goods and services they are ready to use. It would be as much a mistake for an American manufacturer of microwave ovens to seek a market in Nigeria as for Nigerians to seek a market for bullock carts here. On the other hand, American bicycles fetch a premium in Nigeria, and Nigerian palm oil is imported in large quantities into the United States. A nation's readiness for different products and services and its general attractiveness as a market to foreign firms depend on its economic, political-legal, cultural, and business environment.

Economic Environment
The nations of the world exhibit great variation in *industrial structure* and *national income,* both of which critically influence the goods and services they are likely to need and their ability to buy.

[1] See Warren J. Keegan, "Multinational Product Planning: New Myths and Old Realities," in *Multinational Product Management* (Cambridge, Mass.: Marketing Science Institute, 1976), pp. 1–8.

Economies classified according to industrial structure   It is useful to distinguish among four types of industrial structure that a nation can have:

1. *Subsistence economies.* In a subsistence economy the vast majority of people are engaged in simple agriculture. They consume most of their output and barter the rest for simple goods and services. For obvious reasons, they offer few opportunities for exporters.

2. *Raw-material-exporting economies.* These economies are rich in one or more natural resources but poor in other respects. Much of their revenue comes from exporting these resources. Examples are Chile (tin and copper), the Congo (rubber), and Saudi Arabia (oil). These countries are good markets for extractive equipment, tools and supplies, materials-handling equipment, and trucks. Depending on the number of foreign residents and wealthy native rulers and landholders, they are also a market for Western-style commodities and luxury goods.

3. *Industrializing economies.* In an industrializing economy, manufacturing is beginning to play a role of some importance, probably accounting for somewhere between 10 and 20 percent of the country's gross national product. Examples include Egypt, the Philippines, India, and Brazil. As manufacturing increases, the country relies more on imports of textile raw materials, steel, and heavy machinery, and less on imports of finished textiles, paper products, and automobiles. The industrialization tends to create a new rich class and a small but growing middle class, both demanding new types of goods, some of which can be satisfied only by imports.

4. *Industrial economies.* Industrial economies have built up their industrial base to the extent that they become exporters of manufactured goods and investment funds. They trade manufactured goods among themselves and also export them to other types of economies in exchange for raw materials and semifinished goods. The large and varied manufacturing activities of these industrial nations and their sizable middle class make them rich markets for all sorts of goods.

Economies classified according to national incomes   The products and services consumed by a nation are also affected by its level and distribution of national income. These goods can be distinguished for five different national income profiles:

1. *Very low family incomes.* Subsistence economies tend to be characterized by very low family incomes. The families spend long hours at hard work eking out a bare living from the soil. Homegrown food and homemade clothing and simple services constitute the bulk of consumer goods and services.

2. *Mostly low family incomes.* Economies that are seeking industrialization along Marxist lines are characterized by low family incomes, to allow as much as possible for capital formation. Most consumer goods are produced domestically by state-owned enterprises. These nations present some opportunities for trade.

3. *Very low, very high family incomes.* Several countries of the world are characterized by extremes of income, where most of the population is very poor and a small minority is very rich. This makes the market for consumer goods very bizarre. The masses live on subsistence farming, supplemented by the import of needed foodstuffs and textiles, and the rich import expensive cars, appliances, and Western amenities.

4. *Low, medium, high family incomes.* Industrialization tends to be accompanied by the rise of a middle class. The very low and very high income classes tend to persist along with their distinct consumption patterns. The middle class is able to afford basic necessities and have something left over to purchase amenities.

5. *Mostly medium family incomes.* The advanced industrial nations tend to develop institutions that reduce the extremes of income. The result is a large and comfortable middle class confronted with a wide array of branded products, able to own automobiles and major appliances, as well as to enjoy leisure and take vacations.

Political-Legal Environment

Nations differ greatly in the favorableness of their political-legal environment for imports and foreign investment. At least four factors should be considered by the prospective marketer who is evaluating whether to do business in another country.

1. *Attitudes toward international buying.* Some nations are very receptive, indeed encouraging, to foreign firms, and others are very hostile. As an example of the former, Mexico for a number of years has been attracting foreign investment by offering investment incentives, site-location services, and a stable currency. On the other hand, India has required the exporter to deal with import quotas, blocked currencies, stipulations that a high percentage of the management team be nationals, and so on.

2. *Political stability.* One must consider not only the host country's present political climate but also its future stability. Governments change hands, sometimes quite violently. Even without a change in government, a regime may decide to respond to new popular feelings. At worst, the foreign company's property may be expropriated; or its currency holdings may be blocked; or import quotas or new duties may be imposed. Where political instability is high, international marketers may still find it profitable to do business with the host country, but the situation will affect their mode of entry. They will favor export marketing to direct foreign investment. They will keep their foreign stocks low. They will convert their currency rapidly. As a result, the people in the host country end up paying higher prices, have fewer jobs, and get less satisfactory products.

3. *Monetary regulations.* Sellers want to realize profits in a currency of value to them. In the best situation, the importer can pay either in the seller's currency or in hard world currencies. Short of this, sellers might accept a blocked currency if they can buy other goods in that country that they need or that they can sell elsewhere for a needed currency. In the worst case they have to take their money out of the host country in the form of relatively unmarketable products that they can sell elsewhere only at a loss. Besides currency restrictions, a fluctuating exchange rate also leads to unusual risks for the exporter.

4. *Government bureaucracy.* A fourth factor is the extent to which the host government runs an efficient system for assisting foreign companies: efficient customs-handling procedures, market information, and other factors conducive to doing business. Perhaps the most common shock to American business executives is the extent to which various impediments appear to stand in their way, all of which disappear if a suitable payment (bribe) is made to some official(s).

Cultural Environment

Perhaps the most difficult aspect of international markets is the consumer buying preferences and patterns, which are full of surprises:

The average Frenchman uses almost twice as many cosmetics and beauty aids as does his wife.

The Germans and the French eat more packaged, branded spaghetti than the Italians.

French and Italian housewives are not as interested in cooking as their counterparts in Luxembourg and Belgium.

Women in Tanzania will not give their children eggs for fear of making them bald or impotent.

Chevrolet's Nova would be an inappropriate brand name for Spain, where *no va* means "it doesn't go"!

Colors for packaging have varying connotations in different countries: green suggests illness in Malaysia, white indicates mourning in China, while blue connotes femininity in Holland and masculinity in Sweden.

And industrial buying styles vary tremendously:

South Americans are accustomed to talking business in close physical proximity with other persons, in fact almost nose to nose. The American business executive retreats, but the South American pursues. And both end up being offended.

In face-to-face communication Japanese business executives rarely say no to an American business executive. Americans are frustrated and don't know where they stand. Also, Americans tend to come to their point quickly and directly in business dealings. Japanese business executives tend to find this offensive.

In France, wholesalers just don't care to promote a product. They simply ask their retailers what they want today, and they deliver it. If an American company builds its strategy around the French wholesaler, it is almost bound to fail.

Each country (and even regional groups within each country) has cultural traditions, preferences, and taboos that must be carefully studied by the marketer.

In contemplating international marketing a company faces five major types of decisions. (1) The *international marketing decision* determines whether the foreign opportunities and the firm's resources are attractive enough to justify a general interest in marketing abroad. (2) The *market-selection decision* determines *which* foreign markets to enter. (3) The *entry and operating decision* determines the best way to enter and operate in an attractive foreign market. (4) The *marketing-mix decision* develops an appropriate product, price, distribution, and promotion program for that market. (5) The *marketing-organization decision* determines the best way for the firm to achieve and maintain control over its international business operations. We shall examine each of these decisions on the following pages.

THE INTERNATIONAL MARKETING DECISION

Companies initially get involved in international marketing in one of two ways. In some cases, someone—a domestic exporter, a foreign importer, a foreign government—approaches the company. In other cases, the company starts to think on its own about overseas marketing. It might face overcapacity or simply forecast better opportunities abroad than at home.

Before going abroad, the company should try to define its *international marketing objectives and policies.* This involves a number of component decisions.

1. *Proportion of foreign sales to total sales.* Most companies will start small when they venture abroad. Some will plan to stay small, seeing foreign operations as a small part of their business. Other companies will have more grandiose

international-expansion plans, seeing foreign business as ultimately equal to or even more important than their domestic business. Of the more than fifteen thousand American firms engaged in international trade, several companies sell more abroad than at home: Standard Oil (N.J.) (68 percent), United States Machinery Company (59 percent), Colgate Palmolive (55 percent), and Singer (50 percent). Other American companies selling over 30 percent of their output abroad are Pfizer, Kodak, Gillette, 3M, National Cash Register, International Harvester, Caterpillar, and Heinz.

2. *Few countries or many countries.* A company with a fixed budget for international expansion has a choice of entering only a few foreign markets and developing them well *(market concentration)* or entering several markets each on a smaller scale *(market diversification).* For example, Koor, a large Israel company, chose market diversification and set up sales offices in seven countries in one year with disappointing results. Ayal and Zif analyzed the product/market factors that favor market concentration versus market diversification.[2] Market concentration makes sense if market response is S-shaped rather than concave; each market has high growth potential and relative stability; each market needs high product and communication adaptation; each market has high constraints and needs high program control; each market has high economies of scale in distribution; the competitive lead-time is long; and the spillover effects on other markets are low. If the opposite conditions prevail, the firm should consider market diversification.

3. *Types of countries.* The types of countries that are attractive will depend on the product, geographical factors, income and population, political climate and numerous other factors. The seller may have a predilection for certain country groups or parts of the world. For example, the oil-producing countries are experiencing rapid growth and are key markets for construction equipment, luxury automobiles, electrical equipment, and other things. Mainland China is gradually opening its markets to foreign trade, and although trading arrangements are difficult, the gains would be very high.[3] Eastern European countries provide another growing market opportunity. Brazil is an example of a country with high potential. Other less-developed nations (LDNs) have the necessary population but often lack the incomes to be good markets for foreign manufacturers and in addition often impose severe manpower and currency requirements that lower profit opportunities. The company has to decide whether to cultivate opportunities in safe countries or in those countries that offer the chance for higher returns at somewhat high risks.

MARKET SELECTION DECISION

After developing a preliminary list of possible countries in which to market, the company will have to find some procedure for screening and ranking them. Consider the following example:

> CMC's market research in the computer field revealed that England, France, West Germany, and Italy offer us significant markets. England, France, and Germany are about equal-size markets, while Italy represents about two thirds the potential of any one of those countries. . . . Taking everything into consid-

[2] Igal Ayal and Jehiel Zif, "Market Expansion Strategies in Multinational Marketing," *Journal of Marketing,* Spring 1979, pp. 84–94.

[3] Bohdan O. Szuprowicz and Maria R. Szuprowicz, *Doing Business with the People's Republic of China: Industries and Markets* (New York: John Wiley & Sons, 1978).

> eration, we decided to set up first in England because its market for our products is as large as any and its language and laws are similar to ours. England is different enough to get your feet wet, yet similar enough to the familiar U.S. business environment so that you do not get in over your head.[4]

The market choice seems relatively simple and straightforward. Yet one can question whether the reason given for selecting England—the compatibility of its language and culture—should have been given this prominence. Normally the candidate countries should be ranked on several criteria, such as: (1) market size; (2) market growth; (3) cost of doing business; (4) competitive advantage; (5) risk level.

The core of the ranking procedure is to try to determine the probable rate of return on investment in each market. Five steps are involved:

1. *Estimate of current market potential.* The first step is to estimate current market potential in each candidate market. This *marketing research task* calls for using existing published data supplemented by primary data collection through company surveys and studies of various kinds. The rub is that foreign marketing research is more difficult, as a general rule, than domestic market research, for at least four reasons. (1) Published census and market data are usually scarce and somewhat unreliable in several countries, especially the poorer ones. (2) Many trade associations do not make their data public. (3) Marketing research firms are not always of high quality. (4) Buyers in other countries are less used to cooperating in interviews. Yet there are some signs of improvement. The U.S. Department of Commerce and several large banks are increasing the amount of information available about foreign markets. The United Nations publishes statistical data and market information. Foreign governments, banks, chambers of commerce, and private companies are increasingly responding to the problem of better market information.

2. *Forecast of future market potential.* The firm also needs a forecast of future market potential. This is complicated because the market analyst is usually insufficiently versed in the economic, political, cultural, and business currents of another country. Many foreign countries do not show the stability of government, currency, or law that permits reliable forecasting.

3. *Forecast of sales potential.* Estimating the company's sales potential requires forecasting its probable market share. The normal difficulties of forecasting market shares are compounded in a foreign marketing environment. The foreign company will find itself competing against other foreign companies as well as against home-country firms. It has to estimate how the buyers will feel about the relative merits of its product, selling methods, and company. Even if the buyers are impartial, their government may put up barriers in the form of quotas, tariffs, taxes, specifications, or even outright boycotts.

4. *Forecast of costs and profits.* Costs will depend on the company's contemplated entry strategy. If it resorts to exporting or licensing, its costs will be spelled out in the contracts. If it decides to locate manufacturing facilities abroad, its cost estimation will require an understanding of local labor conditions, taxes, trade practices, and stipulations regarding the hiring of nationals as key employees. After estimating future costs, the company subtracts them from estimated company sales to find company profits for each year of the planning horizon.

5. *Estimate of rate of return on investment.* The forecasted income stream must be

[4] James K. Sweeney, "A Small Company Enters the European Market," *Harvard Business Review*, September–October 1970, pp. 127–28.

related to the investment stream to derive an implicit rate of return. The estimated rate of return should be high enough to cover (1) the company's normal target return on its investment and (2) the risk and uncertainty of marketing in that country. The risk premium has to cover not only the chance that the basic estimates of sales and costs may be wrong but also the chance that unanticipated monetary changes (devaluation, blocked currency) and political changes (future discrimination against foreign business firms, or even expropriation) may occur.[5]

ENTRY AND OPERATING DECISION

Once a company decides that a particular foreign market represents an attractive opportunity, its task is to determine the best mode of entering that market. Here it has three major options: *exporting* (home production and selling abroad), *joint venturing* (joining with foreign companies in some way), or *direct investment* abroad.[6]

Export   The simplest way for a company to get involved in a foreign market is to arrange to sell some of its present output abroad. Its manufacturing facilities remain located in the home country. The company may or may not modify its product for the foreign market. Exporting allows the company to enter foreign markets with a minimum of change in its product line, company organization, investment, or company mission.

A company can decide to export its product in two broad ways. It can hire independent international marketing middlemen (indirect export), or it can assume direct responsibility for selling to the foreign buyers or importers (direct export).

Indirect export   Indirect export is the more popular of the two for the firm that is just beginning its exporting activity. First, it involves less investment. The firm does not have to develop an overseas sales force or set of contacts. Second, it involves less risk. International marketing middlemen presumably bring knowhow and services to the relationship, and the seller will normally make fewer mistakes.

Three types of domestic middlemen arrangements are available to the exporting company:

1. *Domestic-based export merchant.* This middleman buys the manufacturer's product and sells it abroad on its own account. The exporting company makes its sales simply to the export merchant.

2. *Domestic-based export agent.* In this case the company retains some of the chores and all of the risk, because the agent simply agrees to seek foreign buyers for a commission. Within the agent class there are several variants: *export buying agents* reside in the manufacturer's country, represent foreign buyers, place orders with the manufacturer, take care of shipments, and make payment; *brokers*

---

[5] See David S. R. Leighton, "Deciding When to Enter International Markets," in *Handbook of Modern Marketing*, ed. Victor P. Buell (New York: McGraw-Hill Book Company, 1970), section 20, pp. 23–28.

[6] The discussion of entry channels in this section is indebted to the discussion in Gordon E. Miracle and Gerald S. Albaum, *International Marketing Management* (Homewood, Ill.: Richard D. Irwin, 1970), chaps. 14–16.

exist to find buyers, are paid a commission, and do not handle the products; and *manufacturers' export agents* represent several exporters whose interests are non-competing and carry out selling and other services.

3. *Cooperative organization.* A cooperative organization carries on exporting activities on behalf of several producers and is partly under the administrative control of the producers. This form is often used by producers of primary products—fruits, nuts, and so on—for foreign sales. Another form consists in piggyback arrangements between two or more domestic manufacturers trying to develop a complementary product line for a foreign market.

Direct export Sellers who are approached by foreign buyers will most likely undertake direct export instead of paying service charges to middlemen. So will larger sellers or those whose market has grown to sufficient size to justify undertaking their own export activity. The investment and risk are somewhat greater, but so is the potential return.

Here, too, there are several ways in which the company can carry on direct exporting activity.

1. *Domestic-based export department or division.* This consists of an export sales manager with some clerical assistants. They carry on the actual selling and draw on regular company departments for marketing assistance in such areas as advertising, credit, and logistics. It might evolve into a self-contained export department or sales subsidiary carrying out all the activities involved in export, and may possibly be operated as a profit center.

2. *Overseas sales branch or subsidiary.* This may be established in addition to, or instead of, a domestic export department. An overseas sales branch allows the manufacturer to achieve greater presence and program control in the foreign market. The sales branch handles sales distribution, and it may handle warehousing and promotion as well. It often serves as a display center and customer-service center.

3. *Traveling export sales representatives.* The company can decide to have one or more home-based sales representatives travel abroad at certain times to take orders or find business.

4. *Foreign-based distributors or agents.* Foreign-based distributors would buy and own the goods, foreign-based agents would sell the goods on behalf of the company. They may be given exclusive rights to represent the manufacturer in that country or only general rights.

Joint Venturing A second broad method of entering a foreign market is to join with nationals in the foreign country to set up production and marketing facilities. Joint venturing differs from exporting in that a partnership is formed that leads to some production facilities abroad, and it differs from direct investment in that an association is formed with someone in that country. Four types of joint venture can be distinguished.

Licensing Licensing represents a comparatively simple way for a manufacturer to become involved in international marketing. The licensor enters an agreement with a licensee in the foreign market, offering the right to use a manufacturing process, trademark, patent, trade secret, or other item of value for a fee or royalty. The licensor gains entry into the market at little risk; the licensee gains production expertise, or a well-known product or name, without having to start from scratch. Gerber introduced its baby foods in the Japanese market through a licensing arrangement. It did not have the staff to develop and operate its own production facility, nor did it want to risk the capital loss if the Japanese were not receptive to its products. Coca-Cola has carried out its international marketing activities by licensing bottlers around the world—or, more technically, *franchising* bottlers, because it supplies the syrup needed to produce the product.

Licensing has potential disadvantages in that the firm has less control over the licensee than if it had set up its own production facilities. Furthermore, if the licensee is very successful, the firm has foregone these profits, and if and when the contract ends, it may find it has set up a competitor. To avoid these dangers the licensor must establish a mutual advantage in working together, and a key to doing this is to remain innovative so that the licensee continues to depend on the licensor.

Contract manufacturing   Instead of licensing a foreign company to manufacture and market its products, the firm may wish to retain the marketing responsibility. But it may not be ready to invest in its own foreign production facilities. Under these conditions, an excellent option is to contract with local manufacturers to produce the product. Sears has used this method in opening up department stores abroad, as in Mexico and Spain. Sears enters into contracts with qualified local manufacturers to produce many of the products it sells. Procter & Gamble resorted to contract manufacturing of soap in entering the Italian market, where it faced Colgate and Unilever, who were not only longer entrenched but also owned their production facilities. Contract manufacturing allowed P&G to move in fast and get the feel of the market.

Contract manufacturing has the drawback of less control over the manufacturing process and the loss of potential profits on manufacturing. On the other hand, it offers the manufacturer a chance to get started faster, with less risk, and with the opportunity to possibly form a partnership or buy out the local company if its manufacturing facility operates efficiently.

Management contracting   Here the domestic firm agrees to supply the management know-how to a foreign company that is willing to supply the capital. Thus, the domestic firm is really exporting management services rather than its own products. This arrangement is used by the Hilton hotel system in undertaking to manage hotels throughout the world.

Management contracting is a low-risk method of getting into a foreign market, and it starts yielding income right from the beginning. The arrangement is especially attractive if the contracting firm is given an option to purchase some share in the managed company within a stated period. On the other hand, the arrangement is not sensible if the company can put its scarce management talent to better uses or if there are greater profits to be made by undertaking the whole venture. Management contracting prevents the company from setting up its own operations for a period of time.

Joint-ownership ventures   An increasingly popular arrangement is for foreign investors to join with local investors to create a local business in which they share joint ownership and control. The foreign investor may buy an interest in a local company, a local company may buy an interest in an existing operation of a foreign company, or the two parties may form a new business venture.

From the point of view of the foreign investor, a joint venture may be necessary or desirable for economic or political reasons. Economically, the firm may find it lacks the financial, physical, or managerial resources to undertake the venture alone. Or the foreign government may require joint ownership with local companies as a condition for entry.

Joint ownership can have certain drawbacks for the foreign firm. The partners may disagree over investment, marketing, or other policies. Whereas many American firms like to reinvest earnings for growth, local firms often like to pay out these earnings. Whereas American firms tend to accord a large role to marketing, local investors may see marketing as simply selling. If the American firm has only a minority interest, then its views are overruled in these disagreements. Furthermore, joint venturing can hamper the plans of a multinational company seeking to carry out specific manufacturing and marketing policies on a worldwide basis. The agreement may also make it difficult for the foreign firm to enter other markets where its partner already operates.

Direct Investment

The ultimate form of involvement in a foreign market is investment in foreign-based assembly or manufacturing facilities. Companies just starting out in the market would be well advised to avoid this scale of participation at the outset. However, as experience is gained through export channels, and if the foreign market appears large enough, foreign production facilities offer distinct advantages. The company may secure these advantages partially through licensing or joint-ownership ventures, but if it wants full control (and profits), it may give serious consideration to direct investment.

The advantages of direct investment are several. First, the firm may secure real cost economies in the form of cheaper labor or raw materials, foreign government investment incentives, freight savings, and so on. Second, the firm will gain a better image in the host country because it demonstrates its concern with that country's future. Third, the firm develops a deeper relationship with government, customers, local suppliers, and distributors, enabling it to make a better adaptation of its products to the local marketing environment. Fourth, the firm retains full control over the investment and therefore can develop manufacturing and marketing policies that serve its long-term international objectives.

The main disadvantage is that the firm has exposed a large investment to certain risks, such as blocked or devalued currencies, worsening markets, or expropriation. In some cases, however, the firm has no choice but to accept these risks if it wants to operate effectively in the host country.

Multinational Marketing

We have been examining the nature, advantages, and disadvantages of different modes of entry into a particular foreign market that appears attractive. If the company eventually gets involved in several foreign markets, it will want to begin thinking about its entire system for operating abroad rather than making ad hoc adaptations in each individual market. In fact, it may stop thinking of itself as a national marketer that ventures abroad and instead think of itself as a *global marketer* that operates in many countries, including the "home" country. At this point the company begins to think about developing a worldwide network of production facilities and serving a plurality of markets through a global marketing strategy. Such companies are called multinational corporations. According to Baker:

> The multinational corporation is defined as a company which has a direct investment base in several countries, which generally derives from 20–50 percent or more of its net profits from foreign operations, and whose management makes policy decisions based on the alternatives available anywhere in the world. Approximately 300 such companies are operating and most of these are American.[7]

Multinational corporations include such giants as Unilever, Philips Electric, the Beecham Group, Nestlé, Olivetti, IBM, and Massey-Ferguson. Such corporations must decide very carefully how standardized their marketing should be from country to country. For example, Nestlé strives for uniform quality, branding, labeling, and packaging of its chocolate products; however, its advertising policy is largely decentralized. Beecham, on the other hand, tries to make its advertising policy uniform: if a campaign or idea works well in one country, it will be used elsewhere. A recent survey of twenty-seven leading multinationals in consumer packaged-goods industries reached the following conclusion:

> To the successful multinational, it is not really important whether marketing programs are internationally standardized or differentiated; the important thing is that the *process* through which these programs are developed is standardized. At the heart of this process is the annual marketing-planning system they use.[8]

MARKETING-MIX DECISION

Companies that operate in one or more foreign markets must decide how much, if at all, to adapt their product and marketing mix to local conditions.

Product and Promotion

Keegan distinguished five possible strategies involving the adaptation of product and marketing communications to a foreign market (Figure 25–1).[9]

The first strategy, *straight extension,* means introducing the product in the foreign market in the same form and with the same communications that the company uses at home. It has been used successfully by Pepsi-Cola to introduce its soft drinks everywhere in the world, but it has failed for some other producers, for instance, Philip Morris in the Canadian market and Campbell's tomato soup in the British market. The strategy is a tempting one because it involves no additional expense of research and development, manufacturing retooling or setup, inventory control, or marketing communication reprogramming.

In the second strategy, *communication adaptation,* the company introduces its unchanged product but modifies its communications. For example,

---

[7] James C. Baker, "Multinational Marketing: A Comparative Case Study," in *Marketing in a Changing World,* ed. Bernard A. Morin (Chicago: American Marketing Association, 1969), p. 61.

[8] Ralph Z. Sorenson and Ulrich E. Wiechmann, "How Multinationals View Marketing Standardization," *Harvard Business Review,* May–June 1975, p. 54.

[9] This section relies heavily on Warren J. Keegan, "Multinational Product Planning: Strategic Alternatives," *Journal of Marketing,* January 1969, pp. 58–62.

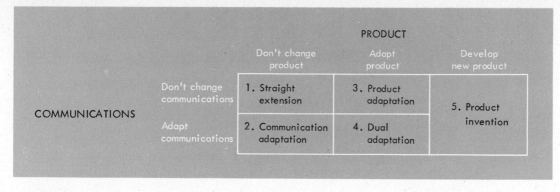

FIGURE 25–1
Five Multinational Product-Marketing Strategies

American bikes are advertised abroad for their transportation rather than pleasure qualities, since bikes are a basic mode of transportation in many other countries. Logic rather than fancy is used in advertising copy in Scandinavia; big, colored illustrations and terse copy in Spain; sex appeal is avoided in Pakistan; and a hundred other communication adaptations are made. The appeal of a communication-adaptation strategy is its relatively low cost of implementation.

The third strategy, *product adaptation*, involves altering the product to meet local conditions or preferences without altering the marketing communications. Thus Heinz varies its baby food products: in Australia, it sells a baby food made from strained lamb brains and in the Netherlands, a baby food made from strained brown beans. Many manufacturers vary the size or contents of their foods, fertilizers, clothing, or appliances to meet local conditions. This strategy involves extra engineering and production cost but may be better than introducing an unaltered product possessing less appeal.

The fourth strategy, *dual adaptation*, involves altering both the product and the communications to increase the product's acceptability. For example, the National Cash Register Company took an innovative step backward by developing and advertising a crank-operated cash register that could sell at half the cost of a modern cash register. This unit caught on greatly in the Philippines, the Orient, Latin America, and Spain. It confirms the existence of *international product life cycles* where countries stand at different stages of readiness to accept a particular product.[10] Dual adaptation is an expensive strategy but is worthwhile if the target markets are large enough.

The last strategy, *product invention*, involves creating a new product to meet a need in another country. For example, there is an enormous need in less-developed countries for low-cost high-protein foods. Companies such as Pillsbury, Swift, and Monsanto are researching the food needs of these countries, formulating new foods, and developing mass-communication programs to gain product trial and acceptance. Product invention would appear to be the costliest of all strategies, but the payoffs to the successful firm also appear to be the greatest.

[10] Louis T. Wells, Jr., "A Product Life Cycle for International Trade?" *Journal of Marketing*, July 1968, pp. 1–6.

Distribution Channels

The international company must take a *whole-channel* view of the problem of getting its products to the final users or consumers. It must see the channel of distribution as an integrated whole, from the manufacturer on one end to the final user or buyer on the other end.[11] Figure 25–2 shows the three major links between the seller and ultimate buyer. The first link, *seller's headquarters organization,* supervises the channels and is part of the channel itself. The second link, *channels between nations,* does the job of getting the products to the overseas markets. The third link, *channels within nations,* is extremely pertinent. Too many American manufacturers think of their channels as ending with the channels between nations, and they fail to observe what happens to their product once it arrives in the foreign market. If the channels within the foreign market are weak or inefficient, then the target customers fail to achieve satisfaction, and the company fails to achieve its international objectives.

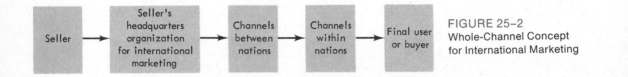

FIGURE 25–2
Whole-Channel Concept
for International Marketing

With respect to consumer goods, within-country channels of distribution vary considerably from country to country. There are striking differences in the *size distribution of retailing units.* For example, food channels in the United States are dominated by the large supermarket chain; in France, supermarkets are growing in number, but food retailing is still dominated by small merchants with modest stores; in India, food is sold mainly through thousands of individual tradesmen squatting in open markets or selling in tiny shops. Second, the *services offered* by retailers vary considerably, with much more personal attention and bargaining in countries such as India as compared with the United States. Third, there tends to be greater specialization in the *assortment of goods* handled by retailers in the lower-income economies. Fourth, the retailing system in other countries tends to be more *stratified* according to class structure; thus selecting the retailer is tantamount to selecting the social class the product will reach.[12]

With respect to industrial goods, within-country channels in advanced countries resemble those found in the United States. In the less-developed countries, importers are strong, and the foreign company must often leave its products in their hands. If it seeks its own distributors, it must carefully sort out the good ones from the poor ones. Often the company has to offer exclusive distribution to a local distributor, and its fate in this market is tied up with how well it has chosen its distributor.

Pricing

Manufacturers often price their products lower for the foreign market than for the domestic market. This may be a response to lower incomes abroad, keener competition, or the use of the foreign market as a dumping ground for surpluses. Although the price quoted to merchants abroad may be lower, these merchants

[11] See Miracle and Albaum, *International Marketing Management,* pp. 317–19.

[12] These retailing variations are discussed in John Fayerweather, *International Marketing* (Englewood Cliffs, N.J.: Prentice-Hall, 1965), p. 63.

may not lower the retail price. Foreign middlemen often prefer high unit margins, even though they lead to a smaller volume. They also like to buy on credit, although that increases the manufacturer's cost and risk.

INTERNATIONAL-MARKETING-ORGANIZATION DECISION

Firms manage their international marketing activities in many different ways. The different organizational arrangements often parallel their degree of involvement and experience in international marketing and their international marketing objectives.

Export
Department

A firm normally gets started in international marketing by responding to a few orders that come in fortuitously. At first it simply ships out the goods. If its international sales expand, the company usually organizes an export department consisting of a sales manager and a few clerical assistants. As sales increase further, the staff of the export department is expanded to include various marketing services so that it can go after business more aggressively and not depend on the domestic staff. If the firm moves beyond exports into a program of joint ventures or direct investment, the export department will no longer serve these purposes.

International
Division

Many companies eventually become involved in a number of different international markets and ventures. A company may export to one country, license to another, have a joint-ownership venture in a third, and own a subsidiary in a fourth, and it may eventually create an international division or subsidiary with responsibility for all of its international activity. The international division is headed by a president (who usually ranks as one of the corporation's divisional vice presidents). The president has goals and budgets and is given total responsibility for the company's growth in the international market.

International divisions, like domestic divisions, are organized in a variety of ways. Usually the international division's corporate staff consists of functional specialists in marketing, manufacturing, research, finance, planning, and personnel. This staff will plan for, and provide services to, various operating units. The operating units may be organized according to one or more of three principles. First, the operating units may be *geographical organizations*. For example, reporting to the international division president (in addition to the division staff) may be vice presidents for different areas, such as North America, Latin America, Europe, Africa, and the Far East. Each area vice president is responsible for a sales force, sales branches, distributors, and licensees in his or her area. Or the operating units may be *product-group organizations*, with a vice president responsible for worldwide sales of each product group. The vice presidents may draw on corporate staff area specialists for expertise on different areas. Finally, the operating units may be *international subsidiaries*, each headed by a president. The various subsidiary presidents report to the president of the international division.

A major disadvantage of the international-division concept is that the corporation's top management may think of it as just another division and never really get involved enough to fully appreciate and plan for global marketing. Top management may not give the division the attention it deserves, and in difficult times may deprive it of adequate supplies or budget.

Multinational Organization

Several firms have passed beyond the international-division organization into a truly multinational organization. This means the top corporate management and staff are involved in the worldwide planning of manufacturing facilities, marketing policies, financial flows, and logistical systems. The various operating units around the world report directly to the chief executive or executive committee, not to the head of an international division. The company trains its executives in worldwide operations, not just domestic *or* international. Management talent is recruited from many countries; components and supplies are purchased where they can be obtained at the least cost; and investments are made where the anticipated returns are greatest.

There is good reason to believe that major companies will have to go multinational in the 1980s if they are going to grow. As foreign companies continue to invade the home market with some success, home companies will have to move aggressively into those international markets that are best suited to their distinctive products and competencies.

SUMMARY

International marketing does not involve any principles not found in domestic marketing, but nevertheless it deserves special attention because of (1) its growing importance as an area of marketing opportunity and (2) its greater level of risk and uncertainty stemming from the marketer's unfamiliarity with other cultures. Doing business abroad requires learning about quite different economic, political, and cultural environments. The company should make a decision in favor of international marketing only when the opportunities appear attractive relative to those at home and the resources are available for carrying out international marketing.

In moving abroad, the first step is to compare the various foreign markets and make market selections on the basis of a hard evaluation of the probable rate of return on investment. Given an attractive market, it can be entered in three ways: export, joint venturing, and direct investment. Many companies start as exporters, move to joint venturing, and finally undertake direct investment as their overseas business expands. A few become multinational corporations with worldwide markets and operating strategies. Companies must also decide on the extent to which their products, communications, distribution, and pricing should be adapted and individuated to individual foreign markets. Finally, they must develop an effective organization for pursuing international marketing. Most firms start with an export department and graduate to an international division. A few pass this stage and move to a multinational organization, which means that worldwide marketing is planned and managed by the top officers of the corporation.

QUESTIONS AND PROBLEMS

1. Develop a list of American products that might have a good reception in Greece. Select one of these and discuss the major problems you anticipate.

2. Pepsi-Cola has used the advertising theme "Now It's Pepsi for Those Who Think Young" quite successfully in the United States. Do you think the same theme makes sense in the Netherlands? Liberia? Hong Kong?

3. A U.S. heavy equipment manufacturer operating in Western Europe has been using Americans as salesmen. The company feels that it could reduce its costs by hiring and

training nationals for salesmen. What are the advantages and disadvantages of using Americans versus nationals for selling abroad?

4. A large American tire company decided to enter the French tire market some years ago. The company produced tires for medium-sized trucks designed to meet the official rear-axle weights. Its subsequent experience was bad, many of its tires blowing out. The company acquired a poor image in France as a result. What went wrong?

5. Select one of the following nations—Italy, Japan, or U.S.S.R.—and describe its marketing institutions and practices.

Nonbusiness Marketing

> *Man does not live by GNP alone.*
> PAUL SAMUELSON

Most of the examples of marketing presented in this book have been drawn from the business sector of the economy. That is because marketing theory and practice began and reached its highest level of development in this sector. Starting in the 1970s, however, there has been a "broadening of marketing" to cover all organizations, on the grounds that all organizations have marketing problems that can be aided by the application of marketing principles.[1] The public and non-profit sectors in particular account for more than a quarter of the American economy and are badly in need of improved management and marketing practices.

Marketing in the public and nonprofit sectors, like marketing in the international economy, does not involve new marketing principles so much as new and challenging applications of these principles. Weinberg and Lovelock have

---

[1] See Philip Kotler and Sidney J. Levy, "Broadening the Concept of Marketing," *Journal of Marketing*, January 1969, pp. 10–15; David J. Luck, "Broadening the Concept of Marketing—Too Far," *Journal of Marketing*, July 1969, pp. 53–55; Philip Kotler, *Marketing for Nonprofit Organizations* (Englewood Cliffs, N. J.: Prentice-Hall, 1975); Christopher H. Lovelock and Charles B. Weinberg, *Cases in Public and Nonprofit Marketing* (Palo Alto, Calif.: Scientific Press, 1977); and Ralph M. Gaedeke, ed., *Marketing in Private and Public Nonprofit Organizations: Perspectives and Illustrations* (Santa Monica, Calif.: Goodyear Publishing Co., 1977).

identified four major characteristics of the nonbusiness sector that call for special attention in seeking to apply marketing principles.[2] They are:

1. **Multiple publics.** Nonbusiness organizations normally have at least two major publics to work with from a marketing point of view: their clients and their funders. The former pose the problem of resource allocation and the latter, the problem of resource attraction.[3] Besides these two publics, many other publics surround the nonbusiness organization and can be dealt with in marketing terms. Thus a college can direct marketing programs toward prospective students, current students, parents of students, alumni, faculty, staff, local business firms, and local government agencies. It turns out that business organizations also deal with a multitude of publics, but their tendency is to think about marketing only in connection with one of these publics, namely, their customers.

2. **Multiple objectives.** Nonbusiness organizations tend to pursue simultaneously several objectives rather than pursuing only one, such as profits. As a result, it is more difficult to evaluate strategic alternatives facing the organization. The management must do its best to explicate the organization's multiple objectives and their relative weight so that some useful evaluation of strategies and resource allocations can be made. Business organizations also have multiple objectives, but these tend to be dominated by the drive for profits.

3. **Services rather than physical goods.** Most nonbusiness organizations are engaged in the production of services rather than goods. As such, they need to draw primarily upon marketing principles used in the marketing of services.

4. **Public scrutiny and nonmarket pressures.** Nonbusiness organizations are usually subject to close public scrutiny because they provide needed public services, are subsidized, are tax exempt, and in many cases are mandated into existence. They experience political pressures from various publics and are expected to operate in the public interest. This means that any marketing activity they engage in will come under public scrutiny.

This chapter will examine how managers of nonprofit and public institutions can apply marketing thinking to the problems of their institutions. We will first examine major types of nonbusiness organizations, then examples of marketing problems and solutions facing colleges, hospitals, and other types of nonbusiness organizations, and finally steps that can be taken to introduce formal marketing responsibility into these nonbusiness organizations.

TYPES OF NONBUSINESS ORGANIZATIONS

Of the various ways to classify organizations in a society, we are primarily interested in two distinctions: (1) whether the organization is privately or publicly owned and operated and (2) whether the organization is organized for profit or nonprofit purposes. These two distinctions lead to the four types of organizations shown in Figure 26–1.

[2] Christopher H. Lovelock and Charles B. Weinberg, "Public and Nonprofit Marketing Comes of Age," in *Review of Marketing 1978*, ed. Gerald Zaltman and Thomas V. Bonoma (Chicago: American Marketing Association, 1978), pp. 413–52.

[3] See Benson P. Shapiro, "Marketing for Nonprofit Organizations," *Harvard Business Review*, September–October 1973, pp. 123–32.

	Private	Public
Profit	**I** Single proprietorships Partnerships Corporations	**II** State-owned airlines State-owned telephone co.
Nonprofit	**IV** Private museums Private charities Private universities Private associations Private hospitals	**III** Government agencies Public schools Public hospitals

FIGURE 26–1
Four Types of Organizations

Quadrant I shows private, for-profit firms and is called, at least in the United States, the *first sector* because it has been entrusted with doing most of society's economic work—producing food, clothing, shelter, and so on.

Quadrants II and III make up the *second sector* (or public sector) and include all of the government organizations set up to carry on residual societal functions that do not yield a profit, have to be performed, and warrant public control. Included are such classic governmental functions as defense, public works, public education, and justice. Most of the public sector organizations are in Quadrant III. However, the government may also own and operate a few enterprises for profit (or at least cost recovery), and these are shown in Quadrant II. Government organizations may be further classified into the following four types:[4]

1. *Business type.* Government organizations that perform economic work, such as the U.S. Post Office or a municipal bus company.
2. *Service type.* Government organizations that provide public services not normally provided by private enterprise, such as public schools, public libraries, police and fire departments, military service organizations, sanitation and water departments, parks and recreation departments, public health and hospital agencies, museums, and symphonies.
3. *Transfer type.* Government organizations that transfer income or aid from one group to another, such as social security administration, city and state welfare departments, and internal revenue service.
4. *Regulation type.* Government organizations that regulate the conduct of other organizations or individuals, such as penitentiaries, courts, and regulatory commissions.

Quadrant IV covers the remaining organizations in the society, those operated privately and not for profit. It is called the *third sector* (or nonprofit sector).

[4] For an alternative classification of government organizations, see William L. Shanklin, "New York City: A Portrait in Marketing Mania," *California Management Review,* winter 1975, pp. 34–40.

Nonprofits perform those societal functions that do not yield a profit, are desirable to perform, and need not be under public control. Third sector organizations represent a *middle way* for meeting social needs, without resorting to the profit motive on the one hand or government bureaucracy on the other. These organizations specialize in the delivery of societal services that are not adequately provided by either business or government. The third sector contains tens of thousands of private not-for-profit organizations, ranging from The Society for the Preservation and Encouragement of Barber Shop Quartet Singing in America to major foundations, colleges, hospitals, museums, charities, social agencies, and churches. In fact, nonprofit organizations can be classified into eight groups:

1. *Religious organizations.* Churches, church associations, evangelical movements.
2. *Social organizations.* Service clubs, fraternal organizations.
3. *Cultural organizations.* Museums, symphonies, opera companies, art leagues, zoos.
4. *Knowledge organizations.* Private grade schools, private colleges and universities, research organizations.
5. *Protective organizations.* Trade associations, trade unions.
6. *Political organizations.* Political parties, lobbyist groups.
7. *Philanthropic organizations.* Private welfare organizations, private foundations, charity hospitals, nursing homes.
8. *Social-cause organizations.* Peace groups, family-planning groups, environmental groups, racial rights groups, consumerist groups, women's rights groups, antivice groups.

ENTER MARKETING

Of all the classic business functions, marketing has been the last to arrive on the public and nonprofit scene. Some years earlier, managers of nonbusiness organizations began to get interested in accounting systems, financial management, personnel administration, and formal planning. As long as these organizations operated in the seller's market of the 1960s, marketing was largely ignored. This situation changed, however, when the same organizations began to experience a decline in clients, members, or funds. Consider the following developments:

More than 170 private colleges have closed their doors since 1965, unable to get either enough students or funds, or both. Tuition at the top private universities is now over $6,000. If college costs continue to climb at the current rate, the parents of a child born today will have to put aside $82,830 to buy that child a bachelor's degree at one of the better private colleges.[5]

Hospital costs continue to soar, leading to daily room rates of $300 or more in some large hospitals. Many hospitals are experiencing underutilization, particularly in the maternity and pediatrics sections. Some experts have predicted the closing of 1,400 to 1,500 hospitals in the next ten years.

The Catholic Church drew as many as 55 percent of all adult Catholics under

[5] See Donald L. Pyke, "The Future of Higher Education: Will Private Institutions Disappear in the U.S.?" *The Futurist*, December 1977, p. 374.

thirty years of age to church in a typical week in 1966. By 1975, the figure had fallen to 39 percent, and further declines in weekly attendance were expected.

Many performing-arts groups cannot attract large enough audiences. Even those that have seasonal sellouts, such as the Lyric Opera Company of Chicago, face huge operating deficits at the end of the year.

Many third-sector organizations that flourished in earlier years—the YMCA, Salvation Army, Girl Scouts, and Women's Christian Temperance Union—presently are reexamining their mission in an effort to reverse membership declines.

In a word, these organizations have marketplace problems. Their administrators are struggling to keep them alive in the face of rapidly changing societal needs, increasing public and private competition, changing client attitudes, and diminishing financial resources. Board members and supporters are asking administrators tough questions about the organization's mission, opportunities, and strategies. As a result, these organizations are now showing a growing interest in marketing. Here is what is happening in a few select "nonbusiness" industries.

Colleges

Colleges are facing an increasingly grim marketing scenario. (1) The annual number of high school graduates will decline from a peak of 3.2 million in 1977 to 2.8 million in 1982–83. (2) The proportion of high school students electing to go to college might decline. (3) A higher proportion of college-bound students are electing to attend community colleges instead of four-year colleges. (4) The absolute and relative future level of tuition will deter college going in general and hurt private colleges in particular.[6]

What are college administrators doing about these problems? One group is doing nothing. Either enrollment hasn't slipped, or if it has, the administrators believe the decline is temporary. Many believe it is "unprofessional" to go out and "sell" their colleges.

A second group has responded by increasing the budget of the admissions office, which serves as the college's sales department. The admissions office then dreams up new ways to attract more applicants. For example:

The admissions office at North Kentucky State University planned to release 103 balloons filled with scholarship offers.

The admissions staff of one college passed out promotional frisbees to high school students vacationing on the beaches of Fort Lauderdale during the annual Easter break.

St. Joseph's College in Renssalaer, Indiana, achieved a 40 percent increase in freshmen admissions through advertising in *Seventeen* and on several Chicago and Indianapolis rock radio stations. The admissions office also planned to introduce tuition rebates for students who recruited new students ($100 finder's fee) but this plan was cancelled.

Bard College developed a same-day-admission system for students who walk into their office and qualify.

Worcester Polytech offers negotiable admission in which credit is negotiated for previous study or work experience to shorten the degree period.

[6] See *A Role for Marketing in College Admissions* (New York: College Entrance Examination Board, 1976), p. 54 and elsewhere.

The University of Richmond has spent $13,000 to create a twelve-minute film for showings to high school students and other interested publics.

Drake University advertised on a billboard near O'Hare Airport in Chicago that "Drake is only 40 minutes from Chicago" (if one flies).

Promotional competition has not yet led to premiums given to students for enrollment (free radio, typewriter) or offers of "satisfaction guaranteed or your money back," but these may come.

In equating marketing with intensified promotion by the admissions office, these colleges may create new problems for themselves. Aggressive promotion tends to produce strong negative reactions among the school's constituencies, especially the faculty, who regard hard selling as offensive. Also, promotion may turn off as many prospective students and families as it turns on. Aggressive promotion can attract the wrong students to the college—students who drop out when they discover they don't have the ability to do the work or decide that the college is not what it was advertised to be. Finally, this kind of marketing creates the illusion that the college has undertaken sufficient response to declining enrollment—an illusion that slows down the needed work on "product improvement," which is the basis of all good marketing.[7]

A genuine marketing response has been undertaken by a relatively small number of colleges. Their approach is best described as *market-oriented institutional planning*. In this approach, marketing is recognized as much more than mere promotion, and indeed, the issue of promotion cannot be settled in principle until more fundamental issues are resolved. These institutions are analyzing their environment, markets, and consumer behavior; assessing their existing resources and resource needs; and developing a clear sense of mission, market targets, and market positioning. By doing its homework on market, resource, and missions analysis, a college is in a better position to make decisions that improve student and faculty recruitment and institutional fund raising.

As an example, the University of Houston recently completed an intensive institutional audit using several faculty task forces. The final report presented recommendations on the university's mission, strategy, and portfolio. The portfolio section recommended which components of the university's "product mix" (schools and departments) should be built, maintained, phased down, or phased out. The criteria included: (1) the centrality of that academic program to the mission of the university, (2) the program's academic quality, and (3) the program's market viability. Thus, a department of women's studies that is marginal to the mission of the school, of low national reputation, and unable to attract an adequate number of students would be slated for phasing down or out.

Hospitals Hospitals are beginning to treat marketing as a "hot" topic. A few years ago, health professionals scorned the idea of marketing, imagining that it would lead to ads such as "This week's special—brain surgery—only $195." Hospital administrators also argued that patients didn't choose hospitals, their doctors did; so marketing, to be effective, would have to be directed to doctors.

Nevertheless, some hospitals began to take their first steps toward market-

[7] See "Rest in Pace," *Newsweek*, April 11, 1977, p. 96.

ing. A few rushed into marketing with more enthusiasm than understanding, believing it to consist of clever promotional gimmicks. For example:

> Sunrise Hospital in Las Vegas ran a large advertisement featuring the picture of a ship with the caption, "Introducing the Sunrise Cruise, Win a Once-in-a-Lifetime Cruise Simply by Entering Sunrise Hospital on Any Friday or Saturday: Recuperative Mediterranean Cruise for Two."

> St. Luke's Hospital in Phoenix introduced nightly bingo games for all patients (except cardiac cases), producing immense patient interest as well as a net annual profit of $60,000.

> A Philadelphia hospital, in competing for maternity patients, let the public know that the parents of a newborn child would enjoy a candlelight dinner with steak and champagne on the eve before the mother and child's departure from the hospital.

> A number of hospitals, in their competition to attract and retain physicians, have added "ego services," such as saunas, chauffeurs, and even private tennis courts.

Fortunately, some hospitals are now beginning to apply marketing to a broader set of problems. Where should the hospital locate a new branch or ambulatory care unit? How can the hospital estimate whether a new service will draw enough patients? How can the hospital attract more consumers to preventive care services, such as annual medical checkups and cancer-screening tests? How can a hospital successfully compete in the recruitment of highly trained specialists who are in short supply? What marketing programs can attract nurses, build community goodwill, attract more contributions?

The marketing naiveté of the typical hospital is illustrated in the following episode:

> A medium-size hospital in southern Illinois decided to establish an adult day-care center as a solution to its underutilized space. It designed a whole floor to serve senior citizens who required personal care and services in an ambulatory setting during the day, but who would return home each evening. The cost was $16 a day, and transportation was to be provided by the patient's relatives. About the only research that was done on this concept was to note that a lot of elderly people lived within a three-mile radius. The center was opened with a capacity to handle thirty patients. Only two signed up!

An increasing number of hospital administrators are now attending marketing seminars to learn more about marketing research and new-service development. The Evanston Hospital of Evanston, Illinois, a major 500-bed facility, appointed the world's first hospital vice president of marketing. Recently, MacStravic published a book devoted entirely to hospital marketing,[8] and many articles are now appearing on health-care marketing.[9]

Other Institutions   In addition to colleges and hospitals, other institutions are paying more attention to marketing. The YMCA is taking a fresh look at its mission, services, and

[8] Robin E. MacStravic, *Marketing Health Care* (Germantown, Md.: Aspen Systems Corporation, 1977).

[9] See, for example, the special issue on marketing of *Hospitals, Journal of the American Hospital Association*, June 1, 1977.

clients in order to develop new services and markets for the 1980s. Major charities like the Multiple Sclerosis Society, the American Heart Association, and the March of Dimes are investigating marketing ideas that go beyond selling and advertising. Marketing successes have been reported by arts institutions.[10] It is likely that within ten years, most of the third sector and a good part of the second sector will have some understanding and appreciation of the marketing concept.

SOCIAL MARKETING

The term *social marketing* was first introduced in 1971 to describe the use of marketing principles and techniques to advance a social cause, idea, or practice.[11] More specifically:

> *Social marketing* is the design, implementation, and control of programs seeking to increase the acceptability of a social idea, cause, or practice in a target group(s). It utilizes market segmentation, consumer research, concept development, communications, facilitation, incentives, and exchange theory to maximize target group response.

Other names for social marketing are *social-cause marketing* or *idea marketing.*[12] Examples of social marketing would include public health campaigns to reduce smoking, alcoholism, drug abuse, and overeating; environmental campaigns to promote wilderness protection, clean air, and resource conservation; and a myriad of other campaigns, such as family planning, women's rights, and racial equality.

Social marketing, in contrast to ordinary business marketing, is more a change technology than a response technology. For example, an anticigarette-smoking group is attempting to get people to stop doing something they want to do. To this extent, social marketing seems to be based on the selling concept rather than the marketing concept. Yet the lesson of a consumer orientation is not lost on the social marketer. The social marketer tries to understand why smokers smoke, what pleasures they get, and what difficulties they have in trying to stop smoking. All of this is important in trying to formulate an effective marketing plan that will encourage people to give up smoking.

Social marketing may aim to produce one of four types of change in a target market. The first is a *cognitive change,* that is, a change in the target group's knowledge or understanding of something. An example would be a campaign to increase the public's understanding of the nutritional value of different foods. The second is an *action change,* that is, an effort to get a target market to carry out a specific action in a given period, such as showing up for a vaccination or

---

[10] See Danny Newman, *Subscribe Now! Building Arts Audiences through Dynamic Subscription Promotion* (New York: Theatre Communications Group, 1977). This book deals primarily with the use of promotion as a marketing tool rather than with overall marketing strategy.

[11] See Philip Kotler and Gerald Zaltman, "Social Marketing: An Approach to Planned Social Change," *Journal of Marketing,* July 1971, pp. 3–12.

[12] The term *social marketing* has subsequently acquired other usages. For instance, it is used in referring to "socially responsible marketing" by business firms or to any marketing done by nonprofit organizations. Hence more specific terms may be needed.

voting in a referendum. The third is a *behavioral change,* seeking to get the target market to change a certain pattern of behavior, such as using an auto seatbelt or giving up smoking. The fourth is a *value change,* that is, attempting to alter a target group's deeply felt beliefs or values toward some object or situation. An example would be to change people's ideas about family planning or abortion. Social marketing gets progressively more difficult as one goes from trying to produce a cognitive change to trying to produce a value change.

The following things should be noted about social marketing:

1. *Social marketing is more than social advertising.* There is a long history of ad campaigns to promote public-interest causes. But social marketing goes beyond communication efforts and incorporates other elements of the marketing mix, such as product, price, and place to increase the likelihood of achieving the desired response. Wiebe, in his study of four social campaigns, showed how their differential success was related to how closely they resembled the conditions of selling a normal product or service.[13] The great success of the Kate Smith radio marathon to sell bonds one evening during World War II was due, in Wiebe's opinion, to the presence of *force* (patriotism), *direction* (buy bonds), *mechanism* (banks, post offices, telephone orders), *adequacy and compatibility* (many centers to purchase the bonds), and *distance* (ease of purchase). These easily translate into such factors as product, price, place, and promotion. The other three social campaigns studied by Wiebe—recruiting Civil Defense volunteers, stimulating people to take steps to help juvenile delinquents, and arousing citizens against crime—met with much less success because of the lack or mishandling of product, price, place, or promotion variables.

2. *Social marketing can be carried out by any group or organization.* Any organization with a cause can approach its task through developing a marketing plan. Thus social marketing can be said to take place if Procter & Gamble sponsors a campaign in a developing nation aimed at encouraging people to take better care of their teeth or Coca-Cola sponsors a campaign calling upon people not to carelessly throw away their used soft-drink containers in public places.

3. *Social marketing is possible with any side of an issue.* The concepts and techniques making up social marketing are available to all sides of an issue. We cannot call it social marketing if we agree with the cause and propaganda if we disagree with it. Proabortion groups and antiabortion groups can both use social marketing.

Social marketing is only one of several strategies available to change agents. The other change strategies are: (1) violent action, (2) legal action, (3) social engineering, (4) social propaganda, (5) social advertising, and (6) economic action. Social marketing is substantially different in form and content from violent action, legal action, and social propaganda. On the other hand, it builds on the idea of social engineering, social advertising, and economic action. Social marketing is not a pure approach but rather a higher-order integration of the functions of incentivization, facilitation, and communication as applied to the problem of influencing the free and voluntary behavior of individuals and groups in an open society. It represents a democratic change technology that is positioned between the extremes of force on the one hand and brainwashing on the other.

[13] G. D. Wiebe, "Merchandising Commodities and Citizenship on Television," *Public Opinion Quarterly,* winter 1951–52, pp. 679–91.

The social marketer, in designing a social-change strategy, goes through a normal marketing-planning process. The first step is to define the social-change objective. Suppose the objective is "to reduce the number of teenage smokers from 60 to 40 percent of the teenage population within five years." The next step is to analyze the beliefs, attitudes, values, and behavior of the target group, here teenagers, and to identify key segments of the target market who would respond to different marketing approaches. An analysis is also made of the major competitive forces that support teenage smoking. This is followed by concept research in which the social marketer generates and tests alternative concepts that might be effective in dissuading teenagers from smoking. The next step is channel analysis, in which the social marketer identifies and assesses the most effective communication and distribution approaches to the target market. This is followed by the formal development of a marketing plan and a marketing organization to carry it out. Finally, provision is made to continuously monitor results and take corrective action when called for.

Social marketing is still too new to evaluate its effectiveness in comparison with other social-change strategies. Social change itself is hard to produce with any strategy, let alone one that relies on voluntary response. So far, the ideas of social marketing have been mainly applied in the areas of family planning,[14] environmental protection,[15] improved nutrition, auto driver safety, and public transportation, with some encouraging successes. Evaluating the full effects of social marketing campaigns is not an easy task.

Social-marketing campaigns, when completely successful, would have the following six attributes: (1) high incidence of adoption; (2) high speed of adoption; (3) high continuance of adoption; (4) no major counterproductive consequences; (5) low cost per unit of successful adoption; and (6) open and moral means.

IMPLEMENTING MARKETING IN NONBUSINESS ORGANIZATIONS

The interesting thing about marketing is that all organizations carry on marketing whether they know it or not. When this dawns on a nonprofit organization, the response is much like Moliere's character in *Le Bourgeois Gentilhomme* who exclaims: "Good Heavens! For more than forty years I have been speaking prose without knowing it." Colleges, for example, search for prospects (students), develop products (courses), price them (tuition and fees), distribute them (announce time and place), and promote them (college catalogs). Similarly, hospitals, social agencies, cultural groups, and other nonprofit organizations also carry on marketing in some fashion.

For nonbusiness organizations that would like to improve their marketing effectiveness, several alternatives are available, including appointing a marketing committee, setting up marketing task forces, hiring outside marketing specialists, and setting up an internal marketing position (see chap. 22, pp. 596–99).

For example, from time to time the organization should engage the

---

[14] Eduardo Roberto, *Strategic Decision-Making in a Social Program: The Case of Family-Planning Diffusion* (Lexington, Mass.: Lexington Books, 1975).

[15] Karl E. Henion, II, *Ecological Marketing* (Columbus, Ohio: Grid, 1976).

services of marketing specialist firms. A marketing research firm might be hired to survey the needs, perceptions, preferences, and satisfaction of the client market. An advertising agency might be hired to develop a corporate identification program or an advertising campaign. As a further step, the organization might hire a marketing consultant to carry out a comprehensive *marketing audit* on the problems and opportunities facing that organization.

Eventually the organization might be ready to appoint a director of marketing. The job is conceived as a middle-management position, created primarily to provide marketing services to others in the institution. A major issue is, What is the marketing director's relationship to those responsible for such related functions as planning, public relations, and fund raising? A good case could be made for locating the marketing director within the planning office, where he or she reports to the vice president of planning. It would not make sense for the marketing director to report to public relations or fund raising because that would overspecialize the use made of marketing.

The ultimate solution is the establishment of a vice president of marketing position in nonprofit organizations. This is an upper-level management position, which gives more scope, authority, and influence to marketing. A vice president of marketing not only coordinates and supplies analytical services but also has a strong voice in the determination of where the institution should be going in terms of its changing opportunities. The vice president of marketing would be responsible for planning and managing relations with several publics of the institution. The person's title may be altered to that of vice president of institutional relations or external affairs to avoid unnecessary semantic opposition.

SUMMARY   Marketing is beginning to attract the attention of nonbusiness administrators. There is a growing body of literature on college, hospital, and other nonbusiness marketing, as well as increased attendance at conferences on marketing for nonbusiness organizations. The interest is precipitated by changing societal needs, increasing public and private competition, changing client attitudes, and diminishing financial resources.

Nonbusiness marketing does not involve new principles so much as it challenges applications, given that nonbusiness organizations tend to have multiple publics, multiple objectives, a service rather than goods technology, and greater public scrutiny and nonmarket pressures.

In becoming interested in marketing, some nonbusiness organizations see it primarily as a promotion function and increase their budgets for advertising, sales promotion, and personal selling. Others recognize it as a planning approach calling for better competitive positioning, product development, and consumer-need satisfaction. Hospitals, colleges, YMCAs, art institutions, and churches are among those organizations currently showing the most interest in marketing.

Social marketing refers to the use of marketing principles to increase the acceptability of a social idea, cause, or practice in a target group(s). Social marketing may aim at producing a change in beliefs, action, behavior, or values. It differs from social advertising by utilizing all four elements of the marketing mix. It can be carried out by any group regardless of its ideological position. Social marketing is a higher-order integration of social engineering, social advertising, and economic action that is undertaken to effect a voluntary change in behavior by members of the target audience.

Nonbusiness organizations can introduce marketing through appointing a marketing committee or marketing task force, hiring outside marketing specialists, and setting up a position of marketing director or marketing vice president. A marketing audit will reveal the many opportunities for the application of marketing in that institution, and the marketing executive can proceed to tackle those problems that are most urgent, significant, and feasible.

QUESTIONS AND PROBLEMS

1. A major university has decided to hire a director of marketing. You are asked to prepare a job description for this position. Describe the scope, functions, and responsibilities of this position.

2. The Samaritan Hospital has appointed a new vice-president of marketing. The vice-president holds meetings with hospital physicians and nurses, describing his skills and inviting them to suggest projects. He receives more than enough suggestions and in fact has to prioritize them. What criteria might he use to rank the proposed projects so that he can attend to the more "important" ones first?

3. An anti-smoking group is preparing to launch a major campaign to get people to quit smoking. A representative of the cigarette industry complained that the campaign, if it succeeds in getting people to quit smoking, will have the effect in many cases of shortening people's lives. What could he possibly have in mind?

4. In the early days of family planning in India, a commission was paid to "agents" who would find men who would be willing to be vasectomized. The commission rate was attractive enough to lead to certain abuses. What are some of the potential abuses and how can they be prevented?

5. In a million-dollar campaign to get people to snap on their auto seat belts while driving, it was estimated that the campaign saved one hundred lives, at a cost-per-life-saved of $10,000. This seemed like a very worthwhile use of public money. Do you agree that more public money should be put into seat belt campaigns?

6. The executive director of a private philanthropic organization saw an advertisement for a book entitled *Marketing for Nonprofit Organizations*. He decided against ordering a copy because his business is to give away money, not to market anything. Would you agree that a private philanthropic organization does not need to understand marketing concepts?

7. The conductor of a symphony orchestra states: "If we adopt a marketing orientation and give the audiences just what they want to hear, we'd be putting on some pretty conventional music. We'd never get a chance to play anything new and daring." Should the conductor adopt the marketing concept?

8. Develop a social marketing campaign to influence people to buy two-way bottles instead of the convenient throwaway bottles. What appeals would you use? What pricing mechanism? How much funding would you need? Do you think the campaign has much chance of success?

9. The New York Metropolitan Museum of Art is seeking to increase its membership, which begins at $15 a year. It believes that persons would respond more to selfish reasons for joining the museum than to broad social appeals. In this connection, the Met is trying to develop at least five tangible benefits that would go with museum membership. Can you suggest five benefits and prepare an ad that displays them?

Marketing in the Contemporary Environment

Marketing is a constantly evolving craft and discipline. As society changes, so do our ideas of what constitutes effective and socially responsible marketing. Starting in the mid-1960s, several forces arose to challenge some of the major premises of marketing practice. These forces constitute a new marketing environment and pose challenging questions about the appropriate character of effective and socially responsible marketing in the years ahead. In this chapter we shall consider seven of these forces: consumerism, environmentalism, shortages, inflation, recession, government regulations, and marketing ethics.

CONSUMERISM

Starting in the 1960s, American business firms found themselves the target of a growing consumer movement.[1] Consumers had become better educated; products had become increasingly complex and hazardous; discontent with American institutions was widespread; influential writers accused big business of wasteful and manipulative practices; presidential messages of Kennedy and Johnson dis-

---

[1] The discussion in this section is adapted from the author's "What Consumerism Means for Marketers," *Harvard Business Review,* May–June 1972, pp. 48–57.

cussed consumer rights; congressional investigations of certain industries proved embarrassing; and finally Ralph Nader appeared on the scene to crystallize many of the issues.

Since these early stirrings, many private consumer organizations have emerged, several pieces of consumer legislation have been passed, and several state and local offices of consumer affairs have been created. Furthermore, the consumer movement has taken on an international character with much strength in Scandinavia and the Low Countries and a growing presence in France, Germany, and Japan.

But what is this movement? Put simply, *consumerism is an organized movement of concerned citizens and government to enhance the rights and power of buyers in relation to sellers.* The traditional sellers' rights include:

1. The right to introduce any product in any size and style, provided it is not hazardous to personal health or safety; or, if it is, to introduce it with the proper warnings and controls
2. The right to price the product at any level, provided there is no discrimination among similar classes of buyers
3. The right to spend any amount of money to promote the product, provided it is not defined as unfair competition
4. The right to formulate any product message, provided it is not misleading or dishonest in content or execution
5. The right to introduce any buying-incentive schemes they wish

The traditional buyers' rights include:

1. The right not to buy a product that is offered for sale
2. The right to expect the product to be safe
3. The right to expect the product to be what is claimed

Comparing these rights, many believe that the balance of power lies on the sellers' side. It is true that the buyer can refuse to buy any product. But it is generally felt that the buyer is really without sufficient information, education, and protection to make wise decisions in the face of highly sophisticated sellers. Consumer advocates therefore call for the following additional consumer rights:

4. The right to be adequately informed about the more important aspects of the product
5. The right to be protected against questionable products and marketing practices
6. The right to influence products and marketing practices in directions that will enhance the "quality of life"

Each of these proposed rights leads to a whole series of specific proposals by consumerists. The right to be informed includes such things as the right to know the true interest cost of a loan (*truth-in-lending*), the true cost per standard unit of competing brands (*unit pricing*), the basic ingredients in a product (*ingredient labeling*), the nutritional quality of foods (*nutritional labeling*), the freshness of products (*open dating*), and the true benefits of a product (*truth-in-advertising*).

The proposals related to additional *consumer protection* include the strengthening of consumers' position in cases of business fraud, the requiring of more safety to be designed into products, and the issuing of greater powers to existing government agencies.

The proposals relating to *quality-of-life* considerations include regulating the ingredients that go into certain products (detergents, gasoline) and packaging (soft-drink containers), reducing the level of advertising and promotional "noise," and creating consumer representation on company boards to introduce consumer welfare considerations in business decision making.

Implications for Marketing Management

A number of business firms at first balked at the consumer movement. They resented the power of strong consumer leaders to point an accusing finger at their products and cause their sales to plummet, as, for instance, when Ralph Nader called the Corvair automobile unsafe, when Robert Choate accused breakfast cereals of providing "empty calories," and when Herbert S. Denenberg published a list showing the wide variation in premiums different insurance companies were charging for the same protection. Businesses also resented consumer proposals that appeared to increase business costs more than they helped the consumer. They felt that most consumers would not pay attention to unit pricing or ingredient labeling and that the doctrines of advertising substantiation, corrective advertising, and counter advertising would stifle advertising creativity.[2] They felt that the consumer was better off than ever, that large companies were very careful in developing safe products and promoting them honestly, and that new consumer laws would only lead to new constraints and higher seller costs that would be passed on to the consumer in higher prices. Thus many companies opposed the consumer movement and lobbied vigorously against new legislation.

Many other companies took no stand and simply went about their business. A few companies undertook a series of bold initiatives to show their endorsement of consumer aims. Here are two examples:

> Giant Food, Inc., a leading supermarket chain in the Washington, D.C., area, took the initiative and introduced unit pricing, open dating, and nutritional labeling. They assigned home economists to their stores to help consumers buy and prepare food more intelligently. They invited Esther Peterson, formerly the president's advisor on consumer affairs, to join the board of directors and provide guidance on consumer-oriented retailing.
>
> Whirlpool Corporation adopted a number of measures to improve customer information and services. They installed a toll-free corporate phone number for consumers to use who were dissatisfied with their Whirlpool equipment or service. They improved the coverage of their product warranties and rewrote them in basic English.

In adopting a "we care" leadership role, these companies increased their market shares and profits substantially. Competitors were forced to emulate them, without, however, achieving the same impact enjoyed by the leader.

---

[2] *Advertising substantiation* is the requirement that advertisers should be able to prove any of their claims to the Federal Trade Commission. *Corrective advertising* is the ordering of an advertiser whose ad was deceptive or misleading to publicly announce this fact and make a correction. *Counter advertising* is the encouragement of parties of opposite persuasions to put out counter messages.

At the present time most companies have come around to accepting the new consumer rights in principle. They might oppose certain pieces of legislation on the ground that such measures are not the best way to solve a particular consumer problem. But they recognize the consumers' right to information and protection. Those who take a leadership role recognize that business's response to consumerism involves more than public relations and a few new products or services that meet neglected consumer needs. Consumerism involves a total commitment by top management, middle-management education and participation, new policy guidelines, marketing research, and company investment. Several companies have established consumer affairs departments to help formulate policies and deal with "consumerist" problems facing the company. All of these steps should improve customer satisfaction and company sales and profits.

Product managers are finding their role changing as a result of consumerism. They have to spend more time checking product ingredients and product features for safety, preparing safe packaging and informative labeling, substantiating their advertising claims, reviewing their sales promotion, developing clear and adequate product warranties, and so on. They have to check an increasing number of decisions with company lawyers. They have to develop a sixth sense about what the consumers really want and may feel about the product and various marketing practices.

On the other hand, consumerism is actually, in a profound way, the ultimate expression of the marketing concept. It will compel the product manager to consider things from the consumers' point of view. It will suggest needs and wants that may have been overlooked by all the firms in the industry. The resourceful manager will look for the positive opportunities implicit in the doctrine of consumerism rather than brood over its restraints.

ENVIRONMENTALISM

Whereas consumerists focus on whether the marketing system is efficiently serving consumer needs and wants, environmentalists focus on the impact of modern marketing on the surrounding environment and the costs that are borne in serving these consumer needs and wants. *Environmentalism is an organized movement of concerned citizens and government to protect and enhance man's living environment.* Environmentalists are concerned with strip mining, forest depletion, factory smoke, billboards, and litter; with the loss of recreational opportunity; and with the increase in health problems due to bad air, water, and chemically sprayed food.

Environmentalists are not against marketing and consumption; they simply want them to operate on more ecological principles. They do not think the goal of the marketing system should be the maximization of *consumption,* or *consumer choice,* or *consumer satisfaction* as such. The goal of the marketing system should be the maximization of *life quality.* And life quality means not only the quantity and quality of consumer goods and services but also the quality of the environment.

Environmentalists want environmental costs formally introduced into the decision calculus of producers and consumers. They favor the use of tax mechanisms and regulations to impose the true social costs of antienvironmental business activity and consumption. Requiring business to invest in antipollution devices, taxing nonreturnable bottles, banning high-phosphate detergents, and other measures are viewed as necessary to lead businesses and consumers to move in directions that are environmentally sound.

Environmentalists in some ways are more critical of marketing than are consumerists. They complain that there is too much wasteful packaging in the United States, whereas consumerists like the convenience offered by modern packaging. Environmentalists feel that mass advertising leads people to buy more than they need, whereas consumerists worry more about deception in advertising. Environmentalists dislike the proliferation of shopping centers, whereas consumerists welcome new stores and more competition.

Implications for Marketing Management

Environmentalism has hit certain industries hard. Steel companies and public utilities have been forced to invest billions of dollars in pollution-control equipment and costlier fuels. The auto industry has had to introduce expensive emission-control devices in cars. The soap industry has had to research and develop low-phosphate detergents. The packaging industry has been required to develop ways to reduce litter and increase biodegradability in its products. The gasoline industry has had to formulate new low-lead and no-lead gasolines. Naturally, these industries are inclined to resent environmental regulations, especially when those are formulated and imposed too rapidly to allow the companies to make the proper adjustments. These companies have had to absorb large costs and later pass them on to buyers.

Companies that did not experience direct environmental regulation found themselves paying more for their fuels and materials. Thus environmentalism touches everyone and reflects itself in higher costs. As a result, many business firms have attacked these regulations, using inflation, the energy crisis, and declining profits as their argument for a slower rate of implementation.

At the same time, many companies have taken positive steps to respond to the spirit and implications of environmentalism:

1. Companies have appointed plant-wide committees to review methods of production with an eye toward spotting wasteful procedures and identifying sources of polluton that critics or government agencies may point out.

2. Companies are introducing environmental criteria in their decision making on product ingredients, design, and packaging. Some companies direct their R&D toward finding ecologically superior products as the major selling point of the product. Sears developed and promoted a phosphate-free laundry detergent; Pepsi-Cola developed a one-way, plastic soft-drink bottle that is biodegradable in solid-waste treatment; and American Oil pioneered no-lead and low-lead gasolines.

3. Some companies moved directly into the rapidly expanding market for environmental products, such as pollution-control equipment and recycling plants.

4. Marketing managers are improving their research into buyer attitudes toward environmental issues to help guide their decisions.[3]

[3] For further reading on the implications of environmentalism for marketing, see George Fisk, "Criteria for a Theory of Responsible Consumption," *Journal of Marketing*, April 1973, pp. 24–31; Norman Kangun, "Environmental Problems and Marketing: Saint or Sinner?" in *Marketing Analysis for Societal Problems*, ed. J. N. Sheth and P. L. Wright (Urbana, Ill.: University of Illinois, 1974), pp. 250–70; and Karl E. Henion II, *Ecological Marketing* (Columbus, Ohio: Grid, 1976).

The gloomy predictions of the environmentalists that mankind would use up the earth's natural resources took on an air of frightening reality in 1973 when the world was plunged into alarming shortages of oil, various minerals, and even food. Business firms found themselves facing marked shortages of oil, chemicals, electricity, natural gas, cement, aluminum, copper, textiles, paper, glass, and furniture. Ironically, as late as 1972 most of these firms were spending the greater part of their time trying to dispose of surpluses.

One business columnist saw in shortages the possible end of marketing:

> There is little doubt that the energy crisis will force an alteration in the role of the marketing man. In some industries, it may alter him out of existence.... When demand exceeds supply marketing men can be replaced by order-takers. The art of selling is unnecessary. There also is no need for advertising, sales promotion, incentives, sweepstakes, trading stamps, free road maps or even windshield cleaning.[4]

What is the proper marketing response of companies to widening shortages? The two most common responses to shortages are both short-sighted.

The first is an *aggressive demarketing response.* The company rushes to buy supplies wherever it can get them, at any cost. It raises its own prices sharply, cuts product quality and new-product development, eliminates weaker customers, reduces customer services, allocates to the remaining customers according to ability to pay, cuts marketing budgets for research, advertising, and sales calls, and drops low-profit items. All of these steps have the positive effect of creating instant profits for the company. At the same time, the company is playing dangerously with its only asset, its customers. Their goodwill is sorely taxed, and when normal times return, many of them will have found other vendors and other ways to meet their needs.

The second is a *marketing-as-usual approach.* Here the company expects shortages to be temporary. The company continues to buy its supplies carefully. It maintains the same product line and sells to the same customers. It raises prices a little to keep up with cost increases. but not excessively. It maintains the same expenditures on advertising, sales force, and marketing research, with minor changes in its messages. These steps at best maintain the company's profit margins and customer goodwill. On the other hand, they smack too much of "Nero fiddling while Rome burns" and do not implement necessary steps to improve the company's position in the long run.

Implications for Marketing Management

A period of deep shortages calls for a third response, which can be characterized as *strategic remarketing.* It calls for the appointment of a top-management committee to review the company's basic policies on its *customer mix, product mix,* and *marketing mix,* and to make a set of recommendations. This committee studies the following questions:

[4] Joe Cappo, "Will Marketing Run Out of Energy?" *Chicago Daily News,* November 27, 1973, p. 34. The columnist makes the mistake of equating marketing with demand stimulation rather than demand management.

1. Which markets will be the most profitable in the coming years?
2. Which customers in these markets will be the best ones to serve?
3. What principles should be used to allocate scarce supplies to existing customers?
4. How many new customers can be cultivated without diluting the interest of present customers in receiving adequate supplies?
5. What products might the company drop from its line, and what products should the company try to add to its line?
6. How much price increase can the company take and justify to its customers?
7. What should the company be communicating to its customers, and what will this require in the way of an advertising and public relations budget?
8. How many sales representatives does the company need, and what kind of retraining should they receive?
9. What can be done to bring down costs to customers and assist them in solving their problems?

Although the answers to these questions will vary from company to company, the guiding principle should be one of customer orientation. The major asset that a firm has in the long run is its loyal customers. Loyal customers are not created by serving them royally during good times and charging what the traffic will bear during bad times. Loyal customers are created by companies that are considerate of their customers at all times. During a shortage period, the market-oriented company strives to help its customers solve their problems.

This philosophy can be translated into specific marketing tasks and activities:

1. *Sales representatives* will find their selling role diminished but their other roles increased: customer counseling, order expediting, and intelligence gathering. Even their *selling role* has not entirely vanished because they must turn some attention to selling slower-moving company products that are in adequate supply.
2. *Advertising* should probably be reduced somewhat but by no means abandoned. It can be redirected to building up demand for company products that are in oversupply: to create buying interest in new products and product modifications; to educate buyers in more economical uses of the scarce product; and to keep customers informed of steps the company is taking to solve the shortages.
3. *Marketing research* should be maintained at a level that permits the monitoring of competitive market changes and interpretation of evolving buyer practices and needs.
4. *Product development* should be alert to new-product opportunities created by the shortage. To a resourceful firm, a shortage means a need for substitute products. A shortage of gasoline expands the market for bikes and mass transportation; a shortage of heating oil expands the market for sweaters, fireplaces, and electric blankets.
5. *Purchasing* must be considerably strengthened as a company function. It must do a better job of finding alternative sources of supply and arranging long-term contracts. Purchasing departments need to utilize marketing principles to "sell" the company's neediness to the vendor's sales representatives. Some companies have transferred some sales representatives into the purchasing department to improve their effectiveness in attracting suppliers and supplies.[5]

[5] For additional steps, see the author's "Marketing during Periods of Shortage," *Journal of Marketing,* July 1974, pp. 20–29.

Ever since the Middle East war of 1973, with the attendant oil crisis, the nations of the world have experienced persistent inflation, sometimes at a double-digit rate and other times at a high single-digit rate. Several forces make it likely that inflation will continue to be a major economic and social problem for years to come. They include:

> Raw-material-exporting countries are engaging in more price fixing of oil, coffee, cocoa, and various minerals and metals.

> The rate of consumption of certain goods, such as energy, paper, and aluminum, is racing ahead of the level of supply.

> Wage settlements are exceeding productivity gains in most developed countries. Industrial discipline is eroding in many countries. The trend toward a shorter workweek contributes to inflation.

> Affluent economies with a growing services sector are subject to more inflationary pressure because of the greater difficulty in achieving productivity gains in service industries.

> Increased government legislation and regulations covering antipollution investment, product liability, consumerism, and environmentalism raise the costs of doing business and are passed on to consumers in the form of higher prices.

> The lengthening of the educational and life span tends to increase the proportion of nonproductive workers in an economy.

Implications for Marketing Management

High inflation poses a number of challenges to marketing management that have no easy answers. The company should establish a high-level *profit protection committee* to forecast the expected rate and duration of inflation, how their customers are responding to inflation, and the government's likely program. Then the company should consider the following possible moves:

1. An effort should be made to hold down purchase costs through such measures as considering new suppliers and searching for substitute ingredients.
2. Manufacturing processes should be reexamined for opportunities to increase efficiency.
3. The company should reexamine customer-account profitability and increase prices or reduce service to the smaller accounts.
4. The company should move more aggressively into those markets that are better able to absorb higher prices.
5. The company should place greater emphasis on its higher marginal products. It should also examine opportunities for improving profit margins on individual products through reducing packaging costs, ingredient costs, and other costs.
6. The company should consider introducing more economical versions of products for customers who need to save money.
7. Price increases should be sufficient but not so high as to drive away customers. The company should consider different ways of passing on price increases and explaining them to customers.
8. Advertising messages might incorporate price appeals, such as "more value for your money" or "buy now and save."
9. Companies should consider using price deals more aggressively, since customers are more responsive to them during high inflation.

10. The sales force should be trained to be effective in explaining price increases to customers and in helping customers find ways to economize.

11. The company should put more emphasis on lower-cost distribution channels, such as mass distributors and discount operations, since these will be increasingly favored by customers.

RECESSION

American consumers of the 1950s and 1960s believed in the American dream: continuous rising real income, a home in the suburbs, two cars, and money to travel. In the early 1970s this dream was shaken. American consumers confronted shortages, then inflation, and then recession. Their real incomes deteriorated.

Consumers exposed to income deterioration go through a number of stages in adjusting to the new economic realities:

1. At first they maintain their old spending patterns, refusing to take their real-income loss seriously.

2. As things get worse, they start to cut certain items from their budget and search for less expensive goods.

3. At a further point, they get angry and blame certain forces for the economic downturn: big business, unions, government.

4. Still later they start despairing because the situation continues to worsen, and no remedies seem to work.

5. Finally, consumers begin to take stock of their new situation and adopt consumer values matched to their economic realities.

Not all consumers pass through all these stages, but many of them make several adjustments of great importance to sellers. The dominant goal of consumers is to find ways to economize. That takes a number of forms:

1. Increased preference for *store brands* over manufacturer brands because of their lower prices, similar quality, and prominent display

2. Increased *multiple shopping* and *discount store patronage* to find lower prices

3. Increased *trading down* toward substitute products. Consumers go from steak to chicken to tuna fish to rice and beans

4. Increased *do-it-yourself* in the area of home repair services, clothing, and food production

5. Increased patronage of *secondhand markets* (used-clothing stores, flea markets, garage sales).

6. Increased interest in *functional product features* and *durability* and less in product aesthetics and convenience

7. Increased elimination of *impulse buying* and *nonnecessities*[6]

These changes result in the emergence of three distinct consumer life-style

---

[6] Industrial buyers go through similar changes. Their steps include (1) search for additional suppliers, (2) search for better terms, (3) movement toward self-production, (4) search for cheaper materials, and (5) product simplification. Industrial sellers must take these evolving customer needs into account in formulating their marketing program.

groups. The majority group, the *intense consumers*, still retain high consumption values. They want to spend freely, buy the latest products, and not worry about waste. The second group, the *sensible consumers*, concentrate on functional product values and economy. They buy small cars, practical clothes, simple appliances. The third and smallest group, the *austere consumers*, turn against material values and start "deconsuming." They may give up their cars, reduce the number of their appliances, wear simple clothes, make their own furniture, grow some of their own food, and eat less.

Implications for Marketing Management

Many of these consumer changes call for new marketing thinking. Traditional marketing is based on "more is better." At the same time, there is a growing market for goods that are less extravagant and conspicuous and more durable and economical. This market segment constitutes a growing market opportunity for manufacturers and retailers. It calls for a different emphasis in product design, distribution, pricing, and marketing communication. Companies may bemoan the decline of the old values, which were based on insatiable demand and never-ending product elaboration and replacement. But the alert marketer knows that there is always work to do as long as there are people, and it is only a question of finding out and offering what they need and want.[7]

GOVERNMENT REGULATIONS

All of the previous developments—consumerism, environmentalism, shortages, inflation, and recession—have increased the role of government in society. Businesses face an increasing number of government regulations affecting marketing practices, employee relations, manufacturing decisions, and a host of other things. Often laws of bewildering complexity are passed—such as OSHA legislation—that few people, including the lawyers, understand. This climate, combined with a growing propensity for people and business firms to sue other business firms for a variety of practices, is creating a highly litigious society. Managers are cautioned by their company not to make major decisions without clearing them with the company's lawyers.

Marketing executives, in particular, have to be keenly aware of the law as it affects marketing decisions in the areas of competitive relations, products, price, promotion, and channels of distribution. The major issues are reviewed here.

Competitive-Relations Decisions

The firm must be careful in the use of different competitive instruments to expand its market size or share. This includes attempts to grow through acquisition or merger, to develop cooperative relations with competitors, or to adopt certain hard tactics against competitors.

Expansion In reviewing acquisitions, the law holds it is a question not of the good or bad intentions of the acquiring firm but only of the effects of the acquisition on competition. The courts have rejected such defenses as competitive intent, growth needs, declining position of acquiring company, lack of com-

---

[7] For further discussion of marketing under different economic climates, see Avraham Shama, "Management and Consumers in an Era of Stagflation," *Journal of Marketing*, July 1978, pp. 43–52.

petition, rapid expansion of an industry, ease of entry, and so forth. If there is a reasonable probability that the acquisition will substantially lessen competition "in any line of commerce in any section of the country," then the acquisition may be prevented by the government. The case hinges on how the relevant market is defined and how the acquisition will affect competition in this market.

Cooperative relations The law also bears down hard on any signs of collusive relations between presumably competing companies. Such joint actions as price fixing, splitting up markets, excluding new competitors, agreeing on various customers, and so forth, would constitute a conspiracy. Price agreements are held to be illegal per se; that is, no defenses are acceptable. This applies to obvious violations, such as rigged bids or the use of common basing points in quoting price, and even such apparently minor actions as exchanging price lists for information purposes, or parallel pricing action.

Competitive tactics The law will condemn a firm that uses hard or predatory tactics against its competitors. This includes cutting off a competitor's source of supply, disparaging a competitor's products or ability, or threatening or using actual intimidation.

Product Decisions Marketing management must take cognizance of the law in making decisions respecting product additions and deletions, product design, product quality, and labeling.

Product additions and deletions The firm's product mix changes through the process of adding new products and dropping old ones. Decisions to add products, particularly through acquisitions, may be prevented under the Antimerger Act if the effect threatens to lessen competition. Decisions to drop old products must be made with an awareness that the firm has legal obligations, written or implied, to its suppliers, dealers, and customers who have a stake in the discontinued product.

Product design The firm must design its new product in the context of the complicated U.S. patent laws. The patent laws are both a constraint and an opportunity for any firm. They are a constraint in the sense that a firm is prevented from designing a product that is "illegally similar" to another company's established product. This may be quite difficult to determine, the definition of "similar" resting on whether consumers consider the design or outward appearance to be the same. After a patent is granted, the patent laws represent an opportunity, because the firm's new product is protected against "illegally similar" products for three and a half, seven, or fourteen years, depending on the patentable period. The firm may license manufacturing rights to others in return for a royalty but is under no legal compulsion to do so.

Product quality, safety, and labeling Manufacturers of foods, drugs, cosmetics, and certain fibers must comply with specific laws in establishing product quality, safety, and labeling. The Federal Food, Drug, and Cosmetic Act was passed to protect consumers from unsafe and adulterated food, drugs, and cosmetics. Various acts provide for the inspection of sanitary conditions in the meat and poultry processing industries. Safety legislation has been passed to regulate fabrics, chemical substances, automobiles, toys, and drugs and poisons. In 1972, the Consumer Product Safety Act was passed, establishing a Consumer Product Safety Commission. As for labels, they must identify the manufacturer or distributor and the package contents and quality, and contain warnings if the product is dangerous or habit-forming.

Price Decisions   Pricing is one of the major marketing-decision areas where a knowledge of the law is essential. Management must avoid price fixing (except for resale price maintenance), price discrimination, charging less than the minimum legal price, raising prices unduly, or advertising deceptive prices.

Price fixing   Price-fixing agreements among competitors, called horizontal price fixing, are prosecutable. The courts have even ruled that a company cannot fix the prices charged by its subsidiaries, where they may be in competition. The only exceptions occur where the price agreements are carried out under the supervision of a government agency, as is the case in many local milk industry agreements, in the regulated transportation industries, and in fruit and vegetable cooperatives.

Price discrimination   Under the Robinson-Patman Act, management must be careful in developing its price differentials for different classes of customers and conditions of sale (as well as any differentials in advertising allowances, facilities, and services). Price differentials are justified to some extent where the products are not of like grade and quality, particularly in the buyers' minds. Otherwise, these differentials must be based on cost differences. Usually it is easiest to justify discounts based on the size of orders because of the obvious savings in the cost of manufacturing, selling, or delivering of larger orders. Discounts based on the amount purchased over a specified period, while not specifically outlawed, are harder to justify under the cost-savings argument. Marketing management may also employ price differentials where the purpose is to "meet competition" in "good faith," providing the firm is trying to meet competitors at its own level of competition and that the price discrimination is temporary, localized, and defensive rather than offensive.

Minimum prices   Wholesalers and retailers face laws in over half the states requiring a minimum percentage markup over their cost of merchandise plus transportation. Called Unfair Trade Practices Acts, they are designed to protect smaller merchants from larger merchants who might otherwise sell certain items at or below cost for a while to attract customers.

Price increases   In contrast to price floors, there is normally no legislation that places price ceilings on sellers' goods, except in times of price control. The company is generally free to increase the price of its goods to any level, the major hurdle being economic. The major exception occurs in the case of public-regulated utilities. Since they have monopoly power in their respective areas, their price schedules are regulated and approved in the public's interest. The executive branch of the government has used its influence from time to time to discourage major-industry price increases because of inflationary concerns.

Deceptive pricing   Deceptive pricing is a more common problem in the sale of consumer goods than business goods, because consumers typically possess less information and buying acumen. In 1958, the Automobile Information Disclosure Act was passed, requiring auto manufacturers to affix on the windshield of each new automobile a statement giving the manufacturer's suggested retail price, the prices of optional equipment, and the dealer's transportation charges. In the same year, the FTC issued its *Guides Against Deceptive Pricing*, admonishing sellers not to claim a price reduction unless it is a saving from the usual retail price, not to advertise "factory" or "wholesale" prices unless they are genuine, not to advertise comparable-value prices on imperfect goods, and so forth.

Promotion Decisions

The company must develop its promotion program in a way that does not invite charges of deception or of discrimination. Advertising is more vulnerable to legal action than personal selling because it leaves a clearer record of itself. Nevertheless, actions have been brought against sales representatives when the evidence indicated conscious deception of their customers.

False and misleading advertising   Marketing executives have to worry about false advertising and misleading advertising. They can avoid the former by refraining from deliberate misrepresentation. Misleading rather than false advertising is the major headache for sellers. The FTC can issue a temporary restraining order against any advertisement that seems to have the capacity to deceive, even though no one may be deceived. The problem is one of distinguishing between puffery in advertising, which is normal, and distortion.

Bait advertising   Bait advertising, where the seller attracts buyers' interest on false pretenses, comes under FTC surveillance. The seller offers or advertises an exceptionally good buy but then finds some excuse for not selling the advertised item and pushes something else instead. Tactics include refusing to sell the product, disparaging its features, demonstrating a defective one, or imposing unreasonable delivery dates or service terms.

Promotional allowances and services   In planning its promotional program, the company must be sure to make promotional allowances and services available to all customers on proportionately equal terms. However, it is difficult to establish what constitutes proportionately equal terms where small and large customers are involved.

Channel Decisions

By and large, manufacturers are free under the law to develop whatever channel arrangements suit them. In fact, much of the force of the law affecting channels is to make sure they are not foreclosed from using channels as the result of the exclusionary tactics of others. But this places them under obligation to proceed cautiously in their own possible use of exclusionary tactics. Most of the law is concerned with the mutual rights and duties of the manufacturer and channel members once they have formed a relationship.

Exclusive dealing   Many manufacturers and wholesalers like to develop exclusive channels for their products. The policy is called *exclusive distribution* when the seller enfranchises only certain outlets to carry its products. It is called *exclusive dealing* when the seller requires these outlets to agree to handle only its products, or conversely, not to handle competitors' products. Both parties tend to draw benefits from exclusive dealing, the seller enjoying a more dependable and enthusiastic set of outlets without having to invest capital in them, and the distributors gaining a steady source of supply and seller support. However, the result of exclusive dealing is that other manufacturers are excluded from selling to these dealers. This has brought exclusive-dealing contracts under the purview of the Clayton Act, although such contracts are not made illegal per se. They are illegal only if they tend to lessen competition substantially or create a monopoly.

Exclusive territorial distributorships   Exclusive dealing often includes territorial agreements as well as exclusive-source agreements. The seller may agree not to sell to other distributors in the area, and/or the buyer may agree to confine sales to its own territory. The first practice is fairly normal under franchise systems, being regarded as a way to promote increased dealer enthusiasm and dealer investment in the area. The seller is under no legal compulsion to establish more outlets than it wishes. The second practice, where the manufacturer tries to restrain each dealer to sell only in its own territory, has become a major legal issue. This comes close to dividing up the market, even though in this case it is the market for a brand (vertical market division) rather than a product (horizontal market division).

Tying agreements   Manufacturers with a brand in strong demand occasionally sell it to dealers on condition they take some or all of the rest of the line. In the latter case, this practice is called *full-line forcing*. Such tying arrangements are not illegal per se, but they do run afoul of the Clayton Act if they tend to lessen competition substantially. Buyers are prevented from exercising their free choice among competing suppliers of these other goods.

Dealers' rights   Sellers are largely free to select their dealers, but their right to terminate dealerships is somewhat qualified. In general, sellers can drop dealers "for cause." But they cannot drop dealers, for example, if the latter refuse to cooperate in a dubious legal arrangement, such as exclusive-dealing or tying arrangements.

MARKETING ETHICS

The law defines what the company cannot do. This does not mean that everything else, because it is legal, is right. Here top management enters as an additional force in developing policies that define proper marketing conduct. Policies are "broad, fixed guidelines that everyone in the organization must adhere to, and that are not subject to exception."[8] They cover distributor relations, advertising standards, customer service, pricing, product development, and ethical standards.

There is little defense for the failure of a company's top management to develop formal policies. Their executives will inevitably face difficult moral di-

[8] Earl L. Bailey, *Formulating the Company's Marketing Policies: A Survey*, Experiences in Marketing Management, No. 19 (New York: Conference Board, 1968), p. 3.

lemmas. Even if they have the finest consciences, the question of the best thing to do is often unclear. Since not all of their executives will in fact have the finest moral sensitivity, the company is taking even more risk that its reputation may be compromised by improper executive behavior.

Even the best set of guidelines cannot anticipate or resolve all the ethically difficult situations that the marketer will face. Consider Howard Bowen's classic question about the responsibilities of marketers:

> Should he conduct selling in ways that intrude on the privacy of people, for example, by door-to-door selling? . . . Should he use methods involving ballyhoo, chances, prizes, hawking, and other tactics which are at least of doubtful good taste? Should he employ "high pressure" tactics in persuading people to buy? Should he try to hasten the obsolescence of goods by bringing out an endless succession of new models and new styles? Should he appeal to and attempt to strengthen the motives of materialism, invidious consumption, and "keeping up with the Joneses"? [9]

Table 27–1 lists fourteen ethically difficult situations that marketers could well face during their careers. If marketers decide in favor of the immediate sales-producing actions in all fourteen cases, their marketing behavior might well be described as immoral or amoral. On the other hand, if they refuse to go along with *any* of the actions, they might be ineffective as marketing managers and unhappy because of the constant moral tension. Obviously managers need a set of principles that will help them determine the moral gravity of each situation and how far they can go in good conscience.

TABLE 27–1
Some Morally Difficult Situations in Marketing

1. You work for a cigarette company and up to now have not been convinced that cigarettes cause cancer. A recent report has come across your desk that clearly establishes the connection between cigarette smoking and cancer. What would you do?

2. Your R&D department has modernized one of your products. It is not really "new and improved," but you know that putting this statement on the package and in the advertising will increase sales. What would you do?

3. You have been asked to add a stripped-down model to the low end of your line that could be advertised to attract customers. The product won't be very good, but the sales representatives could be depended upon to persuade buyers to buy the higher-priced units. You are asked to give the green light for developing this stripped-down version. What would you do?

4. You are interviewing a former product manager who just left a competitor's company. You are thinking of hiring him. He would be more than happy to tell you all the competitor's plans for the coming year. What would you do?

5. One of your dealers in an important territory has had family troubles recently and is not producing the sales he used to. He was one of the company's top producers in the past. It is not clear how long it will take before his family trouble

---

[9] Howard R. Bowen, *Social Responsibilities of the Businessman* (New York: Harper & Row, 1953), p. 215.

straightens out. In the meantime, many sales are being lost. There is a legal way to terminate the dealer's franchise and replace him. What would you do?

6. You have a chance to win a big account that will mean a lot to you and your company. The purchasing agent hinted that he would be influenced by a "gift." Your assistant recommends sending a fine color television set to his home. What would you do?

7. You have heard that a competitor has a new product feature that will make a big difference in sales. He will have a hospitality suite at the annual trade show and unveil this feature at a party thrown for his dealers. You can easily send a snooper to this meeting to learn what the new feature is. What would you do?

8. You are eager to win a big contract, and during sales negotiations you learn that the buyer is looking for a better job. You have no intention of hiring him, but if you hinted that you might, he would probably give you the order. What would you do?

9. You have to make a choice between three ad campaigns outlined by your agency for your new product. The first (A) is a soft-sell, honest informational campaign. The second (B) uses sex-loaded emotional appeals and exaggerates the product's benefits. The third (C) involves a noisy, irritating commercial that is sure to gain audience attention. Preliminary tests show that the commercials are effective in the following order: C, B, and A. What would you do?

10. You are a marketing vice president working for a beer company, and you have learned that a particularly lucrative state is planning to raise the minimum legal drinking age from 18 to 21. You have been asked to join other breweries in lobbying against this bill and to make contributions. What would you do?

11. You want to interview a sample of customers about their reactions to a competitive product. It has been suggested that you invent an innocuous name like the Marketing Research Institute and interview people. What would you do?

12. You produce an antidandruff shampoo that is effective with one application. Your assistant says that the product would turn over faster if the instructions on the label recommended two applications. What would you do?

13. You are interviewing a capable woman applicant for a job as sales representative. She is better qualified than the men just interviewed. At the same time, you suspect that some of your current salesmen will react negatively to her hiring, and you also know that some important customers may be ruffled. What would you do?

14. You are a sales manager in an encyclopedia company. A common way for encyclopedia representatives to get into homes is to pretend they are taking a survey. After they finish the survey, they switch to their sales pitch. This technique seems to be very effective and is used by most of your competitors. What would you do?

All ethical philosophies deal with one or more of three characteristics of the *act*. They judge either the act itself (moral idealism), the actor's motives (intuitionism), or the act's consequences (utilitarianism).

Moral idealism is the most rigid in that it postulates certain acts to be bad under all (or most) circumstances. Moral idealism gives marketing managers the most definitive answers to most of the questions raised in Table 27–1. They would refuse to hear privy information or spy on competitors, deceive customers, and so on. By refusing to let the ends justify the means, they would derive a greater feeling of right conduct.

Intuitionism is less rigid, leaving it up to the individual managers to sense the moral gravity of the situation. If managers feel their motives are good, that they are not out to hurt anyone, they are taking an intuitive approach to these morally difficult situations.

Utilitarianism is the most deliberative of the three systems, seeking to establish the moral locus not in the act or the motives but in the consequences. If the consequences of the act to the individual and society, both the good ones and bad ones, represent a net increase in society's happiness, the act is right.

Ultimately each executive must choose and work out a philosophy of proper behavior. Every moral system is predicated on some conception of the good life and the relation of one's welfare to that of others. Once the executive works out a clear philosophy and set of principles, they will help cut through the many knotty questions that marketing and other human activities pose.

Truly, marketing executives of the 1980s will find their job full of challenges. They will face abundant marketing opportunities opened up by technological advances in solar energy, home computers and robots, cable television, modern medicine, and new forms of transportation, recreation, and communication. At the same time, forces in the socioeconomic environment will increase the constraints under which marketing can be carried out. Those companies that are able to pioneer new values and practice societally responsible marketing will have a world to conquer.

SUMMARY

Marketing is an evolving discipline that must develop new answers as new problems arise. The marketing principles of the 1950s and 1960s are being challenged by new factors in the marketing environment—consumerism, environmentalism, shortages, inflation, recession, government regulation, and marketing ethics. *Consumerism* calls for a strengthening of consumers' rights and power in relation to sellers. Resourceful marketers will recognize it as an opportunity to serve consumers better through providing more information, education, and protection. *Environmentalism* calls for minimizing the harm done by marketing practices to the environment and quality of life. It calls for intervening in consumer wants when their satisfaction would create too much environmental cost. *Shortages* have made real the possibility of running out of resources in the absence of their wise use. Marketers must avoid responding to shortages with either aggressive demarketing or marketing-as-usual. Shortages call for strategic reprogramming of the customer mix, product mix, and marketing mix. *Inflation* raises the company's costs and the company has to determine how much to pass on to the buyer. Resourceful marketers will not simply pass on higher costs but will seek ways to offset them to hold customer costs down. *Recession* and the preceding developments lead to changing consumer life style, characterized by more sensible or austere consumption. Some firms recognize a marketing opportunity to serve the needs of the growing segment of sensible consumers. *Government regulation* continues to grow without any sign of abatement. This requires marketers to check many of their decisions on competitive relations, products, pricing, promotion, and distribution with the company's legal department. Finally, *marketing ethics* is a major concern in that company employees often have to choose between what is in their immediate self-interest, their long-run self-interest, and the interest of society as a whole. Companies have to formulate clear policies to guide the marketing decision making of their employees in socially responsible directions.

1. Consumerists have suggested that public schools should train students in how to view television commercials critically. Students should be taught to recognize objectively what the advertising is trying to do. As a business person, would you support this proposal? Why or why not?

2. The following products satisfy individual wants but at the same time have certain undesirable societal consequences: (a) detergents, (b) automobiles, (c) disposable paper diapers. Discuss what the manufacturers can or ought to do about each product.

3. Distinguish four alternative advertising strategies by an oil company in the event of another major fuel shortage.

4. Two companies, A and B, account for virtually 100 percent of the sales in a certain industry. Company A is the high-price, high-quality company and company B is the low-price, low-quality company. During the period of rising real incomes, company A enjoyed a 60 percent market share and company B had the rest. In the subsequent period of high inflation and recession, several buyers switched to company B because of their need to economize. What are some of the strategies available to company A to avoid losing further market share?

5. Suppose your company has sold 40,000 sets of a particular television set model. A company engineer has just discovered that a switch in the set will not stand up under constant use. There is a very small chance that the set could catch fire. You are the marketing vice-president. What would you do?

6. A group called Action for Children's Television is urging the following guidelines for children's television programs: (a) that there be no commercials on children's programs. (b) that hosts on children's shows should not sell. (c) that stations provide 14 hours a week of programs for children of different age groups. Suppose you are a marketing executive in a toy company. Would you lobby against guidelines?

Indices

Company Ind&ex

Name Index

Subject Index